HECTOR BERLIOZ, BY COURBET

Memoirs of Hector Berlioz

from 1803 to 1865

comprising his travels in Germany, Italy, Russia, and England

TRANSLATED BY RACHEL (SCOTT RUSSELL) HOLMES
AND ELEANOR HOLMES
ANNOTATED, AND THE TRANSLATION REVISED BY

Ernest Newman

DOVER PUBLICATIONS, INC., NEW YORK

Published in Canada by General Publishing Company, Ltd., 30 Lesmill Road, Don Mills, Toronto, Ontario.
Published in the United Kingdom by Constable and Company, Ltd., 10 Orange Street, London, W.C. 2.

This Dover edition, first published in 1966, is an unabridged republication of the work originally published by Alfred A. Knopf, Inc., in 1932.
This edition is published by special arrangement with Alfred A. Knopf, Inc.

International Standard Book Number: 0-486-21563-6
Library of Congress Catalog Card Number: 66-10735

Manufactured in the United States of America
Dover Publications, Inc.
180 Varick Street
New York, N. Y. 10014

Editor's Foreword

W$_E$ have to remember that the *Mémoires* are rather a compilation than a work planned with the specific object of narrating its subject's life in full. As Berlioz's *Preface* indicates, the book was begun as early as 1848, with the purpose of correcting many misstatements concerning him that had already got into print. It was a period of profound discouragement for Berlioz. The failure of *La Damnation de Faust* in December 1846 had not only dealt him what was so far the cruellest blow of his whole career as an artist but had ruined him financially. He had once more to leave Paris to seek his fortune elsewhere. After tours in Russia and Germany he found himself, in the winter of 1847–1848, in London, attached to the Opera at Drury Lane. This venture of the speculator Jullien ended in disaster. In February 1848 the Revolution broke out in Paris. Louis Philippe was in flight: with the collapse of the monarchy the official *Journal des Débats* was in danger: and Berlioz not only happened to be the musical critic of the *Débats* but was further compromised, in the eyes of the revolutionaries, by the fact that he was known to be the particular protégé of Bertin, the proprietor of the journal. There seemed to be no future for him in Paris: he felt he might even lose his small stipend as Librarian of the Conservatoire. It was with a feeling that his world was crashing to ruin around him that he embarked upon the project of leaving posterity his own account of himself.

Always reluctant to scrap anything he had once written, whether music or literature, instead of commencing a formal autobiography on new lines he reverted to matter he had already published. In 1844 he had brought out a work entitled *Voyage musical en Allemagne et en Italie: Études sur Beethoven, Gluck, et Weber: Mélanges et Nou-*

velles. The latter part of the title explains itself: the *Voyage musical* was that of Berlioz himself in Germany in 1843: the Italian chapters dealt with his experiences as Prix de Rome in the French Academy in Rome (and out of it) in 1831 and 1832. By 1848 this work was out of print. Berlioz took from it, for the purpose of his *Mémoires,* the ten letters that now form Chapters LII–LXI of the present edition of the latter work. Another letter, originally addressed to Mlle. Louise Bertin, was later used for the chapter entitled *Un début dans le Freischütz* in the *Soirées de l'orchestre,* issued in 1852. The more formal essays on musical subjects — the article on Music and the studies of Beethoven and Weber's *Freischütz* — went later into the volume *A travers chants* (1862). Another chapter of the *Voyage musical* became Chapter XV of the *Mémoires,* only the five introductory words being omitted.

The Italian portion of the *Voyage musical* contained an appendix consisting of five " *Variétés.*" Four of these — (1) *Le premier opéra,* (2) *Tribulations d'un critique,* (3) *Le suicide par enthousiasme, nouvelle vraie,* (4) *Le ténor, astronomie musicale, ses révolutions, son lever, son coucher, etc.,* — were later incorporated in the *Soirées de l'orchestre;* while the essays on *Le système dramatique de Gluck* and the two *Alcestes* went into *A travers chants.* Of the other fourteen chapters of the second volume of the *Voyage musical,* thirteen were worked into Chapters xiv, xxiii, xxx, xxxi, xxxii, xxxiii, xxxiv, xxxvi, xxxvii, xxxviii, xxxix, xli, xliii of the *Mémoires;* the remaining one, containing the story of Vincenza, was reserved for the *Soirées de l'orchestre.* In addition to all this material for the *Mémoires,* there were six letters to Humbert Ferrand, dealing with Berlioz's second tour in Germany (in the spring of 1846), which had already seen the light in the *Débats,* and an account of his trip to Russia in the spring of 1847, an opportunity for the publication of which had not yet presented itself. Other chapters for the autobiography, such as the account of Lesueur, had been published in the *Gazette musicale* between 1834 and 1842. So that all Berlioz had to do in 1848 was to add the sketch of his earliest years, up to the date of his settling in Paris, and to fill in a blank here and there. As M. Edmond Hippeau says, " of the 109 pages of the *Mémoires* dealing with Berlioz's life from 1803 to 1830, only 44 are new." "Of the 433 pages that tell the story down to 1848, he has only 115 to write; while another 23 pages will suffice for the six years between 1848 and the first ' final ' date, 18 October 1854, especially as he mentions none of the artistic events of this period of his career, but confines himself to three events in his private life — the deaths of his father, his sister, and his wife. With the addition of a letter addressed to his biographer in 1858, which he reproduces as a *Postscript,* and the *Postface* added in 1864 and amplified by the copies of his *correspondance sentimentale,* there is enough matter for an octave volume of 500 pages."

The compilation of the *Mémoires* as he had planned them in 1848 seems to have occupied him fairly continuously from that year until 1854. The *Postscript* is dated 25 May 1858, and in that year some extracts from the work were issued in the *Monde illustré.* The *Postface* and the account of his journey to Dauphiné, with the copies of his letters to Mme. Fournier, complete the work, which bears the final date 1 January 1865. The pages were sent to the printer not long after this: 1200 copies were struck off at Berlioz's expense, and the whole of them stored in his librarian's room at the Conservatoire. The book was not to be published till after his death: this occurred on 8 March 1869, and the *Mémoires* appeared in 1870.

The present edition of the *Mémoires* owes its origin to a suggestion by Mr. Alfred Knopf, some years ago, that I should write for him a new life of Berlioz. That I declined to do, on the ground that no life by any other hand will ever be able to bear comparison, as a piece of literature, with the autobiography; all the other Berlioz Lives we have are merely, for the most part, a watering down into the author's inferior style of the sparkling prose of Berlioz himself. I brought Mr. Knopf round to my own view that all that was needed was a re-issue of the *Mémoires* with the gaps in the story filled in, a few necessary dates added, and the occasional inaccuracies corrected in the light of the fuller knowledge afforded by the composer's letters and by other contemporary documents. I have kept my own contributions down to the indispensable minimum. The reader will bear in mind that this is not a new *Life and Times of Hector Berlioz* but a fresh edition of the *Mémoires.* Had I expanded the story and the references to contemporaries as they might have been expanded at a thousand points, at least another volume would have had to be added to the present one. My general object has been to let Berlioz speak for himself, only correcting or supplementing him where that is absolutely necessary. Much valuable work has been done during the last twenty years in the way of reconstructing Berlioz from his autobiography and letters. But even more valuable than all this is the self-portrait given us in the *Mémoires*. Of the highest interest and value, again, are the pictures given of the European musical world during the fifty years or so of Berlioz's working life; when we have noted, with due respect, the opinion of this modern biographer or that on the errors and extravagancies of the romantic and post-romantic periods, we turn back, with keener interest than ever, to the picture of those periods as they presented themselves to a highly sensitive artist and incomparable writer who lived through them.

Messrs. Macmillan and Company were kind enough to waive their rights in the Misses Holmes' translation of the *Mémoires,* which appeared in 1884. I found, however, when I commenced work on the present edition, that it was utterly impossible to reprint these ladies' version as it stood. It teems with linguistic errors; it often weakens Berlioz's vivid and pungent prose by a tepid English half-equivalent; and there are sundry vital omissions — passages that were a little too realistic for the chaste Victorian pen. While, therefore, the basis of the older version has been maintained in this edition, I have had to subject almost every paragraph to a drastic revision.

The few notes of the Misses Holmes that I have retained are indicated by an [H.], and Berlioz's own notes by a [B.]. The remaining notes are mine.

E. N.

Author's Preface

THE notices of my life which have from time to time appeared are so crowded with errors and inaccuracies as at length to suggest to me that I myself should record those portions of my agitated and laborious career which may be interesting to the lovers of art. Such a retrospective study will afford me the opportunity of giving my opinion on the difficulties which at present beset the career of a composer, and of tendering some useful advice to my brethren.

Portions of my travels have been already included in a book published many years ago, which also contained some fragments of criticism; but this is now out of print.[1]

I have been often urged to rearrange and complete these rough notes; and if at length I yield to the request it is not from any misconception of the value of such work. I have no belief that the public at large cares at all what I may do, or feel, or think. But a certain number of musical artists and amateurs have shown some curiosity on the subject, and it is certainly better to tell them the truth than to allow them to believe what is wrong. I have not the least wish either *to appear before God book in hand as the best of men,* or to write "*Confessions.*" I shall say only what I choose to say; and if the reader refuses me his absolution he must be of a severely orthodox turn, as I have none but venial sins to confess.

But time presses, and I must conclude. Republicanism is at this moment passing like a vast roller over the face of the Continent. Musical art, which has been long dying, is now dead, and will soon be

[1] *Voyage musical en Allemagne et en Italie. Études sur Beethoven, Gluck, et Weber. Mélanges et Nouvelles.* Par Hector Berlioz. Paris: Jules Labitte, Libraire-Éditeur, No. 3, Quai Voltaire. 1844. 2 vols. 8vo.

buried, or thrown on the dust-heap. For me France and Germany exist no longer. Russia is too remote, I can never go there again. England, since my first visit, has shown me much noble and cordial hospitality. But with the first shocks of that earthquake which has overturned so many European thrones, England became the centre for streams of terrified artists, arriving from all points of the compass, like frightened sea-birds before a storm. How long will the metropolis of Great Britain be able to maintain so many refugees? Will not their mournful accents be drowned by the acclamations of the neighbouring nations, as each sovereign people is crowned? Nay! how long will the English themselves resist the contagion? *Jam proximus ardet Ucalegon!* who knows what resort may be left to me before a few months are over? There is no longer any certain subsistence for myself and my family. Every minute is precious, and before long I may have to imitate the stoical resignation of the Indians of Niagara, who, finding their best efforts against the current useless, measure with steady glance the short distance which separates them from the edge, and disappear over the cataract into the abyss beneath, with a song in their mouths.

H. B.

London, *March 21st*, 1848.

Life's but a walking shadow; a poor player,
That struts and frets his hour upon the stage,
And then is heard no more : it is a tale
Told by an idiot, full of sound and fury,
Signifying nothing.

SHAKESPEARE (*Macbeth*).

Contents

Contents

~~~~~~

Second Visit to Germany

(AUSTRIA—BOHEMIA—HUNGARY)

Russian Journey

$\mathscr{I}$llustrations

xxiii

HECTOR BERLIOZ IN 1867
(from a photograph made in St. Petersburg)

Memoirs of
Hector Berlioz

BERLIOZ'S BIRTHPLACE, AT LA CÔTE-SAINT-ANDRÉ

Memoirs of Hector Berlioz

CHAPTER I

LA CÔTE-SAINT-ANDRÉ — FIRST COMMUNION — FIRST MUSICAL EXPERIENCE

[LONDON, March 21, 1848.

I WAS born on the 11th of December, 1803, at La Côte-Saint-André, a very small town in France, situated in the department of the Isère, between Vienne, Grenoble, and Lyons. During the months which preceded my birth, my mother never dreamt, as Virgil's did, that she was about to bring forth a branch of laurel. However painful to my *amour propre* this confession may be, I ought to add that neither did she imagine, like Olympias, the mother of Alexander, that she bore within her a fiery brand. Strange, I admit, but true. I came into the world quite naturally, unheralded by any of the signs which, in poetic ages, preceded the advent of remarkable personages.

La Côte-Saint-André is built, as its name indicates, on the slope of a hill, overlooking a rich, golden, fertile plain, the silence of which has an unspeakable, dreamy majesty, intensified by the chain of mountains bounding it on the east and west. Behind these again rise, in the distance, the gigantic snow-capped peaks of the Alps.

I need scarcely state that I was brought up as a member of the Holy Catholic and Apostolic Church of Rome. Since she has ceased to inculcate the burning of heretics, her creeds are charming. I held them happily for seven years; and, though we quarrelled long ago, I still retain the tenderest recollections of that form of religious belief. Indeed, I feel such sympathy for it that had I had the misfortune to

be born in the midst of one of those ponderous schisms evolved by
Luther or Calvin, my first rush of poetical enthusiasm would have
driven me straight into the arms of the beautiful Roman faith. I made
my first communion on the same day as my eldest sister, and in the
Convent of the Ursulines, where she was being brought up. It is
probably owing to this curious circumstance that I retain so tender a
recollection of that religious ceremony. The almoner came to fetch
me at six o'clock, and I felt deeply stirred as we crossed the threshold
of the church. It was a bright spring morning, the wind was murmuring softly in the poplars, and the air was full of a subtle fragrance.
Kneeling in the midst of a multitude of white-robed maidens we
awaited the solemn moment, and, when the priest advanced and
began to intone the service, all our thoughts were fixed on God. I was
rudely awakened by the priest summoning me to take precedence of
all those fair young girls, and go up to the altar first. Blushing at this
act of discourtesy, I went up to receive the sacrament. As I did so the
choir burst forth into the eucharistic hymn. At the sound of those
virginal voices I was overwhelmed with a sudden rush of mystic
passionate emotion. A new world of love and feeling was revealed
to me, more glorious by far than the heaven of which I had heard so
much; and, strange proof of the power of true expression and the
magical influence of real feeling, I found out ten years afterwards
that the melody which had been so naïvely adapted to sacred words
and introduced into a religious ceremony was Nina's song, *Quand le
bien-aimé reviendra!* What joy filled my young soul, dear Dalayrac!
And yet your ungrateful country has almost forgotten your name.

This was my first musical experience, and in this manner I suddenly became religious; so religious that I attended mass every day
and the communion every Sunday; and my weekly confession to the
director of my conscience was, " My father, *I have done nothing* "; to
which the worthy man always replied, " Go on, my child, as you have
begun "; and so I did for several years.

CHAPTER II

MY FATHER—LITERARY EDUCATION—PASSION FOR
TRAVELLING—VIRGIL—FIRST POETICAL
IMPRESSIONS

MY father, Louis Berlioz,[1] was a doctor. It is not for me to estimate his abilities; but I may say that he inspired great confidence both in our own and in the neighbouring towns. He was keenly sensitive to the responsibilities of his profession, and believed that in the practice of so dangerous and difficult an art as medicine it behoved him to devote every spare moment to mastering it, since the life of his fellow-creatures was dependent on his skill. He was a credit to his profession, which he regarded more as an opportunity for doing good to the poor than as a means of emolument to himself. In 1810 my father gained the prize offered by the medical society of Montpellier for an essay on " Chronic Diseases." It was published in Paris, and several cele-brated physicians appropriated his ideas without acknowledgment. My father was aware of this, and it astonished him; but he always said, " What matter, so long as truth triumphs? " He is too old to practise now, and passes his time in reading and meditation.

He is a free-thinker — that is to say, he has no prejudices, social, political, or religious; but he promised my mother so solemnly to do nothing to unsettle the faith which she regarded as indispensable to my salvation, that he sometimes even heard me my catechism. I

[1] Hector's father, Louis (9 June, 1776–August, 1848), was the son of Louis Joseph Berlioz (1747–1815). Louis married the twenty-one-year-old Marie Antoinette Josephine Marmion on 6 February, 1802. Their children were:
  1. Hector (b. 11 December, 1803, d. 8 March, 1869).
  2. Marguerite Anne Louise ["Nanci"] (b. 17 February, 1806, d. 1856).
  3. Louise Virginie (b. 29 November, 1807, d. 16 April, 1815).
  4. Adèle (b. 9 May, 1814, d. 2 March, 1860).
  5. Louis Joseph Félix (b. 15 December, 1816, d. 29 May, 1819).
  6. Prosper (b. 25 June, 1820, d. 15 January, 1839).
Berlioz's favourite sister all his life was Adèle. She married a notary of Vienne, M. Suat. To her two little daughters Berlioz dedicated the first part of *L'Enfance du Christ*. Nanci married, in 1832, a Grenoble magistrate, M. Pal. She had literary pretensions, and from 1824 to 1832 kept a Journal to which we are indebted for sundry details concerning Hector and his friend Humbert Ferrand.
Prosper was a child whose eccentricities bordered at times on the degenerate. There was a good deal of Hector in him, without Hector's saving quality of a sanity that generally maintained its control in the maddest episodes.

confess that I am quite incapable of acting with such loyalty or philo-
sophic indifference towards my own son. My father has an incurable internal disease, which has often brought him to death's door. He eats
scarcely anything, and only keeps himself alive by constant and ever-
increasing doses of opium. Once, years ago, he was so maddened by
pain that he took thirty-two grains at a dose. " I don't mind telling
you," he said to me afterwards, " it was not to cure myself that I took
it." Instead of killing him, however, so large a dose relieved him instantly of his pain.

At ten [1] years old I was sent to a small school on the hill to learn
Latin; but my father soon took me away again and taught me himself.
My poor father! What a patient, unwearied, careful, clever teacher
of languages, literature, history, and geography he was! He even
taught me music, as we shall see presently.

What love is necessary to carry out such a task, and how few
fathers there are who could and would do it! Still I cannot but think
that a home education has in many respects fewer advantages than
that of a public school. Children are thrown almost exclusively into
the society of relations, servants, and a few chosen companions, instead
of being inured to the rough contact of their fellows; they are utterly
ignorant of the world and of the realities of life; and I know perfectly
well that at twenty-five I was still an awkward, ignorant child.

For a long time my father could not give me a taste for the classics,
and I hated having to learn even a few lines of Horace and Virgil by
heart every day. It was an immense mental effort, and I found it impossible to keep my mind fixed on my task. On the other hand, I spent
hours in studying maps, and in mastering the complicated contours
of the islands, capes, and straits of the southern seas and the Indian
Archipelago, pondering on the aspect of those remote regions, their
vegetation, their inhabitants, and their scenery, and longing intensely
to see them. It was the beginning of my love of travel and adventure.

My father often said to me that, though I knew the name of
every one of the Sandwich Islands, Moluccas, or Philippines, and the
Straits of Torres, Timor, Java, and Borneo, I did not know how
many departments there were in France. My interest in foreign countries, especially those in the other hemisphere, was whetted by reading all the books of travel, both ancient and modern, which I could

---

[1] According to M. Boschot, the records of the district show that this should be *six*. Hector
returned to his home about November, 1811.

lay hands on at home; and, had I chanced to live in a seaport town, I should certainly have run away to sea. My son has inherited my tastes. He is now in the navy, and I trust that he may distinguish himself in his profession.

Further acquaintance with La Fontaine and Virgil, however, caused my sea-dreams to pale before the beauties of poetry. The epic passion of the Latin poet first kindled my smouldering imagination. How often have I felt my heart throb and my voice quiver and break when construing the fourth book of the *Æneid* to my father! . . . One day I was intensely affected by the sound of my own voice uttering the translation of the line:

> At regina gravi jamdudum saucia cura.

I struggled on bravely till I came to the crisis, where Dido expires on her funeral pile, with the gifts and weapons of her betrayer heaped round her and the familiar couch bathed in her blood. But when I came to the despairing cries of the dying queen, " thrice rising on her elbow, thrice falling back," and had to describe her wounds, and the anguish of her heart rent with its fatal passion; the cries of her distracted sister and nurse, and all the details of her death of torture, which moved even the gods to pity — my lips quivered, I could scarcely stammer out the words; and when I reached the line:

> Quæsivit cœlo lucem, ingemuitque reperta,

the sublime vision of Dido, " seeking light from heaven, and moaning as she found it," overwhelmed me, and I broke down utterly.

With kind tact my father rose and shut the book, saying, " That will do, my boy, I am tired." I was intensely grateful to him for taking no notice of my emotion, and rushed away to vent my Virgilian grief in solitude.

CHAPTER III

MEYLAN — MY UNCLE — THE PINK SHOES — THE
HAMADRYAD OF SAINT EYNARD — LOVE AT
TWELVE YEARS OF AGE

I WAS twelve years old before the magic of music was revealed to me; but earlier than that I had experienced the pangs of that great passion which Virgil depicts with so much power. It came about in this wise. My maternal grandfather, who bore the same name as Walter Scott's hero, Marmion, had a country house at Meylan, three miles from Grenoble, near the frontier of Savoy. The village and the neighbouring hamlets, with the Isère valley winding below them, and the mountains of Dauphiné rising beyond, form one of the loveliest views I have ever beheld. My mother and sisters and I used to pay my grandfather a three weeks' visit at the end of the summer, and were sometimes joined there by my uncle, Felix Marmion. He was then deep in the brilliant vortex of the great Emperor, and came among us perfumed with gunpowder, and bearing on his person tangible traces of the battlefield. One time it was a bullet-wound in his foot, another time a splendid sabre-cut across his cheek, and then again a mere lance-thrust which needed healing. Our young cavalry adjutant never doubted that the Emperor's throne was as immovable as Mont Blanc; he was intoxicated with glory, and would gladly have laid down his life for his hero; he was a joyous, gallant, accomplished young fellow, who played the violin admirably, and sang opéra-comique music to perfection.

Above Meylan, and close under the steep wall of the mountain, lies a little white villa buried in gardens and vineyards, with a far-reaching outlook over the valley of the Isère; it is surrounded by rocky hills and woods; behind it rises the bold mass of the great St. Eynard rock; close by is a ruined tower, and it looks as if it were made to be the scene of a romance. This villa belonged to a Madame Gautier, who used to spend the summer there with two nieces, the younger of whom was called Estelle.[1] The name of itself would have attracted me because of its association with Florian's idyl (*Estelle et Némorin*),

---

[1] Her surname was Dubœuf. In later years she was Madame Fornier.

which I had discovered in my father's library and devoured in secret. The real Estelle was a tall, slight girl of eighteen, with splendid shining eyes, a mass of hair which might have waved on the casque of Achilles, and the feet — I will not say of a Spaniard, but of a thoroughbred Parisian — clad in a pair of pink shoes! You laugh? Well, I had never seen a pair of pink shoes before! I have forgotten the colour of her hair (I think it was black); but whenever I think of her I see a vision of large brilliant eyes and equally brilliant pink shoes.

The moment I set eyes on her I felt an electric shock; in fact, I fell in love with her, desperately, hopelessly. I had no wishes, no hopes, I had no idea what was the matter with me, but I suffered acutely and spent my nights in sleepless anguish. In the daytime I crept away like a wounded bird and hid myself in the maize-fields and the orchards. I was haunted by Love's ghostly companion, Jealousy, and suffered tortures when any man approached my idol; and it makes be shudder even now when I recall the ring of my uncle's spurs as he danced with her.

The spectacle of so young a child overwhelmed with a feeling so far beyond his years, seemed to afford all our neighbours the keenest amusement. Estelle was the first to discern my feelings, and she was, I am sure, more amused than anyone. One evening there was a large party at my aunt's; prisoner's base was proposed, and the guests were divided into two parties, the men choosing their companions. I was purposely called up first, but I dared not choose, and stood motionless with downcast eyes and beating heart, while they all laughed at me. At last Estelle took me by the hand and said, " Well then, I will choose. I take Mr. Hector! " Alas! the cruel girl, too, was laughing at me, as she stood looking down on me in her beauty. . . .

No, time itself is powerless . . . no after-loves can blot out the first. . . . I was but thirteen when I ceased to see her . . . I was thirty when, on my return from Italy, I caught sight of St. Eynard in the distance, the little white villa and the old tower, through a mist of tears. . . . I still loved her. . . . I heard that she was . . . married . . . and all the rest of it . . . and even that did not cure me. My mother used often to tease me about my childish love, and one day played me a trick which was scarcely kind. A few days after my return from Rome she handed me a letter, which she said she had been asked to deliver to a lady who was to pass through, in the Vienne diligence, in about an hour's time. " Go to the coach office, and, while they are changing the horses, ask for Mdme. F., and give her the letter. It is seventeen years since you saw her, but I am sure if you look at her carefully you will recognise her." . . . I had no suspicion of what awaited me, and when the coach drew up I went to the door and asked for Mdme. F. " It is I," said a voice, which I at once recognised with a throb of pain. Estelle! Estelle! still beautiful, Estelle, the nymph, the hamadryad of St. Eynard and the wooded hills of Meylan! It is indeed she, with her magnificent hair and her winning smile; but ah! where are the little pink shoes? She took the letter. Did she recognise me? Who can tell? The coach drove off, and I returned quivering with excitement to my mother, who, on seeing my face, said, " Ah, I see, Némorin has not forgotten his Estelle! " *His* Estelle! cruel mother!

CHAPTER IV

FIRST MUSIC-LESSONS FROM MY FATHER — ATTEMPTS
AT COMPOSITION — ANATOMICAL STUDIES —
ANTIPATHY TO MEDICINE — DEPAR-
TURE FOR PARIS

WHEN I stated that love and music had been revealed to me at twelve years old, I should rather have said " composition," because my father had already taught me to read music at sight and to play two instruments. I had discovered a flageolet hidden away in a drawer, and made the most futile efforts to pick out the popular air of *Malbrouk* upon it. My father, annoyed at this tiresome tooting, begged me to lay aside the instrument until he could find time to teach me how to play the heroic strain I had selected, less discordantly. He did so; and I showed such aptitude that in two days I was able to perform my *Malbrouk* tune to the assembled family.

Does not this clearly prove my instinctive feeling for the great capabilities of wind instruments? . . . What thoroughbred biographer would fail to draw the inevitable conclusion from such an incident? . . . This induced my father to teach me to read music; he initiated me into its first principles, and gave me a clear idea of musical signs and their meaning. He then explained the mechanism of the flute, and taught me to play it by means of Devienne's method, and I worked so hard that in seven months I could play fairly well.

My father then combined with some other families of the Côte to get a master from Lyons, and the services of the second violin of the Théâtre des Célestins were secured. He played the clarinet also; and the promise of a certain number of pupils, and of a fixed salary as conductor of the military band of the Garde Nationale, tempted him to come and settle in our Philistine town and be the pioneer of musical culture among us. His name was Imbert,[1] and he gave me two lessons every day; I had a pretty soprano voice, and soon became a fearless reader and a fair singer, and could play Drouet's most complicated concertos on the flute. I had struck up a friendship with my master's son, who was a little my senior, and an accomplished cornet player. One morning, when I was going to Meylan, he came to see me. " You were going away without saying good-bye. I may never see you again." I marvelled at the strange solemnity of his leave-taking; but the delight of seeing Meylan and the radiant *Stella montis* once more soon drove all other thoughts away. What sad tidings greeted my return! On the very day of my departure young Imbert had hanged himself in the house while his parents were out, and the motive for his suicide has never been fathomed.

I had discovered Rameau's treatise on harmony, annotated and simplified by D'Alembert, among some old books, and spent sleepless nights in fruitless efforts to unravel its mysteries. I have since discovered that, in order to grasp the author's meaning, the student must not only have completely mastered the theory of chords, but must also have deeply studied the subject of experimental physics, on which the system is based. It is therefore a treatise on harmony solely for the use of those who already know harmony.

Still, I was longing to compose. I arranged duets and trios with impossible basses and more impossible chords; but by dint of listening to Pleyel's quartets, as played by our local amateurs on Sundays, and studying Catel's treatise on harmony, I at last, and as it were suddenly, obtained some insight into the mystery of the formation and connection of chords. I instantly wrote a *pot-pourri* in six parts on a collection of Italian airs which I possessed. The harmony seemed tolerable, and I undertook the composition of a quintet for flute and strings, which was performed by three friends, my master, and myself.

[1] He came to the Côte in 1817. Dorant succeeded him in July 1819.

My triumph was great; but my father did not seem to share in the general enthusiasm. Two months later another quintet was produced. My father was like many people who think they can judge of a quartet by hearing the first violin part, and asked me to play him over the flute part beforehand. I did so, and at a particular passage he called out, " Bravo! that *is* music! " But this quintet, which was much more ambitious than the first, was also much more difficult, our amateurs were unable to cope with it, and the viola and 'cello blundered about most hopelessly.

As I was twelve and a half years old at this time, it is evident that the biographers who have lately asserted that I did not know my notes when I was twenty are curiously mistaken. I burnt the two quintets some years later,[1] but it is a remarkable fact that long afterwards, when composing my first orchestral work in Paris, the phrase my father approved of came back to me, and I embodied it in my new composition. It is the melody in A flat major given out by the first violins soon after the beginning of the *allegro* in the *Francs-Juges* overture.[2]

Shortly after his son's sad and mysterious death poor Imbert returned to Lyons, where I think he died. He was soon replaced at

[1] The youthful Berlioz never lacked assurance. In March 1819, at the age of fifteen and a quarter, he suggested to the Paris publishers Janet and Cotelle that they should publish at their expense a quintet of his for two violins, viola, cello and flute. "Reply as quickly as possible," he exhorts them . . ."while you are engraving this work I can send you some romances with piano accompaniment . . . on the same conditions." Twelve days later he makes a similar assault on Pleyel, of Paris: "Monsieur, As I am thinking of having some musical works of my own composition engraved, I turn to you, hoping you will be able to fulfil my purpose. I should like you to take from me a *pot-pourri concertant*, composed of selected pieces, and arranged for flute, horn, two violins, viola and bass. See if you can do this, and how many copies you can give me. Please tell me as soon as possible, if you are agreeable, how long it will take you to engrave the work, and if it is necessary for me to frank the parcel."

From each publisher he seems to have met with a polite refusal of the intended honour.

[2] The melody runs thus:

The reader will note a certain family resemblance to the theme of the *idée fixe* in the *Symphonie fantastique*. The resemblance between the two themes, says Mr. Tom Wotton in his admirable booklet on Berlioz (Oxford University Press), "is unmistakable, though of course no proof that the two melodies are contemporaneous, however strong the probability. But there is nothing improbable in the *idée fixe* being connected with Estelle. Towards the end of his life (in 1865) Berlioz told both Mme Fornier (Estelle) and the Princess Sayn-Wittgenstein that the former the Côte by a far more talented man named Dorant.[1] Dorant was an Alsatian from Colmar, and could play almost every instrument, though he excelled on the clarinet, double-bass, violin, and guitar. He taught my elder sister, who had a good voice but absolutely no musical gift, to play the guitar. She is fond of music, but has never been able to read or make out even the simplest air. I used to be present at her lessons: then I wanted to take some myself: and at last Dorant, who was an honest man and a true artist, said one day to my father, " Sir, I cannot go on teaching your son to play the guitar ! " " Why? Has he annoyed you? or is he so lazy that he won't learn? " " Neither; but it is useless to go on teaching him when he already plays as well as I do myself."

I was thus a past-master on those majestic and incomparable instruments, the flageolet, the flute, and the guitar. Does not this fortuitous choice look like the instinctive action of nature urging me towards the most powerful orchestral effects and the Michael Angelesque in music? . . . The flute, the guitar, and the flageolet ! ! ! These are the only instruments I play, but they seem to me by no means contemptible. No, I am wrong: I can also play the drum.

My father did not wish me to learn the piano,[2] otherwise I should doubtless have swelled the ranks of the innumerable army of famous pianists.

He had no intention of making an artist of me; and I dare say he thought that if I learnt the piano I should devote myself too

---

had inspired certain striking phrases of long ago, when she was far from thinking of him. To the latter he instanced the principal theme of the Love Scene of the *Romeo and Juliet* symphony as one of those phrases."

For the reader's guidance I append the *idée fixe* from the *Symphonie fantastique:*

[1] We meet with Dorant again in *Les Grotesques de la Musique.* In 1845 Berlioz was giving a concert in Lyons. He ran into Dorant in the street, and, at the latter's request, drafted him into the orchestra. At the rehearsal next day, Berlioz introduced him thus: "Gentlemen, I have the honour to present to you M. Dorant, a very able professor from Vienne. Among us there is a grateful pupil of his — myself. Perhaps you will soon be able to decide for yourselves that I am no great honour to him, but all the same, please welcome M. Dorant as if you thought otherwise, and in the way he deserves."

[2] It is said there was not a single piano at Côte-Saint-André.

passionately to it, and become more absorbed in music than he wished or intended me to be. I have often felt the want of this accomplishment, and it might have been of the greatest use to me; but when I consider the appalling number of miserable musical platitudes to which the piano has given birth, which would never have seen the light had their authors been confined to pen and paper, I feel grateful to the happy chance which forced me to compose freely and in silence, and has thus delivered me from the tyranny of the fingers, so dangerous to thought, and from the fascination which the ordinary sonorities always exercise on a composer, more or less. Many amateurs have pitied me for this deprivation, but that does not affect me much.

My youthful compositions all bore the stamp of profound melancholy;[1] almost all my melodies were in minor keys; and although I knew this to be a defect, I could not help it. My thoughts seemed to be veiled in crape; they had all been tinged by the Meylan love affair. As, during this state of mind, I was for ever reading Florian's *Estelle,* I was pretty certain to end by setting to music some of the numerous romances in this pastoral, the insipidity of which seemed to me at that time so sweet. As a matter of fact, I did. Among my settings was one very sad one, to some words which expressed my despair at leaving the woods and the spots which had been " honorés par les pas, éclairés par les yeux," and, I might add, by the pink shoes of my cruel fair one. And as I sit here in London, absorbed in business of importance, harrowed with anxiety, raging against the absurd obstacles which pursue me even here, a faint ray of sunshine recalls the sickly words to my mind. Here is the first verse:

> Je vais donc quitter pour jamais
> Mon doux pays, ma douce amie,
> Loin d'eux je vais traîner ma vie
> Dans les pleurs et dans les regrets !
> Fleuve dont j'ai vue l'eau limpide,
> Pour réfléchir ses doux attraits,
> Suspendre sa course rapide,
> Je vais vous quitter pour jamais.[2]

[1] There exists in Côte-Saint-André a manuscript of romances with guitar accompaniment, made by Berlioz at this period. The majority are copies of romances by Dalayrac, Berton, Boieldieu and others. Six are signed *** in place of a composer's name. M. Boschot, however, does not believe these to be compositions of Berlioz himself; printed music, especially in the remote provinces, was scarce in those days, and it is possible that the asterisks merely indicate that Berlioz copied from a manuscript copy in which the composer's name was not given.

Another manuscript, presumably in the handwriting of Dorant, contains a copy of the then celebrated romance, *Fleuve du Tage*, "accompagnement de guitare par Hector Berlioz."

The song was burnt, with the sextet and the quintets, before I went to Paris; but when I began to write my *Symphonie fantastique,* in 1829, the melody came back to me, and, as it seemed to express the overwhelming grief of a young heart in the pangs of a hopeless passion, I welcomed it. It is the air for the first violins at the opening of the *largo* in the first part of the work — *Rêveries, Passions;* I put it in just as it was.[1]

While engaged in these experiments, and absorbed in reading, geography, religion, and the storms and calms of my first love affair, the time approached for me to choose a career. My father intended me to follow his profession, which he considered the finest in the world; and had told me so long before. I had often expressed my contrary views on the subject most emphatically, and he thoroughly disapproved of them. I had as yet no very definite ideas; but I felt a strong presentiment that I was not intended to spend my life at the bedsides of sick people, in hospitals, or in dissecting-rooms, and was firmly determined to resist all attempts to make a doctor of me. About this time I read the lives of Gluck and Haydn in the *Biographie universelle,* and they excited me immensely. " What a glorious existence! " I said to myself, as I thought of their illustrious careers; " what an art, and what happiness to be able to live for it! " An apparently trifling incident strengthened my bent in this direction, and shot a sudden light into my soul that revealed to me a thousand strange and splendid musical horizons.

I had never seen a full score. The only pieces of music I knew were *solfeggios* accompanied by a figured bass, solos for the flute, or bits of

There appears to be no doubt that the harmonisation of this is the first essay in composition by Berlioz that has survived.

    [2] La Fontaine. *Les Deux Pigeons.* [B.] The quotation, however, is from Florian's *Estelle et Némorin.*

    [1] The melody runs thus:

M. Julien Tiersot has shown that the words of the poem can be fitted to the notes, except at the finish, where "the end of the musical phrase is lost in the symphonic development."

It is significant that when Berlioz, in his old age, was preparing his *Mémoires* for the Press, he placed under his photograph a transcription of the opening bars of this melody in his own handwriting.

operas with pianoforte accompaniment. One day, however, I found
a sheet of paper with twenty-four staves ruled upon it. I realised in a
moment the wondrous instrumental and vocal combinations to which
they might give rise, and I cried out, "What an orchestral work one
might write on that!" From this moment the musical fermentation in
my head went on increasing, and my distaste for medicine redoubled.
But I was far too much afraid of my parents to venture to impart
my wild dreams to them, and one day my father suddenly determined to
use my love of music as a lever for removing what he called a " childish
aversion," and by one masterstroke to embark me at once on the study
of medicine.

In order to familiarise me with the things I was soon to have constantly before my eyes, he spread out in his study Munro's enormous
treatise on osteology, with life-size illustrations of the structure of
the body.

" This is the work you are to study," he said to me. " I do not
suppose you will persist in your prejudice against medicine, for it is
unreasonable and wholly unfounded, and if you promise to work earn-
estly at osteology I will get you a splendid flute, with all the new keys,
from Lyons."

I had long coveted such an instrument, and what could I say? . . .
The earnestness of the proposal, the mingled respect and fear with
which, in spite of all his kindness, my father inspired me, and the
promised reward, were too much for me. I stammered out a faint
Yes, fled into my room, and threw myself on my bed overwhelmed
with grief.

Become a doctor! study anatomy! dissect! witness horrible operations! instead of throwing myself heart and soul into the glorious and
beautiful art of music! Forsake the empyrean for the dreary realities
of earth! the immortal angels of poetry and love and their inspired
songs for filthy hospitals, dreadful medical students, hideous corpses,
the shrieks of patients, the groans and death rattle of the dying! . . .
It seemed to me the utter reversal of the natural conditions of my life;
horrible and impossible. Yet it came to pass.

My osteological studies were undertaken in company with my cousin
A. Robert, since become a great Paris doctor, who had also become my
father's pupil. Unfortunately Robert played the violin very well, and
was one of my performers in the quintets, so that we spent more time at
music than at anatomy. But he worked so hard at home that he always

knew his demonstrations much better than I did. This called forth severe rebukes and even fierce bursts of anger from my father. Still, partly by my own efforts, partly by coercion, with the aid of prepared skeletons, I at last learnt in a kind of way all my father could teach me about anatomy; and at nineteen,[1] encouraged by my fellow-student, I decided to go with him to Paris, and there enter upon my medical studies in earnest.

10th April, 1848. — Here I pause for a moment before beginning the story of my Parisian life and of the bitter war against men, ideas, and things which I waged almost from the moment I arrived there, and have carried on ever since. The reader will grant me breathing-time. Besides, the demonstration of the two hundred thousand English Chartists is to take place to-day, and perhaps in a few hours England will have undergone the same upheaval as the rest of Europe, and even this shelter will be denied me. I am going out to watch the course of events.

8 P.M. — Well, the Chartists are a good type of revolutionists. Everything went off well. The cannons, those powerful orators, those mighty logicians whose irresistible arguments get right into the masses, were in the chair. But they had no necessity to make their voices heard; their mere presence was enough to convince everyone of the inexpediency of a revolution, and the Chartists dispersed in perfect order.

Excellent creatures! About as fit to carry out an insurrection as the Italians are to write symphonies! The Irish are probably just the same, as O'Connell well knew when he used to say to them, " Agitate, agitate, but don't act."

12th July. — I have found it impossible to go on with my memoirs during the last three months. I am just going back to the unhappy country which is still called France, and which is, after all, my native land. I am going to see how an artist can live there, or how long it will take him to die amidst the ruins which have crushed and buried the flower of art. Farewell, England! . . .

France, 16*th July*, 1848. — Here I am back again! Paris has buried her dead. The paving-stones from the barricades are laid down in their places again, only, perhaps, to be up again to-morrow.

---

[1] The date was the end of October 1821, so that Hector was not quite eighteen. He took out his passport on 26 October: he is there described as "about five feet three or four inches in height, blond hair, blond eyebrows, beginning to grow a beard, forehead ordinary, eyes grey, complexion high." His hair was really red.

The moment I arrived I rushed off to the Faubourg St. Antoine. What a sight! what hideous ruins! Even the Genius of Liberty on the top of the column of the Bastille has a bullet through her body. The fallen trees, the crumbling houses, the squares, the streets, the quays, seem still quivering with the murderous struggle! . . . Fancy thinking of Art at such a period of wild folly and bloody orgies! . . . All the theatres are closed; all the artists are ruined; all the teachers are idle, all the pupils have fled; poor pianists play sonatas in the squares; historical painters sweep the streets; architects are mixing mortar on the public works. . . . The Assembly has just voted fairly considerable sums towards the opening of the theatres, and in addition has granted some slight relief to the more unfortunate among the artists. But how inadequate this to meet the wants especially of musicians! Some of the first violins at the Opéra only had thirty-six pounds a year, and were hard put to it to live even by giving lessons in addition. They could not possibly have saved much; and now that their pupils are gone, what is to become of the poor creatures? They will not be transported (although for the most part their only chance of gaining a livelihood would be in places like America, India, or Sydney), for it would cost the Government too dear; to get a free passage one must have deserved it, and all our artists fought against the insurgents, and charged the barricades. . . .

Is not this horrible confusion of justice and injustice, of good and evil, truth and falsehood, in which words seem perverted from their original meaning, enough to drive one mad? . . .

I may as well go on with my autobiography: I have nothing better to do, and in recalling the past I may forget the present.

CHAPTER V

A YEAR OF MEDICAL STUDIES—PROFESSOR AMUSSAT
—A PERFORMANCE AT THE OPÉRA—THE CON-
SERVATOIRE LIBRARY—IRRESISTIBLE
ATTRACTION TOWARDS MUSIC—MY
FATHER REFUSES TO LET ME
ADOPT IT AS A PROFESSION
—FAMILY DISCUSSIONS

WHEN I arrived in Paris in 1822 [1] with my fellow-student, Alphonse
Robert, I gave myself up entirely to preparation for the career which
had been forced upon me, and faithfully kept the promise given to
my father at parting. But I was sorely tried when Robert announced
one morning that he had bought a *subject* (a corpse), and asked me
to accompany him to the dissecting-room at the Hospital de la Pitié.
When I entered that fearful human charnel-house, littered with fragments of limbs, and saw the ghastly faces and cloven heads, the bloody
cesspool in which we stood, with its reeking atmosphere, the swarms
of sparrows fighting for scraps, and the rats in the corners gnawing
bleeding vertebræ, such a feeling of horror possessed me that I leapt
out of the window, and fled home as though Death and all his hideous
crew were at my heels. It was twenty-four hours before I recovered
from the shock of this first impression, utterly refusing to hear the
words anatomy, dissection, or medicine, and firmly resolved to die
rather than enter the career which had been forced upon me.

Robert wasted much eloquence in combating my disgust and
demonstrating the absurdity of my plans. But he finally induced me
to make another effort, and I consented to return to the hospital and
face the dread scene once more. How strange! I now merely felt cold
disgust at the sight of the same things which had before filled me
with such horror; I had become as callous to the revolting scene as a
veteran soldier. It was all over. I even found some pleasure in rum-
maging in the gaping breast of an unfortunate corpse for the lungs,
with which to feed the winged inhabitants of that charming place.[2]

[1] See note on p. 17.
[2] In one of his curious volumes—*Mœurs intimes du passé*, 4th series—Dr. Cabanès

" Well done! " cried Robert, laughing; " you are growing quite humane! *Aux petits des oiseaux tu donnes la pâture.*"

" *Et ma bonté s'étend sur toute la nature,*" I retorted, casting a shoulder-blade to a great rat who was staring at me with famished eyes. And so I went on with my course of anatomy, stoically, if not enthusiastically. I was strongly attracted by Professor Amussat, who seemed possessed by the same passion for medicine that I felt for music, and was an artist in anatomy. The fame of this bold scientific explorer has spread all over Europe, and his discoveries have aroused the wonder and opposition of the learned world. Day and night are not long enough for his researches, and, although exhausted by his labours, he pursues his dangerous way with dogged determination. All his traits are those of a man of genius: I often see him, and I love him.

I afterwards found complete compensation in the classes of Thénard, the professor of chemistry, and of Gay-Lussac, professor of physics in the Jardin des Plantes, and in a course of literature in which Andrieux captivated his audience by his subtle simplicity, and in which I took ever-increasing interest. I was thus in a fair way to swell the ranks of the medical students, and might have added another name to the long list of bad doctors but for a visit I paid to the Opéra. There I saw *Les Danaïdes,* by Salieri. The gorgeous splendour of the spectacle, the rich fulness of the orchestra and the chorus, the wonderful voice and pathetic charm of Madame Branchu, Dérivis' rugged power, the air of Hypermnestre, in which I seemed to trace the features of Gluck's style, according to the ideal I had formed from some fragments of his *Orfeo* in my father's library, finally the crashing bacchanal and the voluptuously dreamy dance-music added by Spontini to the score of his countryman, filled me with excitement and enthusiasm. I was like a lad with the inborn instincts of a sailor, who, never having seen anything but fishing-boats on a lake, suddenly finds himself transported

---

reprints an interesting contemporary document descriptive of the life of a Paris medical student in 1830, a life which, we may be sure, is that of the young Berlioz down to the smallest detail. We see the medical student in the lecture room, at the hospital, acquiring, by more or less devious devices, his "subject" for dissection, in his sordid lodgings in the Rue Saint-Jacques or Rue de la Harpe, somehow or other supporting life on an incredibly small allowance from his family, taking his grisette to a ball, and even treating himself to an occasional performance by Talma or a hearing of *Robert the Devil* or *Sylphide.* These last expensive luxuries he obtains by joining the claque for the evening.

to a three-decker in mid-ocean. I hardly slept a wink the night after that performance, and my anatomy lesson the next morning suffered in proportion. I sang the air of Danäus, *Jouissez du destin propice,* while sawing away at the skull of my " subject "; and when Robert, irritated by my constantly humming *Descends dans le sein d'Amphi-trite* when I should have been reading a chapter of Bichat, cried, " Do attend to your work; we are not getting on at all, our subject will be spoiled in three days; eighteen francs wasted. You must really be sensible!" I retorted by singing the hymn of Nemesis, *Divinité de sang avide!* and the scalpel fell from his hands.

I went to the Opéra again the following week, and saw Méhul's *Stratonice,* and Persuis ballet of *Nina.*[1] I admired the overture to *Stratonice* very much, and also the air for Seleucus, *Versez tous vos chagrins,* and the quartet in the conference; but as a whole the work seemed to me rather cold. I was, however, delighted with the ballet, and greatly touched by hearing the hymn which my sister's companions had sung at the Convent of the Ursulines, on the day of my first communion, played on the *cor anglais* by Vogt, during Mademoiselle Bigottini's harrowing pantomime. It was the song, *Quand le bien-aimé reviendra.*[2] The man next me, who was humming the words, told me the name of the opera and the author from whom Persuis had borrowed

[1] He also heard, and was delighted with, Boïeldieu's *Les Voitures versées,* and Dalayrac's *Azémia ou les sauvages.*

[2] See p. 4. Dalayrac's one-act opera *Nina, ou la Folle par Amour,* dealing with the story of a young girl who lost her reason because she believed her lover, who had been beaten in a duel, to be dead, was produced at Paris on 15 May, 1786. The work was eclipsed by Paisiello's later setting of an Italian version of the text (1787). Milon and Persuis turned it into a ballet in three acts (Paris, 23 November, 1813).

The reader may like to make the acquaintance of the melody that so affected a whole generation of French susceptibles:

Quand le bien - ai - mé re - vien - dra, Près de sa lan - guis - san - te a - mi - e, Le prin -

temps a - lors re - nai - tra, L'herbe se - ra tou - jours fleu - ri - e. Mais, je re -

gar - de, mais, je re - gar - de, hé - las! hé - las! Le bien - ai -

mé ne re - vient pas, Le bien - ai - mé ne re - vient pas! Hé - las! Hé - las!

the tune, and thus [1] I learnt that it was taken from Dalayrac's *Nina.*

However great may have been the power of the singer who created the part of Nina,[2] I find it difficult to believe that that song as sung by her could ever have made as true and touching an effect as the combination of Vogt's instrument and Bigottini's acting produced on me.

In spite of these temptations, and the hours I spent every evening in meditating on the melancholy contrast between my tastes and my studies, I persisted in this distracted life for some time longer without either making much progress in my medical studies, or sensibly increasing my scanty musical knowledge. I had given my promise and I kept it. But when I learnt that the library of the Conservatoire, with its wonderful wealth of scores, was open to the public, I could not resist the longing to become better acquainted with Gluck's works, for which I had an instinctive love, and which were not then being played at the Opéra. Once I entered that sanctuary I never quitted it. It was the death-blow to my medical career, and the dissecting-room was finally abandoned.

I was so completely absorbed by my love of music that, with all my admiration for Gay-Lussac and the fascinations of the experimental electricity which I had begun to study with him, I never went near him again.

I read and re-read Gluck's scores, copied them, learnt them by heart, in my enthusiasm forgot either to eat, drink, or sleep; simply raved about them. One day, after weary waiting, I at last succeeded in hearing the *Iphigénie en Tauride,* and I vowed as I left the Opéra that I would be a musician come what might, despite father, mother, uncles, aunts, grandparents, and friends. I actually wrote off on the spot and told my father how irresistibly strong my bent was, and besought him not to oppose it needlessly. He answered me by gentle arguments, assuring me I should soon see the folly of my ways, and quit the pursuit of a chimera to follow in the beaten track of a regular profession. But my father was wrong. The more he argued the more my determination was confirmed, and the correspondence became more angry and threatening on his side and hotter and hotter on mine, until it culminated in a perfect fury of passion.

---

[1] His memory seems to have been at fault on this point. According to M. Boschot, Berlioz had copied it some time previously into the manuscript of romances with guitar accompaniment that he had left at Côte-Saint-André.

[2] Madame Dugazon. [B.]

As Berlioz follows no settled plan in the chapters that follow, the chronology of them is confused and confusing. *The true sequence of events is as follows:*

1823, Spring:	*Berlioz writes to Kreutzer.*
June:	*The episode with Andrieux.*
August to	*Gerono writes libretto of* Estelle et Némorin.
December:	*Berlioz writes* Le Passage de la Mer Rouge. *A performance is planned for December 28, but the work gets no further than the first rehearsal.*
1824, January:	*Berlioz becomes* bachelier ès sciences physiques.
June:	*His father summons him to Côte-Saint-André. He writes to Lesueur that he has tried to compose a Mass, but the Credo and the Kyrie have left him so cold that he puts it on one side and retouches* Le Passage de la Mer Rouge, *which he hopes to give in the Church of St. Roch, Paris, on his return.*
July:	*Returns to Paris.*
Autumn:	*Writes a Mass, and works over* Le Passage de la Mer Rouge *once more. Probably some of the music of this is used for the Mass.*
December:	*Tries to borrow 1200 francs from Chateaubriand to perform his Mass.* Robin des Bois *in Paris.*
1825, January:	*Writes* La Révolution Grecque, *which he hopes to have performed at the Concerts spirituels.*
Spring:	*Completes the Mass. He is anxious to get a performance in order to impress his father, and so ensure the continuance of his allowance. Borrows 1200 francs from Pons for this purpose. The performance takes place on July 10th, 1825.*
December:	*Castil-Blaze produces his* La Fôret de Sénart *— a travesty of Weber's* Euryanthe.
1826, February:	*Weber in Paris.*

March: *Tries to get* La Révolution Grecque *produced
                    at the Concerts spirituels. Ferrand publishes
                    his libretto.
                    Berlioz fails at the first trial for the Prix de
                    Rome. His father stops his allowance and or-
                    ders him to return to the Côte; then he relents,
                    and Berlioz returns to Paris about the end of
                    July. His allowance of 120 francs a month is
                    continued, but Berlioz has to submit to priva-
                    tion in order to pay off his debt to Pons, which
                    now amounts to over 600 francs. (He had told
                    his father that the debt was only one quarter
                    of the actual amount, and that sum his father
                    had liquidated.)*

CHAPTER VI

I BECOME ONE OF LESUEUR'S PUPILS — HIS KINDNESS
— THE CHAPEL ROYAL

WHILE this bitter controversy was raging I had been busy composing, and had written among other things a cantata with full orchestral accompaniments on Millevoye's poem *Le Cheval Arabe*.

One of Lesueur's pupils, Gerono, whom I used often to meet at
the Conservatoire library, suggested that I should try to obtain
admission to his master's composition class, and offered to introduce
me to him. I was delighted at the idea, and went to M. Lesueur one
morning, armed with the score of my cantata and a canon for three
voices, which I regarded as an appropriate selection for this solemn
occasion. Lesueur was kind enough to read through the first of these
crude efforts carefully. He returned it to me with the remark: " There
is a good deal of power and dramatic feeling in your work, but you
don't know yet how to write, and your harmony is one mass of blunders. Gerono will teach you our principles of harmony, and when
you have mastered them sufficiently to follow me, I shall be glad to
receive you as a pupil." Gerono willingly accepted the task thus confided to him, and in a few weeks had indoctrinated me into the whole
system of Lesueur's theory of the production and succession of chords,
which is based on Rameau's system, and on his speculations on the

vibrations of a string. I inferred at once from the manner in which
Gerono laid down these principles that it was no use disputing their
value, for they constituted an article of religion in Lesueur's school, to
be accepted with unquestioning faith. Such is the force of example, however, that I soon became not only one of Lesueur's favorite pupils but
one of his most ardent disciples.[1] I am by no means ungrateful to the excellent and worthy master who guided my first tottering steps so kindly,
and remained my warm friend to his life's end. But what precious hours
I wasted — first, in studying his antediluvian theories, then in practising them, and, finally, in unlearning them, and beginning all over again
at the beginning! And now, when I come across one of his scores, I involuntarily avert my eyes with the same sort of instinctive impulse with
which one avoids the portrait of a lost friend. I had so admired
those little oratorios of Lesueur's at the Chapel Royal, and was so
grieved when I found my admiration failing! I feel so old and worn-
out and disenchanted as I recall the distant days when I used to go
every Sunday to the Tuileries to listen to them. How few of the celebrated artists I met there are alive now! How many others have descended into an oblivion that is worse than death! What struggles
and trials and troubles since that time! Those were the days of vast
enthusiasms, great musical passions, long dreams, unspeakable joys!
. . . When I entered the orchestra at the Chapel Royal, Lesueur
used to employ the interval before the service began in explaining the
plan and purpose of the music to me. Some knowledge of the composer's intention was indeed necessary, for it had rarely any connection with the words of the service. Lesueur wrote a vast number of
masses, and had also a particular affection for the beautiful stories of
the Old Testament, such as Naomi, Ruth and Boaz, Rachel, Deborah,
etc. . . ; these he rendered with so much truth of antique colouring
that in listening to them one forgot the thinness of their musical fabric,
the persistent imitation of the airs, duets, and trios of the old Italian
school, and the childish feebleness of the instrumentation. Lesueur
owes more of the development of his special talent to the Bible than
anything else, except, perhaps, Macpherson's poem (which he persisted in attributing to Ossian). I shared his tastes, and my imagination was possessed by the East — the calm of its vast deserts, the
grandeur of its immense ruins, its historic past, and its wonderful
legends.

[1] Berlioz became a pupil of Lesueur at the beginning of 1823.

The *Ite missa est* was followed by King Charles X's withdrawal, to a grotesque flourish of an enormous drum and a fife, in 5-time, worthy of the barbaric Middle Ages which had given it birth; and after this my master used often to take me for a long walk. Those were days of precious counsels and curious confidences. For my encouragement Lesueur used to tell me strange stories of his youth, of his first beginnings as conductor at Dijon, his admission to the Sainte Chapelle, his competition for the conductorship of the school at Notre Dame; of Méhul's enmity; the ill-treatment he met with from the *rapins* of the Conservatoire; the cabals against his opera, *La Caverne,* and Cherubini's noble conduct on that occasion; the friendship of Paisiello, who preceded him at the imperial chapel; the intoxicating favours lavished by Napoleon on the author of *Les Bardes*,[1] and the great man's historical *mots* on the subject of that work. My master told me also what difficulties he had in getting his first opera performed; his anxiety the first night it was played; the sadness and lassitude which followed its success; his desire to try his chance in the theatre again; his completion of the opera *Télémaque* in three months; Madame Scio's proud beauty when she appeared as Diana at the chase, and her irresistible impetuosity as Calypso. Then we had long arguments about his theory of fundamental bass and modulation, for he allowed me to argue with him when alone, and I sometimes abused this privilege. When we had exhausted musical topics we discussed philosophy and religion, and on these subjects also we generally differed. But there were some things about which we were both enthusiastic, and on which we were always certain to agree — Gluck, Virgil, and Napoleon. After these long talks by the Seine, or in the shady gardens of the Tuileries, I used to leave him, that he might indulge in the long, silent reveries which had become a necessity to him.

[1] The inscription engraved inside the gold casket which Lesueur received after the first performance of the opera runs thus: "The Emperor Napoleon to the Author of *Les Bardes*." [B.]

CHAPTER VII

A FIRST OPERA — M. ANDRIEUX — A FIRST MASS — M. DE CHATEAUBRIAND

SOME months after I had been admitted into Lesueur's special class (I had not yet got into the Conservatoire) I took it into my head to write an opera, and ventured to ask M. Andrieux,[1] the able professor with whom I had studied literature, for a book. I don't know what I said to him, but here is his answer:

" Your letter interested me keenly. Your love for your glorious art is the guarantee of your success; I wish you may achieve it with all my heart. I should be only too glad if I could contribute towards it; but I am too old for the work you propose; my ideas and studies all lie in another direction; and you would call me a savage if you knew how long it is since I have set foot in the Opera-house, or the Feydeau. I am sixty-four, and it would therefore ill become me to write love-poems; and in the matter of music, I am afraid a requiem is all that now concerns me. I am sorry you were not born thirty or forty years earlier, or I thirty or forty later — then we could have worked together. You will, I am sure, accept these excellent excuses and my kindest and most affectionate regards.

" ANDRIEUX."

"17th June, 1823."

He was his own messenger, and we had a long talk. When we parted he said, " In my youth, I too was a passionate lover of music, and raved first about Piccinni . . . and then about Gluck."

Somewhat damped by my failure to secure the co-operation of a literary celebrity, I had recourse to Gerono, who dabbled in poetry. I asked him (please admire my ingenuousness) to dramatise for me

---

[1] M. Boschot suggests that the ever-practical Berlioz went to Andrieux because the latter had influence with the jury at the Opéra that "sat upon" libretti.

A fuller version of the affair is given us by Daniel Bernard, who had it from a friend to whom Berlioz told the story in later years. The old academician found Berlioz cooking a rabbit with onions. The conversation turned on Gluck. Andrieux having declared his passion for Gluck, the delighted Berlioz turned to embrace him and emptied the contents of the casserole on the floor. "Yes," continued Andrieux, leaning on his cane, "and I like Piccinni too." "Ah!" said Berlioz coldly, picking up his dinner again.

Florian's *Estelle*. He did so, and I set his *poem* to music. Fortunately
no one ever heard a note of this offspring of my Meylan memories.
Impotent past! My music was as feeble as Gerono's text. This wishy-
washy composition was followed by a gloomy work taken from Saurin's
drama, *Beverley, ou le Joueur*.[1] I was delighted with this bluster-
ing fragment, written for a bass voice, with orchestral accompaniment, and I wished to have it sung by Dérivis, for whom it seemed to
me peculiarly adapted. The difficulty was to discover a suitable occasion for its performance, and I fancied I had found one when I saw
that *Athalie* was to be performed, with Gossec's choruses, at the
Théâtre Français, for Talma's benefit. As there is to be a chorus,
thought I, there must be an orchestra to accompany it; and as my
scena is an easy one, Dérivis will certainly sing it if Talma puts it in
his programme. I will go to Talma. — But the idea of addressing the
great tragedian and of facing Nero awed me. As I neared the house
my heart began to beat in the most deadly manner; at the sight of the
door I tremble, and pause irresolute on the threshold. Dare I go in?
. . . Shall I give up the idea? Twice I raise my hand to ring the bell,
twice I let it fall. . . . I blush scarlet, there is a singing in my ears;
I feel dizzy and faint. My fear masters me. I turn, or rather rush,
away as fast as my legs can carry me. Who can understand this?
Only a half-civilised young enthusiast such as I was then.

Soon afterwards, M. Masson, the conductor at the church of
Saint Roch, asked me to write a Mass for the Innocents' Day,[2] the
feast-day of the choir-children. We were to have a hundred picked musicians in the orchestra, and a still larger choir, with a month for practice. The copies were to be made gratis by the Saint Roch choir-
children, etc., etc. I set to work heart and soul at my Mass, which was a
bad copy of Lesueur's style, with the same casual inequality of colour.[3]

Like most masters, Lesueur, when he had looked over the score,
praised most the passages in which his own manner was most faithfully reproduced. As soon as it was finished I gave my manuscript to
M. Masson, who handed it over to his young pupils to copy and study.
He swore by all his gods that the performance should be grand and
perfect. We only wanted a good conductor, as neither he nor I was
accustomed to direct such a large body of performers. Valentino was
at that time the leader at the Opéra, and was anxious to obtain the

----

[1] Known in England as *The Gamester*. [H.]
[2] Dec. 28 (1823).
[3] The work was not a Mass but an oratorio — *Le Passage de la Mer Rouge*.

leadership of the Chapel Royal. It was therefore very unlikely he
would refuse my master, who was superintendent of the chapel.[1] He
accordingly acceded to Lesueur's request and promised to help us,
although he evidently felt no confidence in the material I had at my
disposal. On the day of our full rehearsal, our *great choral and instrumental forces* resolved themselves into a choir of twenty singers (consisting of fifteen tenors and five basses), twelve children, nine violins,
a viola, an oboe, a horn, and a bassoon. Imagine my shame and despair
at having to introduce Valentino, the celebrated conductor of one of
the first orchestras in the world, to such a phalanx of musicians! . . .
" Never fear," persisted Masson, " they will all be here at the performance to-morrow. Let us begin." Valentino took up his baton with
a resigned air, tapped his desk, and began; but he was obliged to stop
almost immediately, because of the endless mistakes in the parts; flats
and sharps were missing from the key-signatures; a pause of ten bars
was left out in one place, and thirty bars omitted in another. It is a
miserable hash; I suffer the torments of the damned; and at last am
forced to resign my long-treasured hope of hearing one of my works
performed by a large orchestra.

But the lesson was not lost. The little I had heard of my unfortunate composition had shown me its principal defects, and I immediately resolved to rewrite almost the whole work. Valentino strengthened me in my resolution by promising to help me when the time came
for my revenge; and I set to work at once. In the meanwhile, however,
my parents had heard of my failure, and seized the occasion to point
out the futility of my hopes and the absurdity of my supposed
vocation. This was the lees in my cup of bitterness: I swallowed them
in silence, and went on all the same.

When the new score was ready, taught by my recent painful experience, I set to work myself (as I could not afford to pay anyone
else to do it) to copy, double, triple, and quadruple the parts; and in
three months they were ready. But I found myself in much the same
position as Robinson Crusoe, with the canoe which he was unable to
launch. I had absolutely no hope of getting it performed. I was not
such a fool as to trust to M. Masson's *musical forces* again. As I knew
none of the artists I wanted personally, I could not ask them to perform; and finally, as regarded the Chapel Royal, my master had told

---

[1] The superintendents were present when their works were performed, but did not conduct
in person. [B.]

me once and for all that the thing was impossible.[1] It was then that my friend Humbert Ferrand, about whom I shall have more to say presently, conceived the rather bold idea of my addressing myself to M. de Chateaubriand, as the only man capable of understanding and entertaining such a request, and asking him to enable me to get up a performance of my Mass by lending me twelve hundred francs. Here is his answer :

"Paris, 31st December, 1824.

" You ask me for twelve hundred francs. Sir, I would send them to you if I had them. I cannot assist you as regards the ministry.[2] I sympathise most truly with your troubles. I love art, and I honour artists ; but genius often owes its triumphs to its trials ; and the day of success compensates for all that one has suffered. Accept my deep regrets ; they are very real.

" CHATEAUBRIAND."

CHAPTER VIII

AUGUSTIN DE PONS ; LENDS ME TWELVE HUNDRED
FRANCS — MY MASS PERFORMED FOR THE
FIRST TIME AT ST. ROCH — SECOND
PERFORMANCE AT ST. EUSTACHE —
I BURN IT

I WAS greatly discouraged, and found myself wholly unable to give any satisfactory answer to the letters which poured in from home, threatening to withdraw the small allowance that enabled me to live in Paris. Luckily for me, I met a clever young amateur at the Opéra one night when Piccinni's *Dido* was being played. He was of a generous, ardent nature, and had been an indignant spectator of the collapse at Saint Roch. He was a member of an aristocratic family in the Faubourg St. Germain, and was then well off, but afterwards lost all his money, and married, against the wish of his mother, a second-rate

[1] I did not then know why. If Lesueur had proposed that the whole choir of the Chapel Royal should transport itself to Saint Roch to perform a work by one of his pupils, the proposal would have been regarded as quite natural. But he was probably afraid that some of my fellow-students would claim the same privilege, which would have led to all sorts of complications. [B.]

[2] I must have also asked M. de Chateaubriand for an introduction to the powers of the day. When one asks an inch one may as well ask an ell. [B.]

singer who had been educated at the Conservatoire; she went on the stage, and he became an actor, and accompanied her through France and Italy. When, after a few years, his prima donna deserted him, he returned to Paris, and supported himself there by teaching singing. I have since been enabled to give him some assistance in the *Débats;* but I deeply regret having been able to do so little, for the service he spontaneously rendered me had a great influence on my career, and I shall never forget it. His name was Augustin de Pons. Last year he was barely able to support himself by his lessons. What his fate has been since the February Revolution, which must have deprived him of all his pupils, I shudder to think!

When we met in the foyer of the Opéra he called out to me in his stentorian voice, " What news of the Mass? Is it rewritten yet? and when is it to be performed in real earnest? " " Goodness knows! it is rewritten and copied, but how am I to get it performed? " " How? why, by paying for it. How much do you want? Let us see. Will twelve hundred francs do it? or fifteen hundred — or two thousand? I will lend it to you." " Pray lower your voice, I beseech you! If you mean what you say, I shall be only too glad to accept your offer, and twelve hundred francs will be enough." " All right. Come to me to-morrow, and we will settle it. We will engage the chorus from the Opéra, and a strong orchestra. Valentino must be satisfied, we must be satisfied, and by heaven it shall succeed! "

And it did succeed. My Mass was conducted by Valentino, and splendidly performed before a crowded audience at Saint Roch. The papers praised it, and thus, thanks to Pons, I succeeded in obtaining a public performance of a work of my own, the difficulty and importance of doing which in Paris every composer knows.

The Mass was performed again long afterwards (in 1827) in the church of St. Eustache, on the day of the great outbreak in the Rue St. Denis. This time the orchestra and chorus of the Odéon had offered me their services gratuitously; I ventured to conduct them myself, and got through it pretty well, in spite of some blunders caused by my excitement. But how little I then possessed of the qualities necessary to produce a good conductor! Precision, flexibility, passion, sensitiveness and coolness combined, together with an indefinable subtle instinct! How much time, practice, and thought have I spent in acquiring even a few of these! We often mourn over the paucity of good singers; good conductors are rarer still, and in most cases are of far greater importance, for good or ill, to a composer.

This second performance convinced me of the inferiority of my Mass, and, reserving the *Resurrexit*,[1] which seemed to me better than the rest, I burnt it, in company with *Beverley* (for which my enthusiasm had cooled), the opera *Estelle,* and a Latin oratorio, *The Passage of the Red Sea,* which I had just completed. After an impartial criticism, I ruthlessly condemned it also to a place in this *auto-da-fé*.

A strange coincidence! Last night, after writing the above, I went to the Opéra-Comique. There I met a musician who greeted me with these words: " When did you return from London? " " Some weeks ago." " Well; how about Pons? . . . Have you heard? " " No; what? " " He poisoned himself last month." " Good God! " " Yes; he said that he was weary of life; but I fear the truth of the matter is that he could not live. The Revolution had dispersed his pupils, and the sale of his furniture did not produce enough even to pay his rent." Poor creature! Poor forsaken artists! What a republic of rag-pickers and pickpockets!

" *Horrible! horrible! most horrible!* " and now the *Morning Post* brings me details of the death of the unfortunate Prince Lichnowsky, vilely assassinated at the gates of Frankfort by some brutes of German peasants, worthy rivals of our June heroes! They stabbed him all over with knives, hacked him to pieces with scythes, tore him limb from limb! riddled him with bullets, *but so as not to kill him!* and then stripped him and left him naked and dying by the roadside! . . . He lived for five hours, and died without a murmur![2] Noble, clever, brave, enthusiastic Lichnowsky! I knew him well in Paris, and met him in Berlin last year on my return from Russia. It was just at the beginning of his successes as a speaker. Filthy dregs of humanity! a

---

[1] I destroyed this also afterwards. [B.] Berlioz was mistaken. He not only preserved the *Resurrexit* but worked it up afresh in Rome in 1831. In this later form the work has been published in Series IV of the complete edition of his works, edited by Malherbe and Weingartner. A few years later still he used the material for the big ensemble at the end of the second act of *Benvenuto Cellini,* which expresses the horror of the Roman crowd at the murder of Pompeo by Cellini: the original melody of *Et iterum venturus* is now sung to the words *Assassiner un capucin! Un camaldule, ah, c'est infâme!* while the melody of *Cujus regni non erit finis* is fitted to the words *Ah, cher canon du fort Saint Ange,* and *Ah, quelle nuit noire et profonde!* The old accompaniment figure to *Et in unam sanctam apostolicam* now accompanies the words *À l'aide, au meurtre!* At a still later stage the *Et iterum venturus* was used for the *Tuba mirum* of the *Requiem.*

[2] Prince Lichnowsky was one of the members of the German National Assembly that met at Frankfort-on-the-Main in 1848. He and General von Auerswald were brutally murdered by Hessian villagers just outside the town on 17 September 1848.

hundred times more stupidly brutal in your revolutionary outbreaks and antics than the baboons and orang-outangs of Borneo ! . . .

Oh ! I must go out, walk, run, shout in the open !

CHAPTER IX

FIRST INTERVIEW WITH CHERUBINI — HE TURNS ME OUT OF THE CONSERVATOIRE LIBRARY

Now that I had made some progress in the study of harmony, Lesueur wished me to have a recognised position as one of his pupils in the Conservatoire. He spoke to Cherubini, who was then director, and I was admitted. Fortunately no one suggested that I should be introduced to the terrible author of *Médée,* for the previous year I had put him into one of his white-heat furies by opposing him in a matter which I shall now narrate, and which he probably had not forgotten.

No sooner was Cherubini appointed director, after the death of Perne, than he at once set to work to signalise his accession to power by the introduction of all sorts of restrictions in the internal economy of the school, which had not, up to that time, been organised on exactly puritan principles. In order to prevent the intermingling of the two sexes, except in the presence of the professors, he issued an order that the men were to enter by the door in the Faubourg Poissonnière, and the women by that in the Rue Bergère; the two being at opposite ends of the building.

Wholly ignorant of this moral decree, I betook myself one morning to the library, entering as usual by the Rue Bergère, the female door, and was making my way to the library when I found myself suddenly confronted by a servant, who stopped me in the middle of the courtyard, and ordered me to go back and return to the very same spot by the other entrance. I thought this so absurd that I sent the liveried Argus about his business, and went on my way. The rascal, hoping to find favour in the eyes of his new master by emulating his severity, ran off to report the circumstance. I had forgotten all about it, and had been absorbed in *Alceste* for a quarter of an hour, when Cherubini entered the reading-room, his face more cadaverous, his hair more bristling, his eyes more wicked, and his steps more abrupt than ever. He and my accuser made their way round the table, examining several unconscious students, until the servant stopped in front of me and cried, " Here he is! " Cherubini was in such a passion that he could not utter a word. " Ah! ah, ah, ah! " he cried at last, his Italian accent comically intensified in his anger, " and so you are the man who, who, who dares to come in by the door by which I forbid you to enter? " " I was not aware, sir, of your order, and another time I will obey it." " Another time! another time! What — what — what are you doing here? " " As you see, sir, I am studying Gluck's scores." " And what — what — what — are Gluck's scores to you? and who allows you to — to — to enter the library? " " Sir! (I was getting angry) Gluck's is the grandest dramatic music I know, and I need no one's permission to come here to study it. The Conservatoire library is open to the public from 10 till 3, and I have the right to use it." " The — the — the right? " " Yes, sir." " I — I forbid you to come here! " " Nevertheless, I shall return." " What — what — what is your name? " he cried, trembling with passion. I was, by this time, white with anger too. " Sir, perhaps you may hear my name some day . . . but you will not hear it now! " " Sei — sei — seize him, Hottin " (that was the servant's name), " seize him, and — and — take him away to prison! " Then, to the astonishment of everyone, master and servant pursued me round the table, knocking over stools and reading-desks in the vain effort to catch me, until at last I escaped, calling out with a laugh as I vanished: " You shall neither have me nor my name, and I shall soon come back and study Gluck's scores again! "

This was my first interview with Cherubini. I do not know whether he remembered it when, later on, I was presented to him officially. But it is curious that, twelve years afterwards, I should have been appointed, against his wish, to the charge of the library out of which he tried to turn me. As regards Hottin, he is now porter to the orchestra, devoted to me, and a most zealous partisan of my music; he used even to declare, before Cherubini died, that I was the only man who could take his place at the Conservatoire. M. Auber apparently thought otherwise.

I shall tell many more stories about Cherubini, from which it will be seen that though he gave me some bitter pills to swallow, he had to accept some unpalatable draughts in return from me.

CHAPTER X

MY FATHER WITHDRAWS MY ALLOWANCE — I RETURN
TO THE CÔTE — PROVINCIAL IDEAS OF ART AND
ARTISTS — DESPAIR — MY FATHER'S ALARM —
HE ALLOWS ME TO RETURN TO PARIS — MY
MOTHER'S FANATICISM — HER CURSE

THE partial success of my mass had for a time silenced the distressing opposition of my family; but unfortunately this was soon re-awakened.

I had entered as a competitor in the annual musical examination at the Conservatoire. For this there was a preliminary examination, which I unfortunately failed to pass. The moment my father heard of this he peremptorily informed me that he would withdraw my allowance if I remained in Paris. My kind master at once wrote, begging him to reconsider his decision, and assuring him that there could be no question as to my musical future, inasmuch as *I exhaled music at every pore.* Unfortunately the religious principles which he invoked to support his argument in favour of my being allowed to fulfil my vocation were the most unlucky he could have selected. My father's reply was stiff, rough, and almost rude, and offended and pained Lesueur on his most sensitive points. It began: " Sir, — I am an unbeliever! " and the rest may be imagined.

I had a dim hope that, by resigning myself for a time and pleading my own cause, I might yet prevail, and I therefore returned to the Côte.[1]

I met with a chilling reception, and was left for some days to my own reflections. Then my parents called upon me to choose some other profession, since I did not choose to be a doctor. I replied that my sole desire was to be a musician, and that I could not believe they would refuse to let me return and pursue my career at Paris.

" You may as well make up your mind on that score," replied my father, " for you shall never go back."

From that moment I lapsed into almost complete silence, barely answering when spoken to, scarcely eating, wandering about the

[1] At the beginning of June 1826.

woods, or else shutting myself up in my room. To tell the truth, I
had no plans; my mind seemed paralysed by the dull ferment in my
brain and the constraint to which I had to submit. I had not even
strength to be angry; I was perishing for want of air. One morning
early I was awakened by my father.

"Get up," he said, " and, when you are dressed, come into my
study; I want to speak to you."

I obeyed, without any presentiment of what was coming. My
father was grave rather than angry; but nevertheless I stood expecting another attack, when these words fell on my startled ears:

"After several sleepless nights I have made up my mind. You
shall go to Paris and study music; but only for a time. If after further trials you fail, you will, I am sure, acknowledge that I have done
what was right, and you will choose some other career. You know
what I think of second-rate poets; second-rate artists are no better,
and it would be a deep sorrow and profound humiliation to me to see
you numbered among these useless members of society."

My father was, it may be remarked, far less intolerant of second-
rate doctors, who are not only quite as numerous as bad poets or
artists, but are also not merely useless but positively dangerous. It is
always so even among clever men; they use the most powerful arguments in combating the prejudices of their neighbours, and are wholly
unconscious that their weapons can be turned with deadly effect against
their own most cherished opinions.

I threw myself into my father's arms, and promised all he asked.
" Seeing how radically your mother's ideas and mine differ on this
subject," he continued, " I have thought it better, in order to avoid
painful scenes, not to inform her of my determination; so I wish you
to keep it secret and to start for Paris without telling her." The first
day, therefore, I was most careful to keep my own counsel; but it
was impossible to conceal from my sisters this sudden and extraordinary change, from silent, morose sadness to delirious and exuberant
joy. Nanci, the eldest, besought me so constantly to reveal the cause
to her, that I did so, with many injunctions not to tell. She kept the
secret just as well as I had done; and in a short time the whole house-
hold, all our friends, and finally my mother, were informed of it.

In order to understand what follows, it is necessary to realise that,
in addition to her religious prejudices, my mother held strong opinions with regard to all arts connected with the stage, opinions unfor-

tunately shared by many people in France even in our own day. She looked upon all actors, actresses, singers, musicians, poets, and composers as abominable creatures excommunicated by the Church, and therefore predestined to eternal damnation. *À propos* of this, an aunt of mine — she now loves me very dearly, I hope, and even esteems me — whose head was full of my mother's strange *liberal* ideas, one day made the following astounding remark. We had been arguing, and I said, " To hear you speak, dear aunt, one would think you would be ashamed to own Racine as a member of the family? " "Ah, my dear, *respectability* before everything! " Lesueur was convulsed with laughter when I repeated this story to him in Paris. As he could only conceive of such a speech emanating from a mind verging on second childhood, whenever he was in a good humour he used to ask after Racine's enemy, *my old aunt,* although she was then young and as beàutiful as an angel.

So, when my mother got wind of what was happening, her whole soul was roused to anger. She was convinced that, in adopting music as a career (at that time music and the theatre were inseparably connected in the minds of Frenchmen), I was pursuing a path which leads to discredit in this world and damnation in the next. The moment I saw her angry face I knew that she knew, and tried to avoid her until the moment of my departure. But I had scarcely found a hiding-place when she discovered me, and, with flashing eyes and exciting gestures, exclaimed: "Your father [1] has been weak enough to allow you to return to Paris, and to encourage your wild, wicked plans; but I will not have this guilt on my soul, and, once for all, I forbid your departure." "Mother! " "Yes, I forbid it, and I beseech you not to persist in your folly, Hector. See; I, your mother, kneel to you, and beg you humbly to renounce it." " Good heavens, mother; do not kneel to me! Rise, I entreat you! " " No; I will kneel." After a moment's pause: "Wretched boy! you refuse? You can stand unmoved, with your mother kneeling at your feet? Well, then, go! Go and wallow in the filth of Paris, sully your name, and kill your father and me with sorrow and shame! I will not re-enter the house till you have left it. You are my son no longer. I curse you! "

It is almost incredible that bigotry, backed up by even the most fanatical provincial contempt for the life of an artist, could have led to such a scene between so tender a mother and so grateful and

---

[1] She addressed me as *vous*, not *tu.* [B.]

respectful a son. It is possible that the recollection of this painful, unnatural, horrible scene, which I can never forget, has inspired me
with my deep hatred for those stupid doctrines which, having their
origin in the Middle Ages, are so common in provincial France even
in the present day.

The trial was not yet over. My mother had vanished; she had
taken shelter in a country house, called Le Chuzeau, near the Côte,
which belonged to us. When the hour for my departure had arrived,
my father wished me to make with him a last effort to induce her to
bid me good-bye, and retract her cruel words. We arrived at Le
Chuzeau with my two sisters. My mother was reading under a tree
in the orchard. When she saw us, she rose and fled. We waited for a
long time; we followed her; my father called her; my sisters and I
stood there crying. All in vain; I had to leave without bidding her
good-bye, without a word or a look, and with her curse on my head.[1]

CHAPTER XI

I RETURN TO PARIS — GIVE LESSONS — ENTER
REICHA'S CLASS AT THE CONSERVATOIRE —
DINNERS ON THE PONT NEUF — MY FATHER
AGAIN STOPS MY ALLOWANCE — RE-
LENTLESS OPPOSITION — HUMBERT
FERRAND — RODOLPHE KREUTZER

WHEN I was back in Paris[2] and had resumed my music with Lesueur, my first object was to repay Pons the money he had lent me.
The debt weighed upon me, and I did not see my way to paying it off
out of my monthly allowance of one hundred and twenty francs. I
was fortunate enough to get some pupils, to whom I taught singing,
the flute, and the guitar; and the money I thus obtained, with what I
saved out of my allowance, enabled me to pay back my kind creditor

---

[1] In 1919 M. J. G. Prod'homme discovered two hitherto unknown letters of Berlioz relating
to this period. They were addressed to his uncle Victor Abraham Berlioz, the youngest brother of
Dr. Louis Berlioz. The second is dated Paris, Feb. 18, 1825; the first, which is headed merely
"Friday," clearly belongs to August or September 1824. The two letters are eloquent justifications
of his having chosen music as a career, and the arguments in them were obviously intended to
be passed on by his uncle to his father. The letters are given in full in the *Musical Quarterly* for
July 1919.

[2] He left the Côte at the end of July 1826.

six hundred francs in a few months. You may wonder how I managed
to save anything out of my small allowance, and this is how I did it.
I took a cheap little room on the fifth storey, in the Cité, at the corner
of the Rue de Harley and the Quai des Orfèvres, and, instead of dining at a restaurant as before, I restricted myself to a frugal meal
which only cost me fourpence, and usually consisted of dry bread and
raisins, prunes, or dates.

As it was summer-time I used to buy my delicacies at a neighbouring grocer's, and carry them to the little terrace on the Pont Neuf, at
the foot of the statue of Henry IV. There I ate my frugal meal, without a thought of the *poule au pot* which the good king desired all his
peasants to have for their Sunday dinner, watching the sun's course
towards Mount Valérien, revelling in the shining waters of the river
as it flowed beneath me, my mind full of Moore's beautiful poems, of
which I was then reading a translation. Unfortunately Pons, in distress at the privations I was obliged to incur, which, as we were intimate, it was impossible to conceal from him, and being also probably
in urgent need of the money, wrote to my father, telling him the whole
story, and asking for the remaining six hundred francs. The step was
disastrous. My father had already bitterly repented of his kindness;
I had been five months in Paris, my position was unchanged, and my
musical career seemed to be at a standstill. He had imagined, no
doubt, that by that time I should have obtained the *grand prix* at the
Conservatoire, have composed an opera in three acts, which would
have been performed with unprecedented success, received the Legion
of Honour, a pension from the Government, etc., etc. Instead of this,
he was dunned for a debt! It was a heavy blow, and it rebounded on
me. He paid Pons, and told me that if I did not renounce the pursuit of
my musical chimera he would give me no assistance, and would leave
me to provide for myself. But I had my pupils, I did not want much
to live on, and my debt was paid. So I at once made up my mind to
remain. As a matter of fact, I was working very hard at music. Cherubini, whose love of routine was all-pervading, knew that I had not
been through the usual Conservatoire course before I entered Lesueur's class, and he therefore put me into Reicha's class for counterpoint and fugue, which precede composition in the hierarchy of studies.
I was thus working with both masters at the same time. Besides this I
had struck up a friendship with a clever, warm-hearted young fellow whom I am still proud to number among my friends, Humbert

Ferrand. He had written the book of an opera for me, the *Francs-Juges,* and I was setting it to music with intense enthusiasm. The poem was afterwards refused by the Royal Academy of Music,[1] and my music was consigned to a limbo from which it has never emerged. The overture only has been played. I have used and developed some of the best ideas of this opera in subsequent compositions, and the remainder will either be treated in the same way or burnt. Ferrand had also written a grand scena, with choruses, on the Greek Revolution, a subject of which all men's minds were at that time full, and this I had set to music, without much interruption to my work on the *Francs-Juges.* It was through this work, every page of which bore traces of Spontini's powerful influence, that I first became acquainted with the hard egotism which one encounters in almost all celebrated artists, but of which I had no previous knowledge, and which showed me how little even the obscurest young composer has to hope for from them.

Rodolphe Kreutzer was the conductor-in-chief of the music at the Opéra. The season for the concerts of sacred music which take place in Passion Week, and are given in the Opera-house, was drawing near. The decision as to whether my scena should be performed lay with him. I went to him myself about it. He had been prepared for my visit by a letter from M. de Larochefoucauld, the Superintendent of Fine Arts, who had been induced to write to him about me by one of his secretaries, a friend of Ferrand's. Besides this, Lesueur had verbally recommended me to Kreutzer most warmly; so there was good ground for hope. This, alas! was soon dispelled. Kreutzer, the great artist, the author of *The Death of Abel* (a fine work, on which I had written the most enthusiastic panegyric a few months before) — Kreutzer, whom, because I admired him, I had always pictured as kindly and genial, like my master — received me with contemptuous rudeness. He barely returned my salutation, and, without looking at me, threw these words at me over his shoulder: " My good fellow " (he did not even know me!), " we cannot perform new pieces at these concerts of sacred music. We haven't time to get them up; Lesueur is well aware of this." I left him with a heavy heart. On the following Sunday, Lesueur and Kreutzer had an explanation at the Chapel Royal, where the latter merely played the violin. When pressed by my master, he answered, without attempting to conceal his annoy-

[1] The official name of the Grand Opéra of Paris. [H.]

ance: "Good heavens! what would become of us if we were to help on the young fellows like that?" He was frank enough, at any rate.[1]

CHAPTER XII

I COMPETE FOR A PLACE AS CHORUS-SINGER, AND GET IT—A. CHARBONNEL—OUR BACHELOR ESTABLISHMENT

BUT winter was approaching. In my eagerness to finish my opera I had somewhat neglected my pupils. A raw, cold, damp atmosphere had replaced the sunny warmth of my dining-hall on the Pont Neuf, which was no longer a fitting spot for my Lucullus feasts. I needed firewood and warmer clothes. Where was the money for these necessaries to come from? My lessons at a franc each were wholly insufficient for my needs, and even they seemed likely to fail me. Should I return to my father, contrite and vanquished, or die of hunger? These were my alternatives. The mere notion aroused such an indomitable determination never to yield, as to inspire me with new energy for the struggle; and I resolved to do anything — even quit Paris, if necessary — rather than return meekly to vegetate on the Côte. My old passion for travel joined up with that for music, and I determined

---

[1] Berlioz's letter to Kreutzer has survived: it was probably written after a hearing of some fragments from the opera at a concert, for *The Death of Abel* does not seem to have been given in its entirety after its first production in 1810. In view of the general soundness of Berlioz's taste in music, one cannot repress the suspicion that his enthusiasm for Kreutzer's mediocre opera was prompted, in part at any rate, by the knowledge that the composer could be of use to him. The letter runs thus:

"O genius!

I succumb! I die! My tears choke me! *The death of Abel!* Ye gods!

This wretched public! It feels nothing! What would it take to move it?

O genius! And what will happen to myself, if some day my music were to paint the passions? No one would understand me, for they do not crown, they do not carry in triumph, they do not prostrate themselves before, the writer of everything that is beautiful!

Sublime, heart-rending, pathetic!

Ah! I can bear no more: I must write! And to whom shall I write? To the genius? No, I dare not.

I will write to the man, to Kreutzer . . . He will laugh at me . . . What does that matter? . . . I would die . . . if I were to remain silent. Ah if I could only see him, speak to him, he would understand me, he would see what is in my lacerated soul; perhaps he would restore to me the courage I lost at the sight of the insensibility of those sordid blackguards who barely deserve to listen to the buffooneries of the buffoon Rossini.

I could not finish if the pen did not fall from my hands.

AH! GENIUS!!!"

to apply to the agents for foreign theatres, and try for an engagement
as first or second flute in an orchestra in New York, Mexico, Sydney,
or Calcutta. I would have gone to China, and become a sailor, fili-
buster, buccaneer, or savage, sooner than own myself defeated. Such
is my nature. It is as futile and dangerous to thwart my will, when I
am resolved on anything, as it is to try to prevent gunpowder from
exploding by compressing it.

Fortunately my efforts to obtain employment abroad failed, and
I was at my wits' end, when I suddenly heard that the Théâtre des
Nouveautés was about to open, and that vaudevilles and a certain
class of opéra-comique would be played there. I rushed off to the
manager and applied for a place as flute-player in the orchestra. There
was no vacancy. I then tried for the chorus; that was full too. Death
and fury! . . . However, the manager took down my address,
promising to let me know if they enlarged their chorus. The hope
was a very slight one; but it buoyed me up for some days, until I received a letter saying that I might compete for the appointment. The
examination of the candidates was to take place in the Freemasons'
Hall in the Rue de Grenelle St. Honoré. I went there, and found five
or six poor devils like myself, awaiting the advent of their judges in
silence and anxiety. Among them were a weaver, a blacksmith, an
actor who had been dismissed from a small theatre on the boulevards,
and a chorister from the church of St. Eustache. Bass voices were
wanted, and my voice was at the outside a passable baritone; but I
hoped our examiner would not be too particular.

It was the manager himself. He entered, followed by a musician
called Michel, who still plays in the Vaudeville orchestra. There was
neither piano nor pianist; Michel's violin was to be our sole accompaniment. The trial begins. My rivals sing as best they can the particular song they have carefully learnt. When my turn comes the
colossal manager, whose name oddly enough is St. Léger, asks me
what I have brought.

" Brought? Nothing."

" Nothing? Then what do you mean to sing? "

" Anything you like. Is there nothing here? No *solfège,* no score,
no book of exercises? "

" No; we have none of these. And besides," added the manager
contemptuously, " I don't suppose you can read at sight? "

" Pardon me, I can; anything you like to give me."

" Ah, that is another matter! But as we have no music of any sort, don't you know any popular song by heart? "

" Yes; I know by heart the *Danaïdes, Stratonice, La Vestale, Cortez, Œdipe,* the two *Iphigénies, Orphée, Armide.* . . ."

" That will do. The devil! What a memory! Well, come now, as you are so learned, sing the song *Elle m'a prodigué,* from Sacchini's *Œdipe.*"

" Certainly."

" Can you accompany him, Michel? "

" Of course; only unfortunately I forget what key it is in."

" In E flat. Shall I sing the recitative? "

" By all means; let us hear the recitative."

The accompanist gave me a chord in E flat, and I began:

> Antigone me reste; Antigone est ma fille, etc.

The other competitors cast despairing glances at one another as the glorious melody rolled forth; evidently conscious that, although I was neither a Pischek nor a Lablache, they had sung like crows in comparison; and, to use a piece of theatrical slang, I saw by a little signal from the big manager that they were *enfoncés jusqu'au troisième dessous.* The next morning I received the official notification of my appointment. I had beaten the weaver, the blacksmith, the actor, and even the chorister from St. Eustache, and was to enter upon my duties at once at fifty francs a month.

So behold me, while on my way to become an accursed dramatic composer, sunk to the level of a chorus-singer in a second-rate theatre, despised and excommunicated to the innermost core of my being. I could not help admiring the success which had crowned my parents' efforts to save me from the pit of destruction!

Blessings never come singly. I had scarcely achieved this brilliant success when the sky rained down two pupils upon me; and I also made the acquaintance of a compatriot, Antoine Charbonnel, who was studying chemistry. He wanted to live in the Quartier Latin, to be near his classes, and wished, like me, to practise a Spartan economy. No sooner had we calculated the amount of our joint fortunes than, parodying the words of Walter, in *La Vie d'un Joueur,* we both cried out: " *Ah! tu n'as pas d'argent; eh bien, mon cher, il faut nous associer!* "

We took two little rooms in the Rue de la Harpe. Antoine, who

was accustomed to furnaces and retorts, undertook the duties of head
cook, and used me as a mere scullion. Every morning we sallied forth
to the market to buy our own provisions, which I carried home in the
most unblushing way, to my companion's disgust, under my arm. And,
oh, chemical proprieties! we actually once had words on the subject.

So we lived like two princes — in exile — on thirty francs a month
each. I had not known such luxury since I arrived in Paris. I was
actually extravagant; I bought a piano [1] — and what a piano! I hung
framed pictures of my musical deities on the walls, and presented
myself with a copy of Moore's *Loves of the Angels*. Antoine, who
was as clever as a monkey with his fingers (which is a very poor simile,
for monkeys can only destroy), spent his spare moments in manu-
facturing all sorts of ornamental and useful trifles. He made us each
a pair of well-conditioned clogs out of some of our firewood; and in
order to vary the monotony of our frugal repasts, he contrived a net
and a decoy bird, with which, when the spring came, he caught quails
in the plain of Montrouge. The funniest part of it all was that, in
spite of my periodical absence in the evening (the Théâtre des Nouveautés was open every night), Antoine never found out during all
the time we lived together that I had the misfortune to belong to the
stage — for I was not proud enough of my position as a chorus-singer
to boast of it. While at the theatre I was supposed to be giving lessons
in a remote part of Paris. My pride was on a par with his! I could
not bear to let my companion know how I gained my living, and he
blushed scarlet and could scarcely bear to be seen with me in the
streets when I was carrying the bread earned by my honest labour.
But to tell the truth, and in justice to myself, I must acknowledge that
my reticence did not arise from foolish pride. In spite of my parents'
severity and their desertion of me, I would not for the world have
caused them the anguish (which to them with their ideas would have
been intense) of knowing what I had done; and indeed there was no
reason for doing so. I was therefore doubly careful lest by any indiscretion on my part my secret should be revealed to them, and I kept
my own counsel. And so, like Antoine Charbonnel himself, they were
only informed of my *dramatic career* seven or eight years after it had

[1] It cost me one hundred and ten francs. I have said already that I could not play the piano;
but still I like to have one, and occasionally to crash out some chords on it. Besides, I like to have
musical instruments in the room with me; and if I were rich, I would always have by me, while
I worked, a concert grand piano, two or three of Erard's harps, some of Sax's trumpets, and a
collection of Stradivari violins and violoncellos. [B.]

come to an end, through the biographical notices of me which appeared in various papers.[1]

CHAPTER XIII

FIRST COMPOSITIONS FOR THE ORCHESTRA — STUDIES AT THE OPÉRA — LESUEUR AND REICHA

IT was at this period that I wrote my first grand instrumental work, the *Francs-Juges* overture, that was soon afterwards followed by *Waverley*. I was at that time so ignorant of the mechanism of some of the instruments that, after I had written the trombone solo in the introduction to the *Francs-Juges* in the key of D flat, I feared it might be too difficult to play. So I took it to one of the trombone-players at the Opéra. He examined it, and reassured me by saying: " The key of D flat is, as it happens, one of those best suited to this particular instrument, and you may count on the passage producing a grand effect."

I was delighted at this, and was so absorbed in thinking of it that I walked home as in a dream, without looking where I went, and sprained my ankle in consequence. I get a pain in my foot now when I hear that piece. Perhaps it gives others a pain in their heads.

Neither of my masters taught me anything about instrumentation. Lesueur's ideas on the subject were most limited. Reicha understood the qualities of most of the wind instruments; but I don't think he had any real conception of grouping them in larger or smaller bodies. Besides, his department was counterpoint and fugue, and he had nothing to do with this other branch of music, which is not, even now, represented in the Conservatoire. Before my engagement at the Théâtre des Nouveautés I had become acquainted with a friend of

---

[1] Berlioz is not exaggerating. The register of his and Charbonnel's housekeeping expenses from September 6th, 1826 to May 22nd, 1827 has survived. The main expenditure was on leeks, vinegar, mustard, cheese, lard, and bread. There was evidently an extra financial stringency towards the end of each month. On September 29th the pair lived entirely on a few grapes: on the 30th the account runs:

Bread	o fr. 43 c.
Salt	o fr. 25 c.
Total	o fr. 68 c.

On New Year's Day Charbonnel seems to have feasted with friends: Berlioz, left alone, regaled himself with a dry crust (40 centimes) and the poems of Thomas Moore.

Gardel, the celebrated ballet-master. Thanks to the pit-tickets he gave me, I was able to go regularly to the Opéra. I used to take the score of the work with me, and read it during the performance. By this means I grew to understand the handling of an orchestra, and recognise the accent and timbre of most of the instruments, even though I could not grasp their mechanism or their range.

By a careful comparison of the means used with the effects produced, I perceived the subtle connection which subsists between musical expression and the special art of instrumentation; but no one ever pointed this out to me. It was by studying the methods of the three modern masters, Beethoven, Weber, and Spontini; by an impartial examination of the regular forms of instrumentation, and of *unusual* forms and combinations; partly by listening to artists, and getting them to make experiments for me on their instruments, and partly by instinct, that I acquired the knowledge I possess. Reicha's lessons in counterpoint were singularly lucid; he did, in a short time, teach me a great deal, without waste of words; and, unlike most masters, he generally explained to his pupils the meaning of the rules he wished them to obey.

Reicha was neither an empiric nor a conservative. He believed in progress in certain departments of art; and his respect for the fathers of harmony had not degenerated into fetish-worship. Hence his perpetual discussions with Cherubini. The latter pushed his idolatry for musical authority so far as to submit his own judgment to it, as when he says in his *Treatise on Counterpoint:* " This arrangement of harmony seems to me preferable to the other; but the old masters thought otherwise, *and we must obey them.*" In his composition, however, Reicha followed the routine he despised. I once asked him to tell me what he thought of whole fugues composed on the word *Amen,* or on *Kyrie Eleison,* with which the masses and requiems of the greatest composers of every school are infested. " Oh," cried he quickly, " it is barbarous." " Then, sir, why do you write them? " " Ah! because all the world does." *Miseria!*

Lesueur was more logical in this respect. Those monstrous fugues, which, resembling as they do the shouts of a crowd of drunkards, seem like a parody on the sacred texts, he regarded as remnants of a barbaric age; he never wrote them himself, and the occasional fugues which are found in his sacred compositions have nothing in common with such grotesque abominations. On the contrary, one of his fugues, which opens with the words *Quis enarrabit cælorum gloriam?* is a masterpiece of dignified style and harmonic science; and, what is more, it is a masterpiece of expression, to which the fugal form is here conducive. When, after the exposition of the *subject* (broad and beautiful) in the dominant, the *answer* comes dashing in in the tonic with a repetition of the words *Quis enarrabit,* it seems as if the one part of the choir, fired with the enthusiasm of the other, rushed off in its turn to sing with redoubled joy of the glories of the firmament. And then how the brilliant instrumentation floods the voices with gladness! With what power the basses are heard through the tracery of the violins, which shine like stars in the higher registers of the orchestra! What a thrilling *stretto* on the pedal! This fugue in its glorious beauty is justified by the meaning of the words and wholly worthy of them! It is the work of a musician who is inspired by his subject, and of an artist who understands his art! But as for the fugues of which I spoke to Reicha, *low tavern fugues,* I could cite numbers signed by masters far greater than Lesueur; but in writing them simply because it was customary to do so, those masters, be they who they may, turned their talent to base uses, and were guilty of an unpardonable outrage against musical expression.

Before he came to Paris, Reicha had been a fellow-student of Beethoven at Bonn.[1] I do not think they ever cared much for one another. Reicha was very proud of his mathematical attainments. "It is by the study of mathematics," he once said to us, in one of his lessons, "that I have succeeded in achieving a complete mastery over my ideas; by this means I have subdued and tempered my imagination, which used to run away with me; and, now that it is controlled by reason and reflection, it has doubled its power." I don't know whether Reicha's theory is as true as he thought, or whether his musical faculties were really much strengthened by his study of exact science. It is possible that to it he owed his taste for abstract combinations and clever tricks in music, and the actual charm he used to find in solving some of those difficult propositions which really divert art from its true path, by concealing the high end towards which it should evermore be tending. On the other hand, this love of numbers probably marred much of his work by robbing it of its harmonious or melodious

---

[1] Not a "fellow-student." They were both members of the Elector's band, where Beethoven played the viola and Reicha the flute, while Reicha's uncle was conductor of the band. Beethoven was much attached to young Reicha. [H.]

expression — that is to say, of its pure music; and what it gained
by its laborious combinations, conquest of difficulties, and strange
effects, was more calculated to affect the eye than the ear. However,
Reicha regarded neither praise nor blame; he seemed to care for
nothing but the success of the young artists at the Conservatoire over
whose studies he presided, and whom he taught with all possible care
and attention. He grew fond of me at length; but at first I observed
that my asking him the why and wherefore of all the rules annoyed
him; he could not tell me the reason of some of them — because they
had none. His quintets for wind instruments were the fashion for a
time in Paris. They are interesting, but rather cold. On the other
hand, I remember hearing a magnificent duet, full of fire and passion,
in his opera, *Sappho,* which was played several times.

CHAPTER XIV

COMPETITION AT THE CONSERVATOIRE — MY CAN-
TATA DECLARED UNPLAYABLE — ADORATION FOR
GLUCK AND SPONTINI — ARRIVAL OF ROSSINI
— THE ''DILETTANTI'' — MY FURY —
M. INGRES

THE period of the Conservatoire examinations had come round; I
went up again, and this time was admitted. We were given a scena to
write for full orchestra, on the subject of the death of Orpheus.

I think my piece was not devoid of merit; but the mediocre pianist
(it will be seen presently how extraordinary the organisation of these
competitions was) who had to play the orchestral accompaniments
on the piano, was unable to get through the *Bacchanale,* whereupon
the musical section of the Conservatoire, consisting of Cherubini,
Paër, Lesueur, Berton, Boïeldieu, and Catel, pronounced my work
unplayable, and thereby excluded me from the competition.

I had already seen how musicians, in their selfish dread of competition, discourage young artists; I now realised how the ridiculous
tyranny of our conservatoires strangles them. Kreutzer denied me an
opportunity of success which was of immense importance to me; the
academicians, by carrying out an absurd rule to the letter, robbed me
of my chance of winning a prize which, though not brilliant in itself,

would have encouraged me; whereas the rebuff overwhelmed me with rage and dumb despair.

I had got a fortnight's leave from the Théâtre des Nouveautés in order to attend the competition; when the time had expired I had to resume my fetters. But just then I became seriously ill, and was nearly carried off by an attack of quinsy. Antoine, who was running after grisettes, left me alone all day and part of the night. I had no servant and no nurse. I think I should certainly have died one night if I had not, in a paroxysm of agony, made a desperate cut with my penknife at the abscess in the back of my throat, which was choking me, and lanced it. This unscientific operation saved my life. I was almost well again when my father, who was probably vanquished by my persistence, and must have felt some anxiety as to my means of livelihood, restored my allowance. Thanks to this unexpected revival of the paternal tenderness I was able to give up my situation as chorus-singer — no slight advantage; for, apart from the over-powering physical fatigue of the work, I was utterly sick of the wretched music to which I was obliged to listen, and which would in-fallibly have brought on an attack of cholera, or driven me into an asylum. Any true musician who knows the music of these little vaude-ville operas, and of the larger vaudevilles which ape real operas, will realise what I went through.

I was now free to revel in my evenings at the Opéra, which I had been obliged to give up on account of my dreary work at the Théâtre des Nouveautés, and to plunge entirely into the study and culture of grand dramatic music. The only other serious music I had ever heard was at the concerts in the Opera-house, where the execution was so poor and thin as to awaken no enthusiasm in me. I had, therefore, never paid much attention to purely instrumental music. The sym-phonies of Haydn and Mozart (which are, speaking generally, of an essentially *intimate* character), played by a feeble orchestra on far too large a stage, and with very bad acoustic arrangements, produced about as much effect as if they had been performed on the plain of Grenelle; they sounded confused, poor, meagre. I had read through two of Beethoven's symphonies and had heard an andante [1] played, which made me feel dimly that he was a great luminary, but a luminary

---

[1] Doubtless the slow movement of the Seventh Symphony, which Berlioz elsewhere tells us was for long the only orchestral movement of Beethoven that would go down at Paris, and which is known to have been introduced into the Second Symphony in its performance at the Paris Concerts to make the latter work float. [H.]

only faintly discernible through dark clouds. Weber's masterpieces
had not then seen the light, and his name was wholly unknown. As to
Rossini and the rage for him which possessed the fashionable Parisian
world, it aroused my passionate indignation, all the more because the
new school was the antithesis of that of Gluck and Spontini. I could
conceive of nothing more grand, sublime, or true than the works of
those great composers; and Rossini's melodious cynicism, his contempt for the traditions of dramatic expression, his perpetual repetition of one kind of cadence, his eternal puerile crescendo, and his
crashing big drum, exasperated me to such a degree as to blind me
to the dazzling qualities of his genius and the real beauties of his
masterpiece, the *Barbiere,* with its delicate instrumentation and *no*
big drum. I used often to speculate on the possibility of undermining
the Théâtre-Italien, so as to blow it and its Rossini-worshippers into
space. And when I met one of those hated *dilettanti,* I used to mutter
to myself as I eyed him with Shylockian glance, " Would that I might
impale thee on a red-hot stake, thou scoundrel! " I must confess that
time has not tempered the murderous violence of my feelings, or
caused me to change the strong views I hold on this subject. Not
that I now desire to impale anyone *on a red-hot stake,* or that I would
blow up the Théâtre-Italien, even if the mine were laid and the match
ready to my hand; but I echo Ingres' words with all my heart and
soul when I hear him speak of some of Rossini's music as " the work
of an underbred man." [1]

CHAPTER XV

EVENINGS AT THE OPÉRA — PROSELYTISM —
SCANDALS — A SCENE OF ENTHUSIASM — A
SENSITIVE MATHEMATICIAN

My evenings at the Opéra were solemn occasions, for which I generally prepared myself by serious study and examination of the works
which I was to see performed. The fanatical admiration of myself and

[1] M. Ingres and I are not alone in our opinion of several of Rossini's serious Italian operas.
But this does not prevent the illustrious painter of the *Martyrdom of St. Symphorien* from regarding me as a vile musician, a monster, a brigand, and an Antichrist. However, I forgive him
most heartily, because of his admiration for Gluck. Is enthusiasm the opposite of love? it makes
us love those who love what we love, even when they hate us. [B.]

some of my companions in the pit for our favourite composers was only equalled by our intense detestation of the others. The Jupiter of our Olympus was Gluck; and not even the most ardent musician of the present day can conceive of the intensity with which we worshipped our idol. But if some of my friends were faithful votaries of this musical religion, I may say without vanity that I was its high priest. When I saw any wavering in their devotion I sought to rekindle it by addresses worthy of the St. Simonians. I dragged them off willy-nilly to the Opéra, and even went so far as to buy tickets for them myself, which I pretended had been given to me by someone belonging to the theatre.

After having thus succeeded in getting my man into the theatre when one of Gluck's masterpieces was to be played, I placed him on a seat in the pit, conjuring him not to change his place, seeing that others were not equally good for hearing, and that I had tried every one. Here you were too near the horns, there you could not hear them; on the right the trombones were too loud, on the left the repercussion from the stage-boxes produced a disagreeable effect; nearer to the stage you were too close to the orchestra, and the voices were drowned; higher up you were too far from the stage, and the words were inaudible, or you could not follow the facial expression of the actors; the instrumentation of this work was best appreciated from such a place, the chorus from another; in one act the scene was laid in a sacred forest, which was so vast that the sound was lost in most parts of the theatre, therefore it was necessary to go nearer; in another, which represented the interior of a palace, and was what is called, in the language of the theatre, a *salon fermé,* the force of the sound being doubled by this seemingly trifling change, it became advisable to move to the back of the pit, where the voices would seem to blend in more complete harmony.

When I had instructed my neophytes thus far, I asked them if they were familiar with the piece they had come to hear. If they were not, I produced the libretto, and spent the time before the rising of the curtain in reading it to them, interpolating such remarks as I imagined would facilitate their apprehension of the composer's meaning. We always came early so that we might get good places, hear the first notes of the overture, and indulge in the delight of anticipating a great pleasure one is certain to enjoy. One of our treats was to watch the empty orchestra, which seemed at first like a stringless piano, fill

gradually with music and musicians. First there came the attendant
who put the parts on the desks. That was always an anxious moment;
some accident might have happened, another piece might have been
substituted, and instead of one of Gluck's masterpieces we might have
some *Rossignol,* or *Prétendus,* or *Caravane du Caire,* or *Panurge,* or
Devin du Village, or *Lasthénie,* or other thin, sickly piece, more or
less dreary and poor — for we regarded them all with the same sovereign contempt.

The name of the opera inscribed in huge letters on the double-bass
parts, which were nearest to the pit, either relieved or confirmed our
fears. In the latter case we rushed out of the place, swearing like a
marauding trooper who has found water in what he took to be a cask
of brandy, and anathematising alike the author and the piece, the
manager who palmed it off on the public, and the Government which
sanctioned its performance. Poor Rousseau, who valued his score of
the *Devin du Village* as highly as the masterpieces of eloquence which
have made him immortal, who thought he had utterly eclipsed Rameau, and even the trio of *Les Parques,*[1] by the little songs, little
roulades, little rondos, little solos, little pastorals, and all the little
drolleries of which his little intermezzo is made up; to whom the
Holbachians so grudged this musical achievement, and who was so
worried about it; he who was so often accused of not being its real
author; he whose music was sung by everyone in France, from Jéliotte
and Mdlle. Fel[2] to Louis XV, who was never tired of singing *J'ai
perdu mon serviteur,* more out of tune than any of his subjects; he
whose favourite work was in fact a most complete success in every
possible sense — what would poor Rousseau have said if he could have
heard our curses? How could he dream that his precious opera,
which was received with such enthusiasm, would one day suddenly
disappear and be obliterated under a huge peruke thrown at Colette's
feet by some insolent scoffer? Oddly enough I was present at the
last performance of the *Devin* (it was never given at the Opéra after
that evening of joyous memory), and therefore many people have laid
the *scene of the peruke* to my charge; but I protest mine innocence.
Besides, I recollect feeling quite as much indignation as amusement at

---

[1] A once celebrated and very remarkable piece from an opera by Rameau, *Hippolyte et
Aricie.* [B.]

[2] The actor and actress at the Opéra who created the parts of Colin and Colette in the
Devin. [B.]

so grotesque a piece of irreverence, and cannot make up my mind whether I could have perpetrated it.[1]

But imagine Gluck — Gluck himself — going so far as to write and print, some fifty years ago, *à propos* of this wretched *Devin*, in a perfectly serious letter addressed to Queen Marie Antoinette, such words as these : " *France, which has so little to boast of in the way of music, has, however, produced some remarkable compositions, among which may be cited M. Rousseau's Devin du Village.* " Who would have credited Gluck with such a sense of humour ? By this one sentence the German has borne away the palm for facetious perfidy from the Italians themselves.

But to return to my narrative. When we saw, by the title-page of the orchestral parts, that no change had been made in the opera, I went on with my lecture, singing the principal passages, explaining the instrumental devices to which certain effects were due, and so enlisting the sympathy and enthusiasm of the members of our little club beforehand. Our excitement caused a good deal of surprise among our neighbours in the pit, for the most part good country folks, whose expectations, being keenly excited by my preliminary perorations, were generally much more disappointed than gratified by the reality. I then named each performer as he entered the orchestra, adding a running commentary on his habits and talents.

" There's Baillot. *He* does not reserve himself for the ballets, like the other solo violins ; *he* does not consider it a disgrace to play Gluck's accompaniments ; he will play a passage on the fourth string presently ; and you will hear it through all the rest of the orchestra.

" That fat, red fellow yonder is the double-bass, Father Chénié. He is a robust old fellow, in spite of his years ; a host in himself, and worth four of the others. You may be sure his part will be played as the composer wrote it ; he does not belong to the school of simplifiers.

" The conductor ought to keep an eye on Guillon, the flute-player, who is just coming in. He takes the strangest liberties with Gluck. In the religious march in *Alceste,* for example, the composer has written for the low register of the flutes, so as to obtain the special effect of the deep flute tone. Guillon does not approve of this ; he must take the lead ; he *will* be heard ; and so what does he do but play his part an

---

[1] Berlioz is indulging his talent for picturesque fiction here. The period of which he is writing is about 1824. *Le Devin du Village* remained in the repertory until 1829, when it disappeared for reasons with which Berlioz and his band had no connection.

octave higher, destroying the author's effect, and turning an ingenious idea into a common and puerile one."

The three taps which announced that the opera was about to begin put an end to our critical review of the orchestral notables. We sat with beating hearts, silently awaiting the signal from Kreutzer or Valentino. When the overture had begun it was criminal to speak, beat time, or hum a bar; if anyone did so, we at once made use of the well-known saying, "Confound those musicians who are preventing me from hearing this gentleman!"

As I was intimately acquainted with every note of the score, the performers, if they were wise, played it as it was written; I would have died rather than allow the slightest liberty with the old masters to pass unnoticed.[1] I had no notion of biding my time and coldly protesting in writing against such a crime — oh dear no! — I apostrophised the delinquents then and there in my loudest voice, and I can testify that no form of criticism goes so straight home as that. For example, I once remarked that in *Iphigénie en Tauride* cymbals had been put into the first dance of the Scythians, in B minor, where Gluck has only strings; and that in Orestes' great recitative, in the third act, the trombone parts, which, in the score, are so exquisitely adapted to the situation, had been left out altogether. The next time the opera was played I was resolved that if these errors were repeated I would show them up. Accordingly, when the Scythian ballet began I lay in wait for my cymbals; they came in just as they had done before. Boiling with anger, I nevertheless contained myself until the piece was finished, and then, seizing the occasion of the momentary lull which preceded the next piece, I shouted out with all my might, "There are no cymbals there; who has dared to correct Gluck?"[2]

The hubbub may be imagined. The public, who are not very sharp-sighted in matters connected with art, and to whom changes in an author's work are matters of complete indifference, could not understand what made the young lunatic in the pit so angry. But it was

---

[1] Ernest Legouvé's account of his first meeting with Berlioz confirms all this. Legouvé was at a performance of the *Freischütz*. Suddenly, in the middle of the ritornello in Caspar's aria, he saw a young man leap up and yell at the orchestra, "Not two flutes, you scoundrels! Two piccolos! Two piccolos!! Oh, what brutes!" The young man "was trembling with rage; his fists were clenched; his eyes were blazing; and his mop, oh, his mop! It looked like a huge umbrella, overhanging and waving about the beak of a bird of prey. It was at the same time comic and diabolic." The next day Legouvé discovered that this was Berlioz.

[2] There are no cymbals except in the Scythian chorus, *Les dieux apaisent leur courroux*. The character of the ballet being quite different, it is of course differently scored. [B.]

worse in the third act, where the trombones in Orestes' monologue were suppressed, just as I feared they would be; and the same voice was heard shouting out, " Not a sign of a trombone; it is intolerable ! "

The astonishment of both orchestra and audience was only equalled by Valentino's perfectly legitimate indignation. I learnt afterwards that the unfortunate trombones were only carrying out a distinct order [1] to be silent in that particular passage, which stood in their parts exactly as it does in the score.

As to the cymbals, which Gluck has introduced so happily in the first Scythian *chorus,* I do not know who had taken upon himself to import them into the dance, thus falsifying the colour and marring the sinister silence of that weird ballet. But I know that in all subsequent performances order was restored; the cymbals were silent, the trombones were heard; and I listened content, muttering through my teeth, " All right."

Soon afterwards de Pons, who was just as rabid as I, and who objected to the substitution of someone else's ballet music for that of Sacchini in the first act of *Œdipe à Colonne,* suggested to me that we should put an end to the interminable solos for horn and violoncello which had been inserted in its stead. Could I refuse my help in so just a cause? The means we had employed in the case of the *Iphigénie* were equally successful in that of the *Œdipe;* and the result of a few well-timed words from the pit was the permanent withdrawal of the objectionable dance airs.

Only once, however, did we succeed in carrying the public with us. It had been announced in the bills that Baillot would play the violin solo in the ballet in *Nina.* The evening arrived, and, either because he was indisposed, or for some other reason, he did not perform, and the managers deemed it sufficient to acquaint the public with the fact by means of a minute piece of paper pasted on the theatre door, and seen by no one. The greater part of the spectators, therefore, expected to hear the great violinist.

Even Mdlle. Bigottini's pathetic pantomime, when she comes to her senses in the arms of her father and her lover, failed to make us forget Baillot. The scene was almost over. "So far good," said I, loud enough to be heard, " but where is the violin solo? " "That is true," said one of the public; " it looks as if they were going to leave it out. Baillot, Baillot! the violin solo! "

---

[1] So much the worse for whoever issued the order. [B.]

The pit took fire at once; and then a thing which I had never seen at the Opéra happened. The entire house rose and loudly demanded that the programme should be carried out according to the bill.

The curtain fell in the midst of this hubbub. The uproar redoubled; the musicians fled; the angry public dashed into the orchestra, overturning chairs and music-desks, and smashing the drums. In vain did I cry: " Gentlemen, gentlemen, don't smash the instruments! What vandalism! Don't you see that you are destroying Father Chénié's beautiful double-bass, with its infernal tone? " My words fell unheeded, and the rioters never rested till they had overturned the whole orchestra and smashed I don't know how many seats and instruments.

This was the seamy side of the active criticism we exercised so despotically at the Opéra. Its good side was our enthusiasm when all went well. Then you should have seen with what a frenzy of applause we greeted the passages which no one else noticed — a fine harmonic bass, a happy modulation, a right accent in a recitative, an expressive note in the oboe, etc. The public took us for *claqueurs* out of work, whereas the real chief of the *claque,* who was only too well aware of the true state of affairs, and whose cunning combinations were deranged by our thunders of applause, looked as furious as Neptune when he uttered his *Quos ego.* Then when Mdme. Branchu excelled herself there were shouts and stampings of feet such as are never heard in these days, even in the Conservatoire — the only place in France in which true musical enthusiasm is still to be found.

The most curious scene of this sort that I remember took place one evening when *Œdipe* was being played. Though Sacchini held a far lower place in our esteem than Gluck, we nevertheless admired him greatly. I had dragged one of my friends,[1] who cared for no art but that of billiards, but of whom I was nevertheless determined to make a musical proselyte, to the Opéra. To my disgust, my friend was but moderately affected by the sufferings of Antigone and her father, so after the first act I gave him up as hopeless and went to a seat in front, where I should not be disturbed by his insensibility. As though to throw his impassibility into further relief, however, chance had placed on his right hand a spectator who was as impressionable as he

---

[1] Léon de Boissieux, my fellow-student at the little school on the Côte. He figured for a time in the *Illustrations du Billard de Paris.* [B.]

was the reverse. I soon became aware of this. Dérivis had made a great hit in his fine recitative:

Mon fils? tu ne l'es plus!
Va! ma haine est trop forte!

Absorbed though I was by the beauty and truly antique character of the scene, I could not help overhearing the dialogue which was going on behind, between my man, quietly peeling an orange, and his unknown neighbour, who was evidently suffering from the most intense emotion.

"Good God, sir, be calm."

"No, it is too much; it is overwhelming! — it is terrible!"

"But, sir, you are wrong to give way like this. You will be ill."

"No; let me be. . . . Oh!"

"Sir, come sir, cheer up! After all *it is only a play.* Will you have a piece of this orange?"

"Ah! how sublime!"

"It is Maltese!"

"What heavenly music!"

"Do not refuse."

"What music!"

"Yes; it is very pretty."

During this discordant discourse we had got to the fine trio, *O doux moments,* which follows the scene of reconciliation; I was deeply affected by the penetrating sweetness of the simple melody, and, hiding my face in my hands, was weeping silently. Scarcely was the trio ended when I felt myself raised from my seat by two powerful arms which clasped me like a vice; they belonged to the unknown enthusiast, who, perceiving that I alone of all his neighbours shared his feelings, and unable any longer to control his emotion, was embracing me with wild enthusiasm, exclaiming convulsively, " *Sac-r-r-re Dieu, monsieur,* how beautiful it is!" Without expressing any surprise, and turning my face all blurred with tears towards him, I said, " Sir, are you a musician?" . . . " No! but I could not love music more if I were." " What matter? shake hands; you are a right good fellow."

And thereupon, regardless of the jeers of the spectators who had formed a circle round us, and of the flabbergasted look of my orange-eating friend, we whispered to each other our names and professions. He was an engineer! a mathematician! In what strange soils can keen susceptibility thrive! His name was Le Tessier. I never saw him again.

CHAPTER XVI

WEBER AT THE ODÉON — CASTILBLAZE — MOZART —
LACHNITH — "ADAPTERS" — "DESPAIR
AND DIE!"

WHILE thus absorbed in my musical studies, and while my fever
for Gluck and Spontini and my aversion from the Rossinian forms
and doctrines were alike at their height, Weber appeared on the scene.
The *Freischütz* was given at the Odéon, not in its own beautiful form,
but in a distorted, disfigured, vulgar " adaptation " bearing the title
of *Robin des Bois*. The orchestra, which was a young one, was excellent, and the chorus fair, but the singers were atrocious. One of
them alone, Mdme. Pouilly, who played the part of Agatha (re-
christened Annette by the translator), possessed a fair amount of execution, but nothing else, the result being that the part, being sung
without intelligence, passion, or fervour, was virtually annihilated.
She sang the grand air in the second act with as much feeling as if it
had been one of Bordogni's exercises, and it was not until long afterwards that I discovered what a mine of beauty it contains.

The first performance was greeted with a storm of laughter and
hisses; but on the second night the waltz and the huntsmen's chorus,
which had excited attention from the first, created such a sensation
that they saved the rest of the work, and it drew full houses every
night. Then the bridesmaids' chorus and Agatha's prayer (cut in half)
became popular. Then, by degrees, the public became aware of a certain *racy charm* in the overture, and Max's song was allowed to be
not *wholly wanting in dramatic feeling*. Lastly, the devilries in the
Wolf's Glen were tolerated as *comic*. All Paris flocked to see so *out-
landish* a piece; the Odéon throve on the proceeds; and M. Castilblaze received over a hundred thousand francs for mutilating a
masterpiece.

Prejudiced as I was by my exclusive and intolerant idolatry for the
great classics, I was nevertheless overwhelmed with surprise and delight at Weber's music. Even in its mutilated form I was positively
intoxicated by its delicious freshness and its wild, subtle fragrance.
To a man sated by the staid solemnity of the tragic muse, the rapid

action of this wood-nymph, her gracious brusqueries, her dreamy
poses, her pure maidenly passion, her chaste smile, and her sadness,
brought a torrent of new feelings and emotions. I forsook the Opéra
for the Odéon, and, as I had a pass to the orchestra, I soon knew the
Freischütz (as there given) by heart.

The composer himself at this time — it was twenty-one years ago
— paid his first and only visit to Paris on his way to London, where
he was to witness the failure of one of his greatest works, and die.
How I longed to see him! How my heart beat as I followed him about
on the evening of the revival of Spontini's *Olympie,* shortly before he
left for London! He was ill, but he wanted to see it. My pursuit was
in vain. In the morning Lesueur had said to me: " Weber has just been
here, and if you had come five minutes sooner you would have heard
him play me whole acts of our French operas; he knows them all."
Entering a music-shop a few hours later I heard: " Do you know who
has just been sitting there? " " Who? " " Weber! " When I reached
the Opéra, I heard whispers on all sides, " Weber has just passed
through; he crossed the foyer, and is in the first row of boxes." I was
in despair at not being able to find him. But all my efforts were vain;
no one could point him out to me. He was the inverse of Shakespeare's
apparitions, in that, being visible to all, he was invisible to me alone.
And so I missed making his acquaintance, because, unknown as I was,
I dared not write to him, and I knew no one who could have introduced me.

If men of genius only knew what love their works inspire! If they
only realised with what an intense, concentrated devotion a hundred
thousand hearts yearn towards them as one, how they would rejoice
to receive and surround themselves with such kindred spirits, and how
such worship would console them for the bitter envy, petty hatred,
and careless indifference which they meet with elsewhere!

In spite of his popularity, the stupendous success of the *Freischütz,*
and his consciousness of his genius, Weber would probably have appreciated such silent, sincere adoration more than anyone. He had
written beautiful things which had been coldly received by artists and
critics alike. His last opera, *Euryanthe,* had obtained only a moderate
success; and he could not but feel anxious as to the fate of *Oberon,*
for he must have known it to be a work which could only be truly appreciated by an audience of poets and thinkers. Even Beethoven, the
king of kings, had long misunderstood him, so it is easy to realise how,

at times, he lost faith in himself, and how it was that the failure of
Oberon killed him.[1]

The striking contrast between the fate of this glorious work and
that of its eldest brother, the *Freischütz,* is not due to any defects in
the favourite of fortune; it is neither vulgar nor petty in form, it owes
its brilliancy to no sham effects, to nothing turgid or exaggerated in
its expression; in neither the one work nor the other has the composer made the smallest concession to the puerile exigencies of fashion, or to those, still more imperious, of the singers. He was as simply
true, as fearlessly original, as independent of precedent, as regardless
of the public, and as determined not to truckle to them, in the *Freischütz* as in *Oberon.* But the former is full of poetry, passion, and contrast. The supernatural element introduces strange and sudden effects.
The melody, harmony, and rhythm alike thunder, burn, and illumine;
everything combines to fetter the attention. The characters also are
taken from daily life, and appeal strongly to the general sympathy;
the depiction of their feelings and their manners calls for a less exalted style of music, which, combined with exquisite workmanship, has
a peculiar fascination even for minds which are wont to disdain melodious trifles; while by their very enrichment they become, to the popular mind, the perfect ideal of art, and marvels of originality.

In *Oberon,* on the other hand, although human passion plays a
considerable part there also, the fantastic element is supreme; but it
is the fantastic in a calm, fresh, graceful form. Instead of monsters
and terrible apparitions we have choruses of spirits of the air, sylphs,
fairies, and water-nymphs. And the language of this gentle people —
a language entirely their own — which owes its chief charm to its harmonies (its melodies being capriciously vague, with a strange veiled
rhythm difficult to follow), is almost unintelligible to the general
public, and is only to be fully appreciated, even among musicians, by
those who have studied it deeply, and possess, moreover, the gift of a
vivid imagination. This exquisite poetry is, no doubt, better suited to
the dreamy German temperament than to ours; I fear that, having
studied it as a curiosity, we should soon weary of it.[2] This was proved

[1] It was not the non-success of *Oberon* that killed Weber, but a disease of long standing,
aggravated no doubt by his exertions over the production of the opera. Even before he quitted
Germany for England his frequent expression was, "Whether I go or stay, in a year I shall be
a dead man." See Benedict's *Weber*, p. 111. [H.]

[2] The truth of this statement has been controverted by the performance of *Oberon* at the
Théâtre-Lyrique (1857), and the sensation it created. It was a complete success, and proves that
the Parisian public has made notable progress in music. [B.]

in 1828, when a company came over from Karlsruhe to perform at the Théâtre Favart. There are only two short verses in the mermaids' chorus, the soft cadence of which is a beautiful rendering of pure, perfect happiness. But after a few bars of this softly monotonous rhythm, the interest of the public flagged. At the end of the first verse a murmur arose in the theatre, the end of the chorus was barely audible, and it was cut out altogether at the next performance.

When Weber saw what a hash Castilblaze, that veterinary surgeon of music, had made of his *Freischütz,* he was very angry, and his just indignation found vent in a letter which he published before leaving Paris. Castilblaze had the audacity to reply that it was very ungrateful of M. Weber to reproach the man who had popularised his music in France, and that it was *entirely* owing to the modifications of which the author complained that *Robin des Bois* had succeeded!

The wretch! . . . and to think that a miserable sailor is punished with fifty lashes for the least act of insubordination! . . .

It was some years before this that, in order to ensure the success of Mozart's *Magic Flute,* the manager of the Opéra produced that marvellous travesty of it, *Les Mystères d'Isis,* the libretto of which is a mystery as yet unveiled by no one. When he had manipulated the text of this masterpiece to his liking, our intelligent manager sent for a *German* composer to help him patch up the music. The German proved equal to the occasion. He stuck a few bars on to the end of the overture (the overture to the *Magic Flute!*), turned the soprano part of a chorus [1] into a bass aria, adding a few bars of his own; transplanted the wind instruments from one scene to another; changed the air and altered the instrumental accompaniment in Sarastro's glorious aria; manufactured a song out of the slaves' chorus, *O cara armonia;* and converted a duet into a trio. Not satisfied with the *Magic Flute,* this harpy must next glut himself on *Titus* and *Don Giovanni.* The aria *Quel charme à mes esprits rappelle* is taken from *Titus,* but only the *andante* is there, for the *allegro,* with which it ends, does not seem to have pleased our *uomo capace;* so he decreed a violent divorce, and, in its stead, put in a patchwork of his own, interspersed with scraps of Mozart. No one would dream of the base uses to which our friend put the celebrated *Fin ch' han dal vino,* that vivid outburst of libertinism in which Don Giovanni's whole character is epitomised.

---

[1] The chorus *Per voi risplendi il giorno.* [B.]

He turned it into a trio for a bass and two sopranos, with the following sweetly sentimental lines:

> Heureux délire!
> Mon cœur soupire!
> Que mon sort diffère du sien!
> Quel plaisir est égal au mien!
> Crois ton amie,
> C'est pour la vie
> Que mon sort va s'unir au tien.
> O douce ivresse
> De la tendresse!
> Ma main te presse,
> Dieu! quel grand bien!

When this wretched hotch-potch was ready it was dubbed *The Mysteries of Isis,* was played in that form, and printed and published in full score with the name of that profane idiot Lachnith [1] (which I publish that it may be perpetuated with that of Castilblaze) actually bracketed with Mozart's on the title-page.

In this wise, and at twenty years' interval, two beggars in filthy rags came masquerading before the public in the rich robes of the kings of harmony; and in this sordid fashion two men of genius, disguised as monkeys, decked in flimsy tinsel, blinded, mutilated and deformed, were presented to the French people, by their tormentors, as Mozart and Weber!

And the public was deceived, for no one came forward to punish the miscreants or give them the lie.

Alas! how little the public recks of such crimes, even when it is cognizant of them! In Germany and England, as well as in France, such adaptation (which means profanation and spoliation) of masterpieces by the veriest nobodies is tolerated.

Theoretically it is recognised as an axiom that when any alteration in a great work is required it should be made by the very greatest artists only; that, in fact, correction should come from above, never from below. Practically what takes place every day without protest is the exact opposite. Mozart was murdered by Lachnith; Weber, by Castilblaze; Gluck, Grétry, Mozart, Rossini, Beethoven, and Vogel were all mutilated by this same Castilblaze; [2] Beethoven saw his

---

[1] Not Lachnitz; there should be no error in the spelling of the name of so great a man. [B.]

[2] There is scarcely a work by any of these masters which he has not botched to his fancy; he must surely be mad. [B.]

symphonies corrected by Fétis,[1] Kreutzer, and Habeneck; Molière and Corneille were hacked about by the obscure familiars of the Théâtre-Français; in England, adaptations of Shakespeare by Cibber and others are still played. It does not look as if the corrections came from above, but rather from below, and very perpendicularly at that!

It is futile to assert that, in botching masterpieces, these adapters have sometimes made lucky hits; no exceptions can condone such abominable desecration. No, no, no; a thousand times, no; musicians, poets, prose-writers, actors, pianists, conductors of the third, second, or even of the first order, have no right to meddle with Beethoven or Shakespeare, or to bestow their *scientific* or *æsthetic* alms on them.

No, no, no; a hundred thousand times, no. No man, be he who he may, has any right to compel any other man, be he who he may, to wear a mask not his own; to speak in tones not his own; to take a shape not of his own choosing; to become a puppet, subject to his will; or to be galvanised after he is dead. If he was not a great man, let him lie. If he was a great man, let his equals — nay, even his superiors — respect him; and let his inferiors bow down humbly before him.

No doubt Garrick invented the *dénouement* of *Romeo and Juliet,* which is the most touching thing ever played, and substituted it for the one Shakespeare wrote, which is less effective. But on the other hand, what insolent rogue perpetrated the ending to *King Lear* which is often played instead of the scene Shakespeare wrote, and put those coarse tirades into Cordelia's mouth, expressing passions so foreign to her gentle, noble nature? Where is he? Tell us, so that every poet on earth, every artist, every father, every lover, may flog him, pillory him, and say to him, " Detestable idiot! you have committed an atrocious crime, the most odious, the most enormous of crimes — an assault on that combination of man's highest faculties that is called *Genius!* Curses on you! *Despair and die!!* "

And how *Richard the Third* was distorted! And the *Tempest;* were not a crowd of additional personages thrust into it? And *Hamlet* and *Romeo?* Such is the result of Garrick's experiment! Everybody wanted to give Shakespeare a lesson! [2]

[1] I will show how. [B.] (See chapter xliv.)

[2] This is too true as to England. *The Barber of Seville* is thus announced in the bill of Covent Garden, October 13th, 1818: "A comic opera in two acts, called *The Barber of Seville* (founded on the opera of that name), in which will be introduced part of Rossini's and Paesiello's celebrated music from *Il Barbiere di Siviglia.* The overture and new music composed, and the whole adapted to the English stage, by *Mr. Bishop.*"

On February 28th, 1819, we find that " *The Marriage of Figaro* has been long in rehearsal,

And to return to music. At the last *concerts spirituels* at the Opéra, Kreutzer cut out ever so many passages from one of Beethoven's symphonies,[1] and Habeneck profited by his example to suppress some of the instruments in another.[2] And does not one hear strange big drum, ophicleide, and trombone parts in London which Mr. Costa has stuck into the scores of *Don Giovanni,* the *Nozze di Figaro,* and the *Barbier de Séville?* And if conductors are permitted according to their fancy to suppress or add instruments in such works as these, who shall prohibit violin- or horn-players, or any back-desk musician, from following their example? And what is to restrain translators, editors, or even copyists, engravers, and printers from doing the same thing?[3]

Does not this lead to the utter ruin and destruction of all Art? And is it not the bounden duty of those of us who love Art and glory in her beauty to guard the liberty of the human mind, and to prosecute the culprit who violates its unwritten laws, and denounce him with all possible wrath, crying: "Your crime is ridiculous. *Despair!* Your stupidity is culpable. *Die!* Be thou rejected, derided, accursed of men. *Despair and die!*"

CHAPTER XVII

PREJUDICE AGAINST OPERAS WITH ITALIAN WORDS —THE INFLUENCE PRODUCED BY THIS FEELING ON MY APPRECIATION OF SOME OF MOZART'S WORKS

I HAVE stated that when I went up for my first examination at the Conservatoire I was wholly absorbed in the study of dramatic music of the grand school; I should have said of lyrical tragedy, and it was

---

and will be produced" (at Covent Garden) "early in the week after next. The music selected chiefly from Mozart's operas."

Eight years later, Mozart's *Entführung* was produced in the same disgusting fashion, also at Covent Garden: "November 29th, 1827, will be performed a new grand opera, called *The Seraglio.* The music arranged and adapted from Mozart's celebrated opera, with additional airs, etc., composed by Mr. Kramer."

Cenerentola, again, was thus presented: "*Cinderella; or, The Fairy and the Little Glass Slipper.* The music composed by Rossini, containing selections from his operas of *Cenerentola, Armida, Maometto Secondo,* and *Guillaume Tell.* The whole arranged and adapted to the English stage by Mr. Rophino Lacy." [H.]

[1] The Second Symphony, in D major. [B.]

[2] For the last twenty years the Symphony in C minor has been played at the Conservatoire without the double basses at the beginning of the *scherzo,* because Habeneck cut them out. He thinks they don't sound well! A lesson for Beethoven! [B.]

[3] And they do it too. [B.]

owing to this cause that my admiration for Mozart was so lukewarm. Only Gluck and Spontini could excite me. And this was the reason for my coolness with regard to the composer of *Don Giovanni*. *Don Giovanni* and *Figaro* were the two of Mozart's works oftenest played in Paris; but they were always given in Italian, by Italians, at the Italian Opera; and that alone was sufficient to prejudice me against them. Their great defect in my eyes was that they seemed to belong to the ultramontane school. Another and more legitimate objection was a passage in the part of Donna Anna which shocked me greatly, where Mozart has inserted a wretched vocalise which is a perfect blot on his brilliant work. It occurs in the allegro of the soprano aria in the second act, *Non mi dir,* a song of intense sadness, in which all the poetry of love finds vent in lamentation and tears, and which is yet made to wind up with such a ridiculous, unseemly phrase that one wonders how the same man could have written both. Donna Anna seems suddenly to have dried her tears and broken out into coarse buffoonery. The words of this passage are, *Forse un giorno il cielo ancora sentira-a-a-a-* (here comes an incredible run, in execrable taste) *pietà di me.* A truly singular form of expression for a noble, outraged woman, of the *hope that heaven will one day have pity on her!* . . . I found it difficult to forgive Mozart for this enormity. Now I feel that I would shed my blood if I could thereby erase that shameful page and others of the same kind which disfigure some of his work.[1]

I therefore received his dramatic doctrines with distrust, and my enthusiasm fell to just one degree above freezing point. Still I felt the warmest admiration for the religious grandeur of the *Magic Flute;* though I had only heard it in its travestied form as *The Mysteries of Isis,* and it was not until afterwards that I was able to compare the original score in the Conservatoire library with the wretched French *pot-pourri* played at the Opéra.

As I first heard the works of this great composer under such disadvantageous circumstances, it was only many years later that I was able to appreciate their charm and suave perfection. The wonderful beauty of his quartets and quintets, and of some of his sonatas, first converted me to the worship of this angelic genius, whose brightness was slightly dimmed by intercourse with Italians and contrapuntal pedagogues.

[1] Even the epithet "shameful" scarcely seems to me strong enough to blast this passage. Mozart has there committed one of the most flagrant crimes recorded in the history of art against passion, feeling, good taste, and good sense. [B.]

CHAPTER XVIII

SHAKESPEARE — MISS SMITHSON — FATAL LOVE —
MORAL LETHARGY — MY FIRST CONCERT —
CHERUBINI'S DROLL OPPOSITION — HIS
DEFEAT — HIS FIRST DOSE

I HAVE now come to the grand drama of my life; but I shall not
relate all its painful details. It is enough to say that an English company came over to the Odéon to perform Shakespeare's plays, then
entirely unknown in France. I was present at the first performance
of *Hamlet,*[1] and there, in the part of Ophelia, I saw Miss Smithson,
whom I married five years afterwards. I can only compare the effect
produced by her wonderful talent, or rather her dramatic genius, on
my imagination and heart, with the convulsion produced on my mind
by the work of the great poet whom she interpreted. It is impossible
to say more.[2]

This sudden and unexpected revelation of Shakespeare overwhelmed me. The lightning-flash of his genius revealed the whole
heaven of art to me, illuminating its remotest depths in a single flash.
I recognised the meaning of real grandeur, real beauty, and real
dramatic truth, and I also realised the utter absurdity of the ideas
circulated about Shakespeare in France by Voltaire:

Ce singe de génie,
Chez l'homme, en mission, par le diable envoyé,[3]

[1] On 11 September 1827.

[2] Berlioz calls Miss Smithson Henrietta, but her true names were Harriet Constance. She
was born at Ennis, County Clare, on March 18, 1800. She seems to have taken to the stage in
1815, in consequence of the failure of the health of her adoptive father, the Rev. Dr. James Barrett,
of Ennis. Her first appearance was at the Crow Street Theatre, Dublin. After various appearances
in Ireland and Birmingham we find her at Drury Lane in January 1818: she was described in the
Press as "tall and well formed, with a handsome countenance, and a voice distinct rather than
powerful." Another critic said that her voice had "tremulous and thrilling tones, giving an
irresistible charm to expressions of grief and tenderness." She practised her art for some years
in London and the English provinces without ever being accepted as first-rate, though at one time
she played Desdemona to Kean's Othello.

She made her first appearance in France in October 1824, at the English theatre in Boulogne,
of which her brother was manager. After further appearances in Calais she returned to England.
It was not until September 1827 that she went to Paris, with Kemble. There she was more successful than she had been in her own country: we are told that "her Irish accent, an obstacle to
her success in London, was unperceived in Paris," where she made her effect by means of her
fine presence and the natural expressiveness of her voice.

[3] Victor Hugo, *Chants du crépuscule.* [B.]

and the pitiful pettiness of our old poetic school, the offspring of pedagogues and *Frères ignorantins.* I saw . . . I understood . . . I felt . . . that I had risen from the dead and that I must get up and walk.

But the shock was too great, and it was a long while before I recovered from it. I became possessed by an intense, overpowering sense of sadness, that in my then sickly, nervous state produced a mental condition adequately to describe which would take a great physiologist. I could not sleep, I lost my spirits, my favourite studies became distasteful to me, I could not work, and I spent my time wandering aimlessly about Paris and its environs. During that long period of suffering I can only recall four occasions on which I slept, and then it was the heavy, death-like sleep produced by complete physical exhaustion. These were one night when I had thrown myself down on some sheaves in a field near Ville-Juif; one day in a meadow in the neighbourhood of Sceaux; once on the snow on the banks of the frozen Seine, near Neuilly; and lastly on a table in the Café du Cardinal at the corner of the Boulevard des Italiens and the Rue Richelieu, where I slept for five hours, to the terror of the *garçons,* who thought I was dead and were afraid to come near me.

It was on my return from one of these wanderings,[1] in which I must have seemed like one seeking his soul, that my eyes fell on Moore's *Irish Melodies,* lying open on my table at the song beginning, " When he who adores thee." I seized my pen and then and there wrote the music to that heartrending farewell, which is published at the end of my collection of songs, *Irlande,* under the title of *Élégie.* This is the only occasion on which I have been able to vent any strong feeling in music while still under its influence. And I think that I have rarely reached such poignant truth of melodic expression, combined with such sinister harmony.

The song is immensely difficult both to sing and to accompany, and takes two accomplished artists [2] to render it adequately; above all, a singer gifted with a sympathetic voice and intense power of feeling to enable him to express the deep, tender, passionate despair Moore must have experienced when he wrote the words, and which

[1] Berlioz is in error here: the *Lettres intimes* show that the *Élégie* was written in 1830, whereas the events narrated in this chapter belong to 1827. The *Élégie* may, however, have been originally written before 1829, and re-cast in 1830. See the reference to the burning of "my Élégie en prose" in his letter of 1829 to Hiller (No. 4 of the *Correspondance inédite*).

[2] If Pischek could play his own accompaniment, that would realise my ideal of a performance of the song. [B.]

I felt when I married them to music. It would give me intense pain
to hear that song feebly sung. In order to avoid such a trial, I have
never, in all the twenty years since it was written, asked anyone to
sing it to me. Alizard once saw it in my room, and tried it over without accompaniment, transposing it (into B) to suit his bass voice, and
this upset me so completely that I was obliged to beg him to stop. He
understood the song; I saw that he would sing it perfectly, and so I
determined to arrange the accompaniment for an orchestra. But I
then considered that works of this nature are not suited for the ear
of the concert-public, and that to expose them to its indifference would
be sacrilege; so I stopped short, and burnt what I had done.

As good luck would have it, the French prose translation of
Moore's poetry is so good that I was able, afterwards, to adapt the
original words to my music. If this elegy ever becomes known in England and Germany, it may possibly find some few admirers among
those who have known what grief is. But it would be incomprehensible
to most Frenchmen, and simple insanity to an Italian.

When I left the theatre after seeing *Hamlet,* I was so shaken at
what I had experienced that I determined never again to expose myself to the fire of Shakespeare's genius.

The next day *Romeo and Juliet* was announced. . . . I had a
pass to the orchestra of the Odéon, but so afraid was I that the doorkeeper might have had orders to suspend the free-list, that the moment I saw the advertisement I rushed off to the ticket-office to buy
a stall and secure a seat at any cost.[1] From that moment my fate was
sealed. After the melancholy, the harrowing sufferings, the tearful
love, the bitter irony, the black meditations, the heartrending sorrows,
the madness, the tears, mourning, catastrophes, and malign fortune
of Hamlet — the dark clouds and icy winds of Denmark — the change
was too great to the hot sunshine and balmy nights of Italy — to the
love, quick as thought, burning as lava, imperious, irresistible, illimitably pure and beautiful as the smile of an angel; the raging revenges,
delirious embraces, and desperate struggles between love and death.
And so, at the end of the third act, scarcely able to breathe, stifled with
a feeling as though an iron hand held my heart in its grip, I cried out,
"Ah, I am lost!" I must add that I did not then know a syllable of
English, that I only dimly discerned Shakespeare through the misty

---

[1] *Romeo* was first given on 12 September: Berlioz attended the second performance on the
15th.

medium of Letourneur's translation, and had no conception of the exquisite poetry in which his wonderful creations were clothed. Nor indeed am I much better off even now. It is far more difficult for a Frenchman to sound the deeps of Shakespeare's style than it is for an Englishman to appreciate the subtlety and originality of Molière or La Fontaine. Our two poets are rich continents, Shakespeare is an entire world. But the play of the actors, and especially of the actress, the succession of scenes, the action, and the tones of voice, penetrated me with the Shakespearian ideas and passions as the poor, pale translation never could have done. It was stated last winter in an article in the *Illustrated London News,* that after seeing Miss Smithson as *Juliet* I cried out, " I will marry that woman! and I will write my greatest symphony on that play!" I did both; but I never said anything of the kind. My biographer has endowed me with a vaster ambition than I possessed. This narrative will show what strange circumstances brought about a result which I was too completely overwhelmed even to dream of at the time.

The success of Shakespeare in Paris, which was in great measure due to the enthusiastic support of the new school of literature, led by Victor Hugo, Alexandre Dumas, and Alfred de Vigny, was, however, surpassed by that of Miss Smithson. No actress in France ever touched, stirred, and excited the public as she did; no one ever received such rapturous eulogies from the French press as were published in her honour.

After these two performances of *Hamlet* and *Romeo* I had no difficulty in keeping away from the English theatre; more experiences of that kind would have killed me; I shrank from them as one shrinks from physical pain; and the mere thought of exposing myself to such a trial made me shudder.

I had spent some months [1] in the kind of hopeless stupor of which I have only faintly indicated the nature and the cause, dreaming ceaselessly of Shakespeare and of the fair Ophelia of whom all Paris raved, and contrasting her splendid career and my own miserable obscurity, when all at once I rose up and determined that the light of my obscure name should flash up even to her, where she stood. And so I resolved to do what no composer had ever ventured to do in France. I resolved to give a great concert in the Conservatoire, in which only my own

[1] Berlioz forgets to mention that on the 22nd November 1827 he gave, in the Saint Eustache Church, a second performance of his Mass.

works should be played. " I will show her," I said, " *that I also am an artist.*" To achieve this, three things were necessary — copies of my music, the room, and the performers.

The moment my mind was made up, I set to work to copy out the orchestral and choral parts of the pieces I had selected, and this took me sixteen hours a day.

My programme included the *Waverley* and *Francs-Juges* overtures; a song and trio, with chorus, from the *Francs-Juges;* the *Scène héroïque Grecque;* and my cantata, *La Mort d'Orphée,* which the jury of the Institute had pronounced unplayable.

While copying indefatigably I managed by rigid economy to add a few hundred francs to my former savings, and with these I proposed to pay my chorus. With regard to the orchestra, I was certain of obtaining the gratuitous services of that of the Odéon, and of portions of those of the Opéra and of the Théâtre des Nouveautés. The chief difficulty was, as is always the case in Paris, the room. In order to get the use of the hall of the Conservatoire, which was the only perfectly satisfactory one, it was necessary to obtain the sanction of the Superintendent of Fine Arts, M. Sosthènes de Larochefoucault, and the consent of Cherubini.

M. Larochefoucault at once granted my request; but the moment I spoke of my plan to Cherubini he burst into a passion.

" You want to give a concert? " he began, with his usual courtesy.

" Yes, sir."

" You will have to obtain the sanction of the Superintendent of Fine Arts."

" I have got it."

" M. de Larossefoucault consents? "

" Yes, sir."

" But — but — but, *I* don't; a — a — a — and I object to your having the room."

" But, sir, you have no right to refuse; because the Conservatoire has nothing to do with it at present, and it is not in use during the next fortnight."

" But I tell you that I don't want you to give this concert. Everybody is in the country, and you won't make any money."

" I don't want to make any. I only want to be known."

"There is no necessity for your being known. Besides, you will want money for your expenses. Have you any? "

"Yes, sir."

"Ah! And wha — wha — what music are you going to play at this concert?"

"Two overtures, selections from an opera, and my cantata *La Mort d'Orphée.*"

"That competition-cantata that I would not have? It is bad; it — it — it — is unplayable."

"So you thought, sir; but I am very glad to have an opportunity of judging for myself. . . . If a bad pianist could not play it there is no reason why a good orchestra should not."

"So you want to — to — to — insult the Academy?"

"No, sir; I only want to try an experiment. If, as is probably the case, the Academy was right in pronouncing my cantata unplayable, it is quite evident that it won't be played. If, on the other hand, the Academy was mistaken, it will be said that I took its advice and corrected my work."

"You can only give your concert on a Sunday."

"It shall be on a Sunday."

"But Sunday is the only holiday for the attendants of the Conservatoire; and surely you don't want to kill these poor creatures, to — to — to — kill them with work?"

"You must be joking, sir; these poor creatures, for whom you feel such pity, are only too delighted to have the opportunity of making some money, and you would do them a great injury if you deprived them of the means of doing so."

"I won't have it, I won't! and I shall write to the superintendent and ask him to withdraw his sanction." [1]

"You are very kind, sir; but M. de Larochefoucault will not break his promise. Besides, I shall write to him myself and send him an accurate account of our conversation. He will then understand your reasons and mine."

And I did send it just as it is given here. I heard some years afterwards from one of the secretaries of the Fine Arts Department that the superintendent had laughed over it till he cried. Cherubini's consideration for the poor Conservatoire attendants, whom I wanted to *kill with work* by my concert, struck him as peculiarly touching; and so he replied at once, as anyone with any common sense must have

---

[1] These dialogues lose half their drollery in translation, owing to the impossibility of representing Cherubini's Italian pronunciation of French, which is conveyed in the original. [H.]

done, renewing his authorisation and adding these words, for which I shall always feel grateful to him: " I advise you to show this letter to M. Cherubini, who has received the necessary *orders* with regard to you." The moment I receive this official document I rush off to the Conservatoire and hand it to the director, asking him to read it. Cherubini takes the paper, reads it carefully, re-reads it, turns first pale and then green, and hands it back to me without a word.

That was the first dose he received from me in return for the mortification I endured when he turned me out of the library after our first interview.

I left him with a kind of feeling of satisfaction, muttering to myself, in irreverent imitation of his own soft tones: " Come, sir, it is only a tiny dose, swallow it quietly; and gently, gently, please! It will not be the last, my man, if you do not let me alone!"[1]

[1] The original documents, now in the Archives nationales, show that Berlioz's account of the episode has been slightly coloured by his feelings. Instead of first procuring La Rochefoucault's consent and then approaching Cherubini, as he says, Berlioz first sounded the latter, who, no doubt wanting to get rid of him in what he thought the simplest way, referred him to the Superintendent of the Fine Arts. Berlioz then set his protectors in political high places to work — the Comte de Chabrillant and President Chenavaz, the deputy for the Isère—assuring them that Cherubini had authorised him to ask for the hall.

La Rochefoucault, on the 2nd May, replied that the matter would have his consideration. On the 3rd, Berlioz himself wrote to La Rochefoucault, telling him that his "whole musical existence" depended on the granting of this favour. On the 6th, La Rochefoucault wrote to Cherubini, saying that he would like to oblige the influential persons who had approached him in the matter, and asking if the Director of the Conservatoire had any objection. Cherubini thereupon sent for Berlioz and discussed the details of such a concert with him — the heavy financial responsibility and so on — and then wrote to La Rochefoucault to dissuade him from granting the use of the hall, partly for administrative reasons, partly in Berlioz's own interest, the season, in his opinion, being too far advanced for the concert to have any chance of success. He told Berlioz what he had done; whereupon the young man cleverly played his Director and the Superintendent off against each other, flattering the latter's vanity and stiffening his back by making it appear that his "subaltern" Cherubini was frustrating his will; and on the 13th permission was given to the composer for the use of the hall of the Conservatoire. The delays, however, had made a change in the date necessary. Berlioz now asked for the hall on the 26th instead of the 18th, and this request was granted by La Rochefoucault.

Berlioz's letters reveal him as a diplomatist of the first order. It will be seen that he is not quite ingenuous in his statement, in the *Mémoires*, that La Rochefoucault "at once" granted his request for the hall, and that it was *after* securing this permission that he approached Cherubini. His assertion that he sent the Superintendent an account of his interview with Cherubini "just as it is given here" is hardly borne out by the letter itself, which contains nothing whatever, for example, about the "unplayableness" of the cantata. The main facts of the affair are indeed as given in the *Mémoires*; but the facts have been liberally embroidered by his imagination. Whether La Rochefoucault "laughed over the letter till he cried," and especially over Cherubini's assumed concern for the overworked attendants, is extremely doubtful, seeing that there is nothing about these attendants in Berlioz's letter, which, indeed, has none of the humorous touches of the account given in the *Mémoires*.

CHAPTER XIX

A FUTILE CONCERT — A CONDUCTOR WHO CANNOT CONDUCT — A CHORUS WHICH CANNOT SING

Having got my orchestra and chorus together, and forced a concession of the hall from the *burbero Direttore,* I had still to provide myself with solo singers and a conductor. As I was afraid to conduct myself, Bloc, the leader of the Odéon orchestra, kindly undertook to do so; Duprez, who had only just left Choron's class, and was almost unknown, consented to sing the aria from the *Francs-Juges,* and Alexis Dupont was determined, in spite of his illness, to make another attempt at *La Mort d'Orphée,* for which he had already tried to obtain a hearing from the jury of the Conservatoire. For the soprano and bass parts of the trio from the *Francs-Juges* I was obliged to get two singers from the Opéra who had neither voices nor talent.

The rehearsal shared the fate of all gratuitous performances; a great many players were absent at the beginning, and they nearly all vanished before the end.

Still, the aria, the cantata, and the two overtures went fairly well; that of the *Francs-Juges* was warmly applauded by the orchestra, and a still greater sensation was produced by the finale of the cantata.

In this piece I had made the wind instruments repeat the air of Orpheus' hymn to Love, in accordance with the unexpressed but palpable meaning of the words after the *bacchanale,* the orchestra accompanying it with a vague, dreamy, rushing sound like the faint murmur of the river as it bears along the pale head of the murdered poet, while a dying voice from time to time utters the despairing cry re-echoed from the river-banks : " Eurydice ! Eurydice ! Unfortunate Eurydice ! "

I had had these five lines from the *Georgics* in my mind:

> Tum quoque, marmoreâ caput a cervice revulsum
> Gurgite quum medio portans Oeagrius Hebrus,
> Volveret, Eurydicen, vox ipsa et frigida lingua.
> Ah ! miseram Eurydicen, animâ fugiente vocabat;
> Eurydicen ! toto referebant flumine ripæ.

The strange sadness of this musical picture, the poetical meaning of which was sure to be missed by three-fourths of an ordinary uneducated audience, sent a shiver through the whole orchestra, and was received with a storm of applause. I am sorry now that I destroyed the score; I ought to have kept it for the sake of its last pages.[1] With the exception of the *bacchanale*,[2] which the orchestra rendered with splendid fury, the rest of the cantata did not go well. Dupont was so hoarse that he could scarcely sing his upper notes at all, and warned me not to count upon him for the performance.

So, to my great disgust, I was unable to insert the scena — which I had entitled in the programme, "*La Mort d'Orphée, the scena which was voted unplayable by the Academy of Fine Arts, and was played on the . . . May, 1828.*" And no doubt Cherubini, ignoring the true reason of its withdrawal, maintained that the orchestra had endorsed his verdict.

During the rehearsal of this unlucky cantata, I noticed how incapable conductors who are unaccustomed to handling grand opera are of following the capricious time of recitative. At the Odéon, Bloc only conducted operas interspersed with dialogue; and so, when he came to the recitative after Orpheus' first song which is interspersed with concerted orchestral passages, he always failed to bring in the instruments at the right moment. Seeing this, an antique amateur, who was present at the rehearsal, made the remark: " Ah, talk to me of the old Italian cantatas! That is music which does not tax a conductor; it leads itself." "Yes," I retorted, " like old donkeys, which find their way home alone." That was how I made friends for myself.

However, the cantata was replaced by the *Resurrexit* from my Mass, which was well known to both chorus and orchestra, and the concert took place. The overtures and the *Resurrexit* were well received and applauded; and the aria was well rendered by Duprez, whose voice was at that time gentle and soft. It was an invocation to sleep. But the trio and chorus were pitifully sung, and *without chorus,* for they failed to come in at the right time, and prudently kept silence till the end. The public did not appreciate the Greek scene, which requires a large chorus to produce a proper effect. It was never performed again, and I destroyed it.[3]

[1] As these pages are passing through the press, I learn that the score has been found by M. Boschot in the National Library.

[2] The piece in which the Conservatoire pianist broke down. [B.]

[3] But a manuscript of the score, not in the composer's handwriting, has survived, and the work will be found in Series V of the Malherbe-Weingartner edition of Berlioz's complete works.

Still, the concert did me some good;[1] first, by introducing me to the artists and the public, which, in spite of Cherubini's opinion to the contrary, was necessary; and then, in bringing me face to face with the enormous difficulties which beset a composer when he undertakes the performance of his own works, and showing me what a task I had before me. It is scarcely necessary to add that the receipts barely covered the expenses of lighting, the advertisements, the *droit des pauvres,* and my priceless chorus, with their judicious gift of silence.

The concert was warmly praised by some of the papers. Fétis (who afterwards . . .), Fétis himself — spoke most flatteringly of me in a drawing-room, as a man whose appearance before the public was a great event.

Would the tidings of my success reach Miss Smithson, in the intoxicating whirl of her own triumphs? Alas! I learnt afterwards that, absorbed in her own brilliant career, she never even heard of my name, my struggles, my concert, or my success!

CHAPTER XX

BEETHOVEN AT THE CONSERVATOIRE — VINDICTIVE
RESERVE OF THE FRENCH MUSICIANS — IMPRES-
SIONS PRODUCED ON LESUEUR BY THE SYM-
PHONY IN C MINOR — HIS PERSISTENT
ADHERENCE TO HIS FORMER
CONCLUSIONS

IT sometimes happens that in the life of an artist one thunderclap follows another as swiftly as it does in those great storms in the physical world, where the clouds, charged with the electric fluid, seem

---

[1] Although Berlioz, in his letters after the concert, spoke of it as a great success, the hall was almost empty. The programme consisted of the *Waverley* overture, a *Mélodie pastorale,* for solo and chorus, taken from the second act of the *Francs-Juges,* the *Marche religieuse des Mages,* the *Resurrexit* (i.e. the *Et iterum venturus* from his Mass), the *Francs-Juges* overture, and *La Révolution Grecque.*

With his usual energy and address, he had secured liberal preliminary advertisement of the concert in the Press, and in spite of the poor attendance he certainly achieved the result he had aimed at — to get himself talked about. Fétis, who was afterwards to become one of his most obstinate opponents, hailed him as a young innovator of genius, though, "carried away by his youthful and ardent imagination, he exhausts himself in combinations of an original and passionate effect . . . his originality often becoming bizarrerie . . . and his exaggeration causing him to overshoot his mark."

literally to sport with the thunder, while they hurl it to and fro as if exulting in the effect they produce.

I had scarcely recovered from the visions of Shakespeare and Weber when I beheld Beethoven's giant form looming above the horizon. The shock was almost as great as that I had received from Shakespeare, and a new world of music was revealed to me by the musician, just as a new universe of poetry had been opened to me by the poet.

A society for the performance of orchestral works had been organised at the Conservatoire, under the active and ardent leadership of Habeneck.[1] We must not allow the defects and shortcomings of this conductor with regard to the great master whom he worshipped, to blind us to his good intentions, his undoubted ability, or the fact that to him alone is due the glorious success of Beethoven's works in Paris. It is to his ceaseless exertions that the great society, the Société des Concerts, which has attained world-wide celebrity, owes its existence. He had to inspire other musicians with his own enthusiasm, and he found that their indifference turned to active opposition when they saw what a vista of unremunerative labour opened before them, and when they realised the ceaseless rehearsals which were necessary to secure a satisfactory performance of a class of music which was then chiefly noted for its eccentricity and its difficulty.

Not the least of Habeneck's obstacles lay in the silent opposition, ill-concealed dislike, and ironical reserve of the French and Italian composers, who were but ill-pleased to see an altar erected to a German, whose works they deemed monstrosities, and regarded as fraught with danger to themselves and their school. What abominable nonsense I have heard them talk about these marvels of learning and inspiration!

My master Lesueur, a thoroughly honest man, without malice or jealousy, a lover of his art, but a devoted adherent of certain musical dogmas, which I call stupid prejudices, made a characteristic remark to me about Beethoven's music. A rumour of the sensation which the performance of Beethoven's symphonies, at the first series of the Conservatoire concerts, had produced on the Parisian musical world, reached him even in his retirement. His surprise was all the greater in that, in common with the most of his fellow-academicians, he regarded instrumental music as a respectable, but distinctly inferior,

[1] The Société des Concerts was founded in February of 1828: it was in the spring of that year that it gave the Beethoven performances referred to by Berlioz.

branch of the art, and believed that Haydn and Mozart had achieved all that could be looked for in that direction.

Like Berton, who regarded the whole of the modern German school with contemptuous pity; like Boïeldieu, who did not know what to make of it, and expressed the most childish surprise at any combination of harmonies outside the three chords with which he had trifled all his life; like Cherubini, who dissembled his bile, not daring to vent it on the master whose success exasperated him and sapped the foundations of all his pet theories; like Paër, who, with Italian astuteness, went about disseminating stories about Beethoven, with whom he professed himself acquainted — stories which were always more or less discreditable to the great man and advantageous to himself; like Catel, who had quarrelled with music and was entirely devoted to his roses; like Kreutzer even, who shared Berton's contemptuous disdain for everything German; — like all these masters, Lesueur remained obstinately silent and resolutely deaf, and persistently absented himself from the Conservatoire concerts, in the face of the fever of enthusiasm with which he saw that all artists in general, and I myself in particular, were possessed. Had he gone he would have been obliged to come to some conclusion about Beethoven, and to give expression to that conclusion; he would have been a reluctant witness of the wild enthusiasm which his works had aroused; and this was just what Lesueur dreaded, though he did not acknowledge it even to himself. I left him no peace, however, and insisted so strongly on the necessity for his understanding and appreciating an event of such importance as the introduction of this new style and these colossal forms, that he reluctantly yielded, and allowed himself to be taken to the Conservatoire on a day on which Beethoven's Symphony in C minor was to be performed. He wished to listen to it conscientiously and undisturbed; so he sent me away, and seated himself among strangers in one of the lower boxes. When it was over I went down to find out what effect the marvellous work had produced on him.

I met him striding up and down the passage with flushed cheeks. " Well, dear master? " . . . " Hush! I want air; I must go outside. It is incredible, wonderful! It stirred and affected and disturbed me to such a degree that when I came out of the box and tried to put on my hat I could not find my own head! Do not speak to me till to-morrow." . . .

I was victorious! The next day I rushed off to his house, and we at once fell to talking of the masterpiece which had stirred us so deeply. He allowed me to run on for some time, assenting in a constrained manner to my enthusiastic eulogies. It was easy to see that I was talking to a quite different being from the man of the day before, and that the subject was painful to him. But I persisted until Lesueur, after again admitting how deeply the symphony had affected him, shook his head with a curious smile, and said, " All the same, such music ought not to be written." To which I replied, " Don't be afraid, dear master, there will never be too much of it."

Poor human nature! . . . poor master! . . . His words, which men are evermore uttering under one form or another, express obstinacy, regret, envy, and dread of the unknown, and an implicit confession of impotency. To say, " Such music ought not to be written," after having felt its power and beauty, is tacitly to acknowledge that you will not produce such because you could not if you would.

Haydn had already said much the same thing of Beethoven, of whom he always spoke obstinately as *a great pianist*.[1]

Grétry gave utterance to some equally inept criticisms regarding Mozart, who had, he said, *placed the statue on the orchestra and the pedestal on the stage.*

Handel said *his cook was a better musician than Gluck.*[2]

Rossini, speaking of Weber's music, says *that it gives him the colic.*

But the aversion of Handel and Rossini for Gluck and Weber is, I think, due to a different cause; it is impossible for two men of stomach to understand two men of heart. The feeling of bitter hatred, on the other hand, displayed against Spontini by the whole French school and the greater part of the Italian musicians, was certainly caused by the wretched, contemptible, complex feeling to which I adverted above, and which has been scourged so ruthlessly by La Fontaine in his fable of the fox and the sour grapes.

The persistency with which Lesueur strove against the evidence of his own senses gave the death-blow to my wavering faith in the

---

[1] This is more than doubtful. Haydn and Beethoven were antagonistic in many respects, but there is no trace of any expression of the kind given in the text. Even if Haydn had said what is attributed to him, it need not have been in depreciation; for Beethoven *was* a great pianist, the greatest in Vienna *at the time* when he and Haydn were there together; and Haydn had ceased to go to public performances before Beethoven became known as a great orchestral writer. [H.]

[2] This is always misunderstood. Handel said nothing of the kind. He said: "Gluck knows no more counterpoint than my cook, Waltz." Counterpoint was never Gluck's *forte*, and the sting of the comparison with the cook is very much reduced when it is recollected that Waltz was a musician, and a very good singer, and took the part of Polyphemus in *Acis and Galatea*. [H.]

doctrines with which he had striven to imbue me; I at once forsook the old beaten track and took my way over wood and meadow, mountain and valley. But I hid my defection as well as I could, and Lesueur only became aware of it long afterwards, when he heard some of the new compositions I had taken care not to show him.

I shall return to the subject of the Society's concerts and Habeneck when I come to the period of my intercourse with that clever but unsatisfactory and capricious conductor.

CHAPTER XXI

FATALITY—I BECOME A CRITIC

I MUST here mention the circumstances by which I became involved in the complications of musical criticism. Messrs. Humbert Ferrand, Cazalès, and de Carné, names well known in the world of politics, had just started a periodical review as an organ for their religious and monarchical opinions. It was called the *Revue Européenne,* and they wanted to complete their staff.

Humbert Ferrand asked me to undertake the musical critiques; but I told him I could not write, that my style would be abominable, and that, in fact, I dared not. " You are mistaken," he replied; " I have read your letters, and you will soon acquire the requisite knack; besides, we will look over your articles before they are printed, and point out anything which needs correction. Come and see de Carné, and he will tell you the terms of your agreement."

I was immensely attracted by the idea of wielding such a weapon in the defence of beauty, and for attacking what I deemed unbeautiful, and the opportunity of adding slightly to my limited resources was very welcome. So I went with Ferrand to Carné's, and it was all arranged.

I never feel much confidence in myself until I have proved my power; but on this occasion my natural diffidence was increased by the recollection of a former unsuccessful excursion into the field of musical polemics. It was in this wise. I had been wrought into a condition of absolute fury by the blasphemies which the Rossinian papers were uttering against Gluck, Spontini, and the entire school of feeling and common sense, by their exaggerated laudations of Rossini and his sensual system of music, and by the hopeless absurdity of the reasoning by which they endeavoured to demonstrate that the only end of music, dramatic or other, is to charm the ear, and in no wise to give expression to ideas and passions, together with a great deal more of arrogant nonsense uttered by men ignorant of the very A B C of music.

One day, after reading the ramblings of one of these lunatics, I was seized with a sudden impulse to answer them. I wanted a respectable organ, so I wrote to M. Michaud, the editor and proprietor of the *Quotidienne,* which was then a popular paper. I explained my wish, my object, and my opinions, and promised to hit fair as well as hard. My letter, which was half jest, half earnest, pleased him, and his reply was favourable. My proposal was accepted, and my first article eagerly looked for. " Ah, wretches ! " I cried, leaping with joy, " I have got you." I was mistaken; I had got no one — nothing. My inexperience in the art of writing, in the usages of the world, and the etiquette of journalism, coupled with the intensity of my musical feelings, culminated in a regular fiasco. The article I took to M. Michaud was not only badly conceived and worse written, but it exceeded all bounds, even of polemics. M. Michaud listened, and, shocked at my audacity, he said: " It is all true, but you smash everybody's windows; I could not insert such an article in the *Revue Quotidienne.*" I went away, promising to alter it; but I was too lazy, and too much disgusted at the idea of so many precautions, and so I left it alone.

When I talk of my laziness, it only applies to the writing of prose. I have often sat up all night over my scores, and have spent eight hours at a time labouring at instrumentation, without once changing my position; but I have to fight with myself to begin to write a page of prose, and about the tenth line or so I get up, walk about the room, look out into the street, take up a book, and strive by any means to overcome the weariness and fatigue which instantly overpower me. I have to return to the charge eight or ten times before I can finish an article for the *Journal des Débats,* and it takes me quite two days to write one, even when I like the subject and am interested by it. And then, what erasures, and what scrawls ! You should see my first draft ! Musical composition comes naturally to me, and is a delight; but prose-writing is a labour. Nevertheless, incited and encouraged by Ferrand, I wrote several laudatory articles on Gluck, Spontini, and Beethoven; after touching them up according to some hints of M. de Carné's, they were printed and well received; and I began to understand the difficulties of this dangerous task, which has since played so important and so deplorable a part in my life. My readers will see how impossible it was for me to avoid this, and in how many ways it has influenced my career as an artist in France and elsewhere.

CHAPTER XXII

THE COMPETITION FOR MUSICAL COMPOSITION — THE
CONSTITUTION OF THE ACADÉMIE DES BEAUX-
ARTS — I GAIN THE SECOND PRIZE

IT was in the month of June,[1] in the year 1828, that I presented my-self for the third time at the competition of the Institute. I was haunted by my Shakespearean passion, which had been painfully intensified by the effect produced on me by Beethoven; and was at that time a dreamy, savage creature, silent to the verge of dumbness, disorderly in my attire, as great a burden to my friends as to myself, and my only occupation the occasional production of a small and shapeless article on music. I succeeded in obtaining the second prize.

The privileges it bestows are: a laureate crown and a gold medal of no great worth — both publicly bestowed — a free pass to all the opera-houses, and many chances of obtaining the first prize at the next examination.

The first prize confers much higher privileges. It secures the artist a yearly pension of three thousand francs (£120) for five years, on condition of his spending the first two in the French Academy at Rome, and the third in travelling through Germany. The remainder is paid him in Paris, where he does his best to make himself known and to keep the wolf from the door.

I will now give a *résumé* of what I wrote in various papers, fifteen or sixteen years ago, regarding the curious way in which these exami-nations are organised.

The intention of the Government, in establishing the Prix de Rome, was, first, to bring forward year by year the most promising among the young French composers; secondly, to enable them, by

---

[1] Really July. The cantata to be set was *Herminie*. Berlioz's setting was not published till long after his death: he employs in it the *idée fixe* theme that was later to figure so strongly in the *Symphonie fantastique*.

means of a pension, to devote themselves entirely for five years to the
study of music. These being the objects in view, we shall now consider
what means were, until lately, taken to secure them.

Things have changed somewhat since then, but only slightly.[1]

To most readers the facts I am about to relate may seem strange
and improbable; but as I obtained both the second and first prizes at
the Conservatoire, I shall merely state what I saw myself and know
to be true. My success enables me to speak my mind quite unreservedly,
without any fear that what I utter from pure love of my art, and from
my innermost conviction, will be attributed to the bitterness of
wounded vanity.

Cherubini, who is the most academic of academicians, past, present, and future, and, therefore, the most susceptible to my remarks,
has already reproached me with " striking my nurse," the Academy.
Had I failed in obtaining the prize, he could not have taxed me with
ingratitude; but he and others would have declared that I was aveng-
ing my own defeat. So that there is apparently no way in which I can
approach this sacred topic. Yet I do approach it, and I intend, moreover, to treat it as I would any other topic.

According to the rules, all Frenchmen or naturalised Frenchmen
under the age of thirty were and are eligible for the competition.
When the date of the competition had been fixed, the candidates entered their names at the *secrétariat* of the Institute. They underwent
a preparatory examination called *concours préliminaire,* the object of
which was to designate the five or six most advanced pupils.

The subject for the great competition was to be a serious lyrical
scena for one or two voices *and orchestra;* and, in order to show that
they possessed the requisite feeling for melody and dramatic expression, and also a sufficient knowledge of instrumentation, to produce
such a work, the candidates were called upon to write *a vocal fugue.*
They were given a day to do this, and *each fugue was to be signed.*
On the following day the members of the musical section of the
Institute assembled, looked through the fugues, and made their choice,
which was not altogether impartial, seeing that a certain number of
them bore the signatures of their own pupils.

Then when the votes had been registered and the competitors des-

---

[1] They are completely altered now. The Emperor has just suppressed that section in the
Conservatoire rules, and it is no longer the Académie des Beaux-Arts that awards the prize for
Musical Composition (1865). [B.]

ignated, the latter were called in to hear the text they were to set, and to enter their " boxes." The permanent secretary of the Academy then dictated the words of a classic poem which usually began thus:

"Déjà l'aurore aux doigts de rose." Or:
"Déjà le jour naissant ranime la nature." Or:
"Déjà d'un doux éclat l'horizon se colore." Or:
"Déjà du blond Phœbus le char brillant s'avance." Or:
"Déjà de pourpre et d'or les monts lointains se parent." Etc. etc.

The candidates were then shut up, with some such luminous poem and a piano, in separate rooms called "boxes," until their score was finished. At eleven and at six the jailer unlocked the doors and the prisoners met for their meals; but they were forbidden to leave the building. All papers, letters, clothes, or books sent from the outside world were carefully examined, to guard against the least chance of external assistance or advice. But they were allowed to receive visitors in the courtyard of the Institute from six to eight each evening, and even to invite their friends to festive dinners, where there was no limit to the communications, verbal or otherwise, which might pass between the Burgundy and the champagne. Twenty-two days was the period allowed for the completion of the work, and those who finished before that time were allowed to go away, after they had handed in their manuscript, *numbered* and *signed*.

When all the scores were ready the lyric Areopagus reassembled, their numbers being strengthened by the addition of two members from the other sections of the Institute; a sculptor and a painter, for example, or an engraver and an architect, or a sculptor and an engraver, or an architect and a painter, or even two engravers, two architects, two sculptors, or two painters. The important thing was that they should not be musicians. They had votes, and were there to pass judgment on an art of which they were wholly ignorant. The scenas were gone through one after another, and, though written for orchestra, they were accompanied *on the piano*. . . . And this is still the case.

Can anyone conceive the absurdity of trying to judge of the merits of an orchestral work thus mutilated? The piano can give an idea of an orchestral work to anyone who has already heard it played by an orchestra, because memory supplies what is lacking and recalls the full performance. But in the present state of music it is utterly impossible to convey any adequate idea of a new work in that way.

A score such as Sacchini's *Œdipe,* or any work of that school, in which there is no instrumentation, loses very little by being heard on the piano. But with any modern music — that is supposing, of course, the composer has availed himself of the means now at his disposal — it is quite another matter. Take the Communion march from Cherubini's Mass *du Sacre,* for example. What would become of those wonderful prolonged notes of the wind instruments which fill you with mystic ecstasy? or of those delicious interlacings of flutes and clarinets to which almost the whole effect is due? They would disappear completely, because the piano can neither hold nor swell a note. Try to accompany Agamemnon's song in Gluck's *Iphigenia in Aulis* with the piano! In the passage,

> J'entends retentir dans mon sein
> Le cri plaintif de la nature,

there is a most masterly and touching solo for the oboe, which, when played on the piano, sounds like a meaningless bell, instead of a plaintive wail. In this way the *idea,* the *thought,* the *inspiration* are either marred or destroyed. It is unnecessary to mention the great orchestral effects which are lost on the piano; the piquant exchanges between the wind and string instruments; the sharp contrasts of colour between the brass and wood; the mysterious and gorgeous effects of the percussion instruments when employed *piano;* of their enormous power when employed *forte;* of the striking effects which are achieved by placing one instrumental group at a distance from another; or a hundred other details upon which it would be superfluous for me to enlarge. The injustice and absurdity of the whole thing are self-evident. By destroying the instrumental effects the piano at once reduces all composers to the same level, and places the clever, profound, ingenious orchestrator on the same platform with an ignorant dunce who knows nothing of that branch of his art. The dunce may have put trombones for clarinets, ophicleides for bassoons; may have committed the most outrageous blunders, and not know even the compass of the various instruments; while the work of the other may be a masterpiece of ingenious instrumentation — and yet on the piano it will be impossible to distinguish the difference. The piano, for the orchestral writer, is a guillotine that severs the head of noble and of churl with the same impartial indifference.

To continue: when the pieces have been performed in this manner then comes the ballot (I speak in the present tense, as this still remains unchanged), and then the prize is awarded. Do you think it is all over? Not at all. A week afterwards all the sections of the Académie des Beaux-Arts assemble for the final decision. This imposing jury of thirty to thirty-five members is made up of painters, sculptors, architects, engravers, etchers, not excluding even the six musicians. These six members are to some extent able to supplement the inadequacy of the pianoforte accompaniment by looking over the scores; but that resource is not available for the other academicians, to whom music is a sealed book.

When the performers — that is, the singers and the pianoforte player — have gone through all the compositions a second time, after the manner of the first, the fatal urn is handed round, the votes are counted, and the choice of the musical section, made a week earlier, is either confirmed, modified, or upset by the majority. In this way, then, the prize for music is adjudged by men who are not musicians, and who have not even had a chance of hearing a proper performance of the compositions between which, by an absurd rule, they are required to make a choice.[1]

It is only fair to add that, if painters and engravers have to decide musical questions, musicians are, in their turn, summoned to award prizes for painting, engraving, etc.; all prizes, for all branches of art, being adjudged in precisely the manner described — by a collective jury of all the art sections of the Academy. I must, however, confess that, if I were a member of that august body, I should find it very difficult to state my grounds for awarding a prize for painting or engraving, and should testify my perfect impartiality by drawing lots.

On the solemn day when the prizes are distributed, the cantata thus chosen by painters, sculptors, and engravers is adequately performed. It is somewhat late in the day, and it would probably have been better to summon the orchestra before pronouncing the verdict. It seems rather a waste of money to have this tardy performance at all, as the decision is beyond recall; but the Academy is curious; it really wishes to *hear* the work to which it has adjudged the prize. What more natural?

[1] Berlioz forgets to mention that the musicians on the jury had awarded the second prize to one Margeot, a pupil of Reicha, and that it was the painters, sculptors, architects, and engravers whose votes reversed this judgment, the prize going to Hector Berlioz.

CHAPTER XXIII

THE ACADEMY PORTER — HIS REVELATIONS

In my day there was an old porter, named Pingard, at the Institute, whose indignation at all this procedure was very funny. It was his duty to shut us up in our boxes during the competition, to open our doors morning and evening, and to watch over our intercourse with visitors during play-hours. He also acted as usher to the academicians, and was therefore present at all the private and public sittings, where he had made some curious observations.

He had gone out as a cabin-boy, at the age of sixteen, on board a frigate, and visited the East Indian islands; and was the only one of the crew who survived the pestilential fevers of Java.

I never weary of listening to travellers' tales of distant lands; their digressions never tire me, and I follow them into all the endless intricacies of episode within episode; so, when the narrator loses himself in a digression, strikes his forehead, and cries, " Good heavens! where was I ? " I am always able to put him on the right track, and give him the name and date he wants, and then he says, " Ah, yes, that was it." So old Pingard and I were great friends, and he liked me because I enjoyed talking to him about Batavia, the Celebes, Amboyna, Coromandel, Borneo, and Sumatra, and because I was very curious about the Java women, whose love is fatal to Europeans and with whom our buck had had such a good time that for a while it looked as if consumption were going to do for him what cholera morbus had left undone. I rose greatly in his esteem one day by speaking of Volney, " that excellent simple creature, Count de Volney, who always wore blue woollen stockings "; and his enthusiasm knew no bounds when I asked him if he had known the celebrated traveller, Levaillant.

" M. Levaillant! M. Levaillant! " he cried, delighted; "know him? I should rather think so. Look here: one day, when I was walking up and down the quay at the Cape of Good Hope, whistling . . . I was waiting for a little negress who had given me an assignation on the shore, because, between you and me, there were reasons why she could not come to my house. I will tell you . . ."

" Never mind that, you were going to tell me about Levaillant."

" To be sure. Well, one day when I was walking about whistling at the Cape of Good Hope, a big, sunburnt man with a bushy beard stopped and turned round; he had evidently heard me whistling in French, and that was how he recognised me. ' I say, my boy, are you French?' ' I should rather think so,' I said. ' I come from Givet, in the Ardennes, Méhul's[1] part of the country.' ' Ah! You're a Frenchman?' ' Yes.' ' Ah!' And he turned away. It was M. Levaillant. So now you see I do know him!"

Thus it will be seen that old Pingard was my friend, and he showed his confidence in me by telling me things he would not have dared to reveal to anyone else. I remember a very animated conversation we had the day that I received the second prize. That year the subject we were to set to music was an episode taken from Tasso — the faithful and unhappy Herminia disguising herself in Clorinda's armour, and being thus able to leave Jerusalem and go to nurse the wounded Tancred.

In these academic cantatas there were always three arias — first, the rising of the inevitable dawn; then the first recitative and the first aria; then the second recitative and the second aria; and then the third recitative and the third aria, all for the same person. In the middle of the third aria came these words:

> Dieu des chrétiens, toi que j'ignore,
> Toi que j'outrageais autrefois,
> Aujourd'hui mon respect t'implore,
> Daigne écouter ma faible voix.

I was audacious enough to think that although the last aria was marked *agitato,* yet, this verse being a prayer, the trembling Queen of Antioch would hardly implore the God of the Christians with melodramatic cries to the accompaniment of an agitated orchestra. So I turned it into a prayer, and that *andante* was certainly the best part of my cantata.

When I reached the Academy on the night of the final decision, to learn my fate, and to see whether, in the eyes of the painters, sculptors, and engravers, I was a bad musician or a good one, I met Pingard on the stairs.

" Well," I ask, " who has got it?"

---

[1] Méhul belonged to Givet, but I doubt whether he was born at the time Pingard pretends to have mentioned his name to Levaillant. [B.]

" Ah! It's you, Berlioz. Good. I was looking for you."

" What have I got? Tell me quickly. The first prize, the second, honourable mention, or nothing? "

" Oh, look here! I am quite upset. Just think, you only missed the first prize by two votes."

" This is the first I have heard of it."

" But I tell you it is so! . . . You have got the second prize, that's good; but you only missed the first by two votes. Oh! look here. I *am* sorry, for, you see, though I am neither a painter, an architect, nor an engraver, and consequently know nothing about music, still your *Dieu des chrétiens* brought a great lump into my throat. And, by Jove! look here, if I had met you then I would . . . I would have stood you *a small cup of coffee!* "

" Thanks, thanks, Pingard, you are very kind. You understand it all; you have good taste. By-the-bye, have you not been on the Coromandel coast? "

" I should say so. Why? "

" And to Java? "

" Yes; but —— "

" And Sumatra? "

" Yes."

" Borneo? "

" Yes."

" You knew Levaillant *well?* "

" I should think so, as well as I know myself."

" You have often spoken to Volney? "

" The Count de Volney who had blue stockings? "

" Yes — well, you know, Pingard, you are a good judge of music."

" I don't quite understand."

" It is not necessary that you should; only if anyone should by any chance say to you, ' What right have you to judge between one composer and another? Are you a painter, engraver, architect, or sculptor? ' you must say, ' No; I am a sailor, a traveller, a friend of Levaillant and of Volney.' That is enough. Ah! by-the-way, how did the meeting go? "

" Oh! look here, don't talk to me of that; it is always the same thing. If I had thirty children I should take precious good care not to make one an artist. You see I know all about it. You can't conceive what a confounded job it all is. . . . For instance, they give

away and even sell their votes to one another. Look here: once, at a
competition for painting, I heard M. Lethière ask M. Cherubini to
give him his vote for one of his pupils. 'We are such old friends,' he
said, 'that you cannot refuse. Besides, my pupil is clever, and his
picture is very good.' 'No, no, no, I will not, I will not,' says the
other; 'your pupil promised my wife an album she wanted, and he
has not even drawn her a tree. I will not vote for him.' 'Ah, you are
wrong,' said M. Lethière; 'I give you my votes and you will not give
me yours!' 'No, I will not.' 'Then I will do the album for you myself — I cannot say more than that.' 'Ah! that is another matter.
What is your pupil's name? I always forget; give me his christian-
name too, and the number of the picture, so that there may be no mistake. I will write it all down.' 'Pingard!' 'Sir!' 'Bring a sheet of
paper and a pencil.' 'Here, sir.' . . . They retire into the em-
brasure of a window, write down something, and then, as they part, I
hear the musician say, 'All right, he shall have my vote.' Well, isn't
that abominable? And if one of my sons were a competitor, and I did
that sort of thing, wouldn't they discharge me on the spot?"

"Come, now, Pingard, don't get excited, but tell me what happened to-day."

"I have told you: you got the second prize, and you only lost
the first by two votes. When M. Dupont had finished singing your
cantata, they brought the *hurn*.[1] A musician near me was whispering
to an architect, and saying: 'Look here, that fellow will never do
anything; don't vote for him, he is a hopeless subject. He admires
nothing but that atrocious Beethoven: we shall never get him back
into the right path.' 'Do you think so?' said the architect. 'Still'
. . . 'Oh, I am sure of it; you have only to ask our great Cherubini.
I daresay you will take *his* opinion; he will tell you that the young
man is mad — he has got Beethoven on the brain.'

"I beg your pardon," said Pingard, interrupting his story, "but
who is this Beethoven? He does not belong to the Academy, and yet
everyone is talking about him."

"No; he is not a member of the Academy. He is a German.
Go on."

"Ah, well, it was soon over. When I handed the *hurn* to the
architect I noticed that he voted for No. 4 instead of for you. Suddenly one of the musicians stood up and said: 'Gentlemen, before

---

[1] Good old Pingard always called the ballot-box by this name. [B.]

we go farther, I wish to point out to you that the orchestration of the second part of the work we have just heard is very remarkable, and must be very effective; but of course the pianoforte score gives no idea of it. It is well you should know this.' ' What on earth are you talking about? ' retorts another musician; ' your pupil has not followed the programme; he has written *two* arias *agitato* instead of *one,* and in the middle he has stuck in a prayer that he shouldn't have done. We cannot have the rules broken in this way; we must make an example of him.' ' Oh, this is too bad! What does the secretary say? ' ' I think our friend is a little severe, and that we may pardon the young man's licence. But it would be as well to let the jury understand what are the merits of this composition which cannot be rendered on the pianoforte.' ' It is all a mistake,' breaks in Cherubini, ' this pretended orchestral effect does not exist, it is a regular hotch-potch, and would sound detestable in the orchestra.' ' There, now you hear,' cry the painters, sculptors, engravers, and architects; ' we can only go by what we hear; and, besides, if you are not agreed ———— ' . . . ' Ah, yes.' ' Ah, no.' ' But, good heavens! ' ' Well, what the devil? ' ' I tell you that ———— ' ' Oh, come now! '

" Well, they were all talking at once, and as M. Regnault and two other painters got tired of that, they declined to vote and went away. Then the votes in the *hurn* were counted, and you missed the first prize by two votes, and so you only got the second."

" Thank you, my good Pingard. Now tell me, do they manage things like that at the academy at the Cape of Good Hope? "

" Oh, come now; that is too much of a good thing. An academy at the Cape! A Hottentot Institute! You know quite well that there isn't one."

" Really? Nor among the Indians at Coromandel? "

" No."

" Nor the Malays? "

" Of course not."

" I see: there's no academy in the East? "

" Certainly not."

" How sad for the Orientals."

" Oh, they don't care."

" What barbarians."

And I left the old porter, thinking what a good thing it would be to send the Academy to civilise the island of Borneo. I had a complete project in my mind which I thought of laying before the academicians in the hope of getting them to go off to the Cape, like Pingard. But we Westerns are such egoists, we have so little love for humanity, that I had soon forgotten all about the poor Hottentots and the unfortunate Malays who have no academy, and never gave them another thought. I got the first prize two years later, as you will hear. Good old Pingard, unfortunately, died in the interval; which was a great pity; for I am sure if he had heard the Burning of Sardanapalus's Palace in my piece he would have stood me a *large* cup of coffee.

CHAPTER XXIV

MISS SMITHSON AGAIN — A BENEFIT — CRUEL FATE

AFTER the examination, and the distribution of prizes which followed it,[1] I relapsed into the state of dreary inaction that had become my normal condition. I was still the same obscure planet revolving unnoticed round my shining luminary! . . . so brilliant then, yet doomed to so dark an eclipse. My beautiful Estelle, the *Stella montis,* my *Stella matutina,* had so paled before my brilliant sun, that I never dreamed she could shine for me again. . . . Though studiously avoiding the English theatre, and turning away my eyes whenever they encountered Miss Smithson's portrait, I continued to write to her — without ever receiving a line in reply. My letters frightened instead of pleasing her, and she gave her maid stringent orders not to take in any more of them. The season was nearly over, it was rumoured that the troupe was to make a tour through Holland, and Miss Smithson's last appearances were announced. I felt that it would be madness to go and see her play Juliet or Ophelia again, so I steadily kept away. But when I saw that Miss Smithson and Abbot were to play two acts of *Romeo and Juliet* at Huet's benefit,[2] at the Opéra-Comique, I

---

[1] Berlioz left Paris on the 30th August 1828, and spent nearly a month at the Côte, returning to Paris towards the end of September. His father, who had withdrawn his allowance when he heard that Hector had borrowed money to give his concert of the 26th May, relented and undertook to allow him another year in which to make good as a musician.

[2] Berlioz's chronology is more than usually confusing here. The story of the first visit of the English actors belongs, as we have seen, to September 1827. Berlioz has told us of the concert of May 1828 and of the examination for the Prix de Rome in July of that year. But this episode of the benefit to Huet took place on 5 December *1827*, while the "last appearances" before the departure for Holland were at the end of 1828.

suddenly resolved that my name should figure beside that of the great
actress on the play-bill. I hoped in this way to attract her attention,
and, possessed with this childish idea, I rushed off to see the manager
of the Opéra-Comique, and to get him to play one of my overtures at
Huet's benefit. As the conductor saw no objection, the manager agreed.
When I went to the theatre for my rehearsal the English actors were
finishing theirs; I came in just as the poor distracted Romeo carries
Juliet off in his arms. As my eyes fell on the Shakespearean group I
gave a loud cry and rushed out of the theatre, wildly wringing my
hands. Juliet had seen and heard me.[1] . . . I had frightened her, and
she asked the actors who were with her to watch me, *as she did not
like the look of my eyes.*

When I returned an hour afterwards the stage was empty, the orchestra were in their places, and my overture was rehearsed. I sat as
in a dream, without saying a word; but when the applause with which
the musicians received it roused me, I hoped that the public might
like it too, and that their enthusiasm might kindle Miss Smithson's.
What madness! Is it not incredible that anyone could be so ignorant of
the ways of the world?

Even if the overture to the *Freischütz* or the *Magic Flute* were
played on a benefit night in France, no one would listen to it. It is a
mere prelude to the rising of the curtain, and even if it were differently received, there is nothing in the feeble performance of an
isolated overture, by a small theatrical orchestra like that of the
Opéra-Comique, to provoke enthusiasm. Besides, the great actors
who play for a benefit generally arrive at the eleventh hour, and are
naturally pre-occupied with their own performance. They have barely
time to dress, and are not found waiting about behind the scenes,
listening to what does not concern them. It had never occurred to me
that, even if my overture had been received with acclamations, and
loudly encored, it would have passed unnoticed by Miss Smithson,
who would be full of her part, and absorbed in the details of dressing. And supposing, even, that she had heard it; what then? She
would have asked what the applause meant, and her maid would
have replied, " It is nothing, madame; they are going to play
the overture again." Let us go farther, and suppose she had heard
the composer's name; would that have changed indifference into
love?

[1] This was the first time Harriet Smithson had set eyes on Berlioz.

My overture was well played and fairly applauded,[1] but not en-cored, and Miss Smithson never heard of it. She left for Holland the following day, after winning fresh laurels in her favourite part. By the purest accident (she never could believe this), I had taken a lodg-ing at No. 96, Rue Richelieu, almost opposite her own, at the corner of the Rue Neuve-Saint-Marc. After lying prostrated on my bed until three in the afternoon, I rose mechanically, and, as usual, went to the window to look out into the street. By one of those gratuitous, cruel freaks of fate, it happened that just at that moment Miss Smithson left her house, stepped into her carriage, and drove away for Am-sterdam. . . .

No words can describe what I suffered; even Shakespeare has never painted the horrible gnawing at the heart, the sense of utter desolation, the worthlessness of life, the torture of one's throbbing pulses, and the wild confusion of one's mind, the disgust of life, and the impossibility of suicide. The great poet has done no more, in *Hamlet,* than to count such suffering as among the most terrible evils of life.

I had left off composing; my mind was paralysed as my passion grew. I could only — suffer.

[1] This seems to be one of the cases in which Berlioz's imagination has outrun the facts. According to M. Boschot, "this overture, the title of which he [Berlioz] does not give us, was *not* performed: there is no mention of either Hector Berlioz or his overture even in the journals that were favorable to him, in which the benefit of Huet was announced. Nor is there any word of it or him in the newspaper accounts of the occasion. Did he rehearse the overture? Did he go to the theatre meaning to suggest its inclusion, and was it then that he saw his Juliet in the arms of another Romeo? Or was it no more than the dream of a project of this kind? Berlioz's dreams had so strong an interior life of their own that they left in him memories as precise as the things we call realities. Moreover, in proportion as he mused upon his dreams, or told them to others, or wrote about them, they spontaneously took the place of the forgotten reality. His dreams conformed to his aspirations, to the profoundest forces of his being. He loved them, caressed them, decorated them with precise details to suit himself. As against them, the truth was a dead thing."

CHAPTER XXV

MY THIRD TRIAL AT THE CONSERVATOIRE — NO FIRST
PRIZE AWARDED — A CURIOUS CONVERSATION
WITH BOÏELDIEU — SOOTHING MUSIC

WHEN June came round again,[1] I once more entered the academic
lists. My success was generally predicted, and it was even rumoured
that the members of the Institute themselves had said I was sure to
obtain the first prize. It was a great advantage to me that I had
already secured a second prize, whereas my competitors were altogether unknown; and, as I felt pretty confident of my success, I resolved on a course of action which subsequent events proved to be
suicidal. As the academicians had virtually decided that I was to have
the prize, I thought it unnecessary to cramp myself by writing the
kind of music I had written the previous year, in order to suit their
special prejudices; and I resolved to let myself go, and write something perfectly original, after my own heart. " I will be a true artist,"
I said, " and write a real cantata."

The subject was Cleopatra after the Battle of Actium. The Queen
of Egypt poisons herself by means of an asp, and dies in convulsions.
But before committing the fatal act she invokes the shades of the
Pharaohs, and questions them in dread awe as to what hope there is
that so dissolute and wicked a woman shall obtain admission to the
giant tombs in which lie buried the sovereigns distinguished for their
valour and virtue.

It was a grand idea to be expressed in music. I had often set
Juliet's wonderful monologue: " But if when I am laid into the tomb,"
in imagination, and it expresses the same feeling of dread which the
French rhymster had put into Cleopatra's prayer. But I stupidly put
Juliet's words as a heading to my score, and that in itself would have
condemned it irrevocably in the eyes of such Voltairean academicians
as my judges.

My task was therefore a congenial one, and I composed a piece,
large in treatment, with rhythm of striking originality, with enharmonic harmony of a solemn sonority, and a melody dramatically de-

[1] Berlioz means June 1829.

veloped in a long-drawn crescendo. I used it just as it was, afterwards, for the chorus (in octaves and unisons) entitled *Chœur d'Ombres,* in my lyrical drama, *Lélio.*

I have heard it performed at my concerts in Germany, and I know the effect it produces, and also know, although I have forgotten what the rest of the cantata was like, that this piece of itself should have secured me the first prize. The jury, however, decided not to award any first prize that year[1] rather than encourage a young composer who *manifested such tendencies.* The day following this decision I met Boïeldieu on the boulevard. I give the conversation just as it took place, for it was so curious that I remember every word. When he saw me he cried out:

" My dear boy, what *have* you done? You had the prize in your hand, and have deliberately thrown it away."

" I assure you, sir, I did my best."

" That is just it. You ought not to have done your best; your best is too good. How could I approve of such music, when soothing music is, above all others, the music I like?"

" It seems to me rather difficult to write soothing music for an Egyptian queen who has poisoned herself and is dying a most painful death in the agonies of remorse."

" Oh! I know you are sure to have plenty of excuses, but that makes no difference; it is always possible to be graceful."

" Yes, I know the gladiators learnt how to die gracefully; but Cleopatra was not so clever, it was not in her line; and besides, she did not die in public."

" Now you are exaggerating; we didn't want her to sing a country dance. But what need was there to drag such extraordinary harmonies into her invocation to the Pharaohs? I am not strong in harmony myself, and I must confess that I could make nothing of those other-world chords of yours."

I bowed silently, for how could I venture upon the patent retort, " Am I to blame because you are no harmonist?"

" And then," he continued, " why introduce a rhythm into your accompaniment, the like of which no one ever heard before?"

" I was not aware, sir, that in composing music it was desirable to avoid unusual forms if they were otherwise applicable, and you were lucky enough to light upon them."

[1] 1829.

" But, my dear fellow, it took all the skill and concentration of
Madame Dabadie to get through your music; and yet she is an accomplished musician."

" I certainly was not aware that music was intended to be sung
without skill or concentration."

" Ah, well, you are sure to have the last word, so good-bye; you
can benefit by this lesson next year. Come and see me before then and
have a chat, and I will argue it out with you, but like a *chevalier
français."* And he walked off delighted at having *made a hit,* as actors
say. In order to appreciate the point, which was worthy of d'Elleviou,[1]
it is necessary to understand that Boïeldieu's parting shaft was a quo-
tation from one of his own works [2] in which the two words in italics
occur.

In this quaint conversation, Boïeldieu was merely expressing the
ideas about music current in France at that time. What the Paris
public wanted was soothing music, slightly dramatic in tone, but simple and colourless, with no unusual harmonies, unwonted rhythms,
strange forms, or unexpected effects; whatever the subject might be
it must be so set as to make no unusual demands on the attention or
talents of either audience or actors. Music was to them simply a pleasing, tasteful art, and they liked the music suited for evening dress,
neither too exciting nor too dreamy, but joyous, troubadour, *chevalier
français* — Parisian music.

Some years ago they wanted something different, and not much
better; now they don't know what they want — or rather, they want
nothing.

What the devil could the Almighty have been thinking of when he
had me born *in this pleasant land of France?* And yet I am fond of
this strange country of mine, when I can forget art and dismiss our
absurd political outbursts. What spendthrifts we are (in words)!
How we laugh, how we amuse ourselves, at times! How we tear the
universe and its Creator to rags with our pretty white teeth and our
polished pink nails! How our wit sparkles! How we play upon words!
How royally and republicanly we *swagger!* This last is the least amusing thing about us.

[1] A celebrated actor at the Opéra-Comique, who was the type of a gallant French cavalier
of the time of the Empire. [B.]
[2] *Jean de Paris.* [B.]

CHAPTER XXVI

I READ GOETHE'S "FAUST" FOR THE FIRST TIME—
"SYMPHONIE FANTASTIQUE"—FRUITLESS EN-
DEAVOURS TO GET IT PERFORMED

ANOTHER of the most remarkable events of my life was the deep
and wonderful impression made on my mind by Goethe's *Faust,* which
I read the first time in a French translation by Gérard de Nerval.[1]
I was fascinated by it instantly, and always carried it about with me,
reading it anywhere and everywhere — at dinner, in the theatre, even
in the streets. The translation was in prose, with some versified fragments of songs, hymns, etc. I yielded to the temptation of setting
these; and no sooner was this difficult task ended than I was foolish
enough to have them printed — at my own expense, without having
even heard a note of them. They were published in Paris under the
title of *Huit Scènes de Faust,* and a copy fell into the hands of Marx,
the celebrated Berlin critic and theorist, who wrote me a very kind
letter about it. This unexpected encouragement, coming as it did
from Germany, gave me the greatest pleasure; but it did not blind
me to the many and grave defects of the work, which was incomplete
and badly written. It had, however, some good points, which I retained and developed in quite a new form in my legend, *La Damnation
de Faust.*

As soon as I became convinced of its worthlessness I withdrew
the work from circulation, and destroyed all the copies I could lay
hands on.

I remember that one of the scenes, for six voices, entitled *Concert
des Sylphes,* was performed at my first concert. It was sung by six
pupils of the Conservatoire, produced no effect, and was pronounced
meaningless, vague, colourless, and *wholly devoid of melody.* Eighteen
years later this very piece, with some slight alterations in the instrumentation and modulations, achieved European popularity. It was

[1] Once more the years have become telescoped in Berlioz's memory. Gérard de Nerval's
translation had appeared in December 1827. Precisely when Berlioz became acquainted with it
we cannot say, but it was certainly before he paid his short visit to the Côte in September 1828.
It was there that he made his setting of the ballad of the King of Thule. Apparently his first
intention was to write a descriptive *Faust* ballet for the Opéra. The hoped-for commission for
this having failed him, he wrote the *Eight Scenes from Faust* in the autumn of 1828.

encored whenever it was given, either in St. Petersburg, Moscow, Berlin, London, or Paris, and is now declared to be perfectly intelligible and deliciously *melodious*. It is true that it is now always sung by a chorus, for as I was unable to find six good solo singers I took twenty-four chorus singers, and the idea of the piece consequently becomes clearer; the form and colour stand out, and the effect is tripled. A good many pieces of this kind that are spoiled by the weakness of the singers would stand out vividly and powerfully if performed by a sufficient number of well trained chorus singers. Where one ordinary voice is detestable, fifty ordinary voices may be ravishing. A soulless singer paralyses the most powerful effects of the best composer, and renders them ridiculous; on the other hand, the average warmth of feeling which always resides in a really musical multitude brings out the inner flame of the work, and now it lives, whereas a single frigid virtuoso would have killed it.

It was immediately after this, my first effort at setting *Faust,* and while I was yet strongly under the influence of Goethe's poem, that I wrote my *Symphonie fantastique.* Some portions cost me great labour, while others were composed with incredible ease. For instance, I laboured for three weeks over the Adagio (*Scène aux Champs*), which always affects the public so keenly — and myself too, for that matter — and two or three times gave it up as hopeless. *La Marche au Supplice,* on the other hand, was written in one night. Still, I kept on adding finishing touches to both numbers, and to the whole work, for several years.[1]

[1] Berlioz does not make it clear that a good deal of the music of the symphony had already been written, and only needed revision and a certain amount of rearrangement to adapt it to his new programme. It is highly probable that the *Ronde du Sabbat* originally figured in the *Faust* ballet already mentioned. The Waltz perhaps came from the same source; even the *Scène aux Champs* may have had a place there. The "Estelle" melody, the *idée fixe* of the symphony, had already been used in the cantata *Herminie.*

His statement that the *March to the Scaffold* was written in a single night has been the subject of some controversy. According to M. Boschot, who has seen the manuscript, the March of the symphony is really the March already written for the unperformed opera *Les Francs-Juges.* To bring it into the programme-scheme of the symphony, all Berlioz had to do was to introduce the *idée fixe* at the end — a matter of four new bars, written on a slip (*collette*) and pasted over the original score. M. Boschot suggests that *this* "was what Berlioz wrote in a single night." Mr. Tom Wotton retorts that "it is to be feared that M. Boschot possesses neither a sense of humour nor the rudiments of logic," for it is difficult to picture to ourselves "Berlioz sitting up all night to copy out four bars of the *idée fixe.*" May it not be possible that here, as in other cases, the years have become telescoped in Berlioz's memory, and that while he certainly did not compose the March in a single night in 1830, he may quite well have written it in a single night for *Les Francs-Juges* in 1826?

Partly out of chivalry, we may suppose, towards the memory of Harriet, partly out of respect for himself, Berlioz has not told us the whole story of the genesis of the *Symphonie fantastique.* In the early part of 1829 Harriet seems to have been inclined to listen to his protestations

The Théâtre des Nouveautés had been playing *opéras-comiques*
for some time, and had a fair orchestra, conducted by Bloc. He advised me to ask the directors to perform my symphony, and to help me
to get up a concert for that purpose. They agreed, because the strange
programme of the work struck their fancy, and seemed to them calculated to excite the curiosity of the public. As I wanted a really great
performance, I invited eighty other musicians, which, added to Bloc's
orchestra, gave us altogether one hundred and thirty performers.
There was, of course, no accommodation for such numbers — neither
seats nor even music-desks. With the calmness of people who have not
realised the extent of a difficulty, the managers replied to all my demands by assuring me that all would be well, and that their machinist
might be relied on. But on the day of rehearsal, when my hundred and
thirty musicians were assembled, there was no room on the stage for
them. The little orchestra below had barely space for the violins, and
there was an uproar on the stage which would have maddened a much
more equable temper than mine. There was a call for desks, and the
carpenters hastily clutched anything which might serve the purpose;
the machinist went about swearing and looking for his flies and
wings; on one side there were cries for chairs, on another for instruments, on another for candles; the double-basses wanted strings; there
was no room for the drums, etc., etc. The porter was hopelessly

---

of passion, though she was still somewhat afraid of this wild, incomprehensible creature; and
Berlioz went so far as to communicate his matrimonial intentions to his family, though he prudently forbears to mention that the woman he proposes to make his wife is an actress.

His ardour persists unabated all through her long absence in London. He works at his grand
symphony, which is to be a sort of musical autobiography; his difficulty is to find the right con-
necting thread for all his emotions and for the fragments of music that already exist. Everyone
in Paris knows of his passion for Harriet; the symphony will be the glorification and the justi-
fication of this passion. But in the very letter (16 April 1830) in which he gives Humbert Ferrand
the plan of the symphony he speaks of his discovery of "frightful truths, as to which there is
no possibility of doubt," regarding Harriet. What had led him to this change of opinion we do
not know: perhaps some theatrical gossip from England had reached his ears. Unfortunately for
Harriet, when she arrived once more in Paris, in the spring of 1830, her vogue had completely
gone. In England she had never been regarded as anything better than a moderate actress.
The combination of her own youth and charm and Shakespeare's dramatic action had imposed
upon Paris in 1827. But between then and 1830, the English public having still refused to take
her seriously, she had found her level even in the theatrical company to which she was attached.
In 1830 she had to submit to a terrible humiliation; before the Parisian public that had once
adored her she was now relegated to dumb "walking-on" parts. How much this fact, which, to
the ironic Parisians, was a humiliation for her lover as much as for her, had to do with Berlioz's
change of feeling towards her it is impossible to say. But whether he had already turned against
her or not, it is certain that just at this time she begins to play a new and horrible part in his
symphony. He rends her and himself; she becomes, *via* a grotesque perversion of the melody of
the *idée fixe*, the Witch whose arrival at the Sabbath is greeted with cries of obscene joy from her
fellow demons.

bewildered. Bloc and I did the work of four, sixteen, thirty-two men, but all in vain; order could not be evolved from such chaos, and it turned into a regular rout — a musical Passage of the Beresina.

Still, in spite of the confusion, Bloc was determined to try two numbers, so as to give the directors "some idea of the symphony"; we went through the *Bal* and the *Marche au Supplice* as well as we could with such a disorganised orchestra, and the latter piece created a perfect *furore* amongst the players. Nevertheless the concert did not take place; the directors were scared by the upset, and withdrew from the enterprise. *They had not realised that a symphony necessitated such elaborate preparations.* And thus my plan fell to the ground for want of a few stools and desks. . . . Since then I have taken the utmost pains about the *matériel* of my concerts, having fully realised the disasters which may ensue from neglect of details.

CHAPTER XXVII

FANTASIA ON ''THE TEMPEST''—ITS PERFORMANCE
AT THE OPÉRA

GIRARD was at this time conductor at the Théâtre-Italien. In order to console me for my mishap, he advised me to compose something shorter than my *Symphonie fantastique,* and undertook to have it properly performed at his theatre. I therefore set to work to write a *fantaisie dramatique,* with chorus, on Shakespeare's *Tempest.* The moment Girard saw it he cried out: " This is on much too large a scale; we cannot perform a work of this kind at the Théâtre-Italien. It can only be done at the Opéra." I instantly rushed off to offer it to M. Lubbert, the director of the Académie Royale de Musique. To my great surprise he agreed to insert it in the programme of a concert in aid of the Artists' Benevolent Society. He had heard my name in connection with my first concert at the Conservatoire, and he trusted me so entirely that, without even looking through the score, he gave me his word, and kept it nobly. He is a *rara avis* among directors. As soon as the parts were copied out, the choruses were taken in hand at the Opéra. There were no hitches; the full rehearsal went off brilliantly, and Fétis, who encouraged me with might and main, was present and expressed the greatest interest both in the work and in its author. But, with my usual luck, a tremendous storm, such as had not been known for fifty years, broke over Paris shortly before the hour of performance! There was a regular waterspout, the streets were flooded and turned into rivers and lakes, and all traffic was suspended, so that, during the first half of the performance, while my *Tempest* (accursed tempest!) was being played, the Opera-house was all but empty. The audience consisted of some two or three hundred people at most — including the performers — and I might be said to have given a regular kick in the air.[1]

CHAPTER XXVIII

A VIOLENT DISTRACTION—F. H.—MADEMOISELLE M.

THESE musical enterprises were not my only sources of excitement. The German pianoforte player and composer H.,[2] with whom I had formed an intimacy since his arrival in Paris, was desperately in love with a young lady who has since become equally celebrated through her talents and her adventures. H., who was the confidant of my great Shakespearean passion, and was deeply distressed by my sufferings, had very imprudently confided the story to Mdlle. M.,[3] telling her at the same time that he had never heard of such a case of infatuation. " I should never be jealous of *him*," he said one day; " I know that he would never fall in love with you."

The effect of this idiotic speech on the mind of a Parisienne may be imagined. She became possessed with the idea of proving to her platonic and too-confiding admirer the error of which he had been guilty.

I had been asked that summer by Mdme. d'Aubrée, the superintendent of a girls' school, to give guitar lessons to her pupils. I accepted the offer, and, oddly enough, my name still figures in the prospectus as professor of that noble instrument. Mdlle. M. gave pianoforte lessons in the same school; she rallied me on my doleful looks, and told me *there was someone in the world who took the deepest interest*

---

[1] As so often happens in the *Mémoires*, Berlioz's chronology in this and the surrounding chapters is very confused. The concert at which the *Tempest* was given took place on 7 November 1830. Chapter xxix takes us back to July of that year, while the performance of *Sardanapalus* described in chapter xxx took place on 30 October.

[2] Ferdinand Hiller.

[3] Camille Moke.

in me. She also spoke to me about H., who, she said, was very fond of her, but *it would never come to anything.*

One day I received a letter from her, in which, under pretext of speaking to me about H., she made an appointment with me for the following morning. As luck would have it, I forgot all about it; which, if it had not been purely accidental on my part, would have been the most subtly diplomatic course I could have adopted. I really forgot the rendezvous, I only remembered it some hours too late. My sublime indifference completed the work of conquest, and after playing the part of Joseph rather rudely for a few days I yielded, and threw myself, with all the ardour of youth, into this liaison with a young and exasperatingly beautiful girl of eighteen, striving to forget my past sorrows in a new passion. If I were to narrate all the strange and romantic details of this little episode, my readers would probably be highly diverted; but as I am not penning my confessions, it will be sufficient to say that I ran through the whole gamut of passion in my intercourse with Mdlle. M. I told everything to poor H., who wept bitterly; but as he could not but acknowledge that he had only himself to blame, he made the best of it, and acquitted me of treachery, bade me farewell with a convulsive clasp of the hand, wished me joy of my good-fortune, and fled to Frankfort. I have always admired his conduct under such trying circumstances. The narrative of my Italian journey will show how dramatically this episode ended, and how nearly Mdlle. M. was to giving tragic confirmation to the truth of the proverb, " It is dangerous to play with edged tools."

The "H." of this chapter was Ferdinand Hiller (1811–1885), the friend of Mendelssohn and, in later years, the opponent of Liszt and Wagner. He has left us his reminiscences of Berlioz on his *Künstlerleben* (1880). He lived in Paris from 1828–1835, and seems to have made the acquaintance of Berlioz early in 1829. His descriptions of the young romantic are very interesting. "He was eight years older than I," he says, "and had lived in Paris for six years. He had learned what the fight for existence meant, and in comparison with myself he seemed a man ripened by hard experience, though his quite youthful nature exhibited the southern animation that never wholly deserted him." He found Berlioz trembling under the revelation of the power of the symphonic Beethoven after his experiences at the Conservatoire concerts, and was able to initiate him into the sonatas also. The pair became very intimate, and Berlioz spoke to Hiller a good deal of his happy Côte-Saint-André days and of his first struggles in Paris. By this time he had mastered his repugnance to morbid anatomy, and in true student style used to regale Hiller with the crudest hospital and dissecting room stories, punctuating them with the wild laughter that was always characteristic of him.

When Hiller met him he was earning his living by teaching the guitar and by correcting proofs for the publishers. "I can still see him," he says, "in a café of the Rue Richelieu (where, in the humane Paris fashion, he was allowed to monopolise a table for a whole half-day at a time) reading the proof sheets of Halévy's first successful opera, *Le Dilettante d'Avignon;* though this kind of thing was tiresome to him, he did not greatly worry over it. Now and then he made a little extra, for instance when he sold the gold medal he had won as second prize at the Conservatoire. It was worth 200 francs."

Hiller goes on to describe the rapid change that had come over Berlioz in Paris: the simple young man from the country had forced himself into a position in which every one talked of him, and in which he mixed on equal terms with all the musical celebrities. He rather shocked the good young German by his freethinking: "he believed in neither God nor Bach," says Hiller. "He was a sort of Mephistopheles; not that I was the Faust — rather the poor scholar!" Hiller's hair stood on end when Berlioz let himself go in conversation. He respected no one but Shakespeare, Goethe and Beethoven. He was at war with all conventions: "if it suited me," he said, "I would marry the natural daughter of a hangman and a negress." But below the surface he was an aristocrat and a conservative: he particularly disliked republicans and the mob.

"I do not think," says Hiller, "that anyone could have met Berlioz without being struck by the extraordinary expression of his face. The high forehead, precipitously overhanging the deep-set eyes, the great curving hawk-nose, the thin, finely-cut lips, the rather short chin, the enormous shock of light-brown hair,* against the fantastic wealth of which the barber could do nothing — whoever had once seen this head could never forget it. The face was peculiarly animated, the eyes alternately brilliant — indeed burning — and dull almost to extinction, the expression of the mouth varying from energy to utter contempt, from the friendliest of smiles to mocking laughter. He was of middle height, slender but not elegant, and utterly careless of his appearance. His voice was rather weak, though of course it varied with the endless variations in his mood. Its timbre was agreeable."

Hiller saw him at close quarters during the Harriet Smithson affair, and was psychologist enough to recognise that his passion for the Irish actress, who was completely ignorant of French, while Berlioz did not know a word of English, "was a matter more of his imagination than of his heart." Berlioz must have been a sore trial to his friends at this time. Hiller tells us that it was not in Berlioz's nature to keep silent about anything that affected him, and it needed all the patience of his friends to bear up under the stream of self-confession that he poured out on them during their walks, "filling the unsympathetic boulevards and the adjacent streets with his love-laments." "Nothing was spared us, neither the description of his sleepless nights, nor his nervous attacks, ending in tears, nor his long prowlings in Paris and the neighbouring country, nor his fugitive hopes, nor his hopeless resignation. 'If it were anyone else,' said Girard (the famous conductor, a sceptical man of the world), 'I would show him the door'."

Although Hiller lived only a few streets away, Berlioz seems to have felt a fatal urge to pour out his sorrows to him through the post. Hiller quotes *in extenso* an extraordinary letter that he received one day — dashed off on paper of folio size, and so spaced and capitalised that it filled four enormous pages:

"My dear Ferdinand!

"I must write to you again this evening——this letter will perhaps be no happier than the others. . . . . But no matter——.

Can you tell me what is this overwhelming might of emotion, this *capacity for suffering* that is killing me? . . . . .

—— . . . . .

let us not groan! . . .

my fire is going out, wait a moment——

O my friend, do you know? . . . . to relight it I have burnt the manuscript of my *prose elegy!* . . . . ., always tears, sympathetic tears; I see Ophelia shedding them, I hear her tragic voice, the rays from her sublime eyes consume me.

O my friend, I am so unhappy! inexpressibly unhappy!

I have spent some time drying the floods that have fallen from my eyes. . . . . . . while I saw Beethoven looking at me severely, Spontini, healed of his woes, regarding me with pity and indulgence——and Weber, who seems to whisper in my ear like a familiar spirit, inhabiting a happy sphere where he awaits me to console me.

All this is mad——completely mad, for a domino player in the Café de la Régence, or a Member of the Institut.

No, I still want to live——

* Other observers describe it as red.

music is a heavenly art, nothing surpasses it but true love——— the one will perhaps make me as unhappy as the other, but at least I shall have lived

> suffering, it is true———
> with madness, cries, and tears
> but I should have———————————
> NOTHING!

My dear Ferdinand! .... I have found in you all the signs of true friendship, my own for you is also true, but I fear it will never bring you the calm happiness that one finds far from the volcanoes———
absolutely beside myself,
incapable of saying anything
RATIONAL
today it is a year since I saw HER for the last time——————— oh! unhappy woman! how I loved you. ... .trembling I write, *HOW I LOVE YOU!*
If there is another world shall we find each other again? ....
Shall I ever see Shakespeare?
Will she know me? ..... Will she understand the poetry of my love? .... oh! *Juliet, Ophelia, Belvidera, Jane Shore,* names that hell repeats unceasingly. ....
truly;
I am a most unhappy man, a being almost alone in the world. ... an animal crushed under an imagination it cannot support, devoured by an illimitable love that is rewarded only with indifference and scorn; yes! but I have known certain musical geniuses, I have laughed in the gleam of their lightnings and I gnash my teeth at the mere remembrance.
Oh! sublime ones! sublime ones! annihilate me! summon me to your golden clouds! deliver me! .....
Reason says to me
'Be tranquil, fool, in a few years there will be no more question of your agonies than of what you call the genius of Beethoven, the passionate sensibility of Spontini, the dreamy imagination of Weber, the colossal power of Shakespeare!
'Go, go, Henriette Smithson
and   Hector Berlioz
will be reunited in the oblivion of the tomb, which will not prevent other unhappy ones from SUFFERING AND DYING . . .'."

The Mlle. M. of this chapter was Camille [This is the name under which she figures in the Berlioz biographies. Riemann gives her Christian names, however, as Marie Félicité Denise] Moke. Her father had been a professor in Ghent, who had come to disaster through speculation. To retrieve the family fortunes, his wife opened a shop for the sale of Dutch lingerie in the Faubourg Montmartre, Paris. The pretty little Camille seems to have cultivated, besides the piano, the more realistically profitable business of her feminine charms. The affair with Berlioz was, as his contemporary letters show, anything but the light-hearted matter he tries to make out in his *Mémoires*. He was madly in love with her — poor Harriet was by now forgotten — and wanted to marry her, "my ravishing sylph, my Ariel, my life," as he calls her in a letter to Humbert Ferrand. So ardent was his passion that it survived such temporary trials as the pianistic embroidery the fair Camille was wont to apply to the music she played, and the confession that she found the Beethoven adagios rather too long. The mother's sole concern was to realise the full commercial value of her pretty daughter in a profitable marriage. Poor student as he seemed to be at the time, Berlioz could not be quite ruled out as a candidate. He came of an old and well-to-do family and had prospects; he had influential protectors in political and literary circles. This was the situation at the period of which Berlioz is speaking in the foregoing chapter: the development will be told later.

Meanwhile it is interesting to compare with Berlioz's account that of Hiller himself in his *Künstlerleben*.

"A young German musician," he says (meaning, of course, himself), had had the friendliest reception from a charming French colleague: the pair made so much and such ardent music under mamma's eyes that the desire arose to meet without mamma and without piano. Nothing was easier to arrange. The young pianist was not only beautiful and sweet; she was decidedly talented and was much sought after as a teacher. Accompanied, rather than watched, by an easy-going duenna, she used to go to the most distant parts of Paris to give lessons in schools or to ladies of quality. So the pair used to meet as far from her house as possible, and not hurry on the homeward way. My young fellow-countryman was acquainted with Berlioz, and as the latter taught the guitar in the same school in which the young lady taught the piano, the German was simple enough to make him his confidant and to employ him as *postillon d'amour*. His inexperience brought him good fortune, in that it contributed to his disillusionment.

"The impressionable young pianist, who had heard of the great Shakespearean passion of the messenger, thought it piquant to turn this to her own profit. One day she told him outright that she loved him, and Berlioz at once planned an abduction *in optima forma*. For that he could have been forgiven, had he not also taken it into his head to lead the bold young lady home as his lawful wife. But mamma would not hear of this. The daughter was now very strictly watched, though the tempestuous wooer could not be wholly forbidden the house.

"Then Berlioz won the Prix de Rome, and Frau Martha (which was *not* her name) * had the game in her hands. She half-consented to an engagement, and rings were exchanged; but she knew that the bridegroom would soon have to cross the Alps, and that this latest fancy of her daughter would last no longer than earlier or subsequent ones. Berlioz gave a concert, at which his newest compositions made a great sensation and were lauded to the skies by at any rate a part of the public. Intoxicated with love and fame, he paid a visit to his family, and then went to Rome.

"He had hardly left Paris when the word went round our little musical world that there was a rival candidate for his bride, a rather old but rich and distinguished man — just what the mother needed for her daughter, and the daughter for her own eccentricity. I had the opportunity of seeing with my own eyes how much or how little the absence of the betrothed mattered. He wrote me the most passionate letters from the Côte-Saint-André, telling me of the joy of his family, the pangs of separation, and his anxieties; and when, with the best intentions, I ventured to hint that these affectionate solicitudes seemed to me to exist only on one side, he abused me roundly. All memory of the frivolous way in which the bond — and what a bond! — had been sealed appeared to have been wiped out: he could not have expressed himself otherwise had his beloved been an Iphigenia."

The remainder of the story will soon be told in Berlioz's own words. The new wooer — an undeniable asset in the mother's eyes, whereas Berlioz was more of a liability — was the forty-two-year-old Camille Pleyel (1788–1855), the head of the Paris firm of piano manufacturers.

CHAPTER XXIX

FOURTH COMPETITION AT CONSERVATOIRE —
I OBTAIN THE PRIZE — THE REVOLUTION
OF JULY — THE TAKING OF BABYLON —
"LA MARSEILLAISE" — ROUGET
DE LISLE

THE annual competition took place this year on the 15th July, a little later than usual. I went up for the fifth time, fully determined never to try again if I failed. It was in the year 1830. I was just finishing my cantata when the Revolution broke out.

* Hiller's facetious reference is to the old go-between in *Faust*.

Et lorsqu'un lourd soleil chauffait les grandes dalles
  Des ponts et de nos quais déserts,
Que les cloches hurlaient, que la grêle des balles
  Sifflait et pleuvait par les airs;
Que dans Paris entier, comme la mer qui monte,
  Le peuple soulevé grondait,
Et qu'au lugubre accent des vieux canons de fonte
  La Marseillaise répondait.[1]

A number of families had taken shelter in the Palais de l'Institut, and it looked strangely transformed — with long-barrelled muskets protruding from the barred doors, and its façade riddled with bullets, the air filled with the shrieks of women, and, in the lulls between the discharges of musketry, the joyous twitter of the swallows. I hurriedly dashed off the last pages of my cantata to the tune of the dry thud of the stray bullets as they described a parabola over the roofs and struck close to my windows or on the walls of my room; and on the 29th I was free to loaf about Paris with the *sainte canaille,*[2] and my pistol in my pocket, till the next day.

I shall never forget the aspect of Paris during those memorable days — the wild bravado of the street arabs, the enthusiasm of the men, the frenzy of the public women, the mournful resignation of the Swiss and Royal Guards, the curious pride which the workmen exhibited in not pillaging Paris though they were masters of the situation, the astounding stories told by young fellows of their exploits, in which the real bravery of the deed was lost in the sense of the ridiculous aroused by the manner in which it was told; as, for instance, when they described the storming of the cavalry barracks of the Rue de Babylone — in which considerable loss had been incurred — with a solemnity worthy of Alexander's veterans, as " the capture of Babylon " — an abbreviation forced on them by the length of the real name. With what pompous prolongation of the " o " the name of " Babylone " was pronounced! . . . Oh Parisians, what buffoons you are! Colossal, if you will, but colossal buffoons! . . .

No words can give any idea of the music, the songs, and the hoarse voices which rang through the streets!

And yet it was only a few days after this harmonious revolution that I received a most extraordinary musical impression, or rather shock. I was crossing the Palais Royal, when I heard a tune which I

---

[1] Auguste Barbier, *Iambes.* [B.]
[2] "Sacred rabble," an expression of Auguste Barbier's. [B.]

seemed to recognise, issuing from among a crowd of people. As I
drew nearer I perceived that ten or twelve young fellows were singing
a war-song of my own, the words of which, translated from one of
Moore's *Irish Melodies,*[1] happened exactly to suit the situation. Delighted at the discovery, and little used to that kind of success, I enter
the circle of singers, and ask to be allowed to join in. I am admitted,
and a superfluous bass is interpolated into the chorus. I did not, of
course, betray my identity; but I remember having a warm discussion
with the man who was beating time as to the tempo in which he was
taking my song. Luckily I recovered his good graces by singing quite
correctly my part in Béranger's *Vieux Drapeau,* which he had set to
music, and which we next performed. During the *entr'actes* of this
improvised concert three National Guards, whose duty it was to keep
the crowd off the singers, went round, shako in hand, to make a collection for those who had been wounded during the Three Days. The
Parisians, struck by the quaintness of the idea, contributed liberally,
and there was a perfect hailstorm of five-franc pieces, which our
music alone could hardly have charmed from the pockets of their
owners. As the audience went on increasing it became more and
more difficult to keep the necessary space clear for the performers,
and our *armed force* soon became impotent to control the curious
crowd. We find great difficulty in escaping; the crowd streams after
us; and at last, when we reach the Galerie Colbert, leading to the
Rue Vivienne, we are hunted out like bears at a fair, surrounded on
all sides, and more songs are demanded of us. The wife of a draper,
over whose shop there is a semicircular glazed gallery, suggests that
we shall go up to her first floor, and pour down our torrents of harmony on our ardent admirers from there, without fear of being
crushed to death. We agree, and begin with the *Marseillaise.* The
noisy crowd at our feet is hushed at once. The air is as still and charged
with solemnity as it is in the Piazza of St. Peter's when the Pope
pronounces the blessing, *urbi et orbi,* from the pontifical balcony. At
the end of the second verse, still the same silence. At the end of the
third again, not a sound. This was not at all what I wanted. When I
beheld that vast concourse I suddenly remembered that I had just arranged Rouget de Lisle's song for full orchestra and double chorus,
and had put in the margin: *For all who have voices, hearts, and blood*

---

[1] *Chant Guerrier* (Op. 2); from Moore's "Forget not our wounded companions, who stood."
[H.]

in their veins. " Ah ! " I said to myself, " that is what we want." So
I was greatly disappointed at this persistent silence, and at the end of
the fourth verse, unable to contain myself, I shouted, " Why on earth
don't you sing ? " Then the people roared out *" Aux armes, citoyens ! "*
with the precision and power of a trained chorus. You must remember that the gallery which opened into the Rue Vivienne was crowded,
so was the one opening into the Rue Neuve-des-Petits-Champs, so
was the area in the middle; and also that these four or five thousand
voices came reverberating back in the enclosed space, from the shut-
tered shops below, the glass frames above, and the pavement beneath
their feet. You must not forget either that the singers, men, women,
and children, were hot with the emotion of the combat of the previous
day, and you can imagine the effect produced by their thunderous
refrain. . . . I can only say that I actually fell prostrate in the midst
of our little band, who stood completely dumbfounded by the explosion,
like birds after a peal of thunder.

I have just said that I had arranged *La Marseillaise* for a double
chorus and full orchestra. I dedicated it to the author of the immortal
song, and received the following letter, which I have carefully kept,
in reply :

"Choisy-le-Roi, 20 Dec., 1830.

" We are strangers, Monsieur Berlioz ; shall we become friends ?
Your head seems to be a volcano in a perpetual state of eruption;
there was a straw fire in mine which is burnt out, and has left a little
smouldering smoke. But the wealth of your volcano and the remains
of my straw fire combined may yet produce something. So I have two
proposals to make to you. But we must see and know each other first.
If you like the idea, tell me what day I can see you; or come to breakfast or dine with me at Choisy. You won't get much; but you are a
poet, and the country air will be the best sauce for you. I should have
endeavoured to make your acquaintance sooner, and thank you for
the honour you have done a certain poor little creature in clothing
her nudity with your brilliant imagination. But I am merely a lame
hermit who rarely visits your great city, and spends three quarters
and a half of the time he is there in doing what he does not want to
do. May I hope that you will not reject my humble offer, but will in
some way or another enable me to thank you personally, and to ex-

press to you the pleasure with which I, like all true lovers of art, welcome your daring genius?

" ROUGET DE LISLE."

I heard afterwards that Rouget de Lisle — who, by-the-bye, has written many fine songs beside the *Marseillaise* — had a manuscript opera, founded on *Othello,* which he wanted to show me. But as I had to leave Paris the day after I received his letter,[1] I told him I must postpone seeing him until after my return from Italy. The poor fellow died in the interval, and I never met him.

When peace was restored in Paris after a fashion, and Lafayette had presented Louis Philippe to the people as the best of all possible republics — when, in fact, the play was played out and the social machine was set going again — the Académie des Beaux-Arts resumed its functions.

Our cantatas were played, on the piano of course, before the two Areopagi, whose working I have already explained. And as my piece (since burned) proved my conversion to the established faith, they at last, at last, at last, awarded me the first prize. I had suffered keenly in previous years at not getting it, and did not feel much elated when Pradier the sculptor came to look for me in the library, where I stood awaiting my fate, and said cordially, with a warm shake of the hand, " You have got the prize! " Seeing him so glad and me so indifferent, you would have thought he was the laureate and I the academician. But I soon felt all the advantages of my position. I could not, with my sense of the manner in which the whole thing was managed, feel much pride in my success, but it set an official seal on my powers which would undoubtedly gratify my parents, and it gave me a pension of a thousand crowns and free admission to the lyric theatres; it was a diploma, a certificate of my ability, and it secured me independence, nay, wealth, for five years to come.

---

[1] Did Berlioz really want to see Rouget de Lisle? He did not leave Paris "the next day," as he says, but ten days later. He returned to Paris at the end of 1832, and Rouget de Lisle did not die until 26 June 1836.

CHAPTER XXX

DISTRIBUTION OF PRIZES AT THE CONSERVATOIRE —
THE ACADEMICIANS — "SARDANAPALUS" — ITS PER-
FORMANCE — THE CONFLAGRATION WON'T
BURN — MY FURY — MDME. MALIBRAN'S
TERROR

Two months afterwards the prizes were distributed, and the successful cantata was performed. The ceremony was precisely the same
then as it is now. Year by year the same musicians play works which
are almost always the same, and the prizes, which are awarded with
the same amount of discrimination, are bestowed with the same
solemnities. Every year, on the same day, at the same hour, the same
academician, standing on the same step of the same staircase, repeats
the same sentence to the successful candidate. The day is the 1st Saturday in October, the hour four in the afternoon, the step the third;
everyone knows who the academician is, and here is the sentence:

"Now, young man, *macte animo;* you are going on a delightful
journey . . . the classic home of the Fine Arts . . . the country of
Pergolesi and Piccinni . . . inspired by those blue skies . . . you
will return with some splendid work . . . the world is at your feet."

In honour of the great event the academicians don their green-
embroidered uniforms; they are radiant, dazzling. They are about
to crown a painter, a sculptor, an architect, an engraver, and a musician. There is great joy in the abode of the muses.

What am I saying? . . . it sounds like poetry. To tell the truth
I was not thinking of the Academy at all, but of some lines of Victor
Hugo's, which, for some reason or another, came into my head:

> Aigle qu'ils devaient suivre, aigle de notre armée,
> Dont la plume sanglante en cent lieux est semée,
> Dont le tonnerre, un soir, s'éteignit dans les flots;
> Toi qui les a couvés dans l'aire maternelle
> Regarde et sois contente, et crie et bats de l'aile,
> Mère, tes aiglons sont éclos!

To return to our laureates, some of whom, by-the-way, are more
like La Fontaine's "surly little monsters," the owls, than young
eagles, but who are all impartially beloved by the Academy.

On the first Saturday in October, then, their radiant mother " flaps her wings," and the successful cantata is at last fully performed. An *entire* orchestra is brought together, complete in all its parts. There are stringed instruments, two flutes, two oboes, two clarinets. (To tell the truth this important section has only been completed recently. When the *grand prix* rose above my horizon, there was only one clarinet and a half, for the old man who had played the first clarinet from time immemorial, having but one tooth left, was only able to produce about half the notes from his asthmatic instrument.) There are four horns, three trombones, and even so modern an instrument as the cornet-à-pistons. Do you call that nothing? It is all true. The Academy on this day is completely transformed; it is off its head; it is guilty of actual extravagance. The maternal bird is pleased; " she screams and flaps her wings"; her owlets (I mean eaglets) are hatched at last. We are all at our posts, and the conductor raises his baton.

The sun rises; violoncello solo, slightly *crescendo*.

The little birds awake; flute solo, violin *tremolo*.

The little brooks murmur; viola *solo*.

The little lambs bleat; oboe *solo*.

And as the *crescendo* increases, it comes to pass that by the time the little birds, little streams, and little lambs have each had their say it must be at least midday. Then comes the recitative:

Already dawning day . . . etc. . . .

Then follow the first aria, the second recitative, the second aria, the third recitative, and the third aria, which generally kills the hero but revives the singer and the audience. The perpetual secretary then gives out the name of the composer in sonorous tones, holding in the one hand the wreath of artificial laurels with which to crown the victor's brow, and in the other the real gold medal (which will enable him to pay his bills before he leaves Rome — it is worth a hundred and sixty francs, I know this for certain).

The laureate rises:

Son front nouveau tondu, symbole de candeur,
Rougit, en approchant, d'une honnête pudeur.

He embraces the perpetual secretary (slight applause). He sees his august master standing close by; pupil and master embrace, as it is right they should (more applause). The laureate's parents are on a bench behind the academicians, shedding silent tears of joy; he vaults over the intervening benches, crushes the toes of one man, treads on the coat of another, and casts himself into the arms of his sobbing parents; nothing could be more natural. But instead of applauding the public is beginning to smile. On the right of this touching group stands a young girl, making desperate signs to the hero of the hour; he dashes towards her, tearing a lady's gauze dress to shreds in his haste, and crushing in a dandy's hat; she is his cousin, and he clasps her in his arms. He sometimes even embraces his cousin's neighbour (much laughter). Another woman, standing in a dim, remote corner, makes sympathetic signals, which the hero is careful not to observe. But he flies to embrace his sweetheart — his betrothed, who is to share his good fortune. He is careless of other women in his anxiety to reach her; knocks one down, gets caught in the footstool of another, and comes down with a heavy fall; he renounces his purpose, and returns to his seat humiliated and bathed in perspiration (loud applause and roars of laughter). How delightful! how charming! This is the crowning moment of the academic *séance,* and I know a great many people who go there solely on purpose to enjoy it. I bear the jesters no ill-will, for it happened that in my case there was neither father nor mother, cousin, *fiancée,* master nor mistress to embrace. . . . My master was ill, my parents absent or angry, and as for my mistress. . . . So I merely embraced the perpetual secretary, and as for my blushes, they were hidden beneath a shock of red hair, which, combined with certain other peculiarities, placed me undeniably in the category of owls.

Besides, I was in anything but an embracing mood that day; in fact, I don't think I ever was in such a passion in my life, and this was the reason for it. The subject of the cantata was *The Last Night of Sardanapalus.* The poem closes at the point where Sardanapalus, feeling himself vanquished, calls for his prettiest slaves, and mounts his funeral pyre with them. I had at first intended to write a sort of symphony descriptive of the conflagration, the shrieks of the reluctant women, the defiant words of the proud voluptuary in the midst of the devouring flames, and the crash of the falling palace. But when I recollected how limited were the means at my disposal I refrained. A glance at this orchestral finale would have caused the academicians to condemn the whole piece; while played on the piano it would have sounded perfectly unintelligible. So I bided my time, and when I had secured

the prize, and knew that my work would be performed by a full orchestra, I wrote my conflagration scene.

It produced such an effect when rehearsed that some of the academicians, quite taken by surprise, came up and congratulated me, not
at all resenting the trap into which I had led them. The hall was full
of artists and amateurs, curious to hear the work of the youth of
whom such strange tales were told. Many of them too had heard such
glowing reports of the sensation produced by the conflagration scene
at rehearsal that an unusual amount of interest was excited.

Before the concert began I placed myself, score in hand, beside
Grasset, the ex-conductor of the Théâtre-Italien, for I had my misgivings as to his powers. Mdme. Malibran, whose curiosity had been
aroused by the reports of the rehearsal, could not find a seat in the
hall, so we got a stool for her near myself, between two double-basses.
I have never seen her since.

The *decrescendo* begins.

(The cantata opens with the words, " Night has already drawn
her veil across the day," so that I had to describe a sunset instead of
the usual dawn, which looks as if I had been predestined to take life
and the Academy against the grain from the beginning.)

The cantata proceeds in due course. Sardanapalus hears of his de-
feat, resolves on death, sends for his women; the conflagration begins.
Those who were present at the rehearsal whisper to their neighbours,
" Now the crash is coming; it is wonderful — astounding! "

A hundred thousand curses on musicians who do not count their
bars! In the score, the horn gives the cue to the kettledrums, the kettle-
drums to the cymbals, the cymbals to the big drum, and the first sound
of the big drum brings in the final explosion. But the damned horn
makes no sign, the kettledrums are afraid to enter, and of course the
cymbals and big drums also remain silent; nothing is heard! nothing! ! ! And all the time the violins and basses carry on their impotent
tremolo, and there is no explosion, a conflagration that goes out before
it has begun; a fiasco instead of the talked-of end of all things. *Ridicu-
lus mus!* No one who has not been through a similar experience can
conceive what a fury I was in! With a cry of horror, I flung my score
right across the middle of the orchestra, dashing down two of the
music-desks. Mdme. Malibran started back as though a shell had
burst at her feet. There was a general uproar at once in the orchestra,
among the scandalised academicians, the mystified musicians, and the

enraged friends of the composer. This was the most disastrous of all my musical catastrophes up to then; would that it had been also the last!

CHAPTER XXXI

MY SECOND CONCERT—THE ''SYMPHONIE FANTAS-
TIQUE''—LISZT PAYS ME A VISIT—THE BEGINNING
OF OUR FRIENDSHIP—THE PARISIAN CRITICS—
CHERUBINI'S MOT—I START FOR ITALY

IN spite of the urgent representations I addressed to the Minister of the Interior to induce him to excuse me from the Italian journey,[1] which as laureate I had to undertake, I was obliged to prepare for going to Rome.

I did not want to leave Paris, however, without giving a satisfactory public performance of *Sardanapalus,* the finale of which had been murdered at the prize distribution. So I got up another concert at the Conservatoire, in which the prize cantata was to figure along with the *Symphonie fantastique.* The latter had not yet been heard. Habeneck undertook to conduct, and all the performers were good enough to offer me their services gratuitously for the third time, for which I cannot sufficiently thank them.

On the day before the concert I received a visit from Liszt, whom I had never yet seen. I spoke to him of Goethe's *Faust,* which he was obliged to confess he had not read, but about which he soon became as enthusiastic as myself. We were strongly attracted to one another, and our friendship has increased in warmth and depth ever since. He was present at the concert, and excited general attention by his applause and enthusiasm.

The performance was by no means perfect, as two rehearsals are wholly insufficient for such complicated works; but they went well enough for their principal features to be appreciated. *Le Bal, La Marche au Supplice,* and *Le Sabbat* created a great sensation; the march especially carried the audience by storm. The *Scène aux Champs*

---

[1] It was mainly because he did not want to leave Mlle. Moke that Berlioz tried to evade the obligation to go to Rome. Failure to do so, however, would have meant forfeiting the benefits and privileges attached to the prize— the 3000 francs a year for five years, free maintenance in Rome, and all the rest.

fell flat; but it was very different in those days from what it is now. I made up my mind on the spot to re-write it. Hiller, who was in Paris at the time, gave me some admirable hints, by which I hope I profited.[1]

The cantata was well performed; the conflagration took place, the great crash followed, and the success was immense. Some days later, articles appeared in the newspapers fiercely attacking or passionately praising my music. But instead of pointing out, as they might easily have done, the palpable defects in both works (defects which it took me years of work to eradicate from my symphony), my hostile critics fell foul of me for my absurd ideas (which were not mine at all), the crudeness of certain modulations (which did not exist), my systematic contempt for certain fundamental rules of art (which I had religiously obeyed), and my neglect of certain musical forms (which were the only ones employed in the very passages cited to the contrary)! On the other hand I am bound to confess that my partisans have often credited me with aims of which I was wholly unconscious, and which were utterly absurd. The amount of nonsense, folly, and rubbish, the extravagant theories and ridiculous systems which the critics of the French press have perpetrated on my behalf pass all belief. Only two or three writers have discussed me with intelligent self-restraint. It is not easy, even nowadays, to find critics who possess the requisite knowledge, imagination, feeling, and impartiality to pass a sound judgment on my works, and to appreciate my aims and the tendency of my mind. They certainly did not exist when I began my career; and the few and imperfect performances of my works would necessarily have left much to their imaginations.

I was far better understood and appreciated in Paris by the young men who possessed some musical training, and what we may call the sixth, or artistic, sense, than by the prosy, puffed-up, pretentious, ignorant clique of critics. I became a regular bugbear to the composers whose landmarks I so ruthlessly removed, and my undisguised contempt for certain scholastic articles of faith goaded them to exasperation. God knows that there is nothing on earth so ruthless and violent as such fanaticism.

---

[1] Berlioz omits to tell us that he arranged his concert for the day on which Harriet Smithson, who had lost 6000 francs by the failure of the Opéra-Comique, was to take a benefit at the Opéra. It was the 5th December 1830. His concert took place at the Conservatoire at two o'clock: everyone in the audience must have known the connection of the symphony with Harriet, and the performance was over in time for them to be at the Opéra by seven, when the benefit commenced. Harriet appeared as the dumb girl, Fenella, in Auber's opera *Masaniello*.

Cherubini's indignation at this storm of heterodoxy, and the sensation it awakened, may be imagined. His followers had informed him of the effect produced by the last rehearsal of the " abominable " symphony; on the day of performance he passed the door of the concert-room as the audience was trooping in, and someone stopped him and said, " Are you not coming to hear Berlioz's new work? " " Ze n'ai pas besoin d'aller savoir comment *il né faut pas faire!* " (" I don't want to be taught *how not to write!* ") he retorted, with the air of a cat choking down a forced dose of mustard. When the concert turned out a success he looked like the cat *after* its dose of mustard; he was speechless, and could only sneeze. Then, after some days, he sent for me. " Are you going to Italy? " " Yes, sir." " Your studies are at an end, and your name will be struck off the books of the Conservatoire. *Mais il me semble qué, qué, qué, vous deviez venir me faire une visite. On — on — on — on — né sort pas d'ici comme d'une écurie!* " . . . I was on the point of retorting, " Why not, since we are treated like horses? " but I was wise enough to refrain, and assured our amiable director that I should certainly pay him a farewell visit and thank him for his kindness.

So, much against my will, I was forced to go to Rome, and there forget good old Cherubini's gracious encouragement, the rusty lance-thrusts of the *chevalier français* Boïeldieu, the grotesque disquisitions of my newspaper critics, the enthusiasm of my friends, the invectives of my enemies, and the whole musical world and even music itself, at my leisure. No doubt the objects of the Institute were, on the whole, good, and it is not for me to judge how far the intentions of the founders have been carried out as regards the careers of painters, sculptors, engravers, and architects; but as regards musicians, the Italian journey is, to say the least of it, useless for their special study, though the artistic treasures, scenery, and associations of the country may assist in developing their imaginations. This will be clearly proved by a truthful account of the life led by the French artists in Rome.

Before starting, the five or six new laureates assemble to make arrangements for the journey. A *vetturino* undertakes to convoy the cargo (they generally travel together) to Italy in a huge chariot, into which they are thrust, for all the world like a batch of country folk going to a fair. As they never change horses, it takes a long time to traverse France, cross the Alps, and reach Rome; but the tediousness of the journey is doubtless beguiled by the countless incidents certain to befall a cartload of light-hearted young fellows. I cannot, however, speak from personal experience, for I was detained in Paris until the middle of January, and after spending some weeks at the Côte-Saint-André with my parents — who were proud of my success and received me most warmly — I bent my steps towards Italy, feeling lonely and somewhat sad.[1]

CHAPTER XXXII

MARSEILLES TO LEGHORN — STORM — LEGHORN TO ROME — THE ACADÉMIE DE FRANCE IN ROME

THERE was no inducement to cross the Alps at that time of year, so I determined to go round by Marseilles. It was my first sight of the sea. I spent some time in looking for a tolerably clean vessel going to Leghorn; but saw nothing but wretched little ships, with evil-smelling cargoes of wood or oil, or stinking bones for the manufacture of bone-black, and not a hole or corner on board in which a man could sleep, no shelter, and no food. I was to provide my own victuals, and sleep in a filthy little hole with four sailors, with faces like bull-dogs, and of more than doubtful honesty, for my sole companions. I refused the tempting offer, and spent some idle days wandering about the rocks near Notre-Dame de la Garde, which is a very pleasant way of killing time. At last I heard of a Scandinavian brig, which was on the point of sailing for Leghorn. Some nice-looking young fellows, whom I met at La Cannebière, told me they were going in her, and that we should

---

[1] The success of the *Symphonie fantastique*, following on the winning of the Prix de Rome, seems to have determined Mme. Moke to allow Berlioz to become engaged to her daughter: or was it simply that, with Pleyel on the horizon, she wanted to get rid of the young man? Berlioz's family rejoiced over the news of the engagement; only Nanci had a premonition that the sighted oasis might turn out to be merely a mirage. Berlioz left Paris on 29 December 1930, wearing an engagement ring, and leaving with Camille the gold medal of the Institut. He took in the Côte-Saint-André on his way south, arriving there on the 3rd January. He left for Rome a month later.

During his stay at the Côte he poured out his heart to his friends in Paris, among them Hiller; "may all Europe exhaust itself in cries of rage, the children all cut each other's throats, and Paris perish in flames," he cried, "if only I am there, holding *her* in my arms, we two entwined together in the flames!" Hiller, who must have known that the Fates would soon avenge him on Hector for the rape of Camille, smiled ironically to himself and sent Berlioz word that his betrothed was bearing the separation with fortitude; he had seen her at a concert, gay and smiling. Hector, tortured with jealousy, actually took to his bed for some days. By the time he arrived at Rome he was no doubt more than half-prepared for the catastrophe to be narrated in Chapter XXXIV.

be fairly comfortable if we arranged to mess together. The captain would have nothing to do with our commissariat, so we had to look after it ourselves. We laid in a stock of provisions for a week, which was more than enough, as the crossing only took three or four days in fair weather. One's first journey on the Mediterranean is a delightful experience, if the weather is fine, the ship fairly good, and one is not sea-sick. I congratulated myself on my fortunate exemption from the malady by which my fellow-passengers were prostrated during the first two days of our voyage. Our dinners on deck, as we sailed along the Sardinian coast in the brilliant sunshine, were delightful. My fellow-passengers, who were all Italians, told endless stories, most of them wholly incredible, but very interesting. One had fought in the Greek War of Independence, and had known Canaris intimately. We pestered him with questions about the revolutionary hero whose glory seemed to have burned itself out as quickly as the flame of his own fire-ships. A Venetian, an underbred fellow, who spoke abominable French, averred that he had commanded Lord Byron's corvette during the poet's adventurous excursions in the Adriatic and the Grecian Archipelago. He gave us a minute description of the brilliant uniform Lord Byron had insisted on his wearing, and the orgies in which they indulged; and his modesty did not prevent him from re-peating the praises which the illustrious traveller had bestowed on his courage. During a storm, Byron invited the captain to play *écarté* with him in his cabin; and the latter deserted his post and accepted the invitation. While they were playing, the ship gave a lurch, which upset both table and players.

"Pick up the cards, and go on!" cried Byron.

"With pleasure, my lord."

"You are a brave fellow, captain."

I dare say there is not a word of truth in all this; but the gold-laced uniform and the game of *écarté* savour strongly of the author of *Lara*. Besides, the narrator was not clever enough to have invented the local colouring of his stories, and, in my case, I was too much pleased to find myself with a man who had possibly shared Childe Harold's Pilgrimage to question his veracity.

Meanwhile, our progress was slow; we were becalmed in sight of Nice for three days; and though we drifted along a few miles every evening with the light breeze which sprang up after sunset, a counter-current always carried us back again during the night. Every morning, when I went on deck, I asked the sailors what the town on the shore was, and always got the same answer: " *È Nizza, signore. Ancora Nizza. È sempre Nizza.*" I began to think the lovely city must possess magnetic power, and that, though she did not draw out our iron bolts and screws one by one, as the sailors say the North Pole does, she yet held us spell-bound to the spot. But I was disabused by a raging north wind, which rushed down upon us from the Alps like an avalanche. Eager to avail himself of such a chance, the captain put up every rag of sail. Thus caught on the flank, the vessel leaned over horribly, which alarmed me a good deal; but I soon became used to that angle of inclination. Towards evening, however, as we were making for the Gulf of Spezzia, the *tramontana* blew with such violence that the sailors themselves began to quake, seeing that no sail was taken in. It was a regular hurricane, which I shall some day describe in fine academical language. I clung to an iron bar on deck, watching the wonderful scene with a beating heart, while the Venetian hero kept a strict eye on the captain of the ship, who was steering, exclaiming now and again, " What madness! what obstinacy! The fool will drown us all. . . . Fifteen sails set in such a wind!" The captain paid no heed, but stood to the helm, when suddenly an awful gust caught him and threw him down, and the ship heeled right over on her side. It was a terrible moment. Our poor captain lay rolling about among the casks which the shock had sent flying about in all directions, while the Venetian pounced on the helm and assumed temporary command of the ship, an illegal act which was warranted by the circumstances, and accepted by the sailors, who had given themselves up for lost, and were calling upon the Madonna to save them. " What do you want with the Madonna, you fools? Up with you to the topsails, every man jack of you!" The men swarmed up the rigging, and in a few seconds the principal sails were furled, the ship slowly righted herself, more sail was taken in, and we were saved.

We reached Leghorn the following day, with only one sail, all the remainder having been torn to shreds by the wind. Some hours later, while sitting in the Hôtel Aquila Nera, the sailors came in a body to see us, not, as we at first supposed, with a view to *baksheesh,* but simply to congratulate us on our escape. The poor fellows barely earned their miserable rations of salt cod and ship's biscuit, but we could not get them to accept any money, and had even the greatest difficulty in inducing them to share our breakfast. Such delicacy of feeling deserves to be recorded, especially in Italy, where it is unusually rare.

During the journey my companions had confided to me that they were on their way to join the insurrection against the Duke of Modena. They were very enthusiastic, and evidently believed that the hour for the liberation of Italy had struck. Once Modena was in their hands, the whole of Tuscany would rise, and they would march on Rome at once; France would step forward and help the good cause, etc., etc. Alas! two of them were captured by the grand ducal police on their way to Florence, and sent to prison, where they may be languishing still. I heard afterwards that the others had distinguished themselves in the ranks of the patriots at Modena and Bologna, but that they had subsequently shared the fate of brave Menotti. Thus ended their dreams of liberty.

After bidding one another, in Florence, what we little thought would be an eternal farewell, I began to prepare for my journey to Rome. The time was a most unfavourable one, and, as a Frenchman coming from Paris, I had the greatest difficulty in getting into the Papal States. The officials refused to *viser* my passport,[1] as the Academy students were suspected of having fomented the insurrection of the Piazza Colonna, and the Pope by no means desired an increase of the little revolutionary colony. I wrote to our director, M. Horace Vernet, who, after reiterated applications, succeeded in obtaining the necessary permission from Cardinal Bernetti.

I happened, oddly enough, to have left Paris alone, and to be the only Frenchman on board the brig; and now the *vetturino* could find no other passenger going to Rome, so that I arrived there all by myself. I had picked up two volumes of a Life of the Empress Josephine at a bookstall in Siena, which helped me to pass the long hours in that crawling coach. My Jehu could not speak a word of French, and my Italian was limited to such phrases as "*Fa molto caldo.*" "*Piove.*" "*Quando lo pranzo?*" so that our conversation could scarcely be called interesting. The country was not particularly picturesque, and the utter absence of anything approaching to comfort in the towns and villages through which we passed increased my irritation at the absurd decree which had forced this visit to Italy upon me. At last, at ten o'clock in the morning, we arrived at a little cluster of houses called La Storta, and the *vetturino,* who was pouring

---

[1] This was at Florence, where he arrived on the 1st March.

out some wine for himself, remarked casually, " *Ecco Roma,* *signore!* " pointing carelessly over his shoulder to the dome of St. Peter's. No words can express what I felt when I turned and saw the Eternal City lying before me in the centre of that great barren plain.[1] . . . It seemed unutterably grand, poetical, sublime; the imposing majesty of the Piazza del Popolo, through which you enter the city on the road from France, deepened my religious awe, and I awoke as from a dream, when the horses, whose sluggishness I had ceased to revile, stopped in front of a noble palace. It was the Académie.

The Villa Medici, in which the students and the director of the Académie de France live, was built in 1557, by Annibale Lippi, Michael Angelo adding later a wing and some ornaments; it stands on the side of the Monte Pincio that overlooks the city, from which you see one of the finest sights in the world. On the right lies the Pincian Way, the Champs-Élysées of Rome, which is thronged every evening with carriages, equestrians, and pedestrians, defiling in a never-ending stream along the magnificent plateau. They disperse at the stroke of seven like a swarm of flies in the wind, for the Romans have an invincible, almost superstitious, dread of *l'aria cattiva,* and if you see a group of pedestrians lingering to admire the gorgeous glow of the sunset behind Monte Mario, you may feel certain that such rash loiterers are strangers. To the left of the villa the Pincian Way leads into the little piazza of the Trinità del Monte, with an obelisk in the centre, from which a great marble staircase leads down the hill to the Piazza d'Ispagna.

On the opposite side the palace looks out over beautiful gardens laid out in Le Nôtre's style, as all orthodox academy gardens ought to be. It contains a small wood of laurel and oaks, placed on a raised terrace, and running up to the ramparts of Rome on one side, and the French convent of the Ursulines on the other.

In front of the palace, in the middle of the waste lands of the Villa Borghese, stands the dreary, desolate house in which Raphael lived, and beyond it the horizon is bounded by a circle of umbrella-pines, peopled by a swarm of black crows, which enhance the gloom of the scene.

This is a fairly accurate description of the splendid quarters in which the French Government lodges its artists during their sojourn

[1] 12th March, 1831.

in Rome. The director's apartments are sumptuous, and an ambassador might envy them; but the pupils' rooms, with the exception of two or three, are small, inconvenient, and very badly furnished. A quartermaster in the Popincourt Barracks, at Paris, is better off in this respect than I was in the Palace of the Accademia di Francia. Most of the painters' and sculptors' studios are in the gardens; the others are scattered about the interior of the palace, and some are built out on a raised balcony overlooking the garden of the Ursuline Convent, with the Sabine Hills, Monte Cavo, and Hannibal's Camp in the distance. The library contains a fair collection of classical works, but absolutely no modern books. It is open to the students till three, and is a great resource for those who have nothing to do; for it is only fair to say that they enjoy the most complete liberty, and, beyond sending a picture, drawing, engraving, or piece of music once a year to the Académie at Paris, nothing is required of them; they may work as much or as little as they choose. The director's duties are confined to seeing that the rules of the establishment are not infringed; he exercises no sort of control over the students' work. This is inevitable, for no one man could by any possibility superintend five branches of art, since he cannot excel in all, and his criticisms on those he had not mastered would, of course, be perfectly worthless.

CHAPTER XXXIII

THE SCHOLARS OF THE ACADEMY — MENDELSSOHN

THE *Ave Maria* had just sounded when I alighted at the door of the Academy, and, as it was dinner-time, I made at once for the dining-hall, where I was told that all the students were assembled. I was the only one of the number who had not already arrived; and my sudden appearance in the vast hall was greeted with deafening shouts from the noisy group of twenty seated at the well-furnished table.

" Oh, Berlioz, Berlioz! That head; those locks; that nose! Oh, I say, Jalay, your nose *is* put out of joint now."

" And as for you, what is your hair to his? "

" Great gods, what a mop! "

" Hullo, Berlioz! Don't you remember me? Have you forgotten our meeting at the Conservatoire, and your confounded drums, which would not set Sardanapalus' pyre alight? What a rage he was in; but, by Jove! he had a right to be! Don't you remember me?"

"Of course I remember you; but your name?"

"It's Signol."

"Rossignol, you mean!"

"What an atrocious pun!"

"Ridiculous!"

"Let him sit down."

"Who, the pun?"

"No; Berlioz."

"Here, Fleury, bring some punch; . . . the very best; that will be better than the atrocities of this punster."

"At last our musical section is completed."

"I say, Montfort,[1] here is your colleague. Embrace him."

"Let us embrace."

"They shall not embrace!"

"They shall!"

"They shall not!"

"Yes!"

"No!"

"Oh, I declare, while they are making this noise you are gobbling up the macaroni. Please leave me some."

"Let us all embrace him, and there will be an end of all this."

"End? Why, it's only the beginning. Here is the punch; don't drink your wine."

"No more wine for us!"

"Down with the wine!"

"Here go the bottles. Look out, Fleury!"

Crash! bang!

"Gentlemen — gentlemen! Spare the glasses! You will want them for the punch; for I don't suppose you will care to drink it out of small glasses."

"Small glasses — never!"

"Well done, Fleury! You were just in time."

Fleury is the factotum of the establishment; a capital fellow, who deserves the confidence the director has in him. He has waited on the boarders for years, and is so used to scenes like the present that he

---

[1] The laureate who had gone to Rome before me. As no prize was awarded in 1829, the Academy awarded two in 1830, and Montfort obtained the lesser one, which entitled him to the pension for four years. [B.]

watches them unmoved, and his cool demeanour is a charming contrast to the uproar around him. When I had recovered from the shock
of my reception, and had time to look about me, I noticed that the
dining-hall was a very strange-looking place. One wall was decorated
with life-size portraits of about fifty former students; on the other,
which it was impossible to look at without laughing, was a series
of frightful life-size frescoes, monstrously grotesque caricatures of
former inhabitants of the Academy. Unfortunately want of space has
prevented the continuation of this strange portrait gallery down to
the present time.

In the evening, after I had paid my respects to M. Vernet, I joined
my companions at the celebrated Café Greco, which was their usual
place of resort. It is a miserable hole — dirty, dark, and damp; and
it is impossible to understand why all the artists in Rome should
flock there. Its only advantage is its proximity to the Piazza di
Spagna and the Lepri Restaurant, which is opposite. You pass your
time there in smoking execrable cigars and drinking worse coffee,
served on wretched little wooden tables the size of a hat, and as
greasy and filthy as the walls of this delectable resort. Nevertheless,
the Café Greco is so much frequented by foreign artists that most of
them have their letters sent there, and fresh arrivals know they are
sure to meet all their countrymen collected there.

The next day I met Felix Mendelssohn, who had been some weeks
in Rome.[1] I will describe our meeting and the incidents to which it gave
rise in my account of my first visit to Germany.

[1] Mendelssohn was a frequent visitor at the Vernets'. The twenty-two-year-old young man,
whose experiences and acquaintances in Germany had authorised him to have a good opinion
of himself, does not seem to have thought much of Berlioz, whom he probably looked down upon
as a pretentious amateur in comparison with himself. He could hardly be expected to grasp the
paradoxical fact that this Prix de Rome, who was scarcely distinguishable from all the other
Prix de Rome except that he seemed a trifle madder to the nicely brought up Mendelssohn, had
already written works, such as the *Francs-Juges* overture, the *Huit Scènes de Faust*, and the
Symphonie fantastique, that would still be in the world-repertory a hundred years hence.
    Mendelssohn's first impressions of Berlioz are given in a letter to his father of 29 March 1831.
"Berlioz is a freak [*verzerrt*, distorted, out of shape], without a spark of talent, fumbling about
in the darkness and imagining himself to be the creator of a new world; he writes the most horrible
things, and dreams and thinks of nothing but Beethoven, Schiller and Goethe. In addition he is
inordinately vain, and looks down from his superior height upon Mozart and Haydn, so that
I suspect all his enthusiasms." Mendelssohn has no higher opinion of the other newcomer Montfort,
though he likes both of them personally and goes long walks with them, during which Berlioz
pours out his adoration of Gluck. Mendelssohn does not take him seriously as an artist: "I fancy
he will marry [no doubt Hector had been inflicting the fair Camille on him]; he is really worse
than the others, because he is more affected. This purely external enthusiasm, this desperation
in the presence of women, this assumption of genius in capital letters, black on white, is insupportable to me, and if he were not a Frenchman, with whom life is always agreeable, and who is always interesting, I could not endure him any longer."

CHAPTER XXXIV

DRAMA — I LEAVE ROME — FROM FLORENCE TO NICE —
I RETURN TO ROME — NOBODY KILLED — UNLOADED
PISTOLS HAVE BEEN KNOWN TO GO OFF — ON THE
OTHER HAND, LOADED PISTOLS OFTEN
MISS FIRE

I T took me a long time to get used to this novel kind of existence, and I had something on my mind which prevented me from taking any interest either in surrounding objects or in the society into which I was thus suddenly thrown. I expected to find letters from Paris waiting for me, and for the next three weeks I watched for them with ever-increasing anxiety.[1]

Unable any longer to control my desire to fathom the reason of this mysterious silence, I determined to return to Paris at once, despite M. Horace Vernet's friendly remonstrances, and his warning that he would be obliged to strike my name off the Academy lists if I persisted in my rash resolve. On my way back I was detained for a week in Florence [2] by an attack of quinsy, which confined me to my bed. While there I made the acquaintance of the Danish architect, Schlick, a capital fellow, who is thought very highly of by connoisseurs. During my illness I re-scored the *Scène du Bal,* in my *Symphonie fantastique,* and added the present coda. It was almost finished when I was allowed out for the first time, and I at once proceeded to the post-office for my letters. The packet which was handed to me contained a letter [3] the tenor of which was inconceivably painful to a man of my years and temperament. I was beside myself with passion, and shed tears from sheer rage; but I made up my mind on the spot what to do. My duty was clear. I must at once proceed to Paris, and kill two guilty women and an innocent man.[4] After that, it would, of course, be incumbent on me to commit suicide. I arranged all the

[1] It was from Camille that Berlioz was vainly expecting to hear. He was tortured with jealousy.

[2] The mortuary episode of the beautiful young Florentine woman, told in Chapter XLIII, belongs to this place.

[3] The letter reached him on the 14th April. It announced the marriage of Camille and Pleyel.

[4] My fair comforter was of course at the bottom of all this. Her worthy mother, who was perfectly well acquainted with the true state of the case, accused *me* of having brought trouble into her family, and announced her daughter's marriage with M. P—. [B.]

details on the spot. Knowing me as they did, my reappearance in Paris would be looked for. . . . A complete disguise and the greatest precautions were therefore necessary; and I rushed off to Schlick, to whom I had already confided my story.

"Good God! what is the matter?" he cried, when he saw my white face.

"Look and see," I said, handing him the letter.

"This is horrible!" he replied, when he had read it; "what are you going to do?"

I knew that, if I told him my plan, he would try to dissuade me from carrying it out.

"What am I going to do? Why, return to France, of course; but to my father's house instead of to Paris."

"That is right, my dear fellow; go home, and in time you will recover from the awful condition into which this unexpected blow has thrown you. Come, cheer up."

"I will, but I must be off at once. I could not answer for myself to-morrow."

"We can easily get you off to-night, for I have friends among the police and the postal officials. I will have your passport ready in two hours, and will get you a seat in the diligence which starts five hours hence. Go to your hotel and get ready, and I will meet you there."

Instead of following his advice, I betake myself to one of the quays on the Arno, where I knew there was a French *modiste*. I enter the shop, look at my watch, and say: "It is now twelve o'clock, madame; I leave by the mail this evening, and I want to know if you can let me have, before five o'clock, a costume such as would be worn by a lady's-maid — robe, hat, green veil, and so on? I will pay you whatever you choose to ask."

After a moment's consideration, it is arranged that I am to have what I want. I deposit part of the price, and return to the Hôtel des Quatre Nations, on the opposite bank of the Arno.

I call the head porter.

"I am going to Paris at six o'clock this evening, Antoine, and I cannot take my trunk, so kindly look after it, and send it after me to my father's house as soon as you can. I have written down the address."

I then took the score of the *Scène du Bal,* and, as the instrumentation of the coda was not quite completed, I wrote across it: "*I have not time to finish this; but, if the Paris Concert Society should take it into its head to perform this work during the* ABSENCE *of the author, I request Habeneck to double the passage for flutes in the bass octave, with the clarinets and horns, the last time the theme is introduced, and to write the chords which follow for full orchestra; that will do for the ending."* [1]

I then seal it up, address it to Habeneck, and pack it in a bag with some clothes. I have a pair of double-barrelled pistols, which I load carefully, and two little bottles of laudanum and strychnine, which I examine and put in my pocket. Then, my mind being at rest with regard to my arsenal, I spend the remainder of my time in wandering about the streets of Florence, with the restless, disturbing demeanour of a mad dog.

At five I adjourn to my dressmaker's and try on my costume, which fits to perfection. In paying for it I put down twenty francs more than the price agreed; the girl at the desk tries to point out my mistake, but is deterred by her mistress, who hastily sweeps the gold into a drawer, saying: "Leave the gentleman alone, you little stupid; don't you see that he is too busy to listen to your chatter? A thousand thanks, sir; I wish you success. You will look your part to perfection." I smiled ironically, and she bowed me gracefully out of the shop.

At last it strikes six, and I bid farewell to my honest friend Schlick, who looks upon me as a lost sheep returning to the fold. I stow away my feminine apparel in one of the side pockets of the coach, give a parting glance at Cellini's Perseus, with the famous inscription, *Si quis te læserit, ego tuus ultor ero,* [2] and we are off.

We leave mile after mile behind us, but not a word passes between me and the courier. I had a great lump in my throat, and sat with my teeth tightly clenched, unable either to sleep or eat. About midnight, however, he said something to me about my pistols, which he prudently uncapped and hid under the cushions. He was afraid we might be attacked, and in that case, said he, it is much better to remain passive, unless you wish to be murdered.

"Just as you please," I replied. "I don't want to raise any difficulties, and I bear the brigands no grudge."

My companion did not know what to make of me, and, as I had

---

[1] This manuscript, with the inscription crossed out, is now in the possession of my friend Joseph d'Ortigue. [B.]

[2] "If any offend thee, I will avenge thee." This celebrated statue stands in the Grand Ducal Square, from which the mails start. [B.]

taken nothing but a little orange juice since we started, he began to regard me as scarcely human. When we arrived at Genoa I discovered that a fresh misfortune had befallen me, and that I had lost my female outfit. We had changed carriages at a village called Pietra Santa, and I had left my disguise behind. " Fire and thunder ! " I said, " it looks as if some damned good angel were bent on hindering my purpose. But we shall see ! "

I sent for a courier who could speak both French and Genoese, and asked him to take me to a dressmaker. It was nearly mid-day, and the next coach started at six. I demand a costume : impossible to finish one in so short a time. We go to another dressmaker, then to a third, and a fourth, without success. At last we find a woman who is willing to try; she accomplishes the task, and my disaster is repaired. Un-luckily, however, upon examining my passport, the Sardinian police take it into their heads that I am a *carbonaro,* a conspirator, a patriot, or Heaven knows what, refuse to *viser* my passport for Turin, and advise me to travel via Nice instead.

" Well, then, *viser* it for Nice, in Heaven's name ! What do I care whether I pass through hell, so long as I pass ? " . . .

I don't know which of us was the greater fool, the police, who saw a revolutionist in every Frenchman, or I, who feared to set foot in Paris except disguised as a woman, lest my purpose should reveal itself in my face; forgetting, like an idiot, that I could have remained quietly in an hotel in Paris for a few hours, and sent for any number of effective disguises at my leisure.

When people are possessed with any single idea they always fancy, in the drollest way, that everyone else is full of it too, and act upon the supposition.

Still in a rage, I set out on my way to Nice, rehearsing on the way every point of the little *comedy* I intended to play in Paris. I would go to my *friends'* house, about nine o'clock in the evening, when the family would be assembled for tea, and send in to say that the Count-ess M.'s maid is waiting with an urgent message; I am shown into the drawing-room; I hand over a letter, and, while it is being read, pro-duce my pistol and blow out the brains, first of number one, and then of number two; and, seizing number three by the hair, throw off my disguise, and finish her off in the same manner, regardless of her shrieks. Then, before this concert of voices and instruments attracts attention, I hasten to deposit the contents of the remaining barrel in

my own right temple; and if the pistol misses fire (which has happened before now), I shall at once resort to my small bottles. A
charming comedy! It is really a great pity it was never put upon the
stage.

And yet there were moments when, in spite of my wrath, I could
not help feeling sorry that my plans, excellent as they otherwise were,
involved my own suicide. It seemed hard to bid farewell to life and
art, to go down to posterity merely as a brute who could not get on
in the world; to leave my unfinished symphony, and all the other
greater works which were seething in my brain. . . . Ah! . . . it is
. . . And then suddenly my fell purpose gained the upper hand once
more. . . . No, no, no, no, no, they must all die, they must, and
they shall! . . . And the horses trotted on, bearing me nearer and
nearer to France. It was night, and we were travelling along the
Corniche road, which is cut out of the steep precipice of rocks overhanging the sea. For more than an hour I had been indulging in bright
dreams of what the future might have had in store for me when the
postilion stopped the horses to put on the drag, and suddenly, through
the stillness, the sound of the roaring breakers dashing against the
foot of the precipice broke on my ear. The raging fury of the waves
raised a corresponding tempest in my breast, fiercer and deadlier than
any I had yet experienced. I sat like a raving lunatic, clutching the
seat with both hands, ready to spring out and dash myself over the
cliff, and uttered such a wild, fierce yell that the unfortunate conductor
started away in horror, evidently regarding me as a devil doomed to
wander on the earth with a piece of the true cross in his possession.

It must be admitted that, although I was not yet out of danger,
the fever was intermittent. When I became aware of this, I reasoned
thus with myself — not altogether foolishly, considering the place
and the hour: Supposing, in one of these lucid intervals (that is to
say, the moments in which life smiled to me; you see I was virtually
vanquished), supposing, in one of these lucid intervals, I said, I were
to prepare myself for the next attack by tying myself up in some way
and having something to cling to . . . I might arrive at some . . .
definite . . . conclusion. Let me see.

We were passing through a little Sardinian village [1] on the sea-
shore (the sea was much calmer), and when we stopped to change
horses I told the conductor to wait while I wrote a letter; I go into a

---

[1] Vintimille, I think. [B.]

little café and write a letter on a scrap of paper to the director of the Académie de Rome, asking M. Horace Vernet *to be so good as not to strike my name off the Academy lists, if he had not already done so, as I had not yet broken through the rules; and I gave him* MY WORD OF HONOUR *that I would not cross the Italian frontier until I had received his answer, which I would await at Nice.*

Now that I had bound myself by a promise I went on my way most peacefully, feeling that if I were expelled from the Academy and launched penniless on the world, I could still fall back upon my murderous plan; and then . . . I suddenly found out that . . . I was hungry, having eaten nothing since I left Florence. Oh, beneficent nature! I was evidently cured!

The struggle was not quite over, however, when I reached Nice. I waited for several days, and then M. Vernet's answer came.[1] It was a friendly, kindly, paternal letter, and touched me deeply. He did not know the cause of my trouble, but he gave me the most kindly counsel, and pointed out to me that work and art were the two greatest remedies for troubles of the soul. He told me my name was still on the lists, that the minister should not hear of my escapade, and that I should be received with open arms when I returned.

" Well, they are saved," I said, with a deep sigh. " And supposing now I were to lead a quiet, happy life, and give myself up entirely to music, would not that be too curious? Let us try."

And so I drink deep draughts of the sunny, balmy air of Nice, and life and joy return to me, and I dream of music and the future. I spend a whole month in Nice wandering in groves of orange-trees, bathing in the sea, sleeping on the heather on the Villefranche hills, and looking down from those glorious heights on the silent coming and going of the distant ships. I live entirely alone. I write the overture to *King Lear.*[2] I sing. I believe in a God. Convalescence!

These were the three happiest weeks in my life. Oh, Nizza!

Once more my peace was disturbed by the King of Sardinia's police.

I had recently made the acquaintance of two officers of the Piedmontese garrison, whom I used to meet at the café; and one day I played a game of billiards with them, which was quite enough to arouse the suspicions of the chief of police.

---

[1] At the beginning of May, 1831.
[2] He also sketched the *Rob Roy* overture.

" It is quite clear that that young musician has not come here to see *Matilda de Sabran* " (the only piece which was then being played), " because he never goes to the theatre. He spends his days on the Ville-franche rocks . . . evidently waiting for a signal from some revolutionary ship. . . . He does not dine at the *table d'hôte* . . . that is to avoid being drawn into conversation by the secret agents. Now he is gradually making the acquaintance of our officers . . . in order to open up the negotiations with which *Young Italy* has entrusted him. The conspiracy is as clear as daylight."

Oh, great man — oh, wily diplomat — thou ravest!

I am summoned to the police-office, and formally interrogated.

" What are you doing here? "

" Recovering from a painful illness. I compose and dream, and thank God for the sunshine, the beautiful sea, and the green hills."

" You are not a painter? "

" No."

" Yet you are always drawing something in an album. Is it plans? "

" Yes; plans for an overture for *King Lear*. The designs and the instrumentation are ready, and I think the beginning will be somewhat formidable."

" What do you mean by the beginning? Whom do you mean by *King Lear?* "

" He is a poor old English king."

" English! "

" Yes. Shakespeare says he lived about eighteen hundred years ago, and he foolishly divided his kingdom between his two wicked elder daughters, who turned him out of doors when he had nothing more to give them. You see there are few kings . . ."

" Never mind the king. . . . What do you mean by instrumentation? . . ."

" It is a musical term."

" Always the same excuse! Now, sir, we are well aware that it is impossible to write music walking silently about the sea-shore, with nothing but an album and a pencil, and no piano. So be good enough to tell us where you want to go, and you shall have your passport. You cannot stay here any longer."

" Then I will return to Rome, and compose there without a piano, if you have no objection."

So the following day I left Nice,[1] reluctant, but full of life and happiness. And in this way it came to pass that my loaded pistols missed fire.

All the same, I liked my *little comedy;* and I sometimes think it is a pity that it was never played.

CHAPTER XXXV

THE THEATRES AT GENOA AND FLORENCE — BELLINI'S "I MONTECCHI ED I CAPULETTI" — ROMEO PLAYED BY A WOMAN — PACINI'S "LA VESTALE" — LICINIUS PLAYED BY A WOMAN — THE ORGANIST AT FLORENCE — THE FEAST OF THE CORPUS DOMINI — I RETURN TO THE ACADEMY

On my way through Genoa I went to hear Paër's *Agnese,* which was regarded as a great opera during the dark ages that preceded the advent of Rossini. It was abominably performed, and perhaps that is why I was so bored by it. I noticed at once that it had been " touched up," and that one of those busybodies, who are unable to produce anything original, and therefore deem it their special province to detect flaws in the creations of others, had reinforced Paër's sober and sensible instrumentation with the thunder of the big drum; the inevitable result being that the orchestra was completely drowned. Madame Ferlotti sang the part of Agnese, and carefully abstained from acting it. As she appraises the market value of her voice to a franc, she replied to her poor father's incoherent ravings with the most imperturbable coolness and self-possession; and sang her part all through as though she were at a rehearsal, anxious to save her voice as much as possible, and not do more than merely give an indication of her part.

The orchestra was tolerable; the violins played in tune; and the wind kept good time. *À propos* of violins. All Paris was raving about Paganini, while I, with my usual luck, was kicking my heels in his native town instead of listening to him. I tried to gather some informa-

---

[1] May 19th. On his way back to Rome he seems to have sketched out the scenario of *Lélio ou le retour à la vie.* The music, mostly compiled from works already written, was put together by July.

tion about their distinguished townsman from the Genoese, but found
that, like other people engaged in commerce, they cared little for the
fine arts, and spoke quite indifferently of the genius whom Germany,
France, and England had received with open arms. They could not
even show me his father's house. I also searched all Genoa for the
temple, pyramid, or monument of some sort which I felt certain must
have been raised in memory of Christopher Columbus, but I never
even chanced upon so much as a bust of the great discoverer to whom
the ungrateful city owes its fame.

Of all the Italian cities, Florence is the one of which I have the
pleasantest recollections. Instead of being overwhelmed with spleen,
as I was afterwards at Rome and Naples, I spent delightful days wandering about in solitude and freedom through the palaces and picture
galleries, dreaming of Michael Angelo and Dante, reading Shakespeare, and venting my enthusiasm in the delicious silence of the
woods. Although my Nice expedition had made a considerable breach
in my fortune, I still possessed a few handfuls of piastres, and was
therefore free from care. I knew very well that I was not likely to
find in Florence what I barely hoped for even in Naples and Milan,
so I never even thought of going to hear any music, until I heard
casually at the *table d'hôte* that Bellini's new opera, *I Montecchi ed
I Capuletti*, was going to be played. Not only the music but the libretto
was warmly praised, at which I was the more surprised because I knew
what little attention the Italians usually pay to the words of an opera.
This must be an innovation! At last, after so many wretched failures,
I shall hear a real *Romeo* opera, worthy of Shakespeare! Such a subject! — actually created for music! . . . First there is the splendid
ball at the Capulets', at which young Montague first sees the "sweet
Juliet," whose love will cost her her life, in the midst of the whirling
bevy of beautiful girls; then those-fierce combats in the streets of
Verona, over which the fiery Tybalt presides like the genius of revenge; the unutterable night scene in Juliet's balcony, in which the
lovers utter their tender love, true and pure as the light of the evening star which shines smiling down upon them; then there is careless
Mercutio's mirthful buffoonery, the old nurse's simple chatter, the
grave hermit, with his fruitless efforts to pour oil upon the troubled
waters in this conflict of hate and love which has penetrated even to
his still, sequestered cell; . . . then the awful catastrophe, the conflict between delirious love and despair, passion dying away into the

death-sob; and finally the solemn, tardy reconciliation of the feudal families burying their hate in the graves of their dead children.

I rushed off to the Pergola Theatre. The stage was crowded with the chorus; their voices were true and clear, and they seemed to me to sing fairly well; a most charming effect was produced by the contralto parts, which were sung by a dozen little boys of fourteen or fifteen years of age. The principal characters appeared in due course, and all except Juliet (who was played by a large fat woman), and Romeo (by a small thin one), sang out of tune. Why, because Zingarelli, Vaccai, and others have done so, continue to make Romeo a woman's part? . . . On what principle is Juliet's hero to be shorn of his manhood? What is there childlike in the *champion fencer* who slays the furious Tybalt in three passes, and who afterwards bursts the gates of Juliet's tomb, and then knocks Count Paris down with one casual blow? And his intense despair on the eve of his exile, his awful resignation when he hears of Juliet's death, his wild delirium after drinking the poison — do such volcanic passions lodge in eunuchs' souls?

Is there some notion that two women's voices sound better together? . . . Then why have tenors, baritones, and basses at all? Why not confine ourselves entirely to sopranos and contraltos, and let Othello and Moses, as well as Romeo, pipe in a high key?

Well, we must not mind this; the rest of the work will compensate. . . .

What a disappointment! There is no ball at the Capulets', no Mercutio, no chattering nurse, no grave, calm hermit, no balcony scene, no sublime soliloquy when Juliet receives the phial from the hermit, no duet in the cell between banished Romeo and the disconsolate hermit; in fact, no Shakespeare, nothing but utter failure. And yet he is a great poet this Felix Romani, who was obliged to boil down Shakespeare's masterpiece into such a bald book to suit the requirements of the contemptible Italian stage!

However, the composer has done full justice to one of the principal situations; at the end of one act, in which the lovers are forcibly separated, they escape for a moment and rush into each other's arms, singing, " We shall meet in heaven." The setting of these words, which is intense, passionate, and full of life and fire, is sung in unison, which, under these special circumstances, intensifies the power of the melody in the most wonderful manner; whether it were owing to the setting of the musical phrase, to the manner in which it is introduced, to the unexpected effect of the unison, or to the actual beauty of the tune itself, I do not know; but I was completely carried away, and applauded frantically. Duets in unison have been done to death since.

I was resolved to drink the cup to the dregs, so I went to hear Pacini's *Vestale* a few days later. From what I knew of it already I gathered that it had nothing in common with Spontini's work except the name; but still I was not prepared. . . . Licinius was played by a woman! . . . After listening for a few painful moments, I cried out like Hamlet, "Wormwood! wormwood!" and, unable to endure any more, I rushed out in the middle of the second act with a fierce parting kick to the floor, from which my big toe suffered for three days. Poor Italy! . . . I shall be told that in the churches at any rate the music is on a par with the grandeur of the ceremonial. Poor Italy! . . . It will be seen presently what sort of music is tolerated in Rome, the capital of the Christian world; meanwhile this is what I myself heard while I was in Florence.

Louis Bonaparte's two sons had taken part in the insurrection which had just been crushed at Modena and Bologna. Their mother, Queen Hortense, escaped with one, the other died in his father's arms, and this was his funeral service. The church was draped in black, and there was a great paraphernalia of priests, catafalques, and torches, which were less calculated to awaken solemn thoughts than were the memories connected with the name of the dead man . . . Bonaparte! *his* name; *his* nephew; almost *his* grandson; dead at twenty; and his mother a fugitive to England, with her only remaining son snatched from the reactionary gibbet, not daring to return to France, where she spent her glorious youth. . . . Glancing back through the corridors of time, I pictured the happy creole child on the deck of the vessel which bore her to the shores of the old world as the daughter of plain Madame Beauharnais; then the adopted daughter of the master of Europe; then Queen of Holland; and now exiled, forgotten, orphaned, a despairing mother, a crownless, realmless queen. . . . Oh Beethoven! . . . where was the great Homeric mind which conceived the *Eroica* — the *funeral march on the death of a hero* — and so much more of the grand poetry of music which elevates the soul while the heart is oppressed with grief? The organist had got out his *little flute* stops and was frolicking about on the upper manual, piping out *gay little tunes,* like a wren on a garden-wall fluttering its wings and chirruping in the pale winter sunshine . . .

The feast of the *Corpus Domini* was close at hand, and I had heard so much of the manner in which it was celebrated at Rome that I hurried on my journey to the capital of the Papal States, in company with several Florentines who were going there for the same purpose. During our whole journey we talked of nothing but the wonders which were in store for us, and my imagination was dazzled by the visions of tiaras, mitres, chasubles, shining crosses, golden vestures, glowing through clouds of incense, which were presented to me.

" *Ma la musica?* "

" *Oh, Signore, lei sentirà un coro immenso!* " Then they relapsed into the clouds of incense, golden vestures, shining crosses, thunders of artillery, clanging of bells, etc. But " Robin always reverts to his flute."

" *La musica?* " I persisted; " *la musica di questa ceremonia?* "

" *Oh, Signore, lei sentirà un coro immenso!* "

Well, at any rate there will be this " huge chorus." I conjured up a vision of Solomon's Temple and the musical magnificence of its ceremonial; and, as my imagination became more excited, I even pictured a scene which might rival the splendours of ancient Egypt. Accursed gift, which turns life into a series of miracles! . . . But for this I might have been charmed with the discordant falsetto of the castrati, giving out an insipid counterpoint; but for this I should not have anticipated the pure, fresh voices and the glowing, enthusiastic faces of a bevy of young virgins pouring forth their pious songs to heaven — the perfume, as it were, of these human flowers; but for this fatal imagination of mine I should not have been so disgusted by the impious, coarse cacophony of those two groups of quacking clarinets, roaring trombones, crashing drums, and circus trumpets. This is what they call *military music* at Rome. Had it ushered in old Silenus, riding on his ass, and escorted by a troupe of coarse satyrs and bacchantes, it would have been highly appropriate; but the Holy Sacrament, the Pope, and the pictures of the Virgin! [1]

This was, however, only one of the many marvels which awaited me. But I will not anticipate.

Here I am, back again in the Villa Medici, kindly received by the

---

[1] Barbarous! barbarous! Like all other sovereigns, the Pope is a barbarian; and, like all other peoples, the Romans are barbarians. [B.]

director, and feasted by my companions, whose curiosity must have been aroused by my pilgrimage, though they one and all refrained from any allusion to it. I must have had some reason for going, and I went; I returned; and all was right; no remarks were made, and no questions asked.

CHAPTER XXXVI

LIFE AT THE ACADEMY — WALKS IN THE ABRUZZI MOUNTAINS — ST. PETER'S — "LE SPLEEN" — EXCURSIONS INTO THE CAMPAGNA — THE CARNIVAL — THE PIAZZA NAVONE

I WAS soon quite at home in the daily routine both inside and outside the Academy. Our meals were heralded by a bell, which was rung up and down the passages and through the gardens; and we all rushed in just as we were, without collars, in straw hats, blouses torn or smeared with clay, slippers — in fact, in our studio undress. After dinner we generally wasted an hour or two in the gardens, playing quoits or tennis, pistol-shooting, killing the unlucky blackbirds in the laurel bushes, or training puppies. M. Horace Vernet, whose relations with us were more those of a pleasant comrade than a stern director, often took part in our sports. In the evening there was the inevitable visit to the Café Greco, when the French artists who did not belong to the Academy, and whom we called *les hommes d'en bas* (the lower orders), smoked the pipe of peace and shared the patriotic punch-bowl with us. After this we all dispersed, those who virtuously returned to the academic barrack generally gathering in the great hall, which opened on to the garden. When I was one of the party, my wretched voice and paltry guitar were often requisitioned; and there, sitting round the marble basin of a little fountain, which splashed and flashed in the moonlight, we sang dreamy songs from *Oberon* and the *Freischütz*, stirring choruses from *Euryanthe,* whole acts of *Iphigénie en Tauride, La Vestale,* or *Don Giovanni;* for I must admit, in justice to my contemporaries at the Academy, that their taste in music was anything but vulgar. True, there was another kind of concert, which followed a somewhat disorderly dinner, and was called the *English concert,* and which had a charm of its own. Each one who could sing

at all had his own special song, and, to make as great a variety as
possible, each man sang in a different key from that of his neighbours.
Duc, the gifted architect, sang his song of *La Colonne;* Dantan, the
Sultan Saladin; Montfort's masterpiece was the march from *La
Vestale;* Signol was always charming in his romance, *La Fleuve du
Tage;* and I was effective in the tender, simple air, *Il pleut, bergère.*
At a given signal the performers started off, one after another, and
this grand *ensemble* for twenty-four performers was shouted out in
a continuous *crescendo,* to the accompaniment of the dismal howling
of all the dogs on the Pincian, while the barbers, standing at their
shop-doors in the Piazza di Spagna below, remarked to each other,
with a contemptuous smile and a shrug, " *Musica francese.*"

Thursday was the director's great reception-day. The most brilliant society in Rome frequented the fashionable *soirées,* at which
Madame and Mademoiselle Vernet presided so gracefully; and of
course we students always attended them. But we generally spent our
Sundays in long excursions in the neighbourhood of Rome; either to
Ponte Molle, where you drink the cloying, oily drug called Orvieto
wine, which is the Roman's favourite beverage; or the Villa Pamphili;
or St. Laurent, outside the walls; or, best of all, to Cecilia Metella's
splendid tomb, where it is the correct thing to awaken the echo till you
are hoarse, so as to have an excuse for moistening your throat with a
coarse black wine, thick with midges, in a neighbouring tavern.

With the director's permission, the students were allowed to make
journeys of indefinite duration, provided they did not quit the Papal
States until the conditions of their agreement enabled them to travel
all over Italy. This is why the full number of students is so rarely to
be found in the Academy. Two or three are always wandering about
to Naples, Venice, Florence, Palermo, or Milan. The painters and
sculptors, who have Raphael and Michael Angelo at Rome, usually
remain there; but the architects are always eager to explore the
temples at Pæstum, Pompeii, and in Sicily, while the landscape painters
spend the greater part of their time in the mountains. As for the
musicians, since the capitals of Italy are all about equally interesting
to them, their only reason for leaving Rome is the desire to see, and
their own restless disposition; and so their destination and the duration of their journeys depend entirely on their personal feelings.

When I was weary of Rome and felt my blood stagnating, I rushed
off in adventurous excursions into the Abruzzi mountains, and but for

this liberty the monotony of our existence would have been intolerable. Neither our noisy artistic gatherings, the brilliant balls at the Academy and the Embassy, nor the freedom of the café, could make me forget that I had left Paris, the centre of civilisation, and that I was suddenly deprived of music, theatres,[1] literature,[2] excitement — in fact, all that made life worth living.

Is it surprising that the shadow of Ancient Rome, which alone casts a glory round Modern Rome, did not compensate me for all I had lost? It must be remembered that the eye so soon becomes accustomed to things on which it rests day after day that they cease to arouse any unusual thoughts in the mind. The only exception was the Coliseum; I could never look upon that unmoved, either by day or by night. Nor did I ever see St. Peter's without a thrill. It is so grand, so noble, so beautiful, so majestically calm! During the fierce summer heat I used to spend whole days there, comfortably established in a confessional, with Byron as my companion. I sat enjoying the coolness and stillness, unbroken by any sound save the splashing of the fountains in the square outside, which was wafted up to me by an occasional breeze; and there, at my leisure, I sat drinking in that burning poetry. I followed the Corsair in his desperate adventures; I adored that inexorable yet tender nature — pitiless, yet generous — a strange combination of apparently contradictory feelings: love of woman, hatred of his kind.

Laying down my book to meditate, I would cast my eyes around, and, attracted by the light, they would be raised to Michael Angelo's sublime cupola. What a sudden transition of ideas! From the cries and barbarous orgies of fierce pirates I passed in a second to the concerts of the seraphim, the peace of God, the infinite quietude of heaven; . . . then, falling to earth again, I sought on the pavement for traces of the noble poet's footsteps. . . .

" He must have come to see that fine group of Canova's," I said to myself; " he must have stood just here; his hands must have rested on these rails; he breathed this air; the echo repeated his words . . . words, it may be, of tenderness and love. . . . Ah yes! he surely must have come here with his friend the Countess Guiccioli,[3] that

---

[1] The theatres at Rome are only open during four months. [B.]

[2] Most of the books I then admired were under the Papal ban. [B.]

[3] I saw her one evening at M. Vernet's, with her long white hair falling round her sad face like the branches of a weeping willow. Three days afterwards I saw her bust, in clay, in Dantan's studio. [B.]

admirable, rare woman, who understood him so thoroughly, and loved him so completely. . . . A poet . . . beloved . . . rich. . . . *He* was all three!" . . . And I ground my teeth so that the walls of the confessional re-echoed and the souls of the damned must have quaked.

One day, when in one of these moods, as I rose to rush out, my footsteps were suddenly arrested, and I stood stock still in the middle of the church. A peasant entered, quietly went up to the statue of St. Peter and kissed his great toe!

"Happy biped!" I murmured bitterly, "what more can you desire? You believe and you hope; once upon a time, the statue you adore was called Jupiter the Thunderer, and held thunderbolts in his hand instead of the keys of paradise; you don't know this, and so are not disenchanted. When you go hence, what will you seek? shade and slumber; you will find both in the shrines in the fields. What are your dreams of wealth? A handful of piastres to buy you a donkey or enable you to marry — and three years' savings will be enough for that. What is a wife in your eyes? A being of another sex. What is art to you? A means of materialising the objects of your worship, and exciting you to dancing or laughter. A virgin, streaked with red and green, fulfils your ideas of painting; marionettes and Punch are your dramas; the hurdy-gurdy and the drum, your music; while I am full of despair and bitterness because I lack everything that I need, and have no hope of ever obtaining it."

After listening for some time to the raging storm within me, I discovered that it was evening. The peasant had departed; I was alone in St. Peter's. . . . I went out. I met some German painters, who carried me off to a German *osteria* outside the town, where we drank countless bottles of Orvieto, talked nonsense, smoked, and ate some small birds we had bought from a sportsman — raw. The others liked this savage meal, and although I thought it disgusting at first, I soon came round to their opinion.

We returned to Rome singing Weber's choruses, which reminded us of musical treats we were not to enjoy for many months to come. At midnight I went to the ambassador's ball, and saw an English girl [1]

---

[1] Mendelssohn mentions this lady in his letters from Rome (Dec. 22, 1830). "I must tell you about a ball to which I went the other day, and where I danced even more than usual. I had given a hint to the master of the ceremonies, and he allowed the *galop* to continue for more than half an hour; so I was in my element, and quite aware that I was dancing in the Palazzo Albani at Rome, and also with the prettiest girl in the room, according to the verdict of Thorwaldsen,

there, as beautiful as Diana, reported to have fifty thousand pounds a year! she had a superb voice, and played the piano beautifully, and I enjoyed it. Providence is so just; its favours are so equally divided! I saw some hideous hags bending over the *écarté* table, their faces flushed with greed — Macbeth's witches! I saw some simpering coquettes, and two sweet young girls, who were making what their mothers call their *first appearance in the world;* delicate, precious flowers whom its breath will soon wither. I was delighted. Three amateurs were disputing on enthusiasm, poetry, and music. They drew comparisons between Beethoven and M. Vaccai, Shakespeare and M. Ducis; asked me if I *had read Goethe,* whether Faust had *amused* me; and a thousand other wonderful things. I was so delighted with the whole business that I left the room, wishing that a thunderbolt as big as a mountain would fall on the Palace, and bury it and all inside it.

As we ascended the steps of the Trinità del Monte on our way back to the Academy, we had to draw our big Roman knives. Some wretches lurking in the shadow demanded our money or our lives; but as there were two of us and only three of them, and as they caught the gleam of our knives in the moonlight, they relapsed temporarily into the path of virtue.

I was often unable to sleep after one of these insipid parties, where hearing vapid songs vapidly sung to a piano accompaniment only whetted my craving for music, and embittered my temper. So I put on my hooded cloak and went down into the garden, where I sat on a block of marble till dawn, buried in sombre misanthropic reveries, and listening to the cries of the owls in the Villa Borghese. If my companions had known of these sleepless nights they would have accused me of affectation (*manière* — the orthodox expression), and

---

Vernet, and other good judges. The way in which I got to know her is now quite an anecdote of Rome. I was at Torlonia's first ball, not dancing, as I knew none of the ladies, but merely looking on. Suddenly someone tapped me on the shoulder, and said, 'So you are admiring the English beauty too? I am quite dazzled.' It was Thorwaldsen, standing in the doorway, lost in admiration. He had hardly spoken when we heard a torrent of words behind us: 'Mais où est-elle donc, cette petite Anglaise? Ma femme m'a envoyé pour la regarder. Per Bacco!' It was clear to me that the little thin Frenchman, with the stiff gray hair and the Legion of Honour, must be Horace Vernet. He and Thorwaldsen then set to work to discuss the young lady in the most earnest and thorough manner, and it was delightful to see the two old masters admiring her, while she was dancing away quite unconcerned. They were then presented to her parents, during which I had to stand aside. A few days afterwards, however, I visited some Venice acquaintances in order to be introduced to some of their friends, and these friends turned out to be the young lady and her parents. So your son and brother was highly delighted." [H.]

perpetrated ceaseless jokes at my expense. But I never mentioned them.

If we include some sport and riding,[1] we get a clear idea of the agreeable routine in which my mental and physical existence was spent during my stay in Rome. If, on the other hand, you include the paralysing effect of the sirocco, the ever-increasing longing for musical pleasures, the sad recollections, the trial of finding myself exiled for two years from the musical world, and the actual, though perhaps inexplicable, impossibility of doing any work at the Academy, you will have some idea of the dejection from which I suffered.

I was as fierce as a chained dog, and the attempts of my comrades to induce me to share in their amusements only increased my irritation. Above all, their enjoyment of the " delights " of the Carnival exasperated me. I never could (and I cannot now) conceive what pleasure there is in the amusements of what are called, both in Paris and Rome, *les jours gras*. Fat days, indeed! Fat with grease, and ointment, and plaster, and stale wine, and filthy jests, and coarse jokes, and street girls, and drunken detectives; vile masks, worn-out hacks, laughing fools, gaping idiots, and weary idlers. In Rome, where the good old traditions of the past still survived, a human sacrifice was offered up during *les jours gras*. I do not know whether this admirable custom, which seems to exhale the subtle perfume of the poetry of the circus, still exists; in all probability it does, for great ideas linger long. In those days some poor devil under sentence of death was retained for the purpose; he, too, was fattened, so as to be worthy of the god (the Roman people) to whom he was to be offered up; and when the hour had struck, and this rabble of fools from all nations (for it is only fair to state that the strangers were as keen after these noble sports as the natives), this horde of well-dressed savages, was weary of watching the races, and pelting one another with plaster sweetmeats, and laughing at the refinement of their wit, they adjourned to see the man die; yes, the *man!* They do well, these worms, to call him such. Generally it is some unlucky brigand who, weakened by his wounds, was half dead when the Pope's *brave* soldiers captured him; and he has

[1] It was during my rides in the neighbourhood of Rome with Felix Mendelssohn that I told him how surprised I was that no one had written a scherzo on Shakespeare's glittering little poem *Queen Mab*. He was equally surprised, and I instantly regretted having put the idea into his head. For several years afterwards I dreaded hearing that he had carried it out. Had he done so he would have made my double attempt (a vocal scherzetto and an instrumental scherzo, both on *Queen Mab*) in the *Romeo and Juliet* Symphony impossible or at any rate highly undesirable. Fortunately he never thought of it. [B.]

been nursed, and cared for, and fattened and shrived for the festival;
and, in my eyes at least, this wretched victim is a thousand times more
worthy of the name of man than that rabble of victors whom the tem-
poral and spiritual head of the Church (*abhorrens a sanguine*), the
representative of God upon earth, is obliged occasionally to gratify
by the sight of an execution.[1]

However, the intelligent, sensitive spectators soon hasten to
cleanse their clothes from the possible blood-stains in the Piazza
Navone. The square is at once transformed from a vegetable-market
to a reeking, filthy pond, with cabbage-stalks, lettuce-leaves, melon-
rind, wisps of straw, and almond-husks floating on its surface instead
of water-lilies. On a raised platform on the shores of this enchanted
lake stand fifteen musicians, with drums, large and small, a triangle,
a Chinese pavilion, and two pairs of cymbals, supported, for the sake
of appearance, by some horns or clarinets, and performing music of
the same degree of purity as the water at their feet. Meanwhile the
most brilliant equipages pace slowly through the pool, while the air
resounds with the ironical acclamations of the *sovereign people*.

" *Mirate! mirate!* there is the Austrian ambassador! "

" No; it is the English envoy."

" Look at his arms — a kind of eagle."

" Not at all; it is some other animal; and besides, I can see *Dieu
et mon droit*."

" There is the Spanish consul with his trusty Sancho. Rosinante
does not seem particularly delighted with this watery promenade."

" What! the French representative here too? "

" And why not, pray? That old man with the cardinal's hat behind him is Napoleon's maternal uncle."

" And that little paunchy man, with the malicious smile, trying to
look serious? "

[1] The Parisians are worthy rivals of the Romans of 1831 in this particular. M. Léon Halévy,
the brother of the worthy composer, has just published in the *Journal des Débats* a letter full of
good sense and good feeling on the subject, demanding the suppression of the ignoble scene
enacted during the Carnival round the *Fat Bull*, which is paraded about the streets for three
days, and finally slain with much pomp at the shambles. I was deeply touched by this eloquent
protest, and could not help writing the following letter to the author:

"Sir,—Allow me to shake you by the hand for your admirable letter on the *Fat Bull*. Never
think for a moment that you have made yourself ridiculous; and even if you had, it would be ten
thousand times better to appear so in the eyes of the frivolous than to be regarded as coarse and
brutal by men of feeling for remaining indifferent to the scenes you have so justly stigmatised,
which transform so-called civilised men into cowardly, hateful brutes.

"7th March, 1865." [B.]

" He is a clever man [1] who has written about art, and is consul at Civita Vecchia; he considers himself forced to come here and loll in his carriage in this slum, because it is the *fashion;* he is now contriving a new chapter for his novel, *Rouge et Noir.*"

" *Mirate! mirate!* here is our great Vittoria, our small- (not so very small) footed Fornarina, reposing from her labours in the Academy studios last week, and showing herself off in her cardinal's dress. There she sits in her chariot, like Venus rising from the waves. Listen! the tritons of the Piazza Navone, who all know her, are going to lift up their voices in a triumphal march. *Sauve qui peut!* What a hullabaloo! What has happened? A shopkeeper's carriage upset? Yes; I see it is the excellent wife of our tobacconist in the Via Condotti. Bravo! she is swimming to shore like Agrippina in the Bay of Pozzuoli; and while she is whipping her little boy as a compensation for his bath, the horses, not being sea-horses, are plunging about in the muddy water. Hurrah! someone is drowned! Agrippina is tearing her hair. Increasing delight on the part of the audience. They are pelting her with orange-peel. How touching are thy frolics, O gentle populace! How sweet are thy pleasures! What poetry in thy sports! What gracious dignity in thy joy! Truly the great critics are right; art is for everyone. If Raphael painted his divine Madonnas, it was because he well knew how exalted is the love of the masses for the beautiful, the ideal, the chaste, the pure; if Michael Angelo wrung his immortal Moses from the stubborn marble, if his powerful hands raised a sublime temple, it was doubtless that he might respond to the demand of the masses for great emotions answering to the needs of their souls; and it was to feed the poetic flame which devours them that Tasso and Dante sang their immortal strains. Yes; let all works which are not admired by the masses be anathema! If they scorn them, it is because they are worthless; if they despise them, it is because they are despicable; if they reject them with hisses, let us reject the author likewise, for he is lacking in respect for the public; he has outraged its vast intelligence and jarred its deep feelings. *Send him to the galleys!*

---

[1] M. Beyle, who wrote Rossini's life under the pseudonym of Stendhal, and also the most irritating lucubrations on music, for which he fancied he had some feeling. [B.]

CHAPTER XXXVII

SPORT IN THE MOUNTAINS — THE CAMPAGNA ONCE
MORE — VIRGILIAN RECOLLECTIONS — WILD ITALY
— REGRETS — THE BALLS IN THE OSTERIA —
MY GUITAR

I FOUND life in town perfectly intolerable, and spent all the time I could in the mountains, waiting for the day when I could return to France. I often went as far as Subiaco, a big village some miles from Tivoli, inside the Papal States, a part of the country which is usually only visited by landscape painters.

This was a favourite remedy for one of my attacks of " spleen," and it always seemed to give me new life. I started off in an old grey shirt, with half-a-dozen piastres in my pocket, and my gun or guitar in my hand, strolling along, shouting or singing, careless as to where I should sleep, knowing that, if other shelter failed me, I could always turn into some grotto or one of the countless shrines by the wayside. Sometimes I went along at racing pace, or I might stop to examine an old tomb; or, standing on the summit of one of the dreary hillocks which dot the arid Roman plain, listen meditatively to the far-off chime of the bells of St. Peter's, whose golden cross gleamed on the horizon; or, halting in pursuit of a lapwing, note down an idea for a symphony which had just entered my brain; always, however, drinking in, in deep draughts, the ceaseless delights of utter liberty.

Sometimes, when I had my guitar with me instead of my gun, a passage from the *Æneid,* which had lain dormant in my mind from childhood, would suddenly rise to my recollection, aroused by some aspect of the surrounding scenery; then, improvising a strange recitative to a still stranger harmony, I would sing the death of Pallas, the despair of the good Evander, of his horse Ethon, unharnessed and with flowing mane and falling tears, following the young warrior's corpse to its last resting-place; of the terror of good King Latinus; the siege of Latium, which once stood on the ground beneath my feet; Amata's sad end, and the cruel death of Lavinia's noble lover. This combination of memories, poetry and music used to work me into the most incredible state of excitement; and the triple intoxication

generally culminated in torrents of tears. The funniest part of it all
was that my grief was so real. I mourned for poor Turnus, whom the
hypocrite Æneas had robbed of his state, his mistress, and his life;
I wept for the beautiful and pathetic Lavinia, forced to wed the
stranger-brigand, bathed in her lover's blood. I longed for the poetic
days when the heroes, sons of the gods, walked the earth, clad in
shining armour, hurling slender javelins at targets framed in bur-
nished gold. Then, quitting the past, I wept for my personal sorrows,
my doubtful future, my spoiled career; and at length, overwhelmed
by this chaos of poetry, would suddenly fall asleep with scraps of
Shakespeare or Dante on my lips: *Nessun maggior dolore. . . . che
recordarsi . . . O poor Ophelia! . . . Good-night, sweet ladies. . . .
vitaque cum gemitu. . . . fugit indignata. . . . sub umbras. . . .*

What folly! many will exclaim. Possibly; but also what joy! *Sensible* people have no conception of the delight which the mere consciousness of living intensely can give: one's heart swells, one's imagination soars into space, life is inexpressibly quickened, and one
loses all consciousness of one's bodily limitations. I did things then
which would kill me now.

One day I left Tivoli in pouring rain, carrying a percussion gun
with which I could defy the damp. I walked my ten leagues, killed
fifteen head of game on the way, and arrived at Subiaco in the evening, having spent the whole day in my soaking clothes.

Now that I am back in the Parisian whirlpool, how vividly I can
recall every aspect of the wild scenery of the Abruzzi mountains: the
strange villages, the ragged villagers with their furtive eyes, and their
old rickety guns that carry so far and so true! How often I was struck
by the mysterious solitude of their sites! and what curious forgotten
memories rise up before me as I think of them! Subiaco, Alatri,
Civitella, Genesano, Isola di Sora, San Germano, Arce, the poor old
deserted convents and their empty chapels. . . . The monks are
gone. . . . Silence reigns alone. . . . Presently the monks and ban-
dits will return together.

Then there are the sumptuous monasteries, inhabited by pious,
kindhearted men, who welcome travellers hospitably and surprise
them with the charm of their intellectual conversation; the Benedictine palace of Monte Cassino, with the dazzling splendour of its
mosaics, its wood-carvings, and its reliquaries; the San Benedetto
convent at Subiaco, with the grotto in which St. Benedict dwelt, and

where the rose-bushes he planted may still be seen. Higher up on the same mountain, at the edge of a deep precipice, rising above the old Anio, stream beloved by Virgil and Horace, is the cell of Beato Lorenzo, bathed in sunshine, where the swallows seek shelter and warmth in winter. Vast woods of dusky-leaved chestnut-trees, with here and there an isolated ruin, on which at evening solitary forms — herdsmen or brigands — perch for a moment, and then vanish in silence. . . . Opposite, on the further bank of the Anio, on a huge hill like a hog's back, stands a little pyramid of stones, which it relieved my utter depression to pile up one bitter day, and to which the French painters who love these solitudes courteously gave my name. Below it lies a cave, the entrance to which can only be reached by dropping down from the rock above, and then crawling in on all fours, at the risk of being crushed to death on the stones five hundred feet below.

To the right lies a field, where I was stopped by some gleaners who, astonished at meeting me in such a place, overwhelmed me with questions, and only allowed me to proceed in my ascent on the assurance that my journey was undertaken in fulfilment of a vow to the Madonna. Far beyond, in a narrow plain, lies the solitary house of La Piagia, built on the banks of the inevitable Anio, where I used to ask for shelter and leave to dry my clothes after shooting through the rainy autumn days. The mistress of the house, a most worthy woman, had a beautiful daughter, who afterwards married our friend Flacheron, the Lyonnese painter. I can still see the strange boy, Crispino, half bandit, half conscript, who used to bring us powder and cigars.

In the evening the gleaners, returning late from their work in the plains below, pass by the row of shrines dotted along the tops of the hills, singing soft litanies to the accompaniment of the sad tinkling of the distant convent bell; the pine-forests resound with the wild refrain of the song of the pifferari; great girls, with dark hair, dusky skins, and noisy laughter, are merciless in their demands on the aching fingers *di questo signore qui suona la chitarra francese,* as an accompaniment to their dancing; while the classical Basque tambourine beats time to my improvised *saltarelli;* the carabineers insist on joining our *osteria* balls, to the indignation of the French and Abruzzian dancers; Flacheron's prodigious fisticuffs; the shameful ejection of the *soldiers of the Pope;* threats of ambuscades and big knives! . . . Flacheron, without saying a word to anyone, betaking himself to the appointed place at midnight, with no other weapon than a stick. No carabineer to be seen; Crispino's enthusiastic delight!

*   *   *   *   *   *   *

And then Albano, Castelgandolpho, Tusculum, Cicero's little theatre, the frescoes on his ruined villa, the lake of Gabia, the marsh I slept in at mid-day, without thought of fever, the remains of the garden of Zenobia, the beautiful dethroned Queen of Palmyra, the long line of ancient aqueducts, reaching as far as the eye could see.

Bitter memories of bygone days of freedom, when heart, mind, soul, all were free; when I was free to idle, not even to think unless I chose; free to ignore the flight of time, to despise ambition, to laugh at glory, to discredit love, to wander north, south, east, or west, to sleep out of doors, to live on little, to wander at will, to dream, to lie exhausted and panting whole days in the soft, hot, murmuring sirocco wind! Perfectly, utterly, illimitably free! Oh, great, strong Italy! wild Italy! unheeding of artistic Italy, thy sister!

The lovely Juliet stretched upon her bier!

CHAPTER XXXVIII

SUBIACO — THE CONVENT OF ST. BENEDICT — A
SERENADE — CIVITELLA — MY GUN —
MY FRIEND CRISPINO

Sᴜʙɪᴀᴄᴏ is a little town of four thousand inhabitants, quaintly built on the slopes of a sugar-loaf mountain. It owes what prosperity it possesses to the Anio, which works the machinery in some not very thriving manufactories, before it forms the celebrated Falls of Tivoli lower down.

In some places its course runs through very narrow valleys. Nero had it dammed up, by a huge wall the ruins of which are still visible, so as to form a deep lake above the village; hence its name, Sub-lacu. The convent of San Benedetto is situated about a league higher up, on the edge of a great precipice, and, as it is almost the only place of interest in the neighbourhood, it has a great many visitors. The chapel altar has been built in front of the entrance to the little cave in which the founder of the Benedictines originally sought refuge.

The interior of the church is most curiously constructed, in two storeys, which are connected by a flight of ten steps.

After you have duly admired St. Benedict's *Santa Spelunca,* and the grotesque pictures on the walls, the monks lead you down into the lower storey, which is filled with rose-leaves from the convent garden. These flowers possess the miraculous power of curing convulsions, and the monks sell immense quantities of them. Three old battered carbines, bent and rusty, hang near the perfumed specifics, as irrefragable testimonies to a wonderful miracle, in which some sportsmen were saved from a gun-accident by a lucky appeal to St. Benedict, *made while the charge was exploding.* Two miles higher up lies the hermitage of Il Beato Lorenzo. The awful solitude of the bare red rocks is enhanced by its complete desertion since the death of the hermit. A huge dog was its solitary guardian, and he lay crouched in the sun, jealously watching my every movement. As I was wholly unprotected, and as he could easily have throttled me, or driven me over the precipice if I had chanced to arouse his suspicion, I did not linger long in the presence of my silent Argus.

Subiaco is not so buried in the mountains as to be removed from all civilising influences. It possesses a café for politicians, and even a Philharmonic Society, the conductor of which is also the parish organist. But I was so depressed by his treating us to the overture to *Cenerentola* on Palm Sunday that I stayed away from the singing academy, lest I might betray my feelings, and thus wound these excellent amateurs. I confined my attentions to the peasants' music, which was at any rate spontaneous and original. One night I was awakened by the most unorthodox serenade I had yet heard. A leather-lunged *ragazzo* was roaring out a love-song beneath the window of his *ragazza,* to the accompaniment of a huge mandoline, a bagpipe, and a little iron instrument of the nature of the triangle, called here a *stimbalo.* His song, or rather shriek, consisted of a progression of four or five descending notes, ending, on the re-ascent, with a long sustained wail from the leading note to the tonic. The musette, the mandoline, and the *stimbalo* struck two chords in regular and almost uniform succession, in the intervals between each stanza; then, when the spirit moved the singer, he started off again, quite careless as to whether his notes were in harmony with the chords of his accompanists, who were as indifferent on the point as he was. He might have been singing to the sound of the sea or a waterfall. In spite of the rusticity of the performance, it pleased me immensely. The rough tones of the mountaineer's voice were softened by distance and the intervening walls. By degrees I was lulled into a sort of dreamy reverie by the monotonous repetition of the short stanzas with their mournful termination, and the silence that followed; and when the *ragazzo* came to the end of what he had to say to his fair one, I suddenly felt a great want. . . . I strained my ears. . . . My thoughts had flowed so gently to the sounds which awoke them, that when the one stopped the thread of the other was broken . . . and I lay till morning—wakeful, dreamless, idea-less. . . .

This melodic phrase recurs all over the Abruzzi mountains; I have heard it sung from Subiaco to Arce, in the kingdom of Naples, more or less modified by the sentiment of the singers and the movement they infused into it. I thought it lovely when I heard it sung slowly and softly one night at Alatri, without accompaniment; it then seemed full of religious feeling that was very different from the sentiment I usually associated with it.

The number of bars in this sort of melodic cry is not always the same in each verse, but varies according to the words improvised by the singer, and the accompaniment follows as best it can. Such improvisation calls for no special poetical gifts in the mountain Orpheus; it is merely a prose in which he expresses the same things he would say in ordinary conversation.

Crispino, the lad I have mentioned, who had the audacity to pretend he had been a brigand, because he had spent two years in the galleys, always greeted me, on my arrival at Subiaco, with the same tune, to these words of welcome, yelled out like a convict:

The doubling of the last vowel at the *sforzando* is indispensable. It is produced by a sound in the throat like a sob, which has a most curious effect.

In the villages round Subiaco, of which it is a kind of capital, I did not glean a single musical idea. Civitella, the most interesting of all, is a miserable, reeking hole, perched, like an eagle's nest, on the summit of an almost inaccessible rock. The reward for the climb is the magnificent view; but painters are also attracted by the strange aspect of the rocks, and the fantastic way in which they are piled on one another; a friend of mine once stayed there for six months.

One flank of the village is built on such huge blocks that it is impossible to conceive how any human power could ever have got them in their places. This Titanesque wall stands in the same relation to " Cyclopean " architecture that that does to ordinary buildings; and yet it seems to be wholly unknown, and I never heard an architect mention its existence.

Besides this, Civitella offers a special attraction to the traveller which he will not find in any other village; namely, an inn, or something approaching to it, at which you are fairly well lodged and fed. The rich man of those parts, one Signor Vincenzo, entertains strangers to the best of his ability; Frenchmen are especially welcome, but he overwhelms them with politics. Moderate in all other respects, he is wholly insatiable in this. Wrapped in a dressing-gown, which he has worn for ten years, he sits cowering by his smoky fireside, and the moment you enter he begins his interrogations. However exhausted you may be with thirst and fatigue, you will not be allowed to drink a drop of wine till you have told him all about Lafayette, Louis Philippe, and the Garde Nationale.[1] All the other villages, Vico-Var, Olevano, Arsoli, Genesano, and twenty others whose names I have forgotten, are exactly alike. The same cluster of little grey houses, perched like swallows' nests on almost inaccessible barren rocks; the same half-naked children running after strangers and crying, *Pittore! Pittore! Inglese! Mezzo baiocco!* [2] (All strangers are either Englishmen or painters in their eyes). Such paths as there are are mere irregular ledges cut in the rocks and just discernible. You meet idle men who eye you suspiciously; women driving pigs, which, with maize, form the sole wealth of the country; and girls carrying heavy copper vessels or faggots on their heads; but all so wretched, so miserable, so tattered, so filthily dirty, that, in spite of the natural beauty of the race and the picturesqueness of their costume, all other feelings

---

[1] This was in 1832. By this time he has probably advanced as far as Changarnier and Napoleon III. [B.]

[2] A small Roman coin. [B.]

are swallowed up in one of utter compassion. And yet I keenly enjoyed wandering through these dens on foot, with or without my gun.

When bent on scaling some unknown peak I was obliged to leave my weapon behind, for the Abruzzians coveted it so much that they would not have hesitated to dispose of its owner by a shot from one of their horrible carbines from behind some old wall. By continually visiting their villages I became quite friendly with the worthy inhabitants. Crispino in particular grew much attached to me, and was useful in many ways. He used to get me scented pipes of a most delicious flavour,[1] bullets and powder, and even percussion caps; and that too in a country devoid of all the products of arts and manufactures. Besides this, Crispino knew all the smart *ragazze* for ten miles round, and the flirtations, the relationships, the love-affairs, the hopes and fears, not only of themselves, but of their families and friends. He kept an accurate account of the temperature and virtue of each, and it was sometimes most amusing to consult this moral thermometer. I first won his affection by conducting a serenade to his mistress, and then by singing a duet with him (it was a song much in vogue at the time among the Tivoli elegants) to the young she-wolf with the accompaniment of the *chitarra francese*. I had further presented him with two shirts, a pair of trousers, and three severe kicks on an occasion when he had treated me with disrespect.[2]

Crispino had not had time to learn to read, and he never wrote to me; but when he had any interesting intelligence from beyond the mountains to give me he used to come to Rome. What were thirty leagues *per un bravo* like him? It was the fashion at the Academy not to fasten the doors of our rooms. One January morning — I had come down from the mountains in October, so that I had had three months of *ennui* — on turning round in bed I found myself confronted by a great swarthy scoundrel, with peaked hat and swathed legs, who was quietly waiting for me to wake.

" Hullo, Crispino! What are you doing in Rome? "

" *Sono venuto — per vederlo!* "

" Well; and what then? "

[1] I was a smoker in those days. I had not then discovered how intensely disagreeable is the excitement caused by tobacco. [B.]

[2] This is not true, and proceeds from the tendency which artists always have to write for effect. I never kicked Crispino; Flacheron was the only one of us who ever ventured to take such a liberty with him. [B.]

" *Crederei mancare al più preciso mio debito, se in questo occasione.*" . . .

" What occasion? "

" *Per dire la verità . . . mi manca . . . il danaro.*"

" I thought so! That is what I call telling the *truth*. So you have no money. And what do you expect me to do for you, you *birbon-naccio?* "

" *Per Bacco, non sono birbone!* "

I will finish his speech in English:

" If you call me a scoundrel because I am penniless, you are quite right; but if you do so because of my two years at Civita Vecchia, then you are wrong. I was not sent to the galleys for stealing, but for the good honest carbine-shots and knife-thrusts I bestowed on the strangers (*forestieri*) in the mountains."

Here my friend was doubtless romancing. He had probably not killed so much as a monk, but he evidently had a keen sense of honour, and was so indignant that, having accepted a mere three piastres, a shirt and a silk handkerchief, he would not wait until I had put on my boots to give him . . . the rest. The poor fellow is dead now: he was knocked on the head two years ago in a quarrel.

May we meet again in a better world! . . .

CHAPTER XXXIX

LIFE OF A MUSICIAN IN ROME — THE MUSIC IN ST.
PETER'S — THE SISTINE CHAPEL — PREJUDICE
AGAINST PALESTRINA — MODERN RELIGIOUS
MUSIC IN THE CHURCH OF ST. LOUIS — THE
OPERA-HOUSES — MOZART AND VACCAI —
THE PIFFERARI — COMPOSITIONS
AT ROME

WITH all my wanderings Rome was my head-quarters, and I became more and more convinced that for a foreign musician who is really in earnest nothing can be sadder than to have to live there. Life is a continual martyrdom, in which one's poetical ideals are successively shattered, and one's beautiful musical dreams dispelled by the grim and hopeless reality; and day by day fresh experiences only bring fresh disappointments. While the other arts are flourishing in all their vividness, grandeur, and majesty, glowing with the splendour of genius, proudly displaying their manifold beauties, music alone is degraded to the level of a poor hunted slave, singing wretched verses with a threadbare voice to earn a crust of bread. I became aware of this state of things after the first few weeks. Directly I arrived I rushed off to St. Peter's. Immense! sublime! overpowering! Michael Angelo, Raphael, Canova on this side and that; under foot, precious marbles and exquisite mosaics. . . . The solemn silence, the cool, still air, the fine, luminous harmony of colour. . . . That aged pilgrim kneeling alone in that vast space. . . . Then a slight sound, rising from some dim corner of the church, rolling through the vast arches like the sound of distant thunder. . . . I felt a sudden fear. . . . It seemed to me that this was really the temple of God, and that I had no right to be there. Then I remembered that this great, grand building had been erected by beings like myself, and I felt a sudden throb of proud joy; and as I thought of the glorious part my cherished art must play there, my heart began to beat with excitement. These pictures and statues and columns, all this gigantic architecture, are, after all, thought I to myself, but the body of the building; music is its soul; through her its being is made manifest, through her the other arts find their consummation, and her mighty voice bears up their burning thoughts to the feet of the Almighty. Where is the organ? . . . The organ — a trifle larger than the one in the Opera-house at Paris — was *on wheels,* and was hidden from me by a pilaster. Perhaps, however, this wretched instrument is only to give the key-note to the voices, and, as all instrumental effects are proscribed here, is enough for that purpose. How many singers are there? . . . I remembered the daily chorus of ninety singers in the little concert-room at the Conservatoire, and seeing that St. Peter's would hold at least sixty times as many, I came to the conclusion that the choir of St. Peter's must number some thousands.

There are *eighteen* on ordinary days and *thirty-two* on solemn festivals! I have even heard a *Miserere* in the Sistine Chapel sung by *five* voices.

An able German critic has recently constituted himself the champion of the Sistine Chapel. " Travellers for the most part," he says, " expect a much more exciting — or I might even say, amusing — kind of music than that which pleases them so much in their own operas;

instead of which they hear an ancient plain-song of simple religious character and without any accompaniment. Then these disappointed dilettanti rail against the Sistine Chapel, and declare that the music is utterly uninteresting, and that all the glowing accounts of it are travellers' tales."

We should not go quite so far as these superficial observers. On the contrary, a musician finds the same interest in this music of the past, handed down to us unchanged in style or form, that a painter does in the frescoes at Pompeii. Far from regretting the absence of the trumpets and big drums which have been introduced by the Italian composers of the day, to such excess that both dancers and singers think no effect can be produced without them, we must confess that the Sistine Chapel was the only place in Italy where we felt safe from that deplorable innovation, and from the artillery of the manufacturers of cavatinas. We grant that the Pope's thirty-two singers, though producing no effect and in fact wholly inaudible in the largest church in the world, suffice for the performance of Palestrina's works in the confined space of the pontifical chapel; we grant that the pure, calm harmony tends to a certain kind of reverie which is not without charm. But the charm is due to the harmonies themselves, and is wholly independent of the so-called genius of the composers, if, indeed, you can dignify by that name musicians who spent their lives in compiling successions of chords like those which constitute a portion of the *Improperia* of Palestrina:

Po - pu - le me - e quid fe - ci ti - bi?

Aut in quo contristavi te? re - spon - de mi - hi.

It is quite possible that the musician who wrote these four-part psalms, in which there is neither *melody* nor *rhythm,* and in which the

harmony is confined to *perfect chords* with a few *suspensions,* may
have had some taste and a certain amount of scientific knowledge; but
genius — the idea is too absurd!

There are, moreover, people who sincerely believe that Palestrina
deliberately wrote in this way in order that his music might be perfectly adapted to his own pious ideal of the words of the text. They
would soon see their mistake if they were to hear his madrigals, in
which the most frivolous or gallant words are set to exactly the same
music as those of the Bible. For example, he has set the words, *"Alla
riva del Tebro, giovinetto vidd' io vago Pastore,"* etc.,[1] to a solemn
chorus, the harmony and general effect of which are identical with
those of his so-called religious compositions. The truth is that he
could not write any other kind of music; and, far from pursuing any
celestial ideal, his works contain a quantity of formulas adapted from
the contrapuntists who preceded him, and of whom he is usually supposed to have been the inspired antagonist. If proof is wanted, look
at his *Missa ad fugam.*

How, then, do such works as these, clever though they may be as
regards their conquest of contrapuntal difficulties, contribute to the expression of religious feeling? How far are such specimens of the
labour of a patient chord-manufacturer indicative of single-minded
absorption in the true object of his work? In no way that I can
see. The expressive accent of a musical work is not enhanced in any
way by its being embodied in a perpetual canon. Beauty and truth
of expression gain nothing by the difficulties which the composer
may have had to overcome in producing them, any more than his
work would be increased in value from the fact that he had been
suffering physical pain while he was writing it. If Palestrina had
lost his hands, and been forced to write with his feet, that fact would
not have enhanced the value of his works or increased their religious
merit.

Nevertheless, the German critic above referred to calls Palestrina's *Improperia* sublime. " The whole ceremony," he says, " the
subject in itself, the presence of the Pope and cardinals, the precision and intelligence of the singers, form one of the most imposing
and touching sights of the holy week." . . . True, but that does not
convert the music into a work of inspiration and genius.

Some gloomy autumn day, when the dreary north wind is howling,

[1] By the banks of the Tiber, a young shepherd wandered, etc. [H.]

read *Ossian* to the accompaniment of the weird moans of an Æolian
harp hung in the leafless branches of a tree, and you will experience a
feeling of intense sadness, an infinite yearning for another state of
existence, an intense disgust with the present; in fact, a regular attack
of " blue devils " and a longing for suicide. This is a much more definite
effect than that produced by the music of the Sistine Chapel, and
yet no one has ever thought of ranking the makers of Æolian harps
among great composers.

It may, however, be said of the musical service at the Sistine
Chapel that it has preserved its solemnity and dignity, whereas the
other churches in Rome have in this respect lapsed from their ancient
traditions into an incredible state of degradation, I may even say
demoralisation. Several French priests have been utterly disgusted by
this disgraceful debasement of religious art.

I was present at a celebration of high mass on the King's birthday,
with full orchestra and chorus, for which our ambassador, M. de St.
Aulaire, had engaged the best artists in Rome. The sixty performers
were stationed in a large amphitheatre in front of the organ, and
began by tuning up as noisily as if they had been in a theatre. The
diapason of the organ being much too low for the wind instruments,
it was impossible to combine it with the orchestra. The only thing to
do was to leave it out, but of this the organist would not hear; he was
resolved to take part in the performance and earn his money, even
though the ears of the audience should bleed with agony. And I must
admit that he fairly earned his pay, for I never laughed so heartily
in my life. Like all Italian organists he used only the high stops, and
so in the *tuttis* his piccolos were drowned by the orchestra; but when
the orchestra had a staccato chord followed by a rest, the organ,
which always drags a little and cannot stop short like other instruments, was left alone with a chord a quarter of a tone lower than
the orchestra, producing the most appallingly comic wail that it is
possible to conceive.

In the intervals between the plain-song of the priests, the orchestra
— unable, as it were, to control the demon of music which possessed
it — tuned up in the coolest way; the flutes played scales in D; the
horns did fanfares in E flat; the violins made cadences and *gruppetti;*
the bassoon rattled its keys and produced its deepest notes; and the
organ twittered over all, and completed a concert worthy of Callot.
And this in the presence of a civilised audience, including the French

ambassador, the director of the Academy, a large body of priests and cardinals, and artists of every nationality.

The music was worthy of the performers. Regular cavatinas, each with its *crescendo, cabaletta,* organ points and roulades; the whole an indescribable monster, with a phrase of Vaccai's for its head, scraps of Pacini for limbs, and a ballet of Gallemberg for body and tail; and, to crown all, the solos in this strange farrago were sung in a soprano voice, proceeding from a big man with a rubicund face and an immense pair of black whiskers.

"Good heavens," I said to my neighbour, who was choking with laughter, "is everything miraculous in this favoured country? Did you ever see a bearded *castrato* before?"

"*Castrato!*" cried an Italian lady who was seated in front of us, and whose indignation was aroused by our laughter and our remarks — "*davvero non è castrato!*"[1]

"Do you know him, madam?"

"*Per Bacco! non burlate. Imparate, pezzi d'asino, che quel virtuoso maraviglioso è il marito mio.*"[2] They were husband and wife!

I have often heard the overtures of the *Barbiere, Cenerentola,* and *Otello* in church. They seemed to be special favourites with the organists, and formed an agreeable seasoning to the service. The music in the theatres is in much the same glorious condition, and is about as *dramatic* as that of the churches is *religious.* There is the same amount of invention, the same purity of form, the same charm of style, the same intensity of thought. The singers I heard during the theatrical season had generally good voices, and that facility of execution which is the special characteristic of the Italians;[3] but they were all mediocre except Madame Unger, the German prima donna, who was a great favourite in Paris, and Salvator, a fair baritone. The chorus is a shade below that of the Opéra-Comique as regards precision, accuracy, and warmth. The orchestra, about as imposing and formidable as the Prince of Monaco's army, has all the qualities which are generally regarded as defects. In the Valle Theatre there is *one* violoncello, a watchmaker by trade — more fortunate in this than one of his colleagues, who has to earn his bread by *mending chairs.*

The words "symphony" and "overture" are used in Rome to

---

[1] "He certainly isn't a castrato!"

[2] "Don't try to be funny! Let me tell you, you great asses, that this marvellous virtuoso is my husband."

[3] Which was *then* their special characteristic. [B.]

designate *a certain noise* which the orchestra makes before the curtain rises, and to which no one ever listens. The names of Beethoven and Weber are scarcely known there. A learned abbé, belonging to the Sistine Chapel, told Mendelssohn *that he had heard someone speak of a young man of great promise called Mozart.* It is true that this worthy ecclesiastic does not often come into contact with the world, and has studied nothing but Palestrina all his life. So he may be regarded as an exceptional being, for though Mozart's music is never played in Rome, still a good many people there have heard something more of him than that he was *a young man of great promise.* The more learned amateurs even know that he is dead, and that though he cannot be classed with Donizetti, he has written some remarkable works. I knew one who had a copy of *Don Giovanni;* and after studying it for some time on the piano, he confided to me that he thought *this old music* was really better than the *Zadig* or *Astartea* of M. Vaccai, which had just been brought out at the Apollo Theatre. Instrumental music is a sealed book to the Romans. They have not the most elementary notion of what we call a symphony.

I noticed only one popular kind of music while I was at Rome, which may be regarded as a remnant of antiquity : that of the *pifferari.* These are wandering musicians who towards Christmas come down from the mountains four or five at a time, with bagpipes and *pifferi* (a sort of oboe), on which they perform sacred music before the images of the Madonna. They generally wear large brown cloth cloaks and pointed brigand hats, and there is a strange, wild air about them which is quite unique. I have spent hours watching them in the streets of Rome, as they stood with heads slightly bent and eyes full of faith and devotion, gazing in rapt adoration at the statue of the Virgin. The bagpipe, accompanied by a large bass *piffero,* gives out a harmony of two or three notes, against which a shorter *piffero* plays the tune ; above all this there are two very small *pifferi,* much shorter than the others, and played by children of from twelve to fifteen years of age, which make shakes and trills, and surround the rustic melody with a shower of quaint ornamentation. After a long series of these gay and refreshing refrains, repeated over and over again, comes a slow, grave prayer, of patriarchal and pious character. As the tune of this has been printed in various Neapolitan collections I shall not give it here. When close by the sound is overpowering, but at a little distance this curious orchestra produces an extremely impressive effect. I heard

the *pifferari* afterwards in their own home, and if I was struck with
them in Rome it may be imagined what an impression they made on
me in the wild mountains of the Abruzzi. Volcanic rocks and black
pine-forests are the natural *mise en scène* for such primitive music;
and when, in addition to this, one has before one the mysterious monuments of a lost era — cyclopean walls, and shepherds clad in rough
sheepskins, with the wool outside (the costume of the ancient Sabine
shepherds) — it is easy to imagine oneself a contemporary of the
ancient people among whom the arcadian Evander, the generous host
of Æneas, settled himself.

It is thus best to give up almost all hope of hearing music when
you go to Rome; in fact the anti-musical atmosphere had reduced me
to a state in which I found it almost impossible to compose. I wrote
only three or four pieces all the time I was at the Academy: 1. An
overture, *Rob Roy,* which was long and diffuse, and, when played in
Paris a year afterwards, was so badly received by the public that I
burnt it the night of the concert. 2. The *Scène aux Champs* of my
Symphonie fantastique, which I re-wrote almost entirely in the grounds
of the Villa Borghese. 3. *Le Chant de Bonheur* of my monodrama
Lélio,[1] which I dreamed lying on the thick clipped hedge, or rather
wall, of our classic garden, lulled by the breezes of my perfidious
enemy the south wind. 4. The song called *La Captive,* the success of
which I little foresaw when writing it.[2] I am wrong, however, in saying it was written at Rome, for it is dated from Subiaco. And I now
remember that one day when I was watching my friend Lefebvre the
architect drawing at a table in the inn at Subiaco, he pushed down a
book with his elbow, which I picked up, and which happened to be
Victor Hugo's *Orientales.* It opened at that delicious poem *La Captive.* I read it, and turning to Lefebvre I said, " If I had some music
paper here I would write the music to this, *for I hear it.*" " If that is
all you want," he said, " I will make you some." And he thereupon
ruled some paper for me, on which I jotted down the air and the bass
of the little song. I then put the manuscript into my pocket-book, and
thought no more about it. A fortnight afterwards, during some music
at our director's, I remembered *La Captive.* " I must show you a song

---

[1] The words, both spoken and sung, of this work, which supplements my *Symphonie fantastique,* I had written on my way back from Nice, on foot, between Siena and Montefiascone. [B.]
    [2] Written in February 1832.

I composed at Subiaco," said I to Mademoiselle Vernet; "I am curious to hear what it is like, for I have quite forgotten."

I scribbled off the pianoforte accompaniment, and we were able to give some idea of it; and it was such a success that a month afterwards M. Vernet, who had been ever since haunted by the air, said to me: "I hope when you go into the mountains again that you will not bring back any more songs with you, for your *Captive* is making life intolerable to me; wherever I go — in the palace, the garden, the wood, on the terrace, or in the corridors, one hears people singing, grunting, or growling, *Le long du mur sombre* . . . *le sabre du Spahis* . . . *je ne suis pas Tartare* . . . *l'eunuque noir,* etc. It is perfectly maddening. I am going to dismiss one of my servants to-morrow, and I shall engage another only on the express understanding that he is not to sing *La Captive*." I afterwards developed the song and scored it for the orchestra, and I think it is one of the most vivid I ever wrote.

I must add one more to this short list of my Roman works, a *méditation religieuse,* for six voices, with orchestral accompaniment, on a prose translation of a poem of Moore's, *Ce monde entier n'est qu'une ombre fugitive* (This world is all a fleeting show),[1] which forms the first number of my Op. 18, called *Tristia*.

As for the *Resurrexit,* for full orchestra and chorus, which I sent to the academicians in Paris, in obedience to the rules, and in which those gentlemen were pleased to discover signs of remarkable *progress,* an evident *proof* of the effect of Rome on my ideas, and the complete reversal of my unfortunate *musical proclivities,* it is nothing but a fragment[2] of the Mass which was performed at St. Roch and St. Eustache, several years, as we know, before I obtained the Academy prize. So much for the opinions of the immortals![3]

---

[1] The manuscript is dated August 4th, 1831.

[2] The *Credo*.

[3] M. Boschot unearthed at the Villa Medicis the official judgment (delivered at the Institut on October 12th, 1833) on the works submitted by Berlioz. The *Rob Roy* overture escaped with the ironic comment that it "had already been judged by the public." The "quartetto" was severely censored for its fragmentariness, its lack of melody, its over-ambitious design, and so on: the learned academicians regretted that "an artist gifted with so rich an imagination should not be willing to rid himself of his bizarre forms"; but they hoped that "the great master, Experience, would conduct him back again to correct principles and that we shall have one good composer the more in M. Berlioz." On the other hand, his colleague Montfort's music received high praise: for Montfort "has not disdained to study the great masters."

CHAPTER XL

THE SPLEEN — ITS VARIETIES — ISOLATION

IT was during this period of my academic life that I once more fell a prey to the miserable disease (mental, nervous, imaginary, if you like), which I shall call *the bane of isolation*. I had my first attack of it when I was sixteen, and it came about in this wise. One beautiful May morning, at the Côte-Saint-André, I was sitting in a meadow under the shade of some wide-spreading oaks, reading one of Montjoie's novels called *Manuscrit trouvé au Mont Pausilippe*. Although absorbed in my book, I was perfectly conscious of a soft sad kind of air which was wafted over the plain at regular intervals. The Rogation processions were being celebrated, and the sound I heard arose from the chanting of the litanies by the peasants. There is something touching and poetical in this idea of wandering through the hills and dales in the spring-time and invoking God's blessing on the fruits of the earth, and I was unspeakably affected by it. The procession halted at a wooden cross covered with creepers. I watched the people kneeling while the priest blessed the meadows, and then they wended their way onwards, singing their mournful song. I could occasionally distinguish our old priest's feeble voice, and some fragments of the words as the pious band drifted farther and farther away:

	. . . Conservare digneris.
The Peasants.	Te rogamus audi nos!
Decrescendo.	Sancte Barnaba
	Ora pro nobis!
Perdendo.	Sancta Magdalena
	Ora pro . . .
	Sancta Maria,
	Ora . . .
	Sancta . . .
	. . . nobis.

Silence . . . the faint rustling of the wheat, stirred by the soft morning air . . . the loving cry of the quail to his mate . . . the cheerful ortolan singing on the top of the poplars . . . the utter calm . . . the slow fall of a leaf from the oak . . . the dull throbbing of my own heart. . . . Life was so far, far away from me. . . . On the remote horizon the Alpine glaciers flashed like giant gems in the light of the mounting sun . . . below me Meylan . . . and beyond the Alps, Italy, Naples, Posilippo . . . the beings of whom I was reading . . . burning passions . . . an unfathomable and secret joy. . . . Oh for wings across the space! I want life and love and enthusiasm and burning kisses, I want more and fuller life! . . . But I am only an inert frame chained to the earth! Those beings are either fictitious or they are dead. . . . What is love? . . . what is fame? . . . what are hearts? . . . Where is my star? . . . the *Stella montis?* Vanished possibly for ever. . . . When shall I see Italy? . . .

And the paroxysm possessed me in full force. I suffered agonies, and, casting myself down on the ground, groaned and clutched the earth wildly, tore up the grass and the innocent daisies, with their upturned wondering eyes, in my passionate struggles against the horrible feeling of loneliness and sense of absence.

And yet what was this anguish compared to the tortures I have endured since, which go on increasing day by day? . . .

I do not know how to convey any adequate conception of this unutterable anguish. A physical experiment alone can give any idea of it. If you put a cup of water and a cup of sulphuric acid side by side under the bell of an air-pump, and exhaust the air, you will see the water bubble, boil, and finally evaporate. The sulphuric acid absorbs the vapour as it evaporates, and, owing to the property possessed by the steam of carrying off the caloric, the water which is left in the cup freezes into a little lump of ice.

The same sort of thing happens when I become possessed by this feeling of loneliness and absence. There is a vacuum all round my throbbing breast, and I feel as if under the influence of some irresistible power my heart were evaporating and tending towards dissolution. My skin begins to pain and burn; I get hot all over; I feel an irresistible desire to call my friends and even strangers to help me, to protect me, to console me and preserve me from destruction, and to restrain the life which is being drawn out of me to the four quarters of the globe.

These crises are accompanied by no longing for death; the idea of suicide is intolerable; it is no wish to die — far from it, it is a yearning for more life, life fuller and completer; one feels an infinite capacity for happiness which is outraged by the want of an adequate object, and which can be satisfied only by infinite, overpowering, *furious* delights proportioned to the incalculable wealth of feeling which one longs to spend upon them.

This state is not *spleen,* but precedes it. It is the ebullition and evaporation of heart, senses, brain, and nervous fluid. The spleen follows, and is the congealing of all this — the lump of ice which remains in the bell of the air-pump.

Even in my calmer moods I feel a little of this *isolation* — for instance, on Sunday evenings, when the towns are still and everyone goes away to the country — because there is *happiness in the distance* and people are *absent.* The adagios of Beethoven's symphonies, some of the scenes in Gluck's *Alceste* and *Armide,* an aria in his opera *Telemaco,* the Elysian fields in his *Orfeo,* bring on fierce fits of the same pain; but these masterpieces contribute their own antidotes; they create tears, and tears bring relief. The adagios of some of Beethoven's sonatas, on the other hand, and Gluck's *Iphigénie en Tauride* pertain wholly to the state of spleen, and induce it; the atmosphere is cold and dark, the sky is grey and cloudy, and the north wind whistles drearily.

There are, moreover, two kinds of spleen — one ironical, scoffing, passionate, violent, and malignant; the other taciturn and gloomy, requiring rest, silence, solitude, and sleep. Those who are possessed by this become utterly indifferent to everything, and would look unmoved on the ruin of the world. At such times I have wished that the earth were a shell filled with gunpowder, that I might set fire to it for my amusement.

On one occasion, when a prey to this kind of spleen, I was lying asleep, rolled up like a hedgehog, on a heap of dead leaves in the laurel-wood of the Academy gardens, when I was wakened by a kick from two of my comrades — Constant Dufeu the architect, and the elder Dantan the sculptor.

" Hullo, old boy! Will you come with us to Naples? "

" Go to the devil! You know quite well that I have no money."

" You great stupid! We have got money, and we will lend you some. Now then, Dantan, help me to put him on his legs, or we shall get nothing out of him! . . . Now then, shake yourself; go and ask M. Vernet for a month's leave, and as soon as your bag is packed we will be off; it is all settled."

And so it was.

With the exception of an amusing but unrelatable scandal we

caused in the small town of Ciprano . . . after dinner, I do not remember that anything noteworthy occurred on our journey, which we
performed prosaically with a *vetturino*.

But Naples! . . .

CHAPTER XLI

NAPLES — AN ENTHUSIASTIC SOLDIER — EXCURSION TO NISIDA — THE LAZZARONI — AN INVITATION TO DINNER — THE CRACK OF A WHIP — THE SAN CARLO THEATRE — RETURN TO ROME ACROSS THE ABRUZZI — TIVOLI — VIRGIL AGAIN

NAPLES [1] — with its vivid sky, its holiday sunshine, its fruitful soil!
Everybody has described this beautiful garden much more effec-
tively than I can hope to do, for the scene is one which must strike
every traveller. Who could help feeling the charm of that still expanse of ocean lying asleep under the rays of the mid-day sun, the soft
folds of its azure robe, and the lulling murmur of its faint pulsation?
Who that has seen the crater of Mount Vesuvius at midnight has not
thrilled with dread at the mysterious roll of its subterranean thunder,
the shrieks of fury which issue from its depths, or the awful splendour
of those masses of molten rock which are hurled like glowing blasphemies towards the starlit heavens, and fall back on the broad breast
of the mountain, to lie like a luminous necklace round its mighty
throat? Who has not lingered sadly among the skeleton remains of
desolate Pompeii, or stood waiting, a solitary spectator, on the steps
of the amphitheatre, for the curtain to rise on a tragedy of Euripides
or Sophocles, for which the stage seems all prepared? Who has not
felt some sympathy for the lazzaroni — those grown-up children,
those merry thieves — with their quick wit and their kindly good-
nature?

I shall not, therefore, follow where so many have trod before,
but I must tell one story, because it illustrates the character of the
Neapolitan fishermen so vividly. It concerns a dinner which the lazzaroni gave me three days after I arrived, and a present which I
received at dessert. It was a fine autumn day; a fresh breeze was

[1] October, 1831.

blowing, and the air was so clear and transparent that it seemed as if, though standing at Naples, you had only to stretch out your hand to pick the oranges off the trees at Capri. I had begged my companions to leave me alone that day, and I went for a walk in the gardens of the Villa Reale. As I passed by a little pavilion, which I had not previously noticed, a sentry, who was posted at the entrance, called out to me roughly in French:

" Take off your hat, sir."

" What for? "

" Look there! "

He pointed to a marble statue inside the pavilion, and the two words, Torquato Tasso, which I saw on the pedestal at once caused me to obey the behest of the enthusiastic soldier. It was right and proper; but I still wonder how the sentinel guessed that I was a Frenchman and an artist, and would readily follow his injunction. He was evidently a clever physiognomist. But to return to my lazzaroni.

I was wandering carelessly along the sea-shore, meditating sadly on the fate of poor Tasso, whose modest tomb in the convent of Saint Onofrio, at Rome, I had visited with Mendelssohn some months before, and was philosophising to myself on the misfortunes of poets whose hearts are too poetical, etc., etc.; and from Tasso I turned suddenly to Cervantes, and his lovely pastoral *Galatea,* and *Galatea* recalled another delicious creation in the same story, called *Nisida,* and *Nisida* made me think of the lovely island of that name in the bay of Pozzuoli, whereupon I was at once seized with a wild desire to see the island.[1]

I rush off through the tunnel of Posilippo down to the shore; I see a boat, I hire it; I demand four rowers; six present themselves; I offer them a reasonable fare, pointing out at the same time that six men are not required to row a nutshell of a boat to Nisida. They insist smiling, and demand thirty francs instead of five, which is their proper fare. Two lads were standing silently by, watching the proceedings with longing eyes. I was in a good humour, and the exorbitant demands of my boatmen struck me as rather comic than otherwise; so, pointing to the two lazzaronetti, I called out, " Well, then, I will give you thirty francs, but the whole eight of you come and row furiously." Such shouts of joy and such antics! We jump into the boat and reach Nisida in a few minutes. Leaving my vessel in charge of the

---

[1] The real name of the island is Nisita, but I was not then aware of the fact. [B.]

crew, I land on the island, and wander all over it; watch the sunset behind the Cape of Misena, immortalised by the author of the *Æneid;* while the sea, unmindful of Virgil, or Æneas, or Ascanius, or Misenus, or Palinurus, sings a brilliant song of her own in a major key. . . .

As I was wandering aimlessly along, a soldier comes up and, in very good French, offers to show me the various places of interest and the finest views, etc. — an offer of which I gladly avail myself. When we part, I take out my purse to give him the customary *buona mano,* but he steps back, looks very much offended, and says:

" What is that for, sir? I want nothing from you except . . . your prayers."

" You shall certainly have them," I said to myself, as I pocketed my purse. " The idea is too comic, and may the devil take me if I fail."

And true to my word, I actually said a *pater* for my excellent sergeant that night, but when I began a second I burst out laughing; so I am afraid I did not do the poor fellow much good, and he has probably remained a sergeant to this day. . . .

I should probably have stayed at Nisida till the following day if one of my sailors, deputed by the *captain,* had not hailed me and told me that the wind was rising and that we should find it difficult to return to shore if we did not speedily weigh anchor. I adopt his advice, we seat ourselves in the ship; the captain, like the Trojan hero:

> . . . Eripit ensem
> Fulmineum   [*unclasps his big knife:*
>   strictoque ferit retinacula ferro.
>   [*and promptly cuts the cable.*
> Idem omnes simul ardor habet; rapiuntque ruuntque;
> Littora deseruere; latet sub classibus æquor;
> Adnixi torquent spumas, et cærula verrunt.
>
> Eager and somewhat afraid, we hasten from the shore;
> The spray splashes from our oars, the sea flies beneath our keel.
>   (*Free translation.*)

There really was some danger, for the nutshell of a boat was bobbing about on the white crests of the big waves in a most singular fashion; my merry men had ceased laughing, and were looking for their rosaries. This seemed to me outrageously absurd, and I said to myself: " After all, why should I drown? Because an intelligent soldier worships Tasso? Less than that even; for a hat. For had I been bareheaded, he would hardly have challenged me; I should not have thought of Tasso, Cervantes, or Nisida; should not have started on this stupid expedition, but should at this moment be quietly sitting in the San Carlo Theatre, listening to Brambilla and Tamburini!" These thoughts and the motion of the doomed boat made me very sea-sick. But Neptune thought it joke enough to frighten us, and we were permitted to land. The sailors, who had sat as mute as fish, now began to chatter like magpies, and their joy was so great that when I paid them the thirty francs out of which they had swindled me, conscience smote them, and they gave me a hearty invitation to dinner, which I accepted on the spot. They took me to a solitary spot, in a plantation of poplars on the Pozzuoli road, so far off that my mind misgave me as to their intentions. Poor lazzaroni! But eventually we arrived at a cottage where they were evidently well known, and my hosts at once issued orders for dinner.

A small mountain of smoking macaroni soon made its appearance, into which I was invited to dive, like them, with my fingers; a can of Posilippian wine was set on the table, from which we all drank in turn, beginning with a toothless old man who alone was allowed to take precedence of me on account of his age, which ranks even before the rights of hospitality in the eyes of these good children. After a most unconscionable draught, the old man launched out into politics, and began to maunder about King Joachim, to whom he was devoted. In order to change the subject and to provide me with some entertainment, the young lazzaroni persuaded him to tell me the story — for which he was famous — of a long adventurous voyage he had once made.

Thereupon the old lazzarone held his listeners spell-bound by the narrative of how, when twenty, he had embarked on a *speronare,* on which, after tossing about *for three days and two nights* on *unknown waters,* he had at length been cast on a *remote island,* to which, *it is said,* Napoleon was afterwards exiled, and which the inhabitants called the Island of Elba. I professed the greatest interest in this breath-catching story, and congratulated the brave sailor on his escape from such awful dangers. The lazzaroni were delighted by my sympathy. A good deal of whispering and mystery and commotion ensued in the cottage, as if some surprise were in preparation. And so it was, for when I rise to depart, the biggest of the young lazzaroni, stepping up to me with a very embarrassed air, begs me to accept a present from the party as a *souvenir*. It is the best they have to offer, and is calculated to draw tears from any eye. A gigantic onion! which I receive with a modest gravity becoming the situation, and bear off to the summit of Mount Posilippo, after many farewells, hand-shakings, and protestations of eternal friendship.

It was almost dark when I left my kind hosts, and started off limping on my way home. I had lamed my right foot in coming down from Nisida; and so, when a fine carriage rolled past me on the Naples road, and I saw that the footboard behind was empty, I leapt up into it, hoping to be carried into the town in this unfashionable manner without fatigue. I had, however, counted without my hostess, a pretty little Parisian woman, lying back luxuriously in a cloud of muslin, who cried out sharply to her coachman, " Louis, there is some-one behind! " whereupon I receive a sharp cut from the whip across my face. Thank you for the gift, my gentle country-woman! A French doll! If Crispino had only been there, you should have spent an uncomfortable ten minutes!

So, meditating on the charms of a brigand's life (which, in spite of its drawbacks, would really be the only satisfactory career for an honest man, if there were not so many stupid, stinking wretches even in the smallest bands), I limped home.

To drown my sorrows I went to the San Carlo, and there, for the first time since my arrival in Italy, listened to music. In comparison with the orchestras I had heard, this one seemed to me excellent. There is nothing to fear from the wind instruments; the violins play fairly well, and the violoncellos are harmonious, though too few. Even the kind of music which the Italian orchestras usually play does not justify their always having fewer violoncellos than double-basses. I must protest against the disagreeable noise which the conductor makes by striking his desk with his bow; but I am assured that but for this some of the players would find it difficult to keep time. . . . This is unanswerable; and after all one must not expect as much from an orchestra in a country where instrumental music is almost unknown as one would in Berlin, Dresden, or Paris. The chorus is hopelessly weak; and a composer who writes for the San Carlo says it is very difficult, indeed almost impossible, to get choruses in the ordinary four parts decently performed. The sopranos cannot sing apart from the tenors, and it is almost always necessary to write for them at the octave.

At the Fondo, the opera buffa is played with such fire, spirit, and *brio* as to raise it above almost every theatre of its class. While I was at Naples they were performing a most amusing farce of Donizetti's, *Le Convenienzi teatrali.*

Still the attraction of the theatres in Naples was not to be compared with that of the country around, and I was oftener outside the town than in it.

One morning when I was breakfasting at Castellamare with the sea-painter Munier, whom we had nicknamed Neptune, he threw down his napkin and said:

" What shall we do? I am tired of this place; let us leave it."

" Let us go to Sicily."

" By all means. I will just finish off a sketch I have begun, and at five o'clock we will go and take our places in the steamer."

" All right. Now let us see how much money we have left."

When we had counted it over we discovered that we had enough to take us to Palermo, but must trust to Providence for the return journey; so, being Frenchmen, and therefore, like true Frenchmen, wholly devoid of the faith which removes mountains, and thinking it wiser not to tempt God, we parted — he to his sketch of the sea, I to make my way on foot to Rome.

I had made up my mind some days before to do this; and that evening, after saying good-bye to Dufeu and Dantan, I met two Swedish officers whom I knew, who told me that they intended walking to Rome.

" By Jove! " I said; " I am going to Subiaco to-morrow. I want to go straight across the mountains, over rocks and streams, like the chamois hunter; let us go together."

They accepted my proposal. We sent off our baggage by a *vetturino,* and prepared to make our way to Subiaco as the crow flies, to stay there for a day, and then proceed along the high road to Rome. So off we started,[1] apparelled in the inevitable gray linen costumes, B —— carrying his sketch-book and pencils, and we walking-sticks, which were our only weapons. It was the time of the vintage, and the first day we lived almost entirely on excellent grapes (not nearly so good, however, as those of Mount Vesuvius). The peasants would not always take our money, and we sometimes forgot to send for the owners of the vineyards. In the evening, at Capua, we found

[1] October 14th, 1831.

a good supper, good beds, and . . . an improvisatore. After a brilliant prelude on his mandoline, he asked us what countrymen we
were.

"French," said K———.

I had heard the improvisations of this Campanian Tyrtæus a
month before, and he had then put the same question to my fellow-
travellers, who answered:

"Poles."

To which he replied enthusiastically:

"I have seen the whole world — Italy, Spain, France, Germany,
England, Poland, Russia; but the bravest of all are the Poles, the
Poles."

Here is the song as he sang it, improvising without a moment's
hesitation, and addressing the so-called Frenchmen:

You can imagine how flattered I felt, and how mortified the
Swedes were.

Before plunging into the intricacies of the Abruzzi mountains,
we stopped for a day at San Germano, so as to see the celebrated
convent of Monte Cassino.

This Benedictine monastery is built, like that at Subiaco, on the
side of a mountain, but the two have no other resemblance. In place
of the quaint simplicity of San Benedetto, you have here the proportions and the luxury of a palace. One's imagination recoils at the
conception of the vast sums which must have been squandered
on it. There is an organ with absurd figures of little angels,

which blow trumpets and clash cymbals when the instrument is set in motion. The pavement is made of the rarest marbles, and the choir-stalls are covered with exquisitely carved scenes from monastic life.

By means of a forced march we reached Isola di Sora the next day. It is a village situated on the frontier of the Kingdom of Naples, and is chiefly remarkable for a little river which, after working some mills, forms a fine cascade. Here a curious mystification awaited us. Both K—— and I had cut our feet, we were all fiercely thirsty, smothered in dust, hot and tired, and the moment we entered the town we asked for the inn.

"Inn? there isn't one," replied the peasants with a derisive assumption of pity.

" But where are we to spend the night? "

" Who can say? "

We asked permission to pass the night in a wretched coach-house; but there was not even a wisp of straw, and besides, the owner objected. We were in a state of boundless irritation, which was not diminished by the sneers and cool unconcern of the peasants. It seemed too ridiculous to arrive in a small commercial town and to have to sleep in the streets; but such must have been our fate but for a sudden happy thought of mine.

I had once before spent a day in Isola di Sora, and I fortunately remembered the name of one M. Courrier, a paper manufacturer and a Frenchman. His brother was pointed out to me; I explained the situation to him, and after a moment's consideration he calmly answered me in French, or I may say, in Dauphinois, for its accent virtually renders it an idiom:

"*Pardi, on vous couchera ben*" (Of course you shall have a bed).

" Hurrah! we are saved! M. Courrier is a Dauphinois, I am a Dauphinois, and all Dauphinois are brothers! "

And so it turned out, for M. Courrier remembered me, and entertained us most hospitably. After a good supper we retired to one of those enormous beds which are found only in Italy, and in which we all slept most comfortably, reflecting that in future it would be wise to ascertain beforehand in what towns there are inns. Our host comforted us the following day with the assurance that we should reach Subiaco in two days, so that in any case we had only one night before us. A lad showed us the way through the vineyards and woods for a few miles, and then left us with rather vague directions as to the course we were to pursue.

Veroli is a large village perched on the top of a hill, and looking in the distance like a town. We dined there very badly on bread and raw ham, and before nightfall reached Alatri, another inhabited rock, which was still barer and wilder-looking. We were followed all down the principal street by a crowd of curious women and children. When we reached the market-place, a house, or rather a kennel, with a shabby signboard, was pointed out to us; and in spite of our disgust we had to spend the night there. Good heavens, what a night! Sleep was impossible owing to the vermin *of all kinds,* which so tormented me as to bring on an attack of fever.

What was to be done? My companions would not leave me be‚ hind; we had to get on to Subiaco. I could not bear the idea of staying in such a hovel; but I was shivering so that it was impossible to warm me, and I felt as if I could not move a step. While I was thus trembling with cold, my friends held a consultation in Swedish, which I did not understand; but it was evident from the expression of their faces that I was causing them great inconvenience. So I determined to make a supreme effort; we started on our way, and after two hours' rapid walking the fever left me.

Before quitting Alatri we called a council of the local geographers to determine our route. There was a great diversity of opinion, but at last they and we decided on one leading through Arcino and Anticoli. This was the hardest day's work of all. There were no proper paths; we had to follow the course of the torrents; and so much climbing of boulders was very tiring.

At length we reached a horrible village, name unknown to me. The loathsome hovels were open but tenantless; the only inhabitants we saw were two young pigs wallowing in the black mud on the broken rocks which formed the pavement of the streets in this wretched hole. Where were the inhabitants? Well might we say, " *Chi lo sa?*"

Several times we lost our way in these rocky labyrinths, and often, after straying into a valley, had no alternative but to climb the hill we had just descended, or, from the bottom of a ravine, to shout to some peasant or other:

" *Ohe! la strada d'Anticoli?* "

To which he would either reply by a laugh, or else by calling out " *Via! via!* " which was anything but reassuring. At last, however, we arrived at Anticoli, and found plenty of ham and eggs, and some maize, which we roasted in the local fashion and rather liked. The local surgeon, a great red-faced man like a butcher, came and honoured us by a few questions about the Garde Nationale of Paris, and by the offer of a *printed book* he had for sale.

We had an immense reach of pasture land to traverse before nightfall, and a guide was necessary. The one we got did not seem very sure of the way, and often stopped in doubt. An old shepherd who was sitting by a pond, and had probably not heard the sound of a human voice for a month, all but fell into the water when we suddenly came upon him unawares and asked him the way to Arcinasso, a pretty village (so our guide said), where we should find *all sorts of refreshments.*

Some *baiocchi* soon relieved him from his terror and proved that our intentions were friendly, but it was almost impossible to make anything of his guttural replies, which were more like *clucking* than a human language. Arcinasso, the *pretty village,* resolved itself into a solitary tavern standing by itself in the midst of desolate steppes. An old woman sold us some wine and some fresh water. B ——— 's sketch-book attracted her attention, so we told her it was a Bible; thereupon she rose delighted, looked at the drawings one by one, embraced B ——— cordially, and blessed us all three.

The utter silence of these great prairies is indescribable. The only inhabitants we saw were the old shepherd and his flock, and one solitary crow stalking gravely about. . . . As we approached he flew away towards the north. . . . I watched his flight for a long time. . . . My thoughts followed him in the same direction — towards England — and I became absorbed in Shakespearean dreams.

But this was no time for gaping at crows and dreaming, for Subiaco had to be reached before nightfall. Our guide had left us, and it was getting dark. We were walking along in dead silence like three spectres, when I suddenly recognised a thicket in which I had killed a thrush seven months before.

" Courage! " I exclaimed; " one effort more; I know where we are: and in two hours we shall be at Subiaco."

Forty minutes later we saw lights shining at a great depth below us; it was Subiaco.

I found Gibert there, and he lent me some clean linen, which I sorely needed. I wanted to go to bed, but I soon heard cries of

" *Oh, Signor Sidoro.*[1] *Ecco questo signore francese chi suona la chitarra.*" [2] Flacheron came running with the beautiful Mariuccia [3] and his *tambour de basque,* and, willy-nilly, I had to dance the saltarello till midnight.

On leaving Subiaco two days later I conceived the wonderful project which I shall now describe.

My two Swedish companions, Messrs. Bennet and Klinksporn, walked too quickly for me. As I could not induce them to go slower, or even to stop occasionally, I let them go on in front, and lay quietly down in the shade, meaning to catch them up afterwards like the hare in the fable.

They had a long start of me, and as I got up I said to myself, " I wonder if I could run all the way from here to Tivoli? " It was about fifteen miles. " Suppose I try." Thereupon I rushed off as if someone were carrying away my mistress. I catch up the Swedes and pass them; I run through first one village, and then another, with all the dogs in the place barking at my heels, scattering flocks of grunting pigs as I fly by, but sympathised with by the inhabitants, who are convinced I have *met with a misfortune.*[4]

Presently a sharp pain in my knee-joint leads to the discovery that I cannot bend my right leg; so I have to hop along on my left, dragging the other after me. The pain was excruciating, but I would not give in, and I reached Tivoli without having stopped once in my absurd race. I deserved to die of heart disease, but nothing happened; so I suppose my heart is tough.

The Swedes reached Tivoli an hour afterwards, and found me asleep. When I awoke, and they had ascertained that I was perfectly sound in body and mind (which I forgive them for doubting), they begged me to show them the sights of the place. So we visited the pretty little temple of Vesta, which is more like a temple of Cupid; the great cascade, the small cascades; Neptune's grotto; and then the immense stalactite, a hundred feet high, under which Horace's celebrated villa, Tibur, lies buried. I left my friends to rest under the grove of olive-trees over the poet's house, and ascended a neighbouring hill in order to pluck some myrtle which grows on the top, for,

---

[1] Isidore Flacheron. [B.]

[2] "The French gentleman who plays the guitar" — their designation for me, as they could not pronounce my name. [B.]

[3] Now Madame Flacheron. [B.]

[4] Assassinated someone. [B.]

like a young goat, I find a green hill irresistible. Then, descending towards the plain, we inspected the Villa of Mæcenas; crossed the great arched wall through which a branch of the Anio now flows, working the machinery of the vast iron foundry, and were almost deafened by the thunder of the huge hammers. These walls once reverberated to the sound of Horace's epicurean odes, or re-echoed the grave sweet voice of Virgil reciting some magnificent fragment of his pastoral poems at a feast presided over by the minister of Augustus.

> Hactenus arvorum cultus et sidera cœli:
> Nunc te, Bacche, canam, nec non silvestria tecum
> Virgulta, et prolem tarde crescentis olivæ.

Farther down we came upon the Villa d'Este, recalling the name of the Princess Eleonora, immortalised by Tasso, and the hopeless love with which she inspired him.

When we reached the plain again, I led my friends through the labyrinth of the Villa Adriana; we visited what remains of its vast gardens, and the valley which an imperious fancy strove to convert into a miniature copy of the Valley of Tempe; looked into the Hall of the Guards, now the haunt of swarms of birds of prey; and saw the site of the Emperor's private theatre, now a field of — cabbages!

Strange transformations! at which time and death must surely laugh.

CHAPTER XLII

INFLUENZA IN ROME — NEW SYSTEM OF PHILOSOPHY — HUNTING — DOMESTIC TROUBLES — RETURN TO FRANCE

I NOW returned to the Academy barracks, and was again a prey to ennui. In the town, a kind of infectious influenza was raging, and people were dying by thousands. Clothed in a long hooded cloak of the sort in which the painters represent Petrarch (a costume which afforded great diversion to the Roman idlers), I accompanied the cart-loads of dead to the yawning vault of the Transteverine church. A stone was removed in the inner court, and the bodies were gently lowered by means of an iron hook into this palace of putrefaction.

Some of the skulls had been opened by the doctors, with a view to discovering why the sick men had refused to get well, and the brains were scattered about the bottom of the cart.

The man who in Rome replaces the gravedigger of other nations then gathered up these *débris* of the organ of thought with a trowel, and shot them dexterously into the abyss. Shakespeare's immortal gravedigger would assuredly never have dreamt of using a trowel, nor of employing this human mortar.

Garrez, one of the architects of the Academy, has made a drawing of this charming scene, in which I figure with my famous hood. The spleen increased after this.

About six months previously, I had made a rough sketch of a new system of philosophy entitled, " System of Absolute Indifferentism in Universal Matter " — a transcendental doctrine which tended to produce in man absolute perfection and the susceptibility of a block of stone. Three of my friends, Bézard and Gibert, painters, and Delanoie, an architect, now formed themselves with me into a society called " The Four," for the purpose of elaborating and completing my grand system. But it did not take. We were met with such objections as the existence of pain and pleasure, feelings and sensations; and treated as if we were mad. It was in vain that we answered with praiseworthy indifference:

" So these gentlemen think us mad, do they? Do you mind, Bézard? . . . What do you think of it, Gibert? . . . And you, Delanoie? "

" It does not matter to anyone." . . .

" But I tell you that these gentlemen look upon us as lunatics."

" Let them! "

We were openly ridiculed; but have not all great philosophers been misunderstood in like manner?

One night I went on a sporting expedition with Debay, the sculptor. We called up the watchman at the Porta del Popolo, who, by a Papal order much to the benefit of sportsmen, had to get up and let us out by virtue of our permits. We then walked till two in the morning. A movement in the bushes by the road seemed to imply the presence of a hare. We both fired, and killed . . . a colleague . . . a rival sportsman . . . an unhappy cat, in the act of stalking a covey of quail, and now stretched bleeding on the ground. At length weariness overpowered us, and we slept for hours on the turf. After this we parted. A drenching rain came on; I gained a little oak wood in a ravine, but it gave me no shelter. I then killed a porcupine, and carried away more than one wound from his quills. At length I came upon a lonely village in which not a creature was to be seen but an old woman washing clothes in the tiny stream. From her I learnt that this silent spot was called Isola Farnese. It is said to be the ancient Veii, the chief town of the Volscians, Rome's formidable enemies. Here, then, Aufidius commanded, and here the impetuous Coriolanus offered his sacrilegious aid against his own country. The old washerwoman was perhaps squatting on the very spot where the sublime Volumnia, at the head of a tribe of Roman matrons, knelt to her son!

All the morning I walked over the sites of the splendid battles which Plutarch has described and Shakespeare immortalised, and which were on the same scale and about as important as a battle would be between Versailles and St. Cloud! I stood lost in my reverie, while the rain poured with greater vehemence than ever. My dogs were nearly blinded by it, and buried their noses in the brushwood. I then killed a stupid snake, which had no business to leave its hole in such weather. Presently Debay called me by firing shot after shot, and I rejoined him for breakfast. I took out of my game-bag a skull, which I had picked up in the cemetery at Radicoffani on my way back from Nice the year before. [It now holds my writing sand.] This we proceeded to fill with slices of ham, and put it into the middle of the rivulet, in order to soak the salt out of the atrocious food. Our frugal repast was seasoned with nothing but a cold rain; we had neither wine nor cigars. Debay had shot nothing, and I had only succeeded in sending one poor robin to keep company with the cat, the snake, and the porcupine. We set out for the inn at Storta, which is the only one in the whole neighbourhood. Whilst my clothes were drying I went to bed, and slept for three hours.

At last the sun shone, and the rain ceased. I dressed with great difficulty and started off after Debay, who was too impatient to wait for me. Presently I fell in with a flight of lovely birds, which are supposed to come from the coast of Africa, but whose name I never could find out. They soar perpetually, like larks, with a little cry like a partridge's, and their plumage is variegated green and yellow. Of these I knocked down about half-a-dozen, and saved my reputation as a sportsman. I could see Debay in the distance firing at a hare and missing it. At last we reached Rome, as muddy as Marius must have been when he came back from the Marshes of Minturnus.

After this came a stagnant week.

At last our Academy became a little more lively, thanks to the comical terror of our comrade L., who, having been caught by Vernet's Italian footman in the act of making love to his wife, lived in perpetual fear of assassination. He dared not leave his room, and when dinner was served we were obliged to go in a body, and escort him to the dining-room. He fancied he saw knives gleaming in every corner of the palace. He grew thin, pale, yellow, blue, and began to vanish into space, and at last suggested to Delanoie the following joke:

" Well, my poor L., are you still worried about *the servants?* " [1]

This *mot* went round the table, and received great applause.

But ennui possessed me more strongly than ever, and I could think of nothing but Paris. I had finished my melodrama, and touched up my *Symphonie fantastique*. I now wanted to get them both performed. Vernet gave me permission to leave Italy before my term had expired. I sat for my portrait, which, in accordance with the rules, was painted by our senior artist, and hung in the gallery of the refectory. I made a final excursion to Tivoli, Albano, and Palestrina; sold my gun, and destroyed my guitar; wrote in several albums; treated my comrades to a large bowl of punch; lavished caresses on M. Vernet's two dogs, my usual sporting companions; and had a moment's unutterable sadness at the thought that I was leaving this poetical country, perhaps for ever. My friends accompanied me as far as Ponte-Molle; there I got into a horrible vehicle, and set off.[2]

[1] L. was a great seducer of housemaids, and he declared that a sure way of winning their affections was *to look sad and wear white trousers!* [B.]

[2] Apart from the weariness induced in him by the wretchedness of music in Italy, Berlioz was anxious to be back in Paris in order to realise his ambitions there. He had been fired by the news of the sensation created by the production of Meyerbeer's *Robert the Devil* in November 1831; and wanted to force an entry into the Opéra himself. *Notre-Dame de Paris* appeared about that time, and he tried to get Hugo to collaborate with him in an opera on the subject: in this, however, he was forestalled by Mlle Bertin, the daughter of the proprietor of the *Journal des Débats*.

He seems to have wheedled Vernet into allowing him to spend the uncompleted time of his Italian stay in Paris, his intention, at the moment, being to proceed in due course to Germany, as required by the terms of the Prix de Rome. He left for France on May 2nd, 1832.

CHAPTER XLIII

FLORENCE — A FUNERAL — LA BELLA SPOSINA — THE
GAY FLORENTINE — LODI — MILAN — THE THEATRE
OF THE CANNOBIANA — THE PUBLIC — MUSICAL
ORGANISATION OF THE ITALIANS — LOVE OF
PLATITUDES AND VOCALISATION —
RETURN TO FRANCE

I WAS very morose, although my ardent desire of seeing France again was on the point of being satisfied. Such a farewell to Italy had something solemn about it, and without being able to account to myself for my feelings, I was oppressed in spirit. The sight of Florence,[1] to which I was now returning for the fourth time, made an overwhelming impression upon me. During the two days of my sojourn in that city, which may be called the Queen of the Arts, I was informed that the painter, Chenavard (whose immense head is bursting with brains), had been looking for me everywhere without success. Twice he had missed me in the Pitti Palace; had asked for me at my hotel, and was evidently most anxious to see me. I felt much gratified at this proof of sympathy from so distinguished an artist, and in my turn tried to find him, but in vain. I left without making his acquaintance, and it was not till five years later that we met in Paris, and I was able to admire the penetration, sagacity, and wonderful lucidity of his mind, even when he applied it to the vital problems of arts, such as music and poetry, that were at the opposite pole to his own.

One evening I had just crossed the cathedral in pursuit of him, and was sitting near a column watching the motes dancing in a splendid ray of the setting sun, as it slanted across the gathering gloom, when a troop of priests and torch-bearers entered the nave for a funeral ceremony.[2] I drew near, and inquired of a Florentine whose funeral it was " *È una sposina, morta al mezzo giorno* " (A young bride, who died this afternoon), he answered in a gay tone. The prayers were

[1] He took ten days over the journey from Rome, arriving in Florence on May 12th, 1832. He stayed there three days.

[2] As I have pointed out already, this episode belongs not to Berlioz's homeward journey but to his stay in Florence in April 1831, when he was awaiting a letter from Camille Moke. See Chapter XXXIV.

astonishingly short, and the priests had hardly begun before they
seemed in haste to finish. Then the body was laid on a sort of open
litter, and the *cortège* proceeded to the place where the corpse was to
remain until the next day, when it would be buried. I followed. On
the way the torch-bearers muttered, for form's sake, some vague
prayers between their teeth, but their principal occupation was to melt
as much as possible of the wax candles with which they had been
provided by the family of the deceased. The reason was this. The
remnant of the candles was to go back to the church, and as they
dared not steal whole pieces, they kept perpetually splitting the wicks,
and then sloping them so as to pour the melting wax upon the pavement. A troop of young rascals followed them along, and, flinging
themselves on the ground, eagerly stripped off the wax from the stone,
and rolled it into a ball, which grew bigger and bigger as they proceeded. Thus at the end of their journey—a fairly long one, for
the dead-house was at one of the farthest extremities of the town —
these miserable hornets had amassed a tolerably good provision of
mortuary wax. Such was the pious occupation of the wretches by
whom the poor *sposina* was borne to her last resting-place.

On reaching the morgue, the same gay Florentine who had answered my inquiry in the cathedral, and who had been in the procession, came up and accosted me in a curious kind of patois French,
seeing that I was looking on with interest.

" Would you like to go in ? "

" Yes. How can I manage it ? "

" Give me three paoli."

I slipped the three coins into his hand; he held a moment's parley
with the doorkeeper, and I was ushered in. The dead woman was
lying upon a table. She was almost entirely covered by a long white
garment, gathered in round the neck and below the feet. Her black hair
was partially plaited, and the rest fell in masses about her shoulders;
she had large blue eyes, half closed; a small mouth, a sad smile, a neck
of alabaster, an air of nobility and candour, young — so young, and
dead! The Italian, with his everlasting simper, exclaimed: " *È bella!* "
and in order to give me a better opportunity of admiring the features,
he raised the beautiful young head, with his dirty hands pushed aside
the hair which had seemed to insist on modestly veiling the ineffable
grace of the countenance, and then roughly let it fall back upon the

table. The whole room re-echoed with the shock. . . . I thought that my very heart would have burst at the impious and brutal noise. . . . Unable to contain myself, I fell upon my knees, seized the hand of the desecrated beauty, and covered it with expiatory kisses, a prey to an intenser anguish than I had ever felt in my life. The Florentine, however, continued to laugh.

But suddenly the thought occurred to me, what would the husband say if he could see that beloved cold hand warmed by the kisses of an unknown stranger? In his indignant horror, might he not have some ground for believing that I was a secret lover of his wife, who, more ardent and faithful than himself, was giving full vent to his Shakespearean despair over her beloved form? Heaven forbid that the unfortunate man should think this, although he almost deserved the torture which such an idea would inflict on him. Oh, apathetic husband! how could you let them tear away from your living arms the dead wife whom you loved so well? " *Addio! Addio! bella sposa abbandonata! Ombra dolente! Adesso, forse, consolata! Perdona ad un straniero le pie lagrime sulla pallida mano. Almen colui non ignora l'amore ostinato ne la religione della beltà.*"

I went away altogether overcome by the whole scene.

But these are very cadaverous stories! My fair readers — if, indeed, I have any — may well ask if it is in order to torment them that I insist on exhibiting such hideous images. Well, no; I cannot say that I have the smallest desire thus to distress them, nor yet to reproduce Hamlet's ironical apostrophe. I have no strong taste for death; I love life a thousand times better. I am merely relating a few of the things which have struck me, and naturally some episodes are more sombre than others — that is all.

I may, however, forewarn those of my lady readers who do not laugh at the idea of their some day playing such a part themselves, that I shall tell them no more ugly stories. Henceforth they may peruse these pages without fear, unless, indeed, as is probable, they prefer to attend to their dress, listen to bad music, dance the polka, talk nonsense, and torment their lovers.

In passing Lodi, I took care to see the famous bridge, and could even fancy that I heard the thunder of Bonaparte's grape-shot and the cries of the flying Austrians.

The weather was superb, but the only person on the bridge was an old man fishing from the parapet. Ah, St. Helena!

When I reached Milan,[1] Donizetti's *L'Elisir d'amore* was being played at the Cannobiana, and to satisfy my conscience I went to see it. I found the theatre full of people talking at the top of their voices, with their backs to the stage; the singers all the time gesticulating and shouting in eager rivalry. So at least I judged by seeing their huge open mouths, for the people made so much noise that it was impossible to hear a sound beyond the big drum. In the boxes some were gambling, and others were having supper. I therefore retired, since it was no use hoping to hear the smallest fraction of the music, which was then quite new to me. It appears, however — so at least I am assured — that the Italians do occasionally listen. But, at any rate, music to the Milanese, no less than to the Neapolitans, Romans, Florentines, and Genoese, means nothing but an air, a duet, or a trio, well sung. For anything beyond this they feel simply aversion or indifference. Perhaps these antipathies are mainly due to the incompetence of their choruses and orchestras, which effectually prevents their knowing anything good outside the beaten track they have so long followed. Possibly, too, they may to a certain extent understand the flights of men of genius, if these latter are careful not to give too rude a shock to their rooted predilections. The great success of *Guillaume Tell* at Florence supports this opinion, and even Spontini's sublime *Vestale* obtained a series of brilliant representations at Naples some twenty-five years ago. Moreover, in those towns which are under the Austrian rule you will see the people rush after a military band and listen with avidity to the beautiful German melodies, so unlike their own insipid cavatinas. Nevertheless, in general it is impossible to disguise the fact that the Italians as a nation really appreciate only the material effects of music, and distinguish nothing but its exterior forms.

Indeed, I am much inclined to regard them as more inaccessible to the poetical side of art, and to any conceptions at all above the common, than any other European nation. To the Italians music is a sensual pleasure, and nothing more. For this most beautiful form of expression they have scarcely more respect than for the culinary art. They like music which they can assimilate at a first hearing, without reflection or attention, just as they would do with a plate of macaroni.

Now we French, mean and contemptible musicians as we are, although we are no better than the Italians when we furiously applaud a trill or a chromatic scale by the last new singer, and miss altogether

[1] He stayed two days in Milan — May 20th and 21st, 1832.

the beauty of some grand recitative or animated chorus, yet at least we can listen, and if we do not take in a composer's ideas it is not our fault. Beyond the Alps, on the contrary, people behave during the performance in a manner so humiliating both to art and to artists that I confess I would as soon sell pepper and spice at a grocer's in the Rue St. Denis as write an opera for the Italians — nay, I would *sooner* do it.

Added to this, they are slaves to routine and to fanaticism to a degree one hardly sees nowadays, even at the Academy. The slightest unforeseen innovation, whether in melody, harmony, rhythm, or instrumentation, puts them into a perfect fury; so much so, that the dilettanti of Rome, on the appearance of Rossini's *Barbiere di Siviglia* (which is Italian enough in all conscience), were ready to kill the young maestro for having the insolence to do anything unlike Paisiello.

But what renders all hope of improvement quite chimerical, and tempts one to believe that the musical feeling of the Italians is a necessary result of their organisation — the opinion both of Gall and Spurzheim — is their love for all that is dancing, brilliant, glittering, and gay, to the utter neglect of the various passions by which the characters are animated, and the confusion of time and place — in a word, of good sense itself. Their music is always laughing,[1] and if by chance the composer in the course of the drama permits himself for one moment not to be absurd, he at once hastens back to the prescribed style, the melodious roulades and *gruppetti,* the trills and contemptible frivolities, either for voice or orchestra, and these, succeeding so abruptly to something true to life, sound like a mockery, and give the *opera seria* all the appearance of a parody or caricature.

I could quote plenty of examples from famous works; but speaking generally of these artistic questions, is it not from Italy that we get those stereotyped conventional forms adopted by so many French composers, resisted by Cherubini and Spontini alone among the Italians, though rejected entirely by the Germans? What well-organised person with any sense of musical expression could listen to a quartet in which four characters, animated by totally conflicting

---

[1] A certain part of Bellini's music, and that of his followers, must, however, be excepted. Their style, on the contrary, is essentially dolorous, and the tone is either groaning or howling. These writers return to the absurd style every now and then only in order that the tradition of it may not be entirely lost. Nor should I be so unjust as to include in these falsely sentimental works many parts of Donizetti's *Lucia di Lammermoor.* The finale of the second act, and the scene of Edgardo's death, have an admirable pathos about them. Of Verdi's works I know none as yet. [B.]

passions, should successively employ the same melodic phrase to express such different words as these: *" O toi que j'adore! " " Quelle terreur me glace! " " Mon cœur bat de plaisir." " La fureur me transporte! "* To suppose that music is a language so vague that the natural inflections of fury will serve equally well for fear, joy, and love, only proves the absence of that sense which to others makes the varieties of expression in music as incontestable a reality as the existence of the sun. But this discussion, which has already been raised hundreds of times, would carry me too far. It is enough to say that after having given a long and unbiassed study to the musical sentiment of the Italians, I regard the course taken by their composers as the inevitable result of the instincts of the public, which instincts react more or less on the composers themselves. They are apparent as early as Pergolesi, who in his famous *Stabat* sets the verse —

> Et mœrebat
> Et tremebat
> Cum videbat
> Nati pœnas inclyti—

as a sort of bravura aria. The learned Martini, Beccaria, Calzabigi, and many eminent writers complain of these incongruities. In spite of his herculean genius and of the colossal success of *Orfeo,* even Gluck has not been able wholly to avoid them; they are kept up by singers, and certain composers in their turn have developed them in the public. In fact they are as indestructible in the Italians as the passion for vaudeville is in the French. As for the feeling for harmony among the Ultramontanes[1] of which people talk so much, I may safely say that the accounts of it have been at least exaggerated. At Tivoli and Subiaco I have heard some of the common people sing second pretty fairly, but in the south of France, which has no reputation of this sort, the thing is exceedingly common. In Rome, on the contrary, I have never once caught a harmonious intonation out of the mouth of any of the people. The *pecorari* (herdsmen) of the Campagna have, indeed, a curious grunt which follows no musical scale, and is absolutely impossible to write down. It is a barbarous style of singing said to be analogous to that of the Turks.

Turin[2] was the first place at which I heard street chorus-singing.

---

[1] By Ultramontanes, Berlioz here means the Italians. [H.]

[2] May 25–27. On his way through Lombardy he sketched out a symphony in two parts, to

But the singers were mostly amateurs who had learned what little they knew by frequenting the theatres. In this respect Paris is quite as well off as the capital of Piedmont, for often and often have I heard very decent harmonies resounding through the Rue Richelieu in the middle of the night. I ought also to say that the Piedmontese choristers strew their harmonies with consecutive fifths which, when given in that way, are odious to all practised ears.

As for seeking for the boasted Italian harmonies in villages which have no church-organs and no relations with large towns, it is mere folly, as there is not the slightest trace of them. Even at Tivoli, where two lads struck me as having sufficient feeling for thirds and sixths to sing pretty couplets together, I was astounded a few months later by the burlesque manner in which a mass of people shouted out their litanies in unison.

Without wishing to create any reputation of this sort for the people of Dauphiné, whom, on the contrary, I believe to be absolutely innocent in all matters connected with music, I cannot help saying that the melody of their litanies is sweet, supplicating, and pathetic, and really like a prayer addressed to the Mother of God, whilst at Tivoli they sound like a song in a guard-house. I give a specimen of each, for the purpose of comparison.

1.— MELODY OF TIVOLI.

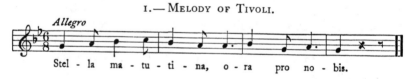

Stel - la   ma - tu - ti - na,   o - ra   pro   no - bis.

2.— MELODY OF LA CÔTE-SAINT-ANDRÉ (Dauphiné), with the bad Latin prosody adopted in France.

Stel - la   ma - tu - ti - na, .   o - ra . . pro no - - bis.

No doubt beautiful voices — not only sonorous and clear, but agile and flexible — are more common in Italy than elsewhere. Such voices facilitate vocalisation, and, by pandering to that natural love of effect which I have already mentioned, must have given birth to

<hr>

be entitled *Le retour de l'armée d'Italie:* 1. *Adieux du haut des Alpes aux braves tombés dans les champs d'Italie,* 2. *Entrée triomphale des vainqueurs à Paris.*

the mania for *fioriture* which deforms the most beautiful melodies, and to those convenient formulas which give all Italian phrases so strong a family likeness. We may thank the same causes for those final cadences which the singer may embellish as he pleases, but which torture many a hearer by their insipid uniformity, as well as for that incessant tendency to buffoonery that obtrudes itself even in the most pathetic scenes; in fact, for all those abuses which have rendered melody, harmony, time, rhythm, instrumentation, modulation, the drama, the *mise en scène,* poetry, the poet, and the composer, all abject slaves to the singer.

On the 12th [1] of May, 1832, as I came down the Mont Cenis, I beheld again in its loveliest spring attire that delicious valley of Grésivaudan, through which the Isère winds, where I had passed the happiest hours of my childhood, where I had been thrilled by my first impassioned dreams — the old rock of St. Eynard, the charming spot from which had gleamed the *Stella montis;* . . . my grandfather's house smiling at me through the blue distance! How beautiful they are! the villas, the rich verdure! how fascinating! There is nothing like them in Italy. But this transport of innocent delight was suddenly stopped by a sharp pang of sorrow. . . . I seemed to hear the rumble of Paris in the distance.

CHAPTER XLIV

THE PAPAL CENSORSHIP — PREPARATIONS FOR CON-
CERTS — RETURN TO PARIS — THE NEW ENGLISH
THEATRE — FÉTIS — HIS CORRECTIONS OF BEET-
HOVEN'S SYMPHONIES — I AM INTRODUCED
TO MISS SMITHSON — SHE IS RUINED —
BREAKS HER LEG — I MARRY HER

𝒜 SPECIAL authorisation from M. Vernet having, as I said, permitted me to leave Rome six months before the expiration of my two years' exile, I went to my father's house for the first half of the time, with the intention of employing the second in organising one or two concerts in Paris before going to Germany, where the rules of the Institut obliged me to spend another year. I employed my leisure at

---

[1] The date is incorrect. He was at Suse, after leaving Turin, on May 28th, and at Grenoble on May 31st; he seems to have arrived at Côte-Saint-André on June 1st or 2nd.

the Côte-Saint-André in copying the orchestral parts of the monodrama which I had written during my wanderings in Italy, and was
anxious to produce in Paris. I had copied the chorus parts in Rome,
and the number called *Les Ombres* caused me a quarrel with the Papal
censorship. The text of this chorus, which I have already mentioned,
was written in an unknown tongue — a dead language, incomprehensible to the living. When I applied to the censor for leave to print
it, the meaning of the words sung by the ghosts puzzled the philologists
a good deal.[1]

What was this language? and what was the meaning of those
strange words? They had in a German, who declared he could not
understand a syllable; an Englishman had no better luck. All the
interpreters — Danish, Swedish, Russian, Spanish, Irish, Bohemian —
were at their wits' end. Great perplexity in the censor's office! The
printer could not proceed, and the publication remained indefinitely
suspended. At last one of the censors, after profound reflection, discovered an argument the justice of which struck his colleagues. " Since
neither English, Russian, Spanish, Danish, Swedish, Irish, nor Bohemian interpreters understand this mysterious language," said he,
" it is very probable that the Roman people will not understand it
either. It seems to me, therefore, that we may fairly authorise the
publication, without any risk either to morality or religion." And
the ghosts' chorus was accordingly printed. Imprudent censors! What
if it had been Sanscrit?

On my arrival in Paris,[2] one of the first visits I paid was to Cherubini. I found him much aged and enfeebled, and he received me with a

---

[1] Since then I have adapted French words to the music, reserving the unknown language
exclusively for the pandemonium in *The Damnation of Faust*. [B.]

[2] Berlioz stayed four months at Côte-Saint-André. In the main he was bored with his relations and with provincial society. Estelle was no longer at Meylan: on the death of her father
she had married M. Fornier, and gone to live at Grenoble. Berlioz did not see her.

It appears from a letter of Hector's to Madame Vernet (25th July) that his father wanted
him to marry a rich young lady of the neighbourhood, but he refused to marry without love.
He tells Mme. Vernet that after he has given a concert in Paris in December he means to go to
Berlin to study as required by the Prix de Rome.

His friend Humbert Ferrand, who had helped him with small loans, and whom he had not
seen for five years, had recently married and settled in Belley. Berlioz visited him there and
tried to get him to write the poem for a grand descriptive musical work, *Le Dernier Jour du Monde;*
but the lymphatic Ferrand could never feel enough confidence in his own powers to complete
the task.

As Berlioz was supposed by the Conservatoire authorities to be in Rome, it was dangerous
for him to show himself in Paris before the end of 1832. Unable to control his impatience, however,
he left Côte-Saint-André on October 28th. He spent two days in Lyons (November 2nd and 3rd),
left there on the 4th, and arrived in Paris on the 7th (1832).

kindliness which I had never observed in him before. This contrast to his former behaviour quite touched me, and I felt disarmed. " Good heavens ! " I said to myself; " I find a Cherubini so unlike the one I left, that the poor man must be going to die." But it will be seen that I very soon received such tokens of his vitality as completely to reassure me on that point.

As the apartment in the Rue Richelieu which I had occupied before going to Italy was no longer vacant, a secret impulse prompted me to take one in the house opposite, where Miss Smithson had formerly lived — Rue Neuve St. Marc, No. 1, and there I established myself. Next morning I encountered the old servant who for a long time had been housemaid to the establishment, and at once inquired if she knew anything of Miss Smithson.

" But, monsieur, don't you know? She is in Paris; she was even lodging in this very house a few days ago. She only left the apartment you are occupying the day before yesterday, for one in the Rue de Rivoli. She is the directress of an English theatre, which is to begin its representations next week."

I was struck dumb by this extraordinary, this fatal concurrence of events. I saw at once that henceforth it would be impossible for me to struggle against my fate. For more than two years I had heard nothing of the fair Ophelia; whether she were in England, Scotland, or America, I knew not; and now I had come back from Italy precisely at the same time that she returned to Paris from the north of Europe! And we had but just missed meeting each other in the same house, and I was in possession of an apartment which she had left only on the previous evening!

Now a believer in magnetic influences, secret affinities, and mysterious promptings would certainly find in all this a powerful argument in favour of his system. Without going so far as that, I reasoned with myself after this manner: " I have come to Paris to produce my new work — the monodrama. If, before giving my concert, I go to the English theatre and see her again, I shall infallibly become delirious about her, lose all my liberty of mind for a second time, and be incapable of making the exertions essential to my success. Let us first of all give the concert, and after that, though Hamlet or Romeo should carry off my Ophelia or Juliet again, I will see her once more, if I am to die for it; and will then give myself up without a further struggle to the fate which seems to pursue me."

In consequence of this determination the Shakespearean bills were placarded about the streets in vain, as far as I was concerned.[1] I resisted their fascination, and the preparations for the concert went on. The programme consisted of my *Symphonie fantastique,* followed by *Lélio, or the Return to Life,* a monodrama which is the complement of that work and forms the second part of the *Episode in the Life of an Artist.* The subject of this musical drama is, as everybody knows, the history of my love for Miss Smithson, my anguish and my distressing dreams. Now wonder at the series of incredible chances about to be opened to your view !

Two days before the concert, which I looked on as a farewell to art and life, I found myself in Schlesinger's music-shop, when an Englishman entered, and went out again almost immediately.

" Who is that man ? " said I to Schlesinger, with a singular curiosity which had really no motive.

" It is Mr. Schutter, one of the editors of *Galignani.* Stay, I have an idea ! " exclaimed Schlesinger, tapping his forehead. " Give me a box ticket. Schutter knows Miss Smithson. I will get him to give her the ticket and induce her to attend your concert."

This proposal made me tremble all over ; but I had not the courage to reject it, and so gave him the box. Schlesinger ran after Mr. Schutter, explained to him, no doubt, the exceptional interest which the presence of the celebrated actress would give to this musical *séance,* and Schutter promised to do his best to bring her there.

You must know that during the whole of my rehearsals and preparations, the unfortunate directress of the English theatre had been occupied in completely ruining herself. Poor innocent thing ! She had been reckoning upon the constancy of Parisian enthusiasm and the support of the new literary school, which only three years ago had lauded Shakespeare and Shakespeare's worthy interpreter up to the skies. But Shakespeare was no longer a novelty to this frivolous and fickle public ; the literary revolution evoked by the romanticists was accomplished, and not only had the chiefs of that school ceased to desire any more apparitions of this giant of dramatic poetry, but, without admitting so much themselves, they even dreaded them on

---

[1] Harriet Smithson's company was at the Théâtre-Italien, with an English repertory that comprised *Jane Shore, Virginius,* and other favorite plays of the time. Her season began on November 21st.

account of the numerous plagiarisms they themselves had made from his masterpieces, with which consequently it was not to their interest to allow the public to become too familiar.

Hence the general indifference to the representations at the English theatre, and the poor receipts, which fell so far short of the expenses that the result was a yawning gulf deep enough to swallow up everything the imprudent directress possessed.

It was under these circumstances that Schutter went to Miss Smithson to offer her a box for my concert, and this is what followed. She herself gave me the details long afterwards.

Schutter found her in a state of profound despondency, and at first his offer was received somewhat ungraciously. " Was it likely that she could think of music at such a moment? " Her sister, however, joined her entreaties to those of Schutter that she would accept this offer of *distraction;* and there was also an English actor present, who appeared desirous on his part of profiting by the box. Accordingly a carriage was sent for, Miss Smithson allowed herself to be put into it almost against her own will, and Schutter triumphantly ordered the coachman to drive to the Conservatoire. On the way the poor thing's eyes fell for the first time on the programme which, till then, she had not looked at. They had not mentioned my name to her, but she now learnt that I was the director of the concert. The titles of the symphony and other pieces in the programme rather astonished her; nevertheless she was still far from guessing that she was herself the heroine of this strange and painful drama.

On entering her box in front of the stage, she found herself in the midst of an immense orchestra, and an object of interest to the whole room. So astonished was she at the unprecedented murmur of conversation of which she was plainly the object, that, without being able to account to herself for it, she was filled with a kind of instinctive terror, which moved her powerfully. Habeneck was conducting. When I came in panting and sat behind him, Miss Smithson, who till then had doubted whether she were not mistaken in the name at the head of the programme, saw and recognised me.

" It is the same," she said to herself. " Poor young man! No doubt he has forgotten me. I hope — that he has ——." The symphony began, and created a tremendous effect. It was a time of great public ardour in that hall from which I am now excluded. This success, and

the passionate character of the work — its burning melodies, its cries
of love, its accesses of fury, and the violent vibrations of such an
orchestra, heard close by, were bound to produce, and did in fact
produce, an impression as profound as it was unlooked-for upon her
nervous organisation and poetical imagination. Then in her heart of
hearts she said, " What if he loved me still! " In the *entr'acte* which
followed the performance of the symphony, the ambiguous speeches
of Schutter and Schlesinger — the latter had not been able to resist
the desire of coming into her box — and their transparent allusions
to the well-known sorrows of this young composer of whom everyone
was talking — all these raised a doubt in her which agitated her
more and more; but when, in the monodrama, Bocage, the actor who
recited the part of Lélio [1] (in other words, my own), pronounced
these words:

" *Ah, could I but find her, this Juliet, this Ophelia whom my heart
is ever seeking! Could I but drink to the full of that mingled bliss
and sadness which true love creates, and on an autumn evening,
cradled with her by the north wind upon some wild moor, sleep my
last sad sleep in her beloved arms!*"

" Good   God!   Juliet — Ophelia — I   can   doubt   no   more! "
thought Miss Smithson. " It is of me he speaks; he loves me still! "
And from that moment, as she has often told me since, it seemed to
her as if the room reeled. She heard no more, and went home like one
walking in her sleep, almost unconscious of all that was happening
around her. This was the 9th of December, 1832.

Whilst this curious drama was being unfolded in one part of the
room, another was preparing on the opposite side, a drama in which
the wounded vanity of a musical critic was to play the principal part,
and create a violent animosity against me, of which he did not fail
to give me many proofs, until a sense of his injustice towards an artist
and critic who, in his turn, had become dangerous, warned him to
practise a prudent reserve. This person was M. Fétis, to whom,
through the medium of my monodrama, I had distinctly addressed a
scathing reproach, dictated by a very natural indignation.

Before my departure for Italy, among my resources for gaining a
livelihood, I must not omit to include that of correcting the proofs
of music. Among other works, Troupenas, the publisher, had given

---

[1] *Lélio* was not performed dramatically, as was done later in Germany, but only as a concert-
piece interspersed with monologues. [B.]

me the scores of Beethoven's symphonies to correct, which M. Fétis had, in the first instance, been employed to edit. I found them full of the most insolent modifications of the very conceptions of the composer, and of annotations still more outrageous. Everything in Beethoven's harmony that did not fit in with the theory of M. Fétis was altered with incredible audacity. Opposite the long-held E flat of the clarinet over the chord of the 6th $\left\{\begin{matrix} \text{B flat} \\ \text{F} \\ \text{D flat} \end{matrix}\right\}$ in the Andante of the Symphony in C minor, M. Fétis had placed this naïve remark in the margin: " This E flat should evidently be an F; it is not possible that Beethoven should have made so gross a blunder." In other words, it is impossible that a man like Beethoven should not entirely agree with M. Fétis in his theories about harmony.

Consequently, M. Fétis had put an F in place of the characteristic E flat, thus destroying the evident intention of the suspension, which does not arrive at the F till it has passed through the E natural, thus producing a little ascending chromatic progression, and a crescendo of remarkable effect. I had already been irritated by other corrections in the same style, which it would be useless to cite, but by this I was simply exasperated. " What? " said I to myself; " they are making a French edition of the most marvellous instrumental works ever brought forth by human genius, and because the publisher has called in the aid of a professor who is drunk with his own vanity, and as capable of making progress within the narrow circle of his own theories as a squirrel in his cage, therefore these monumental works are to be mutilated, and Beethoven is to submit to *corrections* like the veriest pupil in a harmony class. No, indeed, that shall never be." I went at once to Troupenas, and said to him, " Fétis is offering insults both to Beethoven and good sense. His corrections are crimes. The E flat which he wishes to remove from the Andante of the Symphony in C minor is magical in its effect, and celebrated in every European orchestra; the F of M. Fétis is a platitude. I warn you that I shall denounce your edition and M. Fétis' proceedings to all the musicians of the Société des Concerts and the Opéra, and your professor shall soon be treated as he deserves by those who respect genius and distrust pretentious mediocrity." I was as good as my word. The news of these insane profanations incensed the Parisian artists, and not the least infuriated among them was Habeneck, who had indeed himself corrected Beethoven by suppressing an entire repeat of the finale in the same Symphony, and also the double-bass parts at the opening of the Scherzo. So great was the uproar that Troupenas was obliged to cancel the corrections and restore the original text, whilst M. Fétis thought it advisable to publish a stupendous falsehood in his *Revue musicale,* denying that there was the smallest foundation for the rumour which accused him of having corrected Beethoven's symphonies. This first act of insubordination on the part of one who had been throughout his studies encouraged by M. Fétis appeared to that gentleman all the more unpardonable, because he saw in it not only an evident leaning towards heresy, but an act of *ingratitude.*

Many people are thus constituted. From the day that they have been willing to treat you as not wholly devoid of merit, you are bound, for that reason alone, to admire them for ever — without reserve — in all that they may please to do or to leave undone, on pain of being considered *ungrateful.* On this principle many a wretched little composer fancies that, because he has expressed an interest, more or less sincere, in my works, I am therefore necessarily a bad man if at some future time I speak with lukewarmness of the miserable common-places that he has produced under various titles — masses, or operas just as comic.

On my departure for Italy I thus left behind me in Paris the first really active and bitter enemy I had yet made. As for the others, more or less numerous, whom I already possessed, I must say that I had done nothing to deserve their hostility. They sprang into being spontaneously, like the animalcula in stagnant water. However, I troubled myself little about either. Indeed, as for Fétis, I was even more his enemy than he was mine, and I could never think of his attempt on Beethoven without quivering with anger. I did not forget him in composing the literary part of the monodrama, and this is what I put into the mouth of Lélio in one of the monologues of that work:

"*But the worst enemies of genius are the dull inhabitants of the Temple of Routine; fanatical priests who would sacrifice the sub-limest new conceptions — supposing it were ever given to them to have any — to their stupid divinity; young theorists of eighty, living in an ocean of prejudices, and persuaded that the world ends with the shores of their own island; old libertines of every age, who demand of music that it shall caress and divert them, never admitting that the chaste muse could possibly have a nobler mission; but above all, the dese-*

crators who dare to attack original works, submitting them to horrible mutilations which they call corrections and improvements, and for which task, say they, ' much taste is required.' [1] *May they be accursed! They offer a ridiculous outrage to art. They are like the vulgar birds that swarm in our public gardens and perch arrogantly on the most beautiful statues; and when they have fouled the forehead of Jupiter, the arm of Hercules, or the bosom of Venus, strut about with as much pride and satisfaction as if they had laid a golden egg."*

At the last words of this tirade the bursts of laughter and applause were all the more vehement because most of the artists in the orchestra, and many of the audience, understood the allusion. At the words "much taste is required," Bocage even mimicked the affected voice of Fétis, who was actually present in a very conspicuous place in the gallery, and thus received my broadside full in his face. I need not describe his fury and the deadly hatred with which he honoured me from that day forth; it is easy to imagine it. [2]

However, the acrid sweetness which I experienced in having thus avenged Beethoven was completely forgotten on the morrow. I had obtained leave from Miss Smithson to be introduced to her. From that day

---

[1] An expression I had heard from Fétis himself. [B.]

[2] Berlioz repeated the concert on the 30th. The two ventures involved him, of course, in debt, and as early as the 17th of the month we find him petitioning for the payment in advance of his Prix de Rome pension for the first six months of 1833 (1500 francs). Three weeks after the second concert, on January 19th, 1833, he appealed for help to the Ministry of Commerce and Public Works (of which, apparently, the Ministry of Fine Arts was a subsidiary). He pointed out that, in strict logic, music was entitled to as much assistance from an intelligent and enlightened Government as literature or the arts of design. He had just produced a large work of his own at a concert: the artistic success had been stupendous, but unfortunately the expenses had exceeded the receipts. If the Minister could see his way to make him a grant of 500 francs, he would look upon it as an encouragement to go on with his work. The Minister replied that he regretted there was no fund at his disposal for a donation of this kind, and took the opportunity to point out drily that as Prix de Rome, and therefore a pensioner of the King, Berlioz ought to have been in Germany since January 1st. He was told to go there without delay.

Berlioz, however, had other ideas: he was kept in Paris by his newly-awakened passion for Harriet Smithson and by his ambition to force his way into the Opéra. For the latter end he employed, as usual, all the devices of journalism.

He even called in the assistance of the Press to impose himself on the notice of Miss Smithson. He wrote an autobiographical sketch, which was worked up by his friend d'Ortigue and published under the signature of the latter in the *Revue de Paris* of 15 December 1832, i.e., after the concert of December 9, and before that of the 30th. The full story was told there of his love for the Irish actress and the despair to which she had reduced him, and the reader was informed that "Miss S. . . . was present at the last concert of Berlioz, holding in her hand a copy of the *Mélologue*, which she read with close attention."

Berlioz's manuscript, with d'Ortigue's marginal notes and alterations, is in the Library of the Paris Conservatoire. See Charles Malherbe's article *Une autobiographie de Berlioz* in the *Rivista Musicale* for 1906, and J. G. Prod'homme's article *Unpublished Berlioziana* in the *Musical Quarterly* for July 1919.

forth I had not a moment's rest. Terrible fears were succeeded by delirious hopes. What I went through in the way of anxieties and agitations of all sorts during this period, which lasted for more than a year, may be imagined but cannot be described. Her mother and sister formally opposed our union. My parents would not hear of it. Discontent and anger on the part of both families, and all the scenes to which such opposition gives birth in these cases. Meanwhile the English theatre in Paris was compelled to close. Miss Smithson was left absolutely without resources, her whole fortune not being sufficient to pay the debts she had contracted through this disastrous undertaking.

Shortly afterwards the finishing touch was put to all her misfortunes by a cruel accident. As she was getting out of a carriage before her own door, on her return from preparing for a performance which she had been getting up for her own benefit, her foot slipped on the pavement, and she broke her leg.[1] She was with difficulty prevented from falling, and was taken in, half fainting, to her apartments. In England the story was believed to be a ruse of the directress of the English theatre for the purpose of softening her creditors; but the fact was only too real. At any rate it aroused the keenest sympathy in Paris. Mdlle. Mars behaved splendidly. She placed her purse, her influence, all that she had, in fact, at the service of the poor Ophelia who had lost everything; but who, nevertheless, on hearing one day from her sister that I had brought her a few hundred francs, shed tears in abundance, and forced me to take back the money, threatening never to see me again if I refused.

She responded but slowly to our care; both bones had been broken just above the instep; time alone could bring about a perfect cure; indeed, it was possible that she might always be lame. Whilst the poor invalid was thus chained to her bed of suffering, I succeeded in completing the organization of the fatal performance which had been the cause of the accident. Both Liszt and Chopin appeared in an *entr' acte,* and the result was a tolerable sum of money, which was at once applied to the payment of the most pressing debts.[2] At length, in the summer of 1833, though she was ruined and still an invalid, I married her, in spite of the violent opposition of her family.[3] As to

[1] March 1st, 1833.
[2] The benefit performance took place on April 2nd.
[3] It appears from his letters that he at last conquered the reluctant Harriet in August by staging an attempt at suicide in her presence. After two hours' vomiting from the effects of the

HARRIET SMITHSON
(from a lithograph by Francis, 1827)

HECTOR BERLIOZ, BY SIGNOL
(painted at Rome in 1831)

HECTOR BERLIOZ IN 1845
(from a lithograph made in Vienna by Prinzhofer)

MARIE RECIO
(from a photograph made in Paris)

HECTOR BERLIOZ, BY DAUMIER

HECTOR BERLIOZ ABOUT 1863

(lithograph by Fuhn, from a photograph by Pierre Petit)

HECTOR BERLIOZ
(from a photograph)

MADAME FORNIER

my own, I was forced to have recourse to the *sommations respec-*
tueuses. On the day of our marriage she had nothing in the world but
debts, and the fear of never again being able to appear to advantage
on the stage. My property consisted of three hundred francs, borrowed from my friend Gounet, and a fresh quarrel with my parents.
. . . But she was mine, and I defied the world.

CHAPTER XLV

BENEFIT AND CONCERT AT THE THÉÂTRE-ITALIEN—
THE FOURTH ACT OF "HAMLET"—"ANTONY"—DE-
FECTION OF THE ORCHESTRA—REVENGE—VISIT
FROM PAGANINI—HIS VIOLA—"HAROLD EN
ITALIE"—GIRARD'S MISTAKES—I CONDUCT
THE PERFORMANCE—ANONYMOUS LETTER

I HAD one feeble resource left in my prize pension, which had still
another year and a half to run. The Minister had exempted me from
the tour in Germany imposed on me by the Academy.[1] I was beginning
to have some adherents in Paris, and my faith in the future was strong.

---

opium he had taken, and a further three days of illness, even Harriet was compelled to believe
there was some sincerity in this young man's passion for her. She still fought, however, for time;
but Berlioz brought matters to a crisis by declaring he would go to Germany at once unless she
married him. He went, indeed, so far as to apply for his passport. The bans were published at
the end of August, and the pair were married on October 3rd. Harriet had 14,000 francs of debts;
to maintain her, her mother, her sister and himself, Berlioz had the 250 francs per month of his
Prix de Rome pension. The prospect was hardly enticing; but for the moment he found a certain
consolation in an unexpected discovery his marriage had brought him. He tells Humbert Ferrand,
in a letter of October 11th, that in spite of his wife having been so long in a profession and a
milieu where it could not have been easy for her to "résister aux mauvais exemples et aux sé-
ductions de l'or et de l'amour-propre dont elle était sans cesse environnée," he had found that
Harriet was "aussi vierge qu'il soit possible de l'être." And, he thoughtfully adds, "Vous devez
penser quelle sécurité cela me donne pour l'avenir."
    The honeymoon was spent at Vincennes, and from certain standpoints was such a success
at first that even the ardent Hector could avow to his friends that he was "brisé d'efforts."
    [1] In April 1833 he had asked the Ministry to allow him to postpone his over-due journey to
Germany for a year, as he wished to remain in Paris during that time in order to devote himself
to the composition of an opera. His request was granted, but he was warned that he would be
expected to go to Germany in January 1834.
    His reluctance to leave Paris can be understood. His music had made a considerable stir;
he was hailed in several journals as the successor of Beethoven, a young innovator who had
set instrumental music on a new path; he further kept himself in the public eye by means of his
brilliant articles; and it was natural that he should believe that after a brief conflict he would
be able to force his way into the Opéra—the only place where a French composer of that day
could hope to find real fame and fortune.

In order to finish paying off my wife's debts, I resumed the painful task of taking benefits, and, after immense exertions, succeeded in getting up a performance followed by a concert at the Théâtre-Italien. On this occasion my friends again came to my assistance — among others, Alexandre Dumas, who has shown me the greatest kindness all his life.

The evening's programme [1] consisted of Dumas' *Antony,* played by Firmin and Mdme. Dorval; the fourth act of *Hamlet,* by my wife and some English amateurs; followed by a concert, to include my *Symphonie fantastique,* the *Francs-Juges* overture, and *Sardanapalus,* with Weber's *Concertstück,* played by the excellent and admirable Liszt, and one of Weber's choruses — all conducted by myself.

It will be seen that there was far too much acting and music, and that the concert, if it ever reached the end, would not be over till one in the morning.[2]

But for the sake of young artists I must, at any cost to myself, give the exact account of this unfortunate performance. Being but little acquainted with the manners of theatre musicians, I had made a bargain with the leader of the theatre by which he engaged to give me his room and his orchestra, to which I was to add a small number of artists from the Opéra. This was the most dangerous of combinations. The musicians, being obliged by their contract to take part in all concerts given in their theatre, look upon these exceptional soirées as so much extra toil, and bring only ennui and ill-will to the work. If, in addition, they have to play with other musicians, who are paid when they are not, their ill-humour is increased, and the giver of the concert very soon feels the benefit of it.

My wife and I, being both ignorant of such petty stage-tricks, had neglected the precautions usually taken in such cases to ensure the success of the heroine of the fête; we had not given a single ticket to the claque. Mdme. Dorval, on the contrary, believing that there would be a formidable clique in my wife's favour, and that, as usual, everything would be arranged to secure her triumph, had not failed to provide for her own success by filling the pit with the tickets we gave her, those which Dumas got from us, and others which she bought. Mdme. Dorval, who played the part of Adèle admirably, was there-

[1] November 24th, 1833.
[2] It should have commenced at seven: it began at eight. The musical part of the programme should have begun at nine: it commenced at a quarter to twelve.

fore immensely applauded, and recalled. When the fourth act of
Hamlet followed (a fragment altogether incomprehensible, especially
to the French, unless introduced by the preceding acts), the sublime
part of Ophelia, which had produced so deep and poetical an effect but
a few years before, lost three-fourths of its enchantment, and seemed
cold.

The actress was still mistress of her wonderful art, but the exer-
tion displayed when she raised herself from the stage, at the close of
the scene in which she kneels before her black veil as if it were her
father's shroud, was too obvious to escape observation. For herself it
was a cruel discovery. She no longer showed her lameness, but the
certainty and freedom of some of her movements were gone; and
when the curtain went down, and she found that the public, whose
idol she had once been, and who had just given Mdme. Dorval so
great an ovation, did not call her back . . . it was a heart-breaking
disappointment! Every woman and every artist will understand it.
Poor Ophelia! Thy sun was going down. . . . I was touched to the
heart.

Then the concert began. The *Francs-Juges* overture, though most
indifferently performed, was greeted with an amount of applause
which fairly astonished me. Weber's *Concertstück,* played by Liszt
with the overpowering vehemence which he always puts into it, obtained a splendid success. Indeed, I so far forgot myself, in my enthusiasm for Liszt, as publicly to embrace him on the stage; a stupid
impropriety, which might well have covered us both with ridicule,
had the spectators been disposed to laugh. In the orchestral introduction to *Sardanapalus,* my inexperience in conducting was the cause
of the second violins missing an entry; the whole orchestra got out,
and I was obliged to beat the final chord and skip all the rest. Alexis
Dupont sang the cantata pretty well; but the famous conflagration
at the end was badly played and badly interpreted, and produced
little effect. After that nothing went well. I heard only the dull sound
of my own pulse, and felt as if I were gradually sinking into the earth.
It was getting late too, and Weber's chorus and the *Symphonie fantastique* still remained to be done.

The rules of the Théâtre-Italien do not oblige the band to play
after midnight. Consequently, being for the reasons already given
ill-disposed towards me, they were impatiently awaiting the moment
of escape, at any risk; and while the Weber chorus was being sung,

these mean-spirited scoundrels, unworthy of the name of artists, all
furtively disappeared. It was midnight. The paid musicians alone
remained at their posts, and when I turned round to begin the symphony, I found myself reduced to five violins, two violas, four basses,
and one trombone. In my consternation I really did not know what
to do. The public had evidently no wish to go away, and soon began to
get impatient and to demand the symphony. I was not fool enough
to begin. Finally, in the midst of the tumult, a voice called out from
the gallery, "The *March to Execution!*" On which I made answer,
" I cannot perform the *March to Execution* with five violins! It is not
my fault. The orchestra has disappeared. I hope that the public —— "
I was burning with shame and indignation. The audience rose up in
disappointment, and the concert terminated. My enemies did not fail
to turn the event into ridicule, and say that my music *drove musicians
away*. I do not believe that there has ever before been an occurrence
inspired by such ignoble motives. Ah, cursed strummers! miserable
wretches! Your names are protected by their obscurity; but I regret
that I did not collect them.

That wretched evening, however, brought me in about seven
thousand francs,[1] but in a few days it was all swallowed up by my
wife's debts; not that it was enough to discharge them; that was a
work requiring several years and many cruel privations.[2]

I should have greatly liked to give Henrietta the opportunity of
a grand revenge; but there was not a single English actor in Paris.
She would have been obliged again to apply to incompetent amateurs,
and to appear in mere mutilated fragments of Shakespeare. This
would have been absurd, as the event just described proved; so the
plan had to be given up. But I lost no time in endeavouring to reply
to the attacks on myself by an undeniable success. By paying a good
price, I engaged a first-rate orchestra of the very *élite* of Paris musicians, among whom I could reckon many friends, or at the very least
impartial judges of my works; and I announced a concert at the
Conservatoire. The expense was so great that it was quite possible
that it might not be covered by the receipts. But my wife encouraged
me to do it, and thus showed herself, what she has always been since,

[1] In his letter to his sister Adèle of November 28th Berlioz gives the figure as 2,500 francs.
[2] It was about this time that Berlioz began to contribute to the *Rénovateur*, which had just
absorbed the *Revue Européenne*. He used, of course, his articles on other people to bring his own
music before the public eye. In January 1834 he joined the *Gazette musicale*, which had just been
founded by the publisher Schlesinger.

an enemy to all half measures or petty means; and, where the interests of art or the glory of the artist were in question, brave even to rashness.

I was afraid to compromise the performance by again conducting. Habeneck obstinately refused; but Girard, at that time one of my staunch friends, consented to accept the task, and acquitted himself well. The *Symphonie fantastique* again figured in the programme,[1] and took the whole room by storm, being applauded throughout. My success was complete, and the former judgment on me was reversed. My musicians — it may be imagined that I took none from the Théâtre-Italien — looked radiant with delight as they left the orchestra. Lastly, my happiness was crowned when the public had all gone, and a man stopped me in the passage — a man with long hair, piercing eyes, a strange and haggard face — a genius, a Titan among the giants, whom I had never seen before, and at first sight of whom I was deeply moved; this man pressed my hand, and overwhelmed me with burning eulogies that set both my heart and brain on fire. *It was Paganini* (22nd December, 1833). From that day date my relations with that great artist, who exercised such a happy influence upon my destiny, and whose noble generosity to me, as will be seen later, has given birth to such absurd and malicious comments.[2]

Some weeks after the triumphant concert which I have just described, Paganini came to see me.

" I have a wonderful viola," said he, " an admirable Stradivari, and should greatly like to play it in public. But I have no music for it. Would you write me a solo? I have no confidence in anyone but you for such a work." [3]

---

[1] Together with the *King Lear* overture and a couple of songs.

[2] A protégé of Paganini's — the violinist Haumann — played at his concert. But it is extremely doubtful whether Paganini himself was present: there is no mention of this incident in the journals or in Berlioz's letters of the time. He was no doubt confusing this occasion with another — perhaps his concert of December 9th, 1832. But there is this further difficulty, that although in his letter of December 10th, to Adèle, he mentions Paganini as having been at the concert, Berlioz says nothing at all about any episode of this kind.

[3] On January 26th, 1834, the *Gazette musicale* announced that Paganini had just asked Berlioz for "a new work in the style of the *Symphonie fantastique*." It was to be "a dramatic fantasy for orchestra, chorus, and solo viola," with the title, *Les Derniers Instans de Marie Stuart*. M. Boschot throws doubt on the story as told in the *Mémoires;* he will have it that Berlioz thought what an excellent thing it would be if Paganini were to play the viola in a work of his, and then, or later, imagined the rest of the story. It seems hardly likely, however, that with Paganini in Paris at the time, Berlioz and his journalistic friends would have dared to print the account of this "request" had it been pure invention; moreover in a letter of March 19th, 1834, to Humbert Ferrand, Hector says that he is "finishing the symphony with viola solo requested of me by Paganini." But the process is not quite clear by which, nor the reason for which, *Les Derniers*

" Certainly," I answered; " I am more flattered than I can say; but in order to fulfil your expectation, and make a composition sufficiently brilliant to suit such a virtuoso as yourself, I ought to be able to play the viola, and this I cannot do. It seems to me that you alone can solve the problem."

" No," replied Paganini; " you will succeed. I insist. As for me, I am too unwell at present to compose. I could not think of such a thing."

In order to please the illustrious virtuoso, then, I endeavoured to write a solo for the viola, but so combined with the orchestra as not to diminish the importance of the latter, feeling sure that Paganini's incomparable execution would enable him to give the solo instrument all its due prominence. The proposition was a new one. A happy idea soon occurred to me, and I became intensely eager to carry it out.

No sooner was the first movement written than Paganini wished to see it. At sight of the rests, however, in the viola part in the allegro, " That is not at all what I want," cried he. " I am silent a great deal too long. I must be playing the whole time."

" That is exactly what I said," I answered. " What you really want is a concerto for the viola, and you are the only man who can write it."

To this he made no reply, but seemed disappointed, and left me without any further remarks. A few days afterwards, being already a sufferer from that throat affection which was ultimately to prove fatal to him, he went to Nice, and did not return till three years later.

Finding that the plan of my composition did not suit him, I applied myself to carrying it out in another way, and without troubling myself any further as to how the solo part should be brought into brilliant relief. I conceived the idea of writing a series of scenes for the orchestra, in which the viola should find itself mixed up, like a person more or less in action, always preserving his own individuality. The background I formed from my recollections of my wanderings in the Abruzzi, introducing the viola as a sort of melancholy dreamer, in the style of Byron's *Childe Harold*. Hence the title of the symphony, *Harold in Italy*. As in the *Symphonie fantastique,* one principal theme (the first strain of the viola) is reproduced throughout the work, but

---

Instans de Marie Stuart became *Harold in Italy;* though probably M. Boschot is right in his conjecture that the work was pieced together out of fragments of the *Rob Roy* overture and other discarded works, plus a certain amount of new matter.

The final page of the manuscript is dated 22nd June, 1834.

with this difference, that in the *Symphonie fantastique* the theme — the *idée fixe* — obtrudes itself obstinately, like a passionately episodic figure, into scenes wholly foreign to it, whilst Harold's strain is superadded to the other orchestral strains, with which it contrasts both in movement and character, without hindering their development. Notwithstanding its complicated harmonic tissue, I took as little time to compose this symphony as I usually did to write my other works, though I employed considerable labour in retouching it. In the *Pilgrims' March*, which I improvised in a couple of hours one evening over my fire, I have for more than six years past been modifying the details, and think that I have much improved it. Even in its first form it was always completely successful from the moment of its first performance at my concert in the Conservatoire, on November 23rd, 1834.[1]

The first movement alone was feebly applauded, but this was the fault of Girard, who conducted the orchestra, and could not succeed in working it up enough in the coda, where the pace ought gradually to be doubled. Without this progressive animation the end of the allegro is cold and languid. I suffered simple martyrdom in hearing it thus dragged. The *Pilgrims' March* was encored. At its second performance, and towards the middle of the second part — at the place where the convent-bells (suggested by two harp-notes doubled by the flutes, oboes, and horns) are heard afresh after a brief interruption — at this point the harpist miscounted his bars, and lost his place. Girard, instead of setting him right, as I have done a dozen times in the same circumstances (the same mistake is constantly made), called out, " The last chord," which the band accordingly gave, thus skipping some fifty bars. This was a complete slaughter. Fortunately, however, the march had been well played the first time, and the public were under no misapprehension about the cause of the disaster at the encore. Had it happened at first, they would have been sure to attribute the cacophony to the composer. Still, since my defeat

---

[1] As will be seen from all these dates, Berlioz had *not* gone to Germany in January 1834. About the middle of that month he had obtained from the Ministry of Fine Arts six months of his pension (1500 francs) on his assurance that he "was on the point of setting out for Germany." He never had the least intention of going there. When June arrived he asked for, and obtained, a further 1500 francs. The authorities no doubt took into consideration the fact that Harriet was expecting her confinement. (Their son, Louis, was born on August 14th.) But apart from that, they probably thought it prudent to be complaisant towards a young composer and journalist who was not only making his weight felt in Paris but had now come under the protection of Bertin, the proprietor of the all-powerful *Journal des Débats*.

at the Théâtre-Italien, I had such mistrust of my own skill as a conductor that I allowed Girard to direct my concerts for some time
longer; but at the fourth performance of *Harold* he made so serious
a mistake at the end of the serenade (where, if one part of the orchestra does not double its speed, the other part cannot go on, because the
whole bar of the former corresponds to the half bar of the latter)
that, seeing at last that there was no hope of his working up the end
of the allegro properly, I resolved in future to conduct myself, and
not allow anyone else to communicate my ideas to the performers.
From this resolution I only once departed, and my readers will see
how nearly fatal was the result.

 After the first hearing of this symphony, an article appeared in a
Paris musical paper which overwhelmed me with invectives, beginning
in this witty style: " Ha, ha, ha! haro! haro! *Harold!*" On the morning after the appearance of this article I received an anonymous letter
in which, after a deluge of even coarser insults, I was reproached with
not being brave enough to blow out my brains!

CHAPTER XLVI

AN ORDER FOR A REQUIEM—THE DIRECTORS OF THE
FINE ARTS—THEIR OPINIONS ON MUSIC—BREAK
THEIR WORD—THE CAPTURE OF CONSTANTINE—
INTRIGUES OF CHERUBINI, ETC.—MY REQUIEM
PERFORMED—HABENECK'S SNUFF-BOX—I AM
NOT PAID—THEY WISH TO SELL ME THE
CROSS—ALL KINDS OF IGNOMINY—FURY
—THREATS—I AM PAID

It will be seen that Berlioz leaps from November 1834, when *Harold* was produced, to
March 1837, which was the date when he received the definite commission for the *Requiem*.
During that period his chief preoccupation had been with the Opéra; and to gain an entry there
he had mobilised all his resources—the influence of the Bertins, journalistic attacks on, and
suggestions to, the Opéra management by himself and his faithful adherents in the Press, and
so on. He had constituted himself the "musical secretary" of Bertin's daughter; though it is
doubtful whether, as was said in Paris at the time, he had actually written any of the score of
Mlle Bertin's *Esmeralda*, he certainly came to the rescue of the lady's technical amateurishness;
while in superintending the rehearsals of the work he managed to get a footing in the Opéra.
Esmeralda was produced on November 14th, 1836, and soundly hissed, for political as well as
musical reasons, for the *Débats*, as the Government organ, was of course detested by the Opposition. Though Berlioz treated Mlle Bertin with great gallantry in his notice of the production,
the failure of *Esmeralda* left him quite dry-eyed, for with this work out of the way there was one

obstacle the less in the path of his own *Benvenuto Cellini*, at which he had been working ever since the summer of 1836.

In January 1835 he had joined the staff of the *Débats* as writer of concert and theatre notices. It was mainly by his journalism that he had henceforth to support himself; and his small income from this source was depleted by the loss of his post on the *Rénovateur* early in 1836, that journal having amalgamated with the *Quotidienne*, of which d'Ortigue was the musical critic. In January 1835 Berlioz had obtained payment of his Prix de Rome pension for the first half of that year, and in the following July he received his allowance — the final one — for the following six months. He had thus bamboozled the Ministry into paying him the whole of his pension without his carrying out the agreement to complete his studies in Germany. When this source of income had come to an end, Berlioz, weighed down as he still was by debts, had a hard struggle to make both ends meet. His friend Ernest Legouvé lent him 2,000 francs in the spring of 1836 to enable him to get on with the composition of *Benvenuto Cellini*, and about the same time his father relented sufficiently to send him a little money. Harriet, like all actors who have had their day, could not perceive that her evening had come; she made several pitiful attempts to re-establish herself in this small theatre or that, but Press and public would have none of her. All in all, Berlioz's position was now worsening. He kept himself incessantly in the public eye; but it was an expensive business giving an orchestral concert every now and then, the Parisian public of that day was really not interested in serious instrumental music, for which it had neither the training nor the appetite, and obtaining admission to the Opéra was a slow process. Yet the Opéra was the only hope for him as for every other French composer — the only place where there was a machine that would automatically reproduce a work night after night (supposing it to be a success), and so not only spread the composer's fame but fill his pocket. It was upon the Opéra, then, that all Berlioz's thinking was centred during these years: even the *Requiem* was probably planned to force the Director's hand by means of a colossal musical effect of which no other composer of the time was capable.

IN 1836 M. de Gasparin was Minister of the Interior. He belonged to that small section of our statesmen who are interested in music, and to the still more limited number who really have a feeling for it. With the view of restoring sacred music to a position which it had not enjoyed in France for long, he proposed that the Fine Arts Department should give three thousand francs per annum to a French composer who should be appointed by the Minister to write either a mass or an oratorio on a large scale. He proposed also that the Minister should, in addition, charge himself with having the new work performed at the expense of the Government. " I shall begin with Berlioz," said he; " he must write a *Requiem*. I am sure he will succeed." My surprise was equal to my joy when these details were given me by a friend of M. de Gasparin's son, with whom I was acquainted. In order to be sure, I requested an audience of the Minister, who confirmed the correctness of all that I had heard. " I am about to leave my post," added he, " and this will be my musical legacy. You have received the official order for the *Requiem?* " " No, sir; and it is only by accident that I have heard of your kind intentions." " How is that? I gave instructions for the order to be sent to you a week ago. The delay is due to the carelessness of the office, and I will see to it."

Several days, however, passed without the order arriving. In great uneasiness I then addressed myself to M. de Gasparin's son, who put me up to an intrigue of which I had not the faintest suspicion.

The Director of the Fine Arts[1] did not at all approve of the Minister's project, and still less of his choice of me to open the procession of composers. He knew that in a few days M. de Gasparin would leave the Ministry. Now by delaying till then the preparation of the order for founding the institution and calling upon me to compose the *Requiem,* it would be easy afterwards to defeat the project by dissuading his successor from carrying it out. This is what M. le Directeur had in his head. But M. de Gasparin had no intention of being played with, and on learning from his son that nothing had been done on the very eve of his leaving the Ministry, he sent a most peremptory command to the Director to draw up the order immediately and send it to me, which was accordingly done.[2]

Such a check could hardly fail to intensify the ill-feeling of the Director towards myself; it did, in fact, increase it.

This arbiter of the destinies of art and artists did not condescend to recognise real worth in any music but that of Rossini. One day, however, having in my presence reviewed disdainfully all the ancient and modern masters, with the exception of Beethoven, whom he *forgot for the moment,* he suddenly stopped and said: " But surely there must be another — what is his name? A German, whose symphonies they play at the Conservatoire. You must know *him,* M. Berlioz." "Beethoven?" "Ah, Beethoven. Well, *he* was not devoid of talent." I myself heard the Director of the Fine Arts express himself thus, and admit that Beethoven *was not devoid of talent.*

In this he was only the leading representative of musical opinion in the then French official world. Hundreds of connoisseurs of this sort choked up the avenues through which artists had to pass, and set in motion the wheels of the Government machine by which our musical institutions were kept going. In the present day. . . .

Once armed with my order, I set to work. For a long time the text of the *Requiem* had been to me an object of envy, on which I flung myself with a kind of fury when it was put within my grasp. My head seemed ready to burst with the pressure of my seething thoughts. No

---

[1] He has been dead ten or twelve years, but it as well not to give his name. [B.]

[2] Berlioz does not tell us how skilfully, for some time previously, he had been manœuvring to obtain a government commission for a work on this grand scale.

sooner was one piece sketched than another presented itself. Finding it impossible to write fast enough, I adopted a sort of shorthand, which helped me greatly, especially in the *Lacrymosa*. Every composer knows the anguish and despair occasioned by forgetting ideas which one has not time to write down, and which thus escape for ever.

I consequently wrote this work with great rapidity, and it was not till long afterwards that I made the slight changes which are to be found in the second edition of the work, published by Ricordi, at Milan.[1]

The official order guaranteed that my *Requiem* should be performed at the Government expense on the day of the service annually celebrated for the victims of the Revolution of 1830.

As the July day appointed for the ceremony approached, I had the parts of my work copied, and, acting on the advice of the Director of the Fine Arts, began my rehearsals.

Almost immediately afterwards, however, I received an official letter from the Department to the effect that the ceremony was to take place without music, and requesting me to suspend all my preparations. The Minister was none the less indebted for a considerable sum to the copyist and to the two hundred choristers who, on the faith of their agreements, had been working at my rehearsals. For five months I in vain solicited the payment of these debts. As for what was owing to myself, I did not venture even to speak of it, so far did they seem from remembering it. I began to lose patience, when one day, on leaving the Director after an exceedingly animated discussion with him on the subject, the cannon of the Invalides announced the capture of Constantine.[2] Two hours later I was hastily summoned back to the Minister's office.

The Director had found out a way of getting rid of me; at least, so he believed. General Damrémont having perished beneath the walls of Constantine, a solemn service for him and the other soldiers who had fallen during the siege was to be held in the Church of the Invalides. This ceremony was the concern of the Minister of War, and General Bernard, who occupied that post, consented to have my

---

[1] Strange that just at this time, whilst I was writing this work, and after my marriage to Miss Smithson, I should twice have had the same dream. I was in Mdme. Gautier's little garden at Meylan, seated at the foot of a delightful weeping acacia, but alone. Mademoiselle Estelle was not there, and I was saying to myself, "Where is she—where is she?" Who will explain this? Perhaps sailors may, or learned men who have studied the movements of the magnetic needle, and know that those of the human heart are much the same. [B.]

[2] A city in Algeria taken by General Damrémont, Oct. 13, 1837. [H.]

Requiem performed. Such was the unexpected news which greeted me on my arrival.

The plot now thickens, and the most important events rapidly follow each other. I recommend all poor artists who read me to profit by my experience, and meditate on what happened; they will gain from it the doubtful advantage of mistrusting everything and everybody, whenever they shall find themselves in a like position; of putting no more faith in written words than in spoken ones, and of taking precautions alike against heaven and hell.

The news that my *Requiem* was to be performed in a grand official ceremony was no sooner brought to Cherubini than it put him into a perfect fever. It had long been the custom to perform one of his two Requiems under circumstances of this kind, and such an attack, directed against what he considered as his rights, his dignity, his just celebrity, his unquestionable worth, and in favour of a young man just starting his career, with the reputation of having introduced heresy into the school, annoyed him extremely. His friends and pupils, with Halévy at their head, sharing in his annoyance, combined to turn the storm on me, that is to say, to ensure the dispossession of the young man in favour of the old one. One evening I happened to be at the office of the *Journal des Débats,* to the staff of which I had recently become attached, and whose chief, M. Bertin, had always shown me the greatest kindness, when Halévy presented himself. I at once guessed the object of his visit. He was going to invoke the powerful influence of M. Bertin on Cherubini's side. Slightly disconcerted at finding me there, and still more by the coldness with which he was received by the Bertins — father and son — he instantly changed his tactics. The door of the room into which he followed the elder Bertin remained ajar, and I overheard him saying that the shock had been so great as to make Cherubini take to his bed, and that he had therefore come to beg M. Bertin to use his influence in obtaining the Cross of the Legion of Honour for the illustrious master as some consolation. M. Bertin's severe voice here interrupted him with these words: "Yes, my dear Halévy, we will do what you wish to get Cherubini the distinction he so well merits; but if it is a question of the *Requiem,* if they are going to propose any compromise to Berlioz, and if he has the weakness to give in by one hair's breadth, I will never speak to him again as long as I live." Halévy must have felt considerably embarrassed as he retired after receiving this answer.

Thus the excellent Cherubini, who had already sought to make me swallow so many mortifications, was in his turn compelled to receive a far bigger one from my hands which he will assuredly never digest.

Now for another intrigue, still more cleverly contrived, the black depths of which I hardly dare fathom. I incriminate no one; I simply give the naked facts, without the smallest commentary, but with scrupulous exactness. General Bernard having himself informed me that my *Requiem* was to be performed on certain conditions which I shall presently state, I was about to begin my rehearsals when I was sent for by the Director of the Beaux Arts.

"You know," said he, "that Habeneck has been commissioned to conduct all the great official musical festivals?" ("Come! Good!" thought I, "here is another tile for my devoted head.") "It is true that you are now in the habit of conducting the performance of your works yourself; but Habeneck is an old man" (another of them!), "and I happen to know that he will be deeply hurt if he does not preside at your *Requiem*. What terms are you on with him?"

"What terms? We have quarrelled. I hardly know why. For three years he has not spoken to me. I am not aware of his motives, and, indeed, have not troubled to ask. He began by rudely refusing to conduct one of my concerts. His behaviour towards me has been as inexplicable as it is uncivil. However, as I see plainly that he wishes on the present occasion to figure at Marshal Damrémont's ceremony, and as it would evidently be agreeable to you, I consent to give up the baton to him, on condition that I have at least one full rehearsal."

"Agreed," replied the Director; "I will let him know about it."

The sectional and general rehearsals were accordingly conducted with great care. Habeneck spoke to me as if our relations with each other had never been interrupted, and all seemed likely to go well.

The day of the performance arrived,[1] in the Church of the Invalides, before all the princes, peers, and deputies, the French press, the correspondents of foreign papers, and an immense crowd. It was absolutely essential for me to have a great success; a moderate one would have been fatal, and a failure would have annihilated me altogether.

Now listen attentively.

The various groups of instruments in the orchestra were tolerably widely separated, especially the four brass bands introduced in the

[1] December 5th, 1837.

Tuba mirum, each of which occupied a corner of the entire orchestra and chorus. There is no pause between the *Dies Iræ* and the *Tuba mirum,* but the pace in the latter movement is reduced to half what it was before. At this point the whole of the brass enters, first all together, and then in passages that challenge and answer each other — each entry being a third higher than the last. It is obvious that it is of the greatest importance that the four beats of the new tempo should be distinctly marked, or else the terrible explosion, which I had so carefully prepared with combinations and proportions never attempted before or since, and which, rightly performed, gives such a picture of the Last Judgment as I believe is destined to live, would be a mere enormous and hideous cacophony.

With my habitual distrust, I had stationed myself behind Habeneck, and, turning my back on him, overlooked the group of kettledrums, which he could not see, when the moment approached for them to take part in the general mêlée. There are, perhaps, one thousand bars in my *Requiem.* Precisely in that of which I have just been speaking, when the movement broadens out, and the brass burst in with their terrible fanfare; in fact, just in *the* one bar where the conductor's direction is absolutely indispensable, Habeneck *puts down his baton, quietly takes out his snuff-box, and proceeds to take a pinch of snuff.* I had never taken my eyes off him: instantly I turned rapidly on one heel, and, springing forward before him, I stretched out my arm and marked the four great beats of the new movement. The orchestras followed me, each in order. I conducted the piece to the end, and the effect which I had dreamed of was produced. When, at the last words of the chorus, Habeneck saw that the *Tuba mirum* was saved, he said: "What a cold perspiration I have been in! Without you we should have been lost." "Yes, I know," I answered, looking fixedly at him. I did not add another word. . . . Had he done it on purpose? . . . Could it be possible that this man had dared to join my enemy, the Director, and Cherubini's friends, in plotting and attempting such rascality? I don't wish to believe it . . . but I cannot doubt it. God forgive me if I am doing the man injustice! [1]

[1] It is more than doubtful whether any such incident took place, however. There is no mention of it in any of the newspaper accounts of the performance, nor does Berlioz refer to it in his letter of the 17th to Humbert Ferrand: he merely says there that "the *Requiem* was done well." He is equally silent as to the snuff-box crime in his letter of the same day to his mother.

Did Berlioz, I often wonder, in the later years when he was eaten away with disappointments of every kind, *dream* things under the influence of the opium he had to take to dull his pains, and then, in waking hours, transfer his dream to the past as a reality?

The success of the *Requiem* was complete, in spite of all the conspiracies — cowardly, atrocious, officious, and official — which would fain have hindered it.

I alluded a moment ago to the conditions which the Minister of War had attached to its performance. Here they are: " I will give you," said the honourable General Bernard, " ten thousand francs for the performance of your work, but this sum will only be paid on your presenting a letter from my colleague the Minister of the Interior, by which he shall engage to pay what is due to you for the composition of the *Requiem* according to M. de Gasparin's order, and afterwards what is owing to the copyist, and to the choristers for their rehearsals last July."

The Minister had given his word to General Bernard to discharge this triple debt. The letter was drawn up, and wanted nothing but his signature. To obtain this I remained in his ante-room with one of his secretaries, armed with the letter and a pen, from ten in the morning till four in the afternoon. Not till then did the Minister come out, and the secretary, catching him in the passage, made him affix his precious signature to the letter. Without losing a minute I ran off to General Bernard, who, after having carefully read his colleague's letter, paid me the ten thousand francs. I applied the whole of this sum to the payment of my performers. I gave three hundred francs to Duprez, who had sung the solo in the *Sanctus,* and three hundred more to Habeneck, that peerless snuff-taker who had made such an opportune use of his snuff-box. Absolutely nothing remained for myself. I imagined that I should ultimately be paid by the Minister of the Interior, who would feel himself doubly bound to pay off this debt, both by the decree of his predecessor and by the engagement he had contracted in his own person with the Minister of War. *Sancta simplicitas!* as Mephistopheles says. One month, two months, three, four, eight months passed by without my being able to touch a half-penny. By dint of petitions, recommendatory letters from friends of the Minister, constant visits, and written and verbal complaints, the rehearsals of the choristers and the expenses of the copying were finally paid, and I was at length rid of the intolerable persecution I had so long endured from those poor people, who were weary of waiting for their due, and probably had their suspicions of my honesty, the bare idea of which still makes me blush with indignation.

But that the author of the *Requiem* should be supposed to attach any value to filthy lucre! That would indeed have been a calumny, and, in consequence, good care was taken not to pay me. I nevertheless took the liberty to claim the entire fulfilment of the Minister's promises. My need of money was so pressing that I was forced to make a fresh attack on the office of the Fine Arts Director. Several weeks more passed by in useless demands. My anger increased; I grew thin; I lost my sleep. Finally, I went one morning to the office, blue and livid with fury, resolved to make a scene; resolved on any and every extremity. On entering I at once attacked the Director: " Well, it is plain that they are not going to pay me." " My dear Berlioz," replied he, " you know it is not my fault. I have made stringent inquiries, and have found out everything about the affair. The money intended for you has disappeared; it has been put to some other use. I really don't know in what office. If such things took place in mine ——— " " Oh, then the money intended for the Fine Arts can be spent out of your department, and without your knowledge? Is your budget, then, at the disposal of the first comer? But this is nothing to me. Such questions are no concern of mine. A *Requiem* was ordered from me by the Minister of the Interior for the agreed sum of three thousand francs. I want my three thousand francs! " " Good heavens! have a little patience! It shall be considered. Besides, there is an idea of giving you the cross." " A fig for the cross! Give me my money! " " But ——— " " I'll have no buts," cried I, throwing down an arm-chair. " I will give you till twelve o'clock to-morrow; and if at twelve o'clock precisely I have not received the money, I will raise a scandal about you and the Minister the like of which has never been seen before! And you know that it is in my power to raise it." Whereat the Director is quite upset, and, forgetting his hat, rushes down the stairs leading to the Minister's rooms, I behind him, calling out, " Mind you tell him that I should be ashamed to treat my shoe-maker as he treats me, and that his behaviour to me shall soon enjoy a rare notoriety." [1] This time I had found the weak place in the Minister's armour. Ten minutes afterwards the Director returned with a cheque for three thousand francs on the Fine Arts Department. The money had been found. That is how artists ought occasionally to get justice done to them in Paris. There are other ways, still more violent, which I advise them not to overlook. [2]

[1] And yet he was an excellent and well-intentioned man. [B.]
[2] The official documents, however, show that Berlioz received 1000 francs on the 15th December (ten days after the performance), and 4000 francs on the following 23rd January.

At a later date,[1] the excellent M. de Gasparin, having regained possession of the portfolio of the Interior, seemed to wish to make some amends for the intolerable injustice I had endured about the *Requiem,* by giving me the cross of the Legion of Honour, which they had previously as good as tried to sell me for three thousand francs; though when offered in that way I would not have given thirty sous for it. This commonplace distinction was bestowed upon me at the same time with the great Duponchel, Director of the Opéra, and Bordogni, the best singing-master of that period.

When the *Requiem* was afterwards printed I dedicated it to M. de Gasparin, all the more willingly as he was then no longer in power.

What made the behaviour of the Minister so peculiarly galling was that, after the performance of the *Requiem,* after having paid the musicians and choristers, the carpenters who constructed the orchestra, Habeneck, Duprez, and everyone else, and whilst I had only begun to demand my three thousand francs, the opposition newspapers pointed me out as a favourite of the Government, as a silkworm feeding on the revenue, and gravely stated that I had had thirty thousand francs for the *Requiem!* In saying this they merely added a cypher to the sum which I had not received. That is the way in which history is written.

CHAPTER XLVII

PERFORMANCE OF MY ''LACRYMOSA'' AT LILLE—A
LITTLE PILL FOR CHERUBINI—HE PLAYS ME
A NICE TRICK—A ROLAND FOR HIS OLIVER—I
JOIN THE ''JOURNAL DES DÉBATS''—
PAINFUL RESULTS

Some years[2] after the ceremony the events of which I have just narrated, the town of Lille organised its first festival, and Habeneck was engaged to direct the musical part of it. Actuated by one of those kindly impulses which were, after all, not infrequent with him, and wishing perhaps to make me forget, if possible, his famous pinch of snuff, he took it into his head to propose to the committee,

[1] May 10th, 1839.
[2] Some *months* after: the Lille performances of which Berlioz speaks took place on June 25th, 26th and 27th, 1838.

among other pieces, the *Lacrymosa* from my *Requiem*. A *Credo* of
Cherubini's was also included in the programme. Habeneck rehearsed
my piece with extraordinary care, and the performance appeared to
leave nothing to be desired. Its effect, also, was said to be very great;
and in spite of its great length the piece was loudly encored by the
public. Some of the audience were even moved to tears. As the Lille
committee had not done me the honour to invite me, I stayed in Paris;
but after the concert, Habeneck, in great delight at such a success
with so difficult a work, wrote me a short letter something in this style,
which was published in Paris by the *Gazette Musicale:*

" MY DEAR BERLIOZ,
    " I cannot resist the pleasure of telling you that your *Lacrymosa*
was beautifully performed and produced an immense sensation. —
Yours ever,

                                        " HABENECK."

On his return, Habeneck called on Cherubini to assure him that
his *Credo* had been very well done. " Yes," replied Cherubini in a
dry tone, " but you did not write to *me*." [1]
    Here was again a bitter little pill that he was obliged to swallow
about that damned *Requiem,* and he kindly offered me the fellow to
it under the following circumstances.
    The place of Professor of Harmony having fallen vacant at the
Conservatoire, I was advised by one of my friends to become a candidate for it. Without deluding myself with any hope of success, I
nevertheless wrote to our excellent Director, Cherubini, on the subject. On the receipt of my letter he sent for me.
    " You propose yourself for the harmony class? " said he, with
his most amiable manner and sweetest voice.
    " Yes, sir."
    " Ah, well,[2] you will get it. Your present reputation, your
references —— "
    " So much the better, sir; I asked for it in order to get it."
    " Yes, but — but that is just what is troubling me. The fact is,
I wanted to give it to somebody else."

----

[1] I had told him that he would *know my name some day*. [B.]
[2] Here again, to get an idea of Cherubini's odd pronunciation, the reader must see the
original. [H.]

" In that case, sir, I will withdraw my application."

" No, no; I don't want that, because, you see, people would say that I was the cause of your withdrawal."

" Well, then, I shall remain a candidate."

" But I tell you you will get the place if you insist on it, and —— But I did not mean it for you."

" What would you have me do, then? "

" You know that — that — that it is necessary to be a pianist to teach harmony at the Conservatoire; you know that, don't you? "

" It is necessary to be a pianist, is it? Ah, I should hardly have guessed that. Very well, that is an excellent reason. I will write to you that, not being a pianist, I cannot aspire to the professorship of harmony at the Conservatoire, and that I withdraw my application."

" Yes; but — but — but I am not the cause of your —— "

" No; far from it. I ought to withdraw as a matter of course, after having been so stupid as to forget that it was necessary to be a pianist to teach harmony."

" Yes. Come, embrace me. You know how fond I am of you."

" Oh yes, sir; I know it well." And he did, as a matter of fact, embrace me with really paternal tenderness. I went away, wrote to him to withdraw my application, and eight days later he had the place given to a man of the name of Bienaimé, who was no more a pianist than I was. That was what might be called a well-played trick, and I myself was the first to laugh heartily at it.

The reader will admire my self-control in not replying to Cherubini: " Then you yourself, sir, would not be able to teach harmony either? " For the great master himself was also no pianist.

I regret that soon afterwards, though quite involuntarily, I wounded my illustrious friend in the most cruel manner. I was in the pit of the Opera-house at the first performance of his *Ali Baba*. This work, as everyone agreed at the time, is one of Cherubini's feeblest and most insignificant. Towards the end of the first act, tired of hearing nothing striking, I could not help saying, loudly enough to be heard by my neighbours: " Twenty francs for an idea! " In the middle of the second act, still deceived by the same musical mirage, I added to my bid, saying: " Forty francs for an idea! " The finale began: " Eighty francs for an idea! " When the finale was ended I got up, exclaimed: " Upon my word, I am not rich enough. I give it up," and thereupon left.

Two or three young men on the same bench with myself looked at me indignantly. They were pupils at the Conservatoire, who had been placed there that they might admire their Director *to some purpose.* They did not fail, as I heard afterwards, to go next day and tell the Director of my insolent bids and still more insolent criticism. Cherubini was all the more outraged by it because, after having said to me: "You know how fond I am of you," he must doubtless have thought me, as usual, horribly ungrateful. If my former tricks might be called *adders,* this was really one of those venomous *asps* whose bite is so deadly to one's self-love. It somehow escaped me.

I ought now to say how I became attached to the staff of the *Journal des Débats.* Since my return from Italy I had published a good many articles in the *Revue Européenne, L'Europe Littéraire,* and *Le Monde Dramatique* (magazines whose existence was of short duration), in the *Gazette Musicale,* the *Correspondant,* and some other papers that are now forgotten. But these various works of small compass and importance brought me in very little, and did not much improve the state of discomfort in which I was living.

One day, not knowing which way to turn, and anxious to gain a few francs, I wrote a sort of novel called *Rubini à Calais,* which appeared in the *Gazette Musicale.* I was desperately sad when I wrote it, but the story was full of fun; a contrast which is known to occur often enough. The sketch was reproduced in the *Journal des Débats* some days later, with a few words from the editor, full of kindly feeling for the author. I went at once to thank M. Bertin, who proposed that I should edit the musical feuilleton of the *Débats* itself, a much-coveted throne of criticism, which was then vacant through the retirement of Castil-Blaze. At first I was not its sole occupant, and for some time had only to write the critiques of concerts and new compositions. Later on those of the lyrical theatres devolved upon me, though the Théâtre-Italien remained under the protection of M. Delécluse, who has it to this day, while Jules Janin preserved his rights over the Opéra ballets. I then gave up the feuilleton of the *Correspondant,* and limited my critical labours to such as could find a place in the *Débats* and the *Gazette Musicale.*

At present I have almost renounced all work in the last-named paper, notwithstanding its high pay,[1] and write only in the *Débats*

---

[1] They give me 100 francs per feuilleton, that is to say about 1,400 francs in the year. [B.]

when absolutely obliged to do so by what is happening in the musical world.

Such is my aversion to work of this nature, that I cannot learn of a forthcoming first performance without feeling an uneasiness which goes on increasing until my feuilleton is finished.

This never-ending, still-beginning task poisons my life. And yet, independently of the income it gives me, with which I cannot dispense, I find it almost impossible to give it up on pain of remaining defence-less in the face of the furious and almost innumerable animosities which it has stirred up against me. For the Press is, in a certain way, more precious than the spear of Achilles; not only does it occasionally heal the wounds which it has inflicted, but it also serves as a weapon of defence to the person who makes use of it.

And yet what wretched circumspection am I not forced to use! What circumlocution to evade the expression of the truth! What con-cessions to social relations and even to public opinion! What sup-pressed rage, what gulps of shame! And yet I am considered passion-ate, ill-natured, and contemptuous! Oh, you ill-bred fellows who treat me thus! If I spoke my whole mind you would soon see that the bed of thorns on which you believe yourselves to have been laid by me is a bed of roses compared with the gridiron on which I long to roast you!

I ought in justice to myself to say that never for any consideration has it ever happened to me to suppress the most unrestrained ex-pressions of esteem, admiration, or enthusiasm for any works or any men who inspired me with those sentiments. I have warmly praised writers who have done me much harm, and with whom I have ceased to have any relations. Indeed the only compensation which the Press offers me for so many torments is the range it gives to my exaltation in face of the great, the true, and the beautiful, wherever they exist. It is sweet to praise an enemy when that enemy has merit, indeed it is the proud duty of an honest man; while every untrue word written in favour of an undeserving friend causes me heart-breaking anguish. In both cases, however, as critics well know, the man who hates you is so furious at the praise you are likely to obtain by heartily doing him justice in public, that he detests you all the more, while the man who likes you, not being satisfied with the laboured eulogies you bestow on him, likes you all the less. Nor should it be forgotten how sick it makes those who have the misfortune, as I have, to be at once critic and artist, to be obliged to occupy themselves with a thousand

Lilliputian inanities, and to put up with the fawning compliments, meanness, and cringing of people who have, or are likely to have, need of
you. I often amuse myself by following the subterranean operations of
certain individuals as they scoop out a tunnel twenty miles long in
order to get what they call a " good " feuilleton upon a forthcoming
work. Nothing is more laughable than to hear them laboriously dig-
ging away, unless it be the patience with which they clear the passage
and construct the arch — until the moment when the critic, waxing
impatient at all this mole-work, suddenly opens a tap which floods the
mine and sometimes drowns the miner.

When, therefore, the appreciation of my own works is in question,
I do not attach much value to the opinion of any persons who are not
beyond the influence of the feuilleton. Among musicians, those only
whose approbation flatters me are the members of the orchestra and
the chorus, because their individual talent rarely comes up for judgment by the critic, and so I know that they have no reason for paying
court to him. For the rest, the praises dragged out of me from time
to time ought not to gratify those who are the objects of them. The
violence which I do to myself in commending certain works is such
that the truth betrays itself in my sentences in the same way as, in a
hydraulic press, the water oozes out through the pores of the metal.

Balzac in various parts of his admirable *Comédie Humaine* has
said many excellent things upon contemporary criticism, but in showing
up the mistakes and injuries of those who carry on the business, he has
not, as it seems to me, sufficiently brought out the merit of those who
preserve their integrity. Nor does he appreciate their secret miseries.
Even in his *Monographie de la Presse,* notwithstanding the help he
got from his friend Laurent-Jan (also a friend of mine, and one of the
most penetrating minds I know), Balzac has not thrown light on all
the bearings of the question. Laurent-Jan has written in several newspapers, but not regularly, and more as a humorist than a critic, and
neither he nor Balzac could know or see everything.

*　　*　　*　　*　　*　　*　　*

One day M. Armand Bertin — the son of the elder Bertin — who
was much concerned at my embarrassed circumstances, greeted me
with these words, which pleased me all the more for being totally
unexpected:

" My dear friend, your position is now made. I have spoken to the Minister of the Interior, and he has decided that in spite of Cherubini's opposition you shall have a professorship of composition at the Conservatoire, with a salary of one thousand five hundred francs, and a pension of four thousand five hundred francs from the fund at his disposal for the encouragement of the Fine Arts. With six thousand francs a year you will be free from all anxiety, and able to devote yourself without restraint to composition."

The next evening I happened to be in the lobby at the Opéra, when M. X——, whose feeling toward me is no secret, and who was head of the Fine Arts Department at the Ministry, caught sight of me, and, coming forward with studied cordiality, repeated what M. Armand Bertin had said in much the same words. I thanked him, and begged him to bear witness to the Minister of my intense grati‧ tude. This spontaneous promise to one who had asked for nothing was no better kept than all the others, *and from that time forth I never heard a word more about it.*

CHAPTER XLVIII

MDLLE. BERTIN'S "ESMERALDA"—REHEARSALS OF "BENVENUTO CELLINI"—ITS GLARING FAILURE —THE "CARNAVAL ROMAIN" OVERTURE—HABE-NECK—DUPREZ—LEGOUVÉ

THE only thing I did obtain, and that always in spite of Cherubini, was the place of librarian at the Conservatoire,[1] which I have still, and the salary of which is one hundred and eighteen francs a month. Afterwards, when I was in England, after the proclamation of the Republic, certain worthy patriots whom the place suited thought fit to ask for it, on the ground that it was not proper to leave it with a man who was so often absent. On my return from London accordingly I heard that I was to be deprived of it. Fortunately Victor Hugo, at that time a representative of the people, enjoyed a certain amount of authority in the Chamber, in spite of his genius; and he interfered to preserve me my modest situation.

---

[1] February 9th, 1839. The nominal librarian was Bottée de Toulmon, but he drew no salary. This went to Berlioz, the sub-librarian; his official title was "Conservateur Adjoint à la Bibliothèque du Conservatoire."

It was about the same time that M. Charles Blanc occupied the post of Director of the Fine Arts — a sincere and learned friend to art, and brother to the celebrated Socialist. On several occasions he rendered me services, with a warmth and eagerness I shall not forget.

Here is an example of the pitiless hatred that always besets men of the Press, whether literary or political, the effects of which they are sure to feel from the moment they happen to give the least occasion for it.

Mademoiselle Louise Bertin, the daughter of the proprietor of the *Journal des Débats,* and sister of its chief editor, has been remarkably successful both in literature and music. She is one of the ablest women of our time. Her musical talent, to my mind, is rather rational than emotional; but it is a real talent notwithstanding, and, in spite of a certain want of decision, and of the occasionally childish form of her melodies, her opera of *Esmeralda,*[1] to Victor Hugo's words, is of great interest, and certainly contains very fine passages. As Mdlle. Bertin could not herself direct the study of her opera at the theatre, her father commissioned me to do so, and very generously indemnified me for my loss of time. The principal parts — Phœbus, Frollo, Esmeralda, and Quasimodo — were taken by Nourrit, Levasseur, Mdlle. Falcon, and Massol — in other words, by the best singers and actors at the Opéra.

Several pieces — among others the great duet between the Priest and the Gipsy in the second act, a romance, and the very characteristic aria of Quasimodo — were warmly applauded at the general rehearsal. Nevertheless this work, by a woman who never wrote one word of criticism on any human being, good, bad, or indifferent, and whose sole crime consisted in her belonging to a family that owned a powerful journal, the political views of which were detested by a certain section of the community — this work, I say, so far superior to many that succeed daily, or are at any rate accepted, broke down utterly. It was received at the Opéra with unexampled hisses, groans, and cries. At the second attempt, indeed, they were obliged to drop the curtain in the middle of an act, and stop the performance.

Quasimodo's air, known as the *Air des Cloches,* was, however, applauded and encored by the whole house, and as its effect could neither be ignored nor disputed, some of the audience, more hostile

[1] See p. 179.

than the rest against the Bertins, were not ashamed to call out, " It is not by Mdlle. Bertin; it is by Berlioz."

I knew just as much of it as I did of the rest of the score, and I swear upon my honour that not a note of it is mine. But the cabal against the composer was too furious not to take every possible advantage of the pretext offered by my share in the rehearsal of the work, and the *Air des Cloches* continued to be ascribed to me.

This incident showed me what I might expect from such personal enemies as I had made by my criticisms in the *Journal des Débats* and elsewhere, if I should ever appear myself on the boards of the Opéra, where so many acts of cowardly revenge are perpetrated with impunity. My own failure came at last. I had been greatly struck with certain episodes in the life of Benvenuto Cellini, and was so unlucky as to think they offered an interesting and dramatic subject for an opera. So I begged Léon de Wailly and Auguste Barbier — the terrible poet of the *Iambes* — to make me a libretto on the subject.

To believe even our common friends, their libretto did not contain the elements essential to what is called a well-made play. I liked it, however, and I still do not see that it is inferior to many that are performed every day. Duponchel was then Director of the Opéra. He looked upon me as a kind of lunatic, whose music could be nothing but a tissue of extravagances. Still, in order to *please the Journal des Débats,* he consented to hear a reading of the libretto of *Benvenuto,* and appeared to like it. He afterwards went about everywhere, saying that he was getting up this opera not for the sake of the music, which he knew must be absurd, but because of the book, which he thought charming.

He accordingly put it into rehearsal; and never shall I forget the tortures I endured for the three months devoted to it. The indifference and obvious distaste with which most of the actors attended the rehearsals, as if convinced beforehand that it would be a failure, Habeneck's ill-temper, the under-hand rumours circulated in the theatre, the stupid remarks of all these illiterate people about a libretto differing so much in style from the dull rhyming prose of Scribe's school — all this revealed to me a universal hostility against which I was powerless, and of which I had to pretend not to be aware.

Auguste Barbier might perhaps here and there, in the recitatives, have let slip an abusive term belonging to a vocabulary inconsistent with our present prudishness; but it will hardly be believed that the

following words, in a duet written by L. de Wailly, were thought
coarse by most of the singers:

> Quand je repris l'usage de mes sens,
> Les toits luisaient aux blancheurs de l'aurore,
> Les coqs chantaient, etc., etc.

" Oh, the cocks! " said they; " oh, oh, the cocks! Why not the
hens? " etc., etc.

What could be said in reply to such foolery? When we came to
the orchestral rehearsals, the musicians, seeing Habeneck's sulky air,
treated me with the most distant reserve. They did their duty, however, but Habeneck did not do his. He never could catch the lively
turn of the saltarello danced and sung on the Piazza Colonna in the
middle of the second act. The dancers, not being able to adapt themselves to his dragging time, complained to me, and I kept on repeating, " Faster, faster! Put more life into it! " Habeneck struck the
desk in irritation, and broke one violin bow after another. Having
witnessed four or five of such outbursts, I ended at last by saying,
with a coolness that exasperated him:

" Good heavens! if you were to break fifty bows, that would not
prevent your time from being too slow by half. It is a saltarello that
you are conducting! "

At that Habeneck stopped, and, turning to the orchestra, said:

" Since I am not fortunate enough to please M. Berlioz, we will
leave off for to-day. You can go."

And there the rehearsal ended.[1]

Some years afterwards, when I had written the *Carnaval Romain*
overture, in which the theme of the allegro is this same saltarello,
Habeneck happened to be in the green-room of the Herz concert-hall
the evening that this overture was to be played for the first time. He
had heard that we had rehearsed it in the morning without the wind
instruments, part of the band having been called off for the National
Guard. " Good! " said he to himself. " There will certainly be a
catastrophe at his concert this evening. I must be there." On my arrival, indeed, I was surrounded on the orchestra by all the wind
players, who were in terror at the idea of having to play an overture
of which they did not know a note.

---

[1] In France, authors *are not allowed* to direct their own works in the theatres, and therefore
I could not conduct the rehearsals of *Cellini* myself. [B.]

" Don't be afraid," I said. " The parts are correct; you all know your jobs; watch my baton as often as you can, count your bars correctly, and it will be all right."

Not a single mistake occurred. I launched the allegro in the whirlwind time of the Transteverine dancers. The public cried *" Bis! "* We played the overture over again; it was even better done the second time. And as I passed back through the green-room, where Habeneck stood looking a little disappointed, I just flung these few words at him: " That is how it *ought* to go! " to which he took care to make no reply.

Never did I feel more keenly the delight of being able to direct the performance of my music myself; and the thought of what Habeneck had made me endure only enhanced my pleasure. Unhappy composers! learn how to conduct, and how to conduct yourselves well (with or without a pun), for do not forget that the most dangerous of your interpreters is the conductor himself.

To return to *Benvenuto.*

In spite of the prudent reserve maintained by the orchestra in accordance with their conductor's secret hostility towards me, the musicians at the close of the last rehearsals applauded several of the pieces, and some even declared my work to be one of the most original they had ever heard. This came to the ears of Duponchel; and one evening I heard him say: " Did anyone ever know such a sudden change of opinion? They now think Berlioz's music delightful, and these fools of musicians are lauding it up to the skies." Several of them, however, were far from such partisanship. One evening, in the finale of the second act, two were detected playing the air, *J'ai du bon tabac,* instead of their own part, in hopes of flattering Habeneck. These blackguardly tricks were matched on the stage. In this same finale, where the scene is darkened and represents a masked crowd at night in the Piazza Colonna, the male dancers amused themselves by pinching the women, making them shriek and shrieking themselves, to the great disturbance of the chorus. And when I sent for the manager to put an end to the scandal, Duponchel was not to be found, he never condescending to attend a rehearsal!

The opera at last arrived at performance.[1] The overture received

---

[1] It must not be forgotten that this was written in 1850. Since then the opera of *Benvenuto Cellini,* slightly modified as regards the poem, has been successfully put on the stage at Weimar, where it is often given under Liszt's direction. The score for voice and piano was also published

exaggerated applause, and the rest was hissed with admirable energy and unanimity. It was given three times, however, after which Duprez threw up the part of Benvenuto, and the work disappeared from the bills, not to reappear till long afterwards, when A. Dupont spent *five whole months* in studying the part, which he was frantic at not having received in the first instance.

Duprez was very good in any violent scene, such as the one in the sextet, when Cellini threatens to break up his statue; but his voice had already ceased to lend itself to soft airs, long-drawn notes, or calm, dreamy music. For instance, in the air, *Sur les monts les plus sauvages,* he could not sustain the high G at the end of the phrase, *Je chanterais gaîment;* and instead of holding the note for three bars as he should have done, only held it for a moment, and thus destroyed the effect. Madame Gras-Dorus and Madame Stoltz were charming as Teresa and Ascanio, which they had learnt carefully and with a very good grace. Madame Stoltz, indeed, was so much noticed in her rondo in the second act, *Mais qu'ai-je donc?* that that part may be considered as the starting-point for her ultimate high position at the Opéra, from which she was so rudely degraded.

It is fourteen years [1] since I was thus dragged to execution at the Opéra; and on re-reading my poor score with strict impartiality, I cannot help recognising in it a variety of ideas, an impetuous verve, and a brilliancy of musical colouring which I shall probably never again achieve, and which deserved a better fate.

Benvenuto took me a long time to write, and but for the help of a friend I should never have been able to finish it in time. In order to write an opera one must be free from all other work, that is to say, one must have a fixed livelihood for some time, more or less. Well, I was very far indeed from being thus circumstanced. I was living from hand to mouth by the articles I wrote for the newspapers, and which took up nearly all my time. I did, indeed, try to devote two months to my score in the first access of the fever into which it put me; but stern necessity soon tore the composer's pen from my hand, to replace it by that of the critic. It was an indescribable disappointment. But hesitation was out of the question. Could I leave my wife and child in want

with German and French words by Mayer at Brunswick in 1858. It was even published in Paris, by Choudens, in 1865. [B.]

    [1] First performance, September 10th, 1838; second, September 12th; third, September 14th; fourth and last, January 11th, 1839.

of the necessaries of life? In the profound state of melancholy into which I had fallen, equally racked by want and by the musical ideas I was compelled to forego, I had not courage even to fulfil my usual hated task of scribbling.

I was in the deepest depression when I received a visit from Ernest Legouvé. " Whereabouts are you in your opera? " said he.

" I have not finished the first act yet. I cannot find time to work at it."

" But if you had the time? "

" Then, by Jove, I should work from morning till night."

" What do you require to be free? "

" Two thousand francs — which I have not got."

" And if somebody? — if they were? — Come, help me out! "

" With what? What do you mean? "

" Well, if one of your friends were to lend them to you? "

" Of what friend could I ask such a sum? "

"You need not ask. I offer it to you."

My joy may be imagined. Legouvé did, in fact, lend me the two thousand francs next day, and, thanks to that, I was able to finish *Benvenuto*. Noble heart! dear, good fellow! Himself a distinguished writer and artist, he had divined my misery, and, with exquisite delicacy, feared to wound me by proposing to put an end to it. Artists alone can thus understand each other. And I have been happy enough to meet several who have come to my aid in like manner.

CHAPTER XLIX

CONCERT OF DECEMBER 16, 1838 — PAGANINI'S
LETTER AND PRESENT — MY WIFE'S RELIGIOUS
FERVOUR — FURY, CONGRATULATIONS, AND
SCANDALS — MY VISIT TO PAGANINI — HIS
DEPARTURE — I WRITE ''ROMEO AND
JULIET''— CRITICISMS ON
THE WORK

PAGANINI had returned from Sardinia when *Benvenuto* was massacred at the Opéra. He was present at that horrible performance, and indeed went away heart-broken, saying, " If I were manager of the Opéra, I would at once engage that young man to write me three such operas; I would pay him in advance, and should make a capital bargain by it."

The failure of the work, and the effort of restraining my rage during the interminable rehearsals, brought on an attack of bronchitis that forced me to keep my bed and do nothing. Still, we had to live; and, making up my mind to an indispensable effort, I gave two concerts at the Conservatoire. The first [1] barely paid its expenses. To increase the receipts of the second I announced both my symphonies, the *Fantastique* and *Harold,* in the programme, and in spite of my bad health and obstinate bronchitis, I was able to conduct them on the 16th of December, 1838.

Paganini was present; and I will now give the history of the famous occurrence of which so many contradictory versions exist, and about which so many unkind stories have been circulated.

As I have already said, I composed *Harold* at the instigation of Paganini. Though performed several times during his absence, it had not figured at any of my concerts since his return; he therefore was not acquainted with it, and heard it that day for the first time.

The concert was just over; I was in a profuse perspiration, and trembling with exhaustion, when Paganini, followed by his son Achilles, came up to me at the orchestra door, gesticulating violently. Owing to the throat affection of which he ultimately died, he had already completely lost his voice, and unless everything was perfectly quiet, no one but his son could hear or even guess what he was saying. He made a sign to the child, who got up on a chair, put his ear close to his father's mouth, and listened attentively.

Achilles then got down, and, turning to me, said, "My father desires me to assure you, sir, that he has never in his life been so powerfully impressed at a concert; that your music has quite upset him, and that if he did not restrain himself he should go down on his knees to thank you for it." I made a movement of incredulous embarrassment at these strange words, but Paganini, seizing my arm, and rattling out, "Yes, yes!" with the little voice he had left, dragged me up on the stage, where there were still a good many of the performers, knelt down, and kissed my hand. I need not describe my stupefaction; I relate the facts, that is all.

---

[1] November 25th, 1838. Berlioz was too ill to leave his bed: Habeneck conducted the concert for him.

On going out into the bitter cold in this state of white heat, I met M. Armand Bertin on the boulevard. There I remained for some time, describing the scene that had just occurred, caught a chill, went home, and took to my bed, more ill than before.

The next day [1] I was alone in my room, when little Achilles entered, and said, " My father will be very sorry to hear that you are still ill; and if he were not so unwell himself, he would have come to see you. Here is a letter he desired me to give you." I would have broken the seal, but the child stopped me, and saying, " There is no answer; my father said you would read it when you were alone," hastily left the room.

I supposed it to be a letter of congratulations and compliments, and, opening it, read as follows:

" Mɪᴏ ᴄᴀʀᴏ Aᴍɪᴄᴏ,
" Beethoven spento non c'era che Berlioz che potesse farlo rivivere; ed io che ho gustato le vostre divine composizioni degne d'un genio qual siete, credo mio dovere di pregarvi à voler accettare, in segno del mio omaggio, venti mila franchi, i quali vi saranno rimessi dal Signor Baron de Rothschild dopo che gli avrete presentato l'acclusa. Credetemi sempre il vostro affezionatissimo amico,
           " Nɪᴄᴏʟò Pᴀɢᴀɴɪɴɪ.[2]
"Parigi, 18 Dicembre, 1838."

I know enough of Italian to understand a letter like this. The unexpected nature of its contents, however, surprised me so much that I became quite confused in my ideas, and forgot what I was doing. But a note addressed to M. de Rothschild was enclosed, and, without a thought that I was committing an indiscretion, I quickly opened it, and read these few words in French:

" Sɪʀ,
" Be so good as to remit to M. Berlioz the sum of twenty thousand francs which I left with you yesterday.
           " Yours, etc., Pᴀɢᴀɴɪɴɪ."

---

[1] This should be two days afterwards, as is evident from the date of Paganini's letter. [H.]

[2] My ᴅᴇᴀʀ Fʀɪᴇɴᴅ, — Beethoven is dead, and Berlioz alone can revive him. I have heard your divine compositions, so worthy of your genius, and beg you to accept, in token of my homage, twenty thousand francs, which will be handed to you by the Baron de Rothschild on presentation of the enclosed. — Your most affectionate friend, Nɪᴄᴏʟò Pᴀɢᴀɴɪɴɪ. — Paris, December 18, 1838. [H.]

Then only did the truth dawn on me, and I must evidently have grown quite pale, for my wife coming in at that moment, and finding me with a letter in my hand and a discomposed face, exclaimed, " What's the matter now ? Some new misfortune ? Courage ! we have endured as much before."

" No, no; quite the contrary."

" What, then ? "

" Paganini."

" Well, what of him ? "

" He has sent me — twenty thousand francs."

" Louis ! Louis ! " cried Henrietta, rushing distractedly in search of my son, who was playing in the next room, " Come here ! come with your mother; come and thank God for what He has done for your father." And my wife and child ran back together, and fell on their knees beside my bed, the mother praying, the child in astonishment joining his little hands beside her. O Paganini ! what a sight ! . . . Would that he could have seen it ! . . .

My first impulse, as may well be imagined, was to answer his letter, since it was impossible for me to leave the house. My reply has always seemed to me so inadequate and so far from what I really felt, that I dare not reproduce it.[1] Some situations and feelings are quite overwhelming !

Paganini's noble action soon became known in Paris, and for the next two days my room was the rendezvous of numerous artists, all eager to see the famous letter, and learn the particulars of so strange an event. All congratulated me; one, indeed, showed a certain jealousy, not of me, but of Paganini. " I am not rich," he said, " or

---

[1] It ran thus:

                                                                    "18 Dec. 1838.
    "Great and worthy artist:
        "How can I express my gratitude? I am not rich; but, believe me, the approbation of a man of such genius as yours touches me a thousand times more deeply than the royal generosity of your gift.
        "Words fail me; I will hasten to embrace you as soon as I can leave my bed, to which I am still confined today.
                                                                    "H. Berlioz."
    It was said at the time that Paganini, who had been roundly abused in the Paris Press for his avarice, made his gift to Berlioz merely to placate the journalists, knowing that if the campaign against him ceased he could easily make up the sum by a few concerts. Other people asserted that Paganini was merely an intermediary in the matter, the real donor being some benefactor — perhaps Bertin — who preferred to remain anonymous. This latter legend was contradicted by the violinist's son in 1854, and again in 1856. In the absence of anything like evidence to the contrary, we may as well take the simple course of believing that the gift was Paganini's own, wrung from him by admiration of Berlioz's genius.

I would willingly have done as much." He was a violinist; and it is the only example I know of a spirit of honourable envy. Afterwards came out all the remarks, detractions, anger, and falsehoods of my enemies, the transports of delight and triumph of my friends, the letter I received from Jules Janin, his splendid article in the *Journal des Débats,* the abusive language with which I was honoured by certain low wretches, the scandalous insinuations against Paganini, the letting loose and the clashing of a score of good and evil passions.

In the midst of all this agitation and impetuous feeling, I was boiling over with impatience at not being able to leave my bed. At last, at the end of the sixth day, I felt a little better, and, unable longer to contain myself, I dressed, and ran off to the Néothermes, Rue de la Victoire, where Paganini was then living. They told me he was alone in the billiard-room. I went in, and we embraced without a word. After some minutes, as I was stammering out I know not what in the way of thanks, Paganini — whom I was able to understand in the empty room — cut me short with these words:

"Don't speak of that. No, not another word. It is the greatest pleasure I have ever felt in my life. You will never know how your music affected me; it is many years since I had felt anything like it. . . . Ah! now," added he, as he brought down his fist on the billiard-table with a violent blow, "none of the people who cabal against you will dare to say another word, for they know that I am a good judge, and that *I am not easy* " (*Je ne suis pas aisé*).

What did he mean by that? Did he mean, "I am not easily moved by music," or "I don't give my money easily," or "I am not in easy circumstances "?

The sardonic tone in which he uttered the expression makes the last interpretation unacceptable to my mind. Be that as it might, however, the great artist was mistaken. His authority, powerful as it was, could not silence the fools and the knaves. He did not know the Parisian rabble, which only bayed at my heels all the more soon after. A naturalist has said that certain dogs aspire to the state of man: I think far more men aspire to the state of dog!

Having discharged my debts, and finding myself still in possession of a considerable sum, my one idea was to spend it in the way of music. "I must," I said to myself, "leave off all other work, and write a masterpiece, on a grand new plan, a splendid work, full of passion and imagination, and worthy to be dedicated to the illustrious artist to whom I owe so much."

Whilst I was meditating this plan, Paganini's health became so much worse that he was again obliged to go off to Marseilles and then to Nice, whence, alas! he never returned. I wrote him several times about subjects for the grand composition I was meditating, of which I had spoken to him; but his answer was, " I can give you no advice about it. You know what will suit you better than anyone else."

At last, after much indecision, I hit upon the idea of a symphony, with choruses, vocal solos, and choral recitatives, on the sublime and ever-novel theme of Shakespeare's *Romeo and Juliet.* I wrote in prose all the text intended for the vocal pieces which come between the instrumental sections. Émile Deschamps, with his usual delightful good-nature and marvellous facility, set it to verse for me, and I began.

No more feuilletons now! or at least, hardly any. Paganini had given me money that I might write music, and write it I did. I worked for seven months at my symphony, not leaving off for more than three or four days out of every thirty on any pretence whatsoever.[1]

And during all that time how ardently did I live! How vigorously I struck out in that grand sea of poetry caressed by the playful breeze of fancy, beneath the hot rays of that sun of love which Shakespeare kindled, always confident of my power to reach the marvellous island where stands the temple of true art. Whether I succeeded or not it is not for me to decide.

The work, such as it then was, was performed three times [2] running at the Conservatoire under my own direction, apparently with great success. I felt at once, however, that I should have to improve it a great deal, and set myself to study it seriously under all its aspects. To my keen regret, Paganini never either heard or read it. I was always hoping for his return to Paris; and besides, I was waiting to send him the symphony until it was entirely finished off and printed. In the meantime he died at Nice,[3] and to the grief I felt at his death was added that of not knowing whether he would have approved the work undertaken chiefly to please him, and justify him to himself

---

[1] The composition occupied him from January 20th to September 8th, 1839.
On April 2nd his sister Adèle married a notary, Marc Suat. On May 10th Berlioz received the Cross of the Legion of Honour.
[2] November 24th and December 1st and 15th, 1839.
[3] May 27th, 1840.

for what he had done to its author. He also seemed much to regret not having heard the work, as he told me in his letter from Nice, dated January 7, 1840, in which he says, "*Now that all is done, envy cannot but be silent.*"

Poor dear great friend! Happily for him, he never read the horrible nonsense in many of the Paris newspapers about the plan of the work, the introduction, the adagio, Queen Mab, and the allocution of Father Laurence. One regarded it as an extravagance on my part to have attempted this new form of symphony; another could find nothing in the scherzo of Queen Mab but a little grotesque noise like that of *an ill-greased syringe.* A third, speaking of the love-scene — the adagio, the part that three-fourths of the European musicians who know it now rank above all I have written — asserted that *I had not understood Shakespeare!* Toad, swollen with imbecility! if you could prove that to me!

No unlooked-for criticisms ever wounded me more cruelly; and, as usual, none of these aristarchs writing in praise or blame of my work pointed out to me one of its real defects. They left me to discover them in succession, and correct them for myself. M. Frankoski, Ernst's secretary, remarked to me in Vienna on the abrupt ending to the Queen Mab scherzo, and I therefore wrote its present coda, and destroyed the former one. I think it was by the advice of M. d'Ortigue that an important cut was made in the solo of Father Laurence, which suffered from the exaggerated length of the verses supplied by the poet. All the other modifications, additions, and suppressions I made of my own accord, by dint of studying the work, both as a whole and in detail, as I heard it in Paris, Berlin, Vienna, and Prague. If I have struck out no more blemishes, at least I have looked for them in all good faith, and applied such sagacity as I possess to their discovery.

After that, what is left to an author but to avow frankly that he cannot do better, and resign himself to the imperfection of his work? When I had come to that, and not till then, was the symphony of *Romeo and Juliet* published.

As regards execution, it presents immense difficulties of all sorts inherent to its form and style, and only to be overcome by long, patient, and *well-directed* study. To interpret it properly the artists — conductor, singers, and orchestra — must all be first-rate, and prepared to study it as a new opera is studied in good lyrical theatres, that is to say, very nearly as though it were to be played by heart.

It will never, therefore, be played in London, where the necessary rehearsals are not to be had. In that country, musicians have no time to make music.[1]

CHAPTER L

ORDER FROM M. DE RÉMUSAT TO WRITE THE "SYM-
PHONIE FUNÈBRE ET TRIOMPHALE"—ITS PER-
FORMANCE—POPULARITY IN PARIS—HABE-
NECK'S MOT—SPONTINI'S EPITHET FOR THE
WORK—HIS MISTAKE ABOUT THE
"REQUIEM"

IN 1840, as the month of July drew near, the French Government was desirous of celebrating the tenth anniversary of the Revolution of 1830 by a grand ceremonial, and by the translation of the more or less heroic relics of the Three Days to the monument lately erected to their memory in the Place de la Bastille. M. de Rémusat, at that time Minister of the Interior, was, most fortunately, like M. de Gasparin, a friend to music. It was his idea that I should write a symphony for the ceremonial, the form and mode of performance being left entirely to my own choice. For this work the sum of ten thousand francs was guaranteed me, out of which I was to pay the expenses of copying and performance.

I thought that the simplest plan would be best for such a work, and that a large body of wind instruments would alone be suitable for a symphony which was — at least on the first occasion — to be heard in the open air. I wished in the first place to recall the famous Three Days' conflict amid the mournful accents of a solemn march accompanying the procession; to follow this by a sort of funeral oration, or farewell address to the illustrious dead, while the bodies were being lowered into the tomb; and finally to sing a hymn of praise as an apotheosis, when, after the sealing of the tomb, the attention should be concentrated on the column alone, surmounted by the figure of Liberty, with her wings outstretched to heaven, like the souls of those who had died for her.

Scarcely had I finished the funeral march when it was rumoured

---

[1] Since the above was written, the first four parts of *Romeo and Juliet* were played under my direction in London, and never received a more brilliant ovation from any public. [B.]

that the July ceremonies were not to take place. " Good! " said I to myself; " here is the counterpart of the *Requiem* business. I know the people I have to deal with, and will go no further." And I stopped short accordingly. But a few days after, as I was strolling about Paris, I came across M. de Rémusat. On catching sight of me he stopped his carriage, and made me a sign to speak to him. He wanted to know how far I had proceeded with the symphony. I bluntly told him my reason for having suspended my work, adding that I well remembered my torments over Marshal Damrémont's ceremony and the *Requiem*.

" But the rumour that has alarmed you is entirely false," he answered. " Nothing has been changed; the inauguration of the column and the translation of the relics are all to take place, and I reckon upon you. Finish your work as quickly as possible."

This assertion relieved my anxiety, although my mistrust had been but too well founded, and I at once set to work again. When I had finished the march and the funeral oration, and found a theme for the apotheosis, I was delayed for some time by the fanfare, which I wished to bring up by degrees from the very depths of the orchestra to the high note where the apotheosis breaks in. I don't know how many I wrote, but I liked none of them. Either they were too common, or too narrow in form, or not sufficiently solemn, or wanting in sonority, or badly graded. What I imagined was a sound like the trump of archangels, simple but noble, ascending radiant and triumphant and grandly resonant, as it announced to earth and heaven the opening of

the empyrean gates. Finally I decided, not without some trepidation, on the one now in the score; and the rest was soon written. Later on, after my usual corrections and re-touchings, I added a stringed orchestra and a chorus to the symphony, which greatly improves the effect, though neither of them is indispensable. I engaged a military band of two hundred for the ceremony. Habeneck would willingly have conducted again, but I had not forgotten the snuff-box trick, and wisely reserved that task to myself.

I had the happy idea of inviting a large audience to the final rehearsal of the symphony, for no one could have judged of it on the day of the ceremony. Notwithstanding the power of the orchestra, it was scarcely heard at all during the procession.[1] With the exception of what was played as we went along the Boulevard Poissonnière, where the big trees — still standing — served as a kind of reflector for the sound, all the rest was lost. On the Place de la Bastille it was still worse; scarcely anything could be distinguished even ten paces off.

As a finishing stroke, the National Guard, impatient at having to stand so long under arms in the blazing sun, began to march off to the sound of fifty drums, which continued to beat relentlessly throughout the whole of the apotheosis, so that not one note of it could be heard. Music is always thus respected in France at all fêtes or public rejoicings, where they think it ought to figure . . . to the eye.

But I knew this, and the general rehearsal in the Salle Vivienne was my real performance. Such was its effect that the man who managed the concerts there engaged me for four evenings; the new symphony had the place of honour each time,[2] and the receipts were considerable.

On coming out from one of these performances, Habeneck — with whom for some reason or other I had had a fresh quarrel — was heard to say, " Decidedly that beast of a fellow has some grand ideas." A week later he probably said just the contrary.

This time I had no crow to pluck with the Ministry. M. de Rémusat behaved like a gentleman, and promptly sent me the ten thousand francs. When the expenses of the orchestra and copyists were paid, I had two thousand eight hundred francs left for myself. Little enough certainly, but the Minister was pleased; and at each performance of my new work the public seemed to appreciate it beyond any

---

[1] July 28th, 1840.
[2] Four concerts may have been planned, but only two were given — on August 7th and 14th.

of its predecessors, and indeed praised it extravagantly. One evening, at the Salle Vivienne, after the apotheosis some young fellows took it into their heads to smash the chairs against the floor, with shouts of applause. The proprietor immediately gave orders that for the future this novel method of applauding was to be checked. Spontini wrote me a long and curious letter on the subject of this symphony, when it was performed some time afterwards at the Conservatoire with the two orchestras, but without the chorus. I was stupid enough to give it to a collector of autographs, and much regret that I cannot produce a copy here. I only know that it began somewhat as follows: " *Whilst still under the impression of your thrilling music,*" etc., etc.

Notwithstanding our friendship, this was the only time he ever praised any of my compositions. He always came to hear them, but never spoke of them to me. I am wrong! He did so once more, after a great performance of my *Requiem* at St. Eustache. He said to me that day: "You were wrong to blame the Institut for sending its prizemen to Rome; you never could have composed that *Requiem* unless you had seen Michael Angelo's *Last Judgment.*"

In this he was strangely mistaken, for the only effect produced on me by that celebrated fresco in the Sistine Chapel was that of utter disappointment. To me it is a scene of infernal tortures rather than the last great gathering of all mankind. But I know nothing of painting, and am not susceptible to conventional beauty.

CHAPTER LI

BRUSSELS—MY DOMESTIC STORMS—THE BELGIANS—
ZANI DE FERRANTI—FÉTIS—HIS SERIOUS BLUN-
DER—A FESTIVAL AT THE PARIS OPÉRA—
HABENECK'S CONSPIRACY FOILED—
FRACAS IN M. DE GIRARDIN'S BOX
—HOW TO MAKE A FORTUNE—
START FOR GERMANY

I T was towards the end of this year (1840) [1] that I made my first musical excursion out of France; in other words, began giving concerts in foreign parts. M. Snel, of Brussels, having proposed to perform

[1] Berlioz is in error: he did not go to Brussels until September 1842.

some of my works in the concert-room of the Society of La Grande Harmonie, of which he was the head, I determined to make the experiment.

But in order to manage this I had to have recourse to a regular *coup d'état* in my own home. On one pretext or another, my wife had always been opposed to my travelling, and had I listened to her I should never have left Paris to this hour. A mad, and for some time an absolutely groundless, jealousy was at the bottom of her opposition.[1] In order, therefore, to carry out my plan, I was obliged to keep it secret, have my portmanteau and packages of music cunningly conveyed out of the house, and go off suddenly, leaving a letter to explain my departure. But I did not go alone. I had a travelling companion, who always accompanied me from that time forth on my various expeditions. By dint of having been unjustly accused and tortured in a thousand ways, and finding neither peace nor repose at home, I luckily ended by reaping the benefits of a position of which I had hitherto had only the burden, and my life was completely changed.

To cut short the story of this part of my life, and not to enter upon very sad details, I will only say that from that day forth, and after many heart-rending scenes, my wife and I were amicably separated. I often see her; my affection for her has been in no way diminished; her bad health only endears her the more to me. This must suffice to

[1] The main source of what information we possess as to the gradual change that came over the Berlioz-Smithson ménage is Ernest Legouvé, who was intimately associated with the composer during those fatal years. After having described, in his *Soixante Ans de Souvenirs*, how the marriage opened with meridional ardours on Hector's part and coy northern reserve on Harriet's, followed by a rather exacting passion on her side just when his own flame was beginning to die down, the Smithson thermometer, as Legouvé says, rising in proportion as the Berlioz thermometer sank, he shows how jealousy took more and more complete possession of the blonde Irishwoman, who was some years older than her husband, was becoming stouter with the years, was embittered by her failure in the theatre, and was latterly taking to drink for solace. "Berlioz's sentiments changed to a correct and calm good-fellowship; while his wife became imperious in her exigencies and indulged in violent recriminations that were unfortunately justified. Berlioz, whose position as critic and as composer producing his own works made the theatre his real world, found there occasions for lapses that would have proved too much for stronger heads than his; moreover, his reputation as a misunderstood great artist endowed him with a halo that easily tempted his female interpreters to become his consolers. Madame Berlioz searched his feuilletons for hints of his infidelities. And not only there: fragments of intercepted letters, drawers indiscreetly opened, brought her revelations just sufficient to make her beside herself without doing more than half illuminate her. Her jealousy was always outdistanced by the facts. Berlioz's heart went so fast that she could not keep pace with it; when, after much research, she lighted upon some object of his passion, that particular passion was no more; and then, it being easy for him to prove his innocence at the moment, the poor woman was as abashed as a dog which, after having followed a track for half an hour, arrives at the lair only to find the quarry has gone."

explain my subsequent conduct to such persons as have only known me since then, for, I repeat, I am not writing confessions.

I gave two concerts at Brussels,[1] one in the concert-room of the Grande Harmonie, the other in the Church of the Augustines, where Catholic worship has long been abandoned. There is an extraordinary echo in both of them, so much so that, even when but slightly fast, strongly scored music becomes necessarily confused in sound. Only slow and soft pieces, especially in the former room, are unaffected by the echo of the place and preserve their original effect.

Opinions differed as widely about my music in Brussels as in Paris. I was told that a curious discussion took place between M. Fétis (always hostile to me)[2] and another critic, M. Zani de Ferranti, an artist and a remarkable writer, who had declared himself my champion. The latter cited the *Pilgrims' March* in *Harold* as one of the most interesting things he had ever heard. To this Fétis replied, "How can I be expected to approve of a piece in which you constantly hear *two notes out of harmony?*" (He meant the two notes C and B, recurring at the end of each strophe, and imitating bells.)

"Upon my word," answered de Ferranti, "I don't believe in such an anomaly. But if a musician is capable of composing a piece like that, and of charming me throughout by two notes out of harmony, I say that he is not a man, but a god."

"Alas!" I might have answered the enthusiastic Italian, "I am but a simple man, and M. Fétis is but a poor musician, for the two famous notes are really always in harmony. M. Fétis has not noticed that, thanks to their intervening in the chord, the various tonalities terminating the different sections of the march are resolved back into the principal key, and that from a purely musical point of view this very fact constitutes the novelty of the march, and no true musician could be mistaken about it for a moment."

When I heard of this curious misunderstanding I was tempted to point out Fétis's blunder in some newspaper; then I thought better of

[1] September 26th and October 9th, 1842.
[2] Berlioz forgets to mention that in spite of Berlioz's public attack on him in *Lélio*, at the Paris concert of September 9th, 1832, Fétis placed at his disposal the students and the orchestral material of the Brussels Conservatoire, of which he was the Director. Berlioz had an orchestra of 200. Ernst, who played some violin pieces and the viola solo in the *Pilgrims' March* in *Harold* at the first concert, told Liszt, in a letter of October 4th, that while the players were enthusiastic over Berlioz's music at rehearsal, the composer "was not so fortunate at the concert itself, for which the performances, which were anything but irreproachable, were no doubt responsible."

it, and followed my own system — a good one, I believe — of never
answering any criticism, no matter how absurd. When the score of
Harold was published, some years later, M. Fétis could see for himself that the two notes were always in harmony.

This journey was only an experiment. I was planning a visit to
Germany, to last five or six months. I therefore returned to Paris [1] to
make preparations, and give a colossal farewell concert to the Parisians that I had long been meditating.

M. Pillet, then manager of the Opéra, warmly welcomed my proposal of organising a festival [2] in the theatre. I accordingly applied
myself to the work, but allowed none of our plans to transpire. The
difficulty consisted in forestalling Habeneck's hostilities.

He could not fail to object to my directing such a musical solemnity
— the greatest yet seen in Paris — in a theatre where he was conductor. I therefore prepared in secret all the music for the programme
I had selected, and engaged musicians without telling them where the
concert was to take place; and when nothing was left but to unmask
my batteries, I went to M. Pillet and begged him to tell Habeneck that
I was entrusted with the management of the festival. He could not,
however, make up his mind to the annoyance of this step, and left it
to me, so great was his terror of Habeneck. I wrote myself, therefore,
to the awful conductor, informed him of the arrangements I had made
with M. Pillet, and added that, being in the habit of conducting my
own concerts, I trusted not to annoy him by doing so on this occasion.

He received my letter at the Opéra in the middle of a rehearsal,
read and re-read it, walked gloomily about the stage for some time;
then, making up his mind abruptly, went down to the manager's office,
and declared that the arrangement suited him very well, as he was
desirous of spending the day named for the concert in the country.
His vexation, however, was visible, and many of his orchestra soon
sympathised with it, hoping by this means to curry favour with him.
I had arranged with M. Pillet that this orchestra should work under
me, together with the extra musicians I had engaged.

The festival was to be for the benefit of the manager of the Opéra,
who only guaranteed me the sum of five hundred francs for my trouble,

---

[1] Berlioz is completely astray in his chronology. His "festival" at the Opéra took place
not on his return from Brussels in October 1842, but on November 1st, 1840, on which occasion
the programme was as stated in the present chapter.

[2] This word, which I employed on the handbills for the first time in Paris, has become the
commonplace title of the most grotesque exhibitions. We now have dancing or musical "festivals" in the smallest music-halls, with three violins, a drum, and two cornets-à-pistons. [B.]

and gave me *carte blanche* as to the organisation. Habeneck's musicians were bound in consequence to take part in this performance without remuneration. But I recollected the rascals at the Théâtre-Italien, and the trick they had once played me; indeed, my position with regard to the Opéra artists was at this time still more critical. Every evening I witnessed the cabals in the orchestra during the *entr'actes,* the universal agitation, the cold impassibility of Habeneck and his incensed body-guard, the furious glances cast at me, and the distribution of certain numbers of *Le Charivari,* in which I was well cut up. Accordingly, when the grand rehearsals were to begin, seeing the storm increasing, and hearing that some of Habeneck's fanatics had declared they would not march *without their old general,* I tried to induce M. Pillet to pay the Opéra musicians with the others. On his refusal I said to him, " I understand and approve of your motives for refusing; but in this case you are spoiling the performance of the concert. Consequently, I shall apply the five hundred francs you allot me to the payment of those Opéra musicians who do not refuse to help us."

" What! " said M. Pillet; "you will have nothing for yourself, after wearing yourself out with the work."

" That matters little; the chief thing is that it should go off properly. My five hundred francs will quiet the least mutinous; as for the others, pray do not force them into doing their duty, but let us leave them to *their old general."*

So it was arranged. I had a personnel of six hundred performers, choral and instrumental. The programme consisted of the first act of Gluck's *Iphigénie en Tauride,* a scene out of Handel's *Athalie,* the *Dies Irae* and the *Lacrymosa* from my *Requiem,* the apotheosis out of my *Symphonie funèbre et triomphale,* the adagio, scherzo, and finale from *Romeo and Juliet,* and an unaccompanied chorus of Palestrina's. I cannot imagine now how I succeeded in having such a difficult programme learnt so quickly (in one week only) by such a scratch pack of musicians. And yet I did manage it. I ran from the Opera-house to the Théâtre-Italien, where I had engaged the chorus only, from the Théâtre-Italien to the Opéra-Comique and the Conservatoire; here directing a choral practice, and there drilling part of the orchestra; seeing to everything myself, and trusting to no one else. In the foyer of the Opera-house I finally took both my instrumental bodies by turns, the strings rehearsing from eight in the morning till noon, and the wind instruments from noon till four o'clock. In this manner I was on my feet, baton in hand, the whole day. My throat was on fire, my voice nearly extinct, my right arm almost broken. I was ready to faint from thirst and weariness, when one of the chorus was kind enough to bring me a large tumbler of hot wine, and this enabled me to finish this awful rehearsal.

It had been rendered still harder, moreover, by fresh demands on the part of the Opéra musicians. These gentlemen, hearing that I was giving twenty francs to certain extra players, thought themselves entitled to interrupt me, one after the other, with a demand for a similar payment.

" It is not the money," said they; " but the Opéra artists ought not to get less than those at the second-rate theatres."

" Well, well, you shall have your twenty francs," I answered. " I guarantee them; but for God's sake do your work, and leave me alone."

The next day was the general rehearsal on the stage; it went fairly satisfactorily. Everything was quite passable with the exception of the Queen Mab scherzo, which I had imprudently included in the programme. This piece is too rapid and delicate to be played by a large orchestra. In such a case, and with so short a bar, it is nearly impossible to keep all the instruments together. They occupy too large a space; and those who are farthest from the conductor soon lag behind, since they are unable exactly to follow his rapid rhythm. Fretted as I was, it never entered my head to form a little picked orchestra, which I could have grouped round me in the middle of the stage, and so have easily carried out my purpose. Accordingly, after incredible trouble, we had to give up the scherzo and strike it out of the programme. It was on this occasion that I remarked how impossible it was to prevent the little cymbals in B flat and F from coming in late, when placed too far away from the conductor. I had stupidly put the players of these at the back of the stage, beside the kettledrums; and in spite of all my efforts they were sometimes a whole bar behindhand. Since then I have always taken care to have them beside me, and the difficulty has vanished.

The next day I was counting on a little rest, at least until the evening, when a friend [1] forewarned me of certain plots on the part of Habeneck's partisans for ruining my enterprise either wholly or partially. He wrote me word that they intended to slit the kettle-

[1] Léon Gatayes. [B.]

drums, grease the double-bass bows, and call for the *Marseillaise* in the middle of the concert.

This warning, as may be imagined, troubled my much needed repose. Instead of spending the day in bed, I began to wander about the approaches to the Opéra in a perfect fever of agitation. As I was thus panting up and down the boulevard, by good luck I came across Habeneck himself. I ran up and took him by the arm. "I have been warned," I said, "that your musicians are hatching a plot to ruin me this evening; but I have my eye on them."

" Oh," replied the good saint, " there is nothing to be afraid of. They won't do anything. I have made them listen to reason."

" Zounds! it is not I that need to be reassured, but rather you, for if anything were to happen, it would rebound pretty heavily upon you. But never mind; as you say, they won't do anything."

Still I was very anxious as the hour for the concert drew near. I had placed my copyist in the orchestra during the day to guard the kettle-drums and double-basses. Those instruments were intact. But this is what I feared. In the great pieces of the *Requiem,* the four little brass orchestras contain trumpets and cornets in different keys (in B flat, in F, and E flat). Well, it must be understood that the crook of a trumpet in F, for example, differs but slightly from that of a trumpet in E flat, and it is very easy to confuse them. Some treacherous brother might therefore hurl a trumpet passage in F into the *Tuba mirum* for me, instead of one in E flat, counting on excusing himself, after having produced an atrocious cacophony, by saying that he had mistaken the key.

Just before beginning the *Dies Iræ* I left my desk, and, going all round the orchestra, requested each trumpet and cornet player to show me his instrument. I thus reviewed them all, closely examining the inscriptions of the various keys, F, E flat, and B flat. When I came to the brothers Dauverné, Opéra musicians both of them, the elder made me blush by saying: " Oh, Berlioz, you don't trust us; that is not nice. We are honest men, and we are your friends." This reproach embarrassed me, though I might well be excused for having incurred it; and I pushed my inquiries no further.

My brave trumpeters made no mistakes, nothing was wanting in the performance, and the *Requiem* pieces had their proper effect.

Immediately after this part of the concert came an interval. It was during that moment's breathing space that Habeneck's followers thought to strike their blow in the easiest and least dangerous manner. Several voices were heard crying, "*The Marseillaise! The Marseillaise!*" hoping thus to carry away the public, and disturb the whole arrangement of the evening. A certain number of the spectators, charmed at the idea of hearing this celebrated air performed by such an orchestra and chorus, were already joining in the cry, when I went forward to the front of the stage, and said at the very top of my voice: "We will not play the *Marseillaise*. We are not here for that!" At which peace was at once restored.

It was not, however, to be of long duration. Another incident, of which I had had no warning, occurred almost immediately after, and still further excited the house. Cries of " Murder! Shame! Shame! Police!" proceeded from the first gallery, and created a perfect tumult among everyone present. Madame de Girardin, all dishevelled and agitated, was calling for help from her box. Her husband had just been struck at her side by Bergeron, one of the editors of *Le Charivari,* who was reputed to be the first assassin of Louis Philippe — the man whom public opinion had accused of having fired a pistol at the King some years before, on the Pont Royal. This fracas could not but spoil the rest of the concert, which, however, passed off without further interruption, though amidst a universal preoccupation.

Be that as it may, I had solved the problem and checkmated my enemies. The receipts amounted to eight thousand five hundred francs. As the sum I had devoted to pay the Opéra musicians was not sufficient, owing to my having promised them each twenty francs, I was obliged to give the cashier of the theatre three hundred and sixty francs, which he entered in his book with these words in red ink, "*Surplus given by M. Berlioz.*"

Thus, entirely unassisted, I succeeded in organizing the greatest concert yet given in Paris — Habeneck and his crew notwithstanding — by sacrificing the moderate sum allotted to me. The receipts, as I said, came to eight thousand five hundred francs, and my trouble cost me three hundred and sixty. Thus are fortunes made! I have often done the same in my life, and so I have made mine! . . . I never could comprehend how a gentleman like M. Pillet could have suffered it! Perhaps the cashier did not tell him of the circumstance.

A few days later [1] I went off to Germany. In the letters which I addressed on my return to several of my friends (and even to two [2]

---

[1] See note on p. 243.   [2] Habeneck and Girard. [B.]

who cannot claim that title), my adventures and observations on this first journey may be read. True, it was a laborious expedition, but at any rate it was a musical one, tolerably advantageous from a pecuniary point of view, and I enjoyed the pleasure of living in a sympathetic atmosphere, out of reach of the intrigues, the meanness, and the platitude of Paris.

Berlioz had been coquetting since 1837 with the idea of a tour in Germany. He had many friends and influential connections there: he could count, or believed he could, on the assistance of such leading German musicians as Liszt, Mendelssohn, Meyerbeer, Wagner, Schumann, and Hiller, and various Kapellmeisters and instrumental virtuosi. His main object, of course, was to make a sensation in Germany that would have its repercussions in Paris; during his tours he kept the Paris Press fed with publicity matter, as we should say nowadays, and in his letters to his friends he exhorted them to do what they could to spread the flattering news.

As we have seen, he is in error in giving 1840 as the date of his visit to Brussels. He left Paris on September 19 or 20, 1842, his first concert in Brussels taking place on the 26th, his second on the 9th October. The local public was rather puzzled by Berlioz's music, and the financial results of the second concert were very disappointing. He returned to Paris a few days later. Early in December he again went to Brussels, where he planned to give a concert on the 10th: it was postponed to the 17th, and then abandoned. It is this *second* excursion to Brussels to which he refers at the commencement of the foregoing chapter: Harriet had discovered from the reports in the musical journals that Marie Recio had sung at the concerts of 26th September and 9th October, and it was only by a series of ruses that Berlioz managed to get his baggage and his scores out of the house.

On November 7th he had conducted his *Symphonie funèbre et triomphale* at the Opéra. Cherubini had died in the preceding March. For a time, Berlioz hoped that he himself would be elected to the vacant chair at the Institut; but the choice fell upon Onslow (November 19). Berlioz now became more than ever conscious that to establish himself in Paris he would have to win a reputation abroad. Hence the German tour of 1843, which is described in the succeeding chapters.

The "travelling companion" who accompanied him to Brussels was Marie Recio. This was the stage name of Marie Geneviève Martin, the daughter of a French father and a Spanish mother. Berlioz seems to have met her, and fallen victim to her physical charms, in 1841, when she was twenty-seven; she re-kindled the romantic fire that poor Harriet, fat, wretched, alternately maudlin and violent, and tippling away what brains she had ever had, had been unable to keep in being. Marie's mother encouraged the liaison, for Berlioz was a person of importance in the musical world and could presumably help the daughter to procure the engagements that were so necessary to the boiling of the domestic pot. At this time Berlioz was a thorn in the side of Pillet, the Director of the Opéra: he used his influence in the journalistic world not only to further his own interests there as composer but to impose Marie Recio upon an unwilling management. She was engaged for a year from October 9, 1841, at a modest salary, and made her first appearance at the Opéra on November 5, as Ines in *La Favorita*, with decidedly moderate success. As nothing much could be said in praise of her singing, the journals with which Berlioz and his friends were connected laid diplomatic stress on her pleasing appearance.

On January 30, 1842, in his article in the *Débats*, dealing with Marie's appearance as the page Isolier in Rossini's opera *Le Conte Ory*, Berlioz was indiscreet enough to draw a comparison between her graceful figure and the too ample proportions of Mme. Stoltz, one of whose favorite parts was this same Isolier. Mme. Stoltz had been a good friend to Berlioz; she had sung in his *Benvenuto Cellini* and at his concerts, and was not only one of his sincerest admirers but one of his most influential supporters at the Opéra, where her relations with Pillet gave her considerable power. She would have been less than feminine had she not used this power henceforth to the detriment of Berlioz.

The poor composer was no more fortunate in his second love than in his first. The financial strain of keeping up two establishments was serious enough for a man in his position; but even more serious was the fact that the shrill and inartistic Marie insisted on accompanying him every-where and singing at his concerts. Love may be blind, but in Berlioz's case it certainly was not deaf; and we soon find him being driven to the verge of craziness by Marie's insistent co-operation in his musical plans. The story of that tragi-comedy, however, belongs to the next few chapters.

It remains to be added that during 1841 Berlioz was buoyed up with the hope of retrieving the failure of *Benvenuto Cellini*. Scribe supplied him with the first act of an opera entitled *La Nonne sanglante*. The librettist, however, who was before all things a man of business, kept Berlioz waiting indefinitely for the remainder: on calmer reflection he could not see the sense of a commercial partnership with a musician who had failed once at the Opéra and would probably fail again.

$\mathscr{F}irst\ \mathscr{V}isit\ to\ \mathscr{G}ermany$
(1842-1843)

CHAPTER LII

BRUSSELS—MAINZ—FRANKFORT

LETTER I—TO MONSIEUR A. MOREL[1]

WELL, my dear Morel, here I am, back from my long stay in Germany, during which I gave fifteen concerts and had about fifty rehearsals. You may well believe that after such fatigue I need rest and inaction, and you are right, but you would hardly think how strange rest and inaction seem to me.

Often in the morning, when only half awake, I begin to dress furiously, thinking I am late and that the orchestra is waiting for me. Then, after a moment's reflection — as the real state of the case dawns on me — What orchestra? I say to myself. I am in Paris, where the opposite custom prevails, and it is the orchestra that keeps the conductor waiting! Besides, I am not giving concerts; I have no chorus to teach, no symphony to conduct; I shall not see either Meyerbeer or Mendelssohn this morning, nor Lipinski, nor Marschner, nor Bohrer, nor Schlosser, nor Mangold, nor the brothers Müller, nor any of those excellent German artists who welcomed me so kindly and gave me so many proofs of deference and devotion.

There is scarcely any music in France just now, and you, my friend, whom I was so pleased to see again, seem so sad and discouraged whenever I question you about what was done in Paris during my absence, that with a sinking heart I desire to return to

[1] M. A. Morel is one of my greatest friends, and also one of the best musicians of my acquaintance. There is real merit in his compositions. [B.]

Germany, where there is still some enthusiasm left. And yet what unbounded resources we possess in this Parisian whirlpool, the centre of the restless ambition of all Europe! What splendid results might be obtained if all the means at the disposal of the Conservatoire, the Gymnase musical, our three lyric theatres, the churches, and the singing schools could be united! With a judicious selection from these various elements, one might form, if not an irreproachable chorus (the voices are not sufficiently trained for that), at least a matchless orchestra! In order to give the Parisians a chance of hearing a really splendid body of eight or nine hundred musicians, only two things are wanting, a place to seat them, and a little love of art to draw them together. We have not a single large concert-room! The theatre of the Opéra might serve the purpose, if the machinery and decorations required by the repertory did not occupy the stage nearly every day, and so make the preparations for such a ceremony almost impossible.

But should we, even then, find the general sympathy, the unity of sentiment and action, devotion and patience, without which nothing grand or beautiful in this line can ever be produced? One can only hope so. The exceptional order prevailing at the rehearsals at the Conservatoire, and the zeal of its members, are universally admired. Still, only that which is rare is so highly prized. In Germany, on the contrary, I found an almost universal order and attention combined with real respect for the master — or masters. For, in fact, there are several masters: first, the composer himself, who almost always conducts his own rehearsals and performances, without in the least wounding the conductor's self-love; next, the Kapellmeister, usually an able composer, who conducts the principal operas and all important musical works of which the authors are either absent or dead; and the leader, who directs the small operas and ballets, and also acts as first violin when not conducting, in which case he conveys the Kapellmeister's remarks and directions to the further end of the orchestra, superintends the material details of the studies, sees that nothing is wanting either in the way of music or instruments, and sometimes indicates the bowing or phrasing of a passage — a task forbidden to the Kapellmeister, who always conducts with a baton.

In Germany, as elsewhere, there must doubtless be a good deal of hidden and insubordinate vanity among so many musicians of unequal merit; but, with one single exception, I cannot remember ever having seen or heard these come out into the open — possibly because I do not understand German.

I did not meet many able chorus-masters. Most of them were bad pianists; indeed I met one who could not play the piano at all, and only gave the notes by striking the keys with two fingers of his right hand. In Germany, as in France, they still keep up the habit of uniting all the voices in one room under one conductor, instead of having three separate practising rooms and three conductors for preliminary rehearsals, the female voices, the tenors and the basses being taken separately; a proceeding which saves time, and brings about excellent results in the instruction of the different choral parts. The German choristers, especially the tenors, have generally fresher and purer voices than those of our theatres; but one must not be too hasty to award them the palm, and if you care to follow me to the different towns I visited, you will soon see that except at Berlin, Frankfort, and perhaps Dresden, the chorus at all the theatres is bad or at best indifferent. On the other hand, the German Singing Academies must be included among the musical glories of the country. Later on we will try to find out the reason of this difference.

My journey began under unfavourable auspices; mishaps and misfortunes of all sorts succeeded each other in the most troublesome manner, and I assure you, my dear friend, that it needed a stubborn determination to pursue it to the end. When I left Paris,[1] I thought myself sure of three concerts at the outset; the first at Brussels, where I had been engaged by the Society of the Grande Harmonie, and two others were already announced at Frankfort by the manager of the theatre, who seemed to think them of importance, and to be anxious for a good performance. But what resulted from all these fine promises and marked attentions? Absolutely nothing. This is what took place. Madame Nathan-Treillet had kindly promised to come expressly from Paris to sing at the Brussels concert. Just as the rehearsals were beginning, and the concert was heavily billed, we heard that she had been taken seriously ill, and could not therefore possibly leave Paris. Madame Nathan-Treillet has left such recollections in Brussels of the time when she was prima donna of the theatre, that one does not exaggerate in saying that she is simply adored there; she makes a perfect *furore,* and, according to the Belgians, all the symphonies in

---

[1] In the early part of December, 1842. His Brussels concert, originally announced for the 10th, was first of all postponed to the 17th, and then abandoned.

the world are not worth one romance of Louisa Puget's sung by
Madame Treillet.

At the announcement of this catastrophe the Grande Harmonie
collapsed, the smoking-room adjoining the concert-hall became a
desert, every pipe was as suddenly extinguished as if the air were
exhausted, and the Grand Harmonists dispersed with groans. In vain
did I seek to console them by saying, " There will be no concert; make
yourselves easy, you will not have the discomfort of listening to my
music; surely that is compensation enough for so great a misfortune."
Nothing could make it up to them.

Their eyes dissolved in beery tears — *et nolebant consolari* —
because Madame Treillet was not coming. The concert, therefore, fell
through. The conductor of this Grande Harmonie Society, a man of
undoubted merit, and an eminent artist quite devoted to his art, though
not exactly disposed to give way to despair even when Mademoiselle
Puget's romances failed — in a word, Snel himself, who had invited
me to come to Brussels — with shame and embarrassment

> Jurait, mais un peu tard, qu'on ne l'y prendrait plus.

What was I to do? Address myself to the rival society — the Philharmonic, conducted by Bender, leader of the Guides' admirable band?
Collect a brilliant orchestra, by combining that of the theatre with the
Conservatoire? The thing was easy, thanks to the kindly intentions
of Messrs. Henssens, Mertz, and Wéry, who on a former occasion
had all been eager to influence their friends and pupils in my favour.
But this would have been to embark on fresh expenses; and besides,
time failed me, as I thought I was expected at Frankfort for the two
concerts just mentioned. I had to start, therefore, full of anxiety as
to the possible consequences of this dreadful disappointment to the
Belgian *dilettanti,* and of self-reproaches as the innocent and humiliated cause of it. Happily this kind of remorse does not last long — it
vanishes like steam, and I had scarcely been an hour on the Rhine boat,
admiring the river and its banks, before I had forgotten all about it.
The Rhine! ah, that is grand and beautiful! Perhaps, my dear Morel,
you think I should seize this opportunity of enlarging poetically upon
it. Heaven forbid! I know too well that any enlargement of mine
would only be a prosaic diminution; and besides, for your own credit,
I would rather think that you had read and re-read Victor Hugo's
beautiful book.

On my arrival at Mainz, I hastened to make inquiries as to the Austrian military band which had been there the year before, and according to Strauss — the Paris Strauss [1] — had performed several of my overtures with great verve and power, and immense effect. The regiment was gone; no more *musique d'harmonie* (this was really a

[1] The name of Strauss is now celebrated throughout dancing Europe; it is attached to a number of fanciful and piquant waltzes of novel rhythm and a gracefully original gait, that have now gone the round of the entire world. It may be imagined, therefore, that one does not much care to see such waltzes imitated, or such a name forged.

But what is the case? There is one Strauss in Paris — he has a brother; there is another Strauss at Vienna, who has no brother; such is the only distinction between the two. Hence various disagreeable occurrences for our Strauss, who conducts all the balls at the Opéra-Comique, and all the private balls given by the aristocracy, with a *verve* worthy of his name. At the Austrian embassy, a Viennese, obviously a spurious one, recently accosted Strauss in the Austrian language, and said:

"Ah, how are you, my dear Strauss? I am delighted to see you. You don't remember me?"

"Not at all."

"Oh! I know you very well, though you have got a little stouter. Besides, no one but you can write such waltzes. You alone could assemble and conduct such an orchestra for dance music; there is but one Strauss."

"You are very good; but I assure you that Strauss of Vienna is also talented."

"How! Strauss of Vienna? But you are he. There is no other. I know you quite well. You are pale — so is he; you speak Austrian — so does he; you write fascinating dance music."

"Yes."

"You always accentuate the weak beat in the *trois-temps* time."

"Oh, the weak beat is my forte!"

"You have written a waltz called *Le Diamant*."

"Sparkling."

"You speak Hebrew?"

"*Very well.*"

"And English!"

"*Not at all.*"

"That's the man! you *are* Strauss; besides, your name is on the handbills."

"Sir, once more I am *not* Strauss of Vienna. He is not the only man who can syncopate a waltz. I am Strauss of Paris; my brother, a very good violinist (there he is, by-the-way), is likewise Strauss. Strauss of Vienna is also Strauss. There are three Strausses."

"No, there is only one; you are trying to mystify me."

Exit the incredulous Viennese, leaving our Strauss much irritated and puzzled to get his identity verified, so much so that he entreats me to extricate him from this twin dilemma.

I accordingly declare that Strauss of Paris, a pale man, speaking Austrian and Hebrew wonderfully well, French rather badly, and English not at all, writing enchanting waltzes, full of delicious rhythmical coquetteries and exquisitely instrumented, and conducting his gay dance-orchestra with a somewhat melancholy air though with undoubted talent — this Strauss has, I affirm, lived in Paris for a long time, played the viola at all my concerts for ten years past, belongs to the orchestra of the Théâtre-Italien, goes every summer to Aix, Geneva, Mainz, Munich — where he makes a good deal of money — goes everywhere, in fact, except to Vienna, from which he stays away out of consideration for the other Strauss, who, for all that, himself went once to Paris.

Consequently the Viennese have only to stand to what has been said, to keep their Strauss, and let us keep ours. Let everyone, in fact, render to Strauss that which does not belong to Strauss, and cease to attribute to Strauss that which is his; otherwise — such is the force of prejudice — one would end by saying that the paste* of Strauss was better than the diamond of Strauss, and that the diamond of Strauss was only paste. [B.]

* *Strass.*

Grande Harmonie). Concerts were impossible. I had fondly imagined I should be able to entertain the inhabitants of Mainz with that farce *en passant;* still, it must be attempted.

I went accordingly to Schott, the patriarch of music publishers. That worthy man, like the famous beauty in the wood, looks as though he had slept for the last hundred years, and to all my questions he replies slowly, interlarding his words with prolonged pauses: " I don't think . . . you could . . . give a concert . . . here . . . there is no orchestra . . . there is no . . . public . . . we have no money."

As I have not an over-large amount of patience, I quickly made for the station and started for Frankfort. You may think I had not yet had enough to annoy me. Like Schott, the train had also gone to sleep; it hardly went at all, it lounged; that day more especially it made interminable pedal points at each station. Still, every adagio has an end, and I reached Frankfort [1] before nightfall. What a charming, cheerful town it is! An air of wealth and activity reigns everywhere; besides, it is well built, as white and glistening as a new five-franc piece, with a fragrant and verdant girdle of boulevards, planted in the English style with shrubs and flowers. Although it was the month of December, and both verdure and flowers had long since disappeared, the sun gleamed brightly through the bare branches of the trees; and whether from the contrast between those light and airy alleys and the dark streets of Mainz, or from the hope I had of at last beginning my concerts at Frankfort, or from some other cause not to be analysed, a chorus of happy voices started within me, and I took a delicious walk for two hours. " Business may wait till to-morrow," I said to myself as I went back to the hotel.

Accordingly, the following day I went briskly to the theatre, expecting to find it all ready for my rehearsals. On crossing the square where it stands, and seeing some young men with wind instruments, I requested them, as they evidently belonged to the orchestra, to give my card to Guhr, the Director and Kapellmeister. At sight of my name, the indifference of these good honest artists changed at once to a respectful cordiality which did me real good. One of them understood French, and spoke for the others. " We are very happy to see you at last. Herr Guhr announced your arrival to us some time ago; we have twice performed your *King Lear* overture. You will not find your Conservatoire orchestra here, but still, perhaps, you will not be

---

[1] On December 21 or 22.

wholly dissatisfied!" Enter Guhr. A small man with rather a shrewd countenance, keen piercing eyes, rapid gestures, brief and incisive speech. It is plain that he will never err through over-indulgence when at the head of his orchestra; everything about him indicates musical intelligence and will: he is a leader. He speaks French, but not fluently enough to keep up with his impatience, and he interlards every sentence in the funniest manner with great oaths pronounced German fashion. I shall only indicate them by initials. On seeing me: " Oh, S. N. T. T.,[1] is it you, my dear fellow? Then you did not get my letter?"

"What letter?"

"I wrote to you to Brussels to tell you . . . S. N. T. T. . . . Wait a bit. I can't speak properly . . . a misfortune! . . . a great misfortune! . . . Ah, there is the manager, who will act as my interpreter."

And continuing to speak in French: " Tell M. Berlioz how vexed I am; that I wrote to him not to come here yet; that the little Milanollos[2] are filling the theatre every evening, that we have never had such a public *furore* before, S. N. T. T. And that we shall be obliged to keep the good music and the grand concerts for some other time."

The Manager: " M. Guhr desires me to tell you, sir, that " . . .

H. B.: "Don't trouble yourself to repeat it. I understand quite well — too well indeed, seeing that he did not speak German."

Guhr: "Oh! ah! I spoke French, S. N. T. T., without knowing it."

H. B.: " You know it very well, and I know too that I shall have to go back, or else pursue my road at the risk of finding some other infant prodigies to checkmate me elsewhere."

Guhr: "What is to be done, my dear fellow? The children make money, S. N. T. T., French songs make money, French vaudevilles draw crowds; what would you have? S. N. T. T., I am the director; I can't refuse money; but at any rate stop till to-morrow, you shall hear *Fidelio,* done by Pischek and Mdlle. Capitaine, and, S. N. T. T., you shall give me your opinion about our artists."

H. B.: " I am sure they are first-rate, especially under your direction; but my good Guhr, why do you swear so dreadfully? Do you think it is any consolation to me?"

---

[1] "Sacré Nom te Tieu." [H.]   [2] Two young violinists.

"Oh! ah! S. N. T. T. One may do that *en famille*" (he meant to say when one *is familiar*).

Whereupon I burst into an insane fit of laughter, my wrath vanished, and, taking his hand, I said:

"Well, since we are *en famille*, come and drink some Rhine wine. I forgive you for your little Milanollos, and will stay and hear *Fidelio* and Mdlle. Capitaine, to whom I fancy you would like to act as lieutenant."

We settled that I should set off in two days for Stuttgart — where, however, I was not expected — there to try my fortune with Lindpaintner and the King of Württemberg. I was obliged, therefore, to give the inhabitants of Frankfort time to recover their composure, and forget some of the frenzied emotions excited by the violins of those two charming sisters, whom I had been the first to applaud in Paris, but whose presence in Frankfort was singularly inconvenient to me. The next day I heard *Fidelio*. It was one of the finest representations I have ever seen in Germany; Guhr was right to propose it as a compensation for my disappointment, for I have seldom had a more perfect musical treat.

I thought that Mdlle. Capitaine, in the part of Leonora, had all the musical and dramatic characteristics required by Beethoven's grand creation. Her voice has a peculiar timbre, exactly suitable to the deep though repressed feeling of Florestan's heroic spouse. Her singing is simple and perfectly in tune, and her acting is always true to nature. In the famous pistol scene she does not bring down the house as Mdme. Schroeder-Devrient did with her convulsive nervous laugh, when we saw her as a young woman in Paris, sixteen or seventeen years ago; she arrests your attention and moves you by other means. Mdlle. Capitaine is not at all a singer in the brilliant sense of the word, but of all the women I heard in Germany in that kind of opera she is certainly the one I prefer, and yet I had never heard her name before. Others had been mentioned to me as very talented, whom I found simply detestable.

Unfortunately I cannot remember the name of the tenor who took Florestan's part. He certainly had good points, though there was nothing remarkable about his voice. He sang the difficult prison song, not, indeed, so as to make me forget Haitzinger, who rose to great heights in it, but well enough to deserve the applause of a warmer public than that of Frankfort. As for Pischek, whom I appreciated better some months afterwards in Spohr's *Faust,* he taught me the full value of the Governor's part, which we could never understand in Paris, and for that alone I am really grateful to him. Pischek is an artist, and has doubtless studied much, but Nature has also greatly favoured him. He has a magnificent baritone, thrilling, flexible, true, and of considerable compass; a fine face and tall figure; young and full of fire! What a misfortune that he knows no language but German. I thought the chorus of the Frankfort theatre good; their execution was careful, their voices fresh, and generally all in perfect tune. The only thing to desire was that it had been a little larger. When a chorus numbers only about forty voices, it has always a certain harshness that disappears in a larger one. As I did not hear them rehearsing a new work, I do not know whether the Frankfort chorus-singers are good readers and musicians; I can only say that they sang the first Prisoners' Chorus very satisfactorily — a charming piece, which needs *singing;* and the grand finale with the needful enthusiasm and energy. As for the orchestra, looking upon it merely as a theatre orchestra, I should pronounce it first-rate; admirable from every point of view. Not a nuance escapes it; the timbres melt into a smooth and harmonious whole; it never stumbles; it attacks with *aplomb,* one might almost say like one instrument. No doubt Guhr's skill in conducting and his strictness at rehearsals have much to do with this happy result. The orchestra is composed as follows: 8 first violins, 8 seconds, 4 violas, 5 cellos, 4 basses, 2 flutes, 2 oboes, 2 clarinets, 2 bassoons, 4 horns, 2 trumpets, 3 trombones, and timpani. Such a body of 47 musicians is to be found, with very trifling differences, in all the smaller German towns. It is generally disposed in the following manner: the violins, violas, and cellos together occupy the right side of the orchestra; the double-basses are placed in a straight line in the middle, quite close to the footlights, while the wind instruments form a rival group to the strings on the left; the kettle-drums and trombones are placed by themselves at the farthest end on the right-hand side. Not having been able to put this orchestra to the severe test of symphonic studies, I can say nothing about its quickness of conception, aptitude for the irregular or humoristic style, rhythmical solidity, etc., etc., but Guhr assures me that it is quite as good at a concert as in opera. This I can believe, since Guhr is not at all too ready to over-admire his own children. The violins belong to an excellent school; the basses have plenty of tone. I do not know the capacity of the violas, their part being but trifling in the operas I saw. The wind instruments are exquisite as a body. I have only one reproach to make to the horns, who have a defect that is very common in Germany, of often making the tone too brassy, especially when forcing the high notes. This way of giving out the sound spoils the tone of the horn; it may occasionally have a very good effect, but I do not think it could ever be regularly adopted in the school of the instrument.

At the end of this excellent performance of *Fidelio,* about ten or twelve persons condescended to applaud it slightly as they were going out . . . and no more! I was indignant at such coldness, and when someone tried to persuade me that though the audience had applauded so slightly it none the less appreciated the beauty of the work, " No," said Guhr, " they understand nothing — nothing at all — S. N. T. T. He is right, it is a vulgar public."

That evening I saw my old friend, Ferdinand Hiller,[1] in one of the boxes. He lived a long time in Paris, where connoisseurs still talk of his great musical talent. We should soon have renewed our old ways of comradeship. Hiller is engaged on an opera for the Frankfort theatre; two years ago he wrote an oratorio, *The Fall of Jerusalem,* which has been successfully performed several times. He often gives concerts, at which, besides extracts from that work, various instrumental compositions of his have been produced of late years, and are very well spoken of.

Unhappily, whenever I have been at Frankfort it has always so happened that Hiller's concerts took place the day after I had to leave, so that I can only quote the opinion of others about him, which exculpates me entirely from any want of loyalty. At his last concert he gave a new overture, which was warmly received, and several pieces for four male voices and a soprano, which I have been told had a strikingly original effect.

At Frankfort there is a musical institution which I have often heard highly spoken of. It is the St. Cecilia Singing Academy, and has the name of being both rich in numbers and of good material; however, as I was never admitted to it I must maintain the strictest reserve on the subject.

Although the vulgar element prevails in the Frankfort public, yet taking into consideration the great number of persons in the upper

---

[1] Hiller, in his reminiscences of Berlioz in his *Künstlerleben,* says that Guhr had " taken good care" that there should be "no evening free" for Berlioz's concerts.

classes who really study music, it seems impossible that one should not be able to collect an audience intelligent enough to enjoy great works of art. At any rate, I had not time to try the experiment.

Now, my dear Morel, I must call up my recollections of Lindpaintner and the orchestra at Stuttgart. I will make them the subject of a second letter, not, however, to be addressed to you, as I must also answer those of our friends who are as eager as you are to hear the details of my German expedition.   Farewell.

P.S. — Have you published any new songs? Everyone is talking of the success of your latest ones. Yesterday I heard the rondo *Page et Mari,* which you composed to the words of Alexandre Dumas *fils.* I think it very delicate and coquettish, piquant and charming. You never wrote anything so well in that style. That rondo will be intolerably popular. You will be put in the pillory by all the barrel-organs of Barbary, and you will have deserved it richly.

H. B.

CHAPTER LIII

STUTTGART—HECHINGEN

LETTER II—TO MONSIEUR GIRARD

THE first thing I had to do before leaving Frankfort to try my fortune in the kingdom of Württemberg was to find out what were the musical resources of Stuttgart, make a concert programme suited to their powers, and only carry with me the music absolutely essential to its performance. You must know, my dear Girard, that one of the greatest and most unforeseen difficulties of my travels arose from the immense expense attendant on the carriage of my music. You will easily understand this when I tell you that the mass of separate orchestra and chorus parts, manuscript, lithographed, or engraved, was very heavy, and had to follow me almost everywhere by stage-coach [1] at a ruinous cost. This time, however, being uncertain whether I should go to Munich after my visit to Stuttgart, or return to Frankfort on my way northwards, I only took two symphonies, an overture, and some

---

[1] The network of railways with which Germany is now intersected did not exist at that time. [B.]

songs, and left all the rest with that unfortunate Guhr, who was evidently fated to be bothered with my music in one way or another.

There is nothing interesting about the road from Frankfort to Stuttgart, and my impressions of it are not worth telling. I saw no romantic spots, no dark forests, no convents, no lonely chapels, no torrents; no nocturnal sounds, not even from Don Quixote's windmills; neither huntsman, nor milkmaid, nor weeping maiden, nor straying heifer, nor lost child, nor distracted mother, nor shepherd, nor thief, nor beggar, nor brigand; nothing, in fact, but the moonlight, the noise of the horses, and the snoring of the conductor. Here and there some ugly peasants in large three-cornered hats and long dirty linen coats with absurdly long tails that got entangled between their muddy legs; a costume which gave them the appearance of village curés *en déshabille*. Nothing more!

The first person to be seen on my arrival at Stuttgart — indeed, the only one whom I had any reason to suppose would be favourably disposed towards me, owing to the kindness of a mutual friend — was Dr. Schilling, the author of a great many theoretical and critical works on musical art. His title, a very common one in Germany, had made me augur rather unfavourably of him. I imagined some old pedant with spectacles, a reddish wig, and huge snuff-box, always mounted on his hobby of fugue and counterpoint, talking of nothing but Bach and Marpurg; outwardly polite perhaps, but at bottom hating all modern music in general and mine in particular; in a word, an old musical curmudgeon. Now, you see how one may be mistaken. M. Schilling is not old, does not wear spectacles, has fine black hair of his own, is full of animation, speaks loudly and rapidly, almost like pistol shots, and is a smoker, not a snuff-taker. He received me very kindly, at once gave me all the necessary information about my concert, never said a word about fugues or canons, showed no contempt either for the *Huguenots* or *William Tell,* and expressed no aversion to my music before hearing it. Besides, conversation was anything but easy between us when there was no interpreter, M. Schilling speaking French very much as I speak German.

One day, impatient at not being able to make himself understood, he said:

" Do you speak English? "

" I know a few words — and you? "

" I — no! But Italian, do you know Italian? "

" Sì, un poco. Come si chiama il direttore del teatro? "

" Oh bother! not to speak Italian either! "

I believe, heaven forgive me, that if I had declared myself unable to understand either English or Italian, the ebullient doctor would willingly have played the scene in the *Médecin malgré lui* in those two languages with me: *Arcithuram, catalamus, nominativo, singulariter; estne oratio latinas?*

We did try Latin, and understood each other after a fashion, not, however, without some *arcithuram catalamus*. But it may easily be imagined that conversation was rather difficult, and did not deal with Herder's ideas, nor yet Kant's *Critique of Pure Reason*. M. Schilling was able to let me know, however, that I could give my concert either in the theatre or the Salle de la Redoute, a room intended for musical ceremonies of this sort. In the first case, besides the enormous advantage — in a town like Stuttgart — of the royal presence, which he thought he could certainly secure for me, I should have a gratuitous performance, without having to trouble myself either about tickets or advertisements, or any of the other material details of the evening. In the second, I should have had to pay the orchestra and manage everything myself, and the King would not be present — he never went to the concert-room. I accordingly followed the doctor's advice, and hastened to present my request to the Baron von Topenheim, Grand Marshal of the Court, and Intendant of the theatre. He received me with charming urbanity, assuring me that he would speak to the King that very evening about my petition, which he thought would be granted.

" I had better tell you one thing, however," added he, " and that is that the Redoute is the only good room for concerts, and that in the theatre, on the contrary, the acoustic is so bad that for a long time past they have given up playing any important instrumental work there."

I hardly knew what to reply or what to decide upon. " I had better go and see Lindpaintner," I said to myself, " he must be the best judge." My dear Girard, I cannot tell you what good my first interview with that excellent artist did me. At the end of five minutes we felt as if we had been friends for the last ten years. Lindpaintner soon enlightened me as to my position.

" In the first place," said he, " I must undeceive you about the musical importance of our town. True, it is a royal residence, but it has neither money nor a public." (Ah! Ah! I thought of Mainz and Father Schott). "However, as you are here, it must not be said that we let you go without playing some of your compositions, which we are so anxious to know. This is what we must do. The theatre is useless, absolutely useless, for music. The question of the King's presence is of no moment whatever. His Majesty never goes to a concert, and will not appear at yours, no matter where you give it. So take the Redoute room, which is excellent for sound and orchestral effects. As for the musicians, you will only have to expend a small sum of eighty francs for their pension fund, and all without exception will make it their duty as well as feel it an honour, not merely to perform, but to rehearse your works several times under your direction. Come and hear the *Freischütz* this evening. I will introduce you to the band after one of the acts, and you will see if I have done wrong in answering for their good-will."

I took care not to miss this appointment. Lindpaintner introduced me to the artists, and after he had translated a little speech which I thought I ought to address to them, all my doubts and perplexities vanished. I had an orchestra composed much like that at Frankfort — youthful, vigorous, and full of fire. I could easily see this by the way in which all the instrumental part of Weber's masterpiece was performed. The chorus seemed to me rather ordinary, few in number, and not very careful in the interpretation of the well-known nuances of that admirable score. They always sang mezzo forte, and appeared rather bored by their task. As for the actors, they were all respectably mediocre. I do not remember one of their names. The Agatha, the prima donna, has a sonorous but hard voice; the second female singer, the Annette, sings with more flexibility, but often out of tune; the baritone, the Caspar, has, I think, the best voice in the theatre. I heard the same company afterwards in the *Muette de Portici,* without changing my opinion about them. Lindpaintner, in conducting these two operas, astonished me by the rapidity with which he took the time of certain pieces. Afterwards I saw that many German Kapellmeisters are the same in this respect, among others Mendelssohn for example, Krebs, and Guhr. I can say nothing about the tempi of the *Freischütz,* because no doubt they know more about the genuine tradition than I do; but as for the *Muette,* the *Vestale, Moses,* and the *Huguenots,* which were produced in Paris in the presence of their own composers, and the tempi of which have been preserved as they were when they were first performed, I maintain that the tremendous pace at which I heard them performed at Stuttgart, Leipzig, Hamburg, and Frankfort is inaccurate; unintentional, no doubt, but none the less injurious to the effect. And yet in France it is believed that the Germans drag all our movements!

The Stuttgart orchestra is composed of 16 violins, 4 violas, 4 cellos, 4 basses, and the wind and percussion instruments necessary to perform most of the modern operas; there is also an excellent harpist, one Krüger, and this is rare for Germany. The study of that fine instrument is neglected here, for no discoverable reason, in an absurd and even barbarous way. Indeed I am inclined to believe that this was always the case, considering that none of the German masters have ever made use of it. There is no harp part in any of Mozart's works, neither in *Don Giovanni, Figaro,* the *Magic Flute,* the *Seraglio, Idomeneo, Così fan tutte,* nor in his masses or symphonies. Weber also abstained from using it, likewise Haydn and Beethoven;[1] Gluck alone wrote an easy harp part in *Orfeo, for one hand only,* and anyhow that opera was composed and represented in Italy. There is something in this at once amazing and annoying to me. . . . It is a disgrace to the German orchestras, who ought all to have at least two harps, especially now that they perform French and Italian operas, in which they are so frequently employed.

The Stuttgart violins are first-rate; it is plain that most of them have been trained by Molique, the leader, whose vigorous playing, severe though slightly monotonous style, and learned compositions, we admired some years ago at the Conservatoire. Molique, being first violin both at the theatre and at all the concerts, has under him for the most part only his own pupils, who all profess the sincerest respect and admiration for him. Hence a rare correctness in their execution, due as much to oneness of feeling and method as to the attention of the players.

I must make special mention of the second leader, Habenheim, a distinguished artist in every respect. I heard one of his cantatas, written in an expressive and melodious style, well harmonised and orchestrated. The other stringed instruments, if not equal to the violins, might fairly be considered very good. I may say the same for the wind instruments; the first clarinet and first oboe are capital. The elder Krüger, the first flute, unhappily uses an antique instrument that

[1] Not quite correct. There is a harp part in No. 5 of the *Prometheus* music. [H.]

leaves much to be desired in purity of tone and ease of production of the higher notes. Herr Krüger ought also to beware of yielding to the temptation of introducing shakes and turns where the author has abstained from writing them.

Neukirchner, the first bassoon, is a first-rate virtuoso, though perhaps too much disposed to make a parade of great difficulties; besides, he plays on such a bad instrument that one's ears are hurt every moment by questionable intonations which spoil the effect of even the best played passages. Schuncke stands out among the horns; but he, like his compeers at Frankfort, makes the tone of his high notes a little too brassy. At Stuttgart they only use cylinder or chromatic horns. Adolphe Sax, a skilled instrument maker in Paris, has amply proved the superiority of this system over that of pistons, now almost abandoned throughout Germany, while the cylinder system is coming into general use there for horns, trumpets, bombardons, and bass tubas. The Germans give the name of valve-instruments (ventil-horn, ventil-trumpet) to those that are made with this mechanism. I was surprised not to see it adopted for the trumpets in the military band at Stuttgart, otherwise a very fair one; they still use a very imperfect instrument with two pistons, which, for tone and sonority, is far behind the cylinder trumpet, now in general use elsewhere. I am not speaking of Paris; in another ten years we shall have them there.

The trombones have considerable power. The first trombonist, Schrade, who four years ago was a member of the Vivienne concert orchestra at Paris, has undoubted talent. He is thoroughly master of his instrument, revels in difficulties, and produces a magnificent tone from the tenor trombone; I might indeed say tones, for by some inexplicable process he can produce three or four notes at a time, like the young horn player [1] with whom the musical press has lately been occupied in Paris. Schrade, in a pedal point of a fantasia which he performed in public at Stuttgart, caused general astonishment by playing the four notes in the chord of the dominant 7th simultaneously, in this order $\left\{ \begin{matrix} \text{E flat} \\ \text{A} \\ \text{C} \\ \text{F} \end{matrix} \right\}$. It is for those learned in acoustics to account for this new phenomenon in the resonance of tubes, and it is for us musicians to study it well, and profit by it on occasion.

Another merit of the Stuttgart orchestra is the number of intrepid

---

[1] Vivier, the ingenious humorist, an eccentric artist, but one of real merit and rare musical talent.

readers it contains, who are never troubled or put out by anything, who can read at once a note and its nuance, and never even at first sight let a *p* or *f,* a mezzo forte or smorzando, escape them. Moreover, they have been broken in to all the caprices of rhythm and measure, not concentrating on the strong beat, but able to accentuate the weak beat also without hesitation, and go from one syncopation to another without fuss or the air of having performed a difficult feat. In a word, their musical education is complete in every respect. At the very first rehearsal of my concert I recognised all these valuable qualities. I had chosen the *Symphonie fantastique* and the overture to the *Francs-Juges.* You know the rhythmical difficulties of these two works — syncopated phrases sometimes crossing each other, groups of four notes against groups of three, etc., all of which are now boldly thrown at the head of the Paris public at the Conservatoire, but at which we had nevertheless to work long and diligently. I had reason, therefore, to fear a great many mistakes in the overture and in the finale of the symphony. But there was not one. Everything was read and mastered at first sight. My astonishment was extreme; yours will not be less so when I tell you that we got up that damned symphony and the remainder of the programme in two rehearsals. The effect would indeed have been very satisfactory if half the violins had not been kept away on the day of the concert by illness, real or assumed. Can you see me with four first violins and four seconds struggling with all those wind and percussion instruments? For the epidemic had spared the rest of the orchestra, and nothing was wanting except half the violins! I would gladly have imitated Max in the *Freischütz,* and signed a compact with all the devils in hell to get violins. It was all the more vexatious and irritating because, notwithstanding Lindpaintner's prognostications, the King and his Court were present. In spite of the gaps at certain of the desks, the performance,[1] though not a powerful one — that was impossible — was at any rate intelligent, correct, and animated. The most effective pieces in the *Symphonie fantastique* were the adagio (the *Scène aux champs*) and the finale (the *Sabbat*). The overture was warmly received; but as for the *Pilgrims' March* from *Harold,* which also figured in the programme, it was scarcely even noticed. The

[1] On December 29. We must always bear in mind that Berlioz, in his articles relating to his tour, was inclined to exaggerate his successes, for the benefit of his enemies in Paris. In a letter to one of his friends he bewails the miserable financial results of this Stuttgart concert: with low prices and a hall that held only four hundred people, "the return has been practically nothing."

same thing happened at another concert, when I was so imprudent as to give it by itself; whereas where I have played the whole of *Harold,* or at least the first three movements, the march has been as much applauded as it was in Paris, and often encored — a fresh proof of the necessity of not breaking up certain compositions, and of only producing them at the proper time and from the suitable standpoint.

Must I now tell you of all the congratulations I received on the part of the King, through Count Neiperg and Prince Jerome Bonaparte, when the concert was over? Well! why not? Princes are well known to be in general very kindly disposed towards foreign artists, and I should in reality only fail in modesty if I were to repeat what some of the musicians said to me that evening and on the following days. Besides, why should I not fail in modesty? In order that I should not be growled at by a few chained and ill-conditioned curs, that would like to bite anyone who happens to pass in freedom in front of their kennels? Would it be worth my while, for that, to use a lot of old formal phrases, and act a comedy which could deceive no one from such a motive? True modesty would consist not merely in never speaking of oneself, but in never doing anything worthy of being spoken of, in never attracting public attention to oneself, in never saying anything, writing or doing anything, in hiding oneself, in fact — not even living. That would be absurd! . . . Besides, I have made up my mind to confess everything, both in the way of good and ill luck. I began so in my last letter, and am ready to go on with it in the present one. For instance, I am afraid that Lindpaintner, who is a master, and whose approbation I greatly coveted, liked nothing but the overture, and thoroughly abominated the symphony. I would not mind betting that Molique liked nothing whatever. As for Dr. Schilling, I am sure that he thought it all execrable, and was quite ashamed at having taken the first step towards introducing a brigand of my stamp to Stuttgart — one who was strongly suspected of having violated music, and who, if he should succeed in inspiring it with his passion for freedom and vagrancy, would infallibly turn the chaste muse into a sort of gipsy woman, not so much an Esmeralda as a Helen MacGregor, an armed virago with hair floating to the winds, and dark tunic sparkling with gaudy trinkets, springing barefoot over the wild rocks, dreaming to the sound of the wind and tempest, and with her fierce glances terrifying women and troubling men, without inspiring them with love.

Schilling, as counsellor to the Prince of Hohenzollern-Hechingen, took care, however, to write to His Highness, proposing that the curious savage who was more in his element in the Black Forest than in a civilised town should go and amuse him. And the savage, being inquisitive about everything, and having received a courteous invitation from Baron von Billing, another of the Prince's familiar advisers, set forth [1] through the great snow-covered pine woods for the little town of Hechingen, without much troubling himself as to what he should do there.

This excursion into the Black Forest left a curious mixture of recollections behind it — some happy, some sad, some sweet, some painful — which I cannot evoke from the past without an anguish that is almost inexplicable. The cold, the funereal black and white aspect of the mountains, the wind howling through the shivering pine trees, the secret gnawings of heart so powerfully felt in solitude, a sad episode in a melancholy novel I read during the journey. . . . Then the arrival at Hechingen, the gay smiling faces, the amiability of the Prince, the New Year festivities, balls, concerts, wild laughter, projects of meeting again in Paris, farewells and departure.

Oh, how I suffer! What devil prompted me to tell you all this? As you see, there is nothing romantic or touching in it. . . . But I am so constituted that I sometimes suffer without any apparent reason, just as in certain electrical conditions of the atmosphere the leaves on the trees tremble though there may be no wind.

Fortunately, my dear Girard, you have known me for a long time, and so will not think this excursion leading to nothing, this introduction without an allegro, this subject minus a fugue, too absurd. Upon my word, you must confess that a subject without a fugue is a piece of rare good fortune; for we have both of us read thousands of fugues that have no subject, to say nothing of those with bad subjects. Well, well! my melancholy has gone off now, thanks to an interruption by the fugue (an old dotard that has so often bothered us). I am in a better temper, and will now proceed to tell you all about Hechingen.

When I said, a moment ago, that it was a little town, I was exaggerating its importance geographically. Hechingen is only a big village, or, at the outside, a market-town, built on the side of a somewhat steep hill, rather like the upper part of Montmartre, or Subiaco in the Roman States. Above the town, and situated in such a way as to command it entirely, is the Villa Eugenia, the Prince's residence. To the

---

[1] On December 31st. He arrived the following day.

right of this little palace there is a deep valley, and, a little farther away, a bare desert peak crowned by the old castle of Hohenzollern, now only a hunting rendezvous, but formerly the feudal residence of the Prince's ancestors. The present owner of this romantic scenery is a clever young man,[1] lively and kindhearted, with apparently only two ruling ideas in the world, the one being the wish to make the inhabitants of his little states as happy as possible, and the other the love of music. Can you conceive of a happier existence? Everyone about him is contented. His subjects adore him; music smiles on him. He understands it both as a poet and a musician. He composes charming songs, two of which, *Der Fischerknabe* and *Schiffers Abendlied,* really touched me by the expressiveness of their melody. He sings them with the voice of a composer, but with a fire and feeling both of heart and soul that fairly carry you away. Though he has no theatre, he has, at any rate, an orchestra, directed by Techlisbeck, an eminent master, whose symphonies are often[2] creditably performed at the Conservatoire in Paris. Under his direction the simplest of the great instrumental masterpieces are played, not indeed with much parade, but very carefully. Such is the amiable Prince whose invitation to me was so pleasant and his welcome so cordial.

On my arrival at Hechingen, I renewed my acquaintance with Techlisbeck. I had known him in Paris five years before; here he overwhelmed me with attentions, and with all those proofs of true kindness that one can never forget. He very soon acquainted me with the musical resources at our disposal. There were eight violins in all, three of them very feeble, three violas, two cellos, and two basses. Stern, the first violin, is a virtuoso of talent; so is Oswald, the first violoncello. The pastor and registrar at Hechingen plays the first bass in a manner to satisfy the most exacting of composers. The first flute, the first oboe, and the first clarinet are excellent, though the flute does occasionally indulge in those fanciful ornamentations with which I found fault at Stuttgart. The seconds among the wind instruments are passable. The two bassoons and the two horns are not quite all that could be desired. As for the trumpets, the trombone (there is only

[1] Twenty years later, Wagner was the guest of the same amiable princeling: see *Mein Leben* (English edition), p. 877.

Friedrich Wilhelm Constantin, Fürst von Hohenzollern-Hechingen, was born on February 16, 1801, and died on September 3, 1869. He came into the succession in 1838, but surrendered his sovereignty to Prussia in 1850.

[2] Täglichsbeck had the good fortune to have a symphony *twice* played at the Conservatoire. [H.]

one) and the kettle-drum, whenever they play one wishes they were silent — they know nothing. I can see you laughing, my dear Girard, and preparing to ask me what I was able to play with so small an orchestra. Well, by patience and good-will, by arranging and modifying certain parts, by five rehearsals in three days, we got up the overture to *King Lear,* the *Pilgrims' March,* the *Bal* in the *Symphonie fantastique,* and several other pieces, proportioned in size to the framework intended for them. And everything went well, with precision and even *verve.*

I wrote in the viola parts the essential notes belonging to the third and fourth horns, but which had now to be omitted, as we had only first and second. Techlisbeck played the first harp part in the *Bal* on the piano; he had also been anxious to undertake the viola solo in the march in *Harold.* The Prince of Hechingen stood beside the kettle-drummer to count his bars for him and make him come in in time. I suppressed all the passages in the trumpet parts which we agreed were beyond the scope of the two performers. The trombone alone was left to his own devices, but wisely playing only those notes with which he was familiar, such as B flat, D, F, and carefully avoiding all others, he almost shone by his silence. You ought to have seen the wonderful effects produced by this music on the numerous audience assembled by His Highness in this charming concert-room. However, as you may doubtless imagine, the joy I felt at all these demonstrations was mingled with impatience, and when the Prince came up and shook me by the hand I could not help saying: " Ah, monseigneur, I swear that I would give two years of my life to have my Conservatoire orchestra here now, and tackle one of these scores to which you have been so indulgent! "

" Yes, yes; I know," he answered; " you have an imperial orchestra which calls you Sire, and I am only His Highness; but I will go and hear it in Paris. I'll go, I'll go! "

I hope he may keep his promise. His applause weighed on me, it being but ill-deserved.

After the concert we had supper at the Villa Eugenia. The delightful gaiety of the Prince communicated itself to all his guests; he wanted me to hear one of his compositions for tenor voice, piano, and violoncello. Techlisbeck sat down at the piano, the composer undertook the vocal part, and to me was allotted the task of singing the violoncello part, amid the acclamations of the assembly. The piece was much applauded, and the singular timbre of my treble string caused great merriment. The ladies especially could not get over my A. Two days later, after many farewells, I was obliged to return to Stuttgart. The snow was melting on the great weeping pine trees, the white cloak on the mountains was spotted with black . . . it was profoundly melancholy. . . . I began to eat my heart out once more.

The rest is silence.

Farewell.

H. B.

CHAPTER LIV

MANNHEIM—WEIMAR

LETTER III—TO LISZT

O N my return from Hechingen[1] I stayed some days longer at Stuttgart, a prey to new perplexities. To all questions about my plans and the future direction of a journey scarcely yet begun, I could have answered like one of Molière's characters:

Non, je ne reviens point, car je n'ai point été;
Je ne vais point non plus, car je suis arrêté,
Et ne demeure point, car tout de ce pas même
Je prétends m'en aller. . . .

"Go. . . . Where?" I really did not know myself. True, I had written to Weimar, but no answer had come, and I was obliged to wait for it before I could make any decision.

You, my dear Liszt, know nothing of these uncertainties; it matters little to you whether the town to which you go has a good orchestra, whether the theatre be open, or the Intendant be willing to place it at your disposal, etc. Of what use indeed would such information be to you? With a slight modification of the famous *mot* of Louis XIV, you may say with confidence: "I myself am orchestra, chorus, and conductor. I can make my piano dream or sing at pleasure, re-echo with exulting harmonies, and rival the most skilful bow in swiftness. Like the orchestra, it has its harmonies of brass; and like it,

[1] He returned to Stuttgart on January 3.

though without the smallest apparatus, it can throw on the evening breeze a cloud of fairylike chords and vague melodies. Neither theatre nor set-scenes are needed, no vast rows of benches, nor long and fatiguing rehearsals, for I want neither musicians nor music. Give me a large room and a grand piano, and I am at once master of a great audience. I have but to appear before it to be overwhelmed with applause. My memory awakens; from my fingers flow dazzling fantasias which call forth enthusiastic acclamations. I have but to play Schubert's *Ave Maria* or Beethoven's *Adelaïde* to draw every heart to myself, and make each one hold his breath. The silence speaks; the admiration is intense and profound. . . . Then come the fiery shells, a veritable bouquet of grand fireworks, the acclamations of the public, flowers and wreaths showered upon the priest of harmony as he sits quivering on his tripod, beautiful young women kissing the hem of his garment with tears of sacred frenzy; the sincere homage of the serious, the feverish applause wrung from the envious, the intent faces, the narrow hearts amazed at their own expansiveness." And the next day the inspired young genius departs, leaving behind him a twilight of dazzling glory and enthusiasm. It is a dream; it is one of those golden dreams that come to one when one is named Liszt or Paganini.

But the composer who, like myself, must travel to make his works known, has, on the contrary, to nerve himself to a task which is never-ending, still-beginning, and always unpleasant.

Who can imagine the tortures of the rehearsals? First he has to submit to the cold glances of the musicians, who are anything but pleased at all this unexpected upset on his account. " What does this Frenchman want? Why doesn't he stay at home?" Each takes his place, but at the very first glance round the assembled orchestra, the author perceives important gaps. He requests an explanation from the Kapellmeister. " The first clarinet is ill, the wife of the oboe has just been confined, the child of the first violin has the croup, the trombones are on parade — they forgot to ask for an exemption from their military duty for today; the kettle-drum has sprained his wrist, the harp will not come to the rehearsal because he needs time to study his part," etc., etc. Still we begin. The notes are read after a fashion, at about half the right time — a dreadful trial to the composer. Little by little, however, his instinct gains the upper hand; as it warms, his blood carries him away; he insensibly quickens the time. Then, indeed, there is a nice mess, a fearful hubbub, distracting alike to mind and ear. He is forced to stop and resume the slow tempo, and bit by bit repeat those long phrases, the free and rapid course of which he has so often guided in other orchestras.

But, as if this were not enough, he is presently aware of sundry strange discords from some of the wind instruments. What can be the reason? " Let me hear the trumpets alone. What are you doing? I ought to hear a third and you are playing a second. The second trumpet in C has a D; give me your D . . . very good. The first has a C which sounds F; give me your C. Fie! Horrible! you are playing E flat."

" No, sir; I am playing what is written."

" But I tell you no. You are a whole note wrong."

" But I am sure that I am playing C."

" In what key is your trumpet? "

" *In E flat!* "

" Well, there now, there's the mistake; you should have the F trumpet."

" Ah, I had not noticed the signature; excuse me."

Or again, I say, " What the devil are you making that noise for over there, you kettle-drum? "

" Sir, I have a fortissimo."

" Not a bit of it, it is a mezzo forte, there are not two *f*'s, but *m* and *f*. Besides, you are using wooden sticks, and you ought to have them with sponge-heads. It is all the difference between black and white."

" We don't know what you call ' sponge-heads,' " says the Kapell-meister. " We have never seen them."

" I guessed as much, so I brought some from Paris with me. Take the pair that I have put on that table. Now then, where are we? Good heavens! twenty times too loud. And the mutes, you have forgotten the mutes."

" We haven't got them; the boy forgot to put them out. We shall have them to-morrow," etc., etc.

After three or four hours of such anti-harmonious skirmishes, not one single piece has been made intelligible. Everything is broken, inarticulate, out of tune, cold, commonplace, maddeningly discordant, hideous! and you have to send away sixty or eighty tired and discontented musicians under this impression, saying everywhere that they don't understand what it is all about, that it is " an infernal, chaotic sort of music," and that they never tried anything of the sort before. The next day there is little if any progress; only on the third day does it begin to assume a definite shape.

Then at length does the poor composer begin to breathe; the harmony becomes clear, the rhythms dart forth, the melodies smile and weep, and the whole mass gets compacted, and dashes boldly on. After its first stammering attempts, the orchestra walks, talks, becomes man! Acquaintance with the music restores courage to the astonished artists; the composer requests a fourth trial, his interpreters — taking them all round, they are the best people in the world — consent eagerly. This time, *fiat lux*. "Attention to the lights and shades! You are not afraid now?" " No, give us the real tempo." *Via!* And light dawns, art appears, the thought flashes out, the work is understood, and the orchestra rises, applauding and saluting the composer, the Kapellmeister comes up and congratulates him, those inquisitive persons who had hitherto kept themselves hidden in the dark corners of the room now approach, get on the stage and exchange exclamations of surprise and pleasure with the musicians, at the same time casting astonished glances at the foreign master whom at first they had taken for a madman or barbarian. Now is the moment for rest. But let the unfortunate wretch beware of taking any. Far from it, he must now redouble his care and attention, and return before the concert to superintend the arrangement of the desks, and inspect the orchestral parts to be sure they are not mixed. He must go through the ranks, red pencil in hand, and mark the German names for the keys upon the music, instead of those used in France for the wind instruments, such as *C, D, Des, Es,* and *Fis,* for *ut, re, re bémol, mi bémol,* and *fa dièse.* He has to transpose a solo for the cor anglais for the oboe, because the orchestra does not possess the former instrument, and the performer is generally afraid to transpose it himself. He must rehearse the chorus and the solo singers separately, if they are not sure of themselves. But the room fills, the clock strikes, the composer appears at his desk, pale and exhausted with fatigue of body and mind, scarcely able to stand, uncertain, faint, and discouraged, until the applause of his audience, the spirit of the performers, and love for his own work shall transform him into an electrical machine, giving forth marvellous radiations, invisible indeed, but none the less real. And then begins his compensation. Ah! then, I grant you, the composer-conductor has a life unknown to the virtuoso! With frantic delight he abandons himself to the pleasure of *playing on the orchestra!* With what magical influence does he sway that magnificent instrument! Once more his attention embraces everything; his eye is everywhere; with a glance he signals their entries to voice and instrument, up, down, to the right, to the left; with his right arm he flings forth terrible chords that burst in the distance like harmonious projectiles; then, on a pedal point, he arrests all this movement; rivets the attention of all; suspends every arm, every breath, listens for a moment to the silence . . . and then gives freer scope than ever to the whirlwind he has subdued.

> Luctantes ventos tempestatesque sonoras
> Imperio premit, ac vinclis et carcere frenat.

And in the grand adagios, how happy he is, rocked gently on his lovely lake of harmony, listening to the crowd of intermingled voices singing his love songs, or confiding to the solitude of the night his laments for the present and his regrets over the past. Then often, but then only, does the composer-conductor forget the public altogether; listening to himself, judging himself, and touched by the emotion which is shared by the artists around him, he takes no further heed of the impressions produced upon the audience far away behind him. If his heart has been thrilled by contact with poetic melody, if he has felt that secret fervour, the harbinger of the soul's incandescence, his object is attained, the heaven of art is opened to him, and what signifies earth?

Then, when all is over, and success assured, his delight is intensified a hundredfold, since it is shared by the gratified self-love of all his army. You, you great virtuosi, are king and princes by the grace of God, you are born on the steps of the throne; while composers have to fight, to overcome, and to conquer, in order that they may reign. But the very labours and dangers of the struggle only enhance the brilliancy and intoxication of their victory, and they might, perhaps, be even happier than you had they always soldiers at their command.

This, my dear Liszt, is a long digression, and has nearly made me forget that I was giving you an account of my travels. To return to them.

During the few days while I was awaiting my Weimar letters at Stuttgart, the Society of the Redoute, under Lindpaintner's direction, gave a brilliant concert, at which I had an opportunity of observing for the second time the coldness evinced by the German public *en masse* for the most colossal conceptions of the great Beethoven.

The *Leonora* overture, a truly monumental work, performed with rare spirit and precision, was scarcely applauded at all, and that evening at the table-d'hôte I heard a man grumbling that Haydn's symphonies were not given, instead of *this violent music without any tune in it!!!* . . . Really and truly we are not so vulgar even in Paris! . . .

At last I received a favourable answer from Weimar, and started for Carlsruhe. I would willingly have given a concert *en passant,* but Strauss[1] (the Kapellmeister) told me I should have had to wait eight or ten days, on account of an engagement at the theatre with a Piedmontese flutist.

I pressed on, therefore, to Mannheim,[2] with deep respect for the great flute. This is a quiet town, very cold, level, and square. I do not think that a passion for music deprives its inhabitants of their sleep. Still, there is a good-sized Singing Academy, a fair theatre, and a very intelligent little orchestra. Both the orchestra and the Singing Academy are directed by the younger Lachner, brother to the celebrated composer. He is a gentle, diffident, modest, and very talented artist. He soon organised a concert for me.[3] I do not recollect the programme. I only know that I wanted to have my second symphony (*Harold*) in full, and that after the first rehearsal I had to suppress the finale (the *Orgie*) because the trombones were manifestly incapable of playing their part. Lachner was quite vexed about it, being desirous, as he said, to hear the whole of the *tableau.* I was obliged to be firm, however, assuring him that, independently of the trombones, it would be madness to hope to get the proper orchestral effect of this finale with so few violins. The first three parts of the symphony were well played, and made a great impression on the public. I heard that the Grand Duchess Amelia, who was present at the concert, remarked on the colouring of the *Pilgrims' March,* and particularly the *Serenade in the Abruzzi,* where she fancied she again beheld the calm peacefulness of the exquisite Italian nights. The viola solo was played very well by

---

[1] Another Strauss! but this one does not write waltzes. [B.]

[2] On January 9.

[3] On January 13. While the nature of the reception of his music by the Mannheimers can be guessed from his remarks about them, Paris was informed that "M. Berlioz continues his successes in Germany: at Mannheim his symphonies made a sensation."

one of the violas of the orchestra, though he has no pretentions to
being a virtuoso.

I found rather a good harpist at Mannheim, an excellent oboe,
who plays the cor anglais passably, a clever violoncello player (Heinefetter), cousin to the singers of the same name, and some bold trumpeters; but there was no ophicleide. Lachner was obliged to procure a
chromatic trombone, going down to the deep C and B, to replace an
instrument that is now employed in all the big modern works. It would
have been simpler, I should have thought, to send for an ophicleide;
and, speaking from a musical point of view, it would have been far
better, as the two instruments are not in the least alike. I could hear
only one rehearsal at the Singing Academy; its members — all amateurs — have in general good voices, but are by no means all good
musicians or readers.

During my stay at Mannheim, Mdlle. Sabine Heinefetter gave a
representation of Norma. I had not heard her since she left the
Théâtre-Italien, in Paris. There is still a certain power and agility in
her voice, but she forces it a little at times, and her high notes are
becoming difficult to endure; still, such as she is, Mdlle. Heinefetter
is almost unrivalled among German singers, for she knows how to sing.

I was a good deal bored at Mannheim, notwithstanding the kind
attentions of a Frenchman, M. Désiré Lemire, whom I had occasionally met in Paris about eight or ten years before. Doubtless this
was because the very first aspect of the inhabitants, and even of the
town itself, proved plainly that any artistic movement was altogether
unknown to them, and that they only regarded music as a somewhat
agreeable pastime for such leisure moments as could be spared from
business. Moreover, it rained perpetually. There was a neighbouring
clock, too, that always sounded the minor third [1] when it struck, and
a tower inhabited by a nasty hawk, whose shrill discordant cries
pierced my ears from morning till night. Besides this, I was impatient
to see the city of poets, where letters were awaiting me from my

[1] In Germany I was able to make many observations on the different resonances of bells,
and was convinced beyond all doubt that in this, as in all other respects, Nature smiles at our
theories. Certain professors maintain that natural horns give out only the major third; a mathematician has latterly been known to declare, on the contrary, that *all* bells only make the minor
third; and the truth is that they give all sorts of harmonic intervals. Some give the minor third,
some the fourth; one of the bells at Weimar strikes the minor seventh and the octave in succession (its fundamental note F giving off the octave and the E flat); others even give the augmented
fourth. It is plain, then, that the harmonic resonance of bells depends on the form given them by
the moulder, on the different degrees of thickness in the metal at certain points of their curvature,
and on the unknown hazards of melting and casting. [B.]

compatriot Chélard, the Kapellmeister, and also from Lobe, that truly typical German musician, whose merit and ardour of soul I know you quite appreciated.

Here I am back again on the Rhine! I meet Guhr — He begins swearing again! I leave him! I see our friend Hiller for one moment at Frankfort, who tells me he is about to perform his oratorio, *The Fall of Jerusalem.*[1] I set off with a nice sore throat, sleep on the way, have an awful dream — which I shall not tell you! Weimar at last! I am very ill! Fruitless efforts on the part of Lobe and Chélard to set me up. Preparations for the concert. The first rehearsal announced. My spirits rise. I am cured!

Good! Here I can breathe! There is something in the air that tells me this is a literary, an artistic town. Its aspect corresponds exactly to my preconceived idea — tranquil, bright, airy, and peacefully dreamy, with charming surroundings, beautiful streams, shady hills, and smiling valleys. How my heart beat as I went through it! There is Goethe's abode! And there the late Grand Duke used to take part in the learned conversations of Schiller, Herder, and Wieland! This Latin inscription was traced on the rock by the author of *Faust.* Is it possible? These two little windows lighted Schiller's poor garret. In this humble lodging the great poet of every noble enthusiasm wrote *Don Carlos, Marie Stuart, The Robbers,* and *Wallenstein.* There he lived as a poor scholar. Ah! Goethe ought never to have suffered that! He, a rich minister of state, might surely have softened the lot of his friend the poet; or was there no reality in that illustrious friendship? . . . I fear it was genuine only on Schiller's side. Goethe loved

---

[1] In Chapter LII Berlioz tells us that he was unable to hear any of Hiller's works, as they were invariably given the day after he had to leave Frankfort. Hiller's account in his *Künstlerleben,* runs thus: "It so happened that I was giving a concert the next day, and I invited Berlioz to this. 'Impossible,' he replied. You know I am travelling with a concert singer [Marie Recio]. She sings like a cat. That of itself wouldn't matter: the trouble is that she wants to appear at all my concerts. From here I go to Weimar. We have an ambassador there: it's impossible for me to present her, so I have laid my plans. She believes I am invited to Rothschild's this evening. I shall leave my hotel at seven o'clock: my seat in the stage-coach is booked, my luggage has been taken out; I depart, and a few hours later the head waiter will give her a letter from me, 'containing money to pay her fare back to Paris.'"

The resourceful Marie, however, went to the coach office, learned Berlioz's destination, and followed to Weimar. Two or three days later, Hiller, unaware of this, wrote a facetious letter to Berlioz at Weimar. It was answered, in a lofty tone, by Marie: and poor Berlioz had to humble himself to the extent of adding a few lines of his own, to the effect that "he was neither 'captured' nor 're-captured,' but they were reunited."

"Condole with me," Berlioz wrote to his friend Morel. "Marie insisted on singing at Mannheim, Stuttgart and Hechingen. The first two times it was tolerable, but the last. . . ! And at the mere thought of my having another singer she is up in arms."

himself and his accursed son Mephistopheles too well. He lived too long, and was too fearful of death.

Ah, Schiller! Schiller! you deserved a less human friend! I cannot take my eyes off the narrow windows, the dark house, the wretched black roof. It is one o'clock in the morning, the moon is shining, the cold is intense. Silence everywhere . . . they have all passed away. . . . Little by little my breast heaves, and I begin to tremble. Overwhelmed with veneration and regret, and with all those boundless affections with which genius, even from the tomb itself, is capable at times of inspiring an obscure survivor, I prostrate myself before the humble threshold, and in a frenzy of suffering, love, and adoration, I exclaim: Schiller! . . . Schiller! . . . Schiller! . . .

Now, my dear friend, how shall I resume my real narrative, from which I have wandered considerably? Wait! To enable myself to go back to prose and recover my composure, I will think of another inhabitant of Weimar, a man of great talent, who wrote masses and beautiful septets, a severe pianist — in a word, Hummel! . . . There! now I am quite sober.

Chélard, first as an artist and next as a Frenchman and my own old friend, did all he could to help me to attain my object. The Intendant, Baron von Spiegel, entering into his kind and benevolent designs, placed both theatre and orchestra at my disposal. I don't say the chorus, as he would probably not have ventured to mention it to me. I had already heard it in Marschner's *Vampire,* and you cannot imagine such a set of wretches squalling out of tune and out of time. I had never heard anything like it. And the singers — oh, poor women! Let us not speak of them, for the sake of gallantry. But there is a bass who played the part of the Vampire; you can guess that I mean Genast! Is he not an artist in every sense of the word? above all a tragedian? I regretted that I could not stay to see him play the part of Lear in Shakespeare's tragedy, which they were getting up just as I was leaving.

The band is well organised; but Chélard and Lobe tried to get extra strings in my honour, and presented me with an active force of 22 violins, 7 violas, 7 cellos, and 7 basses. The wind was sufficient, with an excellent first clarinet and a wonderfully powerful cylinder trumpet (Sachse); no cor anglais — I had to transpose his part for a clarinet; no harpist — a good-natured young fellow, Montag, a meritorious pianist and perfect musician, offered to arrange the two harp parts for one piano, and play them himself; no ophicleide — this they replaced by a fairly strong bombardon. This was enough, and the rehearsals began. You must know that the musicians at Weimar had quite a passion for my *Francs-Juges* overture, and had already performed it several times. They could not therefore have been better disposed, so, contrary to my usual custom, I was really happy during the rehearsal of the *Symphonie fantastique,* also chosen by their desire. It is an intense though rare delight to be thus immediately understood. I recollect the impression produced on the band and on certain amateurs present at the rehearsal by the first movement (*Rêveries — Passions*), and the third (*Scène aux champs*). The latter in particular seemed to hold every breath during the peroration, and after the last roll of thunder at the end of the forsaken shepherd's solo, when the re-entering orchestra seems to exhale a deep sigh as it dies away, I heard my neighbours also sighing in sympathy amid all their applause. Chélard admired the *March to Execution* more than anything else, but the public seemed to prefer the *Bal* and the *Scène aux champs*. The *Francs-Juges* overture was received like an old and welcome acquaintance. Well, there I am again, verging on lack of modesty; and if I told you of the full room,[1] the prolonged applause, the recalls, the compliments of the chamberlains on the part of their Highnesses, the new friends waiting to embrace me as I left the theatre, and keeping me up till three in the morning — if, in fine, I described a success, I should be voted a ridiculous bore, a . . . Enough! that idea alarms me, in spite of all my philosophy, and I stop there. Farewell!

H. B.

CHAPTER LV

LEIPZIG

LETTER IV — TO STEPHEN HELLER

I HAVE no doubt, my dear Heller, that the blunder I made in my last letter of calling the Grand Duchess Stéphanie " Amélie " was a great source of merriment to you. But I confess that I don't make myself

---

[1] The concert took place on January 25. Marie sang three of his songs to the no great satisfaction of the Weimar critics, who spoke of "the confidence she displayed in the indulgence of German listeners." The receipts were good, and Berlioz was able to send 200 francs to Harriet.

too miserable at the thought of your censure. If I had called the Emperor Napoleon Francis or George, well and good; but one may fairly be allowed to change the name of the sovereign of Mannheim, charming as it is. Besides, as Shakespeare says:

> What's in a name? that which we call a rose
> By any other name would smell as sweet.

At any rate, I humbly beg Her Highness's pardon, and if, as I hope, she grants it, I snap my fingers at your derision.

Leipzig lay most directly in my way after leaving Weimar; still I hesitated to go there, notwithstanding Felix Mendelssohn's dictatorship in that city, and our amicable relations at Rome in 1831. Since then our lines in art have so diverged that I confess I had not expected to find him particularly sympathetic.[1] Chélard, who knows him, made me blush for my doubts, and I wrote to him. His answer, which I give [2] here, was not long delayed:

" MY DEAR BERLIOZ,

" I thank you most heartily for your kind letter, and for your recollection of our Roman friendship. I shall never forget it as long as I live, and I am looking forward to telling you so face to face. All I can do to make your stay at Leipzig both agreeable and happy shall be done, both as a pleasure and a duty. I think I may safely assure you that you will like the town; that is to say, the musicians and the public. I would not write to you till I had consulted several persons better acquainted with Leipzig than myself, and they all confirm me in my opinion that you will have an excellent concert. The expenses of the orchestra, the room, announcements, etc., may be one hundred and ten crowns; the receipts will probably amount to six or eight hundred. You ought to be here and decide on the programme and everything that may be necessary at least ten days beforehand. Besides this, the directors of the Subscription Concerts Society have commis-

---

[1] In a contemporary letter to Moscheles, Mendelssohn had said of Berlioz: "I quite agree with you [as to the French composer's noisy orchestration and 'barbarous counterpoint']. His orchestration is so utterly slovenly and haphazard that one ought to wash one's hands after turning over a score of his. . . . I am sorry, for Berlioz is intelligent, cool and sensible in his judgments, and always thoughtful: but he does not see how much absurdity there is in his works."

[2] The autograph of this letter is in the fine collection of Mr. A. G. Kurtz, of Wavertree, Liverpool. It shows how strangely Berlioz permitted himself to garble a document which he professes to give *verbatim*. He has shortened it by a half, and sadly garbled it by correcting Mendelssohn's French. [H.]

sioned me to ask if you will allow one of your works to be performed at their concert on the 22nd of February for the benefit of the poor. I hope you will accept this proposal after your own concert. I should advise you to come here as soon as you can; I shall be delighted to shake you by the hand and say, 'Welcome to Germany.' Don't laugh at my bad French, as you used to do at Rome, but remain my good friend,[1] as you were then, and as I shall ever be to you. Yours faithfully,

         " FELIX MENDELSSOHN BARTHOLDY."

Could I refuse an invitation couched in such terms ? . . . I set out accordingly for Leipzig, not without regretting Weimar and my new friends there.

My intimacy with Mendelssohn had begun in rather an absurd way at Rome. At our first interview he spoke to me about my prize cantata of *Sardanapalus,* some parts of which had been played to him by Montfort, my co-laureate. On expressing my genuine dislike for the first allegro, he exclaimed in the greatest delight: "Ah, good! I congratulate you on your taste! I was afraid you were pleased with that allegro, and honestly it is wretched!"

We very nearly quarrelled the next day because I had been speaking enthusiastically of Gluck. He replied in a surprised and bantering tone: "Ah, you like Gluck, then, do you?" As much as to say, "How can a musician with your notions have sufficient feeling for grandeur of style and truthfulness of expression to appreciate Gluck?" I soon had an opportunity of revenge for this little affront. I had brought with me from Paris Astoria's aria from Gluck's Italian opera *Telemaco,* a beautiful thing, but not very well known; and one day when Montfort and I were expecting a visit from Mendelssohn, I placed an unsigned manuscript copy of this song on Montfort's piano. On his arrival he at once noticed the music, which he took for a piece out of some modern Italian opera, and proceeded to try it. At those words in the four last bars, *"O giorno! o dolci sguardi! o rimembranza! o amor!"* which are simply sublime in their musical expression, I inter-

---

[1] [25 May, 1864]. I have just seen, in Felix Mendelssohn's letters recently published by his brother, in what his Roman friendship for me really consisted. He writes thus to his mother, plainly alluding to me: "—— *is a regular caricature, without a spark of talent, etc., etc. I sometimes feel inclined to devour him.*" He was then one-and-twenty, and not acquainted with *one* of my scores. I had only produced the first sketch of my *Symphonie fantastique,* which he had not read, and I only showed him my newly-finished *King Lear* overture a few days before he left Rome. [B.]

rupted his grotesque parody of them, *à la* Rubini, by saying with an air of utter astonishment, "Then you don't like Gluck!"

"What! Gluck?"

"Alas, yes! my dear fellow! This piece is by him, and not by Bellini, as you thought. You see I know him better than you do, and am of your own opinion — more so, indeed, than you yourself."

One day I had been speaking of the metronome and its utility.

"What is a metronome for?" exclaimed Mendelssohn. "It is a most useless instrument. A musician who cannot guess the time of a piece at first sight is a blockhead."

I could easily have answered that there were a good many blockheads, but I held my peace.

I had hardly written anything at that time. Mendelssohn knew only my Irish melodies with pianoforte accompaniment. One day he asked me to show him the score of the *King Lear* overture, which I had just finished writing at Nice. First he read it over slowly and attentively, and then, just as he was about to play it on the piano (which he did with matchless ability), "Give me the exact time," said he.

"Why should I? Did you not say yesterday that any musician who could not guess the time of a piece at first sight was a blockhead?"

These repartees, or rather hard hits, annoyed him keenly, though he never allowed his vexation to be seen.[1] He never pronounced the name of Sebastian Bach without adding ironically, "*your little pupil!*" In fact he was a regular porcupine as soon as anyone began to talk about music; one never could be sure of not offending him. He did not mind contradiction on any other point, being very good-tempered and sweet in his disposition; and I, in my turn, abused his forbearance in the philosophical and religious discussions to which we occasionally soared.

One evening we were exploring the baths of Caracalla, and debating the question of the merits or demerits of human actions and of their reward in this life. Just as I had replied by some enormity — I forget what — to his religious and orthodox enunciations, his foot slipped and he rolled violently down a steep ruined staircase.

"Admire the divine justice," said I, as I helped him up; "I blaspheme, and it is you who fall."

This impiety on my part, accompanied by an uproarious laugh,

---

[1] And very likely that was what made him wish to devour me. (1864.) [B.]

was evidently a little too much for him, and thenceforth all religious discussions were tabooed. It was at Rome that I first heard and appreciated that exquisitely delicate and richly coloured work of his, the *Fingal's Cave* overture. Mendelssohn had just finished it, and he gave me a pretty accurate idea of it, such is his marvellous power of rendering the most complicated score on the piano. When the sirocco was overpowering I used often to go and interrupt him in his work, for he was an indefatigable producer. Then he would lay down his pen with the utmost good-humour, and, seeing me bursting with spleen, would try to soothe it by playing anything I chose among such works as we both liked. How often, as I lay there peevishly on his sofa, have I sung the air from *Iphigénie en Tauride, D'une image, hélas! trop chérie,* which he used to accompany, seated properly at his piano. And then he would exclaim: " How beautiful that is; I could hear it all day without being tired." And then we would begin it again.

He was also very fond of making me hum, as I lay, certain songs I had set to Moore's melodies; in fact, he always had a certain liking for my — little songs! After a month of these relations, which had gradually become very interesting to me, Mendelssohn departed without wishing me good-bye, and I saw him no more. His letter, therefore, was an agreeable surprise. It seemed to indicate a gracious kindness of heart which I had not formerly observed in him, and on my arrival at Leipzig I soon discovered that this was in fact the case. At the same time he has lost none of the inflexible rigidity of his artistic principles, but he no longer seeks to force them violently on others; and in the exercise of his functions as Kapellmeister he always limits himself to bringing forward all that he thinks good, and to leaving what is bad and pernicious in the shade. He is still, however, a little too fond of the dead.

The Society for Subscription Concerts of which he had told me is a very large one, and perfectly managed. It has a magnificent chorus, an excellent orchestra, and a perfect concert-room at the Gewandhaus, where I was to give my concert. The moment I arrived I went to see it, and came in just in the middle of the final rehearsal of Mendelssohn's new work, the *Walpurgis Night*. At the very first hearing I was really amazed at the beautiful tone of the voices, the intelligence of the singers, the precision and spirit of the orchestra, and, above all, the splendour of the composition.

I am much inclined to look upon this oratorio (*La Nuit du Sabbat*) as the most finished work [1] Mendelssohn has hitherto produced. The poem is Goethe's, but has nothing in common with the *Sabbat* scene in *Faust*. Its subject is the nocturnal assemblies held on the mountains in the first days of Christianity by a sect which remained religiously faithful to the old customs, though sacrifices on the high places had been prohibited. On the nights destined for this sacred work, armed sentinels in large numbers and strange disguises were placed at all the approaches to the mountain. At a given signal, when the priest mounted the altar and struck up the sacred hymn, this diabolical-looking troop brandished their torches and weapons, uttering all manner of fearful cries and sounds, in order to drown the voices of the religious chorus and deter the profane from interrupting the ceremony. Hence, no doubt, the custom in the French language of employing the word *sabbat* as the synonym for a great nocturnal noise. You must hear Mendelssohn's music in order to have an idea of the varied resources the poem offers to a skilled composer. He has profited immensely by them. His work is perfectly clear notwithstanding its complexity; the vocal and instrumental effects are marvellously intermingled, in an apparent confusion that is the very acme of art. Two magnificent features, in absolute contrast, are the mysterious piece of the placing of the sentinels (" Disperse, disperse "), and the final chorus, where the voice of the priest rises calm and reverent at intervals above the infernal din of the false demons and sorcerers. One scarcely knows what to praise most in this finale, the instrumentation, the choruses, or the whirlwind movement of the whole.

Just as Mendelssohn was leaving his desk, in the utmost delight at having produced this work, I came forward in rapture at having heard it. The meeting could not have been better timed; and yet, after we had exchanged the first greeting, the same sad thought struck us both simultaneously:

" And is it twelve years? twelve years since we dreamed together on the plains of Rome? "

" Yes, and in the baths of Caracalla."

" Ah! always joking! always ready to laugh at me! "

" No, no; I hardly ever jest now; it was only to prove your memory, and see if you had forgiven all my impieties. I jest so little, that

[1] When I wrote this, I had not heard the ravishing score of his *Midsummer Night's Dream*. [B.]

at our very first interview I am going seriously to ask you to make me a present, to which I shall attach the highest value."

"What is that?"

"Give me the baton with which you have just conducted the rehearsal of your new work."

"Willingly, on condition that you send me yours."

"I shall be giving copper for gold, but never mind, I consent."

And Mendelssohn's musical sceptre was brought to me forthwith. The next day I sent him my heavy oaken staff, together with the following letter, which I think would not have been disowned by the Last of the Mohicans himself:

"To the Chief Mendelssohn!

"Great chief! We have promised to exchange tomahawks. Mine is a rough one — yours is plain. Only squaws and pale-faces are fond of ornate weapons. Be my brother! and when the Great Spirit shall have sent us to hunt in the land of souls, may our warriors hang up our tomahawks together at the door of the council-chamber."

Such was the occurrence, in its naked simplicity, out of which malicious gossip did its best to create an absurd scene. Some days later, when it came to organising my concert, Mendelssohn did really treat me like a brother. The first artist whom he introduced to me as his *fidus Achates* was Ferdinand David, the leader of the orchestra, a meritorious composer and a distinguished violinist. He speaks French perfectly, and was of the greatest help to me.

The Leipzig orchestra is not larger than those of Frankfort and Stuttgart; but as there is no lack of instrumental resources in the town, I wished to increase it, and the number of violins was therefore raised to twenty-four — an innovation which, as I afterwards heard, aroused the serious indignation of two or three critics who had made up their minds beforehand. Twenty-four violins instead of the sixteen that had hitherto sufficed for the performance of Mozart's and Beethoven's symphonies! What insolent pretension! . . . In vain did we try to procure three other instruments, marked for use and indeed occupying rather prominent parts in several of my pieces (another dreadful crime!); it was impossible to find a cor anglais, an ophicleide, or a harp. Indeed, the cor anglais was so dilapidated, and so extraordinarily out of tune, that notwithstanding the talent of the artist who played it, we were obliged to substitute the first clarinet.

The ophicleide, or rather the thin copper instrument shown to me under that name, was quite unlike a French one, and had scarcely any tone. It was therefore rejected, and replaced after a fashion by a fourth trombone. As for the harp, it was not to be thought of, for six months previously Mendelssohn had been obliged to get harpists from Berlin for a performance of his own *Antigone*. As I heard he had not been particularly well pleased with them, I wrote to Dresden, and Lipinski (a great artist of whom I shall shortly have occasion to speak) sent me the theatre harpist. The only question now was to find the instrument. At last, after various useless visits to different makers and music sellers, Mendelssohn heard of a certain amateur who possessed a harp, and he obtained the loan of it for a few days. But now admire my ill-luck; when we had got the harp and given it a fine set of new strings, it turned out that Richter, the Dresden harpist who had so kindly come to Leipzig on Lipinski's invitation, was a very clever pianist and quite a good violinist, but scarcely played the harp at all. He had only studied it for a year and a half, so as to be able to perform the very simple arpeggios which usually serve as an accompaniment to the airs in Italian operas. So that his courage failed him entirely at sight of the diatonic touches and melodic outlines so frequent in my symphony, and Mendelssohn was obliged to represent the harp solos at the piano on the evening of the concert, to make sure of their coming in properly. What a fuss about a small matter!

However, be that as it might, the rehearsals began when my mind was once made up to all these difficulties. The orchestral arrangement in this beautiful room is so good, the relations of each performer with the conductor so simple, and the artists, besides being perfect musicians, are so well trained in habits of attention by Mendelssohn and David, that two rehearsals sufficed to get up a long programme, containing, among other difficult compositions, the *King Lear* and *Francs-Juges* overtures, and the *Symphonie fantastique*. David, moreover, agreed to play the violin solo, *Rêverie et Caprice,* which I had written for Artôt two years before, and the orchestration of which is somewhat complicated. He performed it in a masterly manner, amid great applause from the assembly. As for the orchestra, to say that after only two rehearsals its performance was irreproachable, is to give it the highest praise.[1] All Paris musicians, and many others also, would I think be of this opinion.

This soirée disturbed the musical conscience of the inhabitants of Leipzig, and, as far as I could judge from the polemics of the newspapers, the discussions it provoked were quite as violent as those called forth by the same works in Paris some ten years ago.

While people were thus debating the morality of my musical actions, approving some and regarding others as premeditated crimes, I made that journey to Dresden which I shall speak of presently.

But not to interrupt the account of my Leipzig experiences, I must tell you, my dear Heller, what took place, on my return, with regard to the concert for the benefit of the poor, mentioned in Mendelssohn's letter, in which I had promised to take part.

As this soirée was organised entirely by the concert society, the fine Singing Academy, whose well-merited praises I have already sung to you, was placed at my disposal. Of course I readily availed myself of such a grand body of singers, and proposed to the directors the finale of *Romeo and Juliet,* with its triple chorus. A German translation of this had been made in Paris by Professor Duesberg. There was nothing to do, therefore, but to fit the translation to the notes of the voice parts. This was a long and troublesome task. Moreover, owing to the copyists' carelessness in the matter of the allocation of long and short notes to the German words, there were so many difficulties that Mendelssohn was obliged to waste his time in revising the text, and correcting the most glaring blunders. He was also compelled to practise the choir for nearly a week. (In Paris eight rehearsals of so large a chorus would cost four thousand eight hundred francs. And yet I am sometimes asked why I never give *Romeo and Juliet* at any of my concerts!) This Academy consists chiefly of amateurs belonging to the higher classes of Leipzig society, though it also includes artists from the theatre and pupils from the St. Thomas school. A good number of rehearsals can thus be easily obtained whenever any serious work is to be studied. When I came back from Dresden, the studies were, however, still far from being complete, the male choir especially leaving much to be desired. It grieved me to see a great master and virtuoso like Mendelssohn engaged in such a menial task, although it must be said he fulfilled it with unwearied patience, all his remarks being made with perfect sweetness and courtesy, the more gratifying from their rarity

---

[1] The concert was given on February 4. Marie sang.

in like cases. As for myself, I have often been accused of want of politeness by the ladies at the Opéra, and I fear that I deserve my reputation.

Before I even begin a rehearsal with a large choir, before anything has occurred to rouse my ill-temper, I am conscious of a sort of anticipative anger tightening my throat. Indeed, my look must forcibly remind the chorus of the Gascon who kicked an inoffensive little boy in the street, and to the child's remonstrance that *he had done nothing to him,* answered, " Only fancy if you *had.*"

However, after two more attempts the three choruses were learnt, and the finale would doubtless have gone quite well with the support of the orchestra but for one of the theatre singers, who had been exclaiming for days past at the difficulty of his part (Father Laurence), and calmly demolished all the harmonious edifice we had been erecting with such labour and difficulty.

I had already remarked, even at the piano practices, that this gentleman — whose name I have forgotten — was one of that numerous class of musicians who know nothing of music; he miscounted his bars, never entered at the right place, mistook the key, etc.; but I said to myself : " Perhaps he has not had time to study his part; he learns very difficult rôles for the theatre, why should he not master this? " Nevertheless I often thought of Alizard, who always sang this scene so well, and regretted keenly that he was in Brussels, and did not know German. But at the general rehearsal the night before the concert, as this gentleman had made no progress, and moreover was muttering various Teutonic imprecations below his breath whenever we had to stop the orchestra on his account, or Mendelssohn or I had to prompt him, I finally lost patience and dismissed the band, begging it to take no further trouble with my work, the performance of which was thus plainly rendered impossible. On my return home I indulged in some sad reflections. Two composers who for years had applied all their intelligence and imagination to the study of their art, two hundred clever and careful musicians, vocal and instrumental, have wearied themselves in vain for the last week, and are forced to give up their work owing to the inefficiency of one man! Oh, you singers who cannot sing, you also are as gods! . . . The society was greatly perplexed about replacing this finale, which would have occupied a full half-hour; an extra rehearsal, however, kindly given by the orchestra and choir on the very day of the concert, settled the matter.

The *King Lear* overture, with which the orchestra was already
familiar, and the *Offertorium* from my *Requiem,* where the chorus
have only a few notes to sing, were substituted for the movement from
Romeo, and performed in the evening in a most satisfactory manner.[1]

I must not forget to mention one result of the piece from the
Requiem, on which I had not reckoned but to which I attach the highest value, viz., the approbation of Robert Schumann, one of the most
justly renowned and critical composers in Germany.[2]

Some days afterwards the *Offertorium* was the occasion of another
compliment still more unexpected. I had had a return of my illness at
Leipzig, and on asking my doctor what I owed him, as I was leaving
the place, he replied: "Write me the theme of your *Offertorium* on
this piece of paper, with your signature, and I shall still be your
debtor. I have never been so struck by any music." I hesitated a little
at recompensing the doctor's attentions so cheaply, but he insisted,
and when I had a chance of replying to his compliment by one that
was better deserved, would you believe that I was dense enough to
let it slip? I wrote at the head of the page: *To Dr. Clarus.*

" *Carus,*" he said; "you are putting an *l* into my name."

I thought immediately, " *Patientibus* Carus *sed* Clarus *inter doc-
tos,*"[3] but did not dare to write it.

I am sometimes uncommonly stupid.

A virtuoso composer like you, my dear Heller, is keenly interested
in everything connected with his art, and so I think your numerous
questions about the musical resources of Leipzig quite reasonable, and
will proceed to answer some of them. You ask if there is anyone in
Germany to be compared with the great pianist, Madame Clara
Schumann?

I think not.

You request me to tell you if the musical feeling of the big-wigs
at Leipzig is good, or at least inclined to what you and I would call
the beautiful?

I will not.

If it is true that the creed of all who profess to love high and serious
art is: " There is no god but Bach, and Mendelssohn is his prophet "?

---

[1] February 22. Marie sang the song *L'Absence*, which Berlioz had scored for her in Dresden.
[2] At the rehearsal, Schumann, breaking his habitual silence, exclaimed: "That *Offertorium*
beats everything." Mendelssohn himself complimented me on a double-bass entry in the accompaniment to my song, *L'Absence*, which was also sung at this concert. [B.]
[3] *Dear* to patients, but *illustrious* among the learned. [H.]

I must not.

If the theatre is well organised, and if the public is wrong to be amused by Lortzing's little operas, so often performed there?

I cannot.

If I have read or heard some of those old masses for five voices with *basso continuo,* which are thought so much of at Leipzig?

I know not.

Farewell! Go on writing beautiful capriccios like your two last, and Heaven preserve you from fugues for four voices on a chorale.

H. B.

CHAPTER LVI

DRESDEN

LETTER V—TO ERNST

YOU particularly advised me, my dear Ernst, not to stop in the small towns on my way through Germany, because it was in the capitals alone that I should find the necessary performers for my concerts. Others gave me the same advice, and reproached me afterwards with not having followed it, and gone first to Berlin or Vienna. But you know it is always easier to give good advice than to follow it; and if I did not adopt what most people would have considered the wisest plan in my travels, it is because I could not. In the first place, I could not always time my journeys. After my useless visit to Frankfort, I could hardly go back to Paris. I would have started for Munich, had not a letter from Baermann[1] informed me that I could not give a concert there for another month, while Meyerbeer wrote me that the revival of several important works at the Berlin theatre made my presence in Prussia useless just then. I could not, however, remain idle, and accordingly, being anxious to make myself acquainted with the musical institutions of your harmonious country, I resolved to see and hear everything, and greatly to reduce my choral and orchestral pretensions in order to make myself more generally known. I knew that I could not expect to find all the instruments required by some of my works in the second-rate towns, but I reserved these for the end

---

[1] The great clarinet player; friend of Weber and Mendelssohn. [H.]

of my journey, to form the climax to the crescendo, and I thought that, all things considered, this slow but progressive step would not be wanting either in prudence or interest of a certain kind. In any case I have no cause to repent having taken it.

And now to speak of Dresden,[1] where I was engaged for two concerts, and found a chorus, orchestra, wind band, and also a famous tenor. Such treasures as these I had not found since I first came to Germany. Moreover, at Dresden I was destined to meet with a devoted, energetic, enthusiastic friend, Charles Lipinski, whom I had formerly known in Paris. I cannot describe, my dear Ernst, the ardour with which this excellent man seconded me. His position of leader of the orchestra, and the general esteem in which both his office and talent are held, gave him great authority over the members of the band, and good use he made of it. As the Intendant, Baron Lüttichau, had promised me two evenings, the entire theatre was at my disposal, and the only question was to see to the quality of the performance. We succeeded perfectly, although our programme was formidable. It included the *King Lear* overture, the *Symphonie fantastique,* the *Offertorium, Sanctus,* and *Quærens me* from my *Requiem,* the two last parts of my *Symphonie funèbre* — written, as you are aware, for two orchestras and chorus — and several songs. I had no translation of the chorus of the symphony, but the manager of the theatre, M. Winkler, a clever scholar, was so extremely obliging as to improvise, so to speak, the necessary German verses, and thus we were able to begin the practices of the finale. As for the solos, they were in Latin, French, and German. Tichatschek, the tenor, has a pure and touching voice, which becomes very powerful when animated by the dramatic action. His style of singing is simple and in good taste; he is a consummate reader and musician, and undertook the tenor solo in the *Sanctus* at first sight, without reserve, or affectation, or pretension. He might easily, like so many others in like cases, have accepted the *Sanctus* and stipulated for some familiar cavatina for his own benefit; but he did nothing of the kind. That is something like! what I call really good.

The cavatina from *Benvenuto,* which I added to the programme, gave me more trouble than all the rest. We could not propose it to Madame Devrient, as it lay too high, and the vocalises were too delicate for her. Lipinski therefore offered it to Mademoiselle Wüst, the second singer, who thought the German translation bad, the andante

[1] Berlioz went to Dresden on February 6.

too lengthy and too high, the allegro too low and too short. She asked for cuts and alterations, she had a cold, etc., etc. You know by heart the whole comedy of a cantatrice who neither can nor will. At last Madame Schubert, wife of the excellent leader and clever violinist with whom you are acquainted, relieved me from all this bother by accepting the unfortunate cavatina, though not without misgivings, for her modesty made her exaggerate its difficulties. She was immensely applauded. In truth, it would seem as if it were more difficult at times to get up the *Fleuve du Tage* than the Symphony in C minor.

Lipinski had so excited the self-love of the musicians that their ambition to succeed, and especially to surpass the Leipzig performance (there is a kind of hidden rivalry between the two towns), made us work tremendously hard. Four long rehearsals seemed scarcely sufficient, and the band itself would willingly have asked for a fifth if there had been time. The result, accordingly, was a first-rate performance. My only misgivings at the general rehearsal were about the chorus, but two extra practices inspired them with the necessary self-confidence, and the pieces from the *Requiem* were as well done as any of the others. The effect of the *Symphonie funèbre* was the same as in Paris. The next morning, the military band who had played in it came in the greatest delight to serenade me, a proceeding that had the effect of disturbing my sorely needed slumbers, and obliged me to go down and drink some punch with them, though I was suffering from neuralgia in the head, as well as from my everlasting sore throat.

It was at this Dresden concert that I first noticed the predilection of the German public for my *Requiem*. We did not attempt the larger pieces, such as the *Dies Iræ*, the *Lacrymosa,* etc., the chorus not being strong enough. The *Symphonie fantastique* was not so well liked by some of my hearers. I heard that the elegant section of the audience, with the King and Court at their head, were not particularly attracted by the violence of its passions, the melancholy of its reveries, or the monstrous hallucinations of the finale. The *Bal* and *Scène aux Champs* alone found favour in their eyes. The public, properly so called, let itself be carried away by the musical current, and applauded the *Marche au Supplice* and the *Sabbat* more than the three other numbers.

Still it was evident, on the whole, that this composition, though well received at Stuttgart, perfectly understood at Weimar, and discussed at Leipzig, was unsuited to the musical and poetical tastes of

Dresden. The people were puzzled by its unlikeness to the symphonies with which they were familiar, and they were more surprised than charmed by it, more disturbed than stunned.

The Dresden band, formerly directed by Morlacchi, the Italian, and by the illustrious composer of the *Freischütz,* is now conducted by Reissiger and Richard Wagner. In Paris we know scarcely anything of Reissiger's, except his slow melancholy waltz, known as *Dernière Pensée de Weber.* While I was in Dresden they gave one of his compositions, the praises of which had been loudly sung to me. I could not join in these praises, for a severe illness confined me to bed on the day of the performance, and I was consequently unable to be present. As for the young Kapellmeister, Richard Wagner, who lived for some time in Paris without succeeding in making himself known, except by some articles in the *Gazette musicale,* his authority was exercised for the first time in assisting me with my rehearsals, which he did with both zeal and good-will. The ceremony of his installation took place the day after my arrival; and when I met him he was in all the intoxication of a very natural delight. After having endured untold privations in France, and all the mortifications attendant on obscurity, Wagner, on his return to Saxony, had the boldness to undertake and the good fortune to carry out the composition of both words and music of an opera in five acts, *Rienzi.* It had a brilliant success at Dresden, and was soon followed by the *Flying Dutchman,* an opera in three acts, of which he likewise wrote both words and music. Whatever opinion one may have about the merit of these works, it must be admitted that there are very few men capable of twice successfully accomplishing this double task. It was a proof of capacity more than sufficient to attract both attention and interest. The King of Saxony fully understood this, and on the day that he guaranteed Richard Wagner's position by associating him with his principal Kapellmeister, the friends of art might have said to His Majesty what Jean Bart said to Louis XIV when he informed that brave Jack-tar that he had made him a commodore: " Sire, you have done well ! "

As *Rienzi* is far longer than most German operas, it is never represented in full. The first two acts are played one evening, and the three last on the next. I saw only the second part, and hearing it but once, it was impossible to express a decided opinion about it. I only remember a beautiful prayer sung in the last act by Rienzi (Tichatschek) and a triumphal march modelled on the magnificent march in *Olympie,* though by no means an imitation of it. I was much struck by the sombre colouring of the *Flying Dutchman,* and by certain stormy effects perfectly appropriate to the subject; but I also remarked an abuse of the tremolo, the more to be regretted that it had already struck me in *Rienzi,* and that it implied a certain indolence of mind in the author, against which he is not sufficiently on his guard. Of all orchestral effects the sustained tremolo is the most monotonous; and it calls for no inventive power on the part of the composer, unless accompanied by some striking idea either above or below it. Be this as it may, however, one must, I repeat, honour the royal consideration that has, so to speak, rescued a young and most gifted artist by its active and unreserved patronage.[1]

The Dresden theatre left nothing undone that could possibly give *éclat* to the representations of both Wagner's works, the scenery, costumes, and *mise en scène* of *Rienzi* approaching very closely the best Paris style. Madame Devrient, of whom I shall have occasion to speak more fully with regard to her representations at Berlin, plays the part of a youth in *Rienzi;* a costume scarcely suited to the somewhat motherly outlines of her figure. She struck me as better suited to her part in the *Flying Dutchman,* in spite of certain affected poses and *spoken* interjections which she introduced throughout. But the talent that really impressed me as the most genuine was that of Wächter, who played the part of the doomed Dutchman. His baritone is one of the finest I have ever heard, and he uses it like a consummate singer. It is of that rich and vibrant timbre that has such a wonderful power of expression, provided the artist sings with soul and feeling, which Wächter does to a very high degree. Tichatschek is gracious, impassioned, brilliant, heroic, and entrancing in the rôle of Rienzi, in which his fine voice and large fiery eyes are of inestimable service. Mademoiselle Wüst represents the sister of Rienzi, with scarcely anything to do; this part the composer has adapted exactly to the powers of the singer.

Now, my dear Ernst, I should like to tell you something about Lipinski, but I could not tell *you,* a violinist admired and applauded throughout Europe — *you,* the studious and careful artist, anything you did not know already about the talent of your great predecessor.

---

[1] In the original of this Dresden letter (*Journal des Débats,* 12 September, 1843), and again in the reprint of it in the *Voyage musical,* Berlioz pays a tribute to the "energy and precision" with which Wagner conducted his own operas. This passage does not appear in the *Mémoires:* Berlioz seems to have deleted it after the Paris *Tannhäuser* episode of 1861.

You know his singing tone, his lofty, touching, and pathetic style, as well as or better than I do, and long ago you committed the finest passages in his concertos to your infallible memory. Besides, Lipinski was so kind during my stay at Dresden, so warm-hearted and so devoted, that people would think my praises were by no means free from partiality, and would attribute them — though I may safely say quite wrongly — to gratitude rather than to genuine admiration. He was immensely applauded at my concert, in my violin romance, which had been played some days previously at Leipzig by David, and also in the viola solo of my *Harold* symphony.

This second evening was a greater success than the first; the melancholy and religious scenes in *Harold* evidently commanded all sympathies from the very first, and the movements from *Romeo and Juliet* (the adagio and the banquet scene) were equally successful. But that which touched the Dresden public and artists most deeply was the cantata *Le Cinq Mai,* admirably sung by Wächter and the chorus to a German translation, again kindly made for the occasion by the indefatigable Herr Winkler. The memory of Napoleon is now almost as dear to the Germans as to the French, which doubtless explains the profound impression always produced by the piece in every town where it was afterwards performed. The end especially often gave rise to singular manifestations:

> Loin de ce roc nous fuyons en silence,
> L'astre du jour abandonne les cieux.

At Dresden I made the acquaintance of the great English harpist, the Liszt of the harp, Parish-Alvars, whose name has not yet obtained the popularity it deserves. He had come from Vienna. It is inconceivable what graceful and spirited effects he manages to produce with an instrument which is so limited in some respects — what original touches, what unheard-of sonorities! His fantasia on *Moïse,* the form of which has been so happily imitated on the piano by Thalberg, his variations in harmonics on the Naiades' chorus in *Oberon,* and a score of similar pieces charmed me inexpressibly. The advantage which the new harps possess of being able, by means of the double action of the pedals, to tune two strings in unison, gave him the idea of combinations which seem absolutely impracticable on paper.

The only difficulty of them, however, consists in the ingenious use of the pedals, which produce the double notes known as *synonymes.*

Thus he plays chords with astounding rapidity in four parts proceeding by intervals of minor thirds, because the harp-strings, instead of representing the ordinary diatonic scale of C flat, are enabled
by the *synonymes* to give in descending succession the series of
C natural, C natural; A natural; G flat, G flat; E flat, E flat.

Parish-Alvars trained some good pupils during his stay at Vienna.
He has just been playing at Dresden, Leipzig, and Berlin, and in many
other towns also, where his marvellous talent invariably excited enthusiasm. Why does he not come to Paris?

Among other eminent artists in the Dresden orchestra is Dotzauer,
an excellent professor, leader of the violoncellos. He has also to
assume alone the responsibility for the entries of the first desk of the
double-basses, for the bassist who reads with him is too old to be able
to play some of the notes of his part, and indeed can barely support
the weight of his instrument. I have met with many instances in
Germany of this mistaken regard for old men, which leads Kapellmeisters to entrust them with musical duties that have long been
beyond their physical strength, and this, unfortunately, until they die.
More than once I have had to don the armour of all my insensibility
and insist cruelly on the replacement of these poor invalids by other
players.

There is a very good cor anglais at Dresden. The first oboe has
a fine tone, but an old-fashioned style, and an irritating mania for
trills and mordents. He gave himself terrible liberties, more especially
in the solo at the beginning of the *Scène aux champs*. At the second
rehearsal I expressed my detestation of these melodic tricks pretty
sharply, and he abstained from them at the subsequent rehearsals;
but this was only a feint, and on the day of the concert, the perfidious
oboe, knowing that I could not stop the orchestra and remonstrate
with him in public and before the Court, recommenced his little vil-
lainies, giving me at the same time a cunning look that almost laid me
flat with indignation.

The most remarkable of the horn players is Levy, who enjoys a
great reputation in Saxony. He and his colleagues use the cylinder
horn, to which the Leipzig band, unlike almost all the others in the
north of Germany, has hitherto refused admission. The Dresden
trumpets are likewise *à cylindre;* they might with advantage take the
place of our cornets à pistons, which are not known there.

The military band is very good — even the drummers are musicians; but the reeds did not strike me as irreproachable. Their intonation left much to be desired, and the bandmasters of these regiments would do well to order their clarinets from our incomparable Sax. Ophicleides there are none; the deep parts are sustained by Russian bassoons, serpents, and tubas.

I often thought of Weber when conducting this Dresden orchestra, which he led for so many years, when it was even more numerous than now. Weber had trained it so well that he would sometimes just beat the first four bars in the allegro of the overture to the *Freischütz,* and then allow the orchestra to go on alone to the pedal points at the end. Musicians may well be proud when they see their chief fold his arms on such occasions.

Would you believe, my dear Ernst, that during the three weeks I spent in this so musical town, no one ever told me that Weber's family were living in the place? I should have been so happy to make their acquaintance, and to express a little of my respectful admiration for the great composer who has made their name illustrious. . . . I did not know till too late that I had lost this precious opportunity, and I must here, at any rate, express my regret to Madame Weber and her children.

At Dresden I also saw some scores by the celebrated Hasse, who for long ruled the destinies of the band. I found nothing very remarkable in them, except one *Te Deum,* composed for some glorious commemoration of the Saxon Court, which I thought as stately and splendid as a peal of grand bells. To those who are satisfied with powerful sonority, this *Te Deum* must be very fine; but sonority does not strike me as sufficient. What I should especially like to have heard, but really well performed, would be some of the numerous operas which Hasse wrote for the Italian, German, and English [1] theatres, and on which his vast fame rests. Why not try to revive at least one of these at Dresden? It would be a curious experiment, perhaps even a resurrection. Hasse's life must have been very eventful; but except commonplace biographies, which repeated all that I knew and said nothing of what I wanted to know, I could find nothing. He travelled much, and lived long both in the torrid zone and the polar regions, that is to say, in Italy and in England. There must be a curious romance in his relations with the Venetian Marcello, and his passion for Faustina, whom

---

[1] Hasse's only achievement in London was to put on the stage his opera of *Artaserse,* originally written for Venice. [H.]

he married, and who used to sing the principal parts of his operas. There was often war between the composer and the cantatrice, in which the master was the slave, and the right was always wrong. Perhaps nothing of all this ever happened. Who knows? Faustina may have been a very human *diva,* a modest cantatrice, a virtuous wife and a good musician, faithful to her husband and her part, telling her beads and knitting stockings when she had nothing else to do. Hasse wrote, Faustina sang; together they earned a fortune which they did not spend. That is nothing nowadays; and if you ever marry it is what I should wish for you.

When I left Dresden [1] to return to Leipzig, Lipinski, hearing that Mendelssohn was getting up the finale from *Romeo and Juliet* for the concert for the poor, announced his intention of going to hear it if he could get two or three days' leave from the Intendant. I took this promise merely as a compliment; but judge of my vexation when I saw Lipinski turn up at the concert, and the finale could not be performed owing to the occurrence of which I told you in my last letter. He had travelled more than a hundred miles to hear it. There's a lover of music for you! But you, my dear Ernst, will not be astonished at this; I am sure you would do as much yourself. You are an artist. Farewell, farewell!

H. B.

CHAPTER LVII

BRUNSWICK — HAMBURG

LETTER VI — TO HENRI HEINE

I HAVE had all sorts of good luck in this excellent town; and accordingly my first idea was to regale one of my intimate enemies with the following account of it, which would have given him pleasure, whereas it will probably vex you, my dear Heine. Anti-moralists assert that *there is something disagreeable to our best friends in any happiness that befalls us;* but I don't believe it. It is an infamous calumny, and I can swear that the brilliant and unexpected fortunes of certain of my friends have not troubled me at all.

---

[1] His Dresden concerts were so successful that he was able to send 500 francs to his wife He returned to Leipzig for the charity concert mentioned in the preceding chapter.

Enough! Let us not enter upon the thorny fields of irony, where wormwood and euphorbia flourish in the shade of the arborescent nettle, where vipers and toads hiss and croak, where the water of the lake seethes, the earth quakes, the night wind scorches, and silent lightning flashes from the western clouds. For what is the sense of biting one's lips, grinding one's teeth, showing green eyes under half-closed eyelids, and playing bitter practical jokes on one's interlocutor, when one's thoughts, far from being bitter, are full of pleasant memories — when one's heart is overflowing with gratitude and innocent delight, and one would gladly have a hundred trumpet voices to tell those dear to us that for one day at least we were happy? It was a little movement of puerile vanity that induced me to begin like this. I was unconsciously trying to imitate you, the inimitable ironist. It shall not happen again. In our conversation I have only too often regretted that I could never compel you to be serious, nor arrest the convulsive movement of your claws when you were under the impression that you were making them into velvet paws, tiger-cat that you are, *Leo quærens quem devoret!*

And yet what feeling — what imagination without malice, there is in your works! How well you can sing in the major key when you please! How impulsive and abundant is your enthusiasm whenever you are suddenly filled with admiration, and so forget yourself! What infinite tenderness breathes through the secret recesses of your heart for the country which you have so often satirised, this land fruitful in poets, this country of dreaming genius — this Germany, in fact, whom you call your old grandmother, and who loves you so well notwithstanding?

I could see this by the sadly tender way in which you were spoken of during my journey. Yes, she loves you! On you she has concentrated all her affections. Your great elder brothers are dead. She now counts only upon you, and with a smile calls you her naughty child. It is by her, and by the deep romantic songs with which she cradled your first years, that you have been inspired with a pure and high feeling for music; but when you left her to wander through the world, suffering made you mocking and pitiless.

You could, I know, make a fine caricature of the account I am about to give you of my journey to Brunswick, and yet see what confidence I have in your friendship, and how I have lost my fear of your irony, for I address it to you and no other! . . . Just as I was leaving Leipzig I received a letter from Meyerbeer, telling me that they could not attend to my concerts for another month. The great master recommended me to utilise this delay by going to Brunswick, where he said I should find a prize orchestra. I followed this advice, without guessing how much I should have to congratulate myself on doing so. I knew no one at Brunswick; I was completely ignorant both as to the feelings of the artists with regard to myself and as to the public taste. But the bare idea that the four brothers Müller were at the head of the band was enough to inspire me with confidence, independently of the very encouraging opinion of Meyerbeer. I had heard them when they were last in Paris, and I regarded their performance of Beethoven's quartets as one of the most extraordinary prodigies of modern art.

The Müller family, in fact, represents the ideal of the Beethoven quartet, as the Bohrer family represents the ideal of the trio. Nowhere else in the world has perfection of ensemble, unity of sentiment, depth of expression, purity of style, grandeur, force, spirit, and passion been carried to such a pitch. Such an interpretation of these sublime works gives us, I think, the most exact idea of Beethoven's thoughts and feelings while writing them. It is the echo of creative inspiration, the rebound of genius! Moreover, this musical Müller family is more numerous than I had thought; I counted seven artists of that name, brothers, sons, and nephews, in the Brunswick orchestra. George is the Kapellmeister; his elder brother, Charles, is only the first violin, but by the deference with which his remarks are listened to, it is plain that he is looked up to as the leader of the famous quartet. The leader of the second violins is Freudenthal, a violinist and meritorious composer. I had given notice of my arrival to Charles Müller, and on alighting from the stage at Brunswick I was accosted by a most amiable young man, Herr Zinkeisen, one of the first violins in the orchestra, speaking French like you or me, who was waiting to take me to the Kapellmeister the moment I arrived. This attention and cordiality seemed to me to augur favourably. Herr Zinkeisen had sometimes seen me in Paris, and recognised me in spite of the pitiable condition to which I was reduced by the cold, for I had passed the night in a practically open *coupé* to escape the smell of six horrible pipe smokers inside. I admire the police regulations in Germany; you are forbidden under penalty of a fine to smoke in the streets or public squares, where this amiable practice cannot inconvenience anybody; but wherever else

you go, to the café, the table-d'hôte, or in the stage-coach, that infernal pipe pursues you. You are German, my dear Heine, and you do
not smoke! Believe me, it is not the least of your merits; posterity
may not take note of it, but among your contemporaries many men
and all women will be grateful to you.

Charles Müller received me with that calm, serious manner that
occasionally alarmed me in Germany, believing, as I did, that it meant
coldness and indifference; nevertheless, there is less to fear from it
than from the smiling demonstrations and pretty speeches with which
we greet a stranger, and then forget him five minutes afterwards.

The leader of the orchestra, having ascertained my wishes respect-
ing the composition of it, went off immediately to make arrangements
with his brother for collecting the necessary strings, and appealing
to such amateur and independent artists of the Ducal chapel as were
fit to join it. The very next day they had formed for me a fine orchestra, somewhat larger than that of the Opéra in Paris, and composed
of musicians who were not only skilled, but also animated by a rare
zeal and ardour. The question of the harp, ophicleide, and cor anglais
again presented itself, as it had already done at Weimar, Leipzig, and
Dresden. (I tell you all these details in order to give you the reputation of being a musician.)

One member of the orchestra, a Herr Leibrock, an excellent artist, well versed in musical literature, had only studied the harp for
a year, and was therefore a good deal alarmed at the test to which
he was likely to be put by my second symphony. Besides, his harp was
an old-fashioned thing, with pedals of simple action, which do not
admit of the execution of modern harp music. Fortunately the harp
part of *Harold* is extremely easy, and Herr Leibrock worked so hard
for five or six days that he acquitted himself most honourably . . . at
the general rehearsal. But on the evening of the concert he was seized
with a panic at the important moment; he stopped short in the introduction, and left Charles Müller, who was taking the viola solo, to
play alone.

This was our only mishap, and though the public never even perceived it, Herr Leibrock reproached himself bitterly for some days,
in spite of all my efforts to make him forget it.

There was no ophicleide of any sort at Brunswick; and to replace
it I was offered first a bass tuba (a magnificent deep instrument, of
which I shall have occasion to speak in connection with the military

bands of Berlin). The young man who played it did not, however, seem to me thoroughly master of the mechanism, not even knowing its full compass. Then a Russian bassoon, called by the performer a double-bassoon. I had much trouble in undeceiving him as to the nature and name of his instrument, which emits the sound just as it is written, and is played with a mouthpiece like the ophicleide; whilst the double-bassoon, a transposing reed instrument, is simply a large bassoon, reproducing almost the entire bassoon scale an octave lower. Be that as it may, the Russian bassoon was adopted to replace the ophicleide after a fashion. There was no cor anglais; we arranged its solos for an oboe, and began the orchestra rehearsals whilst the choir practised in another room. I must say here that never to this day, in France, Belgium, or Germany, have I seen a body of eminent artists who brought such devotion, attention, and ardour to their task. After the first rehearsal, when they were able to form some idea of the principal difficulties of my symphonies, the watchword was given for the following rehearsals. They agreed to cheat me as to the hour at which they were supposed by rights to begin, and every morning (I did not know this till afterwards) the orchestra assembled an hour before my arrival to practise the risky passages. Accordingly, I was each day more and more amazed at the rapid progress in the performance, and the impetuous assurance with which the whole body attacked difficulties that had long seemed formidable even to my Paris orchestra — that young guard of the grand army.

The only piece that gave Charles Müller much difficulty was the *Queen Mab* Scherzo, which, on the entreaty of Herr Zinkeisen (who had heard it in Paris), I had ventured for the first time since I came to Germany to insert in the programme.

" We will work so hard," he had said to me, " that we shall manage it." He did not overrate the powers of the orchestra, and Queen Mab in her microscopic car, attended by the buzzing insects of a summer's night, and launched at full gallop by her tiny horses, fully displayed to the Brunswick public her lively drollery and her thousand caprices. But you will understand my anxiety on this subject; for you, the poet of fairies and elves, the own brother of those graceful and malicious little creatures, know only too well with what slender thread their veil of gauze is woven, and how serene must be the sky beneath which their many-coloured tints sport freely in the pale starlight.

Well, in spite of our fears, the orchestra identified itself completely with Shakespeare's fascinating fancy, and became so tiny, agile, minute, and soft, that I do not think the imperceptible queen ever threaded her silent harmonies more happily.

In the finale of *Harold*, on the contrary, that furious orgy where wine, blood, joy, rage, all combined, parade their intoxication — where the rhythm sometimes seems to stumble along, sometimes to rush on in fury, and the brass seem to vomit forth curses and to answer prayer with blasphemies; where they laugh, drink, fight, destroy, slay, violate, and utterly run riot; in this brigand scene the orchestra became a regular pandemonium; there was something positively supernatural and terrifying in its frantic life and spirit, and violins, basses, trombones, drums, and cymbals all sang and bounded and roared with diabolical order and concord, whilst from the solo viola, the dreamy Harold, some trembling notes of his evening hymn were still heard in the distance as he fled in terror.

How my heart and my frame shuddered as I conducted that marvellous orchestra, in which I seemed to find my young Paris heroes more hot-blooded than ever. You know nothing like this, you poets; you are never carried away by such hurricanes! I would willingly have embraced the whole orchestra; but all I could do was to exclaim — in French, it is true, but the mere tone must have made them understand me — " Sublime! Gentlemen, you have my thanks and admiration; you are perfect brigands! "

The performance of the overture to *Benvenuto* was equally spirited; and yet the Introduction to *Harold,* the *Pilgrims' March,* and the *Serenade,* which are in a totally opposite style, were never played with calmer grandeur and more religious serenity. As for the piece from *Romeo* (*The Feast at the Capulets'*), its characteristics are also of the whirlwind sort, and it fairly carried one away.

You should have seen the excited look of the band in the intervals between the rehearsals. . . . Schmidt (an astounding double-bass) tore the skin off the forefinger of his right hand at the beginning of the pizzicato passage of the *Orgie;* but he went on, not thinking of stopping for such a trifle, or caring for its bleeding, merely contenting himself with changing the finger.

While we were abandoning ourselves to these delights, the choir on its side was also working diligently at the pieces from the *Requiem,* but with different results. The *Offertoire* and *Quærens me* at last went tolerably, but there was an insurmountable obstacle to the *Sanctus,* namely, the solo, which was to be sung by Schmetzer, the first tenor in the theatre and an excellent musician. The andante of this piece, written for three women's voices, presents certain enharmonic modulations which the fair Dresden singers had understood perfectly, but which were apparently quite beyond the musical comprehension of those at Brunswick. Having tried in vain for three days to grasp its meaning and intonations, these poor disheartened wretches sent a deputation to implore me not to expose them to such a public humiliation, and to strike the dreadful *Sanctus* out of the bill. I consented, but with great reluctance, especially on account of Schmetzer, whose high tenor exactly suits this seraphic hymn, and who, moreover, was delighting in the idea of singing it.

All was now ready, and in spite of Charles Müller's terror about the Scherzo, which he wished to practise once more, we were about to study at the concert the impressions produced by my music. On the advice of the Kapellmeister I had invited some twenty of the leading Brunswick amateurs to the rehearsals. Well, each day they acted as a living advertisement, exciting the curiosity of the public to the highest degree, until the interest even of the common people in the preparations for the concert, and their curiosity about it, rose to the highest pitch. "What happened at the rehearsal this morning? . . . Is he pleased? . . . He is a Frenchman, is he? . . . But surely the French only compose comic operas? . . . The singers think him very cross! . . . Did he really say the women sang like ballet-dancers? Then he knew that the sopranos of the chorus belong to the ballet corps? . . . Is it true that he took off his hat to the trombones in the middle of a piece? . . . The orchestra attendant says he drank two bottles of water, one of white wine, and three glasses of brandy at the rehearsal yesterday. . . . But why is he always saying, 'César! César!' ('*C'est ça, c'est ça!*') to the leader?" etc., etc.

Long before the appointed hour, however, the theatre was filled to overflowing by an impatient crowd already prepossessed in my favour. Now, my dear Heine, draw in your claws, for at this point you might be tempted to make me feel them. When the hour had come and the orchestra was seated, I entered, and, passing the violins, approached the conductor's desk. Judge of my terror when I saw it entirely covered by a huge garland of leaves.

"This is the musicians' doing," I said to myself, "and they will

have compromised me. How imprudent! To sell the bear's skin before
they have killed the bear! And a nice mess I shall be in if the public are
not of their opinion! Such a manifestation would be enough to ruin an
artist in Paris." The overture, however, was received with great
acclamation, the *Pilgrims' March* was encored, the *Orgie* put the
whole room in a fever, the devout were evidently deeply moved by the
Offertoire, with its chorus on two notes, and by the *Quærens me.*
Charles Müller was greatly applauded in the violin romance; *Queen
Mab* created quite a sensation; a song with the orchestra was encored;
and the *Feast at the Capulets'* formed a glowing finale to the evening. Scarcely had the last chord been struck when a terrible noise
shook the entire room, the whole public *en masse* hallooing (from pit,
boxes — everywhere else); the trumpets, horns, and trombones of
the orchestra, some in one key and some in another, made the most
discordant fanfares, accompanied by all the fracas that it was possible
to make with bows on the backs of violins and basses, and with the
percussion. The Germans have a word of their own for this peculiar
way of applauding.[1] On hearing it thus unexpectedly, my first feelings
were anger and disgust; they were spoiling the musical effect I had just
produced; and I almost felt a grudge against the artists for showing
their satisfaction by such a hubbub. But it was impossible not to be
deeply moved by their homage when the Kapellmeister, George Müller, came forward laden with flowers, and said in French: " Permit
me, sir, to offer you these wreaths in the name of the ducal band, and
allow me to lay them on your scores! "

At these words the public redoubled its applause, the orchestra
recommenced its fanfares . . . the baton fell from my hand, and I
was no longer aware of what was going on.

Laugh if you like! It will do you good and me no harm; besides,
I have not finished yet, and it would be too much for you to hear my
dithyramb to the end without putting your claws into me.

Scarcely had I left the theatre, in a perspiration as though I had
just been dipped in the Styx, and in such a bewildered state of delight
that I hardly knew what was being said, when I was informed that a
supper of one hundred and fifty covers had been ordered at my hotel,
to which I was invited by a society of artists and amateurs. I was, of
course, obliged to go. Fresh applause, fresh acclamations on my arrival; toasts and speeches in German and French succeeded each other.

[1] *Tusch.*

I replied as well as I could to such as I understood; and as each health
was drunk, a hundred and fifty voices replied by a hurrah in chorus,
the effect of which was most beautiful. The basses began first on D, the
tenors came in on the A, and the ladies on the F sharp, thus making the
chord of D major, followed immediately by the four chords of the sub-
dominant, tonic, dominant, and tonic, the connection of which thus
forms a plagal and a perfect cadence in succession. This fine salvo of
harmony burst forth with pomp and majesty in its grand movement;
and, at any rate, is truly worthy of a musical people.

What shall I say to you, my dear Heine? Though you may think
me *naïf* and primitive in the extreme, I must confess that all these
kindly manifestations and sympathetic acclamations made me super-
latively happy.[1] Doubtless this happiness does not even approach to
what the composer feels when conducting a magnificent orchestra in
the inspired performance of one of his beloved works; but the two
go very well together, and after such a concert, an evening like this
spoils nothing. I thus owe a great deal to the artists and amateurs of
Brunswick, as I do also to its chief musical critic, Robert Griepenkerl,
who engaged in vehement polemics with a Leipzig paper in a learned
pamphlet about me, and gave a very correct idea, I think, of the force
and direction of the musical current that carries me away.

So give me your hand and let us sing a grand hurrah for Brunswick on its favourite chords.

I am sorry, my dear poet, but here you are committed to being a
musician.

[1] Berlioz had a genuine success at Brunswick: even Marie was encored. In spite of the cheap
prices, he tells his father, he netted 750 francs. He complains he is being ruined by the expense
of carriage of his scores and parts, which weigh 500 lbs.

Now for your native town of Hamburg, that city desolate [1] as ancient Pompeii, which yet rises powerfully from its own ashes, and bravely stanches its wounds! . . . Certainly, I have only praises to bestow upon it, for it has grand musical resources, singing societies, philharmonic societies, military bands, etc. True, the orchestra of the theatre has been reduced, for economy's sake, to very mediocre proportions; but I had made my terms with the manager beforehand, and the orchestra to which I was introduced was quite admirable both in numbers and in talent, thanks to a valuable addition of strings, and to the leave of absence I procured for two or three almost centenarian players, to whom the theatre was devoted. One strange thing I must mention: there is an excellent harpist with a very good instrument! I had begun to despair of finding either the one or the other in Germany. I also found a vigorous ophicleide, but had to dispense with a cor anglais.

The first flute (Cantal) and the first violin (Lindenau) are two virtuosi of the highest order. The Kapellmeister (Krebs) fulfils his functions with talent and a strictness that is excellent in a conductor. He helped me with great good nature during our long rehearsals. The singing troupe of the theatre was pretty well organised; it possessed three meritorious artists, a tenor who, if not gifted with an exceptional voice, had both taste and method; an agile soprano whose name I have forgotten (the young *diva* would actually have done me the honour to sing at my concert if I had been better known — Hosanna in excelsis!); and lastly Reichel, the formidable bass, with his enormous voice of two octaves and a half! Reichel is a superb-looking man, and represents such characters as Sarastro, Moses, and Bertram, to perfection. Madame Cornet, the wife of the manager, a finished musician, with a most striking soprano of unusual compass, was only engaged to appear in a limited number of representations. I applauded her highly as the Queen of Night in the *Magic Flute*. The chorus was small and not strong, but got through its part very decently. The opera-house is very large: I rather dreaded its size, having found it empty at three different representations of the *Magic Flute, Moïse,* and *Linda di Chamounix.* Accordingly, I was most agreeably surprised at finding it full the day I presented myself before the Hamburg public.

An excellent performance, a numerous, intelligent, and very cordial

[1] Hamburg had just been burnt to the ground. [H.]

audience made this one of the best concerts [1] I ever gave in Germany. *Harold* and the cantata of *Le Cinq Mai,* sung with great feeling by Reichel, carried off the honours. After this piece, two musicians close to my desk touched me deeply by these simple words, spoken under their breath, in French: "Ah, monsieur, notre respect, notre respect!" It was all the French they could muster.[2]

In a word, the Hamburg orchestra has ever been my firm friend, and I assure you I am not a little proud of it. Krebs alone displayed a curious reticence in his opinion. " My dear fellow," he said to me, " in a few years your music will be known all over Germany. It will become popular, and that will be a great misfortune! What imitations it will provoke, what a style, what absurdities! It would be better for art that you had never been born." Still, let us hope that these poor symphonies are not so *contagious* as this implied, and that they will breed neither yellow fever nor cholera morbus!

Now Heine, Henri Heine, famous banker of ideas, nephew of Mr. Solomon Heine, author of so many precious poems in ingots, I have no more to say to you, and I . . . salute you.

H. B.

CHAPTER LVIII

BERLIN

LETTER VII — TO MLLE. LOUISE BERTIN

I MUST first of all implore your indulgence, mademoiselle, for the letter I am taking the liberty to write to you; I have but too much to fear from my present state of mind. A fit of black philosophy attacked me some days ago, and God knows to what gloomy notions, or absurd judgments, or strange stories it will impel me . . . if it lasts. You do not, perhaps, know exactly what black philosophy is? It is the contrary of white magic — neither more nor less.

By white magic one divines that Victor Hugo is a great poet; that Beethoven was a great musician; that you are at once musician and poetess; that Janin is a man of intellect; that if a fine and well-

[1] On March 22.
[2] In Hamburg, and in Brunswick, Berlioz had a great success. Marie sang twice.

performed opera fails, the public has not understood it; that if it succeeds, the public has not understood it either; that the beautiful is rare; that the rare is not always beautiful; that might is right; that Abd-el-Kader is wrong, and O'Connell also; that the Arabs are decidedly not Frenchmen; that peaceful agitation is stupidity — and other problems equally intricate.

By black philosophy one is reduced to doubt and wonder at everything, to see all gracious images on the wrong side, and all hideous things in their naked significance; to murmur without ceasing, to blaspheme life, and curse death. Like Hamlet, one is indignant that

> Imperial Cæsar, dead, and turn'd to clay,
> Might stop a hole to keep the wind away.

One would be still more indignant if the ashes of the poor only were put to this ignoble use. One pities " poor Yorick " for not being able to laugh at the senseless grimace he makes after his fifteen years underground, and one throws down his skull with horror and disgust, or else one makes it into a drinking-cup, and poor Yorick, who can drink no more, serves to stanch the thirst of the topers who jeer at him.

Thus, in the solitude of the Roches, where you are peaceably indulging your own thoughts, I should only experience mortal weariness and discontent while a prey to this black philosophy.

Yesterday, mademoiselle, while in this condition, I happened to be in a house where they have a mania for autographs. The lady of the house did not fail to ask me to write something in her album. " But, I beg of you," she added, " no commonplaces." This injunction irritated me, and I immediately wrote:

" *The death penalty is a great misfortune, for, if it did not exist, I should probably have murdered a great many people, and we should now have fewer of those begging idiots who are the plague of art and artists.*"

They laughed a good deal at my aphorism, thinking that I did not mean a word of it.

If you called on me to admire a fine sunset, I should probably prefer the gaslights of the Avenue des Champs-Élysées; if you pointed out your graceful swans on the lake, I should say, " The swan is an idiotic animal; it thinks of nothing but paddling and eating, its only ' song ' is a stupid and horrible rattle." If you were to go to the piano and play something from your favourite composers, Mozart and

Cimarosa,[1] I should probably interrupt you in a pet, saying that it was really time to have done with this admiration for Mozart, whose operas are all exactly alike, and whose *sang-froid* provokes and wearies me. . . . As for Cimarosa, I should pitch to the devil his unique and everlasting *Matrimonio segreto,* which is nearly as tiresome as the *Mariage de Figaro,* without being anything like so musical; I should prove that the comedy of the work resided entirely in the interpolations of the actors; that its melodic invention was extremely limited, that the perpetually recurring perfect cadence took up at least two-thirds of the score; in fact, that it is an opera only for carnivals and fairs. And if, to take an example in the opposite style, you were to produce one of Sebastian Bach's works, I should probably take flight at the sight of one of his fugues and leave you alone with his *Passion.* You see the consequences of this terrible malady! When possessed by it you have neither courtesy, nor *savoir-vivre,* prudence, policy, tact, nor good sense; you say all sorts of enormities, and what is worse, you mean what you say, commit yourself, lose your head.

A plague, then, upon black philosophy! The attack is past. I am now sober enough to speak reasonably, and tell you what I have seen and heard at Berlin;[2] afterwards I shall speak of my own performances.

To begin with the lyrical theatre.

The late German Opera-house, which was burnt down scarcely three months ago, was rather dark and not over clean, but very sonorous and well suited for musical effects. The orchestra was not so near the audience as in Paris; it extended further on both sides, and the noisy instruments — trombones, trumpets, and drums — were somewhat screened by the first boxes, and thus lost some of their excessive resonance. The band — one of the best I ever heard — was composed as follows for the big performances: 14 first and 14 second violins, 8 violas, 10 cellos, 8 double-basses, 4 flutes, 4 oboes, 4 clarinets, 4 bassoons, 4 horns, 4 trumpets, 4 trombones, 1 kettle-drummer, 1 big drum, a pair of cymbals, and 2 harps. The stringed instruments are almost all first-rate; at their head I must specify the brothers Ganz (first violin and first cello of the highest merit), and the clever violinist, Ries. The wood-wind is also very good, and, as you see,

---

[1] Mademoiselle Bertin told me lately that I did her an injustice in regarding Cimarosa as one of her favorite composers. I regret my error; but in any case the calumny, I imagine, is not a very serious one. [B.]

[2] He arrived in Berlin March 28.

double that at the Paris Opéra — a great advantage, since it allows two flutes, two oboes, two clarinets, and two bassoons to come in as ripieni in the fortissimi, and thus greatly soften the harshness of the brass, which would otherwise be too prominent. The horns are very powerful, and all *à cylindre,* to the great regret of Meyerbeer, who still retains the same opinion of the new mechanism which I held myself till quite lately. Several composers object to the horn *à cylindre* because they do not think its tone equal to that of the simple one. I have made the experiment several times with the open notes, and I confess I found it impossible to discover the least difference in timbre or sonority between the ordinary and the cylinder horn. Another objection, apparently better founded, has also been made to the new horn, but it can easily be overcome. Since this instrument (which to my mind is now perfect) has been introduced into our orchestras, some players, while employing the cylinders for the ordinary horn tones, find it more convenient with this mechanism to produce the *stopped* notes (so intended by the composer) as *open* sounds. This is, no doubt, a great mistake, but it is one for which the performer is to be blamed and not the instrument. The cylinder horn in the hands of a clever artist can produce not only all the stopped sounds of the ordinary horn, but even the entire scale without employing a single open note. The only conclusion from all this is that horn players ought to be able to use their hands in the bells as if the cylinders did not exist, and that composers from henceforth should mark stopped notes by some sign, the performer only producing open sounds where there is no mark.

The same prejudice has opposed the use of the cylinder trumpets, now so common in Germany, but with even less reason than in the case of the horn. No composer ever uses stopped sounds for the trumpet, and the question is, therefore, naturally one of no moment. The only complaint was that the trumpet lost much of its brilliancy of tone by the cylinders; but this is not the case, at least to my ear. Well, if a finer ear than mine is wanted to detect a difference between the two instruments, I trust it will be admitted that the inconvenience resulting from this difference is not to be compared with the advantage of being able to go up and down a chromatic scale two octaves and a half in compass, without difficulty and without the slightest inequality of tone. To my mind, therefore, the Germans have done well to abandon the use of the simple trumpet almost entirely. In France we have still very few chromatic (or cylinder) trumpets, the incredible

popularity of the cornet à pistons having so far stood in their way —
wrongly, as I think. The tone of the cornet is far from being so noble
or brilliant as that of the trumpet. At any rate there is no lack of instruments. Adolphe Sax now makes cylinder trumpets in all sizes and
in all possible keys, usual and unusual, the perfection and sonority of
which are undeniable. And yet, will it be believed that this ingenious
young artist has all the trouble in the world in making his way and
maintaining himself in Paris? Persecutions worthy of the Middle
Ages are inflicted on him, corresponding perfectly to those Benvenuto
Cellini had to endure from his enemies. His workmen are enticed away,
his designs stolen, he is accused of madness, and driven to litigation. A
trifle more, and they would assassinate him. Such is the hatred that
inventors always excite amongst those of their rivals who can invent
nothing for themselves. Fortunately the gifted inventor has always
enjoyed the friendship and protection of General de Rumigny; but
will he be able to count for ever on these aids in the wretched struggle?
It is the duty of the Minister of War to place so useful and so gifted
a man in the position to which his talent, his perseverance, and his
efforts entitle him. Our military bands have as yet neither cylinder
trumpets nor bass tubas. These instruments will be absolutely necessary if the French military orchestras are to reach the same level as
those of Prussia and Austria. An order for three hundred trumpets
and a hundred bass tubas, sent to Adolphe Sax by the Government,
would save him.

Berlin is the only German town where I found the deep bass trombone (in B flat). We have none in Paris, the performers there declining the practice of an instrument which tires their chests. Apparently
the Prussian lungs are more robust than ours. The orchestra of the
Berlin Opera possesses two of these instruments, the sonority of
which is such as completely to destroy the tone of the alto and tenor
trombones. The domineering tone of a bass trombone would be
enough to destroy the balance and ruin the harmony of the three trombone parts as written by most composers nowadays. Well, at the Berlin Opera there is no ophicleide, and instead of replacing it by a bass
tuba in the French operas, which nearly all contain an ophicleide part,
they imagined that they could have this part played by a second bass
trombone; but the result of combining these two terrible instruments
— the ophicleide part being often written an octave below the third
trombone — is most disastrous. The deep tone of the brass so pre-

dominates that it is as much as even the trumpet can do to make itself heard. In my own concerts, at which, however, I only employed one bass trombone (for the symphonies), I noticed this, and was therefore obliged to beg the artist who played it to sit so as to turn the bell of the instrument towards the desk, which thus served as a sort of sordine, whilst the alto and tenor trombones played standing, with their bells above the desk. In this way alone could the three parts be heard. Repeated observations at Berlin led me to think that the best way of grouping the trombones in the theatres is, after all, that adopted at the Paris Opéra, where three tenor trombones are employed. The alto one is so shrill that its high notes are of little use, and I should be inclined to vote for its exclusion from theatres, and to allow the presence of a bass trombone only if the music were in *four* parts, and there were *three tenors* capable of holding their own against it.

My speech may not be golden, but at any rate there is plenty of brass about it. I am sure, however, that these details about instrumentation will interest you, mademoiselle, far more than my misanthropic tirades and bad jokes about death's heads. Though both a melodist and a harmonist, you are but little versed in osteology — at least as far as I know. I therefore resume the examination of the musical forces of the Berlin Opera.

The kettle-drummer is a good musician, but his wrists are not supple nor his rolls sufficiently rapid; his kettle-drums also are too small, and have too little tone, and he is only acquainted with one sort of drumstick, which occupies a middle place between the ordinary leather heads and those with sponge. In this respect the Germans are far behind the French. Even as regards execution — with the exception of Wiprecht, the head of the military band at Berlin, who plays the kettle-drums like a clap of thunder — I have not met one player who for precision, rapidity of roll, and delicacy of nuance, can compare with Poussard, our excellent artist of the Opéra.

Am I to tell you anything about the cymbals? All I can say is, that you rarely find a pair of cymbals intact, that is to say, neither cracked nor chipped; neither at Weimar, nor Leipzig, nor Dresden, nor Hamburg, nor Berlin was I so fortunate. This was always a subject of great wrath with me, and I have sometimes kept the orchestra waiting half an hour, and refused to begin a rehearsal until they had brought me two perfectly new cymbals, as vibrating and as Turkish as I desired, to prove to the Kapellmeister that I was not wrong in regarding the broken fragments presented to me under that name as both absurd and detestable. It must be admitted that the inferiority of certain parts of the German orchestras is quite disgraceful. The instruments are poor, and the performers are far from knowing all that can be got out of them: I speak of the kettle-drums, the cymbals, the big drum, the cor anglais, the ophicleide, and the harp. But this defect is evidently due to the style of writing of certain composers, who attach so little importance to these instruments that their successors, who write in another style, are unable to get anything out of them.

But, on the other hand, the Germans are greatly superior to us in their brass in general, and their trumpets in particular. We have no idea of these. Their clarinets are also better; as to oboes, I think the two countries are about on a par. In flutes we beat them, for the flute is nowhere played as it is in Paris. Their double-basses are more powerful than ours; their cellos, violas, and violins have grand qualities; but still, you could hardly without injustice put them on the same level with the unrivalled violins, violas, and cellos of our Conservatoire.

I have given abundant proofs of the scarcity of good harps in Germany; those of Berlin are no exception to the rule, and in that capital there is great room for some pupils of Parish-Alvars. This magnificent orchestra, which is famous for its precision, force, and delicacy, is under the command of Meyerbeer, director-general of the King of Prussia's music — you know him I think; of Hennig (first Kapellmeister), a clever man, and highly esteemed; and of Taubert (second Kapellmeister), a brilliant pianist and composer. I heard one of his piano trios performed by himself and the brothers Ganz, and found it an excellent work, in a new style and full of fire. His choruses to the Greek tragedy, *Medea,* have just been successfully produced at Berlin. Messrs. Ganz and Ries share the title and functions of leader.

Now let us go upon the stage.

On ordinary occasions the chorus contains but sixty voices; but when grand operas are performed before the King it is doubled in numbers. All these voices are excellent, fresh, and sonorous; most of the chorus, men, women, and children, are musicians — not such clever readers as those of our Opéra, but far better trained in the art of singing, more attentive and careful, and better paid. It is the finest theatrical chorus I have yet come across. Its director is Elssler, brother to the celebrated ballet-dancer, a patient and intelligent artist. He might save himself much trouble and accelerate the choir practices considerably if, instead of training all the hundred and twenty in one room at the same time, he were to divide them into three groups (sopranos and contraltos, tenors, basses) in three different rooms, under three sub-leaders, superintended by himself. This analytical method, which is rejected by the theatres for miserable reasons of economy and routine, is, however, the only one that admits of the thorough study of each chorus part, and of a careful and well-shaded performance. I have said this often, and shall never tire of repeating it.

The actor-singers of the Berlin Theatre do not occupy, as virtuosi, so high a place among Europeon musicians as do the choir and orchestra. There is much talent among them, however, more especially in the following:

Mdlle. Marx, an expressive and very sympathetic soprano, whose extreme notes, both low and high, are unhappily already beginning to show signs of wear.

Mdlle. Tutchek, a soprano, with a tolerably pure and flexible timbre.

Mdlle. Hähnel, a contralto of individuality.

Boeticher, an excellent bass, with a grand compass and fine tone, a clever singer, fine actor, consummate musician and reader.

Zsische, a *basso cantante,* with real talent and a voice and method calculated to shine rather in the concert-room than at the theatre.

Mantius, first tenor, voice somewhat wanting in flexibility and not very large in compass.

Madame Schroeder-Devrient, only recently engaged, a soprano somewhat touched in the upper notes, but still brilliant and dramatic. When Madame Devrient cannot force her notes, she now sings flat. Her ornamentation is in very bad taste, and she intersperses her singing with spoken phrases and interjections, like our vaudeville actors in their couplets, the effect of which is execrable. Her school of singing is most anti-musical and trivial, and beginners ought to be warned against imitating it.

I hear that Pischek, the excellent baritone, whom I spoke of in connection with Frankfort, has just been engaged by Meyerbeer.

This, mademoiselle, is all I can tell you of the dramatic and musical resources of the capital of Prussia. I did not attend a single performance at the Italian Theatre, and so abstain from speaking of it.

In another letter, and before giving any account of my own concerts, I shall have to call up my recollections of the performances of the *Huguenots* and *Armide,* of the Singing Academy and of the military bands — most important institutions, though essentially opposite in character, and so magnificent in comparison with anything of ours in the same style, that our national self-love ought to be deeply humiliated.

H. B.

CHAPTER LIX

BERLIN

LETTER VIII — TO MONSIEUR HABENECK

I WAS lately giving Mdlle. Louise Bertin, whose musical science and serious love of art are no strangers to you, an account of the vocal and instrumental resources of the Grand Opera at Berlin. I shall now proceed to tell you of the Singing Academy and the military music of the place; but since you specially wish to know my opinion of such opera performances as I attended, I will reverse the order of my narrative, and give you an account of the Prussian artists in the operas of Meyerbeer, Gluck, Mozart, and Weber. In Berlin, as in Paris and indeed everywhere else, there are, unhappily, certain days when it would seem that a tacit understanding between the artists and the public sanctions more or less carelessness in the performance. Many empty places are then visible in the theatre, and many vacant desks in the orchestra. On such evenings the authorities dine out, give balls, are out hunting, etc. The musicians are asleep, though playing the *notes* of their parts; some do not even play at all, but sleep, read, draw caricatures, play foolish jokes on their neighbours, and chatter loudly; I do not need to tell *you* what goes on in orchestras on these occasions.

As for the actors, they are too much *en évidence* to allow themselves such liberties, though even that sometimes happens; but the chorus-singers indulge themselves to their hearts' content. They straggle on to the stage one after the other, a few at a time; many have arrived late at the theatre and are not yet dressed, and some, having had a fatiguing service at church during the day, are quite worn out when they make their appearance, and fully determined beforehand not to sing a note. Each takes his ease, the high notes are transposed an octave lower, or given *sotto voce;* there are no nuances; the mezzo forte is adopted throughout the evening, no one looks at the baton, and the result is three or four false entries and as many disjointed phrases; but what does it signify? Does the public take any notice? The director knows nothing about it, and if the composer complains he is laughed at openly as a mischief-maker. The ladies in particular amuse themselves in a charming manner by exchanging smiles and signals with the musicians in the orchestra or the *habitués* of the balcony. In the morning they were at the christening of the child of Mademoiselle X., one of their colleagues, and have brought back bon-bons, which they eat on the stage, laughing all the time at the grotesque appearance of the godfather, the coquetry of the godmother, or the delighted countenance of the parson. As they chat they thump the children in the chorus, who are behaving rather too noisily:

" Have done, you mischievous child, or I will call the singing-master."

" My dear, just look at the lovely rose in M. ———'s button-hole; it was Florence who gave it him."

" Is she still mad about her *agent de change?* "

" Yes; but it is a secret. Everyone cannot have *solicitors.*"

" Oh, what a good pun! By the way, are you going to the Court concert? "

" No. I have an engagement that day."

" What is it? "

" I am going to be married."

" What an idea! "

" Take care! there is the curtain! "

And so the act is finished; the public mystified; and the work spoilt! But what then? One must take a little rest; one cannot always be on one's best behaviour; and these disorderly, slovenly representations serve to set off those that are done with care, zeal, attention, and talent. I admit this, but still there is something sad in seeing the great masterpieces treated with a familiarity likely to breed contempt. I admit that one cannot burn incense day and night before the statues of great men; but who could bear to see the bust of Gluck or of Beethoven employed as a barber's block? . . .

Do not philosophise. I am certain it would make you indignant. I

do not wish you to conclude from all this that in the Berlin Opera
these frolics are of very frequent occurrence. No, they go to work with
moderation; in this, as in other respects, the palm remains with us.
A masterpiece may be represented in Paris in the utterly disorderly
manner that I have just described, but in Prussia it would only be permissible to give it in slight undress. I saw *Figaro* and the *Freischütz*
played in this manner. It was not bad; neither was it very good. There
was a certain slackness in the ensemble; vagueness, rather than precision; moderation, instead of *verve;* warmth, instead of fire. The
colour and animation which betoken life, and that luxury which is so
essential to good music, were altogether wanting; as well as something
still more essential, namely, inspiration.

But at the performances of *Armide* and the *Huguenots* the trans-
formation was complete; I could have believed myself to be at one of
those " first nights " in Paris, where you come early in order to see a
little of the performers and make your final suggestions; where each
is at his post beforehand; where the minds of all are on the stretch,
where every face wears a grave, intelligent, attentive look; where, in
a word, you can see that a musical event of some importance is
looming.

In the great orchestra not a desk was empty — strings or double-
wind; the chorus were there to the last of the one hundred and
twenty, and Meyerbeer was in the conductor's seat. I was very anxious
to see him conduct, especially his own work. He acquitted himself as
though he had been at it for twenty years; the orchestra is in his grasp,
he does what he likes with it. As for the tempi at which he takes the
music, they are the same as your own, with the exception of the entry
of the monks in the fourth act, and the march at the end of the
third, which were a little slower. In the first case this difference produced, on me, a slightly chilling effect; but in the second (played on
the stage by the military band) the result was a great improvement in
every respect.

I cannot analyse the orchestral playing in Meyerbeer's masterpiece scene by scene; enough to say that the whole representation was
magnificent, beautiful, perfect in nuance throughout, and with incomparable clearness and precision even in the most intricate passages.
The finale of the second act, with its passages based on the series of
chords of the diminished seventh, and its enharmonic modulations,
was given with extreme clearness and an absolute perfection of intona-

tion. The same for the choir. The vocalised passages, the contrasting double choruses, the answers in imitation, the sudden transition from loud to soft, the intermediate gradations — all these were clearly and vigorously executed with a rare warmth, and a still rarer feeling of true expression. The stretto of the Consecration of the Poignards struck me like a thunderclap, and it was long before I recovered from the shock. The grand ensemble of the *Pré aux Clercs,* the dispute of the women, the litanies of the Virgin, the song of the Huguenot soldiers — formed a musical tissue of marvellous richness, so clearly given that every thread in the complex thinking of the composer could be followed distinctly. This miracle of dramatised counterpoint remains in my recollection as a perfect marvel of choral execution. I do not think that Meyerbeer can hope to hear a better anywhere else in Europe. It must be added that the *mise en scène* is most ingeniously arranged. In the *rataplan* song the chorus imitate a kind of tambour march, thereby greatly enlivening the scene and increasing the effect of the music.

The military band, instead of being placed, as in Paris, at the back of the theatre, separated from the orchestra by the entire depth of the stage, and out of sight of the conductor, so that it cannot follow his beat accurately, commences playing in the front side-scenes to the right, then begins to march, and gradually passes across the stage close to the footlights, and through the groups of the chorus. Thus the musicians remain close to the conductor almost to the end of the piece; they keep the same strict time as the orchestra, and there is never the slightest rhythmical discordance between the two groups.

Boeticher is an excellent Saint-Bris, and Zsische a fairly good Marcel, without, however, possessing any of that dramatic *humour* which makes our Levasseur so true and original in the part. Mademoiselle Marx shows sensibility and modest dignity, qualities essential for Valentine. I must nevertheless reproach her with two or three spoken monosyllables which she was weak enough to borrow from the school of Madame Devrient. I saw the latter in the same part some days later, and if my open opposition to her manner of playing shocked some good judges who, probably from habit, admire the celebrated artist unreservedly, I am bound to state why my opinion differs so entirely from theirs. I had formed no judgment and contracted no prejudice either for or against Madame Devrient. I only remember that at Paris many years ago I thought her admirable in Beethoven's

Fidelio, while quite recently in Dresden, on the contrary, I had noticed certain very bad habits in her singing, and much affectation and exaggeration in her stage action. These defects were all the more obvious in the *Huguenots* because the situations are so thrilling and the music so stamped with grandeur and truth. Accordingly I blamed her severely, both as singer and actress, and for this reason: in the conspiracy scene, where Saint-Bris unfolds to Nevers and his friends his plan for the massacre of the Huguenots, Valentine listens to her father's bloody projects with a shudder, but takes care not to allow her horror to be seen. Indeed, Saint-Bris is not the man to tolerate such opinions in his daughter. Valentine's involuntary spring towards her husband, when the latter breaks his sword and refuses to join the conspiracy, is all the more beautiful because the timid woman has long suffered in silence, and her trouble has been so painfully concealed. Well, instead of masking her agitation and remaining almost passive, like other sensible tragediennes in this scene, Madame Devrient approaches Nevers, forces him to follow her to the back of the stage, and there, striding along beside him, appears to dictate to him both his line of conduct and his reply to Saint-Bris. Hence it follows that the exclamation of Valentine's husband,

> Parmi mes illustres aïeux
> Je compte des soldats, mais pas un assassin,

loses the whole force of its opposition; there is no spontaneity in his movement, and he only looks like a submissive husband repeating the lesson his wife has taught him. When Saint-Bris sings the famous theme, "*À cette cause sainte,*" Madame Devrient so entirely forgets herself as to throw herself into the arms of her father, who is supposed all the while to know nothing of Valentine's feelings. She beseeches, she implores, in fact, she torments him by so vehement a pantomime that Boeticher, who at first was evidently not prepared for these ill-timed transports, could scarcely move and breathe, and by the motion of his head and right arm seemed to say: " For heaven's sake, madame, leave me alone; and let me sing my part to the end."

This is an illustration of the extent to which Madame Devrient is possessed by the desire to assert herself. She would think herself ruined if somehow or other, by any kind of stage trick whatever, she did not attract the attention of the public. She evidently regards herself as the pivot of the drama, the only character worthy to occupy the spectators. "You listen to this actor? You admire the composer? You are taken by this chorus? How stupid of you! Look at *me;* for I am the poem, I am the poetry, I am the music, I am everything! To-night there is no object of interest but me, and you cannot have come to the theatre for anything but me!"

In the great duet that follows this immortal scene, while Raoul surrenders himself to the full madness of his despair, Madame Devrient rests her hands on a settee, and gracefully inclines her head to the left so as to let her beautiful blonde ringlets fall. She says a few words, and then, while Raoul is replying, she adopts another pose and lets the audience admire her hair from the other side. I take leave to doubt whether these puerile coquetries are what would be occupying the soul of Valentine in such a movement.

Madame Devrient's singing, I have already said, is often wanting in exactness and taste. The pauses and changes which she introduces into her parts are in bad style, and awkwardly brought in. But they are nothing to her spoken interjections. She never *sings* such words as O God; yes; no; impossible! They are always spoken, or rather shouted in the loudest voice. I cannot express my aversion for this anti-musical declamation. To my mind it is a hundred times worse to speak in an opera than to sing in a tragedy.

One sees occasionally a phrase in a score marked *canto parlato,* but such phrases are not intended to be hurled forth in the manner I have described; they should be delivered *as music,* with the voice true to the notes. Everyone can remember the way in which Mademoiselle Falcon used to give the words at the end of that same duet, " *Raoul! ils te tueront!* " in *spoken singing,* at once natural and musical, and also immensely effective. How different when, in answer to Raoul's entreaties, Madame Devrient shouts thrice with a powerful cre-scendo, " *Nein! nein! nein!* " One might be listening to Dorval or Georges in a melodrama, and one asks why the orchestra should go on playing when the opera is over. It is really too absurd. I was too furious at hearing a masterpiece like the fourth act thus treated to wait for the fifth. Am I slandering you, dear Habeneck, if I say that I feel sure you would have done the same? I hardly think so. I know your feeling about music; when a fine work is being badly performed, you say what you think; and the more detestable the performance is, the greater your courage! But if all is going well and just a single thing happens to go wrong, you are driven crazy by this solitary exception; you would gladly watch the extermination of the offender, and while the public are amazed at your anger, the true artists share it with you, and I, for my part, gnash my teeth with you.

Madame Devrient has certainly fire and spirit, but these fine qualities, even had they been enough in themselves, never struck me as sufficiently restrained within the natural limits of certain of her characters. The part of Valentine, for example, even independently of what I have just been saying — Valentine the young bride of a day, whose heart though strong is timid, the noble wife of Nevers, who only avows her chaste love to Raoul in order to save him from death — is surely better represented by modest passion, dignified acting, and expressive singing, than by all the exaggerated volleys and detestable egoism of Madame Devrient.

Some days after the *Huguenots* I saw *Armide*. This celebrated work was revived with all the care and respect due to it; the *mise en scène* was magnificent and dazzling, and the public proved itself worthy of the favour granted to it. Of all the ancient composers, Gluck has, I believe, the least to fear from the incessant revolutions of art. He sacrificed nothing either to the caprices of singers, the exigencies of fashion, or the inveterate routine with which he had to contend on his arrival in France, after his protracted struggles with the Italian theatres. Doubtless his conflicts at Milan, Naples, and Parma, instead of weakening him, had increased his strength by revealing its full extent to himself; for, in spite of the fanaticism then prevalent in our French artistic customs, he broke these miserable trammels and trod them underfoot with the greatest ease. True, the clamour of the critics once succeeded in forcing him into a reply; but it was the only indiscretion with which he had to reproach himself, and thenceforth, as before, he went straight to his aim in silence. We all know what that aim was; we also know that it was never given to any man to succeed more fully. With less conviction or less firmness, it is probable that, notwithstanding his natural genius, his degenerate works would not have long survived those of his mediocre rivals now completely forgotten. But truth of expression, purity of style, and grandeur of form belong to all time. Gluck's fine passages will always be fine. Victor Hugo is right: the heart never grows old.

I thought Mademoiselle Marx in *Armide* noble and impassioned, although somewhat overwhelmed by her epic burden. In fact, mere talent does not suffice to represent Gluck's women; for them, as for

Shakespeare's, the greatest qualities of soul, heart, voice, physiognomy, and pose are so indispensable, that there is no exaggeration in asserting that these characters absolutely require both beauty and genius.

What a happy evening I passed listening to that performance of *Armide,* under Meyerbeer's direction! Orchestra and chorus, alike inspired by the composer and the conductor, showed themselves worthy of two such illustrious masters. The famous finale, *Poursuivons jusqu'au trépas,* produced a regular *furore.* The Hatred scene, with the admirable dances arranged, if I mistake not, by Paul Taglioni, the ballet master at the Berlin Theatre, struck me as equally remarkable for its *verve* and for the *infernal* harmony which pervaded its apparent disorder. They suppressed the dance air in A major 6-8, which we play in Paris, and in its stead introduced the great chaconne in B flat, unknown there; it is well worked out and most striking and fiery. What a conception is that Hatred scene! I had never before so fully understood or admired it. I shuddered at this passage in the invocation:

> Sauvez-moi de l'amour;
> Rien n'est si redoutable!

On the first line the two oboes make a cruel discord on the major seventh, like a woman's cry of terror and keenest anguish. But in the following verse,

> Contre un ennemi trop aimable,

how tenderly do those same two voices lament in thirds! A few notes only, but how full of regret; and how one feels the enormous power of the love thus bemoaned! In fact, no sooner has Hatred arrived with her terrible attendants and begun her work, than Armide interrupts her and refuses her aid.

Thereupon the chorus,

> Suis l'amour, puisque tu le veux,
> Infortunée Armide;
> Suis l'amour, qui te guide
> Dans un abîme affreux!

There the act ends in Quinault's poem; Armide goes out with the chorus without a word. But to Gluck this *dénouement* seemed commonplace and unnatural; he desired that the enchantress should remain for a moment alone, and then retire musing on what she had just heard; and one day after a rehearsal at the Opéra he improvised both words and music of the scene as they stand at the end:

> O ciel! quelle horrible menace!
> Je frémis! tout mon sang se glace!
>
> Amour, puissant amour, viens calmer mon effroi,
> Et prends pitié d'un cœur qui s'abandonne à toi!

The music is lovely: full of melody, harmony, vague uneasiness, touching languor — in a word, of the finest dramatic and musical inspiration.

Between each exclamation in the first two lines the basses play a long chromatic phrase (under a sort of intermittent tremolo in the second violins), which continues to growl and menace until, at the word *amour,* in the third line, the semi-obscurity of the preceding bars is relieved by the tender light of a slow, suave melody. After this all dies away. . . . Armide withdraws with downcast eyes, while the second violins, abandoned by the rest of the orchestra, continue their solitary tremolo. Stupendous genius to have created such a scene!

Bless me! My admiring analysis is really naïve; I really might be initiating you, Habeneck, into the beauties of Gluck's work! But you know it is involuntary! I am talking to you now as we do sometimes on the boulevards, after the Conservatoire concerts, when our enthusiasm is too strong to be kept in.

I will make one remark about the *mise en scène* of this piece at Berlin.

The curtain drops too quickly; it ought to wait until the last bar of the final *ritornel,* otherwise we lose Armide's slow exit up the stage accompanied by the gradually diminishing sighs and palpitations of the orchestra. This effect was most beautiful at the Paris Opéra, where the curtain was never lowered at all when *Armide* was performed. On the other hand, although you know I disapprove of the conductor's making any changes in music not his own, where his only business is to secure a good performance, I must compliment Meyerbeer on a happy idea in connection with the tremolo just mentioned. This passage for the second violins being on the low D, Meyerbeer, in order to make it more striking, had it played on two strings in unison, the open D and the D on the fourth string. The natural consequence of this is that the number of the instruments appears suddenly

to have been doubled, while the combination of the two strings produces a certain resonance that is most effective. *Such* corrections of
Gluck are always permissible.[1]

It is like your idea of playing the famous continuous tremolo of
the oracle in *Alceste* close to the bridge of the violin and *smashing the
string*. Gluck did not express this, it is true, but *he ought to have
done so*.

For exquisite expression the performance of the scenes in the
enchanted garden surpassed all the others to my mind. It was a kind
of voluptuous languor, a fascinating *morbidezza* that transported me
into the palace of love dreamed of by Gluck and Tasso, and seemed
to present it to me as an enchanted abode. I closed my eyes, and whilst
listening to the divine gavotte, with its caressing melody and its softly
murmuring monotonous harmony, and to the chorus, *Jamais dans ces
beaux lieux,* so exquisitely graceful in its expression of happiness, I
seemed to be surrounded on all sides by enfolding arms, adorable,
intertwining feet, floating hair, shining eyes, and intoxicating smiles.
The flower of pleasure, gently stirred by the melodious breeze, expanded, and a concert of sounds, colours, and perfumes poured forth
from its ravishing corolla. Is this Gluck, the terrible musician who
chanted all the sorrows, who sang of the horrors of Tartarus, who
painted the desolate shores of Tauris and its savage inhabitants? Is
it he who could thus reproduce in music so marvellous an ideal of
voluptuous reverie, of repose in love? . . . Why not? Had he not
already opened the Elysian fields? Was not he the creator of that immortal chorus of the happy spirits? —

> Torna, o bella, al tuo consorte
> Che non vuol che più diviso
> Sia di te pietoso il ciel!

And as our great modern poet has said, are not the strongest generally
also the gentlest?

But I perceive that the pleasure of talking with you of all these

---

[1] No, these things ought never to be done. I was wrong to write what I did. Gluck knew
the effect of two strings in unison as well as Meyerbeer; and if he did not intend them to be used
no one has any right to introduce them into his works. But Meyerbeer has introduced other
effects into *Armide*, such as that of the trombones in the duet, *Esprits de haine et de rage*, which
are incredible blunders and cannot be sufficiently blamed. Spontini once reproached me for not
having pointed them out. And yet he himself added wind instruments in *Iphigénie en Tauride*. . . .
Forgetting that he had been guilty of this weakness, he exclaimed on another occasion: "It is
dreadful! Will they orchestrate me also after I am dead?" [B.]

beautiful things has carried me too far, so that I cannot speak of the non-dramatic musical institutions flourishing at Berlin. They shall be the subject of a second letter, and shall serve as a pretext for boring someone else with my indefatigable verbosity. You don't bear me too great a grudge for this letter, do you? In any case, farewell!

                                                                H. B.

CHAPTER LX

BERLIN

LETTER IX — TO MONSIEUR DESMAREST[1]

I should never have done with this royal city of Berlin if I were to examine all its musical wealth in detail. Few, if any, capitals can boast such treasures of harmony. Music is in the air. You breathe it; it penetrates you. You find it in the theatre, in church, in the concert-room, in the street, in the public gardens, everywhere; ever great and proud, strong and agile, radiant with youth and beauty, with noble and serious air, like a beautiful armed angel, who sometimes deigns to walk the earth, but whose wings are always vibrating, ready to take flight again to heaven.

The reason is that music in Berlin is honoured by all, and held in equal veneration by rich and poor, artists and amateurs, clergy and soldiers, King and people. The King especially worships it with that genuine fervour which animates his devotion to science and the arts, and that is saying a great deal. He follows with an eager eye the onward progress of modern art, without neglecting the preservation of the ancient masterpieces. He has a prodigious memory, which is indeed embarrassing to his librarians and Kapellmeisters when he calls on them unexpectedly for the performance of certain unknown pieces from the old masters. Nothing escapes him, either present or past; he wishes to hear and to examine into everything. Hence the keen attraction Berlin has for great artists, the extraordinary universality of musical feeling in Prussia, and hence also the choral and instrumental institutions of its capital, which I have always thought so worthy of admiration.

[1] A cellist at the Paris Conservatoire.

One of these is the Singing Academy. Like that of Leipzig and all the other academies of the same nature in Germany, it is composed almost entirely of amateurs; but several of the artists of the theatre, both men and women, also belong to it, and the ladies of the best society do not think it at all derogatory to sing in an oratorio of Bach, side by side with Mantius, Boeticher, or Mdlle. Hähnel. Most of the singers in the Berlin Academy are musicians, and nearly all have fresh and full voices; the sopranos and basses in particular I thought excellent. The rehearsals, moreover, are skilfully directed at great length and with much patience by M. Rungenhagen; and accordingly, whenever a great work is performed, the results are magnificent and far beyond anything of the same sort at Paris.

I was invited by the director to a performance of Sebastian Bach's *Passion.* That celebrated work, with which you are no doubt familiar, is written for two choirs and two orchestras. The singers, at least three hundred, were arranged upon the steps of a large amphitheatre, exactly like that in the chemistry lecture-room at the Jardin des Plantes; a space of three or four feet separated the two choirs. The two orchestras, neither of them large, accompany the voices from the highest steps behind the chorus, and are consequently somewhat distant from the conductor, who is placed below, in front, and close beside the piano. I ought rather to call it a clavecin, for it has almost the tone of the miserable instruments of that name used in Bach's time. I do not know if such a choice is made designedly, but I have remarked in all singing schools, in the foyers of theatres, and in fact everywhere, that the piano intended to accompany the voice is always the most detestable that can be found. The one which Mendelssohn used at Leipzig in the Gewandhaus concert-room is the only exception.

You will want to know what the piano-clavecin can have to do *during the performance* of a work in which the composer has not employed that instrument at all! It accompanies along with the orchestra, and probably serves to keep the first ranks of the chorus in tune, since they are supposed not to be able to hear the orchestra properly in the *tuttis,* as it is too far from them. At any rate, it is the custom. The constant strumming of the chords on this bad piano produces a most wearisome effect by spreading a superfluous layer of monotony over the whole; but that is doubtless one reason for not giving it up. An old custom is so sacred when it is bad! The singers sit while they are silent, and rise for singing. I think there is really an advantage in

singing standing for the proper emission of the voice; but it is unfortunate that the singers should weary of this posture and want to
sit down as soon as each has finished, for in a work like Bach's, where
the two choirs not only carry on dialogues but are interrupted every
instant by solo recitatives, it follows that one side is always rising
and another sitting down, and in the long run this series of ups and
downs becomes rather absurd. Besides, it takes away all unexpected-
ness from certain entries of the choir, because the audience perceive in
advance the direction from which the sound is coming before they
hear it. I should prefer the choristers to be always seated if they could
not remain standing. But this impossibility is among those which vanish instantaneously if the director knows how to say *I will* or *I will not*.

Be this as it may, there was something very imposing in the performance of these vocal masses; the first *tutti* of the two choruses
took away my breath, as I did not expect such a powerful burst of
harmony. It must, however, be admitted that one wearies of this fine
sonority far more quickly than of that of the orchestra, the timbres of
voices being less varied than those of instruments. This is easily understood; there are only four kinds of voices, while the number of
different instruments is upwards of thirty.

You will not, my dear Desmarest, expect an analysis from me of
Bach's great work; such a task would quite exceed my prescribed limits.
Indeed, the fragment of it performed at the Conservatoire three years
ago may be considered the type of the author's style throughout the
work. The Germans profess an unlimited admiration for Bach's
recitatives, but their peculiar virtue necessarily escaped me, as I did
not understand the language, and so was unable to appreciate their
expression.

Whoever is familiar with our musical customs in Paris must witness, in order to believe, the attention, respect, and even reverence with
which a German public listens to such a composition. Everyone follows
the words in the book with his eyes; not a movement among the audience, not a murmur of praise or blame, not a sound of applause; they
are at divine service, they are hearing the gospel sung, and they listen
in silence, not to the concert but to the service. And really such music
ought to be thus listened to. They adore Bach, and believe in him,
without supposing for a moment that his divinity could ever be called
into question. A heretic would horrify them; he is forbidden even to
speak of him. God is God and Bach is Bach.

Some days after the performance of Bach's masterpiece, the Singing Academy announced Graun's *Tod Jesu*. This is another sacred work, a holy book, the worshippers of which are, however, mainly to be found in Berlin, whereas the religion of Bach is professed throughout the north of Germany.

You may judge of the interest I felt in this second evening after the impression made upon me by the first, and of the eagerness with which I would have made acquaintance with the favourite work of the great Frederick's Kapellmeister. Behold my misfortune! Precisely on that day I fall ill; the doctor, although a great lover of music (the learned and amiable Dr. Gaspard), forbids me to leave my room; in vain I am urged to go and admire a famous organist; the doctor is inflexible; and not till after Holy Week, when there are no more oratorios, or fugues, or chorales to be heard, does the Almighty restore me to health. Hence my enforced silence about the famous musical service of the Berlin churches. If I ever return to Prussia, ill or well, I must hear Graun's music; and I will hear it, you may be sure, if I am to die for it. But in that case it would still be impossible for me to tell you anything about it. . . . It is decided, then, that you will hear nothing on the subject *from me;* so you had better take the journey yourself, and it will be for you to give me an account of it.

As for the military bands, one would have designedly to avoid them not to hear at least some, since at all hours of the day, either on foot or on horseback, they are passing through the streets of Berlin. These little isolated bands do not, however, give any idea of the majesty of the grand whole which the head bandmaster of the military bands at Berlin and Potsdam (Wiprecht) can collect whenever he chooses. Imagine, he has a body of upwards of six hundred musicians under his command, all good readers, all well up in the mechanism of their instruments, playing in tune, and favoured by nature with indefatigable lungs and lips of leather. Hence the extreme facility with which the trumpets, horns, and cornets give those high notes unattainable by our artists. They are regiments of musicians, rather than musicians of regiments. The Crown Prince of Prussia, anticipating my desire to hear his musical troops and study them at my leisure, kindly invited me to a matinée organised at his house expressly for me, and gave Wiprecht orders accordingly. The audience was very small — twelve or fifteen at the most. I was astonished at not seeing the orchestra; no sound betrayed its presence, when a slow phrase in

F minor, well known to both you and me, made me turn my head towards the largest room in the palace, which was concealed from our sight by an immense curtain. His Royal Highness had had the courtesy to order the concert to open with the *Francs-Juges* overture, which I had never heard arranged thus for wind instruments. There were three hundred and twenty players, directed by Wiprecht, and difficult as the music was they performed it with marvellous exactness, and that furious fire with which you of the Conservatoire perform it on your great days of enthusiasm and ardour.

The solo for the brass in the introduction was especially startling, performed by fifteen bass trombones, eighteen or twenty tenor and alto trombones, twelve bass tubas, and a host of trumpets.

The bass tuba, which I have already named several times in my former letters, has dethroned the ophicleide in Prussia, if, indeed, it ever reigned there, which I doubt. The bass tuba is a huge brass instrument, derived from the bombardon, and furnished with a mechanism of five cylinders, which gives it an immense compass in the bass. It is true that the extreme low notes of the scale are a little vague, but when doubled in the high octave by another bass tuba part they acquire an incredible roundness and force of vibration. The middle and high tones of the instrument are, moreover, very noble, not at all dull like those of the ophicleide, but vibrant, and very sympathetic to the tones of the trombones and trumpets, of which it forms the true double-bass, and with which it blends perfectly. Adolphe Sax makes admirable tubas, and Wiprecht has introduced them into Prussia.

The clarinets seemed to me equal to the brass: they performed great feats in a grand battle-symphony composed for two orchestras by the English ambassador, the Earl of Westmoreland.

Afterwards came a brilliant and chivalric piece for brass only, written by Meyerbeer for the Court festivals under the title of *Torchlight Dance,* in which there is a long trill on the D, kept up through sixteen bars by eighteen cylinder trumpets, doing it as rapidly as the clarinets could have done. The concert ended with a very fine and well-written funeral march, composed by Wiprecht, and played with only one rehearsal!

In the intervals allowed between the pieces by this terrific orchestra, I had the honour of talking for a few moments with the Crown Princess of Prussia, whose exquisite taste and knowledge in composition make her opinion most valuable. Her Royal Highness speaks our language, moreover, with a purity and elegance that quite abashed her interlocutor. I wish I could draw a Shakespearean portrait of the Princess, or at least give you a glimpse of the veiled outline of her sweet beauty; I might dare to do so, perhaps, were I a great poet.

I was present at one of the Court concerts. Meyerbeer was at the piano. There was no orchestra, and the singers were those of the theatre whom I have already mentioned. Towards the end of the evening, Meyerbeer — who, although a great pianist, and, indeed, perhaps for that very reason, sometimes wearies of his task as an accompanist — gave up his place: guess to whom? — to the King's first chamberlain, the Count de Roedern, who accompanied Madame Devrient in Schubert's *Erl-King,* like a pianist and consummate musician! What do you say to that, and to the amazing spread of musical knowledge which it betokens? M. de Roedern has also another talent, of which he gave brilliant proof by organising the famous masked ball that created such a sensation at Berlin last winter, under the name of " The Festival of the Court of Ferrara," and for which Meyerbeer wrote a host of pieces. These ceremonious concerts always seem cold; but people find them very agreeable when they are over, because they usually bring together some hearers with whom one is proud and pleased to have a moment's conversation. In this way I met, in the presence of the King of Prussia, M. Alexander von Humboldt, so celebrated in scientific literature, and the great anatomist of the terrestrial globe.

Several times in the course of the evening the King and Queen and the Crown Princess of Prussia came and talked to me about the concert[1] I had just given at the Grand Theatre, asking my opinion about the principal Prussian artists, questioning me about my methods of instrumentation, etc., etc. The King declared that I had put a devil into all the musicians of his orchestra.

After supper, His Majesty prepared to return to his apartments, but suddenly coming to me as though he had changed his mind:

" By the way, Monsieur Berlioz, what will you give us at your next concert? "

" Sire, I shall repeat half of the preceding programme, with five pieces out of my symphony, *Romeo and Juliet.*"

" *Romeo and Juliet,* and I am about to make a journey. We must hear that, however. I will come back." And accordingly on the evening

[1] April 20.

of my second concert, five minutes before the appointed hour, the King got out of his carriage and entered his box.

Those two evenings gave me a great deal of trouble, I assure you. And yet the artists were clever and well disposed, and Meyerbeer seemed to multiply himself in order to assist me. The fact is that the requirements of a great theatre like that of Berlin are quite incompatible with preparations for a concert, and Meyerbeer must certainly have used greater pressure and address to overcome all these recurring difficulties than in getting up the *Huguenots* for the first time. Moreover, I had wished to bring out the great pieces from the *Requiem,* the *Prose* (*Dies Iræ, Lacrymosa,* etc.), which I had not yet attempted in the other German towns, and you know what a vocal and instrumental apparatus they necessitate. Fortunately I had warned Meyerbeer of my intention, and before my arrival he had been already searching for the means necessary to carry it out. As for the four little brass orchestras, it was easy to find them — we could have had thirty if necessary — but the kettle-drums and drummers gave a great deal of trouble. However, by the aid of the excellent Wiprecht, we succeeded at last in getting them together.

For the first rehearsals we were put into a splendid concert-room belonging to the second theatre, the sonority of which was unhappily so great that on my first entrance I saw what we should have to endure. The excessive resonance produced an insupportable confusion, and made the practice of the orchestra exceedingly difficult. There was one piece, indeed, the Scherzo from *Romeo and Juliet,* that we were obliged to give up altogether, not having succeeded in doing more than one-half after an hour. And yet, I repeat, the orchestra could not have been better composed. But we had not sufficient time, and were obliged to postpone the Scherzo to the second concert. I got used to the hubbub at last; I found out what the echo would allow to be done and what it would not, and we pursued our studies accordingly without taking into consideration the effect, which, happily, was very different from what we obtained afterwards in the opera concert-room. The overture to *Benvenuto, Harold,* Weber's *Invitation,* and the pieces from the *Requiem* were thus learnt by the orchestra alone, the chorus working in another room. At the special rehearsal which I had called for the four brass orchestras in the *Dies Iræ* and the *Lacrymosa,* I observed for the third time the following fact, which has always remained inexplicable to me:

In the middle of the *Tuba mirum* the four groups of trombones play the four notes of the chord of G major in succession. The bar is a long one; the first group should give the G on the first beat; the second the B on the second; the third the D on the third; and the fourth the octave G on the fourth. Nothing more easy of conception than such a succession, nothing more easily played than each of these notes! And yet, when the *Requiem* was performed for the first time in the Church of the Invalides at Paris, it was impossible to get the passage done. Subsequently, when movements from the work were played at the Opéra, after having in vain practised that one bar for a quarter of an hour, I was obliged to give it up; one or two of the groups always came in wrong, invariably the B or the D — sometimes both. At Berlin, when my eye fell on that part of the score, I thought at once of the stubborn trombones in Paris.

" Let us see," said I to myself, " if the Prussian artists will succeed in smashing in that open door!"

Alas! no! Vain efforts! Neither rage nor patience availed anything! It was impossible to get the second or third group to come in; even the fourth, not hearing its cue, which ought to have been given by the others, did not strike up either. I take them separately.

I ask the second to give the B.

He gives it all right.

Addressing myself to the third, I ask for his D.

He gives it without difficulty.

Now let us have the four notes, one after the other in the order in which they are written. . . . Impossible! Quite impossible! And we must give it up! Can you understand that? And is it not enough to make one knock one's head against the wall? . . .

And when I asked the trombone players at Paris and Berlin why they did not play in the fatal bar, they could not think of an answer, they did not know themselves; the two notes fascinated them.[1] I must write to Romberg, who has given the work in St. Petersburg, and ask him if the Russian trombones have been able to break the spell.

The rest of the programme the orchestra understood, and it carried out my intentions perfectly. We soon managed to have a general rehearsal in the theatre on the stage arranged with steps as for a concert. Symphony, overture, cantata, all went to a wish, but when it

[1] At the last two performances of the *Requiem* in the Church of St. Eustache, in Paris, this passage was given, however, without a mistake. [B.]

came to the selection from the *Requiem* there was a general panic; the
chorus had practised in different tempi from mine, and when they
found themselves combined with the orchestra at the proper speed,
they no longer knew what they were about, they came in wrong or
without confidence, and in the *Lacrymosa* the tenors left off singing
altogether. I did not know what saint to invoke. Meyerbeer was ill and
unable to leave his bed, the choirmaster, Elssler, was ill also, the
orchestra became demoralised by the vocal catastrophe. For one
moment I sat down quite exhausted, and asked myself whether I
should leave them all in the lurch and run away from Berlin that same
evening. And I thought of you at that dreadful moment, and said to
myself: " It is madness to go on ! Oh, if Desmarest were here ! he who
is never satisfied with our Conservatoire rehearsals; and if he could see
me bent on allowing the concert to be announced for to-morrow, I
know very well what he would do; he would lock me up in my room,
put the key in his pocket, and bravely go and inform the manager of
the theatre that the concert could not take place."

You know you would have done so, would you not? Well, you
would have been wrong, as I shall prove to you. After the first trembling fit had passed and the first cold perspiration was wiped off, I
came to a decision, and I said:

" The thing must be done ! "

Ries and Ganz, the two leaders, were close to me, not knowing
really what to say to reassure me.

" Are you sure of the orchestra ? " said I sharply.

" Yes, there is nothing to be afraid of as far as it is concerned; we
are very tired, but we understand your music, and to-morrow you will
be satisfied."

" Very well then, there is only one thing to be done; you must
summon the chorus for to-morrow morning, give me a good accompanist, since Elssler is ill, and one of you bring your violin, and we will
practise the vocal part for three hours if necessary."

" All right ! We will be there. Orders shall be given directly."

Accordingly, next morning we set to work, Ries, the accompanist,
and myself. We took each part of the chorus in succession; made them
sing in groups of ten, then of twenty, then joined two parts, three, four,
and finally all the voices. And like Phaeton in the fable, I exclaimed
at last:

"Qu'est-ce ceci?   Mon char marche à souhait?"

I made a little speech to the chorus, which Ries translated into German phrase by phrase; and behold all our forces reanimated, full of courage, and enchanted at not having lost a battle in which both their honour and mine were at stake. On the contrary, we gained a brilliant victory. It is needless to say that the overture, the symphony, and the *Cinq Mai* cantata were splendidly performed in the evening. With such an orchestra and a singer like Boeticher, it could not be otherwise. But when the *Requiem* came, everyone being very attentive, very earnest, and desirous of pleasing me, the orchestras and the chorus being perfectly placed, everyone at his post, nothing wanting, we began the *Dies Iræ*. No mistakes, no indecision; the chorus sustained the assault of the orchestra without flinching; the fourfold peal of trumpets broke forth from the four corners of the stage, already vibrating with the rolling of the ten kettle-drums and the tremolo of fifty bows; and in the midst of this cataclysm of sinister harmonies and noise from the other world the hundred and twenty voices hurled forth their terrible prediction:

> Judex ergo cum sedebit
> Quidquid latet apparebit!

For one instant the public overwhelmed the opening of the *Liber scriptus* with applause, and we reached the last *sotto voce* chords of the *Mors stupebit* trembling but victorious.

And what delight among the performers! What glances flashed from end to end of the stage! As for me, I had a peal of bells in my heart, a mill-wheel in my head, my knees were knocking against each other; I dug my nails into the desk; and if I had not forced myself at the last bar to laugh and talk very loud and fast with Ries, who aided and abetted me, I am quite sure that, for the first time in my life, I should, as soldiers say, have *turned up my eyes* in a most absurd manner. The first volley once endured, the rest was mere play, and the *Lacrymosa* finished up that apocalyptic evening to the composer's entire satisfaction.

When the concert was over, a great many people came up and spoke to me, congratulated me, and shook me by the hand; but there I stayed, without understanding . . . without feeling anything . . . brain and nerves alike overstrained. I had to become stupid in order to rest. Wiprecht alone, with an embrace like that of a cuirassier, had the power to make me come to. He really cracked my ribs, dear good man, interlarding his exclamations with German oaths to which Guhr's were mere Ave Marias.

Certainly, if anyone had attempted to sound my palpitating joy, they would have found it fathomless. You will admit, then, that it is sometimes wise to commit an act of madness; had it not been for my wild audacity the concert would never have taken place, for the business of the theatre had been so arranged that it would have been impossible to recommence the study of the *Requiem*.

For the second concert I announced, as I said above, five pieces from *Romeo and Juliet*, *Queen Mab* among the number. During the fortnight between the first and second performances Ganz and Taubert had been studying the score of the Scherzo, and when they saw me resolved upon giving it, it was their turn to take fright.

" We shall never manage it," they said. " You know that we can only have two rehearsals; it ought to have five or six, nothing is more difficult or dangerous; it is a musical spider's web, and without an extraordinary delicacy of touch it will be torn into rags."

" Bah! I bet you that we shall get through again. True, we have but two rehearsals, but there are only five new pieces to learn, four of which contain no great difficulty. Besides, the orchestra has already some idea of the Scherzo from our first partial attempt at it. And Meyerbeer has spoken of it to the King, who wants to hear it, and I want the artists to know it, and so it *shall* go." And go it did, nearly as well as at Brunswick. You can venture a great deal with such musicians — musicians who, before being conducted by Meyerbeer, had had a long apprenticeship under Spontini.

This second concert was equally successful with the first; the pieces from *Romeo* were very well played. *Queen Mab* puzzled the public a good deal, including certain learned hearers; witness the Crown Princess of Prussia, who was bent on finding out how I had produced the effect of the accompaniment in the allegretto, and never imagined that it was done with the harmonics of the violins and harps in several parts. The King preferred the *Fête at the Capulets'*, and asked for a copy; but I think that the sympathies of the orchestra were rather with the *Scène d'amour* (the adagio). In that case the Berlin musicians were of the same way of thinking as the Paris ones. At the rehearsal, Mademoiselle Hähnel sang the contralto verses of the prologue with perfect simplicity, but at the concert she thought it her duty at the end of the lines,

> Où se consume
> Le rossignol en longs soupirs,

to embellish the organ point with a long shake in imitation of the nightingale. Oh, mademoiselle! What treason! And you seemed so nice!

Well, well! there are some people who openly prefer the *Cinq Mai* to the *Dies Iræ*, the *Tuba Mirum,* the *Lacrymosa* and *Offertoire* from the *Requiem,* the *Benvenuto* and *King Lear* overtures, *Harold,* the *Serenade, Pilgrims,* and *Brigands, Romeo and Juliet,* the concert and ball at the Capulets', the witcheries of Queen Mab, to everything, in fact, that I performed at Berlin!

I know that impressions are as varied as faces; but when they told me this I was obliged to make a grimace. Happily these opinions are quite exceptional.

Farewell, my dear Desmarest; you know that in a few days we shall have to perform an anthem at the Conservatoire; assemble your sixteen grand violoncellos, those splendid singers. I shall be very happy to hear them again, and to see you at their head. It is so long since we have played together. And in order to give them a treat, tell them I shall conduct with Mendelssohn's baton. Yours ever,

H. B.

CHAPTER LXI

HANOVER — DARMSTADT

LETTER X — TO MR. G. A. OSBORNE

ALAS! alas! my dear Osborne, my journey is drawing to a close.[1] I am leaving Prussia, full of gratitude for the welcome I received there, for the warm sympathy of the artists, and the indulgence both of the critics and the public; but weary and exhausted by this life of excessive activity and the continual rehearsals with fresh orchestras. So weary am I that I shall give up Breslau, Vienna, and Munich for the present, and get back to France. A certain vague uneasiness, a fever in my blood, an aimless restlessness in heart and head, already tell me that I am again in communication with the electric current of Paris.

---

[1] He left Berlin towards the end of April.

Paris! Paris! as our great poet, Auguste Barbier, has but too truly
depicted it:

> . . . . Cette infernale cuve,
> Cette fosse de pierre aux immenses contours,
> Qu'une eau jaune et terreuse enferme à triples tours;
> C'est un volcan fumeux, et toujours en haleine,
> Qui remue à long flot de la matière humaine.
>
> .   .   .   .
>
> .   .   .   .
>
> Là personne ne dort, là toujours le cerveau
> Travaille, et, comme l'arc, tend son rude cordeau.

It is there that our art now lies dormant, and then again bursts into a
flame; there music is at once sublime and commonplace, lofty and
mean, beggar and king, exalted and despised, adored and insulted.
In Paris music finds faithful, enthusiastic, intelligent, and devoted
disciples; and in Paris also it appeals too often to the deaf, to idiots,
and barbarians. At one time it moves and soars in freedom; at another, its glorious limbs are so fettered by the bonds of the hag
Routine as hardly to allow of even a slow and ungraceful walk. It is in
Paris that music is crowned and deified — always provided that no
sacrifice of any value is required for its altars. It is in Paris too that
her temples are inundated with magnificent presents — on condition
that the goddess shall become a mortal, not to say a mountebank. In
Paris, too, Commerce, Art's scrofulous and bastard brother, clad in
gaudy tinsel, displays its vulgar insolence before all eyes; while Art
itself, like the Pythian Apollo, in its divine nudity, scarcely deigns to
interrupt its lofty meditations with a smile of contempt. Sometimes —
shame that it should be so! — the bastard obtains such incredible
favours from his brother as to insinuate himself into the chariot of
light, seize the reins, and attempt to force backwards the immortal
car; till the real driver, startled by such stupid audacity, tears him
from his seat and hurls him to the ground. And it is money that brings
about this fleeting and odious alliance, it is the love of immediate and
hastily-gotten lucre which thus sometimes poisons the souls of the
elect.

> L'argent, l'argent fatal, dernier dieu des humains,
> Les prend par les cheveux, les secoue à deux mains,
> Les pousse dans le mal, et pour un vil salaire
> Leur mettrait les deux pieds sur le corps de leur père.

And such noble souls generally fall only because they have overlooked the sad but incontestable truth that, with our form of government and with our present habits, the more artistic the artist, the more he has to bear; the greater and more original his work, the more severely does he suffer from the consequences it entails; the more elevated his thoughts, the further is he removed from the dim eyes of the crowd.

The Medicis are dead. They will hardly be replaced by our deputies. You remember the profound remark of a provincial Lycurgus on hearing some poetry by one of our greatest poets (the one who wrote *La Chute d'un ange*). "Yes," he said, opening his snuff-box with a paternal air — "Yes, I have a nephew who writes little trifles like that." After this, will you look for encouragement for artists from the *colleague of the poet?*

You virtuosi who do not work in musical masses, who only write for the orchestra of your two hands, and are independent of vast rooms and large choirs, you have less to fear from contact with vulgar habits, and yet you also feel their effects. Scribble some brilliant bit of silliness, and the publishers will cover it with gold and scramble for it; but if you have the misfortune to develop a serious idea under a grand form, then you are done for; the work remains on your hands, or at any rate, if it is published, no one buys it.

It is only fair to say, in order slightly to justify Paris and constitutionalism, that it is the same almost everywhere. At Vienna, as here, a fashionable manufacturer is paid a thousand francs for a song or a waltz, while Beethoven was obliged to give the Symphony in C minor for less than half that sum.

You have published in London trios and various pieces for piano solo, grand in design and elevated in style; and even without searching through your full repertory, your solo songs, such as *The beating of my own heart, My lonely home,* or *Such things were* — which your sister, Mrs. Hampton, sings so poetically — are fascinating things. Nothing excites my imagination more vividly and makes it fly more rapidly to the green hills of Ireland, than those simple, original melodies, which seem wafted by the evening breeze over the gently rippling waves of the Lake of Killarney; those hymns of resigned love, to which one listens inexplicably moved, dreaming of solitude, of grand nature, of beloved beings who are no more, of the heroes of ancient times, of one's suffering country, even of death itself, " *dreamy and calm as the night,*" according to the expression of your national poet,

Thomas Moore. Well, put all these inspirations, all this melancholy-smiling poetry in the balance with some turbulent caprice devoid alike of mind and heart, such as music-sellers often commission you to write on the more or less vulgar themes of the new operas, where the notes jostle, pursue, and roll over one another like a handful of bells shaken in a bag, and you will soon see on which side the monetary success would be.

No, one must make up one's mind that — except for certain chance circumstances and certain associations with the inferior arts, always more or less degrading, music is not productive in the commercial sense of the word; it addresses itself too exclusively to the exceptions of intelligent society, it demands too much preparation, too many appliances. There must therefore of necessity be a sort of honourable ostracism for those who cultivate it without being in any way pre-occupied by foreign interests. Even the greatest nations are, with regard to artists pure and simple, like the deputy of whom I spoke just now; side by side with the giants of human genius, they place their *nephews who also write, etc., etc.*

In the archives of one of the London theatres is a letter addressed to Queen Elizabeth by a troupe of actors, and signed by twenty obscure names, among which is that of William Shakespeare, with the collective designation of *Your poor players*.[1] Shakespeare was one of those *poor players*. . . . And yet dramatic art in the time of Shakespeare was more appreciated by the masses than it is in our day by those nations which lay most claim to possess a feeling for it. Music is essentially aristocratic; it is a daughter of noble race, such as princes only can dower nowadays, who must be able to live poor and virginal rather than form a *mésalliance*. All these reflections you have doubtless made to yourself a hundred times, and I imagine you will be obliged to me to cut them short, and give you an account of my two last concerts in Germany, after leaving Berlin.

This account will, however, offer you nothing of great interest as far as I am concerned. I shall be obliged again to speak of works which I have probably already mentioned too frequently in previous letters; the same everlasting *Cinq Mai, Harold,* selections from

[1] It is a pity to destroy the force of this neat and apposite illustration, but unfortunately it is an entire fiction. The "letter" referred to was a petition, purporting to be from the Burbages, Shakespeare, and their fellow-players owning the Blackfriars and Globe Theatres, to the Lords of the Queen's Privy Council. It was to be found, not in "the archives of a London theatre," but in the State Paper Office; and on attention being directed to it some years ago it was proved to be a forgery, and has now disappeared. [H.]

Romeo and Juliet, etc. The same deficiencies in certain instruments and players, the same excellence in other parts of the band, constituting what I shall call the old orchestra — Mozart's orchestra; and also the same faults, invariably reproducing themselves at the first attempt in the same pieces, to disappear at last after careful practice.

I did not stop at Magdeburg, where, however, I met with rather an original success. I was very nearly insulted for having had the audacity to call myself by my own name, by an employé of the mails, who, on registering my luggage and examining the address it bore, asked with an air of suspicion:

" Berlioz? The composer? "

" Ja."

Whereupon, great anger on the part of this worthy man, caused by my impertinence in trying to pass for Berlioz, the composer.

He had imagined, doubtless, that this astounding musician could only travel upon a hippogriff in the midst of a whirlwind of flames, or, at any rate, with a paraphernalia of sumptuous luggage and respectful menials. So that on seeing a man arrive, looking like any other man who has been at once frozen and smoked in a railway carriage, a man who had his trunk weighed for himself, who actually walked, and spoke French, and only knew the word " Ja " in German, he concluded at once that I was an impostor. As you may easily think, his murmurs and shrugs quite fascinated me; the more scornful his gestures and tone became, the more proudly I bore myself; if he had struck me, I should certainly have embraced him.

Another employé, who spoke my language very well, was more disposed to allow me to be myself, but his gracious speeches flattered me infinitely less than the incredulity and frank ill-humour of his *naïf* colleague.

Just consider, half a million of money would have lost me that success! I shall be careful in future to take nothing with me, and always travel as I am now doing. This was not the opinion, however, of our witty and jovial dramatic censor, Perpignan, when he exclaimed, *à propos* to a man who was saved in a duel by the bullet being stopped by a five-franc piece in his waistcoat pocket: " These rich fellows are so lucky; I should have been killed on the spot."

I arrived at Hanover, where A. Bohrer was expecting me. The intendant, Herr von Meding, had kindly put both band and theatre at my disposal, and I was just beginning my rehearsals when the death of the Duke of Sussex, the brother of the King, threw the Court into mourning, and the concert had to be postponed for a week, which gave me a little more time to make acquaintance with the principal artists who were about to suffer from the bad character of my compositions.

I could not become particularly intimate with the Kapellmeister, Marschner, as his difficulty in expressing himself in French made our conversations rather laboured, besides which he was extremely busy. He is now one of the first composers in Germany, and everyone appreciates the eminent merit of his works, *Der Vampyr* and *Der Templer*. Bohrer I knew already. Beethoven's trios and quartets had brought us into contact at Paris, and our mutual enthusiasm for these had not cooled since. Bohrer is one of those men who strike me as best able to understand such of Beethoven's works as are commonly reputed eccentric and unintelligible. I can still see him at quartet rehearsals, where his brother Max (the celebrated violoncello player, now in America), Claudel (the second violin), and Urhan (the viola) seconded him so well. Max, as he studied that transcendent music, smiled with pride and pleasure; he seemed to be in his natural element, and to breathe perfect happiness. Urhan adored in silence; lowering his eyes, as though before the sun, he seemed to say: " God has willed that there should be a man as great as Beethoven, and that we should be permitted to contemplate him. God has willed it! " Claudel especially admired this profound admiration. As for Antoine Bohrer (the first violin), it was passion at its zenith, it was love in ecstasy. One evening, in one of those superhuman adagios where Beethoven's genius soars upwards, immense and solitary as the colossal bird of the snowy heights of Chimborazo, Bohrer's violin, whilst singing the sublime melody, seemed animated by epic inspiration; his tone acquired a twofold power of expression, and broke forth in accents unknown even to himself; inspiration shone out on the countenance of the virtuoso. We held our breath with swelling hearts, when Antoine, suddenly stopping short, laid down his fiery bow, and rushed into an adjoining room. Madame Bohrer followed anxiously, but Max said, still smiling:

" It is nothing; he could not contain himself. We will leave him for a little to get calm, and then begin again. We must excuse him."

Excuse him? Beloved artist!

At Hanover, Antoine Bohrer fulfilled the duties of orchestral leader. He now composes but little, his dearest occupation being to direct the musical education of his daughter, a charming child of twelve, whose marvellous organisation fills her friends with not unnatural fears. In the first place, her talent as a pianist is most extraordinary; while her memory is such that in the concerts she gave last year at Vienna, her father, instead of a programme, printed a list of seventy-two pieces — sonatas, fantasias, fugues, variations, studies by Beethoven, Weber, Cramer, Bach, Handel, Liszt, Thalberg, Chopin, Döhler, etc. — which the little Sophie knew by heart, and could, without hesitation, play from memory just as the assembly might desire. It is enough for her to play over a piece three or four times, no matter how long or complicated, never to forget it. So many combinations of different kinds engraving themselves thus in this young brain! Is there not something prodigious in it, and calculated to inspire as much terror as admiration? We must hope that when little Sophie has become Mdlle. Bohrer she will return to us in a few years, and that the Parisian public may then become acquainted with that phenomenal talent of which, as yet, it has but a very feeble conception.

The orchestra at Hanover is good, but has not sufficient stringed instruments. There are only seven first violins, seven seconds, three violas, four violoncellos, and three double-basses. Some of the violins are weak, the violoncellos are skilful, the violas and double-basses good. The wind instruments deserve all praise, especially the first flute, the first oboe (Eduard Rose, whose pianissimo playing is matchless), and the first clarinet (with an exquisite tone). The two bassoons (there are only two) play in tune, which is, unhappily, a very rare thing. The horns are not first-rate, but they pass muster. The trombones are steady, the old-fashioned trumpets pretty good. There is one splendid cylinder trumpet; the name of the player is Sachse, like that of his rival at Weimar; and I hardly know which is the better of the two. The first oboe plays the cor anglais, but his instrument is very much out of tune. There is no ophicleide, but the bass tubas in the military band can be used with advantage. The kettle-drummer is mediocre; the *musician* who takes the big drum is *no musician at all;* the cymbal player is uncertain, and the cymbals are so broken that only a fragment of each is left.

There is a lady in the chorus who plays the harp fairly well. Though not a virtuoso, she is mistress of her instrument, and she, and the harpists of Stuttgart, Berlin, and Hamburg, are the sole exceptions I have found in Germany, where harpists in general cannot play the harp. Unfortunately she is very timid, and not a particularly good musician; but with a few days to study her part, you may count on her exactness. She produces the harmonics very well; her harp is a fine one with a double action.

The chorus is small, containing only about forty voices, not, however, devoid of merit, as they all sing in tune; the tenors in particular have a very good tone. The solo troupe is more than mediocre. With the exception of the bass, Steinmüller, an excellent musician with a fine voice, cleverly managed, though now and then forced, I heard nothing that I thought worthy of mention.

We could have only two rehearsals; even that was considered unusual, and certain members of the band murmured loudly. This was the only time that anything so unpleasant occurred in Germany, where the artists invariably welcomed me as a brother, without ever complaining of the time or trouble entailed by my rehearsals. A. Bohrer was in despair; he would have had four, or at least three, rehearsals; but we could not get them. The performance [1] was passable but cold and somewhat feeble. Only think! Three double-basses, and six violins and a half on either side! The public was polite, and that was all. I believe it is still wondering what the devil it all meant. Dr. Griepenkerl had come from Brunswick express; he was obliged to admit that there was a notable difference in the artistic spirit of the two towns. We amused ourselves — he and I and some Brunswick officers — in tormenting poor Bohrer by describing the musical *fête* they had given me at Brunswick three months before. The details broke his heart. Dr. Griepenkerl then made me a present of his work about myself, and in return asked me to give him the baton with which I had just conducted the *Cinq Mai*. Let us hope that these batons, thus planted in France and Germany, will take root and become trees under which I may some day find shelter. . . .

The Prince Royal of Hanover was present at this concert. I had the honour of conversing with him for a few moments before my departure, and I think myself lucky to have had this opportunity of becoming acquainted with his gracious and affable manners and his distinguished mind, the serenity of which has been in no wise disturbed by the dreadful misfortune of the loss of his sight.

---

[1] The concert took place on May 6. The financial results were meagre, the profit being only 84 thalers (a little more than £12).

Now for Darmstadt. I pass Cassel at seven in the morning. But Spohr is asleep and must not be awakened.[1]

To continue. I return to Frankfort for the fourth time. There I again find Parish-Alvars, who magnetises me by his fantasia in harmonics on the chorus of the Naïades from *Oberon*. The man is a wizard, and his harp is a siren with a beautiful curved neck and long dishevelled hair, breathing forth the fascinating sounds of another world under the passionate embrace of his powerful arms.

There too is Guhr, very much exercised by the workmen who are repairing his theatre. Ah, by Jove! you must excuse me, Osborne, if I leave you to say a few words to that formidable Kapellmeister. I will return immediately.

My dear Guhr,

Do you know that many people have made me fear that you took amiss the little jokes I permitted myself to make at your expense when describing our first interview? I doubted it greatly, knowing your mind, and yet the doubt troubled me.

I now hear that far from having been annoyed at the discords I lent to the harmony of your conversation, you were the first to laugh at them, and that you had a German translation of my letter printed in one of the Frankfort newspapers. That's right. You understand a joke, and besides, no one is lost for a little swearing. Hurrah! *Terque quaterque vivat!* S. N. T. T. Regard me as really one of your best friends, and accept a thousand fresh compliments on your Frankfort band — worthy of being conducted by an artist like yourself. Farewell! Farewell! S. N. T. T.

Here I am again.

Well! Let us see. The question now is about Darmstadt. There we shall find some friends; among others, L. Schlosser, the leader, formerly my fellow-student at Lesueur's during his stay in Paris. Besides, I brought letters from M. de Rothschild, of Frankfort, to Prince Emile, who gave me the most charming welcome and obtained from the Grand Duke more solid assistance for my concert than I had dared to hope. In most of the German towns where I had hitherto given concerts, the arrangement with the Intendants of the theatres had been almost always identical, the management undertaking most

---

[1] Spohr was Kapellmeister at Cassel. [H.]

of the expenses and I receiving half the gross receipts. The Weimar Theatre alone courteously allowed me all the proceeds. As I have said before, Weimar is an artistic town, and the ducal family know how to honour the arts.

Well, at Darmstadt, the Grand Duke not only granted me the same favour, but wished further to exempt me from every kind of expense. This generous sovereign certainly has no *nephews who also write, etc.*

The concert [1] was speedily organised, and far from having to ask for rehearsals from the orchestra, it would fain have had an additional week's study. We had five rehearsals. All went well, with the exception of the double chorus of young Capulets at the beginning of the love scene in *Romeo and Juliet*. The performance of this piece was a regular vocal rout; the tenors of the second choir went nearly a semi-tone flat, and those of the first came in wrong at the return of the theme. The chorus-master was in a fury, the more so because he had taken infinite pains with the singers for a week past.

The Darmstadt orchestra is a little larger than that of Hanover. It has an exceptionally good ophicleide. The harp part is given to a *painter,* who, in spite of all his efforts and good will, is never sure of giving much *colour* to his performance. The remainder of the instrumental body is well arranged, and animated by the best spirit. There is one remarkable virtuoso. He is named Müller, — not, however, a member of the celebrated Müller family of Brunswick. His almost colossal stature permits of his playing the true four-stringed double-bass with marvellous facility. Without trying, as he easily might, to execute turns and trills of needless difficulty and grotesque effect, he makes this enormous instrument sing out broadly and nobly, drawing forth tones of the greatest beauty, which he shades with much art and feeling. I heard him play a most beautiful adagio, composed by the younger Mangold, brother to the Kapellmeister, in such a manner as profoundly to move a very severe audience. It was at a soirée given by Dr. Huth, the leading musical amateur in Darmstadt, who in his sphere does for art what Mr. Alsager [2] does in London, and whose

---

[1] May 20.

[2] Mr. Alsager, one of the proprietors of *The Times,* was also one of the most distinguished musical amateurs of London at the time of Berlioz's visit. The concerts at his house in Queen Square were the best performances attainable of music, such as Beethoven's quartets, then unknown except to a very narrow circle. They were the seed from which the Musical Union, the Monday Popular Concerts, and all similar institutions in London may be said to have grown. [H.]

influence is therefore great over the musical mind of the public. Müller must be a very tempting prize to composers and conductors, but the Grand Duke will certainly dispute it with them with all his might.

The Kapellmeister, Mangold, a clever and excellent man, received much of his musical education in Paris, where he was reckoned among Reicha's best pupils. For me he was accordingly a fellow-student, and he treated me as such. As for Schlosser, the leader already mentioned, he showed himself so good a comrade and seconded me with such zeal that it is really impossible to speak of his compositions as they deserve; I should seem to be thanking him for his hospitality, when really I should only be doing him justice. A fresh proof of the truth of the anti-proverb, " A benefit is always lost! "

At Darmstadt there is a military band of about thirty musicians, for which I envied the Grand Duke. They play in good tune, with style, and with such a feeling for rhythm that even the drum parts are interesting.

Reichel (the splendid bass who was of such use to me at Hamburg) happened to have been some time at Darmstadt when I arrived there, and had won quite a triumph in the part of Marcel in the *Huguenots*. He was again so kind as to sing the *Cinq Mai*, but with a talent and sentiment far beyond what he showed at the first performance. He was especially admirable in the last strophe, which is most difficult to nuance properly:

> Wie? Sterben er? O Ruhm, wie verwaist bist du!
> What! shall he die? O Fame, then art thou widowed!

The air from Mozart's *Figaro, Non più andrai*, which we had added to the programme, showed the versatility of his talent, and exhibited it under a new aspect, which brought him an encore from the whole room, and in the morning a very profitable engagement at the Darmstadt Theatre. No occasion to tell you the rest.

If ever you go to that part of the world, they will tell you that my *naïve* vanity was such that I thought both artists and public very intelligent.

And now here we are, my dear Osborne, at the end of perhaps the most difficult musical pilgrimage ever undertaken by a musician, and the memory of which I know will hover over the remainder of my life. Like the religious men of ancient Greece, I have been consulting the oracle of Delphi. Have I rightly understood its reply? Can I think it favourable to my wishes? Are there no false oracles? The future — the future alone will decide. Be this as it may, I must now return to France and bid my final farewell to Germany, that noble second mother of all the sons of harmony. But where can I find expressions adequate to my gratitude, my admiration, and my regret? . . . What hymn could I sing worthy of her greatness and her glory? . . . On leaving her, I can only bow with reverence and say in a voice broken with emotion:

" Vale, Germania, alma parens! "

H. B.

CHAPTER LXII

I GET UP ''FREISCHÜTZ'' FOR THE OPÉRA—MY RECITATIVES—THE SINGERS—DESSAUER—M. LÉON PILLET—HAVOC MADE BY HIS SUCCESSORS IN WEBER'S WORK

I HAD just returned[1] from this long peregrination in Germany, when M. Pillet, the Director of the Opéra, formed the plan of getting up the *Freischütz* for the stage. But in that work the different numbers are preceded and followed by prose dialogue, as in our opéras-comiques; and since the usages of the Opéra require that everything in its dramas or lyrical tragedies shall be sung, the spoken text had to be put into recitative.[2] M. Pillet offered me this task.

" I do not think," I answered, " that the recitatives you wish for ought to be added to the *Freischütz* at all. However, since it can only be performed at the Opéra on that condition, and as you would probably, if I declined the task, give it to someone less familiar with Weber than myself, and certainly less devoted to the glorification of his masterpiece, I accept your offer on one condition: the work shall be played exactly as it is, without any alteration either in the book or the music."

---

[1] Berlioz returned to Paris towards the end of May 1843. His articles in the *Débats*, dealing with his German tour, commenced on the 13th August.

[2] The distinction between a *grand opéra* in France and any other kind is that the *grand opéra* must be sung from beginning to end. The mixture of spoken dialogue with the music constitutes an *opéra-comique* — not necessarily a *comic* opera. [H.]

" That is my intention," replied M. Pillet. " Do you think me capable of renewing the scandal of *Robin des Bois?* "

" Very well; in that case I shall set to work. How do you think of distributing the parts? "

" I shall give Agatha to Mdme. Stoltz, Annette [1] to Mdlle. Dobré: Duprez will sing Max."

" I bet you he won't." I interrupted.

" Why not? "

" You will soon know why."

" Bouché will make an excellent Gaspard." [2]

" And whom have you for the Hermit? "

" Oh," replied M. Pillet, in some embarrassment, " that's a useless part, and one that drags heavily; my intention was to leave it out altogether."

" Oh, is that all? Is that the way you intend to respect the *Freischütz* and not imitate M. Castil-Blaze? We are very far indeed from being agreed. Permit me to withdraw; it is impossible for me to have anything to say to your new *correction."*

" Good heavens! how obstinate you are. Very well, we will keep the Hermit, we will keep everything; I give you my word."

Emilien Paccini, who was to translate the libretto, having given me the same assurance, I consented, though not without misgivings, to undertake the composition of the recitatives. The feeling which had urged me to insist on the preservation of Weber's work in its integrity, a feeling which many would call fetichism, removed all pretext for the manipulations, derangements, suppressions, and corrections, which otherwise would have been eagerly made.

But one grave inconvenience was a necessary result of my obstinacy: the spoken dialogue, when set to music, seemed too long, notwithstanding all my precautions to render it as concise as possible. I never could make the actors alter their slow, heavy, and emphatic manner of singing the recitative; and in the scenes between Max and Gaspard especially, the essentially simple and familiar flow of their conversation had all the solemnity of a scene from a lyrical tragedy. This rather marred the general effect, but the success was nevertheless very striking. I did not wish to be known as the author of these recitatives, notwithstanding that both artists and critics discovered dramatic qualities in them and especially praised the style, which they said

---

[1] Aennchen.　　　[2] Caspar.

harmonised exactly with Weber's, and the reserve in the instrumentation which even my enemies themselves were forced to admit.

Just as I had foreseen, Duprez, who, ten years before, had in his then weak tenor voice sung Max (Tony) in the pasticcio of *Robin des Bois* at the Odéon, could not adapt this same part — which lies rather low in general, it is true — to his great first-tenor organ. He proposed some singular transpositions, necessitating, of course, the most senseless modulations and grotesque transitions. . . . I cut short all these follies by assuring M. Pillet that Duprez could not sing this part without, by his own showing, ruining it completely. It was then given to Marié, the second tenor, whose voice was not wanting in tone in the lower register, a very good musician but a thick and heavy singer.

Neither could Mdme. Stoltz sing Agatha without transposing her two principal airs. I had to put the first (which is in E) into D, and to lower the prayer in the third act from A flat to F, which deprived it of three-fourths of its delicious colouring. On the other hand, she was able to maintain the sextet at the end in its proper key, and sang her part with a spirit and enthusiasm that made the whole theatre ring with applause each night. There is about one quarter of real difficulty, another quarter of ignorance, and a good half of caprice in the objections raised by singers to rendering certain parts as they are written.

I remember that Duprez, in the romance in my opera, *Benvenuto Cellini, La gloire était ma seule idole,* obstinately refused to sing a middle G, the easiest note in his voice, *and in all voices.* To G D, placed on the word " protège," which led up to the final cadence in a graceful and piquant manner, he preferred D D, which makes a horrible platitude. In the air, *Asile héréditaire,* in *Guillaume Tell,* he never would give the G flat (the enharmonic of F sharp), which Rossini had placed there so skilfully and appositely in order to bring back the theme in its first key. He always substituted an F, which produced an insipid harshness and destroyed the whole charm of the modulation.

One day I was returning from the country with Duprez, and as I sat in the carriage by his side, the idea occurred to me to murmur in his ear Rossini's phrase *with the G flat.* Duprez looked me in the face with a slight blush and said :

" Ah, you are criticising me."

" Yes, certainly I am criticising you. Why the devil don't you sing the passage as it is written ? "

" I don't know. . . . That note puts me out, it bothers me."

" Come, come, you are joking. How could it possibly bother you, when it does not bother artists who have neither your voice nor your talent?"

" Well, perhaps you are right."

" By Jove! I am quite certain that I am right."

" Very well; I will do the *G flat* in future *for you.*"

" Not at all; do it for yourself and for the composer, and for the sake of that musical good sense which it is strange to see an artist like yourself sinning against."

Bah! Neither for me, nor for himself, nor for Rossini, nor for music, nor for common sense did Duprez ever do the *G flat* in any performance of *Guillaume Tell*. Neither saints nor devils could make him give up his abominable F. He will die impenitent.

Serda, the bass who had undertaken the Cardinal's part in *Benvenuto Cellini,* maintained that he could not give the high E flat in the aria, *À tous péchés pleine indulgence;* transposing that note to the lower octave, he went down by a leap of a sixth instead of going up a third, which absolutely perverted the melody.

One day, as it was impossible for him to attend a rehearsal, Alizard was asked to replace him. The latter, with his magnificent voice, the expressive power and beauty of which had not as yet been recognised, sang my air at sight without the slightest alteration, and in such a manner that the chorus-singers round him applauded vehemently.

Serda heard of this success, and the next day he found the E flat. Observe that this same Serda, who pretended not to be able to give that note in my aria, afterwards attained not merely to the *E natural,* but to the high F sharp in the part of Saint-Bris in the *Huguenots.* What a race these singers are!

To return to the *Freischütz*.

Of course they wanted to introduce a ballet, and as all my efforts to prevent it were useless, I proposed to write a choregraphic scene, indicated by Weber himself in his rondo for the piano, *Invitation à la Valse,* and I scored that charming piece for the orchestra. But the ballet-master, instead of following the plan traced in the music, could invent nothing better than commonplace dance figures and dull combinations little likely to attract the public. To replace, therefore, quality by quantity, an addition of three other dances was insisted upon. Well, there were the dancers, who took it into their heads that I had some pieces in my symphonies very well suited for dancing, which would finish off the ballet beautifully. They spoke of this to M. Pillet, who fully agreed with them, and asked me to introduce into Weber's score the ball scene out of my *Symphonie fantastique* and the *fête* from *Romeo and Juliet.*

The German composer, Dessauer, happened to be in Paris at the time, and was a constant frequenter of the side-scenes of the Opéra. To the Director's offer I contented myself by replying:

" I cannot consent to introduce music which is not by Weber into the *Freischütz;* but to prove to you that it is not from any exaggerated or unreasonable respect for the great master, let us go to Dessauer, who is walking about at the back of the stage, and submit your idea to him: if he approves, I will conform to it; but if not, I beg that you won't mention it again."

At the Director's first words, Dessauer, turning quickly to me, said:

" Oh, Berlioz, don't do that."

" You hear ! " I said to M. Pillet; and consequently nothing more was said on the subject. We took the dance-tunes in *Oberon* and *Preciosa,* and the ballet was thus finished off with Weber's own compositions.

But after a few representations the airs from *Preciosa* and *Oberon* disappeared, then they cut the *Invitation à la Valse* at random, though, transformed into an orchestral piece, it had obtained a very great success. After M. Pillet gave up the directorship, and whilst I was in Russia, they went so far as to cut off a piece of the finale in the third act of the *Freischütz;* in fact, to suppress, in this same third act, all the first tableau, containing Agatha's sublime prayer, as well as the *Bridesmaids' Chorus* and Annette's romantic air for alto solo. And in this dishonoured shape the *Freischütz* is given in Paris! This masterpiece of poetry, originality, and passion serves merely as a curtain-raiser to the most wretched ballets, and has to be mutilated to make room for them. If some new choregraphical work should arise, more developed than its predecessors, they will, without hesitation, clip the *Freischütz* afresh.

And how they perform what is left of it! What singers! What a conductor! What sleepy indolence in the tempi! What discordance in the ensembles! What a flat, stupid, revolting interpretation of everything by everybody! You have but to be an inventor, a torch-bearer, an inspired man, a genius, to be thus tortured, soiled, and vilified! You coarse salesmen! Till the scourge of a new Christ shall chase you from the temple, be assured that everyone in Europe who has the smallest feeling for Art holds you in the most profound contempt.

Berlioz returned to Paris to find that his position had been only slightly, if at all, improved by his desperate and exhausting assault on Germany. His financial and domestic situation was an anxious one. Life with Harriet was impossible, though an appearance of friendly relations was still maintained, and he called on her occasionally. He was fretted by the spectacle of the environment in which his delicate little son was growing up. He himself was well cared for physically by Marie Recio and her mother, but the expenses of the two establishments were a serious matter for a man who could count on little in the way of regular and certain income beyond his salary as Librarian of the Conservatoire (about 125 francs a month), and his articles in the *Débats* (100 francs each), supplemented by an occasional article in the *Gazette musicale*. His concert-giving, even when it did not result in a loss, rarely brought him anything to compensate him for the time expended and the strain endured.

Yet it was imperative that he should keep his name before the public by any and every means in his power. He was a musical phenomenon for which France, and indeed Europe in general, was not yet quite prepared. Habeneck's jealousy — no doubt motived in large part by Berlioz's manifest desire to replace him at the Opéra if he could — barred him both from the Conservatoire concerts and from the use of the hall of the Conservatoire for his own purposes. Paris, then and for a long time after, possessed no public concert hall suitable for large-scale operations. The result was that Berlioz had to give his concerts either in a theatre or in buildings utterly unsuitable for the purpose, such as the Champs-Élysées Circus and the Industrial Exhibition building. It was often difficult for him to collect the huge orchestral and choral forces required by music such as his, while the presence of so many amateurs in the orchestra must have made for poor performances, and the rehearsals must have been generally inadequate. The marvel is that his works should have made the effect they did under such circumstances.

His object in everything he did was so to impress himself on the Paris public that a solid position, such as the conductorship of the Opéra, would be offered him as his mere due, and he himself be placed in a situation in which he could perform his own music regularly and convincingly. It was mainly to bring about these results that he clung so desperately to his journalism. His very ability as a composer was sufficient to make enemies for him everywhere in the official world of music. He could counteract their machinations only by making himself a power in the Press: most people would think twice before openly falling foul of a writer so brilliant and so audacious as he. But though he thus drove a good deal of the opposition underground, it was no less active and unscrupulous there; while his caustic pen raised a fresh crop of enemies for him each month. His constant insistence, in his articles, on his own doings and his future plans — the only means of "publicity" open to him in those days — necessarily made him appear to be a rather pushing egoist; and he became in consequence the regular butt of witty and malicious writers in other Paris journals.

Marie Recio, useful as she was to him in his home-from-home, was a perpetual trouble to him in public. Having failed to establish herself at the Opéra, she tried to get a footing in the Opéra-Comique. She made her début there on 18 August, 1843, and failed so badly that Berlioz could not have the performance discussed even in the papers with which he was connected.

In addition to all this, Paris was yearly becoming more Philistine, and the romanticism of 1830, of which Berlioz had seemed to be the incarnation in music, had lost its appeal for the bourgeois.

In the next few chapters we see him striving desperately to break down the growing indifference of the Paris public towards him as a composer. He makes another flank attack on it by way of Vienna, Prague, and Pesth, completes and produces his *Damnation of Faust*, finds himself ruined after it, and is once more driven abroad, this time to Russia and England. While he is in London in 1848 the February Revolution breaks out in Paris, and Berlioz' world seems to have crashed to ruin about him.

CHAPTER LXIII

I AM FORCED TO WRITE ARTICLES — MY DESPAIR —
THOUGHTS OF SUICIDE — FESTIVAL OF INDUSTRY —
1022 PERFORMERS — RECEIPTS, 32,000 FRANCS —
PROFIT, 800 FRANCS — M. DELESSERT, PREFECT OF
POLICE — CENSORSHIP OF CONCERT PROGRAMMES
ESTABLISHED — HOSPITAL COLLECTORS — DR.
AMUSSAT — JOURNEY TO NICE — CON-
CERTS IN THE CIRCUS OF THE
CHAMPS-ÉLYSÉES

MY existence after this period presents no musical event worthy of
mention. I stayed at Paris, occupied almost entirely by my *métier,* I
will not say of critic, but of feuilletonist, a very different thing. The
critic (I assume him to be honest and intelligent) only writes if he has
an idea, if he wants to elucidate a question, combat a system, bestow
blame or praise. Then he has motives, which he believes to be valid,
for expressing his opinion and distributing blame or praise. The unhappy feuilleton writer, compelled to write on everything within the
domain of his feuilleton (a sorry domain, a morass full of toads and
grasshoppers!), desires only to accomplish his task. He has often no
opinion whatever about the *things* on which he is forced to write; those
things excite neither his anger nor his admiration — they *do not exist.*
And yet he must *seem* to believe in their existence, seem to have a reason for bestowing attention on them, seem to take part either for or
against them. Most of my colleagues can extricate themselves, not only
without difficulty, but with charming facility, from this embarrassment.
As for me, when I do succeed in getting out of it, it is by efforts as
tedious as they are painful.

I once remained shut up in my room for three whole days, trying to
write a feuilleton on the Opéra-Comique, and not able even to begin it.
I do not recollect the name of the work of which I had to speak (a
week after its first representation I had forgotten it for ever), but the
tortures I went through during those three days before finding the first
three lines of my article, those indeed I can recall. My brain seemed
ready to burst; my veins were burning. Sometimes I remained with my

elbows on the table, holding my head with both hands. Sometimes I strode up and down, like a soldier on guard in a frost twenty-five degrees below zero. I went to the window, looking out on the neighbouring gardens, the heights of Montmartre, the setting sun . . . and immediately my thoughts carried me a thousand leagues away from that accursed opéra-comique. And when, on turning round, my eyes fell upon the accursed title inscribed at the head of the accursed sheet of paper, still blank and so obstinately waiting for the other words with which it was to be covered, I felt simply overcome by despair. There was a guitar standing against the table; with one kick I smashed it in the centre. . . . On my chimney two pistols were looking at me with their round eyes. . . . I stared at them for a long time. . . . I went so far as to bang my head again and again with my fist. At last, like a schoolboy who cannot do his lesson, I tore my hair and wept with furious indignation. The salt tears seemed slightly to soothe me. The barrels of my pistols were still looking at me, so I turned them to the wall. I took pity on my innocent guitar, and, picking it up, tried it with some chords which it gave forth grudgingly. At that moment, my little boy, then aged six, knocked at my door. In consequence of my illhumour, I had scolded him unjustly that morning. As I did not answer him he called out: " Father, won't you be friends? " I ran to open the door. " Yes, my boy," I said, " let us be friends. Come."

I took him on my knees, I laid his fair head on my shoulder, and we both went to sleep. It was the evening of the third day, and I had just given up trying to find a beginning for my article. Next morning I succeeded, I know not how, in writing I know not what on I know not whom. . . .

It is fifteen years since then! . . . and my punishment continues still. Destruction! Always to be at it! Oh, let them give me scores to write, orchestras to conduct, rehearsals to direct; let me stand eight or ten hours at a time, baton in hand, training choirs without accompaniments, singing their refrains myself, and beating time till I spit blood and till my arm is paralysed by cramp; let me carry desks, basses, harps, remove steps, nail planks like a commissionaire or a carpenter, and, by way of a rest, let me correct proofs or copies at night. All this I have done, I do, I will do. It is part of my life as a musician, and I can bear it without a murmur or even a thought, as the sportsman endures cold, heat, hunger, thirst, the sun, rain, dust, mud, and the thousand fatigues of the chase. But everlastingly to have to write feuilletons for one's bread! to write nothings about nothings! to bestow lukewarm praises on insupportable insipidities! to speak one day of a great master and the next of an idiot, with the same gravity, in the same language! to employ one's time, intelligence, courage, and patience at this labour, with the certainty of not even then being able to serve Art by destroying a few abuses, removing prejudices, enlightening opinion, purifying the public taste, and putting men and things in their proper order and place! This indeed is the lowest depth of degradation! Better be Finance Minister in a republic! Had I but the choice!

I submitted with less resignation than ever to the irksomeness of my position when the Industrial Exhibition took place in Paris in 1844.[1] It was just about to close. Chance (that unknown god who has played so large a part in my life) brought about a meeting in a café between Strauss, the fashionable ball-conductor, and myself. The conversation turned upon the approaching close of the Exhibition, and the possibility of giving a regular festival in honour of the exhibiting manufacturers, in the immense premises so soon to be left vacant.

" I have long thought of it," I said; " but after all my musical statistics have been worked out, there is one difficulty that hinders me — that of obtaining the use of the premises."

" That is not at all an insurmountable difficulty," replied Strauss promptly. " I know M. Sénac, the Secretary to the Minister of Trade, very well; he directs all affairs connected with French industry, and can put us in the way of carrying out the idea."

Notwithstanding the enthusiasm of my friend, I remained rather indifferent. The only agreement we came to before parting was that we should go together the next day to see M. Sénac, and if he gave

[1] There is a gap in Berlioz's story here. He gave a successful concert of his own works at the Conservatoire on the 19th November, 1843, that yielded a profit of 549 francs. During the autumn of this year he was working at his *Traité d'instrumentation*, which was published, in part by subscription, in the spring of 1844. In January 1844 he wrote the *Carnaval romain* overture; this was performed for the first time and encored at a concert he gave in the Salle Herz on the 3rd February. In August he published his *Voyage musical*, made up out of the articles which from time to time had described his experiences in Italy and Germany.

On the 6th April he conducted the Concert spirituel at the Opéra-Comique, six of the twelve works on the programme being his own. On the 12th April he conducted the *Carnaval romain* overture at a concert given by Herz and Sivori. On the 4th May he gave a concert at the Théâtre-Italien at which Liszt appeared as pianist.

The concert in the building of the Industrial Exhibition, referred to in the text above, took place on the 1st August.

us the slightest hopes of the building being placed at our disposal, we would go into the matter more seriously.

Without absolutely binding himself there and then, M. Sénac did not at all discourage us. He promised a speedy reply, which, in fact, we received a few days later, and which proved favourable. All that was now needed was the authorisation of M. Delessert, the Prefect of Police.

We acquainted him with our plan, which consisted of a three days' festival in the Exhibition building, to consist of a concert, a ball, and a banquet for the exhibitors. Strauss's idea of having dancing and eating and drinking after the concert would doubtless have brought us in a great deal of money, but M. Delessert, as Prefect, was constantly possessed with the idea of risings and plots, would hear of neither feast, nor ball, nor music, and in short flatly prohibited the festival.

This prudence appeared to me to savour of absurdity. I spoke about it to M. Bertin, who was of the same opinion, and he took care to tell M. Duchâtel, Minister of the Interior. The latter immediately sent an order to the Prefect to allow us at all events to have the music, and M. Delessert found himself compelled to authorise a grand concert of a serious character for the first day, and a so-called popular concert for the second, under the direction of Strauss, a promenade concert, at which dance music was to be played — waltzes, polkas, and galops — but at which there was to be no dancing. This would have deprived us of the certain profits arising from the undertaking. However, M. Delessert still dreaded the danger which might accrue to the State from our orchestras, our chorus, and the amateurs assembled in broad daylight in the Champs-Élysées, too much to listen to us. Who indeed could tell whether Strauss and I were not ourselves conspirators disguised as musicians? . . . However, I was well pleased to be able to organize and conduct a gigantic concert, and limited my desires to a musical success, without risking everything I possessed.

My plan was soon drawn up. Leaving Strauss to occupy himself with his dance orchestra, destined to accompany no dancing, I engaged nearly everyone in Paris of any worth, either as a chorus-singer or instrumentalist, for the grand concert, and succeeded in collecting a body of one thousand and twenty-two performers. All were paid, with the exception of the solo singers from the lyrical theatres. To these I had made an appeal in a letter, beseeching them to join my vocal forces in order to *guide them with soul and voice.*

Duprez, Madame Stoltz, and Chollet alone refused; but their absence was noticed, and severely commented on by the press the next day. Nearly all the members of the Conservatoire concerts likewise thought it their duty to stay away and sulk again with their *old general.* Habeneck, naturally enough, looked upon this grand ceremony, of which *he was not to have the direction,* with a very evil eye.

In order not to raise the expenses to an exorbitant sum, I only asked for two rehearsals, one partial and the other general. I hired the Herz hall, and there practised the violins, the violas and cellos, the basses, the wood-wind instruments, the brass, the harps, the percussion, the women and children of the chorus, and the men successively.

These nine practices, in which each individual only took part once, produced results which would certainly not have been obtained by five general rehearsals. That of the thirty-six double-basses was especially curious. When we came to the Scherzo of Beethoven's Symphony in C minor, it was like the grunting of about fifty ferocious pigs; such was the incoherence and want of precision in the performance of this passage. Little by little, however, it got better, the whole went together, and the phrase came out clearly in all its wild ruggedness.

> D'abord on s'y prit mal, puis un peu mieux, puis bien,
> Puis enfin, il n'y manqua rien.

We repeated it some eighteen or twenty times, which would have been impossible if the whole orchestra had been present. This is the advantage of partial rehearsals. You can pass rapidly over such parts of the programme as present no difficulties to that section of the performers with which you have to do, and, on the other hand, can give all the necessary time and attention to the awkward and difficult passages; the only result being extreme fatigue to the conductor. But, as I have already said, I have exceptional strength in such cases, and my endurance rivals that of a cart-horse.

I had, as may be imagined, arranged that my programme should only consist of pieces of great breadth of style, or such as the performers were already familiar with.

It was as follows:

The overture to *La Vestale* (Spontini).

The prayer from *La Muette* (Auber).

The Scherzo and Finale from the Symphony in C minor (Beethoven).

The prayer from *Moïse* (Rossini).

The *Hymne à la France,* which I had composed expressly for the occasion.

The overture to *Der Freischütz* (Weber).

The hymn to Bacchus, from *Antigone* (Mendelssohn).

The *March to Execution,* from my *Symphonie fantastique.*

The *Chant des Industriels,* written for this *fête* by M. Adolphe Dumas, and set to music by M. Méraux.

A chorus from *Charles VI* (Halévy).

The chorus of the consecration of the poignards, from *Les Huguenots* (Meyerbeer).

The pleasure-garden scene from *Armide* (Gluck).

The apotheosis from my *Symphonie funèbre et triomphale.*

We were to have the general rehearsal in the Exhibition building, where I had selected the great central square, known as the machinery hall, for the concert.

The room was not empty even on the evening before this important trial, and the carpenters were still working at my platform during the rehearsal. A number of iron machines blocked up the space intended for the public. They had not even taken the necessary steps to remove these monstrous implements. I will not attempt to describe my anxiety at the sight.

The walls of Paris were covered with placards announcing the festival. I was bound for a considerable sum, and I found myself arrested in my undertaking by the most insurmountable and unforeseen of obstacles! We could not delay the concert for a day, for the order for demolishing the edifice by the 5th of August at the latest had already been given, and the proprietors of the building materials, having the right to begin pulling it down on the 1st of August, the day of the first concert, only consented to let it stand a few hours longer for a pecuniary consideration. They were the real masters of the premises, and proved to us in a peremptory manner that the Minister of Trade had lent us what did not belong to him. I lost my head for a moment, and was about to rush out and have placards posted up to countermand the festival, when Strauss prevented me almost by force, assuring me that fifty carts would clear the space next day. As ruin seemed to threaten me from every point, I let things take their course. On the morrow my thousand performers assembled for the general rehearsal, which took place amid the cries of carters, cracking of whips, and neighing of horses. At last, by the exertions of the carters and the horses, the machinery was carried off and the space left clear, and I breathed more freely. After the rehearsal a fresh nightmare arose. The numerous listeners came to me and declared unanimously that the platform must be rebuilt, and that it was *impossible* to hear a sound from the instruments, because of the chorus being placed in front of the orchestra. Fancy an orchestra of five hundred instruments *not being heard!* Sixty workmen immediately set to work and cut the platform in two; they then lowered the front portion, reserved for the chorus, by ten feet, thus bringing into view the orchestra, the back rows of which were also raised. This new arrangement allowed the instruments to be heard, notwithstanding the want of sonority in the hall, an irremediable and undeniable defect.

No sooner had this second cause for anxiety disappeared than a third, no less serious, presented itself. Strauss and I, profiting by a few hours' respite which we managed to snatch from all this uproar, rushed off in a cab to the various music-sellers who held the concert tickets, in order to find out what sort of a sale they had had. After adding everything up, we discovered to our horror that the amount, twelve thousand francs, would not defray half of our general expenses. All we could reckon on would be an extraordinary receipt at the doors next day, and if it failed we must be prepared to make up the deficit. The night we both passed after this discovery!

But no withdrawal was possible. The next day (August 1st), I got to the Exhibition building about noon. The concert was announced for one. The first thing I noticed, with a delight to which I did not dare to give vent, was the extraordinary number of carriages converging towards the centre of the Champs-Élysées. I went in and found everything in perfect order, my instructions having been carried out to the letter. The musicians, choir, and sub-conductors of orchestra and chorus were quietly taking their places. With a glance I consult my librarian, M. Rocquement, a man of rare intelligence and indefatigable activity, whose friendship for me, sincere as mine for him, has made him render me unforgettable services on many an occasion of this kind. He assures me that the music is all set out, and that *nothing is wanting.* Then the musical fever begins to rush through my veins. I think no more either of the public, the receipts, or the deficit. I was just about to give the signal for beginning the overture, when a violent noise was heard of cracking wood, accompanied by a prolonged roar. This was the ticket-holding crowd breaking down a barrier and bursting joyously into the hall.

" Just look at the inundation ! " said one of the musicians, showing me how the room was filling. " We are saved ! " cried I, striking my desk with the baton in greater delight than I had ever done before. " Now we shall do something fine."

We begin. The introduction to the *Vestale* unfolds its grand periods, and from this moment the majesty, power, and unanimity of the immense vocal and instrumental body became more and more remarkable. My thousand and twenty-two artists went all together, like the performers in a first-rate quartet. I had two sub-conductors; Tilmant, of the Opéra-Comique, who led the wind instruments, and my friend Auguste Morel, now Director of the Conservatoire at Marseilles, in command of the percussion. I had also five choirmasters, one in the centre and the others at the four corners of the choral body. To these was entrusted the task of conveying my movements to those singers who were unable to observe them in consequence of having their backs turned to me. Thus there were seven conductors, who never lost sight of me for a moment, and our eight arms, although far removed from each other, rose and fell simultaneously with incredible precision. Hence the miraculous unanimity which so astonished the public.

The most effective pieces were as follows: The overture to the *Freischütz,* with the Andante played by twenty-four horns; the prayer from *Moïse* (encored), in which the twenty-five harpists, instead of playing the arpeggios in simple notes, played them in chords in four parts, and, by thus quadrupling the number of the strings, gave the effect of a hundred harps; the *Hymne à la France,* likewise encored, but not repeated; and, lastly, the chorus of the consecration of the poignards, from the *Huguenots,* which electrified the audience. I had multiplied the soli of this sublime piece by twenty, and consequently there were eighty bass voices for the parts of the three monks and of Saint-Bris. The impression it made on the performers and those nearest to the orchestra exceeded anything hitherto experienced. As for me, I was seized with such a fit of nervous trembling that my teeth chattered as

though I were in a violent fever. Notwithstanding the acoustic defects
of the place, I do not think that such an effect in music has often been
produced, and I regretted that Meyerbeer was not present. This terrible piece, which one might say had been written with electric fluid,
by a gigantic galvanic pile, seemed to be accompanied by thunder-
claps and sung by tempests.

I was in such a state after this scene that the concert had to be
stopped for some time. They brought me some punch and a change of
clothes. Then they formed a kind of little room on the platform itself,
by putting together a dozen harps in their linen cases, and, by slightly
stooping, I was able to undress and even change my shirt, in the very
face of the public, without being seen.

Of the remaining pieces, the most successful were the *Oraison
funèbre* and the *Apotheosis* from my *Symphonie funèbre et triomphale* (the solo trombone played with remarkable talent by Dieppo),
and the scene from *Armide,* which gave great delight by its voluptuous
calmness.

The *March to Execution,* the instrumentation of which is so noisy
and the effect so spirited in an ordinary concert-room, seemed quite
muffled and feeble in sound, as also did the scherzo and finale from
Beethoven's Symphony in C minor. Mendelssohn's *Hymn to Bacchus*
sounded dull and heavy; one of the papers, a few days later, said
that the priests of this Bacchus had doubtless imbibed beer instead
of Cyprus wine.

The *Chant des Industriels* was very badly received, especially by
the performers. I had engaged to compose myself the music for
Adolphe Dumas' words, but could not possibly manage it, and I was
obliged to consent to their being set by any composer he chose. He
nominated his brother-in-law, Amédée Méreaux, a piano professor in
Rouen. The overture to the *Vestale* was warmly applauded, as also
the unaccompanied chorus from the *Muette.* As for the song from
Halévy's *Charles VI,* which I had introduced as an after-thought into
the programme at the request of Schlesinger, who published the work,
its effect was peculiar. It awoke that senseless spirit of opposition
always fermenting in the Parisian mob, and at the well-known refrain,

> Guerre aux tyrans, jamais en France,
> Jamais l'Anglais ne régnera!

three-fourths of the audience began to sing with the chorus. It was a
plebeian protest of grotesque nationalism against the then policy

of Louis Philippe, and seemed to give some grounds for the objections of the Prefect of Police. This absurd incident had consequences of which I shall have to speak presently.

Thus my *Musical Exhibition* took place not merely without a mishap but with brilliant success, and the applause of an immense audience. On going out, I had the pleasant satisfaction of seeing the *toll-gatherers of the hospital dues* busied in counting the sum total of the receipts at a huge table. It amounted to thirty-two thousand francs.[1] Of this sum they took the eighth part, viz., *four thousand francs*. The receipts of the dance-music conducted by my partner Strauss, two[2] days after, were so scanty, and the *fête* itself so far from successful, that we had to make up the deficiency from the profits of the concert, and the upshot of all my trouble and risk in accomplishing so great a labour was a net profit of eight hundred francs for myself, against the four thousand taken by the hospital collectors.

Charming land of liberty, whose artists are serfs, receive their sincere benediction, and their admiring homage for thine *equal, noble,* and *liberal* laws!

Scarcely had Strauss and I paid off our musicians, copyists, printers, instrument makers, masons, slaters, joiners, carpenters, upholsterers, officials, and inspectors, when the Prefect of Police, who had charged us the modest sum of one thousand two hundred and thirty-eight francs for his agents and municipal guards (the police service for the Opéra only costs eighty francs), summoned us to his office on pressing business.

" What is it about ? " asked Strauss. " Have you any idea ? "

" Not the slightest."

" Does M. Delessert feel remorse at having charged such an exorbitant sum for his useless agents ? Is he going to return us some of the money ? "

" Oh, very likely indeed ! "

We reached the Prefecture of the Police.

" Sir," said M. Delessert, addressing himself to me, " I regret to have to make you a serious reproach."

" What for ? " replied I, in utter astonishment.

" You secretly introduced into your programme a piece calculated

---

[1] M. Boschot, relying on the journals of the period, gives the figure as 37,000 francs. The King's son, the Duc de Montpensier, sent Berlioz "a magnificent porcelain vase"; and apparently by the Duke's influence 1000 francs were knocked off the sum originally deducted by "the tollgatherers of the hospital dues."

[2] Really three days later, on the 4th August.

to excite those political passions which the Government is endeavouring to repress and extinguish. I allude to the chorus from *Charles VI,* which did not appear at all in the first announcement of the festival. The Minister of the Interior has reason to be much displeased at the manifestations it provoked, and I entirely agree with him on the subject."

" Sir," I answered, with all possible calmness, " you are completely mistaken. It is true that the chorus from *Charles VI* did not appear in my first programme; but hearing that M. Halévy was hurt at the absence of his name, I consented, by his publisher's wish, to admit the chorus from *Charles VI,* on account of its facility of performance by a large body of musicians. This reason alone decided my choice. I do not in the smallest degree sympathise with a national outbreak in 1844 over a scene of the time of Charles VI; and so little did I think of introducing the piece into my programme clandestinely, that its title figured in the bills for more than a week, and moreover those bills were affixed to the very walls of this Prefecture. Let me beg of you, sir, to entertain no doubt on this point, and to disabuse the mind of the Minister of the Interior."

M. Delessert, slightly embarrassed by his own blunder, declared himself satisfied with my explanation, and even went so far as to excuse himself for having reproached me unjustly. Nevertheless, from that day forth the censorship of concert programmes was established; and no one can now sing a song by Bérat or Mdlle. Puget in public without a permit from the Minister of the Interior, *visée* by a Commissioner of the Police.

I had just brought this mad enterprise to a conclusion — an enterprise which I should take good care not to undertake now — when my old anatomy-master and kind friend, Dr. Amussat, called on me. At sight of me he fell back a step or two.

" Hallo! what's the matter with you, Berlioz? You are as yellow as an old parchment. You look uncommonly irritated and exhausted."

" You talk of irritation," said I. " Why should I be irritated? You attended the festival; you know what took place there. I have had the pleasure of paying away four thousand francs to the hospital collectors. I have eight hundred francs left. What have I to complain of? It's all right, isn't it? "

Amussat (feeling my pulse): " My dear fellow, you are on the verge of a typhoid fever. You must be bled."

" Very well, don't put it off till to-morrow. Bleed me now ! "

I took off my coat immediately. Amussat bled me freely, and said :

" Now be kind enough to leave Paris as quickly as possible. Go to Hyères — Cannes — Nice — where you will; but go south, and breathe sea air, and think no more of all these things that are inflaming your blood and over-exciting your nervous system, which is quite irritable enough already. It is not a case for delay, so good-bye."

I took his advice, and went to Nice [1] for a month — thanks to the eight hundred francs from the festival — to try as far as possible to repair the injury done to my health.

Not without emotion did I behold again the places I had known thirteen years before, on the occasion of another convalescence, when I first went to Italy. . . .

I swam a great deal in the sea; made numerous excursions in the environs of Nice, Villefranche, Beaulieu, Cimiès, and Phare. I resumed my explorations of the rocks on the sea-shore, where I found my old acquaintances the cannon still sleeping in the sun. I saw once more the fresh and smiling little creeks, carpeted with soft seaweed, where I had formerly bathed. The room in which I had written the *King Lear* overture, in 1831, was occupied by an English family, so I established myself in a tower built against the rock of the Ponchettes, just above the house.

There I enjoyed with delight the exquisite view of the Mediterranean, and a calm that I valued more than ever. Then, having been cured after a fashion of my jaundice, and having spent my eight hundred francs, I left the always fascinating Sardinian coast, and returned to Paris to resume my Sisyphean labours.

Some months after this journey, the director of the Franconi Theatre, tempted by the extraordinary receipts from the Industrial Festival, proposed that I should give a grand series of musical performances in his circus in the Champs-Élysées.[2] I do not recollect our arrangement; I only know that it turned out badly for him. There were four concerts, for which we engaged five hundred musicians; and the expenses of this enormous *personnel* were not entirely defrayed by the receipts. The room, moreover, was worthless for musical purposes.

[1] On the 20th August. At Nice he wrote an overture, originally entitled *La Tour de Nice*, that afterwards became *Le Corsaire rouge*, and ultimately *Le Corsaire*. He returned to Paris about the middle of September.

[2] The concerts were planned for December 1844, but had to be postponed. They ultimately took place in January, February and March, 1845.

The sound rolled slowly about the circle of the building in a maddening manner, causing a most deplorable confusion of harmony in even
the most slightly intricate composition. One piece alone produced a
great effect, and that was the *Dies Iræ* from my *Requiem*. The
breadth of its harmonies and its movement made it less out of place
than anything else in this vast enclosure, which resounded like a
church; and its success obliged us to include it in the programme of
each of the concerts.

This undertaking was by no means a lucrative one, and quite
wearied me out. I had a fresh opportunity for recovering my health
on the beneficent shores of the Mediterranean, thanks to two concerts
I was persuaded to give at Marseilles [1] and Lyons, the proceeds of
which were at any rate sufficient for my travelling expenses. I was
thus enabled for the first time to produce my own compositions in some
of the French provinces.

The letters I addressed to my coadjutor Edouard Monnais, in the
Gazette musicale in 1848, notwithstanding their somewhat comic
tone, give an exact account of all my adventures on this excursion, and
of another which I made shortly afterwards to Lille. They are to be
found, under the title of *Correspondance académique,* in my book, *Les
Grotesques de la Musique.*

Some months later [2] I went for the first time through Southern
Germany — Austria, Hungary, and Bohemia. The following letters to
my friend Humbert Ferrand, from the *Journal des Débats,* give an
account of my travels there.

---

[1] Two concerts at Marseilles, on June 19th and 25th. The Lyons concert was on July
20th: it was repeated, at lower prices, on the 24th. In the Lyons orchestra was the M. Dorant
who had taught Berlioz the guitar twenty-five years before. See Chapter IV.

[2] In August 1845 Berlioz attended the Festival of the inauguration of the Beethoven me-
morial at Bonn, a full account of which he gives in his *Soirées de l'orchestre.* He returned to Paris
about the middle of the month, and set to work on *La Damnation de Faust.* This subject engrossed
him throughout his Austrian tour.

He left Paris for Vienna, accompanied by Marie Recio, on October 22nd, 1845. He arrived
in Vienna on November 2nd.

Second Visit to Germany
(Austria—Bohemia—Hungary)

CHAPTER LXIV

VIENNA

LETTER I—TO MONSIEUR HUMBERT FERRAND

I HAVE again returned from Germany, my dear Humbert, and no sooner am I back than I feel compelled to give you an account of all my doings there. You have so often sustained me in the heat of the struggle, buoyed me up in discouragement, reassured me about the future by comparing it with the past; you have so keen and noble a feeling for the beautiful, so profound a veneration for the true, such a conviction of the power and greatness of art, that the account of my adventures, discoveries, and experiences in Europe will, I hope, interest you, and could not possibly be given to a more sympathetic and intelligent mind than your own. Notwithstanding the serious passions preoccupying your heart, and in spite of your labours in that sweet retreat with which royal benevolence has provided you, I know that you never forget either poetry or music for a single day. Your love for those two heavenly sisters is too deep and pure ever to swerve; and I am sure that, from the summit of your island mountains, you often lend an ear to the musical and literary murmurs wafted on the north wind from Paris. And yet how sad and mournful Paris seems to me, especially since this last trip! And in these stifling dog-days, how I envy you your perfumed reveries under the great orange-groves in the island of Sardinia, the nightly harmonies of the Mediterranean, and even the simple songs of your Sardinian labourers, the Africans of

Europe, the ancients of the present day! " Non nobis Deus hæc otia
fecit."

I find our capital again absorbed with material interests, indifferent and inattentive to all that is dear to the poet and the artist, devoted to scandal and banter, and laughing sarcastically whenever that
strange taste is satisfied. I came back to the smell of its infernal
asphalte-boilers, the acrid odours of its bad excise cigars, its bored
countenances and boring faces, discouraged artists, wearied men of
understanding, swarms of fools, extenuated, starving, dying, or
defunct theatres; the same barrel-organ coming, as it was wont, at
the same hour, to play me the same everlasting old tune. I hear the
same barbarous opinions put forth and defended, the same barbarous
men and works extolled.

In fact, on the whole, things seem rather gloomy, besides which,
I am not in a mood to see things with rose-coloured spectacles. Do
you recollect the utter melancholy that used to afflict us in our youth,
the day after the ball? A certain uneasiness of soul, a vague suffering
of heart, an objectless sorrow, causeless regrets, ardent aspirations
towards the unknown, an inexpressible restlessness of the whole being
— that was what we felt. I am ashamed to confess it, but that is what
I feel now. I feel as if it were the day after a great *fête,* given in my
honour by strangers. I miss the great orchestras; the grand choruses,
full of ardour and devotion, which I used daily to have such delight in
conducting; I miss that courteous, brilliant, attentive, and enthusiastic
public; I miss those impetuous emotions experienced at a great concert,
when I address myself to the crowd, through the thousand voices of
orchestra and chorus; I miss the study of the various impressions
made on an unprejudiced audience by the recent essays of modern art.
In a word, I feel so wretched from this stagnation after so much harmonious movement, that since my return I have been possessed by one
idea day and night — that of embarking on board a ship, and going
round the world. And just as though fate also were conspiring against
my good resolutions, whom should it have thrown in my way yesterday, to tempt me by his example, but one of my old friends, Halma,
the virtuoso, who has just come straight from Canton. You may guess
how I questioned him about all the places he had visited — China, the
Malay islands, Cape Horn, the Brazils, Chili, Peru — and with what
avidity I examined all the rare and curious things he had brought
back! My heart came into my mouth, and if I had been a king I

should certainly have parodied Richard III and cried, " My kingdom for a ship ! "

But having neither ship nor kingdom, I remain in this little town, which extends, as our charming poet Méry says, from the Rue du Mont Blanc to the Faubourg Montmartre, and is called Paris; and there I walk about of an evening, repeating this line of *Ruy Blas* in every imaginable key and to every imaginable rhythm:

Ah, ça! mais on s'ennuie horriblement ici!

Happily the proverb is not wrong, "L'ennui porte conseil"; it suggested to me a way of forgetting Paris without leaving it. It is to revisit in thought all the distant parts where I have travelled, the foreign artists I have known, the great buildings I have seen, the institutions I have studied; in one word, to write to you, choosing, however, a time when I am free from spleen, in order not to weary you more than I can possibly help. But how do I know that you will even read my letter? Methinks I see you slumbering beneath the shade of a grove of citron-trees, like the happy old man of whom the Roman poet speaks, to the sweet murmur of the busy bees who are plundering the flowers around you. A Virgil or Horace lies open in your hand; that immortal poetry is rocking your slumbers, and you will not care for my prose. Fortunately I know a way of awakening you without incurring your reproaches. Listen. I am going to tell you something of Gluck — Gluck, do you hear? — of his country, which I have just visited; and of Mozart, and Haydn, and Beethoven, who, like Gluck, all lived at Vienna. . . . I knew well that those magical names would make you forgive my unseasonable summons. Now to begin.

Only two striking souvenirs remain of my journey from Paris to Vienna, one being a violent pain (not a mental pain, so look for no romance; only a very prosaic pain in the side), which forced me to stop at Nancy, where I thought I should have died; not so very wonderful an incident, seeing that in truth we live but to die. And the other, a divinity whom I saw through the window of an inn at Augsburg. The worthy man, who has just founded a sort of Neo-Christianity already somewhat in vogue in Bavaria and Saxony, was getting into his carriage when the innkeeper, pale with emotion, pointed him out to me. I have forgotten his name, but he seemed to me to have a lively, intelligent face, and in fact looked rather a good sort of fellow.

This journey, made, like my Italian travels, in a carriage, was all the more tedious because the last steamboat had left Ratisbon before I arrived, and being obliged to stay two days in that large little town I was heartbroken at being slowly wheeled along the banks of the Danube as far as Lintz, instead of rapidly descending the current of the stream in a cloud. How many centuries separate these two methods of travelling? On leaving Ratisbon, I could have believed myself to be a contemporary of Frederick Barbarossa; at Lintz, as soon as I set foot on the deck of a swift and graceful steamboat, I found myself once more in the year 1845.

The names of those two towns recall an observation I have often made about our senseless mania for distorting and changing the names of places, when transplanting them from one language to another. For example, we say Londres, instead of London; and what business have the Italians to say Parigi, instead of Paris? I had a map of Germany which I frequently consulted on this journey. I found out Lintz easily enough, because in France we are kind enough to write and pronounce the name as the Germans do; but I never could make out Ratisbon, for the simple reason that this name is an invention of us French, and has no likeness whatever to Regensburg, the real name of the town I was looking for.

We honour certain names, and those the most difficult to pronounce, by preserving them intact. Others we distort without knowing why. We say Stuttgart, Karlsruhe, Darmstadt, the kingdom of Württemberg, quite correctly; and the next moment we say Bavière for Baiern, Munich for München, Danube for Donau. But at least there is some distant resemblance between these French translations and the original names, whereas there is none whatever between Regensburg and Ratisbon. And yet we should think it extremely absurd of the Germans if they took it into their heads to call Lyons, Mittenberg, and Paris, Triffenstein.

On landing at Vienna, I very soon discovered the passion of the Austrians for music. One of the custom-house officers, whilst examining the luggage coming from the steamboat, caught sight of my name, and immediately exclaimed (in French, be it understood) :

" Where is he? Where is he? "

" Sir, here I am."

" Oh, good heavens, M. Berlioz, what has happened to you? We have been expecting you for the last week. Your departure from Paris, and your approaching concerts at Vienna, have been advertised in all our papers. We were quite uneasy at not seeing you."

I thanked the worthy official with all my heart, saying to myself that most certainly I should never occasion such uneasiness to the officers at the *octroi* of Paris.

No sooner was I established in this gay city than I was invited to attend the first annual concert at the Riding School. It is given for the benefit of the Conservatoire, and the immense body of performers, more than a thousand in number, is almost entirely composed of amateurs. As the Government does little or nothing to support the Conservatoire, it is but right that the true friends of music should come to its assistance. But just for that very reason I was profoundly astonished by it. At the same time each year the Emperor places this immense hall at the disposal of the Society of Amateurs. Lists are opened at the music shops for the inscription of the performers' names, and so great is the number of more or less skilled amateurs at Vienna, both vocalists and instrumentalists, that more than five hundred have to be refused, and there is a real difficulty in selecting the chorus of six hundred and the orchestra of four hundred performers. The receipts from these gigantic concerts (there are always two) are very large, as the hall is capable of seating nearly four thousand people, notwithstanding the immense space taken up by the raised stage for the performers. The room is generally full, however, only for the first concert; the second is not so well attended, the programme being only a recapitulation of the first. Are the Viennese, then, unable to hear the same masterpieces twice in a week without being bored? . . .

In this respect nearly all audiences are alike. It is true that the programmes of these musical festivals are almost always made up from the best known works of the old masters, and the public would probably attend a second concert with no less eagerness than the first, provided they were likely to hear some new work composed expressly for so immense a body of performers. And this, indeed, would be a musical proposition of great interest. No doubt grand music like the oratorios of Handel, Bach, Haydn, and Beethoven gains very much by being thus performed; but after all, in this case it is only a question of more or less doubling the parts, whereas a composer writing for such a colossal orchestra and choir, and acquainted with their manifold resources, would inevitably produce something as novel in detail as it would be grand in its entirety. This has never yet been done. In all

works considered as monumental, the form and tissue are alike. They
are produced with all pomp in huge halls, but would not lose much
if heard in a smaller room, with fewer performers. They do not im-
periously demand an unusual number of voices or instruments, which
may, indeed, give a more marked emphasis to the music, but produce
no effect that is either remarkable or unforeseen. Still, I must admit
that I was much impressed by this concert, more especially by the
choral effects. The soprano voices were of surpassing beauty, and the
general effect first-rate. When I saw the overture to Mozart's *Magic
Flute* in the programme, I was afraid that that wonderful piece, the
time of which is so rapid, and the texture so closely and delicately
woven, could not be properly played by so vast an orchestra, composed entirely of amateurs; but my anxiety did not last long, and it
was executed with a precision and *verve* rarely found even among
artists.

The programme consisted of one of Mozart's motets, another by
Haydn, an air from the *Creation,* the overture just mentioned, and
Beethoven's oratorio, the *Mount of Olives.* Staudigl and Madame Barthe-Hasselt sang the solos. Staudigl's bass is velvety and
impressive, at once sweet and powerful, more than two octaves in
compass (from the low E to the high G), which he emits without the
slightest forcing, filling even so immense a room as the Riding School.
His voice is a most touching one, though he himself is in general but
little moved; it penetrates and charms you. Moreover, Staudigl,
though he sings with the simple good taste that characterises virtuosi who have the secret of breadth of style, has also a great
facility in vocalises and rapid runs. In short, he is a thorough musician,
and reads anything you give him at first sight with an imperturbable
aplomb that is sometimes quite provoking. He is rather inclined to
gratify his self-love by parading this accomplishment, and never, therefore, so much as looks over a piece he is not bound to sing by heart,
until he presents himself before the orchestra. Accordingly, at a general rehearsal, he takes his book, at which he has not yet glanced, and
sings off both words and music without a mistake either of word or
note. He reads it as if it were a book that had been put into his hands
for the first time, but he never reads it any better, and that better is
just what is indispensable at a general rehearsal, where not only
literal exactness, but also an intelligent and animated execution of the

composer's work is required. But how is a performer to put this fire, and soul, and life into his reading when he has prepared nothing beforehand, and knows nothing of the general spirit, the nuances, or even the tempi of the composition? This slight criticism, not so much of the talent as of the habits of this great artist, was made in Vienna in my hearing by composers who had often been annoyed by it on important occasions. Louis XVIII used to say: " Il ne faut pas être plus royaliste que le roi." One might say to Staudigl: " One must not try to be more of a musician than the music." His singing of the D major aria from the *Creation* at the Riding School concert evoked such enthusiasm that, on the point of leaving the hall, where his presence was no longer required, he was forced to return and sing it again.

Staudigl is at once the manager and the first singer of the Theatre an-der-Wien, which is so well directed by M. Pokorny. His magnificent bass voice, in spite of the exquisite beauty of its tone, is not one of those delicate organs requiring hygienic precautions and especial régime. So far from this, he can hunt for days together in the snow, in the coldest weather, bare-necked, and return in the evening to sing the part of Bertram, Marcel, or Caspar without the slightest difficulty. This Theatre an-der-Wien, so called because it stands on the little river of that name, was opened scarcely three years ago, and is already paying well enough to give grave cause for uneasiness to its rival, the Kärntnerthor Theatre.[1] Nearly all the celebrated artists who desire to be known in Vienna go to it. Pischek made his début there in the winter of 1846, and Jenny Lind some time afterwards; and heaven only knows the fury of enthusiasm which they excited, and the fortunes they made.

The chorus, though by no means numerous, has a good deal of force; it is composed almost entirely of young men and women with fresh, fine-toned voices. They are not all very good readers. The orchestra, which I had heard much abused from the moment of my arrival, certainly cannot be put on a level with that of the Kärntnerthor Theatre, of which I shall speak presently; but it does very well notwithstanding, and the young artists composing it are full of that ardour and goodwill which occasionally work miracles. In the singing troupe I remarked one woman whose talent for tender and

[1] The Theatre an-der-Wien may have been reopened at the date given by Berlioz; but it existed at the time of Mozart, and, in fact, the *Zauberflöte* was brought out there. [H.]

impassioned parts was of a most superior order, and I am sorry that I cannot tell you her name, which has escaped me in spite of all my efforts to recall it. She excelled in the part of Agatha, in the *Freischütz*.

I must also mention Mademoiselle Treffz, a graceful cantatrice, and Mademoiselle Marra, the prima donna, whose talent is at once striking and attractive; her voice, though not well adapted to certain vocalises, is both light and brilliant, but unfortunately she is a very poor musician, and consequently sometimes makes such serious blunders in the time as to put out an entire ensemble, notwithstanding all the conductor's care and skill. Mademoiselle Marra excels in Donizetti's *Lucia;* she has had a great success this winter in the north of Germany, and in some Russian towns.

But the tenors! the tenors! Ah, there is the weak side of this theatre, as of nearly every theatre in the world nowadays; and I am very much afraid that, in spite of all his efforts, M. Pokorny will not find it easy to fill up this gap in his *personnel* of singers.

In this respect the Kärntnerthor is more fortunate; it has Erl, a high " white " tenor, somewhat cold, better in calm scenes than in passionate ones, and in purely musical rather than dramatic singing. This theatre is managed by an Italian, one M. Balochino, whose administration is severely criticised both by the city and the court, by artists and amateurs. I cannot appraise the motives for this abuse; its effect seemed to me to be to keep the public away from the theatre, notwithstanding the intelligent efforts of the eminent artist [1] Nicolaï, who manages the musical department, with which M. Balochino, in his capacity of manager of an opera house, is necessarily unacquainted. It is something to be thankful for that M. Balochino has not engaged tailors to play the double-bass,[2] but has engaged violinists for the violins. In France we are still under the cruel necessity of employing musicians to make music; but we are busily trying to solve the problem which will permit us to do without them.

Besides a very deep and sonorous bass, M. Balochino has another singer in his troupe whom I mentioned above, Madame Barthe-Hasselt. Her talent is of the very first order, both from a musical and a dramatic point of view. Her voice has lost some of its freshness, but it is of a large compass, of uncommon power, very true, and with a most touching tone, which may be the result of its being slightly

---

[1] The composer of *The Merry Wives of Windsor*.
[2] I was told that he had been a tailor himself. [B.]

veiled. I heard Madame Hasselt sing the difficult and beautiful soprano scene in *Oberon* in a most triumphant manner, and I do not believe that one prima donna in a hundred could have interpreted that fervid page of Weber's with such fidelity, boldness, fire, and grandeur. At the close of the last allegro, after the burst of delight from Huon's beloved, there was a perfect struggle between the singer and the orchestra. Madame Hasselt came out of it with honour; her ringing voice prevailed above the tempest of instruments and seemed to defy it, without, however, letting one doubtful or exaggerated tone escape her. The impression left upon me by this scene from *Oberon* thus performed in a concert-room was one of the most powerful I can recollect. Some time afterwards I had an opportunity of recognising Madame Hasselt's merit as a tragedienne, in Nicolaï's opera *Il Proscritto,* the last act of which is in every respect admirable, and to my mind exalts Nicolaï to a high rank among composers. In this opera, taken from one of Frederick Soulié's dramas, there is a woman who, under the belief that her husband has died in exile, marries a man whom she loves; and on the return of her first husband, whom she respects without having ever really loved, she is compelled to leave the second in order to return to him. Her strength is not sufficient for so terrible an ordeal. To escape from it the unhappy woman poisons herself, after having reconciled the two rivals, and dies pressing their united hands to her heart. Madame Hasselt plays and sings this part like a consummate lyric tragedienne, and I found in her all those fine emotions and clever calculations, combined with sudden inspirations, which made Madame Branchu's just renown in France forty years ago.

Alas, my dear Humbert, these great tragic singers are disappearing, one by one, like the tenors, and without them the lyrical drama is lost. Judging by the ever-increasing scarcity of artists capable of reproducing the great and noble passions of the human heart by means of our art, it would seem as if those passions were an invention of poets and musicians, and as if nature, having created certain exceptional beings capable of understanding and expressing them, looked upon them as luxuries altogether out of the reach of the human race, and refused henceforth to supply any more.

H. B.

CHAPTER LXV

VIENNA (*Continued*)

LETTER II—TO MONSIEUR HUMBERT FERRAND

WHEN I said that dramatic female singers were becoming as scarce as tenors, and that nature was apparently unwilling to produce any more of them, I did not mean that powerful soprano voices of large compass were, like real tenors, priceless gems. No. Fine and even well-trained female voices are still to be found; but of what use are those organs if not directed by feeling, intelligence, and inspiration? It was of real dramatic talent that I was speaking. We find a fair number of female singers, popular from their brilliant singing of brilliant trifles, and odious to the great masters because utterly incapable of properly interpreting their works. They have voices, a certain knowledge of music, and flexible throats; they are lacking in soul, brain, and heart. Such women are regular monsters, and all the more formidable to composers that they are often charming monsters. This explains the weakness of certain masters in writing falsely sentimental parts, which attract the public by their brilliancy. It also explains the number of bastard works, the gradual degradation of style, the destruction of all sense of expression, the neglect of dramatic proprieties, the contempt for the true, the grand and the beautiful, and the cynicism and decrepitude of art in certain countries.

I have not yet told you of the orchestra or the chorus of the Kärntnerthor Theatre. Both are first-class; the orchestra especially, selected, drilled, and led by Nicolaï, may be equalled but cannot be surpassed. Besides its steadiness, fire, and great mechanical skill, this orchestra has an exquisite sonorousness, owing doubtless to the accurate tuning of the instruments with each other and the perfect purity of intonation in the individual instruments. No one knows how exceptional this quality is, and what evil effects can follow from even a small amount of bad intonation in orchestras otherwise excellent. The Kärntnerthor band can accompany a singer in any style, can lead when it has the principal part, its forte is never noisy except in those wretched masses of sound that compel an orchestra to be as bad as their composer. In the opera, it is perfect; in the symphony, triumphant; and finally, to conclude my panegyric, it contains none of those conceited artists who resent just criticism, regard a comparison between themselves and foreign virtuosi as an insult, and believe themselves to be doing an honour to Beethoven when they condescend to play him.

Nicolaï has enemies in Vienna. It is a pity for the Viennese, for I regard him as one of the best orchestral leaders I ever met. He is one of those men whose influence alone suffices to bestow a marked musical superiority on the town in which they live, when provided with the necessary opportunities. He possesses the three qualities indispensable to a finished conductor. He is a learned composer, skilled and enthusiastic; he has a strong feeling for rhythm; and his technique of conducting is perfectly clear and exact; finally he is an ingenious and indefatigable organiser, grudging neither time nor trouble at rehearsals; one who knows what he is doing because he only does what he knows. Hence the excellent qualities, moral and material, the confidence, devotion, patience, marvellous assurance and unity of action of the Kärntnerthor orchestra.

The intellectual concerts organised and conducted annually by Nicolaï in the Salle des Redoutes form a worthy pendant to our Conservatoire concerts in Paris. There I heard that scene from *Oberon* of which I told you in my last letter, together with the air from *Iphigénie en Tauride, Unis dès la plus tendre enfance,* rather drearily sung by Erl, a fine symphony by Nicolaï, and Beethoven's marvellous and matchless one in B flat. All this was performed with that impassioned fidelity, finish in the details, and power in the whole, which to my mind make such an orchestra, so conducted, the finest product of modern art, and the most genuine representative of what we call *music.*

In this vast and beautiful hall Beethoven's masterpieces — now worshipped throughout Europe — when performed some thirty years ago, were received by the Viennese with the most profound contempt. Count Michel Wielhorski told me he was one of fifty who attended the performance of the Symphony in A, in 1820! At that time the Viennese were thronging to Salieri's operas! Poor pigmies, to whom a giant had been born! They preferred dwarfs.

You may imagine, my dear Humbert, that my legs trembled under me when I stepped for the first time on the platform formerly trodden by his mighty foot. Nothing had been changed since Beethoven's time.

The conductor's desk of which I made use had once been his; there was the place occupied by the piano on which he used to improvise; he descended those steps leading to the artists' green-room, when certain far-seeing enthusiasts, after the performance of his immortal poems, gave themselves the delight of recalling him amidst transports of applause, to the utter astonishment of the rest of the audience, who had been brought there by idle curiosity, and could see nothing in the sublime outbursts of his genius but the convulsive movements and brutal eccentricities of a delirious imagination. Some secretly approved of the enthusiasts, but dared not join them. They did not wish to come into collision with public opinion. They must wait. And meanwhile Beethoven suffered. Under how many Pontius Pilates was this Christ thus crucified!

The great Salle des Redoutes is very good for music. It is a parallelogram, but the angles do not produce an echo. There is only a pit and a gallery. It was at one of my concerts there [1] that the celebrated singer Pischek first sang at Vienna. I was enchanted by his proposal, having known and admired him at Frankfort three years before. He chose for this occasion one of Uhland's ballads, entitled *Des Sängers Fluch,* set to music by Esser, which suited him admirably. As it had a piano accompaniment, I begged of Seymour-Schiff, a clever and spirited German pianist, to play it; to which Seymour-Schiff, like a true artist, agreed. Accordingly we went to Pischek's to rehearse. I need hardly say it was not one of those musical baubles to which we Parisians give the name of ballad. Uhland's is a poem of some length; and Esser's work, which is essentially varied, powerful, and dramatic, in the manner of Schubert, in no way resembles our little couplets, more or less veneered with Gothic polish. I cannot tell you, my dear Humbert, the impression Pischek's incomparable voice and thrilling *verve* made upon me. The progress he had made in three years was simply astounding. It was a kind of intoxication, something like that which Duprez created in the public at the Opéra, the day he made his début in *Guillaume Tell.* You can have no idea of the beauty and power of that baritone, the amplitude of the chest notes, the exquisite sweetness of the high ones, and its flexibility and volume. Moreover the compass is considerable, embracing two octaves in pure chest voice, from the low to the high A flat. And what a fervent inspiration animates it! What passion — sometimes skilfully kept in, sometimes

---

[1] Berlioz's Vienna concerts took place on November 16th, 23rd and 29th, 1845.

bursting forth without restraint. In listening to Pischek, how quickly we recognise the artist — the true musician. He stirs and calms his hearers at will; fascinates and carries them away. The enthusiasm with which he sang his ballad infected me from the very first bar; I felt myself blushing up to the eyes, my veins throbbed as if they would burst, and I exclaimed, almost mad with delight: " There is Don Juan; there is Romeo; there is Cortez!" Moreover, Pischek is greatly favoured as regards his appearance; he is tall and well made, his countenance is full of life and animation. He is an intrepid reader, an excellent pianist, and sufficiently expert in counterpoint to improvise with ease in the fugue style on any theme offered. It is really deplorable, for the sake of our Paris Opéra, that he does not know a word of French. He was born, I believe, at Prague in 1810, and the first language he spoke was Bohemian; afterwards he learnt German, then Italian; now he is studying English, in which language he will sing this winter in London.

His success in Esser's ballad at my concert was spontaneous and universal. A romance which he also sang, to his own accompaniment, at the request of the public, put the finishing touch to their frenzy of delight; and, in fact, nothing more delicious could possibly have been heard. A few days later he appeared at the An-der-Wien Theatre, first in Lortzing's *Zimmermann,* then in the *Puritani,* where the famous duet gave him an opportunity of competing with Staudigl. He was about to play Don Giovanni when I left for Prague. I regretted keenly not being able to hear him in that part, of which I am convinced he is the ideal personified. There were, however, many among the highest Viennese authorities who criticised Pischek severely for affectation and mannerisms in his way of singing. I confess that I never observed anything in it to merit so grave a reproach, which, for that matter, has also often been incurred by Rubini. And I repeat that if Pischek could learn French, and a part at once brilliant and impassioned were written for him, he would bring down the house at the Opéra, and the Parisians would be his slaves.

The Salle des Redoutes derives its name from the great balls often given there during the winter season. There the Viennese youth abandons itself to its passion for dancing, a very real and delightful passion, which has led the Austrians to make a regular art of drawing-room dancing, as far above the routine of our balls as the orchestra and waltzes of Strauss are superior to the polkas and strummers in the dancing-saloons of Paris. I have passed whole nights watching thousands of incomparable waltzers whirling about, and admiring the choregraphical order of the country dances, composed of two hundred persons in two ranks, and the piquant look of the characteristic steps, which for originality and precision I have never seen surpassed, except in Hungary.

And then there is Strauss, conducting his fine orchestra; and when the new waltzes he writes expressly for each fashionable ball turn out successful, the dancers stop to applaud him, the ladies approach the platform and throw him bouquets, and he is recalled at the end of the waltz. Thus there is no jealousy between dancing and music; each shares with the other in its pleasure and success. This is only fair, for Strauss is an artist. The influence he has already exercised over musical feeling throughout Europe in introducing cross rhythms into waltzes is not sufficiently appreciated. So piquant is the effect that the dancers themselves have already sought to imitate it by creating the *deux-temps* waltz, although the music itself has kept the triple rhythm. If, out of Germany, the public at large can be induced to understand the singular charm frequently resulting from contrary rhythms, it will be entirely owing to Strauss. Beethoven's marvels in this style are too far above them, and act at present only upon exceptional hearers; Strauss has addressed himself to the masses, and his numerous imitators have been forced, whilst imitating, to second him.

The simultaneous employment of the various divisions of the bar and syncopated accentuations of the air, even in a regular and invariable form, is to simple rhythm what the harmonies of parts in motion are to plain chords; I might even say, what harmony itself is to the unison and the octave. But this is not the place in which to examine the question. Some twelve years ago I ventured to moot it in a study on rhythm, which cost me the anathemas of many persons, most of whom had certainly no idea of my meaning. You know, my friend, that, without being quite so behindhand as Italy, France is still the centre of resistance to any progress in the emancipation of rhythm. A minute section of the Parisian public is beginning to suspect, thanks to having heard Weber and Beethoven at the Conservatoire, that the constant use of only one rhythm is monotonous, and occasionally very commonplace. But I have no longer the slightest wish to torment those who are behindhand on this subject. Our French peasants sing only in unison. I am quite convinced that if the furious partisans of simple rhythm — phrases of eight bars, with a bang from the big-drum on the strong beat of each bar — ever come to feel the *harmonies of rhythm,* it will not be until the same peasants are able to sing in six parts; and this is equivalent to saying they will never do so. Let us therefore leave them to their primitive enjoyments.

At one of the nocturnal festivals, I was once in a mournful reverie — for Strauss's waltzes, with their fervid airs resembling love voices, have the gift of putting me into a profound melancholy — when a small man, with a clever, intelligent face, made his way to me through the crowd. It was the day after one of my concerts.

" Sir," he said briskly, " you are French, and I am Irish; so there is no national *amour-propre* in my opinion, and " (seizing my left hand) " I beg your permission to grasp the hand that wrote the symphony of *Romeo.* You understand Shakespeare ! "

" Certainly," I answered, " but you are mistaken in the hand, as I always write with this one."

The Irishman smiled, took the right hand I offered him, pressed it very cordially, and went off, saying :

" Oh, these Frenchmen ! these Frenchmen ! They must laugh at everything and everybody; even at their own admirers."

I never knew the name of this kindly islander, who thus took my symphonies for left-handed children.

But I have told you nothing of Ernst, who made such a sensation in Vienna about this time. I shall reserve all mention of him for my Russian travels; for I met him again at St. Petersburg, where his success is daily increasing. He is now reposing on the shores of the Baltic, and taking lessons from the grandiose and sublime sounds of the sea. I hope to meet him again in some other part of the world; for Liszt, Ernst, and myself are, I think, among musicians the three greatest wanderers ever impelled by curiosity and restless temper to leave their own country.

It requires a talent as prodigious as that of Ernst even so much as to attract attention in a town like Vienna, where such superior violinists have performed and still perform. Among the latter I may mention Mayseder, whose great and well-merited fame has long been established; the young Joachim,[1] whose name is beginning to appear; and Hellmesberger junior, son of the leader at the Kärntnerthor.

---

[1] Joachim is now the first violinist in Germany, indeed one might say in Europe, and is a finished artist. [B.]

Mayseder is a brilliant violinist, correct, graceful, irreproachable, always sure of himself; the two others, Joachim especially, are, as befits their age, rash and impetuous, ambitious of producing novel effects, indefatigably energetic, and refusing to believe in the impossible. Mayseder is the leader of Prince Czartoryski's excellent quartet; his second violin is Strebinger, his viola Durst, and his cello Borzaga. All of them belong to the imperial band. This quartet is among the fine things to be heard at Vienna; and its interpretations of Beethoven, Haydn, and Mozart are well worthy of the religious attention with which they are listened to once a week by the Prince and a select audience. The Princess Czartoryski, a perfect musician and distinguished pianist, sometimes takes an active part in these concerts.

After one of Hummel's quintets, which she had just been playing in a masterly manner, someone said to me:

" Decidedly there are no more amateurs."

" Oh," I answered, " if you look well, you may perhaps find them, even among artists. But, in any case, the Princess is an exception."

The imperial chapel, composed of picked instrumentalists and singers, is of course first-rate. There are some children in the choir with lovely voices. The orchestra is not large, but it is exquisite. Most of the solos are entrusted to Staudigl. The chapel recalled to my mind that of the Tuileries in 1828 and 1829, when it was at its prime. I heard it perform a mass composed of fragments from various masters, such as Assmayer, Joseph Haydn, and his brother Michael. They sometimes did these *pot-pourris* in Paris, for the service at the Chapel Royal, but not often; probably this was also the case at Vienna, but I consider myself out of luck, in spite of the remarkable beauty of the pieces I heard.

If I am not mistaken, the Emperor had three Kapellmeisters at that time: Eybler and Assmayer, learned masters of counterpoint, and Weigl, who died a few days before I left Vienna. Weigl is known to us in France by his opera of *The Swiss Family,* performed in Paris in 1828. It was not very successful; musicians thought it insipid and colourless, and the wits described it as a pastoral written in milk.

One thing at Vienna struck me painfully, and that was the incredible ignorance prevailing with respect to Gluck's works. From how many musicians and amateurs have I not inquired if they knew *Alceste,* or *Armide,* or *Iphigénie,* and the reply was always the same: " They are never performed at Vienna; we do not know them." But, you wretched creatures, whether they are performed or not, you ought to know them by heart! It is very plain that contractors like Messrs. Balochino and Pokorny, who are more solicitous of large receipts than of fine works, will never imitate the King of Prussia, and indulge in the luxury of producing antique masterpieces, when they can offer such modern works to the public as *Indra* or *Alessandro Stradella*.

They even spoke of the recent discovery of Gluck's tomb as one of the remarkable events of the season! The discovery! Can you imagine such a thing? It was unknown, then? Exactly so. Oh, my dear Viennese! you are quite fit to inhabit Paris! Still, there is nothing strange in the fact, if one remembers that to this day no one knows the spot where Mozart's ashes are reposing.

I said something in my first letter which can hardly have given you a very brilliant idea of the Conservatoire at Vienna. Notwithstanding all the merit of its director, Herr Preyer, and the much-appreciated talent of Joseph Fischhoff, Boehm, and certain other excellent professors, the Conservatoire is not what would be naturally expected from a capital like Vienna, either in importance or numbers. A few years ago, indeed, it seems to have been in such decay that, but for the energy and devotion of Dr. J. Bacher, it would not now be in existence. Dr. Bacher is not an artist; he is one of those lovers of music, of whom there are some two or three in Europe, who undertake and carry out the hardest tasks, for pure love of art, acquire a real authority over opinion by the purity of their taste, and often succeed in doing by their own strength what monarchs fail to undertake. Active, persevering, willing, and generous beyond all expression, Dr. Bacher is the most staunch supporter of music at Vienna, and a godsend to musicians.

The Philharmonic concerts take place in the Conservatoire concert-room, which though small is very good. They are under the able direction of the Baron de Lannoye, as are the Academy *réunions* of male singers, a most valuable institution, directed by Herr Barthe with zeal and intelligence. There I heard the astounding pianist, Dreyschock, five or six times, and always with renewed pleasure; a young man, whose talent is fresh, brilliant, and energetic, with immense technical skill and musical feeling of the highest order. He has introduced many novel and effective combinations into his pianoforte music.

I must ask the forgiveness of many remarkable artists for the brevity with which I am forced to speak of them. I should have to write a book to do justice to each, and catalogue all the musical wealth of Vienna in detail.

And as yet I have said nothing of certain of its most eminent minds; more especially of those who compose chamber music, such as quartets and songs with piano accompaniments. Herr Becher is among this number; a dreamy, concentrated soul, whose harmonical audacity goes beyond anything ever yet attempted, who endeavours to enlarge the form of the quartet and give it new turns. Herr Becher is also a distinguished writer, and his criticisms are highly esteemed among the masters of the Viennese press.[1]

Councillor Wesque, of Putlingen, who publishes under the pseudonym of Hoven, gave me many a happy hour with his songs, the style of which is charming, full of fancy, and accompanied by very piquant harmonies. I noticed the same characteristics in some movements from two of his operas, which unfortunately I only heard on the piano.

Herr Dessauer is better known to us from his two years' stay in Paris — I think from 1840 to 1842. He has set to music many pieces by our best poets. He continues to add to his songs, and most of them obtain decided success in the drawing-room. Dessauer's style is exclusively the elegiac; he is only at his ease when dealing with the miseries of the soul; sufferings are his dearest delight, and tears his greatest joy. Both at Vienna and Paris, he was always waging a courteous war with me. His one idea is to convert me to a musical doctrine with which I am not yet acquainted, for he never could make up his mind to impart it to me. Every time we had an opportunity for discussing the matter *thoroughly* — to quote his own word — if I looked at him steadily in my gravest manner, he concluded that I was going to laugh at him, shut his lips, and postponed the conversation. If all preachers had acted thus, we should still be groping in the darkness of paganism.

I must not forget to mention the cordiality with which I was received at Vienna by many writers who, like myself, are labouring in the rugged and flinty soil of criticism, too often to see it produce nothing but thistles and nettles. They treated me as an equal, for which I thank them. One of them, Herr Saphir, gives an annual literary and musical gathering, in which, in spite of the censure, his spark-

---

[1] Unfortunate Becher! I hear that he madly threw himself into the furnace of the last insurrection at Vienna, and was taken, tried, condemned, and shot. [B.]

ling wit contrives to use its scourge, to the great delight of his hearers, who, like the rest of the world, are always enchanted at hearing some-one cut up.

I say nothing of the conductor's baton [1] with which I was so kindly presented by my friends at Vienna, at a supper-party, after my third concert; nor of the handsome present made me by the Emperor; nor of many other things which you will have heard through the news-papers of the day.[2] You are not ignorant of any good fortune that befell me during that journey, and so it would be useless to recur to it.

H. B.

CHAPTER LXVI

PESTH

LETTER III—TO MONSIEUR HUMBERT FERRAND

WHEN travelling in Austria, one must positively visit at least three of its capitals — Vienna, Pesth, and Prague. Certain wayward minds assert that Pesth is in Hungary, and Prague in Bohemia; but none the less do these two states form integral parts of the Austrian Empire, to which they are attached and devoted — soul, body, and estate — much as Ireland is to England, Poland to Russia, Algeria to France; much as all conquered nations have always been to their conquerors. Let us start accordingly for Pesth, a great Austrian town in Hungary.

I am not fortunate in my relations with the Danube. As I told you, its last steamboat had been taken off when I wanted to embark at Ratisbon for Vienna; it was covered with fogs, and so prevented me from going down it as far as Pesth; and you will soon see that the old river did not stop its ill-natured proceedings there. Apparently it objected to my entering its dominions, and wished not merely to throw difficulties in my way, but even to hinder me altogether. And yet how I

---

[1] This baton is silver-gilt, inscribed with the names of the numerous subscribers. It is wreathed with a spray of laurel, on the leaves of which are inscribed the titles of my works. The Emperor, after having attended one of my concerts in the Salle des Redoutes, sent me a hundred ducats (eleven hundred francs). But he accompanied it with this extraordinary compliment: "Tell Berlioz that I was *very much amused!*" [B.]

[2] The supper was given on December 10th, the eve of his birthday.

On January 2nd, 1826, his *Romeo and Juliet* was given in the Theater an der Wien. Berlioz did not conduct, but was in the audience.

admired it! How often have I eulogised that majestic and powerful river! It ought to have been grateful for my admiration. But far from this, the more I went into ecstasies over its grandeur, the more hostile did it show itself, and I might say of it what La Fontaine said of his lion:

> Ce monseigneur du lion-là
> Fut parent de Caligula.

Before leaving Vienna,[1] I expressed a wish to be introduced to Prince Metternich, but even those friends who were in a position to enable them to procure me this honour seemed so much put out by my request that I was on the point of withdrawing it. It was a question of seeing an official acquainted with a Privy-councillor who would speak to some member of the cabinet influential enough to introduce me to a secretary of the embassy, who would get the ambassador to speak to a minister, so that he might introduce me. I found this circumlocution infinitely too prolonged, and at last the idea occurred to me of dispensing with the officer, the councillor, the chancellor, the secretary, the ambassador, and the minister, and introducing myself. My friends, seeing that I was resolved on trying the experiment, very probably regarded me as a madman *in petto,* or, at any rate, as a Frenchman and a half. Be that as it may, however, I braved Austrian etiquette, or the opinion entertained at Vienna about its strictness, and took my way to the Prince's palace. I go up, find an officer on guard in the drawing-room, and, presenting my card, made known my wishes. He goes to the Prince, and returns in a moment to inform me that His Highness will be disengaged in a few minutes, and be much pleased to receive me. Accordingly I was admitted without further preamble. The Prince was most amiable; he questioned me much about music, especially my own, of which, as it seemed to me, His Highness had formed beforehand a most curious notion, which I endeavoured to correct. Finally I withdrew, enchanted with my welcome, immensely surprised at the facility with which I had thus flouted the laws of German etiquette, and quite proud of having for some minutes exercised the functions of officer, councillor, chancellor, ambassador's secretary, and minister, without any trouble whatever. And thus I again recognised the truth of the evangelical precept, " Knock, and it shall be opened unto you," and also the exquisite tact with which on occasion certain princes can say, " *Sinite parvulos venire ad me,*" on condition, of course, that the

[1] Early in January, 1846.

parvuli shall be foreigners, no matter how unskilful, and that they belong to that class of useless folk, always interesting to see close at hand, called in these days poets, musicians, painters — in a word, artists, and in the Middle Ages more rudely styled minstrels, troubadours, stage-players, and gipsies.

Perhaps you will be surprised to hear, my dear Humbert, that I did not exercise my powerful influence to obtain admission to the Imperial Family, in order to pay my respects to them — and you will have some grounds for astonishment. There was, in fact, a reason of state for my coyness, which I will tell you in the strictest confidence. It had come to my ears, in the first days of my stay at Vienna, that the Empress, that angel of piety, sweetness, and devotion, held even stranger opinions about me than Prince Metternich did about my music. Certain passages out of my *Voyage en Italie,* somewhat too uncivilised in style, and which, moreover, had been skilfully commented on to Her Majesty by kind friends (one is a prey to friends everywhere, even at the Austrian Court), had gained me the reputation of a regular brigand in these high places, neither more nor less. Well, I was not merely flattered — that would be saying too little — but really proud of this eccentric renown which had thus fallen upon me from the heavens. I said to myself, what you would certainly have said in my place, that a slight aureole of crime is too distinguished a thing, since Byron has made it fashionable, not to be carefully preserved when one has had the good fortune to gain it, even if it be placed upon a forehead altogether unworthy of it. Accordingly I reasoned thus: " If I *present myself* at Court, the Empress may not impossibly condescend to address a few words to me. I shall necessarily have to answer her to the best of my ability, and once engaged in conversation, heaven knows where I may be led. Her Majesty may lose her original opinion of my individuality, and only see in me, as in many others, a worshipper of her own grace and goodness. She will find nothing fierce or sinister in my countenance; nothing tigerish in my voice. True, my nose will always be slightly aquiline; but, on the whole, *my appearance will not betray my employment,* and I shall pass for a plain, honest man, incapable of *doing any harm,* or of even stopping a coach, and thus my reputation would be lost. No, by Jove! I would rather remain a brigand, and vanish as quickly as possible, since distance would only serve to increase and embellish my aureole."

That is why I obstinately declined to do myself the honour of being presented at the Austrian Court, and went off suddenly one fine morning into Hungary. I must here give you an account of my quarrels with the Danube. Each day it enveloped itself in a cloud, like Homer's gods when about to commit some evil action; hence the interruption to navigation and the necessity laid upon travellers of taking the land way to Pesth. This is a very polite way of putting it. You must know, my friend, that the most ordinary pebbles are as scarce as emeralds on the surface of the immense plain that extends from Vienna to Pesth; the soil is composed of a fine dust, as fine as if it had been sifted, and which, when soaked by rain, forms quagmires that you can only cross by the aid of a grand supply of horses, and in which you are always being engulfed at the risk of never being able to get out again. I ought therefore rather to have said the mud way than the land way. Imagine the charms of such a journey! But still all this was nothing. What should the Danube do but overflow its banks, and overwhelm with its angry waters the black ditch in which we had been paddling for the last fifteen hours, and which in that country they persist in calling *the grand road!* At midnight I was roused from my slumbers by the carriage coming to a stand-still, and by the sound of crashing, rolling water. The coachman, going on at random, had driven us into the bed of the river, and dared not move a step forward.

All this time the water was rising. A Hungarian officer in the *coupé* had spoken to me two or three times through a small window in the intermediate compartment of the unhappy carriage.

" Captain," said I in my turn.

" Sir."

" Don't you think we shall be drowned? "

" Yes, sir, I do! May I offer you a cigar! "

His insolent *sang-froid* made me feel much inclined to strike him, and in a fury of rage I accepted his cigar and began promptly to smoke it.

The water continued to rise.

Then the coachman, making a desperate effort, turned sharply round at the risk of upsetting us into the stream, succeeded in climbing up the right bank, to which we were fortunately pretty near, drove across country and brought us . . . straight into a lake. This time I thought it was all up with us, and again calling to the officer, I said:

" Captain, have you got a cigar left? "

" Yes."

" Well, give it me quick, for this time we shall really be drowned ! "

Fortunately a worthy peasant was passing (where the deuce was he going at such an hour, on such a road?), who helped us out of the lake, and gave our unlucky Phaëton some directions, thanks to which he succeeded in finding the road. We arrived at Pesth next day, having gone from ditches to quagmires, amid jolts and starts, alternately driving into the water out of the mud, and into the mud out of the water. I should say we arrived opposite Pesth, on the right bank of the Danube, which was kind enough to allow us to cross it in a boat for lack of a bridge.

On this same right bank a tolerably large town is situated, and I asked my captain its name.

" That is Buda," said he.

" Buda ? But on my map the town opposite to Pesth bears quite a different name. It is called Ofen."

" Precisely, that is Buda. Ofen is a very free German translation of the Hungarian word."

" I understand." The German maps are apparently drawn up with no less ingenuity than the French ones. Only on the latter they should put " *Ratisbonne,* pronounced *Regensburg,*" and on the former " *Ofen,* pronounced *Buda.*"

On my arrival I had a treat which I had promised myself the night before, if I should escape from the mud and the Danube. I took a bath, drank two glasses of tokay, and slept for twenty hours, though not without dreaming of inundations and lakes of mud. After which I had to make preparations for my first concert, arrange with the managers, look for violinists, see the Kapellmeister, singers, etc., etc.

Thanks to the kindly influence of Count Radaï, the Intendant of the National Theatre, where I had been advised to give my concerts in preference to the German Theatre, the principal difficulties were soon overcome. I had a momentary uneasiness about the composition of my orchestra, for that of the National Theatre is so small that it was impossible to think of getting up my symphonies with its little band of violins only. On the other hand, it was impossible to have recourse to the artists at the German Theatre, owing to a regulation which will give you some idea of the touching affection of the Hungarians for everything German. The admission of any artist from the German Theatre into the National Theatre, whether singer, chorister, or instrumentalist, is strictly forbidden, no matter how greatly his assistance may be needed. More than this, at the Hungarian Theatre the use of all languages ancient and modern in singing is permitted, with the single exception of German, which is formally prohibited. This strange and daring exception in a country subject to Austria is somewhat of an imitation of Napoleon's Continental system, practised towards Germany in general and Austria in particular by the Hungarian nation. Accordingly the products of German industry are commonly rejected, and it is considered a duty in all classes of the population to make use of Hungarian manufactures only. Hence the frequent use in large letters on the windows of most of the Pesth shops, even those of the modistes, of the word *hony*, which puzzled me so much the first day, and which means *national.*

Henry Müller, the music publisher at Vienna (the most obliging of men, who overwhelmed me with marks of attention during my stay in Austria), had fortunately given me a letter to a colleague at Pesth, one Herr Treichlinger, one of the great violinists produced by the ancient German school. He put me into communication with the principal members of the Philharmonic Society of Pesth, and very speedily obtained for me an extra dozen excellent violinists, whom he begged to be allowed to lead himself. They acquitted themselves marvellously of the task which they had so courteously undertaken, and the performance of my programme was, I fancy, one of the best that had been heard at Pesth for a long time. Among the pieces was the march which now forms the finale to the first part of my legend of *Faust.* I wrote it the night before my departure for Hungary.[1] A Viennese amateur, well up in the ways of the country which I was about to visit, had brought me a volume of old airs. "If you wish to please the Hungarians," said he, "write a piece on one of their national themes; they will be delighted with it, and when you come back you shall give me an account of their *eljen* (hurrahs) and applause. Here is a collection in which you have only to choose." I took his advice and chose the theme of Rákóczy, on which I wrote the grand march you know.

No sooner had the announcement of this new piece of *hony* music spread through Pesth, than the national imagination began to ferment. They wondered how I should treat that famous — one might

---

[1] This statement must perhaps not be taken too literally; Berlioz had probably thought the March out after his return from Bonn in the preceding August. It has been conjectured that the idea of it was given him by Liszt during the Beethoven Festival.

say almost sacred — theme, which had long set all Hungarian hearts beating with enthusiasm for liberty and glory.

There was even some anxiety on the subject; they dreaded a profanation. . . . Certainly, I was so far from being offended at this misgiving that I even admired it. Besides, it was only too well justified by a host of pitiable *pots-pourris* and arrangements in which melodies worthy of the highest respect had been horribly outraged. Perhaps, also, more than one Hungarian amateur had witnessed in Paris the impious barbarity with which we drag our immortal *Marseillaise* through the musical gutter on national fête-days.

At last a Herr Horwath, chief editor of a Hungarian paper, being unable to restrain his curiosity any longer, came to the publisher with whom I was in treaty about the organisation of the concert, found out the address of the copyist who had been commissioned to write the orchestral parts from the score, ran off to this man, asked for my MS., and examined it carefully. Herr Horwath was but ill pleased with the result of his inquiry, and on the morrow could not disguise his anxiety.

" I have seen your score of the *Marche de Rákóczy,*" said he.

" Well? "

" Well, I have my fears."

" Bah! "

" You have begun the theme piano, and we, on the contrary, are accustomed to hear it played fortissimo."

" Yes, by the Zingari. Besides, is that all? Never fear; you shall have a forte such as you have never heard in all your life. You have not read it properly. The *end* must be considered in everything."

Still, on the day of the concert I felt a certain tightening in my throat when the moment came for producing the piece. After a trumpet phrase based on the rhythm of the first bars of the melody, the theme appears, you will remember, performed piano by the flutes and clarinets, and accompanied pizzicato by the stringed instruments. To this unexpected exposition the public listened in silence; but when, after a long crescendo, fugued fragments of the theme reappeared, interrupted by dull beats of the big drum, simulating the effect of distant cannon, the room began to seethe with an indescribable sound, and when at length the orchestra burst out in a furious *mêlée,* and hurled forth the long delayed fortissimo, it was shaken by the most unheard-of cries and stampings; the concentrated fury of all this burning audience exploded in accents that made me shiver with terror. I felt as if my hair were standing on end, and from the moment of that fatal bar I had to bid farewell to the peroration of my piece, the orchestral tempest being quite incapable of contending with the eruption of this irresistible volcano. We had to recommence, as you may imagine; and the second time it was with the greatest difficulty that the public could contain itself two or three moments longer than before in order to hear a few bars of the coda. Herr Horwath was throwing himself about his box like one possessed; I could not help laughing, as I threw a glance at him which said: " Well, are you still afraid? Are you satisfied with your forte? " It was a lucky thing for me that I had placed the *Rákóczy-induló* (that is the Hungarian title of the piece) at the end of the concert, for anything played afterwards would have been entirely lost.

I was violently agitated, as may be believed, after such a hurricane, and was wiping my face in a little room behind the stage, when I experienced a singular rebound from the emotion of the concert-room. It happened in this wise. A poorly dressed man, with a strangely agitated face, dropped in upon me unawares in my small retreat. The moment he caught sight of me he flung himself upon me and embraced me with fervour; his eyes were full of tears, and with difficulty he stammered out these words:

" Ah, sir, sir! I Hungarian — poor devil — not speak French — un poco l'italiano. Forgive — my — ecstasy. Ah, I understood your cannon. Yes, yes — the great battle — German dogs! " And striking himself a great blow on the chest with his fist, " In my heart here — I shall bear you — ah, you Frenchman — you revolutionist — you *do* know how to make revolutionary music."

I cannot attempt to describe the terrible excitement of this man, his tears and gnashings of teeth. It was something almost appalling; it was sublime.

You can well believe, my dear Humbert, that after that the *Rákóczy-induló* was put into all the programmes, and always with the same result. Indeed, on leaving I was obliged to bequeath my manuscript to the town of Pesth, by its own desire, and a month later I received a copy of it at Breslau. To this day it is performed in Hungary on all great occasions. But I must take this opportunity of informing Herr Erckl, the Kapellmeister, that I have made various alterations in it since then by putting about thirty bars more into the coda, which, I think, add to its effect.

I shall make a point of sending him the revised score, corrected and augmented, as soon as my publisher will allow.[1]

Herr Erckl is a most excellent man of great talent. I heard an opera of his during my stay at Pesth, cleverly conducted by himself, and entitled *Hunyady*, the subject of which is taken from the heroic annals of Hungary. It contains many things remarkable for their originality, and more especially for the depth of feeling which dictated them. Moreover it is written in a pure style, and instrumented in a very refined and intelligent manner, by which I am far from meaning that the instrumentation is lacking in energy. Madame Schodel, a genuine lyrical tragedienne of the school of Madame Branchu — an extinct school of which I little expected to find an offshoot in Hungary — played and sang the principal part beautifully.

I must also mention a very meritorious tenor named Feredy in the Hungarian troupe. He sings the Hungarian romances and national songs marvellously, with a charming and original accentuation that would certainly make them attractive to all nations. The orchestral leader is a violinist of great talent, named Kohne, who resided for a long time in Paris, and, if I am not mistaken, attended the Conservatoire.

The chorus of the National Theatre of Pesth is but feeble, both as regards the numbers and the quality of the voices. The Hungarian language is by no means unfavourable to music; indeed in my opinion it is much less hard than German. A wonderful language! which no one can understand . . . unless he learns it. It would be useless to

---

[1] (March 6th, 1861.) I have just sent the score to Hungary. A few weeks ago a body of young Hungarians sent me a silver crown of most exquisite workmanship, bearing these words on the coat-of-arms of the town of Gior (Raab in German): "The Young Men of Gior to Hector Berlioz." This present was accompanied by a letter, to which I replied thus:

"Gentlemen, — I have received your handsome present, together with the flattering letter accompanying it. This proof of sympathy, from a country of which I have always preserved such tender memories, has touched me deeply.

"The effect of my work is doubtless due to the feelings which your national air awakens in you, whom, according to your own poetical expression, it must lead *to life* — in you of whom one may say with Virgil,

'Furor iraque mentes
Præcipitant, pulchrumque mori succurrit in armis.'

"But if in my music you have found even one spark of the enthusiasm which kindles in all noble Hungarian breasts, I must consider myself only too fortunate, and regard this success as one of the rarest that any artist can obtain.

"Receive, gentlemen, my most cordial greetings, together with this expression of my gratitude. — Yours faithfully,

"Hector Berlioz.

"February 14th, 1861."

try to discover any resemblance between Hungarian and any other known tongue; there is none. Even certain musical terms derived from the Italian, which have been preserved almost intact everywhere else, are replaced by peculiar terms in Hungarian, either composite or simple, but entirely different. For example, take the word *concert,* which is to be found almost exactly the same whether in Italian, Spanish, French, German, English, or Russian. You would never guess that on the Hungarian placards it becomes *hangverseny,* neither more nor less. This strange word means literally *concourse of sounds.*

My musical preoccupations did not prevent me from attending two balls during my stay at Pesth, as well as a grand political banquet given by the Hungarian nobility. Never have I seen anything so magnificently original as these balls, as much from their prodigious display of luxury as from the singular picturesqueness of the national costumes, and the beauty of the proud race of Magyars. The dances are essentially different in character from those known throughout the rest of Europe. Our cold French country dances play no great part in them. Mazurkas, tarsalgos, keringos, and csardàs reign triumphant. The csardàs especially, a rustic importation, danced by the Hungarian peasants with a charming exuberance of delight and spirits, seemed in particular favour with the aristocratic dancers, notwithstanding the timid remarks of an unlucky newspaper critic, who took it into his head to criticise the figures and movements of the csardàs as slightly improper, and compared them, most inaccurately, to the eccentricities of the unmentionable dance interdicted by the Parisian sergents-de-ville. Heaven only knows with what a volley of reproaches he was greeted, and what withering glances he received from the ladies, when he dared to appear at the ball after the publication of his article. The *hony* writer was *honni.* That pun I hatched just forty-eight hours ago! The political banquet gave me the opportunity of hearing the celebrated orator Deak, the O'Connell of Hungary, whose name is in every mouth, and his portrait in every house. Like the illustrious defender of Ireland, M. Deak only desires to bring about the reforms necessary for his country gradually and legitimately, and has much difficulty in restraining the quivering impatience of his party. He spoke but little, and very calmly, and I understood the subject of his speech from the exclamation which escaped my neighbour, like an aside, " Fabius *cunctator!* "

Among the guests, a young man with a very expressive face was pointed out to me. " He is an Atlas," said Herr Horwath. " How an Atlas ? " " Yes, he is a poet, and bears the name of Hugo."

During dinner, a small orchestra of dark Zingari performed some national airs after a fashion of its own — that is to say, an extremely *naïve* and wild one — and these alternating with the speeches and toasts, and amply seconded by the burning wines of Hungary, excited the revolutionary fever of the guests to excess.

Next morning, I had to bid farewell to my Hungarian hosts. I departed, still quivering with various emotions, and full of sympathy with so ardent, chivalrous, and generous a nation. During my stay at Pesth the Danube had calmed down, all expression of ill-temper had disappeared from its venerable face, and it now allowed me to follow its course as far as Vienna without let or hindrance. No sooner had I arrived than I received a visit from the amateur whose officious advice had persuaded me to write the *Rákóczy* march. He was a prey to the most comical uneasiness.

" The fame of your piece has spread even here," he said, " and I hasten to implore you not to say a word about me in the matter. If it were known in Vienna that I had contributed in any way whatever to its composition I should be gravely compromised, and I might come to grief about it."

I promised to keep his secret. If I tell you his name now, it is only because I think there has been time since then for so serious a matter to be hushed up. It was . . . ah, well, it would certainly be indiscreet if I told you. I only wanted to frighten him.

H. B.

CHAPTER LXVII

PRAGUE

LETTER IV — TO MONSIEUR HUMBERT FERRAND

I HAD already gone all over Germany before it came into my head to visit Bohemia. When at last I thought of it at Vienna, I ought in prudence to have rejected the idea at once, according to the advice of several apparently well-informed persons. " Don't go to Prague," said they; " it is a city of pedants, where the works of the dead alone are respected. The Bohemians are excellent musicians, it is true, but only after the manner of professors and schoolmasters; all novelty is detestable in their eyes, and the chances are that you won't care for them."

I had accordingly made up my mind to give up the journey, when someone brought me a Prague *Gazette musicale,* containing three long articles on my *King Lear* overture. I had them translated, and, far from finding that they savoured of malevolence and pedantry, I recognised with delight exactly the opposite characteristics. The author, one Dr. Ambros,[1] seemed to combine real learning with judgment and imagination. I wrote to thank him, and to sound him as to his countrymen's disposition of mind with regard to myself.

His answer quite dispelled my doubts, and my desire to visit Prague became as great as the fear I formerly had of showing myself there. When the Viennese heard that I had made up my mind to go, they did not spare their witticisms at my expense. " The inhabitants of Prague claim to have discovered Mozart; they swear by him, care for no symphonies but his. They will give it you finely," etc. But Dr. Ambros had inspired me with a confidence which nothing could shake, and I set off, notwithstanding the gloomy forebodings of the mockers.

Is it not pleasant, five hundred leagues away from your home, to find an unknown friend waiting for you when you alight in a foreign town, who recognises you, by your *charmingly characteristic countenance,* as the man he is looking for, accosts you, shakes you by the hand, and tells you in your own language that everything has been prepared for your reception? This is exactly what happened to me with Dr. Ambros when I arrived at Prague. The only thing was that, as my *charmingly characteristic face* completely failed in its effect, he did not recognise me. It was I, on the contrary, who, on catching sight of a small man with a quick, kindly countenance, and hearing him say in French to someone, " How on earth do you expect me to make out M. Berlioz in this crowd? I have never seen him " — it was I, I repeat, who had the amazing acuteness to guess that he was Dr. Ambros, and going up abruptly to the two friends:

" Here I am," I said.

" M. Berlioz ? "

" Neither more nor less."

" Well, good-day to you; we are very glad to see you at last. Come

[1] The author of the celebrated *History of Music.*

along; we have got a room all ready for you, and an orchestra too; both very warm. You will be well pleased with them. Rest yourself to-night, and to-morrow we will set to work."

Accordingly we began our preparations for my first concert the very next day, after first making acquaintance with the musical authorities of the town. Dr. Ambros introduced me to the director of the Conservatoire, Herr Kittl, who in his turn made me known to the brothers Scraub, Kapellmeisters of the theatre and the cathedral respectively, and also to the orchestral leader, Herr Mildner. Then came the turn of the singers, journalists, and principal amateurs; and when all these visits were over I said to Dr. Ambros, " Now, supposing you were to introduce me to the town. I perceive a hill literally covered with monumental buildings, and, contrary to my usual habit, I have the greatest curiosity to examine it all thoroughly."

" Well, come along," said the obliging doctor.

Perhaps it was the only time that I did not mind the trouble of such an ascent (of course I except that of Vesuvius; and as for Etna, I never saw it). Joking apart, the climb is a hard one; but how wonderful it is, that continuous succession of temples, palaces, battlements, steeples, towers, colonnades, courts, and arches! What a view when you get to the top of the mountain, so adorned with marble! On the one hand, a forest extending to the great plain below; on the other, a cascade of houses descending like a smoky torrent to the Moldau, which sweeps majestically past the town to the sound of the mills and factories which are worked by it, leaps a barrier that Bohemian ingenuity has erected to modify the course of its waters, and then, passing by two small islands, loses itself in the far distance, amidst the windings of a chain of red hills which lead it carefully towards the horizon.

" That is the Huntsmen's Island," said my guide, " so named, doubtless, because there is no game there. Behind it, as you go up the river, you may see Sophie's Island, in the centre of which is the Sophie concert-room where you are to give your concert, and which is devoted to the meetings of the Singing Academy, Sophie's Academy."

" And who may this Sophie be, in whose room and academy and island I am to have the honour of giving my concert? Is she a nymph of the Moldau, the heroine of some romance of which this island was the scene, or is she merely a rough, red-handed washerwoman who, like a modern Calypso, makes it resound to her songs and to the thumping of her washing-bat? "

"Your last supposition is, I fancy, the more correct. Tradition does not say, however, that her hands were chapped."

"Ah, doctor, you seem to me to have been playing the part of Ulysses with this Sophie! Is there a Eucharis there? Let us see. Suppose I turn Telemachus and look for you in the island of Calypso." A blush was the doctor's only answer, and I saw that it would not do to harp too long on that string. . . . And so it befell that I heard nothing definite about this Sophie, who was the patroness of a Singing Academy, a concert-room, and an island.

Unhappily that delicious retreat in the midst of the Moldau's flowing waters, which in summer is shaded by a verdant girdle and garlanded with flowers, conceals, somewhere in the vicinity of its Temple to Harmony, two or three abominable *guinguettes,* where bad musicians make execrable music in the open air, and ill-conditioned young people abandon themselves to rollicking dances, bad tobacco, worse beer, and still worse gossip. What a deplorable idea, thus to depoetise a flowery and leafy bower, to mingle such nauseous odours with its perfumes, such noises with its gentle melodies! Is not the Huntsmen's Island there with its taverns, its mills, its tanneries? Does not this go better in every way with these popular merry-makings? Between ourselves, I am afraid Sophie really had chapped hands.

To return abruptly to the subject of music, though reserving to myself the right of wandering again at will, I hope, my dear friend, that you do not expect me to write you a dissertation more wearisome than learned, equally pretentious and tiresome, and more *futile* than *utile* (it is plain that I am a poet: I beg you to observe the facility with which rhymes drop from my pen), on the revolutions of music in Bohemia, on the special tendencies of the Slav mind, and on the probable date at which the old masters of this country allowed the use of the dominant seventh without preparation. On these deep and grave questions I must confess my incurable ignorance, and if my indolence were but less obstinate with regard to the study of history or of *histoires,* I should certainly prefer to make researches about the famous ivory guitar which the philosopher Koang-fu-Tsée, commonly called Confucius, used in preaching morality to the Chinese Empire. For I also play the guitar, and yet I never preached morality even to the population of a bedroom ten feet square; quite the contrary. True, my guitar is very simple, and the elephant's tusk does not enter into its ornamentation. No matter! The following passage, which I re-read yesterday for at least the hundredth time, is a very good subject of meditation for philosophical musicians — not musical philosophers; there have been none since Leibnitz. I believe I have already quoted it elsewhere. "Koang-fu-Tsée, having accidentally heard the song called Li-po, which everyone says is fourteen thousand years old (after that let no one call music a modern art), was filled with such admiration that he remained seven days and nights without either sleeping, eating, or drinking. He then formulated his sublime doctrines, and promulgated them without difficulty, singing all the precepts to the air of Li-po, and thus preached morality to China with a five-stringed ivory guitar."

Alas for me! My guitar has not only five strings like that of Confucius, but sometimes even six; and yet I have not the smallest fame as a preacher. Ah! if it had only been ivory, what blessings might I not have scattered, what errors dissipated, what truths inculcated, what a beautiful religion I should have founded, and how happy we should all be! But no, it is impossible that a strip of ivory the less should lead to such misfortunes! No doubt it has its share in them; but there must be another cause of these calamities, a cause beyond my perceiving, and one more worthy, perhaps, of being the subject of investigation by one philosopher after another than the questions relating to the Bohemians and the dominant seventh.

Modern European music deprives no one of food or sleep, as the ancient Chinese melopœia did, and yet it has its value. That is to say, be it clearly understood, it does not prevent anyone from eating and drinking; though I have often heard it said by excellent musicians that whilst practising their art they had not even water to drink, and that such and such a celebrated composer or musician was dying of hunger. As for preventing sleep, the most ancient compositions of our old masters have certainly never had the slightest claim to that distinction. But now the question is, what is my opinion about the musical institutions of Prague, and the taste and intelligence of its inhabitants. I should have to live longer in that beautiful capital to know it thoroughly in this respect; however, I will try to gather up my recollections and only speak of what really struck me. I will tell you, therefore, of its Theatre and the singing troupe, the orchestra and the chorus;

Of its Conservatoire, the able composer who directs it, the masters and pupils I had the privilege of knowing;

The Singing Academy;

The *Maîtrise,* or cathedral school;

The military bands;

The virtuosi and composers independent of the aforesaid institutions;

And finally the public.

When I saw the theatre (in 1845) [1] it struck me as dark, small, dirty, and very bad for sound. It has, I know, since been restored, and its new manager, Herr Hoffmann, makes the most laudable efforts to restore that prosperity which under his predecessors was fast vanishing. His troupe was superior to most German singing companies of that period. The first tenor, the baritone (Strackaty), Mesdemoiselles Grosser, Kirchberger, and Madame Podhorsky, seemed to me artists of real merit, with rare voices both as to intonation and timbre, and, like all Bohemians, musicians besides . . . one could hardly say more. Unfortunately, the personnel of the orchestra and the chorus matched the scanty dimensions of the room, and seemed rather to reproach the manager with parsimony. With so small a number of performers, it really is not permissible to attempt any masterpieces in a high style, and yet this is just what the Prague Theatre occasionally does. The result was some deplorable mutilations, complained of by all artists. In these cases the splendour of the scenery and the quality of the performance were in perfect harmony. In the finale of the fourth act of Gluck's *Iphigénie en Tauride,* I remember seeing a ship *with a row of artillery* setting sail for Greece. The *mise en scène* of the regular repertory was somewhat better, and suffered little or nothing from the feebleness of the orchestra and chorus; this repertory was composed, in fact, of contemptible little works translated from the French, and long since forgotten at the Opéra-Comique. All managers are alike; their sagacity in the discovery of platitudes is equalled only by their instinctive aversion for any works tending either to refinement of style, grandeur, or originality. In this respect they are more *public* than the public, both in Germany, Italy, England, and elsewhere. I say nothing of France; it is well known that our lyrical theatres, without exception, are and have always been managed by superior men. And whenever the opportunity has presented itself of choosing between two productions, one commonplace and the other distinguished, between a creative artist and a miserable imitator, between bold ingenuity and in-

---

[1] Really 1846.

sipid, prudent stupidity, their exquisite tact has never led them astray. Therefore, glory to them! All friends of art profess a veneration for these men only equal to their gratitude.

I have often wondered why theatrical managers everywhere have such a marked predilection for what genuine artists, cultivated minds, and even a certain section of the public itself persist in regarding as very poor manufacture, short-lived productions, the handiwork of which is as valueless as the raw material itself. Not as though platitudes always succeeded better than good works; indeed, the contrary is often the case. Neither is it that careful compositions entail more expense than " shoddy." It is often just the other way. Perhaps it arises simply from the fact that the good works demand the care, study, attention, and, in certain cases, even the mind, talent, and inspiration of everyone in the theatre, from the manager down to the prompter. The others, on the contrary, being made especially for lazy, mediocre, superficial, ignorant, and silly people, naturally find a great many supporters. Well! a manager likes, above everything, whatever brings him in amiable speeches and satisfied looks from his underlings, he likes things that require no learning, and disturb no accepted ideas or habits, which gently go with the stream of prejudice, and wound no self-love, because they reveal no incapacity; in a word, things which do not take too long to get up.

Other managers, again, are ambitious of doing everything themselves, and for that reason alone are hostile to such as are ill-advised enough to offer them works which cannot be got up without the assistance of the authors. The importance acquired by these indiscreet authors is so much subtracted from that of the manager, who suffers under it and is indignant. The captain of the ship, thus humiliated before his crew, never forgives the pilot for having reduced him to inaction, and degraded him (without considering his feelings) to the rank of lieutenant or sub-lieutenant. Consequently, he hourly curses his own imprudence in venturing into quarters of which he did not know the difficulties, and vows never again to navigate waters that are not in every sense ploughed.

Besides this, some managers are monomaniacs, or, to put it more politely, monophiles. These are extravagantly fond of one particular channel of ideas, a particular class of incident, a particular epoch in history, particular costumes, scenes, and effects in the *mise en scène,* a particular singer, or dancer, or what not. They must insist on introducing their hobby everywhere, in season and out of season. Thus the hobby of M. Duponchel, the director of the Opéra, was, is, and ever will be, a cardinal in a red hat under a daïs. Such operas as have no daïs, no cardinal, and no red hat (and there are many) have never had the smallest attraction for him. And I once heard it said by M. Méry, that if the Almighty had a part in a new work, Duponchel would still insist on His being dressed out in his favourite headgear. It would be in vain for the Almighty to say: "But, my dear director, I am *le bon Dieu,* and I must not appear in the costume of a cardinal." "Pardon me, Eternal One," M. Duponchel would reply; "it is absolutely essential that your Immensity shall deign to put on this fine costume and ascend the daïs, for otherwise *my opera* would not be a success." And *le bon Dieu* would have to give in!!! I say nothing of M. Duponchel's passion for horses, for a passion as profound as this is deserving of respect.

All this, however, has no connection with the former manager of the Prague Theatre; indeed, I ought to have said so sooner. He was an honest man, and, like most of his trade, little versed in musical matters; but, unlike them, he was liked and esteemed by his dependents, and when, in consequence of the bad state of his affairs, he found himself compelled to give up the management of the theatre, he was sincerely regretted. M. Pokorny, the director of the An-der-Wien Theatre, at Vienna, must also be included among the honourable exceptions.

Enterprising managers of their type, who work on their own account and at their own risk, are not numerous in Germany. I have only known five or six, namely, at Leipzig, Prague, Vienna, the German Theatre in Pesth, and Hamburg. The other lyrical theatres are mostly under the direction of titled Intendants, managing on behalf of their sovereigns. It must be admitted in general that no matter what the degree of aristocratic coldness with which many of these counts or barons treat their subordinates, artists much prefer them to the manufacturers who make capital out of them. The former have at any rate, for the most part, exquisitely polite manners, on which the latter do not particularly pride themselves. Moreover, they possess the advantage of education, literary and occasionally musical, a still rarer article with contracting managers. Count von Rödern, who ruled the destinies of the Berlin Opera for a long time, is an example of this class.

At all events, though theatrical managers may be met with in Germany, whether contractors or Intendants, who are extremely stupid and ignorant of everything appertaining to art, I do not think they can be compared to what France has produced in this line during the last thirty years. I would not mind betting that no German manager, either noble or plebeian, is ignorant of the names of Gluck and Mozart, or of their principal works. In France, on the contrary, one might cite a number of incredible blunders. For example, a certain director of the Opéra,[1] on receiving a visit from Cherubini, asked him, in an off-hand way, although the illustrious composer had stated his name, what *was his profession,* if he belonged to the personnel of the Opéra, and if he were attached to the department of the ballet or of the machinery. About the same period Cherubini, who had just had a new mass performed with great triumph, was calling one evening on the Superintendent of Fine Arts,[2] who paid him this extraordinary compliment: " Your mass is very fine, my dear Cherubini, its success is indisputable, but why do you confine yourself to sacred music? *You ought to have written an opera!* " Imagine the indignant embarrassment of the author of *Medée, Les Deux Journées, Lodoiska, Mont Saint-Bernard, Faniska, Les Abencérages, Anacréon,* and many other dramatic works, at so unexpected a blow!

A director[3] of the Théâtre-Français asked once who wrote the comedy entitled *Le Médecin malgré lui,* and was much offended when told, with a burst of laughter, that it was by Molière. . . .

In Paris, moreover, there is one manager whose office is more difficult of access than that of a minister, who never replies when written to, and pushes his audacity so far as to request those persons whom he needs to be so kind as to call upon *him,* whoever they may be. The director has a favour to ask of them, and so he thinks it quite natural that they should put themselves out for him. It is true he does not always boast of the answers he receives in such cases. . . .

Still, it must be admitted that at the head of some of the theatres in Paris there are men who combine good sense, intellect, and literary merit (I do not say musical; that is never to be seen) with genuine politeness. Among the most intelligent of these, if not the most lucky and disinterested, may be mentioned Harel, who died about two years ago, after having won the prize offered by the Academy for the eulogy of Voltaire. His *bons mots* enjoyed some celebrity. None of them,

---

[1] M. Duplantys. [B.]   [3] M. Buloz. [B.]
[2] M. le Vicomte Sosthène de Larochefoucault. [B.]

however, are to be compared with the one he suggested to Fréderick Lemaître on the following occasion. Harel was manager of the Theatre of the Porte-Saint-Martin. One of our literary *grand-seigneurs* [1] (in the old style), who was very rich, and much enamoured of art and poetry, had had a tragedy [2] performed at this theatre, the *mise en scène* of which cost him a considerable sum. He happened to be in Harel's office in company with Lemaître, having come to pay the bill for the scenery, costumes, accessories, etc., and thought himself at last free, when he was presented by the insatiable manager with an account of three or four thousand francs for the ropes used in the machinery. In vain did M. de Custine rebel against what he had some grounds for calling robbery; he was compelled to pay, and went off in a fury of indignation. Lemaître, who had studied this curious scene in silence, tapped the manager on the shoulder, and said:

" Very careless of you; you left him his watch! "

H. B.

CHAPTER LXVIII

PRAGUE (*Continued*)

LETTER V—TO MONSIEUR HUMBERT FERRAND

To-day I feel sufficiently serious to talk to you about the Conservatoire of Prague, and Conservatoires in general. However imperfect the state of these institutions may be, it seems to me that they alone in connection with musical art have been founded under the influence of good sense and reason. At the present moment every Conservatoire in Europe is directed by a musician, which has not always been the case. At this we can but marvel, and thank Providence. During the reign of that opinion now so universally prevalent, that *the more important an artistic question, and the more difficult of solution, the more necessary it is that the men appointed by Government to deal with it should be strangers to the art in question* — during the reign, I say, of these doctrines, which one would assume to be dictated by madness if envy were not so plainly apparent in them, it is a subject for congratulation that the teaching of the different branches of music should

---

[1] M. de Custine. [B.]   [2] *Beatrix Cenci.* [B.]

be confided to special artists, more or less masters of their particular art. No doubt many people (particularly in Paris) would not fail to say that *this was a misfortune,* that it would be infinitely better to employ mathematicians to teach the violin, to place men of letters at the head of composition classes, and choose medical men as singing-masters. Others (the Academy of the Fine Arts at the Institute is of this opinion) think that music in general is better known, better felt, better understood, and in consequence better judged of by painters, sculptors, architects, and engravers than by anyone else. And finally, many (indeed, the great majority) display quite a touching unanimity in laying down as a maxim that not merely are musicians unnecessary for teaching music, or directing Conservatoires or operatic theatres, but that mathematicians, men of letters, doctors, engravers, painters, sculptors, and architects are a dangerous race, by reason of their intelligence and a certain odious sentiment proper to them all, the respect for art and science.

In the eyes of the upholders of this principle, the best judges and directors of musical art, and those most likely to exercise a beneficent influence upon its present and future state, are the men who are strangers to all science, all art, all feeling for the beautiful, all aspirations towards the ideal, all work, and all thought — men who have never done anything, who know nothing, believe in nothing, love nothing, wish for nothing, can do nothing; and who combine with these indispensable conditions of ignorance, incompetence, and indifference, a certain indolence of mind akin to stupidity. It may be seen that the number of persons interested in supporting this beautiful thesis is so incalculable that one must not be astonished at the multitude of their proselytes. I am only surprised that their triumph should not be more complete, and their progress more rapid. Hence the appositeness of my remark on Conservatoires which are now given over exclusively to musicians.

More than this: the one at Prague, with which I have more particularly to do at present, is directed by a talented composer, full of love for his art, active, ardent, indefatigable, severe on occasion, but lavish of praise when praise is merited . . . and young. Such is Herr Kittl. They might easily have found some heavy piece of mediocrity consecrated by years (for even in Bohemia there are men of this sort), and confided to him the task of gradually paralysing the progress of music in Prague. But no! On the contrary, they got hold of Herr Kittl, aged thirty-five, and so music is alive there, moves and grows. There must evidently have been some spirit of folly among the committee who made such a choice, or else that committee must have been composed exclusively of men with minds and hearts.

A musical Conservatoire ought, in my opinion, to be an establishment for *conserving* the practice of musical art in all its departments, and learning and acquirements connected with it, the monumental works produced by it, and in addition to this, by placing itself at the head of the progressive movement inherent to an art so young as European music, it ought to preserve all good and beautiful work bequeathed to us by the past, whilst advancing with prudence to future conquests.

I shall hardly be giving way to national partiality in saying that of all the Conservatoires with which I am acquainted, that of Paris approaches most nearly to this definition.

Next to it is the Conservatoire at Prague,[1] and if one takes into consideration the naturally immense difference between the resources of a town like Prague and those of the capital of France, it is really praising it highly to put it in the second rank. It cannot be so rich as ours in any respect, there are fewer teachers and pupils, and the efforts of the authorities for its maintenance are not to be compared with the constant and energetic support lent to the Conservatoire at Paris by the Fine Arts Department; still, the study is good, and so is the spirit of the school.

Among the masters under M. Kittl's superintendence, I must make particular mention of Messrs. Mildner and Gordigiani. The former, a clever violinist, who also, as I have already told you, holds the office of leader and solo violinist at the Prague Theatre, has turned out a considerable number of clever pupils. The second, reputed to be one of the best singing-masters that Italy has sent to Germany, is also a composer of merit. I know a *Stabat* by him for two choirs in a very fine style, and an opera, *Consuelo,* of which both words and music are his, remarkable for its natural melodies, and for a graceful sobriety of orchestration, of which few examples are to be found in these days.

It has been said sometimes, and I think rightly, that it is useful to a composer to *know how to sing:* perhaps it is still more necessary for a singing-master to *know how to compose.* In fact, it is in the accurate

---

[1] I am not yet acquainted with the interior organisation of the Conservatoire at Brussels, of which M. Fétis is the skilful director. I only know that it is one of the largest in existence. [B.]

understanding of qualities which the composer can and ought to insist upon from his interpreters, that the singing-master will find his most solid point of support in the proper superintendence of his pupils' studies. A singing-master who composes will not, unless he be detestably mediocre, have any fancy for those eccentricities which are threatening to destroy the art of singing in three-fourths of musical Europe. He will not teach his pupils to despise time and rhythm. He will never allow them to take the insolent liberty of embellishing their songs at random, when an exact reproduction is imperatively required by the expression of the phrase, the character of the personage, and the style of the author. Neither will he allow them to get into the habit of looking upon the private interest of their own vocal organ as the only one to guide them when singing in public. And consequently his pupils will not disfigure the most exquisite works in order to avoid the poor notes in their voices, or to make a long and absurd display of the good ones.

Such a master will not fail to study the art of singing with his pupils, and to convince them that it does not consist in the execution of feats of strength, destitute of reason or musical interest; still less in forcing the larynx to utter sounds which are unnatural, either from their depth, height, violence, or duration. He will require a reason for each of their *accents,* and will show them that if it is shocking to sing out of tune, it is not less shocking to sing with false expression; that if a note hurts the ear when too sharp or too flat, a passage given loud when it ought to be soft, or weak when it should be strong, or pompously when it ought to be simple, is even more painfully irritating to an intelligent hearer, does more serious wrong to the work thus misinterpreted, and proves conclusively that the singer is a mere idiot, however splendid his voice and however exceptional his vocalisation may be. The pupils of such a master will not — as is everywhere the case today — cynically try the patience of the conductor with the most grotesque rhythmical eccentricities; unduly lengthening any bar, slackening the time of a phrase or a single bar in order to hurry the next; keeping the poor man's arm in the air till a favourite note has been prolonged to the utmost; joining in fact in a conspiracy against art and good taste, and becoming the frantic slaves of folly and leather lungs.

Neither will such a master suffer his pupils to enter upon the study of fine works without understanding the subject of the poem, and knowing the historical part; without having reflected upon the passions called into play by the author, and attempted thoroughly to enter into their character. No singer would leave his class without having learnt to respect the language in which he sang, and the rules imposed upon the connection of the words by the very nature of rhythm and euphony. Moreover, he would make his pupils clearly understand that if, in the organ points or elsewhere, they permitted themselves to depart from the lines laid down by the author, such departures must at least be in the same harmony as the accompaniment, and that the virtuoso must never be toying with the notes of the chord of the six-four when the orchestra is sustaining that of the dominant, and vice versâ.

The conversations I had with M. Gordigiani, and the method of such of his pupils as I have heard, showed me that he was entirely of this opinion.

If, as I shall presently show, special classes are wanting in the Conservatoire at Paris, we need not be surprised at finding the same defect at Prague. Indeed, the teaching there is far from being complete. Still, it has produced a fair number of pupils capable at this moment of a satisfactory and wholly unassisted performance of such difficult works as Beethoven's Choral Symphony. This is doubtless one of M. Kittl's greatest results. If a Conservatoire is an institution intended for the maintenance of *all* departments of musical art and the instruction directly pertaining to them, it is strange that not even in Paris should they have yet succeeded in carrying out such a programme. For a long time our instrumental school had no classes for the study of the most indispensable instruments, such as the double-bass, trombone, trumpet, and harp. True, these gaps have been filled up of late years, but unhappily there are many others, which I shall now point out. My remarks will doubtless call forth loud exclamations from many, who will consider them idiotic, absurd, and ridiculous. I hope they may! I shall proceed accordingly to say:

(1) That the study of the violin in Paris is very incomplete; the pupils are not taught the pizzicato, and the result is that many passages, arpeggioed on the four strings, or *hammered* with two or three fingers on the same string, in a quick movement — perfectly practicable passages, since they can be performed by guitar-players on the violin — are declared impossible by violinists, and consequently prohibited to composers. It is possible that in fifty years some director will be bold enough to insist upon having the pizzicato taught in the

violin classes. Then, when artists shall have mastered the novel and piquant effects resulting from such a study, they will have good ground for jeering at the violinists of the last century, who used to cry out, "Take care of the C!" Neither is the use of harmonics properly studied in a business-like manner. The little that our young violinists know about it they have learnt by themselves, since the appearance of Paganini.

(2) It is to be regretted that there is no special class for the viola. This instrument, notwithstanding its family relation to the violin, needs individual study and constant practice if it is to be properly played. It is an antique, absurd, and deplorable prejudice that has hitherto handed over the performance of the viola part to second or third-rate violinists. Whenever a violinist is mediocre, it is said, "He will make a capital viola." From the standpoint of modern music this is false reasoning, for mere filling-in parts are no longer written for the orchestra (at least by the great masters), but each has an interest proportionate to the effect to be produced, and a condition of inferiority in any one part with regard to any other is not recognised.

(3) Another great mistake was never to have taught the *corno di bassetto* in the clarinet classes until now, the absurd and disastrous effect of it being that many of Mozart's pieces could not be performed in France as written. Nowadays the improvements brought into the bass clarinet by Adolphe Sax make it capable of performing anything written for the basset-horn, and indeed more, its bass compass exceeding that of the basset-horn by a minor third. Moreover, its tone is very like that of the basset-horn, only much finer; it ought therefore to be studied in the Conservatoires conjointly with the soprano clarinets and the small ones in E flat, G, and high A flat.

(4) The saxophone, a new member of the clarinet family, and really of value when the performer can bring out its characteristics, ought nowadays to have a separate place in Conservatoire classes, for the time is not far distant when every composer will wish to employ it.

(5) We have no ophicleide class, and the result is that, out of a hundred or a hundred and fifty blowers of that difficult instrument in Paris at the present moment, there are scarcely three fit to be admitted into a well-arranged orchestra. M. Caussinus is the only proficient in it.

(6) We have no class for the bass tuba, a powerful cylindered instrument, differing from the ophicleide in tone, mechanism, and

compass, and taking exactly the same place in the trumpet family that the double-bass does in the violin family. And yet in these days most composers make use of either an ophicleide or a bass tuba in their scores, sometimes of both.

(7) The sax-horn and the cornet à pistons ought both to be taught in our Conservatoire, being now in general use, especially the cornet.

(8) There is no instruction whatever in any percussion instrument; and yet is there a single orchestra in Europe, great or small, that does not boast a kettle-drummer? There is a man in every orchestra who goes by that name, but how many real players are there, that is to say, how many artistic *musicians* familiar with all the difficulties of rhythm, thoroughly masters of the mechanism (less easy than is supposed) of that instrument, and gifted with an ear sufficiently trained to be able to *tune* it and to *change the pitch* with certainty, even during the performance of a piece, and amid all the harmonic murmur of the orchestra? How many kettle-drummers are there of this description? I declare I only know of three in all Europe, besides M. Poussard of the Paris Opéra. And you know how many orchestras I have been allowed to examine during the last nine or ten years! Most of the drummers I have met do not even know how to hold their drumsticks, and consequently find it impossible to produce a real tremolo or roll. Well, a drummer who cannot make a quick roll with every variety of light and shade is good for nothing.

There ought, therefore, to be a class in every Conservatoire for percussion instruments, where first-rate musicians should thoroughly teach the use of the kettle-drum, the tambourine, and the military drum. The now intolerable custom (already abandoned by Beethoven and certain others) of treating percussion instruments in a coarse and unintelligent way, or of neglecting them altogether, has doubtless contributed to the long maintenance of a more or less unfavourable feeling against them. From their having hitherto been employed by composers only to produce more or less unpleasant noises, or merely to mark the accented times in the bar, it was concluded that they were fit for nothing else, had no other mission in the orchestra, and nothing better to claim, and that it was therefore quite unnecessary either to study their mechanism with care, or to be a real musician in order to play them. Now to play certain cymbal or big-drum parts in modern compositions one really ought to be a very good musician; and this brings me to the mention of another gap, perhaps the most serious of all, in the instruction at all Conservatoires, that of Paris included.

(9) *There is no class for rhythm,* devoted to initiating all pupils without exception, whether singers or instrumentalists, into the various difficulties of the division of time. Hence that insupportable tendency of most French or Italian musicians to insist on the loud beats in the bar, and reduce everything to a monotonous phraseology. Hence also the impossibility, as regards most of them, of performing compositions in syncopated style with any nicety; such, for example, as the charming airs so popular in Spain (which we call bizarre). French and Italian singers are very far from being able to *play with the rhythm;* and when they do attempt it they feel puzzled, and show a heaviness and awkwardness which results not in good music but in bad. Hence their hatred for everything that is not what they call *square,* or, as you and I would say, *insipid.* Hence their puerile and absurd ideas about *carrure,* and their astonishment when they come across melodies differing in shape and accent from those invariably adopted in France and Italy. Hence that indolence of performers in general who are used to being supported and guided by the divisions of the time, and by an accentuation that can always be foreseen, like children who cannot walk except by the help of the go-cart. Beethoven's symphonies have forcibly broken a great many of our Paris players of these puerile habits, and given them a taste for piquant and original rhythms. But as nothing of the same sort has ever been attempted with which to wake up singers, to set the blood circulating in their veins, to train them to watchfulness, resource, and vivacity of motion, it follows as a matter of course that their torpor continues, and that in order to get them out of it they must be subjected for some time to a particular régime. For them a *rhythm* class would be of special advantage, though a large number of instrumentalists also might derive much benefit from it.

A perfect Conservatoire, jealous of keeping up the tradition of the interesting facts and remarkable works bequeathed to us by the past, and of the various revolutions in art, should have a professorship of Musical History; and the professor should carry out the objects of his chair not merely by verbal and written instruction, but also by illustrative and adequate performances of such fine works as are worthy of being remembered. Then we should not see students — some of them quite gifted — as ignorant as Hottentots about the most magnificent works of great masters still living; the taste of musicians thus enlightened would become very different, their ideas would grow wider and far more elevated than at present, and finally, we should find more artists than artisans engaged in the practice of music.

H. B.

CHAPTER LXIX

PRAGUE (*Conclusion*)

LETTER VI — TO MONSIEUR HUMBERT FERRAND

THERE is another most important class wanting in all modern con-servatoires, which to my mind is becoming more essential every day, namely, that for instrumentation. That branch of the composer's art has been so greatly developed of late years as to have attracted the attention both of the critics and the public. It has, however, also served only too often to mask the poverty of a composer's ideas, to ape real energy, to counterfeit the power of inspiration, and even in the hands of really able and meritorious writers it has become a pretext for incalculable abuses, monstrous exaggerations, and ridiculous nonsense. It is easy to imagine to what excesses the example of such masters has beguiled their followers. But these very excesses prove the regu-lar and irregular use now made of instrumentation, a blind use in general, and, when not led by chance, guided by the most pitiable rou-tine. For it does not follow that because most composers make more use of instruments than their predecessors, they are better acquainted with the force, character, and action of each member of the instru-mental family, and the various ties of sympathy uniting them. Far from this, many illustrious composers are still quite ignorant of the most elementary part of the science, namely, the *compass* of many of the instruments. One composer, to my certain knowledge, knew noth-ing of that of the flute. Of that of the brass in general and trombones in particular they have but a very vague idea; and accordingly you may remark in most modern as in ancient scores, the prudent reserve with which their authors confine themselves to the middle range of those instruments, avoiding with equal care either an ascent or de-scent, because afraid to overstep the limits of what they know accurately, and ignorant of the advantage to be derived from the notes at either extremity of the scale. Instrumentation in the present day therefore is like a fashionable foreign language, which many people affect to speak without having learnt it, and therefore speak without properly understanding it, and with a great many barbarisms.

Such a class in conservatoires, besides being useful to composition students, would be of great service to such as are called on to become conductors. Indeed, it may readily be imagined that a conductor who is not thoroughly master of all the resources of instrumentation is not very much of a musician, and it is plainly of the greatest necessity that he should at least know as much of the *exact compass and mechanism* of the instrument as the musicians under his direction, if not more. Otherwise he can only offer them timid suggestions, especially when it is a question of some unusual combination, or bold or difficult passage, about which indolence or incapacity would drive the performer to exclaim: " It cannot be done! There is no such note! It is unplayable!" and other aphorisms in use among ignorant mediocrity in such cases. Then the conductor can answer: "You are mistaken. It is quite feasible. If you set about it in such and such a manner you will master the difficulty!" or else: " It is difficult certainly, but if it remains an impossibility to you after having worked at it for some days, I can only conclude that you are not master of your instrument, and shall be obliged to have recourse to a more skilful artist."

In the opposite case — a too frequent one, I must admit — where the composer, for want of proper knowledge, torments the artist, however skilful, by trying to obtain impossibilities, the conductor who is sure of his facts will be able to take part with the musicians against the composer, and correct his blunders.

Indeed, as I am on the subject of conductors, I may as well say that it would not be at all a bad plan in a well organised conservatoire, as far as possible to teach the art of conducting, to composition students especially, so that on an emergency they may at any rate conduct the performance of their own works without making fools of themselves, and distracting the musicians instead of helping them. It is generally supposed that every composer is a born conductor, that is to say, that he knows the art of conducting without having learnt it. Beethoven was an illustrious example of the falsity of this opinion, and one might name a host of other masters whose compositions are held in general esteem, but who, the moment they take up the baton, neither mark time nor nuance, and would indeed literally bring the musicians to grief,[1] if the latter did not quickly perceive the inexperience of their leader and make up their minds to pay no attention to his whirling arms. There are two distinct parts in the work of a conductor; the first and easiest consists simply in conducting the performance of a work already known to the players, and which, to use a phrase in vogue at the theatres, has been *mounted* beforehand. The second consists in directing the study of a work unknown to the performers, clearly setting forth the author's conception and rendering it salient and distinct, obtaining from the band that fidelity, unity, and expression without which there can be no real music, and, the technical difficulties once overcome, identifying the players with himself, exciting them by his own zeal, animating them with his own enthusiasm, and imparting to them his own inspiration.

But to do this, besides the elementary knowledge acquired by study and practice, and those qualities of feeling and instinct which are the gift of nature alone, and the absence or presence of which makes the conductor either the composer's best interpreter or his most formidable enemy, there is one more art indispensable to the conductor, namely, that of *reading the score*.

He who employs a *simplified score,* or a simple first violin part, as is often done in our day, more especially in France,[2] cannot detect half the mistakes in the performance; and if he does point out a fault, exposes himself to some such answer as this from the musician addressed: " What do you know about it? You have not got my part " — one of the least of the inconveniences arising from this deplorable system.

Whence I conclude that if you want to form perfect and genuine conductors, you ought by all means to familiarise them with score-reading; and those who cannot master that difficulty, though they be learned in instrumentation — even composers — and also well up in the mechanisms of rhythmical movement, are really only half masters of their art.

Now I must tell you of the Singing Academy at Prague. Organised much in the same way as all the others in Germany, it consists almost entirely of amateurs drawn from the middle classes. The chorus num-

---

[1] Berlioz indulges in a pun that cannot be translated into English: these bad conductors, he says, do not so much *battre la mesure* (beat the time) as *battre la campagne* (talk nonsense).

[2] Habeneck used only a first violin part, when conducting the Conservatoire concerts, and in this respect his successors have taken care to imitate him. [B.]

bers about ninety, and Herr Scraub, jun., is the director. Most of the members are musicians and readers, with fresh and thrilling voices. The aim and object of the institution is not the study and performance of old works to the utter exclusion of all modern productions, as is the case with so many academies of this kind. These latter — pardon me the expression — are nothing but musical coteries or consistories, where the unknown living are gently calumniated under the pretext of enthusiasm for the dead; where Baal is preached against, and all so-called golden calves, together with their worshippers, are handed over to execration. In these temples of musical Protestantism a cross-grained, jealous, and intolerant worship is maintained — not of the *beautiful*, whatever its age, but of the *old*, whatever its worth. They have their Bible and their two or three evangelists, which the faithful read and re-read exclusively and without relaxation, commenting upon passages in a thousand different ways, the real direct meaning of which is perfectly self-evident; finding a profound and mystical idea where the rest of the world can see nothing but horror and barbarity, and ever ready to sing Hosanna! even when the God of Moses commands them to *crush the heads of little children against the wall, to have their blood licked up by the dogs, forbidding His people to shed one tear of pity at the sight!*

Let us be on our guard against such fanatics, who are enough to destroy the respect and admiration which all pious souls owe to the past.

The Singing Academy at Prague has, I repeat, nothing in common with these, and its leader is an intelligent artist. Accordingly, not merely the modern but the living are admitted within its musical sanctuary. Side by side with the oratorios of Bach or Handel he places the study of *Moses* by Herr Marx, the learned critic and theorist, still living at Berlin, or some piece from an opera, or a hymn, having no pretensions to academical regard merely on account of their age. Indeed, the first time I attended a gathering of the Prague Singing Society, I was struck by a charming and original choral fantasia on national Bohemian airs, composed by Herr Scraub. Never before or since have I heard such piquant combinations performed with so much dash and fire, such unexpected contrasts, unity, and fine sonority. When I thought of the thick and heavy compilations of chords that I had too often been obliged to endure on similar occasions, the performance of that spirited work produced the same effect upon my ear as the fresh balmy air of a forest, on a beautiful summer's night, would have upon the lungs of a prisoner newly escaped from the fetid atmosphere of his dungeon.

The Academy of Sophie (as I have already said, it bore that name) gives a certain number of public concerts annually, conducted by the two Scraubs, on which occasions the theatre orchestra, under the leadership of the elder, is added to his brother's chorus. These grand performances, carefully and patiently prepared beforehand, always draw a numerous and select audience, to whom music is neither a weariness nor a diversion, but a noble and serious passion demanding the whole strength of their intelligence and feeling, and all the enthusiasm of their hearts.

I promised to tell you about the *maîtrise,* or cathedral-school, as well as the military music; but if I mention these, I confess it is only to make the list complete. Religious music! military music! The words make a great figure in an account of musical observations. But I never had the least intention of keeping my promise with respect to those two sources of musical wealth in Bohemia, for this very good reason, that I don't know enough of them to speak of them properly. I have never yet been able to write upon matters of which I know nothing. Perhaps with good examples I may come to it in time. But meanwhile you will excuse me if I hold my tongue. Notwithstanding M. Scraub's repeated invitations, I never set my foot in a church during the whole of my stay at Prague. And yet I am, as you know, very devout, so there must have been some grave reason, which I have forgotten, for my apparent indifference in the matter of sacred music, or I must have been entirely overwhelmed by the terror of gigues for the organ and fugues on the word Amen.

As for military bands, I will tell you a story to justify my silence. On a certain fête-day, I heard the band of the regiment then garrisoned at Prague play Haydn's hymn to the Emperor for four successive hours! This touching, patriarchal, and majestic song is so simple, that I really could not appreciate the merit of the performers as I listened to it. An orchestra not able to play such a piece tolerably must to my mind be composed of musicians who did not know the gamut. These, however, played *in tune,* which is wonderfully rare, especially in military bands. Besides, I do not know if the regiment in question was a Bohemian one, or from some other part of the empire of Austria, and it would be too absurd to establish a theory which well-informed people might ridicule by simply saying: " The Bohemian musicians you are speaking of are Hungarians, or Austrians, or Milanese."

Among the composers and virtuosi of Prague, belonging neither to the theatre, nor to the Conservatoire, nor to the Singing Academy, I must specify Dreyschock, Pischek, and the venerable Tomaschek. The two former enjoy a European reputation. I have often heard both one and the other at Vienna, Pesth, Frankfort, and elsewhere, but never at Prague. Having, it appears, been ill received by their compatriots at their first appearance, Dreyschock and Pischek made up their minds in future never to exhibit their talents to the appreciation or depreciation of the Bohemians. That no one is a prophet in his own country is true of all times and countries. The inhabitants of Prague are now, however, beginning to listen to the murmurs of admiration, which in a hundred different ways and from a hundred points of the horizon are repeating that Dreyschock is an admirable pianist! Pischek is one of the best singers in Europe! and are beginning to suspect that they may possibly have done them injustice.

Tomaschek is well known in Bohemia, and even at Vienna, where his works are greatly appreciated. Not having the same reasons as Dreyschock and Pischek for being severe to the inhabitants of Prague, he allows them occasionally to hear his compositions. I was present at one concert where thirty-one out of thirty-two pieces were by M. Tomaschek. Among them was a new setting of the *Erl-King,* quite unlike Schubert's. Someone (for there are people who find fault with everything) drew a comparison between the accompaniment of this piece and that of Schubert's ballad, in which the furious gallop of the horse is reproduced, and declared that M. Tomaschek had mimicked the placid gait of a priest's nag. An intelligent critic, however, more capable than his neighbours of judging of the philosophy of art, annihilated this irony, and replied with great good sense: " It is just because Schubert made that unlucky horse gallop so wildly that it has foundered, and is now forced to go at a foot pace." Tomaschek has written for the last thirty years at least, and so the list of his works must be rather formidable.

There is one more amiable virtuoso to be mentioned, and her talent, only too rare in Germany, was of the greatest assistance to myself personally. This was Mdlle. Claudius, a first-rate harpist, an excellent musician, and Parish-Alvars' best pupil. Mdlle. Claudius has also a remarkable voice, and often sings solos with marked success at the Singing Academy, of which she is a member.

Of the public, what shall I tell you? . . . Louis XIV, wishing to pay Boileau a compliment about his lines on the passage of the Rhine, is reported to have said: " I would praise you more if you had not praised me so much." I am in the same predicament as the great king; I should write a beautiful eulogium on the sagacity, quickness, and sensibility of the public at Prague if they had not treated me so well. I may say, however — since it is matter of public notoriety — that the Bohemians are the best musicians in Europe, and that the love and feeling for music are universal in all classes of society. My concert was attended not only by the lower classes but even by the peasants, to whom certain places were rendered accessible by the low prices; and I was able to judge of the interest this audience took in my musical efforts by their singularly *naïve* exclamations at the most unexpected effects, a proof that their memory was sufficiently well stocked to allow of their forming comparisons between the known and the unknown, the old and the new, the good and the bad. You will not, my dear friend, insist on my setting forth here my opinions about the public in general; a volume would not suffice for the thorough study of that multiple being — by turns just, unjust, reasonable, capricious, *naïve,* malicious, enthusiastic, and scoffing, at one time so easily led, at another so rebellious. And besides, after devoting an entire volume to the solution of that problem, one would probably be no further advanced at the last stage than at the first. Even Voltaire's irony deserted him on the subject, and after asking *how many fools it took to make a public,* ended his career by allowing himself to be crowned by those same fools at the Théâtre-Français, and being exceedingly delighted with their approbation. So let us say no more about it, and let the public be what it is — a sea always more or less rough, but the dead calm of which is more formidable to artists than its tempests.

I gave six concerts at Prague, either in the theatre or in Sophie's concert-room. At the latter, I remembered to have had the delight of performing my *Romeo and Juliet* symphony, for Liszt, for the first time. Several movements of the work were already known in Prague. It evoked no violent controversy, no doubt because it had already done that at Vienna, the two towns being notoriously rivals in the matter of musical taste. The vocal performance was grand, and only marred by one mishap. The young person who undertook the contralto solo had never yet sung in public. Notwithstanding her extreme timidity, all went well as long as she felt herself supported by other voices or instruments, but when she reached the passage in the prologue:

Le jeune Roméo plaignant sa destinée,

a real solo with no accompaniment, her voice began to tremble, and by the end of the phrase, where the harp comes in on the chord of E natural, she had got into an unknown key, a tone and a quarter lower than E. Mdlle. Claudius, who was sitting close to my desk, dared not touch the strings of her harp. At last, after a moment's hesitation, she asked in a low voice:

"Had I better give the chord of E?"

"Certainly; we must get out of this."

And the inexorable chord rang out, hissing and shuddering like a spoonful of molten lead in cold water. The poor little singer nearly fainted at finding herself so abruptly set right, and as she did not understand French, I could not say anything to reassure her. Happily, however, she succeeded in recovering her self-possession before the *Premiers transports,* which she sang with great feeling and in perfect tune. The rôle of Father Laurence was perfectly interpreted by Strakaty; he showed unction and genuine enthusiasm in the finale.

That day, having already encored several pieces, the public called for another, which the band implored me not to repeat; but as the shouts continued, Herr Mildner took out his watch and held it up to show that the hour was too far advanced to allow of the orchestra remaining till the end of the concert if the piece were played a second time, since there was an opera at seven o'clock. This clever pantomime saved us. At the end of the concert, just as I was begging Liszt to serve as my interpreter and thank the excellent singers, who had been devoting themselves to the careful study of my choruses for the last three weeks and had sung them so bravely, he was interrupted by them with an inverse proposal. Having exchanged a few words with them in German, he turned to me and said:

"My commission is changed; these gentlemen rather desire me to thank you for the pleasure you have given them in allowing them to perform your work, and to express their delight at your evident satisfaction."

That was indeed a day for me; I remember few like it. There was a supper afterwards, at which the artists and amateurs of Prague presented me with a silver cup, a pendant to the silver-gilt baton given me at the banquet at Vienna of which I told you. Most of the virtuosi, critics, and amateurs of the town were present, as well as one of my countrymen, the kindly and intellectual Prince de Rohan. Liszt was unanimously chosen to speak in the place of the president, who was not sufficiently familiar with French. At the first toast he made me a speech in the name of the assembly at least a quarter of an hour in length, with a warmth of heart, a flow of ideas, and a choice of expressions that many orators might have envied, and which had the effect of touching me deeply. Unhappily, if he spoke well he drank well too; the treacherous cup inaugurated by the guests overflowed with such oceans of champagne that all Liszt's eloquence was drowned in it. At two o'clock in the morning Belloni[1] and I were still in the street, trying to persuade him to wait till daylight for a duel which he insisted on fighting with a Bohemian who had drunk *better* than himself.

As the morning advanced we grew rather uneasy about Liszt, whose concert was to take place at noon. He was still asleep at half-past eleven; at last they awoke him, he gets into his carriage, reaches the concert-room, receives a triple volley of applause on his entrance, and plays better I believe than he had ever done before in his life.

Verily, there is a God for . . . pianists.

Farewell, my dear Ferrand; you will not complain, I fear, of the brevity of my letters. And yet I have not said all that I feel of affectionate regret for Prague and its inhabitants; but, as you know, I have a serious passion for music, and you can judge from that whether I like the Bohemians or not.

O Praga! quando te aspiciam!

H. B.

---

[1] Liszt's man of business. [B.]

CHAPTER LXX

CONCERT AT BRESLAU—''THE DAMNATION OF FAUST''
— PATRIOTIC GERMAN CRITICS — PRODUCTION
OF THE WORK AT PARIS — RESOLUTION TO
VISIT RUSSIA — KINDNESS OF FRIENDS

In the preceding letters to M. Ferrand I said nothing of my journey to Breslau. I do not know why I omitted it, for my stay in the Silesian capital was both pleasant and useful. Thanks to the warm assistance of several persons, among others Herr Koettlitz, a young artist of great merit, Dr. Naumann, a distinguished medical man and a real connoisseur among musical amateurs, and Hesse, the celebrated organist, I succeeded in giving a concert [1] in the University hall (Aula Leopoldina), with very happy results. My audience came from all the neighbouring villages and suburbs of Breslau; the receipts far exceeded what I usually made in German towns, and the public gave a most brilliant reception to my compositions. This pleased me all the more as I had attended a concert the day after my arrival, where the audience never relaxed from its coldness for a moment, and dead silence followed the performance of even the Symphony in C minor. When I exclaimed against this reception of Beethoven, a lady, enthusiastic herself about the great master after her own fashion, told me I was mistaken. " The public," said she, " admire that masterpiece as much as it can be admired, and if they do not applaud, it is *from respect.*" I must confess that this word, which would have had so deep a meaning in Paris, and in all places where the disgraceful manœuvres of the claqueurs are prevalent, made me feel very anxious. I was dreadfully afraid of being respected. Happily this was not at all the case, and at my own concert the assembly, to whose respect I was evidently not sufficiently entitled, thought fit to treat me according to the vulgar custom adopted towards popular artists throughout Europe, and gave me most irreverent applause.

During these travels in Austria, Hungary, Bohemia, and Silesia

---

[1] March 20th. He does not mention a final concert, at Brunswick, on April 21st. A few days after this, Berlioz and Marie returned to Paris. In June he attended the festival, at Lille, of the inauguration of the French Northern Railway, to which he had been asked to contribute a short cantata. This — the *Chant des chemins de fer*, words by Jules Janin — was given on the 14th June.

I began the composition of the legend of *Faust,* which I had long been planning. When I had once decided upon undertaking it, I also made up my mind to write nearly the whole of the book myself, as not more than one-sixth of the work was taken up by a translation of fragments of Goethe's poem made by Gérard de Nerval twenty years before and then set to music by me, and by a few more scenes written by M. Gandonnière from notes given him before I left Paris.

Such being my decision, I attempted to write the verses for my music as I rolled along in my old German post-chaise. I began with Faust's invocation to Nature, not trying either to translate or even to imitate Goethe's masterpiece but only to use it as an inspiration, and extract all its musical substance. My attempt gave me hopes of being able to continue:

> Nature immense, impénétrable et fière!
> Toi seule donnes trêve à mon ennui sans fin!
> Sur ton sein tout-puissant je sens moins ma misère,
> Je retrouve ma force, et je crois vivre enfin.
> Oui, soufflez, ouragans; criez, forêts profondes;
> Croulez, rochers; torrents, précipitez vos ondes!
> À vos bruits souverains, ma voix aime à s'unir.
> Forêts, rochers, torrents, je vous adore! Mondes
> Qui scintillez, vers vous s'élance le désir
> D'un cœur trop vaste, et d'une âme altérée
> D'un bonheur qui la fuit.

Once launched, I wrote the rest by degrees, as my musical ideas came to me, and composed the score with a facility I have rarely experienced with any of my other works. I wrote when I could and where I could; in the coach, on the railroad, in steamboats, and even in towns, notwithstanding the various cares entailed by my concerts. Thus I wrote the introduction, *Le vieil hiver a fait place au printemps,* in an inn at Passau. At Vienna I did the Elbe scene, Mephistopheles' song, *Voici des roses,* and the sylphs' ballet.

I have already mentioned my writing a march at Vienna, in one night, on the Hungarian air of Rákóczy. The extraordinary effect it produced at Pesth made me resolve to introduce it into *Faust,* by taking the liberty of placing my hero in Hungary at the opening of the action, and making him present at the march of a Hungarian army across the plain. A German critic considered it most extraordinary in me to have made Faust travel in such a place. I do not see why, and I should not have hesitated in the least to take him anywhere else if it would have benefited my score. I had not bound myself to follow Goethe's plot, and the most eccentric travels may be attributed to such a personage as Faust, without transgressing the bounds of possibility. Other German critics took up the same thesis, and attacked me with even greater violence about my modifications of Goethe's text and plot, just as though there were no other *Faust* but Goethe's,[1] and as if it were possible to set the whole of such a poem to music without altering its arrangement. I was stupid enough to answer them in the preface to *The Damnation of Faust.* I have often wondered why these same critics never reproached me about the book of *Romeo and Juliet,* which is not very like the immortal tragedy. No doubt because *Shakespeare was not a German.* Patriotism! Fetishism! Idiocy!

One night, when I had lost my way in Pesth, I wrote the choral refrain of the *Ronde des Paysans* by the gaslight in a shop. At Prague I got up in the middle of the night to write down a melody I was afraid of forgetting, the angels' chorus in Marguerite's apotheosis:

> Remonte au ciel, âme naïve,
> Que l'amour égara.

At Breslau I wrote the words and music of the students' Latin song: *Jam nox stellata velamina pandit.* On my return to France I composed the grand trio, *Ange adoré dont la céleste image,* while staying on a visit to the Baron de Montville, near Rouen.

The rest was written in Paris, but always improvised, either at my own house, or at the café, or in the Tuileries gardens, and even on a stone in the Boulevard du Temple. I did not search for ideas, I let them come, and they presented themselves in the most unforeseen order. When at last the whole outline was sketched, I set to work to re-cast the whole, touch up the different parts, unite and blend them together with all the patience and pertinacity of which I am capable, and to finish off the instrumentation, which had been only indicated here and there. I look upon this as one of my best works, and hitherto the public seems to be of the same opinion.

To have written it was nothing.[2] I wanted to bring it out; and then

---

[1] Marlowe's, for example, and that of Spohr's opera, neither of which is in the least like Goethe's. [B.]

[2] The Opéra, he now saw, was definitely closed to him. He attacked it in an article in the *Débats,* in which he asked, "Is our first lyrical theatre about to become the second, and the Opéra-Comique the first?" In another article he took off the gloves in a criticism of Mme Stoltz, the friend of the Opéra Director, Pillet.

began all my misfortunes and miseries. The copying of the orchestral
and vocal parts cost me an immense sum, and the numerous rehearsals
on which I insisted, and the exorbitant price of sixteen hundred francs
for the hire of the Opéra-Comique, the only room then at my disposal,[1]
embarked me in an undertaking that was bound to end in ruin. Still I
persevered, being kept up by a specious reasoning that would have
enticed anyone in my place. "When *Romeo and Juliet* was first performed," I reflected, "the eagerness of the public was so great that
we had to issue *corridor tickets* to seat the crowd after the room was
filled, and I had some small profits, notwithstanding the immense
expenses. Since then my name has gone up in public opinion, and besides, my success in foreign parts has been so much talked of that it
now carries a weight in France which was not formerly the case. The
subject of *Faust* is quite as famous as that of *Romeo*. It is generally
believed to be sympathetic to me, and I am thought likely to have
treated it well. Everything combines, therefore, to make me hope
there will be great curiosity to hear this new work, which is on a larger
scale and more varied in effect than any of its predecessors, and its
expenses will at any rate be covered."

Vain hope! Years had elapsed since the first performance of
Romeo and Juliet, during which the indifference of the Parisian public
about everything concerning literature and the arts had made incredible strides. At this period it had already ceased to be sufficiently
interested, more especially in a musical work, to consent to be im-
mured in the daytime (I never could give my concerts in the evening)
in so unfashionable a theatre as that of the Opéra-Comique. It was the
end of November, 1846; snow was falling, the weather was dreadful.
I had no fashionable cantatrice to sing the part of Marguerite. As for
Roger, who did Faust, and Herman Léon, who took the part of
Mephistopheles, they might be heard any day in this same theatre; nor
were *they* the fashion. The result was that *Faust* was twice performed
to a half-empty room. The concert-going Parisian public, supposed to
be fond of music, stayed quietly at home, caring as little about my new
work as if I had been an obscure student at the Conservatoire; and
these two performances [2] at the Opéra-Comique were no better attended than if they had been the most wretched operas in the theatre's
repertory.

[1] The score was finished October 19th, 1846.
[2] On December 6th and 20th — not in November, as stated in the text.

Nothing in all my artistic career ever wounded me so deeply as this unexpected indifference. It was a cruel discovery, but useful in the sense that I profited by it, and from that time forth never risked so much as a twenty-franc piece on the popularity of my music with the Parisian public. I sincerely hope this may never happen again, if I live a hundred years.[1] I was ruined, and in debt for a considerable sum. After two days of inexpressible anguish, I perceived a way of extricating myself from my difficulties by going to Russia. But money was needed for the journey, the more so as I did not wish to leave a single debt behind me. The greatest comfort arose, however, out of these trying circumstances through the cordiality of my friends. I received offers of help on all sides as soon as it was known that I had to go to St. Petersburg, to try to repair my losses from the performance of my last work in Paris. M. Bertin advanced me one thousand francs from the funds of the *Journal des Débats;* some of my friends lent me five hundred francs, others six or seven hundred; one young German, Herr Friedland, whom I had known in Prague, advanced me twelve hundred francs; Sax did the same, though himself in difficulties; and finally Hetzel, the publisher, who has since played a very honorable part in the Republican Government, and was then only one of my ordinary acquaintances, met me by chance at a café and said:

"So you are going to Russia."

"Yes."

"It is a very expensive journey, particularly in winter; if you should want a bank note for a thousand francs, will you allow me to offer it to you?"

I accepted as frankly as the good Hetzel offered it, and thus I was enabled to face everyone and fix the day for my departure.

I believe I have already made this remark, but I do not mind repeating it here, that if I have come across a good many villains and scamps in my life I have also been singularly blessed in the opposite respect, and few artists have met with warmer hearts and more generous devotion than myself. You, good men who have doubtless long since forgotten your noble conduct towards me, let me recall it to you in these pages, thank you for it most heartily, press your hands, and tell you of the secret pleasure with which I think of my obligations to all of you.

[1] I did not keep to this. After having written *L'Enfance du Christ,* I could not resist the temptation of bringing out the work in Paris. Its success was spontaneous, and so great as really to insult my former compositions. I also gave several concerts in Herz's concert-room, which, instead of ruining me, brought me in some thousands of francs. (1858.) [B.]

Russian Journey

CHAPTER LXXI

A PRUSSIAN MUSICAL COURIER — M. NERNST —
SLEDGES — SNOW — THE COUNTS WIELHORSKI
— GENERAL LWOFF — MY FIRST CONCERT — THE
EMPRESS — I MAKE MY FORTUNE — JOURNEY TO
MOSCOW — LUDICROUS OBSTACLE — THE GRAND
MARSHAL — YOUTHFUL MELOMANIACS —
CANNONS AT THE KREMLIN

LENT is the best season for giving concerts at St. Petersburg. It occupies the entire month of March, when the theatres are all closed. I left Paris on the 14th of February, 1847. The ground was covered with snow six inches deep, and during the fortnight that elapsed before I reached St. Petersburg I never once lost sight of it. Indeed, it had fallen so heavily in Belgium that my train was compelled to stop at Tirlemont for several hours, while the rails were being cleared. It may be imagined what I suffered the week after, when I reached the other side of the Niemen.

I only stayed a few hours at Berlin to ask for a letter of introduction from the King of Prussia to his sister the Empress of Russia, which (with his usual kindness) His Majesty sent me immediately. While posting from Berlin to Tilsit I had the ill-luck to have a music-mad courier, who tormented me dreadfully the whole time I was with him. No sooner had this man seen my name on his travelling papers than he conceived the idea of making capital out of me during the journey, and in the following manner. He had a mania for composing polkas and waltzes for the piano. He used to stop at the post-houses sometimes for an unconscionable time, and there, while he was supposed to be reckoning with the landlord, he was engaged in ruling music paper and jotting down the dance tune he had been whistling for the last three hours. After which he was kind enough to give the word of departure, and returning to the carriage at once presented me with his polka or waltz, together with a pencil for me to write the bass and harmony to it. This done, there were endless comments, whys and wherefores, amazements and raptures, which amused me a good deal the first time, but when repeated too often made me curse my brave courier's ignorance of French and music pretty freely. I certainly should never have had such an adventure in France. On arriving at Tilsit I asked for the post-master, M. Nernst (I shall say presently how I came to know his name and reckon on his good-nature). His office was pointed out to me. I went in and perceived a big man in a cloth cap, with a severe countenance, which however betrayed both shrewdness and benevolence. He remained seated on his high stool when I first went in.

"M. Nernst?" said I, with a bow.

"The same, sir; to whom have I the honour of speaking?"

"To M. Hector Berlioz."

"What! Nothing less?" he exclaimed, bounding off his seat, and falling on his feet before me, cap in hand.

Whereupon the worthy man overwhelmed me with all sorts of attentions and civilities, which he redoubled when he knew who had given me my letter of introduction.

"Be sure to ask for Nernst, the post-master, as you pass through Tilsit," one of my Paris friends had said to me. "He is an excellent man, and also well-informed and literary. He may possibly be of use to you." It was no other than Balzac who gave me this advice on the eve of my departure, at the corner where I had met him at eleven o'clock at night. He had himself been in Russia only a short time before. On hearing that I was going to give concerts at St. Petersburg, he said quite seriously: "You will come back with a hundred and fifty thousand francs. I know the country; you can't bring away less." That great mind had the weakness of always and everywhere seeing fortunes to be made, of which he felt so confident that he would willingly have asked a banker to discount them on the spot. His dreams were of millions, and the innumerable deceptions he underwent on that point all through his life could never disabuse his mind of that perpetual mirage. I smiled at his estimate of the result of my travels, without appearing to doubt its correctness. It will soon be seen that if my concerts at St. Petersburg and Moscow produced more than I had hoped for, I succeeded, notwithstanding, in bringing back a good deal less than the hundred and fifty thousand francs predicted by Balzac.

That rare writer and incomparable anatomist of the very heart of modern French society was, as may easily be imagined, a fruitful subject of conversation with M. Nernst and myself. He gave me very interesting details about Balzac, his hopes of marriage and his love affairs in Galicia. For the rest, he is one of that small number of foreigners who may be allowed to admire Balzac passionately, for he knows French well enough to understand him.

I remember that when I told my family about this episode in my journey, my father burst into a fit of laughter at M. Nernst's exclamation, " *Rien que ça!* " on hearing my name. He was already much enfeebled and sadly ailing; but the *naïf* pride he felt, notwithstanding his philosophy, at this original proof of his son's celebrity, displayed itself thus almost involuntarily.

" *Rien que ça!* " he repeated, with renewed laughter. " And you say it was at Tilsit? "

" Yes, on the banks of the Niemen, at the extreme frontier of Prussia."

" *Rien que ça!* "

And his laughter broke out afresh every time he said the words.

Having thus rested for a few hours at Tilsit, I began the most painful part of my journey, furnished with instructions from M. Nernst, and warmed by several glasses of a most delicious curaçoa which he was never tired of pressing upon me. A post-chaise brought me to Taurogen, on the Russian frontier, and there I had to shut myself up in an iron sledge, which I never quitted till I reached St. Petersburg; having undergone tortures, the very existence of which I had never suspected, for four weary days and as many terrible nights. In fact, in this hermetically sealed metal box, into which, however, the snow-dust succeeds in penetrating and powdering your face, you are ceaselessly and violently shaken, like shot in a bottle; the result of which is a great many contusions on the head and limbs, caused by perpetual shocks from the sides of the sledge. I also suffered from an unspeakable discomfort and nausea that may fairly be called *snow-sickness,* on account of its likeness to that produced by the sea.

In our climate it is generally believed that Russian sledges glide over the snow, drawn by swift horses, as over a frozen lake, and so one forms quite a charming idea of this mode of travelling. And this is true when one has the good fortune to meet with even ground, and untrodden or well-trodden snow; the sledge then certainly goes with marvellous rapidity and smoothness. But you do not find a road like this one mile in fifty. The rest of the way is all cut up into transverse ruts, formed by the peasants' carts drawing huge loads of wood, and looks just like a stormy sea solidified by the cold. The spaces between these snowy waves form regular deep ditches, into which the sledge, having first been painfully hoisted up to the summit, falls with a crash enough to split your head; especially at night, when you are less prepared for it, or have dropped off for a few minutes to sleep. If the ruts are less sudden, the sledge follows them with regularity, going up and down like a boat on the waves, and hence the sickness of which I spoke. I say nothing of the cold; but towards the middle of the night, notwithstanding all one's fur bags, cloaks, and pelisses, and the hay stuffed into the sledge, it becomes quite unbearable. One feels as if one's body were being pricked all over by a million needles, and no matter how warmly clad, one trembles as much from the fear of being frozen to death as from the cold itself.

On fine days, when the brilliant sunshine allowed me to see the whole of the sad and dazzling expanse, I could not help thinking of the ever famous retreat of our unfortunate army. I seemed to see the wretched soldiers, destitute of food and clothing, without boots, without brandy, without either mental or physical strength, the majority wounded, dragging themselves along like spectres by day, and stretched shelterless at night like corpses on that terrible snow, in weather even more fearful than that by which I myself was tormented. And I wondered how even one of them had been able to resist such suffering and return alive from that frozen hell. Death must be desperately hard for man.

Then I laughed at the stupidity of the famished crows who followed my sledge on torpid wings, alighting on the road every now and then to feast upon the horse-dung, and then crouching on their bellies and trying to thaw their half-frozen claws, when they might have found at will a mild climate, fertile fields, and abundant pasture without trouble by a flight of a few hours southwards. Is their native country then dear to true-hearted crows? If indeed, to quote our own soldiers, Russia can be called a *country!*

At last, one Sunday evening, a fortnight from the time I left Paris, I arrived, starved with cold, at the proud northern capital called St. Petersburg.[1] From all I had heard in France of the severity of the imperial police, I expected that my bales of music would be confiscated for a week at least; since, at the frontier, they had been scarcely touched. But I was not even asked to state their contents at the police-office, and was allowed to take them off to the hotel at once, which I confess was an agreeable surprise.

I had not been installed an hour in my hot room when I received a visit of welcome from M. de Lenz, an extremely learned and amiable amateur, whom I had met in Paris some years before.[2]

" I have come from Count Michel Wielhorski's," said he, " where we have just heard of your arrival. He is giving a grand soirée, at which all the musical authorities of St. Petersburg are assembled, and the Count has sent me to say how charmed he will be to receive you."

" But how could he know I was here? "

" Well, he does know. . . . Do come."

I only waited to thaw my face, shave, and make my toilette, and then followed my kind friend to Count Wielhorski's. I ought to say the Counts, for there are two brothers, living together, and equally intelligent and eager in their love of music. Their house at St. Petersburg is a little Department of the Fine Arts, thanks to the authority they derive from their justly renowned taste, and to the influence they exercise through their large fortune and numerous connections, and to their official position at Court about the Emperor and Empress.

They gave me a most gracious welcome, and soon presented me to all the principal persons, virtuosi, and men of letters assembled in their *salon*. I made the acquaintance of the delightful Henri Romberg, then conductor at the Italian Theatre, who with rare good-nature immediately constituted himself my musical guide at St. Petersburg, and manager of my body of performers. The day of my first concert was fixed that very evening by General Guédéonoff, director of the imperial theatres. The assembly-room of the nobles was chosen for it, the

---

[1] On February 28th, 1847.
[2] See my analysis of his book on Beethoven in my *Soirées de l'orchestre*. [B.]

price of the places fixed at three silver roubles (twelve francs), and thus, four hours after my arrival, I found myself *in medias res*. Romberg came for me the next day, and we scoured the town together in search of the necessary artists. My orchestra was soon formed. We also soon succeeded in collecting a large and well-formed choir through the good offices of General Lwoff, the Emperor's aide de camp, conductor of the imperial band, and a composer and virtuoso of rare merit, who from the first showed me the most sincere musical fellowship. I now only wanted two solo singers, a bass and a tenor, for the first two parts of *Faust*. Versing, the bass of the German Theatre, undertook the part of Mephistopheles, and Ricciardi, an Italian tenor I had formerly known in Paris, that of Faust; the only drawback was, that he had to sing in French and Mephistopheles in German. The Russian public, being equally familiar with both, did not object to this absurd mixture. I had to have all the voice parts re-copied in Russian for the benefit of the chorus-singers, who knew no other characters, though they sang in German. After the first rehearsal, Romberg assured me that the German translation, which had put me to great expense in Paris, was a detestable one, and so unmetrical that it was impossible to sing it. He hastened to correct the grosser blunders, so that my first concert might not be postponed; but another translator was inevitable for the future, and I was fortunate enough a few weeks later to find one in M. Minzlaff, who was at once a musician and a *littérateur*, and performed the task perfectly. My first concert [1] was a splendid affair. The orchestra and choir were both large and well-trained, and I had also a military band, provided by General Lwoff, and chosen from the musicians of the Imperial Guard.

Romberg and Maurer, the two Kapellmeisters of St. Petersburg, actually undertook the parts of the small antique cymbals in the *Queen Mab* scherzo. My artists were animated throughout with the best of spirits and a zeal that augured well for the performance, and moreover I found a compatriot among them who seconded me with all his might — Tajan-Rogé, a clever cello player and a genuine artist. My programme consisted of the *Carnaval romain* overture, the first two parts of *Faust*, the *Queen Mab* scherzo, and the Apotheosis from the *Symphonie funèbre et triomphale*. The enthusiasm of the vast and brilliant audience filling the immense room exceeded anything I could ever have imagined in that line, more especially for *Faust*. The

[1] On March 15th.

clapping and shouting, encores, and recalls were enough to make one giddy. At the end of the first act of *Faust,* the Empress sent for me by Count Michel Wielhorski, and I was obliged accordingly to appear before Her Majesty as I was, red, out of breath, perspiring, and with loose cravat — in a word, in my musical battle array.

Her Majesty gave me a most flattering reception, presented me to her sons, spoke of her brother the King of Prussia and the interest he took in me, as shown by his letters, praised my music much, and expressed herself astonished at the exceptional performance I had managed to secure. After a quarter of an hour's conversation, she said :

" I must now send you back to your audience, which is too excited to be kept waiting any longer."

I then left, full of gratitude for all these imperial courtesies.

After the sylph-chorus, the public was really almost beside itself. This sort of refined, aerial music, to which you have to listen with all your ears in order to catch its low tones, was evidently quite unexpected, and I confess the moment was an intoxicating one for me. I was a little uneasy with regard to the non-appearance of the military band as the moment approached for the Apotheosis, with which the concert was to finish up. I feared that if they entered the orchestra in the middle of the piece, they would make a noise and spoil the effect. But I little knew Russian discipline. When I turned round at the close of the scherzo, which was played amid the most profound silence, I beheld my sixty musicians at their posts, instruments in hand. They had taken their places unobserved by anyone. That was something like !

At last, when the concert was over, the embraces concluded, and a bottle of beer consumed, I bethought me of inquiring about the financial result of the experiment. Receipt, *eighteen thousand francs;* expenses, six thousand; clear profit, twelve thousand francs. I was saved!

Then I turned mechanically to the south-west, towards Paris, and could not refrain from murmuring :

" You dear Parisians ! "

Ten days afterwards [1] I gave a second concert with similar results. I was a rich man. Then I started for Moscow,[2] where material difficulties of a strange nature awaited me; third-rate musicians,

[1] On March 25th.

[2] On April 1st. The journey took four days.

fabulous choristers, but a public quite as sensitive and enthusiastic as that at St. Petersburg, and to crown all, a clear gain of eight thousand francs.[1] Again I thought of my indifferent and *blasé* fellow countrymen, and again turned towards the south-west and exclaimed: " Oh, dear Parisians ! " Happily, this was not the last time. Often since, in London, have I turned in like manner to the south-east.

A musician, in the eyes of many people, is a man who plays some instrument. It never occurs to them that there are such things as musical composers, still less that they give concerts in order to make their works known. Such persons doubtless imagine that music is to be had at the publisher's like cakes at the confectioner's, and has only to be manufactured by the proper workman. I admit that in many cases there is some foundation for this eccentric idea; still, it is occasionally devoid of either foundation or justice. But there is nothing so droll as the amazement of certain people when you speak to them of a composer.

One day at Breslau I was nearly being insulted by a worthy pater-familias, who wanted, right or wrong, to insist on my giving violin lessons to his son. In vain did I protest that I had never touched a bow in my life. He took everything I said as a joke, and would see nothing in it but a kind of heavy pleasantry.

" Sir, no doubt you are under the impression that I am the celebrated violinist Bériot. His name is certainly very like mine."

" Sir, I have seen your placard. You are giving a concert the day after to-morrow in the University rooms, and so ———— "

" Yes, sir, I am giving a concert, but I shall not play the violin myself."

" Then what will you do ? "

" *I shall have the violin played,* and shall conduct the orchestra; but go to it yourself, and you will see."

My man restrained his anger till the next day, and not till the concert was over and he had reflected on the subject could he realise how a musician might figure in public without being a performer.

At Moscow, a blunder of the same description was nearly proving serious for me. The nobles' assembly-room was, as I have said, the only one suitable for my concert. Wishing to obtain the use of it, I had myself introduced to the grand marshal, a venerable-looking old

---

[1] The concert was on April 10th.

man of about eighty, and proceeded to unfold to him the object of my visit. The first thing he asked me was:

" What instrument do you play? "

" No instrument whatever."

" In that case, how do you propose to give a concert? "

" To have my compositions performed, and to conduct the orchestra."

" Ha! that is an original idea. I never heard of a concert like that. I will willingly lend you our large hall, but, as you no doubt know, artists who make use of it are obliged, in return, to perform at one of the private gatherings of the nobility."

" Has the Assembly an orchestra, then, for the performance of my music? "

" Certainly not."

" How, then, am I to have it done? I suppose I shall hardly be expected to spend three thousand francs in paying the musicians required to perform one of my symphonies at a private concert. That would be rather a high rent to pay for the room."

" Well, I regret to have to refuse you, but I cannot do otherwise."

And there I was, compelled to go away with this curious answer, and with the prospect of my long journey being rendered fruitless by this extraordinary and unforeseen obstacle. A French artist — M. Marcou by name — long settled at Moscow, was much amused at the account I gave of my disappointment; but he knew the grand marshal, and proposed to accompany me to his house next day, and try a fresh attack.

Second visit — second refusal — useless explanations offered by my compatriot. The grand marshal shakes his hoary head, and remains inexorable. Fearing, however, that he did not speak French very well, and so might have failed to understand some term of my proposal, the marshal went off for his wife. Enter Madame la Maréchale, nearly as venerable-looking as her husband, but distinctly less benevolent. She looked at me, heard what I had to say, and cut short the discussion by saying, in very rapid and distinct French:

" We neither can nor will infringe the regulations of the Assembly. If we lend you the room, you will play an instrumental solo at our next *réunion*. If you will not play, the room cannot be lent."

" Good heavens, Madame la Maréchale! I once played fairly well on the flageolet, flute, and guitar; choose one of these instruments for my performance. But as it is about five-and-twenty years since I have touched either of them, I must warn you that I shall play very badly. Or if you will be satisfied with a drum solo I shall probably acquit myself better."

Fortunately for me, one of the superior officers had entered the room during this scene; he soon took in the difficulty, and drawing me aside, said:

" Say no more at present, M. Berlioz, or the discussion may become unpleasant for our good marshal. If you will be so kind as to send in your written demand to me to-morrow, everything shall be arranged. I will make it my business."

I took this advice, and, thanks to the good-natured colonel, they consented to a departure from the regulations *for this once*. My concert was allowed to take place, and I was exempted from playing either the flute or the drum. It was a very lucky escape for the nobles, for, sooner than recross the Volga without having given my concert, I had made up my mind to play the *galoubet*,[1] if necessary. None the less, however, was this extraordinary regulation — of which, unfortunately, I had heard nothing at St. Petersburg — the occasion of rather a large pecuniary loss to me; for though the concert was announced as the *only* one I should give, yet so loud were the demands of the audience for a repetition, that a second would probably have produced more than the first. But where was the room to be found?

When the assembly-room was granted me it was on the strict understanding that the exception to the rule was for once and once only. Besides, a composer . . . a man who could not play any instrument . . . a mere incapable! And yet how many individuals there are, more or less lacking in gifts, in the non-noble classes of society, whose highest aspirations are for this arduous and all but impracticable career!

If the persistence of the musical vocation in certain artistic families is explainable on the natural grounds of education and example, of the ease with which children follow the path traced by their parents, and even by the natural disposition often transmitted from father to son, like the features of the face; how, on the other hand, is one to account for the extraordinary fancies that seem to drop from the skies into the heads of many young people?

Not to mention the amateurs who insist on taking useless and expensive lessons to vanquish a barbarous organisation, with which

---

[1] The *galoubet* is a rustic flageolet. [H.]

neither the talent nor the patience of the most skilled masters can cope, nor yet visionaries who think that you can learn music by pure reasoning as you do mathematics, nor even those worthy fathers who propose to make their sons *colonels* or *great composers* at will, one meets very sad examples of musical madness among people whom one would fancy quite secure from that mental malady.

I will mention two which came under my own observation, and, I fear, were incurable cases. One of these was a Frenchman, the other a Russian.

I was alone one day in Paris, and hard at work, when the first of these knocked at the door of my study, and I bade him enter. A young man of about eighteen came forward, all breathless and agitated, partly from the idea which possessed him and partly from the pace at which he had come.

" Sir," said I, " pray take a seat."

" It is nothing . . . I am a little . . . I have come . . . [then, like a pistol-shot] sir, I have come into an inheritance."

" An inheritance! I congratulate you."

" Yes, I have come into an inheritance, and I want to ask you if you advise me to spend it in becoming a composer."

I opened my eyes. " Pray sit down, my dear sir. But good heavens! you must suppose me to be gifted with a marvellous intuition: prognostications founded even on rather important works are not always fulfilled. However, perhaps you have brought me one of your compositions."

" No, I have brought nothing, but you will see how hard I shall work. I have such a taste for music! "

" You have no doubt written something already: a movement of a symphony perhaps, or an overture, or a cantata? "

" An overture? . . . N — no. Nor a cantata."

" Perhaps you have tried a quartet? "

" Ah, sir! a quartet! "

" Well, you need not turn up your nose at a quartet; of all styles of music it is perhaps the hardest to deal with, and the number of masters who have succeeded in it is curiously limited. However, not to attempt anything so high, have you got a simple song to show me, or a waltz? "

(With an injured air.) " Oh! a song — no, no! I don't do things like that."

" Then you have done nothing? "

" No, but I shall work so hard."

" At any rate you have thoroughly studied harmony and counterpoint; you know the compass of voices and instruments? "

" Well, as to that . . . no, I don't know either harmony or counterpoint, or instrumentation, but you will see —— "

" Pardon me, my dear sir, but you are eighteen or nineteen, and it is very late to begin such studies profitably. I suppose, however, that you can read music at sight and write it at dictation."

" Do I know the solfeggio? . . . Oh, dear me! . . . Well, no! . . . I don't even know my notes. I know nothing at all; but I have such a taste for music. I should so like to be a composer! If you would give me lessons, I would come to you twice a day, and would work all night."

After a tolerably long silence, during which I controlled my desire to laugh, I gave my young composer a faithful but discouraging picture of the difficulties he would have to surmount before he could attain to the merest mediocrity, in other words, before he could write the vilest music. I set out the obstacles awaiting him even when he should have become a composer of a very high order. All to no purpose! He listened angrily and impatiently, and went off with the evident intention of finding another master to whom to offer his vocation and . . . his inheritance. Pray Heaven he may not have found him!

The other example is not absurd at all; quite the contrary. I had just given my concert at Moscow when a letter was put into my hand in very good French, in which an unknown person requested me to give him an interview. I hastened to fix a day and hour. This time my friend had no inheritance; far from it. He was a tall young Russian, of at least twenty-two years of age, with a remarkable but slightly strange face, expressing himself in very select language, and full of that concentrated and fiery ardour that betrays the enthusiast. I felt keenly interested in him from the moment he opened his mouth.

" Sir," he said, " I have an immense passion for music. I have learned it entirely unassisted, but very imperfectly, as you may imagine. Moscow does not offer much in the way of musical advantages, and I am not sufficiently well off to travel. My relations have tried in vain to deter me from this career. Now, however, one of our great Moscow noblemen is willing to assist me. He has assured my father that if a musician in whom he can place implicit confidence should discover me to have a real aptitude for music, he will undertake all the expenses of my complete education in Germany under the best masters. I have come accordingly to beg of you to examine my attempts, and favour me with your honest opinion of my capacities. In any case, I shall owe you an eternal debt of gratitude. But if your opinion is favourable, you will restore me to life, for I am dying, sir; the constraint they are putting upon me is killing me; I feel my wings and cannot unfold them. It is a torture which you ought to be able to enter into."

"Oh, certainly, my dear sir. I can imagine what you are suffering, and all my sympathy is yours. Make what use of me you please."

"A thousand thanks. I will bring the works for your inspection to-morrow." Whereupon he departed, his eyes gleaming in the ecstasy of his delight.

The next day he came back another man. His eyes were mournful and dimmed, and symptoms of discouragement were plainly visible on his pallid countenance.

"I have brought nothing," he said. "I spent the whole night in looking through my manuscripts. They are not fit for you to look at, and honestly not one of them is a fair representation of my capabilities. I am going to set to work to do something better for you."

"Unhappily," I answered, "I must go back to St. Petersburg the day after to-morrow."

"Never mind; I will send you my new work. Ah, sir, if you knew the fire which is consuming my soul, and the inspired voices calling me at times. I cannot remain in the town; however cold it may be I go and wander far away into the woods, and there, alone with nature, I hear a whole world of marvellous harmonies around me, my tears overwhelm me, I utter cries, and fall into ecstasies that are like a foretaste of heaven. They look upon me as a madman, but I am not; I will prove to you that I am not."

I renewed my assurances of the interest the young enthusiast awakened in me, and my desire to be useful to him.

"Good heavens!" I said to myself after he had left me, "are not these the signs of an exceptional organisation? . . . Perhaps he is a man of genius! . . . It would be a crime not to help him. Assuredly I will devote myself heart and soul to him if necessary, if he will only give me the smallest opportunity."

Alas! I waited at St. Petersburg for several weeks in vain, and all

I received at last was a letter in which the young Russian excused himself afresh for not sending me any music. But to his despair, and notwithstanding all his efforts, he could not, he wrote, get any inspiration.

What did it mean, that frigid and poor appreciation of his own works? . . . that avowed incapacity on the part of a man who at other times fancied himself all-powerful and inspired? What is the ideal to which he seeks to attain? What has he as yet done to approach it? What is there in that troubled spirit? . . . God knows. But, also, what is there in common between such ardent aspirations towards music, more or less explained and justified by time, and the mean calculation and prosaic ambition that induce so many lads to enter a Conservatoire and embrace the musical profession, as one would learn the trade of a tailor or shoemaker? . . . Melomaniacs, at any rate, even when akin to madmen, injure no one, and their madness, when not laughable, is touching and poetical; whereas artisan-musicians are detrimental both to art and artists, give rise to tedious and vexatious blunders, and are capable of corrupting the taste of a whole nation by their numbers, no less than by their low instincts. The most musical nation is not that which can show the greatest number of mediocre musicians, but rather that which has given birth to great masters, and in which the feeling for musical beauty has been most cultivated.

In spite of all the curious and interesting architectural features of the semi-Asiatic town of Moscow, I studied it but slightly during my three weeks' stay. The preparations for my concert absorbed me entirely. Thanks, moreover, to the thaw then raging in all its attractiveness, it was really hardly visitable. The streets presented nothing but lakes of water and melting snow, through which the sledges could scarcely penetrate. I saw nothing but the exterior even of the Kremlin. I confined myself to counting the beads of the necklace of cannon that surround it — sad relics of our perishing army. They are of all sorts and calibres, and belong to all nations. Inscriptions in the *French language* (horrible irony) pointed out the regiments to which the various pieces in this mournful collection had belonged. One bears a most peculiar wound; it has the print of a Russian bullet on its lip, which entered the gun after having struck it on the mouth, and ripped up the interior. If the piece were loaded at the moment, I leave you to imagine the amazement of the cartridge it contained, on receiving so rude a blow. . . . It must have fancied, in its pride, that the Emperor had resumed his old task of artilleryman, and was loading it in person.

At Moscow I heard a performance of Glinka's opera, *La Vie pour le Czar.* The immense theatre was empty (is it ever full?), and the scenery was constantly representing snow-covered pine forests and steppes, and men all white with snow. I still shiver when I think of it. There are many graceful and highly original airs in the work, but I could hardly make them out, the performance was so imperfect. The studies in this theatre appeared to be carried on in a very curious manner, notwithstanding the zeal and musical erudition of M. Verstowski, the director. I noticed this when rehearsing the choruses of the first two parts of *Faust.*

When I entered the chorus practising-room, I found some sixty men and women standing about in silent groups, but without either master or accompanist, or even a piano.

" Where is the piano," said I, " and the pianist? "

" They never have one here to teach the choruses," was the reply. " We study without an accompaniment."

" The deuce you do! What musicians you must be! Your chorus must certainly be the best readers in the world."

" Oh, no; certainly not. But such is the custom, and we do as we can."

" You are joking! Pray have the goodness to send for a piano; I must be excused for being so troublesome, but I am a foreigner. We shall soon find an accompanist, and at a pinch I can even strike a few chords myself, which will be better than nothing."

The piano arrived, to the great surprise of the singers. M. Genista, a very good German teacher, who happened to be present, was kind enough to accompany, and we succeeded in reading the *Faust* choruses, which were learnt after a fashion in a few more meetings of the same kind. Russians must be gifted in a way that other nations do not dream of, if chorus singers can really succeed in learning whole operas in this way. They also sang in German, like their compeers at St. Petersburg. But the parts of Faust and Mephistopheles, kindly undertaken by Messrs. Léonoff and Slavik (two Russians), were sung in — *northern* French! It was a step in advance: the two heroes of the drama kept up their dialogue in the same language, at any rate. M. Grassi, a Sardinian violinist settled in Russia, and M. Marcou, already mentioned, were of great use to me in organising my concert; and Max

Bohrer, the celebrated cellist, who arrived in Moscow at the same time as myself, with great cordiality offered to help in the orchestra. It was a gracious and welcome act, seeing how few cellists I had, and considering how fine a one Bohrer is — a piece of artistic simplicity into which virtuosi are not generally in any danger of falling.

I have a grudge against the censorship for their treatment of a couplet from the students' Latin song in *Faust:*

> Nobis subridente lunâ,
> Per urbem quærentes puellas eamus,
> Ut cras fortunati Cæsares dicamus:
> Veni, vidi, vici.[1]

(Under the smiling moon, let us scour the town for young maidens, so that to-morrow we can say, like happy Cæsars, "I came, I saw, I conquered.")

The censor refused to authorise the printing of so scandalous a song. In vain did I assure him that the libretto had undergone censorship at St. Petersburg, and presented him with a copy stamped with the official approbation; he only answered: " The censor at St. Petersburg can do as he pleases, but I do not feel bound to imitate him. The passage in question is immoral, and must be suppressed." And so it was . . . *in the libretto.* I was certainly not going to mutilate my score for mere prudery's sake. The prohibited verse was *sung* at the concert, though in such a way as to be unintelligible. And that is why the population of Moscow has remained the most moral on the face of the earth, and why, in spite of all the moon's smiles, the students do not go round the town at night, looking for young girls — in the winter.

Among the distinguished amateurs at Moscow I must not omit to name M. Graziani, eldest son of one of the best of our former Italian opera singers in Paris.

There is a splendid institution for young ladies, under the immediate patronage of the Empress, where the pupils receive solid and

---

[1] A Dresden critic, in 1854, protested solemnly against this song, maintaining that German students were well-mannered youths, incapable of running after grisettes by moonlight. This same innocent fellow accused me in the same article of *vilifying Mephistopheles* by making him cheat Faust. "The German Mephistopheles was honest," he said, "and carried out every clause of the treaty signed by Faust, whereas in M. Berlioz's work he makes Faust believe that he is bringing him to Margaret's prison, when he is really conducting him to the abyss. It is an insult." Yes, was it not disgraceful on my part? I am convicted of having slandered the spirit of evil and falsehood, of being worse than a demon, of not being so good as the devil. This charming criticism was for long the delight of Dresden, and I believe even still amuses its inhabitants. [B.]

severe musical instruction as a supplement to their general education. Three of the best pianists performed for me an old triple concerto for the harpsichord in D minor by X——,[1] which it must be admitted is decidedly severe. And yet their master, M. Reinhard, is an amiable man and an able musician, and I am sure that he did not intend to annoy me when he chose that piece for performance by his pupils.

There was also a delightful little prodigy at Moscow, the son of the Princess Olga Dolgorouki, aged ten, who really frightened me by the intelligent passion with which he sang dramatic scenes from the great masters, and songs of his own composition.

Although overwhelmed with civilities by several of the Moscow families, and by a French family settled there, I was obliged to return immediately to St. Petersburg, where I was expected to superintend the rehearsals of *Romeo and Juliet,* of which M. Guédéonoff had promised me a splendid performance at the great theatre.

CHAPTER LXXII

RETURN TO ST. PETERSBURG—TWO PERFORMANCES OF "ROMEO AND JULIET"—ROMEO IN HIS CABRIOLET —ERNST—HIS TALENT—RETROACTIVE EFFECT OF MUSIC

ON reaching the banks of the Volga, I witnessed for the first time the breaking up of a Russian river by the thaw. I had to wait five hours on the left bank until the frozen mass had somewhat dispersed; and when at last I crossed in a boat, which was purposely swayed from right to left and from left to right to facilitate its passage through the blocks, the slow but irresistible movement of the icebergs, the mysterious crackling sound produced by their floating, the excessive weight of the boat with its load of luggage, the manifest anxiety and loud cries of our conductors, did not, I confess, particularly delight me, and I breathed a real sigh of pleasure when I landed safely on the opposite bank.

The sun was already shining pretty brightly, but in spite of the feebleness of its rays I frequently saw children playing and rolling about in the snow heaps, with nothing on but their shirts, just as ours

---

[1] Evidently Bach.

would do in summer on the hay. The Russians must have hell-fire in their bodies.

Immediately on my arrival I began the choral rehearsals of *Romeo and Juliet* at the Grand Theatre. When M. Guédéonoff had approved the idea of getting up that work, I asked his excellency how many rehearsals he would allow me.

"As many as you please. Let them rehearse every day, and when you tell me it is all right we will announce the concert, but not before."

"Splendid," said I; "we will take great pains and it shall go well."

In fact, as I have already said, that symphony cannot even be decently performed unless it is studied regularly and connectedly, like an opera to be sung by heart. And that is why it has seldom been performed with such confidence, spirit, and grandeur as at St. Petersburg.[1]

I had a colossal chorus of men, and for the sopranos and contraltos sixty young women with fresh sonorous voices, fairly good musicians taken from the choirs of the Italian Opera, the German Opera, and the theatrical school, a kind of Conservatoire where the pupils are taught music, French, and stage business. The Capulets rehearsed in one room, the Montagues in another, and the prologue was studied in a third. When, at last, each singer knew his part almost by heart, I united the three choirs, and the general effect of the whole body in the grand finale was perfectly satisfactory. Moreover I had Versing for the part of Father Laurence, Madame Walcker for the contralto in the prologue, and Holland (a clever actor, who delivered the recitative with rare intelligence) for the scherzo. It was imperially organised; the performance was bound to be, and in fact was, a marvellous one; I recall it as one of the greatest delights of my life. Besides, I was in such a good mood that day that I was lucky enough not to make a single mistake in conducting, which at that time seldom happened. The great theatre was full; uniforms, epaulettes, helmets, diamonds, glittered and sparkled on all sides. I do not know how often I was recalled. But I confess I did not pay much attention to the public; and such was the impression made on me by that divine Shakespearean poem as I sang it to myself that after the finale I fled for refuge into one of the side rooms, where Ernst found me a few moments later in floods of tears. "Ah, your nerves are unstrung!" he said; "I know well what that is." And he supported my head and let me cry like a hysterical girl for a good quarter of an hour. Can you imagine a

[1] April 23rd, 1847.

respectable tradesman of the Rue St. Denis, or the manager of the Opéra (in Paris, of course), witnessing such a crisis? Try to imagine what they would understand of the summer tempest in the artist's heart, its torrents and electric fires, vague memories of youth, first love, and Italian skies, blooming afresh beneath the burning rays of Shakespeare's genius; the apparition of Juliet, ever dreamt of, ever sought for, and never possessed; the revelation of the infinite in love and sorrow; my joy at having awakened some distant echoes of the voices of that heaven of poetry . . . then measure the roundness of their eyes and their gaping mouths . . . if you can! The first would say, "That gentleman must be ill, I will send him a glass of *eau sucrée*"; and the second, " He is giving himself airs. I will have him put in the *Charivari."*

All said and done, however, I believe that, notwithstanding its warm reception, the symphony slightly wearied the public by the amplitude of its form, and especially by the sad solemnity of the final scenes, and that they preferred *Faust* to *Romeo and Juliet*.

The cashier of the theatre was well pleased with the result of the first concert, but he confided to me that he had doubts as to the second, unless I gave at least two scenes from *Faust* besides *Romeo;* and I had to take his advice.

Among the audience on the second occasion I heard of a lady who was an *habituée* of the Italian Opera, and consented to be bored at this performance with the most exemplary courage. She could not endure to be supposed incapable of liking such music. On leaving her box, she said in a tone of great elation at having stayed to the end, " It is certainly a very serious work, but quite intelligible. In that grand orchestral effect in the introduction, I recognised at once that *Romeo was arriving in his cabriolet"!!!*

The overture to the *Carnaval romain* was the least successful of all my works at St. Petersburg. It passed almost unnoticed on the evening of my first concert, and Count Michel Wielhorski (an excellent musician) having confessed that he did not understand it in the least, I took care not to give it again. A Viennese would hardly credit this, but scores have their destiny, like books and dramas, roses and thistles.

At a concert in the Grand Theatre, for Versing's benefit, I also conducted my *Symphonie fantastique;* and on this occasion Damcke, that able composer, pianist, conductor, and critic, had the amazing good-nature to come and play on the piano the two deep notes (C, G), representing the funeral knell in the finale, as if he had been any ordinary kettle-drummer.

The overture to the *Carnaval romain* was for long the most popular of all my compositions in Austria, and was played everywhere. I recollect that while I was at Vienna it gave rise to various notable incidents. Haslinger, the publisher, gave a musical soirée, at which, among other things, this overture was to be performed, arranged for two pianos and a physharmonica. When its turn arrived, I happened to be near a door opening into the room where the five performers were seated. They took the first allegro far too slowly; the andante went fairly well, but when they resumed the allegro at a still more dragging pace than before, the blood rushed to my head, I grew scarlet, and, unable to keep my temper, cried out: " It is not the Carnival, it is Good Friday that you are playing! "

I leave you to imagine the mirth excited among the audience by this exclamation. It was impossible to restore silence, and the overture was finished amid the laughter and noise of the assembly, but still quite slowly, and apparently without my five placid interpreters having been in the least disturbed.

Some days afterwards, Dreyschock was giving a concert in the concert-room of the Conservatoire, and begged me to conduct the same overture, as a part of his programme. " I want to make you forget Good Friday at Haslinger's," said he. He had engaged all the orchestra of the Kärntnerthor Theatre. Just as the rehearsal was beginning, one of the first violins, who spoke French, whispered: " You will see the difference between us and those little wretches at the Wien Theatre " (where I used to give my concerts). Certainly he was not wrong. Never was the work performed with such fire, precision, spirit, and well-ordered turbulence. And what sonority! What harmonious *harmony!* That apparent pleonasm can alone convey my meaning. And at the concert itself it *exploded* like a mass of fireworks, and was encored with a noise of feet and hands never heard except at Vienna. Dreyschock, whose own personal success was obscured by this tempestuous enthusiasm, tore his gloves in fury and said with a look of rage, as if I had done him a real injury: " Catch me playing *overtures* again at my concerts! " . . . However, his comic ill-temper did not last very long, or prevent him from being most cordial to me at Prague some weeks later.

I mentioned Ernst just now. He arrived at St. Petersburg the same

day as myself, and we met by chance in Russia, as we had already met
at Brussels, Vienna, and Paris, and as we have since met in other parts
of Europe, where the various incidents or accidents of our artistic life
seem to have strengthened the bonds of sympathy already established
between us. I have the warmest and most affectionate admiration for
him. He has such a good heart, is at once a good friend and a great
artist! Ernst has been compared to Chopin. In certain respects there is
ground for the comparison, but in others, and those the most important, there is none whatever. From a purely musical point of view
they differ essentially. Chopin could ill endure the restraint of time,
and to my mind pushed rhythmical independence much too far. Ernst,
though taking such legitimate and reasonable liberties with the time as
passionate expression demands, remains a periodic musician, keeping
strict time, with an imperturbable steadiness in the midst of his most
venturesome caprices. Chopin *could* not play in strict time. Ernst can
forsake it for a moment, but only to make its power felt the more
forcibly when he returns to it. He must be heard in Beethoven's quartets to be appreciated in this respect.

In Chopin's compositions, all the interest is centred on the piano;
the orchestra in his concertos is nothing but a cold and almost useless
accompaniment. Ernst's works are especially distinguished by the contrary qualities. His concerted pieces written for the violin manifestly
combine qualities formerly supposed to be incompatible — namely,
a brilliant mechanism and a sustained symphonic interest. To make the
solo instrument predominate, without suppressing the orchestra, was
the problem which Beethoven was the first to solve successfully. And
perhaps even Beethoven made the orchestra predominate, to the detriment of the solo; whereas the balance seems to me evenly kept in the
system adopted by Ernst, Vieuxtemps, Liszt, and some others. On this
point I insist.

Ernst, who is the most charming humorist of my acquaintance, a
great musician as well as a great violinist, is a thorough artist whose
expressive faculties take the lead, but who is in no way deficient in the
vital qualities of musical art properly so called. He is gifted with that
rare organisation which permits the artist to conceive powerfully, and
to carry out his conception without hesitation. In his zeal for progress,
he makes use of all the resources of art. He writes beautiful poems on
the violin in musical language, of which he is complete master. Chopin
was purely the virtuoso of elegant drawing-rooms and intimate gather-

ings. To Ernst, a theatre, a large room, and a huge audience are always welcome; and, like Liszt, he never seems so powerful as when he has two thousand listeners to subdue. His concerts at the theatre in St. Petersburg would have proved this to me, had I not been convinced of it already. It was marvellous to hear him in his variations on the *Carnaval de Venise,* written after those of Paganini, though not in imitation of them. In this tasteful fantasia, all the caprices of a rich invention are mingled in so skilful and rapid a manner with the eccentricities of a tremendous technique, that at last one loses all sense of surprise, and lets oneself be rocked by the monotonous accompaniment of the air just as though the most variously coloured cascades of melody were not bounding forth from the solo violin in the most diverting and unforeseen manner. In this curious combination of melodic dexterity and almost careless facility, Ernst is simply dazzling and fascinating. He plays with diamonds as with counters. If Krespel, the whimsical owner of the Cremona violin, could have witnessed these incredible feats, the little reason the poor man had left would have speedily disappeared altogether, and he would have suffered less from the death of Antonia.

These variations, which I have often heard Ernst play since then — and quite recently in Baden — now affect me in a strange way. The moment the theme appears beneath that magic bow, it is again midnight for me. I am once more at St. Petersburg in a huge hall, as bright as day; again I experience that strange sweet languor that one feels at the end of a splendid musical soirée; smiles and murmurs of enthusiasm fill the air; I fall into a romantic melancholy which I cannot overcome, nay, which it would be painful to resist. . . .

Music is the sole art that has this retroactive power; no other, not even that of Shakespeare, can thus poetise the past it recalls. For music alone speaks at once to the imagination, the mind, the heart, and the *senses;* and it is the reaction of the senses on the mind and heart, and *vice versâ,* that produces the impressions felt by those who are gifted with the necessary organisation, but of which *others* (the barbarians) can know nothing.

CHAPTER LXXIII

MY RETURN—RIGA—BERLIN—PERFORMANCE OF
"FAUST"—A DINNER AT SANS SOUCI—THE KING
OF PRUSSIA

LENT was over; there was no longer anything to keep me at St. Petersburg, and I made up my mind, though not without much regret, to leave that brilliant capital and its charming hospitality.[1] On my way through Riga, the strange idea occurred to me of giving a concert there.[2] The receipts barely covered the expenses, but it procured me the acquaintance of Schrameck, the Kapellmeister, of Martinson, and of the post-master, and several other distinguished artists and amateurs. This last gentleman did not give much support to my plan for a concert. " Our little town is not like St. Petersburg," said he. " We are all commercial men; everyone is occupied just now with selling corn; you won't have more than a hundred ladies at the outside, and not a single man." He was mistaken. I had a hundred and thirty-two

[1] He left St. Petersburg on May 10th, 1847.
He tells us nothing in his *Mémoires* of a brief idyll with a young woman in St. Petersburg. She was a corset-maker who sang in the chorus at a theatre. She was engaged; but apparently the fiancé, for whom she had no great affection, was absent. She doubtless afforded sorely needed emotional consolation to the unhappy Berlioz amid the torments and fatigues and disappointments of his Russian exile: the intoxication of the Russian spring seems also to have played its part in lending the episode a romance it might not have had elsewhere and in other circumstances. They took walks together in the sunset on the banks of the Neva; the young lady's limited command of French must have made conversation a trifle difficult, but music was a stronger link between them than words. "I crushed her arm against my breast," says Berlioz in a letter to a friend, "and I sang to her the melody of the adagio in *Romeo and Juliet*."
We owe most of the little we know about this affair to Berlioz's friend Tajan-Rogé, the cellist, who was in St. Petersburg at the time. He died in 1876; his book *Mémoires d'un Piano*, in which he deals with the episode, was published in 1878. There he gives in full Berlioz's letter to him from London, on 10 November 1847, which was curtailed by the editor of the *Correspondance inédite* (Daniel Bernard). A second and still more interesting letter, dated 1 January 1848, was omitted from the *Correspondance*. Not having heard from the corsetière on his return to Paris (a letter of hers appears to have gone astray), Berlioz asked Tajan-Rogé to deliver a letter to her personally. Tajan-Rogé, having done this, received a reply which he transmitted to Berlioz. One gathers that the fiancé, who had been in Sweden, had now returned to St. Petersburg, and the young lady had returned to the path of duty, though she assured Berlioz that she would always be grateful to him for his affection. On his part the affair had undoubtedly been taken with the utmost seriousness. See J. G. Prod'homme's article *Une Aventure d'amour de Berlioz*, in the *Zeitschrift der Internationalen Musikgesellschaft*, Heft 4, 1912.
It was probably at this time that he conceived *La Mort d'Ophélie*, for female choir and orchestra, and the *Marche funèbre pour la dernière scène d'Hamlet*. He gave these two works their final form in the summer of 1848.
[2] On May 29th, 1847.

ladies and seven men. I think I had even three roubles (about twelve francs) profit. The post-master also maintained that I had not the proper exterior for my profession. " You don't seem at all bad, sir," he said, " and from your feuilletons, which I read regularly, I should have expected to find you quite another sort of person, for, devil take me! you write with a dagger instead of a pen." At any rate, the point of my dagger is not poisoned, and the " precious villains "[1] whom I am so readily supposed to have murdered are in excellent health. Moreover, I had an unexpected stroke of good luck at Riga. Baumeister, the excellent German actor, was playing, and I saw him in . . . *Hamlet.*

I had received a letter from Count von Rödern at Moscow, five weeks earlier, telling me of the King of Prussia's desire to hear my legend of *Faust,* and advising me to stop at Berlin on my way home for the purpose. The King offered me the Opera theatre and all its resources, and guaranteed me half of the gross receipts. I was much touched by this royal kindness, and remained ten days at Berlin to get up the performance.[2] As far as the orchestra and choir were concerned it was an admirable one, but very feeble in other respects. The tenor who had undertaken the part of Faust, and the soprano who was overwhelmed by that of Marguerite, did me the greatest injury. The ballad of the King of Thule (which till then had been always applauded) was hissed, but whether these manifestations were addressed to the composer or to the singer, or to both, I cannot tell; the latter idea is the most probable. The pit was filled with ill-natured people, indignant, as I heard, that a Frenchman should have had the insolence to set to music a paraphrase of the national masterpiece, and also with partisans of Prince Radzivill, who, with the help of a number of real composers, had set some of Goethe's scenes to music.

Never have I seen anything so absurdly ferocious as the intolerance of certain idolaters of the German nationality. . . . And this time I had a section of the Opera orchestra against me, whose good graces I had forfeited some years before by my letters on Berlin.[3] And yet these letters, as the reader may judge,[4] assuredly contain nothing to wound the Berlin instrumentalists. On the contrary, I have praised them in every way, and only criticise certain minor details in

[1] Othello's expression in speaking of Iago. [B.]
[2] He arrived in Berlin on June 4th. The Berlin performance of *Faust* took place on the 19th.
[3] Translated into German by M. Gathy, and published at Hamburg. [B.]
[4] See letters vii., viii., ix. [B.]

their orchestra and that with great reserve. I call the orchestra *magnificent;* I pronounce it gifted with *precision, unity, force,* and *delicacy;* but, and herein consists my crime, I compare some of its virtuosi with those of Paris, and confess (now shudder with indignation!) that our flautists are superior to theirs! These simple words made the Berlin first flautist furious, and he managed to imbue many of his colleagues with his own feeling, by representing that I had *heaped insults on* the Berlin orchestra. A fresh proof of the danger one runs in writing about players, and of being within reach of their self-love after giving it the slightest wound! In criticising a singer, one does not necessarily expose oneself to the aversion of his competitors; on the contrary, they are more likely to think you have not been sufficiently severe on him. But a virtuoso in a renowned orchestra always asserts that in criticising him you *insult* the whole body to which he belongs, and sometimes succeeds in making his comrades believe his nonsense.

In Paris, during the rehearsals of *Benvenuto Cellini,* it once happened that I had to point out a mistake in an important passage to the second horn (M. Meyfred, a man of sense). At this observation, which was made as calmly and politely as possible, M. Meyfred rose angrily and exclaimed: " I am doing just what is marked! Why should you *mistrust* the *orchestra* in this way?" To which I replied still more calmly: " In the first place, my dear M. Meyfred, it is not exactly a question of the orchestra, but of you alone. In the next place, I do not *mistrust* you, for mistrust implies doubt, and I am perfectly *certain* that you made a mistake."

But to return to the Berlin orchestra. I soon discovered its ill-will towards me during the rehearsals of *Faust.* The icy greeting I received each day on entering, the hostile silence after the best parts of the score, the sour glances darted at me, especially by the flutes, and the revelations of certain still friendly members of the orchestra, left no doubt on my mind. My friends, intimidated by the hostility of their comrades, dared not applaud me, and it was in an undertone that one of them, who spoke a little French, contrived to slip these words into my ear as he passed me on the stage: " Monsieur, la *mousik* . . . elle est souperbe! " . . . As for some of the people who hissed the ballad, I may perhaps be permitted to suspect their acquaintance with the great flautists, the stupendous flautists, the incomparable flautists of the Berlin orchestra. However that may be, I repeat that the playing of the orchestra, like the singing of the chorus, was irreproachably beautiful. Boetticher sang the part of Mephistopheles like a good musician and true artist. The public endeavoured to encore the *Danse des Sylphes,* but I was in a bad temper, and would not obey their wish.

The Crown Princess of Prussia, who had twice come at eight o'clock in the morning to hear my rehearsals in the cold dark opera house, made me all sorts of pretty speeches. The King sent me the Cross of the Red Eagle through Meyerbeer, and invited me to dinner at his château of Sans Souci two days later; and Rellstab, the great critic, so long the bitter enemy of Meyerbeer and Spontini, after various verbal professions of friendship and regard, made *mincemeat* of me in the *Vossische Zeitung.* These were real triumphs, the last, to my thinking, not the least. The dinner at Sans Souci was delightful. Herr von Humboldt, Count Mathieu Wielhorski, and the Crown Princess of Prussia were among the guests. After dessert, we took our coffee in the garden. The King walked about cup in hand, and seeing me on the steps of one of the pavilions, called out:

" Berlioz, come here and tell me something about my sister and your travels in Russia."

I know not what nonsense I talked to my august host, but he took it all in the highest good-humour.

" Did you learn any Russian? " he asked me.

" Yes, Sire, I can say, ' Na prava, na leva ' (to the right, to the left) sufficiently to guide a sledge-driver. I can also say ' dourack ' when the driver loses his way."

" And what does ' dourack ' mean? "

" It means ' stupid fool,' Sire! "

" Ha, ha! Stupid fool, Sire! stupid fool, Sire! that's good! "

And the King burst into such fits of laughter that he upset nearly all the contents of his cup. This merriment, in which I unceremoniously joined, made me an important personage on the spot. Several courtiers, officers, gentlemen, and chamberlains remarked it from the pavilion, and immediately began to think of being on good terms with the man who had made the King laugh so heartily, and who laughed with him in such a familiar manner. Accordingly on my return to the pavilion I found myself surrounded by various noblemen, all perfect strangers to me, who made me the most profound salutations, at the same time modestly mentioning their names. " Monsieur, I am Prince von . . . , and I am happy to make your acquaintance. — Monsieur, I am Count von . . . Permit me to congratulate you on your great success. —

Monsieur, I am Baron von . . . I had the honour of seeing you six years ago at Brunswick, and I am delighted etc., etc." I really could not understand at first my sudden reputation at the Prussian Court, but at last I remembered the scene in the first act of the *Huguenots,* where Raoul, after the receipt of Queen Margaret's letter, is surrounded by people singing in canon on every note of the scale, *" Vous savez si je suis un ami sûr et tendre!"* I was taken for an influential favourite of the King! What queer people courtiers are!

Without being either a favourite or influential, I am at any rate profoundly grateful for the King of Prussia's many kindnesses, and it was with no intention of flattering him that I said, in the course of a few moments' serious conversation that day:

" You are the real king of artists."

" How so? What have I done for them? "

" To speak of musical artists alone, you have done much for them, Sire. You have rewarded Spontini and Meyerbeer regally, and overwhelmed them with honours. You have had their works splendidly performed. You have had magnificent revivals of Gluck's masterpieces, which are no longer heard anywhere but in Berlin. You have had the *Antigone* of Sophocles represented, and commissioned Mendelssohn to write choruses in honour of that resurrection from the antique. You also engaged him to set Shakespeare's fascinating *Midsummer Night's Dream* to music. Moreover, the direct interest you take in all these noble artistic efforts acts as an incentive to the producers, and a ceaseless encouragement to their labours; and the support thus given to the efforts of artists is the more valuable because it is the only one of the sort they obtain in Europe."

" Well, well; perhaps there is some truth in what you say, but you must not talk so much about it."

Certainly it was true. Things are slightly changed now. The King of Prussia is no longer the only sovereign in Europe interested in music. There are two others besides, the young King of Hanover and the Grand Duke of Weimar. Three in all.

CHAPTER LXXIV

PARIS—I HAVE ROQUEPLAN AND DUPONCHEL NOMI-
NATED AS DIRECTORS OF THE OPÉRA—THEIR GRATI-
TUDE—''LA NONNE SANGLANTE''—I GO TO LONDON
—JULLIEN, MANAGER OF DRURY LANE—SCRIBE—
THE PRIEST MUST LIVE BY THE ALTAR

On my return to France I spent a few days with my family, from whom I had so long been separated, and introduced to my father his hitherto unknown grandson. Poor Louis! how he enjoyed the tender welcome of his grandparents and their old servants, and what pleasure he had in running about the fields with me, with his little gun in his hand! In a letter I received from him two days ago, dated from the Aland Islands, he speaks of that fortnight at the Côte-Saint-André as the happiest in his whole life. . . . And now he is a sailor in the Anglo-French fleet, blockading the Russian ports on the Baltic, and constantly expecting that hell on water, a naval battle.

The notion of it upsets my heart and my head. Happy they who love no one! And yet he chose this career himself. Could I oppose him? . . . For after all, it is a grand and noble profession. And who could have foreseen this war! . . . Those terrible and innumerable instruments of destruction! God grant he may escape safe and sound! . . . Those enormous pieces of cannon he is obliged to *serve!* those red-hot balls, those Congreve rockets! that hail of grape-shot! the firing! the leaks! the steam explosions! . . . It drives me mad to think of them! . . . I can write no more!

Two days later. — I am always thinking of it. Let us talk of something else. A modern naval battle . . . my story goes so slowly. It is so tiresome to write, and no doubt also to read. What use is it all? Let us abridge facts as much as possible, without note or comment. Poor dear child!

After that excursion into Dauphiny I returned to Paris. They are bombarding . . . Bomarsund . . . perhaps he is in the very midst of the firing at this moment. . . .

M. Léon Pillet was about to give up the directorship of the Opéra. M. Nestor Roqueplan and that eternal Duponchel had associated themselves together and united all their efforts to obtain the post. They called on me.

" You know," they said, " that M. Pillet cannot remain at the Opéra any longer. We have a chance of getting it " (Duponchel might have said of getting it again), " but the Minister of the Interior is not favourably disposed towards us, and you are the only person who might be able to make him change his mind by interesting the director of the *Journal des Débats*. Would you mind asking M. Armand Bertin to make representations to the Minister? If we are nominated, we shall offer you the chief management of the music at the Opéra, and the post of conductor besides."

" Pardon me, but that place is already occupied by M. Girard, one of my oldest friends, and not for any consideration would I be the means of his losing it."

" Very well, two conductors are wanted at the Opéra. We do not wish to keep the second, who is good for nothing, and so we will have the duties of conductor divided evenly between you and M. Girard. Leave it to us; it shall all be arranged to your satisfaction."

Taken in by these fine speeches, I went to M. Bertin. After some hesitation, occasioned by his want of confidence in the applicants, he consented to speak for them to the Minister. They were nominated.

From the day of their installation I began to be insulted in all sorts of ways at the Opéra. Roqueplan made appointments with me and never kept them. Duponchel followed his example. For two hours they would make me dance attendance; and when, at last, one of the pair arrived, he would regret the absence of his partner, and declare himself unable to talk business without him. I very soon understood what was at the back of the minds of these gentlemen. Such proceedings filled me with indignation, but I restrained myself, being bent on seeing how far they would push their *candour*. I determined to persist till I had got them into a fix, and I succeeded. After I know not how many comings and goings and appointments not kept, it had to end in our all meeting together, and then the recantation began very distinctly: *" They did not exactly see their way to creating a post for me at the Opéra. They might possibly be able to give me the direction of the chorus, but I did not play the piano, and that was essential for rehearsals. Girard would not hear of recognizing anyone as equal to himself in the direction of the orchestra. 'A throne,' said he, 'cannot be*

divided.' " (Roi d'Yvetot!), etc., etc. In short, they were in a difficulty. But now for the climax!

At the request of M. Léon Pillet, I had long since begun a grand
opera, in five acts, entitled *La Nonne Sanglante*, the book of which
had been sketched by Scribe, and the contract signed between M. Pillet,
Scribe, and myself. Will it be believed that in the middle of our conversation Roqueplan had the audacity to throw these words in my
face:

" You have an opera libretto by Scribe? "

" Yes."

" Well, what do you propose to do with it? "

" Hang it all, what is usually done with opera librettos? "

" But you are aware that artists employed in our theatre are prohibited by ministerial regulations from having their works represented
there; and as you are going to occupy a place in it, you will not be able
to write operas."

" Oh, you may be sure I don't intend to write a dozen. If I can
produce two good ones in my life I shall esteem myself very lucky."

" No matter, it won't be possible for you to have even one performed. Your *Nun* will be lost. *You ought to give it to us, and we will
have it set to music by somebody else.*"

I still restrained myself, and in a choking voice answered: " Take
it ! "

From that moment the conversation became more and more useless and muddled. I had found out my men. My suspicions were
evidently well founded. They were aiming at getting rid of me, and not
only had they no intention of keeping any of their promises, but, looking on me as an absurd and dangerous composer, incapable of doing
anything but compromise the theatre, they were firmly resolved not to
allow any work of mine to be played at the Opéra, and even to withdraw a work already begun, and commissioned of me by the previous
manager.

Duponchel did not say a word, being probably put out of countenance by the impudence of his associate. He also had no opinion of
my value, but he seemed to feel that managers who owed their place to
me might at any rate conceal their contempt for me, even if they were
not keen to make a sacrifice by putting on a work of mine the failure
of which seemed to them assured.

It may well be believed that it was not the opinion of these gentlemen on my compositions that made me so indignant. I had often heard them express their sovereign contempt for Beethoven, Mozart, Gluck, and all the great musical divinities; I should rather have been ashamed if I had met with the slightest appearance of sympathy from them. But such colossal ingratitude exceeded anything I had hitherto encountered in that line. Accordingly, the day after this conversation, in which, though nothing was settled, I had learned what I wished to know — the full extent of the gratitude of two men under obligations to me — I accepted the proposal I had by chance received at that time of directing the orchestra of the great English Opera in London. I wrote immediately to Duponchel and Roqueplan to acquaint them with my determination, released them from all their promises, and wished them all sorts of prosperity. Then these gentlemen, in order to exculpate themselves in the eyes of those who knew what I had done for them, and to throw on me the odium of their conduct, went about everywhere saying that I had insisted on having the first conductorship and on Girard's dismissal; a double calumny, because, from the very beginning, I had declared that I would accept nothing that could injure Girard. Girard, of course, believed the falsehood. I took offence at his credulity, and from that day to this we have not been on good terms — which, I confess, does not greatly trouble me. For the rest, I am bound to say that I got very much what I deserved. I was perfectly acquainted with the musical morality of my two aspirants for the directorship of the Opéra; with regard to music they are a couple of Chinese, while all the time they believe themselves to be gifted both with taste and judgment. Consequently they combine the most absolute self-confidence with the most complete ignorance and profoundest barbarism. Instead, therefore, of smoothing their way to the Opéra, I ought to have hampered them as much as possible.

But their promise of the musical direction of the Opéra dazzled me. All the fine things that might be done with such an instrument, when one knows how to use it, and when one's sole aim is the grandeur and progress of art, rushed into my mind. " They," said I to myself, " will administer the finances, they will manage the ballet and the scenery, etc., and as for the Opéra, properly so called, I shall be the real Director ! " And I fell into their net. THE PROMISES SPONTANEOUSLY MADE BY THESE GENTLEMEN HAVE BEEN NO MORE FAITHFULLY KEPT THAN MANY OTHERS, AND THAT WAS THE END OF THE MATTER FROM THAT DAY TO THIS.

I had been some weeks in London when it once more occurred to me to put my two Directors of *La Nonne Sanglante* into a fix. I had certainly told Roqueplan, in reply to his fresh request for this work, to "take it," but it was rather in the tone of Leonidas' reply to Xerxes' order to give up his arms: "Come and take them." The point in question was the regulation forbidding a composer holding any employment at the Opéra to write anything for that theatre. True, M. Dietsch, the director of the chorus, had had his *Vaisseau Fantôme* played;[1] M. Benoist, the accompanist, had had his *Apparition* performed; while Halévy's *Juive, Drapier,* and *Guido et Ginevra* were all played at the very time that he was director of singing at the Opéra! Still, Roqueplan had a ghost of a pretext for refusing me a performance of my *Nonne Sanglante*. But being now settled in London, and out of reach of a regulation which had ceased to apply to me, I wrote to Scribe, begging him to get a final decision. "If they consent," I said, "to carry out the agreement we signed with M. Pillet, pray ask them to let me have the necessary time to finish my score. The direction of the orchestra at Drury Lane leaves me no time for composing, and you yourself have not finished the libretto. I must have plenty of leisure for pondering upon this work, even after it is finished; and I cannot undertake to let it be put upon the stage in less than three years from now. If they will not allow us this latitude, or if, as is more likely, they refuse to sanction our agreement, then I will abuse your patience no longer, but will ask you to take back the poem, and dispose of it as you please."

To which Scribe, after having seen the Directors, replied that, being well aware that we were not nearly ready, they accepted the *Nonne* on condition that they might put it into rehearsal immediately, and he finished his letter thus:

"So I think the chances in our favour are not great, and since you are kind and honourable enough to allow me to dispose of the old poem that has been so long in hand, I don't mind telling you frankly that I take you at your word, and shall try to get rid of it, either at the Théâtre National that has just been opened, or elsewhere."

And so the matter ended. Scribe took back his poem, and, I am told, offered it to Halévy, Verdi, and Grisar, who all had the delicacy

[1] The libretto of this work, written by Richard Wagner, had been purchased from him for twenty pounds and composed by Dietsch, who inspired the manager with much more confidence than Wagner. [B].

to decline his offer, knowing the state of the case, and considering Scribe's treatment of me to have been rather unhandsome. M. Gounod finally accepted it, and his score will soon be performed.[1]

I had written but two acts of it. At the head of what I consider as my best compositions I should put the grand duet containing the legend of the Bleeding Nun, and the finale which follows it. That duet and two airs are fully scored, the finale is not. It will probably never be known.[2]

When I saw Scribe on my return to Paris, he seemed slightly confused at having accepted my offer and taken back his poem. " But, as you know," said he, " Il faut que le prêtre vive de l'autel." ("The priest must live by the altar.") Poor fellow! he could not in fact have waited; he has only some two or three hundred thousand francs per annum, a house in town, three country houses, etc.

Liszt made a capital pun when I repeated Scribe's remark to him. " Yes," said he, " by his *hotel* " — comparing Scribe to an innkeeper.

I shall not enter into details as to my first stay in England, for they would be simply interminable. Besides, it is always the same thing over and over again. I was engaged by Jullien, the celebrated director of the promenade concerts, to conduct the orchestra of a Grand English Opera, which he had the wild ambition of establishing at Drury Lane Theatre. Jullien, in his incontestable and uncontested character of madman, had engaged a charming orchestra, a first-rate chorus, a very fair set of singers; he had forgotten nothing but the repertory. The sole work he had in view was an opera he had ordered from Balfe, called *The Maid of Honour,* and he proposed to open his series with an English version of *Lucia di Lammermoor.* While they were waiting for the *mise en scène* of Balfe's opera, he would have had to take ten thousand francs (four hundred pounds) a night with Donizetti's *novelty,* merely to cover expenses.

The result was inevitable; the receipts from *Lucia* never came near ten thousand francs. Balfe's opera was only a moderate success, and in a very short time Jullien was utterly ruined. I never touched a penny beyond my first month's salary, and to this day, notwithstanding all the fine protestations of Jullien — who, after all, is as honest a man as one can be, consistently with such a depth of folly — I look upon all he owes me as lost without redress. There is a passage on the English

---

[1] It has been only a quarter successful. As for the poem, which was at last finished by Scribe and Germain Delavigne, it is so tame and monotonous that I ought to think myself fortunate not to have kept it. [B.]

[2] It has all been destroyed since, with the exception of the two airs. [B.]

opera in my *Soirées de l'orchestre* that deals with him and his extravagant theatre. It was Jullien I had in view when I spoke of the impresario who was in so desperate a situation that he seriously proposed to me to get up the opera of *Robert le Diable* in *six days,* though he had neither copies, nor translation, nor dresses, nor scenery, and though the singers did not know a note of the work. It was simple madness.

Here is a perfect sample of the insane notions that occur to a man who is used to catering always for the puerile instincts of the mob, and succeeding by the most fatuous means. Being at the end of his resources, seeing that Balfe's opera was bringing in no money, and recognising to a certain extent the impossibility of putting *Robert le Diable* on the stage in six days (even by resting on the seventh), Jullien assembled his committee for deliberation. The committee was composed of Sir Henry Bishop, Sir George Smart, Mr. Planché (author of the libretto of Weber's *Oberon*), Mr. Gye (the manager of Drury Lane), M. Marezzeck (the singing-master), and myself. Jullien stated his perplexities, and spoke of different operas (not translated or copied, of course) which he wished to put on the stage. It was amusing to hear the ideas and opinions of these gentlemen as the various masterpieces were trotted out.

I listened in amazement. When at last they came to the *Iphigénie en Tauride,* which had been announced in Jullien's prospectus (it is the custom of the London managers to announce that work every year, and never give it), the members of the committee, not knowing a note of it, were at a loss what to say. Jullien, impatient at my silence, turned sharply round and said: " Why the devil don't you speak? You must know it? "

" Of course I know it; but what do you want me to say? Tell me, and I will answer you."

" I want to know how many acts there are, the chief characters and their voices, and, above all, the style of the scenery and dresses."

"Well, take a sheet of paper and a pen, and write to my dictation: *Iphigénie en Tauride,* an opera by Gluck, as you probably know, is in four acts. There are three male parts. Orestes (baritone), Pylades (tenor), Thoas (a bass going very high); one grand woman's part, Iphigenia (soprano); another small part, Diana (mezzo-soprano), and several leading chorus parts. The dresses, I fear, you will not think becoming. The Scythians and King Thoas are ragged savages on the shores of the Black Sea. Orestes and Pylades appear in the simple costume of two shipwrecked Greeks. Pylades alone has two costumes; he re-enters in the fourth act with a helmet on his head."

"A helmet?" cried Jullien, in a transport of delight. "We are saved! I shall order a gilt helmet from Paris, with a coronet of pearls and a tuft of ostrich feathers as long as my arm, and we shall have forty performances."

I forget how the meeting ended, but if I were to live a hundred years I should never forget the flashing eyes, the wild gestures, and distracted enthusiasm of Jullien on learning that Pylades has a helmet, or his sublime idea of getting it from Paris, since no English workman could possibly turn out one sufficiently dazzling; or his hope of having forty splendid performances of Gluck's masterpiece, thanks to the pearls, gilding, and feathers in Pylades' helmet. "Pro-di-gious!" as good Dominie Sampson would say, "Pro-di-gious!" I need not add that *Iphigénie* was not even studied. Jullien left London some days after this learned committee meeting, leaving his theatrical undertaking to crash to the ground. Meantime the singers and singing-master had, as might have been expected, pronounced against the *antique score,* and the god-tenor (Reeves) had laughed a good deal when the part of Pylades was proposed to him.

Berlioz's account of his London venture calls for the addition of a few details.

Louis Antoine Jullien (1812–1860) was a semi-musical adventurer who fled from his French creditors in 1838 and settled in London. There he became a great figure with his popular concerts, in which the more respectable compositions of the masters acted as foils to his own quadrilles. He specialised in "monster" orchestras, and understood thoroughly how to exploit his own showman's personality in front of his audiences. The "Mons," as *Punch* called him, "with coat thrown widely open, white waistcoat, elaborately embroidered shirt-front, wristbands of extravagant length turned back over his cuffs, a wealth of black hair, and a black moustache — itself a startling novelty — wielded his baton, encouraged his forces, repressed the turbulence of his audience with indescribable gravity and magnificence, went through all the pantomime of the British Army or Navy Quadrille, seized a violin or piccolo at the moment of climax, and at last sank exhausted into his gorgeous velvet chair. All pieces of Beethoven's were conducted with a jewelled baton, and in a pair of clean kid gloves, handed him at the moment on a silver salver."

His venture at Drury Lane, of which Berlioz gives us so grimly amusing an account, ended in his being adjudged bankrupt in April 1848. He blithely commenced musical operations again in the following year, and had a variety of exciting experiences until May, 1859, when he was put in a French prison for debt. He died in a lunatic asylum near Paris in the following year.

Nothing could have been handsomer, on paper, than his contract with Berlioz. The latter was to receive £400 per quarter as conductor. The engagement was for six years, though Jullien could terminate the agreement, if he wished, at the end of each season. Berlioz was further guaranteed £400 net for a month's concerts. Finally he was to compose an opera in three acts, for which he was to receive £800 in eight instalments.

Early in September, 1847, Berlioz had taken his little thirteen year old son, Louis, to see his father in Côte-Saint-André. The old man was then seventy-one; he and Hector had not met since 1832.

Berlioz returned to Paris about the 20th of the month. He left for London on November 3rd, having with great difficulty persuaded Marie Recio that for reasons of economy he had better go abroad alone this time. In his other establishment, Harriet was steadily deteriorating both in body and in mind. It was obviously no place for a boy of Louis' age; so Berlioz, on his way to London, deposited him in a pension in Rouen.

The composer arrived in London on the 5th, and took up his quarters first of all at 76 Harley Street, removing in the following spring to 26 Osnaburgh Street, Regents Park. The Drury Lane season opened on December 6th with *Lucia di Lammermoor;* Balfe's new opera, *The Maid of Honour*, was produced on the 20th. Berlioz gave a concert of his own works on February 7th, 1848, but apparently the proceeds of this were appropriated by the needy and none too scrupulous Jullien. On February 22nd, Berlioz presided at the annual dinner of the Royal Society of Musicians at the Freemasons' Hall, and proposed a toast. From the 22nd to the 25th, Paris was in the throes of revolution. Berlioz, like most of the French artists, musicians and literary men of the day, now looked upon art as dead; and it was in these dark days, and in a fit of profound depression, that he commenced the compilation of his *Mémoires*. (See his preface to the book.) His financial position was especially precarious just then. Jullien was visibly heading for bankruptcy. The fall of the French monarchy jeopardised its official organ, the *Débats*, and Berlioz had to face the possibility of his income from this source coming to an end just when he needed it most. In addition, there was a strong probability that the Republican government, in its zeal for economy, would abolish his post as librarian at the Conservatoire, which was little more than a sinecure.

In the midst of all these troubles, Marie descended upon him (towards the end of April). There had been hectic scenes between her and Harriet, owing to some promissory notes of Hector's, which had fallen due a little while before, having been presented by the holders at both Marie's apartment and Harriet's. Berlioz had dated them from the former. Marie and her mother referred the creditors to Berlioz's genuine wife Harriet, who sent them back in turn to the other ladies. Harriet had no money, while Marie pointed out that though the notes bore the address of 41 Rue de Provence, the legal tenant of that apartment was her mother, with whom Berlioz and herself merely happened to be living. The end of the long tragi-comedy was an angry scene between Harriet and Marie, following upon which, Mme Martin and her daughter removed to Rue de La Rochefoucauld, and Marie flew to London to distract poor Hector with the story.

On June 29th he gave another concert, in the Hanover Square Rooms, but apparently with no profit worth mentioning. Jullien, finding himself at the end of his resources, disappeared from London. Berlioz tells the whole story of his futile nine months in England in a letter to Liszt of July 23rd. Latterly the situation had become quite hopeless; political and economic causes combined to distract the Londoners' attention from music, and though the town was full of French refugees, these, as Berlioz says, "had too much of the national spirit in them to do anything but resolutely stay at home."

He was back in Paris by the middle of July, and at once had to incur fresh debts to keep his head above water. Fortunately the Conservatoire post was preserved to him, while his *Débats* articles were continued temporarily at half the former rate.

His father died on the 28th July. Hector went to the Côte some three weeks later. His share in the patrimony was nominally about 130,000 francs; but it would have been injudicious to realise the various properties until the French political and financial situation improved, and it was not until some years later that Berlioz was free of anxiety as regards money.

CHAPTER LXXV

MY FATHER'S DEATH — ANOTHER JOURNEY TO THE CÔTE-SAINT-ANDRÉ — EXCURSION TO MEYLAN — DEVASTATING LONELINESS — STELLA DEL MONTE AGAIN — I WRITE TO HER

IN one of the earlier chapters of these memoirs I have already mentioned the state in which I found Paris, on my return from London, after the Revolution of 1848. It was a mournful impression, but I was soon after visited by a grief far more searching and infinitely deeper —my father's death.

I had lost my mother ten years before, and the eternal separation had been a bitter blow. But between my father and myself there existed a friendship altogether independent of natural affection, and perhaps even deeper. Our ideas were entirely alike on many questions, the mere approach to which electrifies the intelligence of certain men. He had such lofty aspirations, was so full of feeling, so entirely and naturally good-hearted. He rejoiced that his prognostics with regard to my career had not been fulfilled.

On my return from Russia he confessed that one of his greatest desires was to hear my *Requiem.*

"Yes, I want to hear that terrible *Dies Iræ,* of which they talk so much; and, having done so, would gladly say my Nunc dimittis."

Alas! I was never able to give him that pleasure, and he died without ever having heard a single note of my music.

He was deeply and sincerely regretted, especially by our poor peasants, to whom he had been so good in many ways. My sister Nanci gave me touching details about them when she told me of his death.

She wrote thus: "We must not regret our dear father's life, for it had become a heavy burden to him. His one wish was to die as soon as possible. He had evidently no further interest in the things of this world, and was in haste to leave it. A glorious procession of the poor and the sick whom he had helped and cured accompanied him weeping to his last resting-place. Two speeches were made over his grave, amid the tears of all present; one by a young doctor, who did homage to his talents, his knowledge and his virtues, and the other by one of the people, the natural interpreter of the class among whom he spent that useful and unobtrusive life of which there are now so few examples. If anything can soften the bitter regret you feel at not being able to receive his last sigh with us, let it be the thought that his extreme weakness prevented him from feeling your absence. He was frequently unconscious, and spoke with difficulty. . . . But he asked me one day if I had any news of you and Louis." . . .

I cannot refrain from giving almost the whole of a letter from my other sister, Adèle, in which the ardent affection of her heart is laid bare without restraint.

"Vienne, Saturday, August 4th, 1848.

"DEAR BROTHER,

"Let us embrace each other in the grief common to us both. It is heart-rending. I knew well how severely you would feel the blow, and pitied you in your loneliness. In such moments of anguish we ought to be together. You would not have arrived in time for our beloved father to recognise you . . . let this console you for our silence, and forgive us for not giving you more timely notice. We did not know whether you were in Paris, and for six days we expected his death every moment. We were overwhelmed with grief from the Sunday till the Friday (July 28th), when he died at noon. He was constantly delirious, recognising no one except at rare intervals. The death-struggle of the last days was terrible. I can only compare him to a galvanised corpse. His head and arms were continually in motion from the irritation of the nerves. . . . His eyes were fixed and full of pain, and his hollow voice was ever asking for impossibilities. Now and then, in the most violent of his crises, I used to clasp him passionately in my arms, and that seemed to calm him. Nanci fled in terror . . . but he did not suffer — at least we hope not. At any rate, the doctor attending him thought so too, and told us his nervous convulsions were the result of the opium which he took to the last. One day, dearest, our good Monica showed him your picture. He called you by name, and asked eagerly for paper and pen, which we gave him. 'Good,' said he, 'I will write presently.' What he wished to say no one knows; but this was the only time that you crossed his mind. I think he recognised us more by instinct than in reality. One day I saw, by his wandering look, that he wanted something; and when, in order to satisfy him, I asked him what, he answered with unspeakable tenderness: 'Nothing, my daughter, I am looking for your eyes.' I burst into tears, and shall never forget those words. My husband remained with him to the last. He had promised me to close his eyes in your place; he kept his word, and my heart will ever be grateful to him for it."

Of course this grief brought me back to the Côte-Saint-André for a few days, to weep with my sisters under the paternal roof.

When I arrived I hurried into the study where my father had passed so many sad hours in sorrowful meditation, where he had begun my literary education and given me my first music lessons, before he frightened me with anatomical studies. I fell half-fainting on his sofa, where my weeping sisters embraced me. I touched everything with trembling hands: his Plutarch, his memorandum-books, his pens, his stick, his gun (an innocent weapon he never used), one of my own letters on his desk. Then Nanci opened one of the drawers. "Look, dearest brother; there is his watch. Keep it. . . . How often he looked at it during his last struggles, as if to know how many hours he had still to suffer." I took the watch. It was going. It was alive, though my father was no longer living.

Before returning to Paris I wished to revisit Grenoble, and my maternal grandfather's house at Meylan. With a strange thirst for sorrow I longed to see again the scene of my first passionate emotions. In a word I wished to embrace my whole past; to intoxicate myself with recollections, however harrowing they might be. My sisters remained at the Côte, understanding that I wished to be alone on this sacred pilgrimage, which was bound to arouse many feelings in me too sacred for the eyes of even my nearest and dearest. I feel my heart beat at the notion of relating the history of that excursion. But I will do it if it be but to prove the persistency of old feelings, apparently so irreconcilable with the new, and the reality of their co-existence in a heart which forgets nothing. So powerful is the inexorable action of memory in me that to this day I cannot see my boy's picture, at the age of ten, without pain. The sight of it makes me suffer as though I had had two sons, and death had taken the charming child, and left me only my grown-up son.

I reached Grenoble at eight in the morning; my uncle and cousins were in the country. In my impatience to get to Meylan, I only crossed the faubourg, and walked straight to the village. . . . It was a beautiful autumn day, full of poetic charm and serenity. When I reached Meylan, and stood before the house that was once my grandfather's, and was now in the hands of one of his tenants, I found it empty. The new proprietor was installed in a fresh building at the other end of the garden.

I made my way into the drawing-room, where the family used to be when we visited our grandfather. The room was just as before, with its grotesque paintings and its fantastic paper birds of all colours gummed on the wall. There was my grandfather's chair, where he slept of an afternoon; there was his game of tric-trac. On the old sideboard I caught sight of a wickerwork cage I had made when a child.

There I had seen my uncle waltzing with the lovely Estelle. . . . I rushed out.

Half the orchard was ploughed up. I looked for the bench where my father used to sit in the evenings, wrapped for hours in his own thoughts, with his eyes fixed on St. Eynard, a colossal limestone rock, the offspring of the last cataclysm of the Deluge. The seat was broken, and nothing left but its two worm-eaten feet. There was the field of maize where I used to hide my melancholy when my love first made me unhappy. At the foot of that tree I began to read Cervantes. Now to the mountain.

Thirty-three years have passed away since I saw it last. I feel like one who has been dead and is alive again, and, on his resurrection, finds all the feelings of his previous life as young and ardent as ever. I clambered up the rugged, deserted roads, in the direction of the white house which I had only seen in the distance, on my return from Italy sixteen years before — the house where the *Stella* once shone.

On I went, and as I mounted I felt my heart beating faster and faster. I thought I recognised an avenue of trees on the left side of the road, and followed it for some way, but it ended in an unknown farm, and was not the one I wanted. I resumed my road; it ended in the vineyards, and I had evidently lost my way. In my mind I could see the real road as plainly as if I had gone over it the night before; there used to be a little fountain, which I had not yet come across. Where was I then? . . . where was the fountain? The mistake only served to heighten my anxiety. I resolved to go and inquire at the farm I had just seen. I went into the barn, where the threshers were at work. They stopped their flails for a moment at sight of me; and trembling like a thief pursued by the gendarmes, I asked if they could show me the way to the house formerly inhabited by Madame Gautier. One of them scratched his head.

"Madame Gautier?" said he, "there is no one of that name in this part of the country."

"Yes, an old lady . . . she had two young nieces,[1] who used to come and visit her every autumn."

"I remember them," interrupted the wife of the thresher; "don't you recollect? . . . Miss Estelle, so pretty that everyone used to stop at the church door on Sundays to see her pass."

"Ah! now it's beginning to come back to me . . . yes, yes;

---

[1] No, not two nieces — I made a mistake — but two grand-daughters. [B.]

Madame Gautier. . . . But it is a long time ago, you see . . . her house now belongs to a Grenoble shopkeeper. . . . It is up there. You will come to the fountain a little way here behind our vineyard, and then turn to the left."

"The fountain? Ah! now I know my way. Many thanks. I am sure not to blunder again."

And crossing a field close by the farm, I struck at last into the right path.

Soon I heard the murmur of the little fountain . . . there I was. . . . And there is the path; and the right avenue at last. I feel that it is there. . . . I shall see her. Heavens! how the air intoxicates me; my head is turning! I stopped for a moment to control the beating of my heart. . . . I reached the avenue gate. . . . A gentleman in a jacket — doubtless the prosaic owner of my sanctuary — stood there, lighting a cigar.

He looked at me with an air of amazement.

I passed him without a word, and continued to climb. I wanted to reach an old tower that used to stand on the top of the hill, and from which my eye could take in all at a glance. I went on without once turning round. I must first reach the top. . . . But the tower, the tower! Where was it? . . . Had they pulled it down? No; there it was . . . they had destroyed the upper part, and the trees had grown so tall as to hide the rest. At last I reached it. Here, where the young beech trees are growing, we had sat together, my father and I, and I had played him *La Musette de Nina* on the flute.

Estelle must have come there. Perhaps I am standing on the very spot. Now, let me see. I turn round, and my glance takes in the whole picture . . . the sacred house, the garden, the trees, the valley below, the winding Isère, the Alps, the snow, the glaciers — all that she saw and admired. I inhale the blue air she breathed. . . . Ah! . . . A cry, that no human language can ever reproduce, is repeated by the echo of St. Eynard. Yes, I see; I see again and I adore; the past is before me; I am once more a boy of twelve — life, beauty, first love, infinite poetry, these are mine! I flung myself on my knees, and I cried to valley, mountains, and skies: "Estelle! Estelle! Estelle!" I clasped the ground in a convulsive embrace, I gnawed the grass, and a feeling of indescribable and terrible desolation surged up within me. "Bleed, my heart, bleed! . . . but leave me the strength to suffer still!"

At length I rose, and as I wandered down I devoured with my eyes all the scattered objects on the hills. I went along, smelling on the right hand and on the left, like a lost dog in search of its master. There is the cliff where I was walking when she called out: "Take care! Don't go so near the edge!" Here is the thicket of brambles where she stooped to gather blackberries. And down there must be the rock where her lovely feet once rested—where I saw her grand, upright figure as she stood gazing at the valley. . . . That day I had said to myself, with the simplicity of childish sentimentality: "When I am grown up, and have become a famous composer, I will write an opera on Florian's *Estelle;* I will dedicate it to her, and bring the score to this very rock, where she shall find it some morning when she comes to see the sun rise." Where is the rock? . . . Nowhere to be found. . . . Disappeared entirely. The vine-dressers have crushed it, or the mountain winds have buried it in sand.

That beautiful cherry tree! Her hand once rested upon its trunk. . . . But what is that close by? . . . Something that seems to recall her more than all the rest. . . . Something that resembled her in grace and elegance. . . . What is it? My memory is failing. Ah! a plant of pink sweet-pea, from which she gathered blossoms. It was at the turn of the path. . . . I rushed to it. . . . Eternal Nature! . . . there are the pink peas still, and the plant, richer and more bushy than of old, is swaying its perfumed blossoms to the breath of the breeze.

Time, thou capricious reaper! the rock has vanished, and the grass remains. I was on the point of tearing it all up. But no, beloved plant, remain and bloom in thy calm solitude, the emblem of that portion of my soul that I left here long ago, and which will abide here till I die! I will but gather two of thy fresh-coloured butterfly-blossoms — perennial butterflies! Farewell! farewell, beloved and beautiful plant; mountains and valleys, old tower, farewell! Old St. Eynard, heaven of my star, farewell! Farewell, my romantic childhood, and the last reflections of a pure love! The current of time bears me onward. Farewell, Stella . . . Stella! . . .

And I descended the mountain, mournful as a spectre returning to the grave. Again I passed the avenue of her home. The gentleman with the cigar had disappeared; he no longer defiled the peristyle of my temple. But still I dared not enter, despite my passionate desire. I went on slowly, slowly, lingering at each step, losing sight of each object with an anguish of regret. No need now to control the beatings

of my heart. I could not hear them. I was dead once more. And everywhere there was sweet sunshine, solitude, and silence. . . .

Two hours later I was crossing the Isère, and a little before sunset
I reached the hamlet of Murianette on the opposite bank, and found
my cousins and their mother. The next day we returned together to
Grenoble. My manner was, no doubt, strange and preoccupied. When
left alone for a moment with my cousin Victor, he could not help
saying: "What's the matter with you? I have never seen you like this."
"What's the matter with me? Well, you will certainly laugh at me;
but since you ask the question I will answer it. . . . Besides, it will
relieve me, for I am stifling. . . . Yesterday I was at Meylan."

"I know. What did you find there?"

"Among other things, Madame Gautier's house. . . . Do you
know her[1] niece, Madame F—— ?"

"Yes, the one they used to call the beautiful Estelle D——."

"Well, I loved her to distraction when I was twelve . . . and I
love her still!"

"But, you idiot," replied Victor, with a burst of laughter, "she is
fifty-one by this time. Her eldest son is twenty-two; he and I went
through our law-course together."

And his laughter broke out again; I joined in it, but mine was as
convulsive and distorted and desolate as the rays of an April sun
through the rain.

"Yes, it is absurd, I know; and yet it is . . . it is absurd, but it is
real. . . . It is puerile, but it is infinite. Don't laugh; or yes, laugh
if you will, it does not signify. Where is she now? where is she? You
must know." . . .

"Since her husband's death, she has been living at Vif." . . .

"Vif! is it far from here?"

"About ten miles."

"I shall go there. I want to see her."

"Are you off your head?"

"I shall find some excuse for presenting myself."

"I beg of you, Hector, not to do such a senseless thing."

"I want to see her."

"You will never have the presence of mind to get through such a
visit properly."

"I want to see her."

[1] Her grand-daughter. [B.]

"You will only make a fool of yourself, and compromise her, that's all."

"I want to see her."

"But do just consider."

"I want to see her."

"Fifty-one years old! . . . More than half-a-century! . . . What will you find? Would it not be better to keep your fresh and youthful memories, and preserve your ideal?"

"O execrable Time! horrible profaner! At any rate, I will write to her."

"Write away. Good heavens, what a lunatic!"

He handed me a pen, and fell into an arm-chair, with a fresh burst of merriment, in which I joined by fits and starts; and in the midst of my sunshine and my rain I wrote this letter, which I was obliged to copy on account of the tears that blurred all the lines:

"MADAME,

"There are certain faithful and persistent admirations that only die when we die. . . . I was twelve years old when I beheld Mademoiselle Estelle for the first time at Meylan. You could not have known then how you overwhelmed that childish heart, that was ready to break beneath the disproportionate burthen of its feelings. I believe that you were even so pardonably cruel as sometimes to laugh at me. Seventeen years later, on my return from Italy, my eyes filled with tears—the silent tears of memory—when I entered our valley, and caught sight of the house where you once lived, on the romantic heights commanding St. Eynard. Some days afterwards, before I knew your new name, I was asked to deliver a letter addressed to you. I waited for Madame F—— at one of the stations of the coach by which she was travelling. I presented her with the letter; a violent shock at my heart made my hand tremble as it approached hers. I recognised the object of my first admiration, the *Stella del monte,* whose radiant beauty illuminated the morning of my life. Yesterday, madame, after long and violent agitation, after far distant travels through Europe, after labours an echo of which may perhaps have reached you, I undertook a long contemplated pilgrimage. Once more I desired to see everything, and I have done so: the little house, the garden, the avenue, the hill, the old tower, the wood, the everlasting rock, and the sublime scenery so worthy of your frequent contemplation. Nothing is changed. Time has respected the temple of my memory. But strangers inhabit it now; your flowers are cultivated by other hands, and no one in the world, not even yourself, could have guessed why a gloomy-looking man, with features furrowed by labour and sorrow, should yesterday have penetrated to its most secret recesses. O *quante lagrime!* . . .

"Farewell, madame, I must return to my whirlwind. You will probably never see me, never know who I am; and I hope you will pardon the strange liberty I am now taking in writing to you. I forgive you beforehand if you smile at the recollections of the man, as you laughed at the admiration of the child.

"DESPISED LOVE." [1]

"Grenoble, December 6th, 1848."

And notwithstanding my cousin's raillery I sent this letter. I know not what became of it. Since then I have never heard of Madame F—— again.

In a few months' time I must return to Grenoble. And then I feel I shall not be able to resist: I shall go to Vif. [2]

CHAPTER LXXVI

DEATH OF MY SISTER—AND OF MY WIFE—HER FU-NERAL—THE ODÉON—MY POSITION IN THE MUSICAL WORLD—IMPOSSIBILITY OF BRAVING THE HATRED FELT FOR ME—CABAL AT COVENT GARDEN—THE COTERIE AT THE PARIS CONSERVATOIRE—A SYM-PHONY DREAMED AND FORGOTTEN—CHARMING WEL-COME IN GERMANY—THE KING OF HANOVER—THE DUKE OF WEIMAR—THE KING OF SAXONY'S INTENDANT—MY FAREWELLS

I MUST have done with these memoirs, which I find almost as weari-some as a feuilleton. When I shall have written the few remaining

---

[1] An expression of Shakespeare's in *Hamlet*. [B.]

[2] I never went. But five years ago I heard that Madame F—— was living at Lyons. Is she still alive? I dare not find out (February, 1854).
She is still living, I find (August, 1854). [B.]

Estelle Dubœuf had married, some thirty years before this, M. Casimir Fornier, the President of the Grenoble Chamber. She was now a widow, and spent her time between Grenoble and her property at Vif. Of six children she had had, two daughters were dead; four sons were still living.

Berlioz returned to Paris about the middle of September 1848.

pages, I think I shall have said enough to give a fairly accurate idea of the principal events in my life, and of the vortex of feeling, labour, and sorrow in which I am destined to revolve, until I shall revolve no longer. The road which remains, whatever its length, must certainly strongly resemble that already passed; everywhere the same deep ruts, the same rough stones, the same broken ground, crossed here and there by some clear brook, shaded by some peaceful grove, and surmounted by some sublime rock which I shall laboriously ascend, and there bathe myself in the evening sunshine, after the cold rain endured all day in the plains. Men and things do indeed change, but so slowly that the change is hardly perceptible in the short span of human existence. To derive benefit from it, I should have to live two hundred years.

I have lost my eldest sister, Nanci.[1] She died of a cancer in the breast, after six months' terrible suffering, that forced the most heart-rending cries from her, day and night. Adèle, my other dear sister, who went to Grenoble to nurse her, and never left her till all was over, very nearly succumbed to the fatigue and distress caused by such pro-tracted agony. And no doctor dared be humane enough to put an end to her sufferings by a dose of chloroform! They give it to a patient to prevent the pain of a quarter-minute surgical operation, and yet refuse to employ it for avoiding a six months' torture, when it is certain that no remedy, not even time, can cure the terrible disease, and when death is obviously the supreme boon, deliverance, joy, happiness! . . .

But the law forbids it, and religion is not less formally opposed to it.

And no doubt she herself would have refused such deliverance had it been proposed to her. "God's will be done." As if everything that happened were not the will of God, and as if deliverance by means of a gentle and speedy death were not just as much the will of God as use-less and execrable torture! . . .

How absurd are all these questions of fatality, divinity, free-will, etc.! Endless absurdity! the human understanding reels under them, and cannot but lose itself. In any case, the most horrible thing in this world for us living and sentient beings is inexorable suffering and un-reasonable torture; and one must either be a barbarian or an idiot, or both, not to employ the sure and gentle means used in these days for ending it. The very savages are wiser and more humane.

My wife is also dead; but at any rate without any great suffering. My poor Henrietta! After being paralysed for four years, and unable

[1] May 4th, 1850.

either to move or speak, she drew her last breath at Montmartre, March 3rd, 1854. My son, then at Cherbourg, was fortunate enough to obtain leave to spend a few hours with her, only four days before her death. The interview sweetened her last moments. I, too, was fortunately in France at the time. I had left her for about two hours, and on my return all was over. . . . Her last breath had been drawn, and she was already covered with the fatal shroud, which I withdrew to kiss her pale forehead for the last time. A year before, I had given her a portrait of herself, painted in the time of her splendour, glowing with beauty and genius; now it hung beside her couch, a sad contrast to the poor disfigured form beneath it.

I will not attempt to give an idea of my grief. It was complicated by a feeling which, though never before so intense, had always been a most painful one for me to bear — *the feeling of pity*. In the midst of all my regret for our dead love, I felt almost overwhelmed by the immense, terrible, infinite pity, inspired by the recollection of my poor Henrietta's sorrows: her ruin before our marriage, her accident, the failure of her last dramatic attempt in Paris, her voluntary but ever-regretted renunciation of her adored art, her eclipsed glory, the rising fame and fortune of her mediocre imitators of both sexes, our domestic differences, her inextinguishable jealousy (in the end not unfounded), our separation, the death of all her relations, the enforced absence of her son, my long and frequent journeys, her wounded pride at being the cause of an endless expense which she knew was crushing me, the mistaken idea that the affection of the English public had been alienated from her by her love for France, her broken heart, her vanished beauty, her ruined health, her increasing bodily sufferings, the loss of speech and movement, the impossibility of making herself understood, the long vista of death and oblivion.

Destruction! Fire and thunder! Blood and tears! My brain shrivels at the thought of such horrors.

Shakespeare, Shakespeare! where art thou? He alone, of all intelligent beings, could have understood me . . . have understood us both. He alone could have looked with pity on two poor artists, at once loving and lacerating each other. Shakespeare, the true man, if he is still in existence, must know how to succour the wretched. He is our father, our father in heaven — if there be a heaven. An almighty being, wrapped in his infinite indifference, is an atrocious absurdity. Shakespeare alone is the good God to the soul of the artist. Receive us into thy bosom, O father, and hide us there. *De profundis ad te clamo!* Death, annihilation, what are they? The immortality of genius — what? "O fool, fool, fool!"

I was unaided in my sad duties. The Protestant pastor required for the ceremony lived at the other end of the town, in the Rue M. le Prince. I went to him at eight o'clock in the evening. A street being closed to traffic, my cab had to make a detour that took me past the Odéon. The theatre was lighted up for a play then in vogue. It was there I saw *Hamlet* for the first time, twenty-six years ago, when the glory of my poor dead wife suddenly burst forth like a brilliant meteor; there I saw a crowd in tears over the grief, the poetic and heart-breaking insanity of Ophelia; there I saw Henrietta Smithson, when recalled after the final catastrophe in *Hamlet* by the most critical audience in France, return trembling to acknowledge the plaudits of her admirers, almost terrified by the stupendousness of her success. There also I saw Juliet for the first and last time. How often, on winter nights, did I pace up and down under those arcades in feverish anxiety. There was the door by which I saw her enter for a rehearsal of *Othello*. She did not then even know of my existence; and had a pale, worn, obscure youth, leaning against one of the pillars of the theatre and devouring her with wild glances, been pointed out as her future husband, she would assuredly have regarded the prophet of evil as a madman.

And yet it is he who is preparing for thy last journey, poor Ophelia, he is on his way to a priest, with Laertes' words in his mouth — "What ceremonies else?" he who so tormented thee, and so suffered through thee, after having suffered for thee; he who, in spite of all his wrongs, might say like Hamlet:

Forty thousand brothers would not have loved her as I loved her.

Shakespeare! Shakespeare! Again I feel my sorrow overwhelming me like a flood, and again I seek thee:

Father! father! where art thou?

The next day, two or three of my literary friends — d'Ortigue, Brizeux, Léon de Wailly — and several artists, the good Baron Taylor, and a few other kind-hearted people, attended Henrietta to her last resting-place, *out of friendship for me*. Twenty-five years before, the whole of intelligent Paris would have attended her obsequies, in admiration and adoration of *her*. The poets, painters, and sculptors, the actors to whom she had just given such noble examples of movement, gesture, and attitude, the musicians who had felt the melody of her tender accents and the lacerating reality of her cries of anguish — lovers, dreamers, philosophers — all would then have followed her coffin in tears. . . .

And now, while she is proceeding thus almost in solitude to the cemetery, ungrateful and forgetful Paris is grovelling in its own smoke; and he who loved her but has not the courage to follow her to the grave weeps in a corner of a deserted garden; while her son, battling against the tempest far away, is rocked on the topmast of a ship on the gloomy ocean.

Hic jacet! She lies in the little cemetery of Montmartre, on the slope of the hill, her face turned towards the England she never wished to see again. Her modest tomb bears this inscription: " Henrietta Constance Berlioz-Smithson, born at Ennis, in Ireland; died at Montmartre, March 3rd, 1854."

The newspapers announced her death in cold, commonplace language. Jules Janin alone had a heart and a memory; he wrote the following lines:

" With what cruel rapidity pass away the divinities of fable! How frail they are, these frail children of Shakespeare and Corneille! Alas! it is not so very long ago, when, one summer's evening, in all the arrogance of youth, we saw her in a balcony overlooking the road to Verona, Juliet with her Romeo, Juliet, trembling in the intoxication of her happiness, listening to the nightingale of the night and the lark of the morning. She was in white, and listening dreamily, with a sublime fire in her half-averted glance. In her low, pure golden voice we heard the prose and poetry of Shakespeare ringing out in triumphant tones, instinct with undying life. A whole world was hanging on the grace, the voice, the enchanting power of this woman.

" Miss Smithson was scarcely twenty when she thus succeeded in winning the sympathy and admiration of an audience enchanted by these new verities. And thus, all unconsciously, this young woman became an unknown poem, a new passion, an absolute revolution. She it was who gave the signal to Dorval, Lemaître, Malibran, Victor Hugo, and Berlioz. She was called Juliet . . . Ophelia. Eugène Delacroix himself was inspired by her when he painted his sweet picture of

Ophelia. She is in the act of falling; one hand, though about to yield, is still clinging to the branch. With the other she presses her last garland to her lovely breast; the hem of her robe already touches the rising waters; all about is sad and gloomy; the wave that is soon to engulf her is gathering in the distance; the unhappy girl, with her sweet songs, is dragged downwards by her heavy garments to the mire and to death!

"This admirable and touching actress at length took another name, one borne also by Malibran, that of Desdemona; and the Moor as he embraced her called her his 'fair warrior.'

"I see her still, even at this distance, pale and wan as the fair Venetian of Angelo, tyrant of Padua! She is alone, listening to the rain and wind howling without, that beautiful maiden, charming and fated, whom the poet Shakespeare surrounded with all his love and respect. She is alone and in fear — her soul troubled by an inexpressible uneasiness, her arms bare, and a little of her white shoulder visible. Saintly nudity of the woman who is about to die!

"Miss Smithson was marvellous, more like a vision from on high than a creature of earth! And now she has been dead a week, still dreaming of that glory which alike came and went so swiftly! Oh, visions! oh, regrets! oh, sorrows! In my youth they used to sing a chorus in praise of Juliet Capulet. The funeral march had a desolating effect amidst the ceaseless refrain, ' Throw flowers, throw flowers!' [1] It brought one down into the gloomy cavern where Juliet lay slumbering, and the mournful melody accomplished its task as it told of the horrors of those mortuary vaults. ' Throw flowers, throw flowers! Juliet is dead,' said the funeral song, after the fashion of a chorus of Father Æschylus. ' Juliet is dead (throw flowers!), death weighs her down like frost on April grass (throw flowers!).' Thus do the instruments of the dance serve as funeral knells, the marriage supper becomes a banquet of the dead, the wedding flowers ornament a tomb." . . .

Soon afterwards Liszt sent me from Weimar an affectionate letter of the sort that he alone could write. "She inspired you," he said; " you sang of her; her task was done." . . .

I have no more to say with regard to the two great passions which

---

[1] Janin alludes here to the chorus of the funeral procession in my *Romeo and Juliet*, where, it is true, those words are constantly chanted. [B.]

influenced my heart and my intellect so long and so powerfully. The one was a memory of childhood. It comes to me radiant with smiles, adorned with all the charms of a perfect landscape, the mere sight of which was sufficient to move me. Estelle was then the hamadryad of my valley of Tempe; and at the age of twelve I experienced for the first time, and together, love and the love of nature.

The other love came to me in my manhood, with Shakespeare, in the burning bush of Sinai, amid the thunders and lightnings of poetry entirely new to me. It prostrated me, and my heart and whole being were invaded by a cruel, maddening passion, in which the love of a great artist and the love of a great art were mingled together, each intensifying the other.

The power of such an antithesis may be imagined, if indeed there be any antithesis. Between Henrietta and myself, my Meylan idyll was no secret. She knew how vividly it remained in my mind. Who has not had his first idyll? Notwithstanding her jealous temper, she had too much sense to be hurt. Indeed, she used sometimes to rally me gently on the subject.

Those who cannot understand this will still less enter into another peculiarity of my nature. I have a vague feeling of poetic love whenever I smell a rose, and for a long time past I have felt the same at sight of a beautiful harp. When I see that instrument, I can hardly restrain myself from falling on my knees and embracing it. Estelle was the rose, " left blooming alone "; Henrietta was the harp, that took part in all my concerts, in all my joys and sorrows; and of which, alas! I broke many strings.

And now, if not at the end of my career, I am at any rate on the last steep decline — exhausted, consumed, but ever ardent, and full of an energy that sometimes revolts with an almost overwhelming force. I begin to know French, to be able to write a page of music, of verse, or of prose fairly well; I can direct and inspire an orchestra; I adore and venerate art under all forms. . . . But I belong to a nation which has ceased to be interested in the nobler manifestations of intelligence, and whose only deity is the golden calf. The Parisians have become a barbarous people. In ten rich houses you will scarcely find a single library. I am not speaking of musical libraries. No; books are no longer bought. Miserable novels are hired from the circulating library at a penny per volume; such is the literary food of all classes of society. In the same way, people subscribe to the music-shop, for a few francs a month, in order to select, from the infinite commonplace rubbish of our day, some masterpiece of the sort which Rabelais has characterised by a contemptuous epithet.

The industrialism of art, followed by all the base instincts it flatters and caresses, marches at the head of an absurd procession, full of stupid disdain for its vanquished enemies.

In Paris, therefore, I can do nothing, for there I am considered only too fortunate to be able to fulfil the task of writing feuilletons — the only one, some would say, for which I was sent into the world. I know well what I could accomplish in the way of dramatic music, but it would be both useless and dangerous to attempt it. In the first place, most of our lyrical theatres are houses of ill fame, musically speaking; the Opéra especially is disgraceful. In the next place, I could not give full scope to my thoughts in this style of composition unless I felt myself to be as absolutely master in a great theatre as I am of my orchestra when conducting one of my symphonies.

I should have to be assured of the goodwill and obedience of all, from the first soprano and the first tenor, chorus, orchestra, dancers, and supernumeraries, down to the scene-painters, machinists, and stage-manager. A lyrical theatre as I take it, is first and foremost a vast musical instrument. I can play on it, but in order to play it well it must be entrusted to me without reserve. That is just what will never take place. The intrigues, conspiracies, and cabals of my enemies would have only too full scope. They dare not come and hiss me in a concert-room, but in a huge theatre like the Opéra they would not fail to do so.

Not only should I have to submit to the hostilities promoted by my criticisms, but also to the fury excited by the tendencies of my music, which, in and by itself, is exceedingly popular. They say, very truly: " The day that the public *en masse* understands or even enjoys such compositions, ours will become worthless." I had a proof of all this in London, when a band of Italians almost drove *Benvenuto Cellini* from the Covent Garden stage.[1] They cried, groaned, and hissed from first to last; they even tried to prevent the performance of the *Carnaval romain* overture, which formed the introduction to the second act, and had often been applauded at the Philharmonic Concerts and elsewhere. Public opinion at any rate, if not mine, placed Costa, the conductor of Covent Garden, at the head of this comically furious

[1] On June 25th, 1853.

cabal. I had attacked him several times in my feuilletons on the subject
of the liberties he takes with the music of the great masters, by cutting, expanding, re-instrumenting, and mutilating them in every con-
ceivable manner. If Costa is the culprit (which is not at all unlikely),
he showed rare skill at all events in lulling my suspicions by his eagerness to be of use to me during the rehearsals.

Two hundred and thirty of the London artists, indignant at this
meanness, expressed their sympathy by offering their services for a
Testimonial Concert at Exeter Hall, but this was never carried out.
Beale, the publisher, now one of my best friends, brought me a sum
of two hundred guineas from a body of amateurs, headed by Messrs.
Broadwood, the celebrated piano-makers. It would have been altogether inconsistent with French habits for me to accept this gift,
though it was dictated by genuine kindness and generosity. We are not
all Paganinis. However, I was far more touched by these proofs of
affection than wounded by the insults of the cabal.

In Germany, no doubt, I should have nothing of this sort to en-
counter. But I do not know German. I should have to compose to a
French text, which would afterwards have to be translated; and that
is an immense disadvantage. The composition of a grand opera would
also take at least a year and a half, during which time I should earn
nothing; nor should I receive any other compensation, since in Germany the composers of operas do not receive fees. Besides, the first
performance of *Faust* in Prussia shows what hostilities I had provoked among the musicians of the Berlin orchestra by a harmless observation published in the *Journal des Débats*. At Leipzig also, although my music is now heard with ears very different from those that
listened to it in Mendelssohn's time (as I saw for myself, and as I am
assured by Ferdinand David), there are still certain small fanatics,
pupils of the Conservatoire, who regard me, without knowing why,
as a destroyer, an Attila of music, and who honour me with a furious
hatred, write me insolent letters, and make faces behind my back in
the corridors of the Gewandhaus. Certain Kapellmeisters also, whose
peace I disturb, play me rather mean tricks now and then.

But this inevitable antagonism, even when joined to the perfectly
natural opposition of a small section of the German press,[1] is as noth-

[1] In the German, as in the Paris press, there are men of fixed ideas, who get into a fury at
the mere sight of my name on a placard or in a paper, like a bull at the sight of a red rag. They
attribute to me a whole world of absurdities that are hatched in their own small brains, imagine
they hear things in my works which do not exist, and do not hear what is to be heard; they fight

ing in comparison with the fury that would be vented against me in Paris if I were to be produced in the theatre.

For the last three years I have been tormented by the idea of a vast opera, of which I should write both words and music, as I did for *L'Enfance du Christ*. I am resisting the temptation, and trust I shall continue to resist it to the end.[1]

To me the subject seems magnificent and deeply touching — a sure proof that to the Parisians it would be insipid and wearisome. Even were I mistaken in attributing to them " a taste so utterly unlike my own " — to quote the great Corneille — I should never find a woman singer sufficiently clever and devoted to interpret the principal part, since it requires beauty, a great voice, real dramatic talent, perfect musicianship, and a heart and soul of fire. Still less could I hope for all the other various resources which must be absolutely at my own disposal, without let or hindrance from anyone. My blood boils at the bare notion of again encountering those senseless obstacles to the mounting of such a work, which I myself have endured, and daily see endured by other composers writing for our grand Opéra. A collision between myself and such malevolent idiots would now be full of risk. I feel quite capable of anything as far as they are concerned, and should slay the rascals like dogs.

I do not feel the least desire to add to the number of useful and agreeable works called opéras-comiques, daily turned out in Paris like tarts from the oven. In that respect I am not like the corporal in the play, whose " ambition was to be a servant." I prefer to remain a simple soldier.[2]

I must also add that Meyerbeer's influence, and the pressure exercised by his immense fortune, not less than by his *genuine* eclectic talent, on managers, artists, critics, and public alike, are such as to render any serious success at the Opéra almost impossible. That deleterious influence will probably continue to be felt ten years after his

---

windmills with a noble zeal, and if asked their opinion of the chord of D major, having been told beforehand that I had written it, they would exclaim indignantly, "A detestable chord!" Those poor wretches are maniacs; there are such, and have been such, everywhere and in all times. [B.]

[1] Alas, no! I could not resist. I have just finished the book and music of *Les Troyens*, an opera in five acts. What is to become of this huge work? . . . (1858.) [B.]

[2] A few years ago, however, notwithstanding the above, I did consent to write a work of that sort. My friend Carvalho, the Director of the Théâtre-Lyrique, had contracted, under a penalty of ten thousand francs, to give me a libretto by a stated time, which I was to set to music for his theatre. But when the time arrived, Carvalho had forgotten his engagement; and consequently that promise was no better kept than all the rest had been! [B.]

death. Henri Heine declares that he *has paid in advance*.[1] As for the
musical concerts which I might give in Paris, I have already said how
I was circumstanced, and how indifferent the public had become to
everything outside the theatre.

Meantime, the coterie of the Conservatoire has shut its doors
upon me. The Minister of the Interior came forward one day at a
distribution of prizes, and announced to the audience that this room
(the only suitable one in Paris) was the exclusive property of the
Conservatoire Society, and was not henceforth to be lent to anyone
for the purpose of concerts. " Anyone," of course, meant me, for,
with some two or three exceptions, no one but myself had given any
big musical performances there for twenty years.

That celebrated society, of which nearly all the performing members are my friends or partisans, is directed by a conductor and a small
clique who are my enemies, and who take good care not to admit the
most insignificant of my compositions into their concerts. Some six or
seven years ago, they indeed asked me for two pieces out of *Faust;*[2]
but, as if to make up for the concession, they placed them between the
finale from Spontini's *Vestale* and Beethoven's Symphony in C minor.
As good luck would have it, these gentlemen were disappointed in their
hope of crushing me, and, in spite of its formidable neighbours, the
sylph scene in *Faust* excited genuine enthusiasm, and was encored.
But M. Girard, who had conducted the work in an exceedingly dull
and awkward manner, pretended that he could not find the place in
the score, and, notwithstanding a unanimous encore, would not repeat
it. Its success, however, was none the less evident. From that time
forth my works have been avoided like the plague. Not one among
the many millionaires of Paris would ever entertain the idea of doing
anything for good music. We do not possess a single good public
concert-room, and it would never enter into the head of one of our

---

[1] I believe I have said elsewhere, and I now repeat, that Meyerbeer has not merely the luck
to have talent, but in a very high degree the talent to have luck. [B.]

[2] Berlioz is apparently referring to the Conservatoire concert of April 15th, 1849, at which
the Hungarian March and the episode of the Gnomes and Sylphs were given. Berlioz is alleged
to have been the dupe of Meyerbeer in the matter. *Le Prophète* was to be produced at the Opéra
on April 16th, and for a long time before the great day Meyerbeer had been paying his usual
flattering attentions to whoever was likely to be either useful or dangerous. Berlioz, of course,
could not be bought in the ordinary way; but Meyerbeer and Girard (who had recently succeeded
Habeneck as conductor of the Conservatoire concerts), paid the musical critic of the influential
Débats the delicate compliment of including two pieces of his in the programme of the 15th.
Their immediate purpose achieved, poor Berlioz had no more to hope for from them.

Habeneck had died on February 8th, 1849; and with Girard impregnably entrenched both at
the Opéra and the Conservatoire there was now no possible chance for Berlioz in official Paris.

Crœsuses to build one. Paganini's example was thrown away, and what that noble artist did for me will remain a unique feature in history.

To be a composer in Paris one must rely entirely on oneself, and produce works of a serious character having no connection with the theatre. One must be content with mutilated, incomplete, uncertain, and consequently more or less imperfect performances, for want of rehearsals for which one cannot pay;[1] inconvenient and uncomfortable rooms; annoyances of all sorts arising from the necessity of employing the players from the theatres, which have of course to consider the interests of their repertory.

One has to endure the robbery of the tax-collectors for the *droits des hospices,* who never take into account the expenses of the concert, and aggravate one's loss by deducting their eighth from the gross receipts. One has further to hear hasty and, necessarily, false judgments on complicated works heard under these conditions, and seldom heard more than once or twice; and, last of all, one has to spend a great deal of time and money, to say nothing of the strength of mind and will which it is humiliating to have to use against such obstacles. The artist, however gifted he may be with these qualities, is therefore like a loaded shell, which goes straight to its point and overthrows everything on its way, but is doomed to burst and perish at the end of its course. Speaking generally, I would make every possible sacrifice; but there are circumstances in which sacrifice ceases to be generous, and becomes in the highest degree culpable.

Two years ago, before my wife's health had become hopeless and when it was the cause of great expense to me, I dreamt that I was composing a symphony. On awaking next morning I recollected nearly the whole of the first movement, which I can still remember was an allegro in 2 time, in the key of A minor.

I had gone to my table to begin writing it down when I suddenly reflected: " If I write this part I shall let myself be carried on to write the rest. The natural tendency of my mind to expand the material is sure to make it very long. I may perhaps spend three or four months exclusively upon it (I took seven to write *Romeo and Juliet*); meantime I shall do no feuilletons, or next to none, and my income will suffer. When

---

[1] The most absurd theatrical puppet-show is rehearsed nearly every day for a month, while I had to produce my *Romeo and Juliet* in public after four rehearsals, and many other works after only two. [B.]

the symphony is finished I shall be weak enough to allow my copyist to copy it out, and thus immediately incur a debt of one thousand or twelve hundred francs. Once the parts are copied I shall be harassed by the temptation to have the work performed; I shall give a concert, in which, as is sure to be the case in these days, the receipts will barely cover half the expenses; I shall lose what I have not got; I shall want the necessaries of life for my poor invalid, and shall have no money either for myself or for my son's keep on board ship!" These thoughts made me shudder! I threw down my pen, saying, " Bah! I shall have forgotten the symphony to-morrow." But the following night the obstinate symphony again presented itself, and I distinctly heard the allegro in A minor, and, what was more, saw it written down. I awoke in a state of feverish agitation, and hummed the theme. The form and character of it pleased me extremely; I was about to rise . . . but the reflections of the preceding night again restrained me. I hardened myself against temptation. I clung to the hope of forgetting. At last I fell asleep again, and when I awoke next day all recollection had vanished for ever.

Some young fanatic — whose contempt I forgive beforehand — will say: "Coward! you should have dared! You should have written! You should have ruined yourself! You have no right thus to banish thought, to force back into nothingness a work of art that is striving to escape from it into life!" Ah, my young friend, you, who call me a coward, would be less severe if you saw the sight that was then too constantly before my eyes. In early days, when the consequences of my bold ventures were still doubtful, I never hesitated. At that time there was a small select audience in Paris. The princes of the house of Orleans and the Queen herself took an interest in music. My wife was then in her prime, and was ever the first to encourage me. " You ought to bring out this work," she would say, " and have it worthily and grandly performed. Fear nothing, we will bear whatever it may cost us. We must! Go on!" And I did go on. But at the time of my dream, when she was lying there half-dead, only able to groan, and requiring three nurses and an almost daily visit from the doctor; when I was certain — as absolutely certain as that the Parisians are barbarians — that every musical enterprise of mine would have the disastrous ending I have just described, it was no cowardice to abstain. No! my conscience tells me that I was simply humane; and while convinced that I am quite as much devoted to art as yourself or anyone else, I believe that I honour it by not treating it as a monster greedy for human victims, and by proving that it has not left me so wholly devoid of reason as not to be capable of distinguishing courage from ferocity. If I have gradually yielded to the allurements of music in writing my sacred trilogy *L'Enfance du Christ,* it is because my position is no longer the same, and that I am no longer bound by such imperative duties. I am also certain to have this work easily and frequently performed in Germany, where I often go, where indeed I have made four journeys in the last year and a half.[1]

My welcome there is heartier every time I go; the German artists are more and more sympathetic. At Leipzig, Dresden, Hanover, Brunswick, Weimar, Carlsruhe, and Frankfort I am overwhelmed with marks of friendship for which I can find no adequate expression of gratitude. On the public also, the intendants of the royal theatres and ducal orchestras, and most of the ruling princes, I can bestow nothing but the highest praise. The charming young King of Hanover and the Queen, his Antigone,[2] were so interested in my music that they used to come to my rehearsals at eight o'clock in the morning, and would sometimes remain there till noon, the better to penetrate, as the King lately said, into the inner meaning of the work, and become familiar with the novelty of the details. He was enthusiastic in his admiration of my *King Lear* overture: " Magnificent, M. Berlioz, magnificent; your orchestra speaks, you have no need of words. I have followed each scene: the entrance of the king into the council-chamber, the storm on the heath, the terrible prison scenes, and the laments of Cordelia. Oh! that Cordelia! how you have painted her! so tender and so timid! it is heartrending, and how beautiful!" [3]

When I last visited Hanover, the Queen begged me to insert two pieces from *Romeo and Juliet* in my programme; one in particular which was a great favourite of hers — the love-scene. The King afterwards formally requested me to return in the winter, to superintend the performance of the whole of *Romeo and Juliet,* which had been

---

[1] Since writing the above, M. Bénazet, the manager at Baden, has urged me more than once to organise and conduct the annual festival there, with everything I could desire for the performance of my works. His generosity far surpassed anything ever done for me by those European sovereigns to whom I have the most reason to be grateful. "I give you *carte blanche,*" he said again this year. "Get all the artists you want from wherever you please, and make any terms you like. I consent to everything beforehand." [B.]

[2] The King of Hanover is blind. [B.]

[3] I never saw my Henrietta in that part, which I can well believe to have been one of her sublimest, but I have heard her recite some of the scenes. [B.]

then only partially given. " If you do not find our resources sufficient," added he, " you shall have artists from Brunswick, Hamburg, and even Dresden."

The new Grand Duke of Weimar said, as I was leaving after my last visit: " Give me your hand, M. Berlioz, that I may press it with sincere and warm admiration; and never forget that the Weimar Theatre is always open to you." Herr von Lüttichau, Intendant to the King of Saxony, offered me the post of Kapellmeister at Dresden on its approaching vacancy. " If you would take it " (I quote his own words), " what grand things we would do with our artists, whom you think so first-rate and who are so fond of you, you who conduct as so few can. Dresden would become the musical centre of Germany." I do not know whether I shall decide on settling in Saxony when the moment comes. . . . It is a matter for much consideration. Liszt is of opinion that I ought to accept. My friends in Paris think differently. I have not made up my mind, and besides, the post is not yet vacant. They are now proposing at Dresden to bring out my *Cellini,* which has already been revived at Weimar by the admirable Liszt.

In that case I must certainly superintend the first performances. But I will not now occupy myself with the future; indeed, I have already expatiated too much on the past, though many curious episodes and sad details are still left untold. I end . . . with fervent thanks to that sacred Germany where the worship of art is still kept pure; to generous England; to Russia, who saved me; to all my kind friends in France; and to all the noble hearts and lofty minds that I have ever known in any nation. I am happy to have known you, and I shall always retain the most tender recollections of our relations. And as for you madmen, more stupid than dogs or bulls, my Guildensterns, my Rosencranzes, my Iagos, my precious Osrics, you reptiles and insects of every species, farewell . . . my friends; I despise you all, and trust to have forgotten you before I die.

Paris, October 18th, 1854.

As has been shown in the Foreword to the present edition of the *Mémoires*, Belioz worked at the compilation of the book in the most haphazard way imaginable. Four-fifths of it had been put together, for the most part out of material that had already appeared in print, by the autumn of 1848. From that time onward not only is there no attempt on Berlioz's part to make the record complete, but he is careless as to the proper sequence of the few events he takes the trouble to narrate. The six years between 1848 and 1854 saw him steadily declining in health — he was practically an old man at fifty — losing heart in the ever more and more hopeless struggle against the apathy of Paris, the rising Philistinism of the epoch, and the enmity of the other French musicians, and consuming himself in futile rage against a world of imbeciles and scoundrels. He saw each of the Paris theatres closed to him, while the crowd flocked every night to the operas of Meyerbeer and of the crowd of mediocrities who followed in his wake. He saw himself excluded from each position of musical power and profit as a vacancy occurred. He saw himself again and again passed over when death or some other cause removed a member of the Institut, the coveted chair being given to an Ambroise Thomas (succeeding Spontini), a Reber (succeeding Onslow), a Clapisson (succeeding Halévy). He could give his own occasional concerts in Paris only by a terrific expenditure of money and energy. Till the liquidation of his father's estate in 1854 he had practically no income but that of his librarianship at the Conservatoire and the proceeds of his feuilletons, plus an occasional windfall from a concert or two in Germany or an engagement in London. With two establishments to maintain, in one of which the paralysed Harriet needed constant medical care and nursing, and with his son to be floated on a career, he could stave off ruin only by incessant journalism. He wrote magnificently, with an endless stream of wit, humour, cynicism, gaiety, and even seriousness when the occasion called for it; but this drudgery left him with little time or energy for composition. He had had, in fact, the imprudence to be born into a not very musical nation in one of its least truly musical periods; and France could find no better use for its greatest composer than to keep him listening to, and scribbling about, the passing trivialities of the ordinary musical life of a big city. The composer of the *Symphonie fantastique*, the *Harold in Italy*, the *Romeo and Juliet*, the *Damnation of Faust*, had to run round night after night reporting the doings of composers who were not fit to black his boots, of conductors who were the merest journeymen in comparison with himself, and of the eternal succession of singers and fiddlers and pianists and all the other small fry of music.

In the first edition (1917) of his life of Berlioz, Julius Kapp gives us a complete list (omitted from the later editions for reasons of economy) of the composer's articles in the *Débats* and elsewhere, from 1823 to 1863. I reproduce the titles of a few of them during these years 1848 to 1854, to give the reader some notion of the causes that led to the concentrated bitterness that finds expression in what he intended to be the final chapter of his biography (chapter LXXVI of the present edition).

1848
An account of the opening of the Théâtre de la Nation.
Notices of the first performances of Clapisson's *Jeanne la folle*, Saint-Georges' *Le Val d'Andorre*, and Bordèse's *Les deux Bambins*.

1849
Notices of Ambroise Thomas's *Le Caïd*, Limnander's *Les Monténégrins*, Meyerbeer's *Le Prophète*, Reber's *La Nuit de Noël*, Adolphe Adam's *Le Toréador*, Bazin's *La Saint-Sylvestre*, Donizetti's *Dom Sébastien*, Halévy's *La Fée aux roses*, Maillart's *Le Moulin des tilleuls*, Adam's *Le Fanal*, and a Mass by Niedermeyer.

1850
Notices of Grisar's *Porcherons*, Thomas's *Songe d'une nuit d'été*, Adam's *Giralda*, Massé's *La Chanteuse voilée*, Auber's *L'enfant prodigue*.

1851
Notices of Halévy's *Dame de pique*, Grisard's *Bonsoir, M. Pantalon*, Rosenhain's *Démon de la nuit*, Gounod's *Sappho*, Thalberg's *Florinda*, St. Jullien's *Serafina*, Boisselot's *Mosquita la sorcière*, Gautier and Heller's *Murdock le bandit*, David's *Perle du Brésil*, Limnander's *La Château de la Barbe-bleue*.

1852
Notices of Boïeldieu's *Le Butte des moulins*, Déjazet's *Le Mariage en l'air*, Grisard's *Le Carillonneur de Bruges*, Villeblanche's *Les Fiançailles des roses*, Adam's *La Poupée de Nuremberg*, Maillart's *La Croix de Marie*, Cadaux's *Les deux Jaket*, Reber's *Père Gaillard*, Gautier's *Flore et Zéphire*, Clapisson's *Les Mystères d'Udolphe*, Auber's *Marco Spada*.

1853
Notices of Verdi's *Luise Miller*, Gastinel's *Le Miroir*, Grisar's *Les Amours du Diable*, Thomas's *La Tonelli*, Prudent's *La Danse des Fées*, Niedermeyer's *La Fronde*, Adam's *Le Roi de Hall*, Duprez's *La Lettre au bon Dieu*, Halévy's *Le Nabab*, Vogel's *La Moissonneuse*, Poise's *Le Voisin*, Adam's *Le Bijou perdu*.

1854

Notices of Bénoit's *Betly*, Meyerbeer's *L'Étoile du Nord*, Boïeldieu's *La Fille invisible*, Clapisson's *La Promise*, Massé's *La Fiancée du Diable*, Reyer's *Maître Wolfram*, Duprato's *Les Trovatelles*, Boulanger's *Les Sabots de la Marquise*, Gevaert's *Le Billet de Marguerite*, Gounod's *La Nonne sanglante*.

In addition to all this, notices of operatic revivals, of concerts, of virtuosi, and articles on general subjects! Paris looked calmly on while the best musical brain in the country was prostituted, year in and year out, to trash and futilities and inanities of this kind. Rightly understood, Berlioz's story is in some respects the most pitiful in the whole annals of music.

The following is a summary of the main events in his outward life between 1848 and 1854.

In January 1849 he began his *Te Deum*, in the hope that it would be chosen for some public ceremonial—a hope that was not fulfilled. He completed it in the following October.

Towards the end of the year, a few friends joined with him in the founding of a Société Philharmonique, mainly for the performance of his own works. It commenced operations on February 19th, 1850, and gave concerts once a month during the winter months of that year and the next. The public was indifferent, there were constant difficulties as regards the engagement of orchestra and chorus, many of the performances, by reason of poor material and insufficient rehearsal, must have been mediocre, and the Society came to an end in November 1851.

In May 1851 he went to London, accompanied by Marie Recio, to perform his duties as a member of the jury at the Great Exhibition. It is to his experiences on this occasion that we owe some of the best chapters of the *Soirées de l'orchestre*. Returning to Paris in July, he recast *Benvenuto Cellini* for a revival of the work projected by Liszt in Weimar; the performance took place on March 20th, 1852. By that time Berlioz was in London, whither he had gone, at the end of January, to assume the conductorship of the New Philharmonic Society, founded by the publisher Beale and others as a rival to the Philharmonic Society already existing. He and Marie stayed at 10 Old Cavendish Street. The first concert took place on March 24th. At the third concert he had a piquant experience; his ancient love Camille Pleyel, who had once moved him to thoughts of murder and suicide, was the soloist in Weber's Concertstück.

He returned to Paris about the end of June, and in November went to Weimar, where a "Berlioz Week" was held in his honour, *Benvenuto Cellini* being given on the 17th and 21st of the month, while at a concert on the 20th the whole of *Romeo and Juliet* and the first two parts of *Faust* were performed. In December he published the *Soirées de l'orchestre*. The book had a success that was mortifying for Berlioz: it was yet another proof that the unmusical French public thought more highly of the journalist than of the composer.

In March 1853, his father's estate still being unliquidated, and the settlement of his son in life being a pressing problem for him, he was compelled to sell the as yet unpublished *Faust* for the derisory sum of 700 francs. In May he was once more in London, where, on June 1st, he conducted for the "Old" Philharmonic Society a concert of his own music. On June 25th *Benvenuto Cellini* was given at Covent Garden by Italian singers, in an Italian version, and failed unmistakably. He returned to Paris in July.

It was only abroad that he could find appreciation; and no doubt it was only his limited acquaintance with English and German that stood in the way of his obtaining a more or less permanent post as conductor in some foreign town. He seems to have found a new admirer about this time in Bénazet, the proprietor of the gaming concession at Baden-Baden. There he went, for the first time, in August of this year, to conduct part of *Faust* and the *Carnaval romain* overture on the 11th. Concerts at Frankfort followed on the 20th and 29th, and after a stay of a few weeks in Paris he set off once again for Germany, conducting at Brunswick on October 22nd and 25th, at Hanover on October 28th and November 8th and 15th, at Bremen on the 22nd, and at Leipzig on December 1st and 10th. On the latter occasion he gave the *Fuite en Egypt*, a new work which ultimately became the second section of the oratorio *L'Enfance du Christ*. He repeated the performance in Paris on the 18th, at a concert of the Société Sainte-Cécile. The unexpected simplicity of style revealed in this work brought it immediate popularity, and the piano score of it soon found a publisher. Berlioz at once planned a prelude and a sequel to it, but, fretted as he was with his journalistic work, it was not until July, 1854 that he could complete the other two portions—*Le Songe d'Hérode* and *L'Arrivée à Saïs*.

Harriet died on March 3rd, 1854, and on the 26th Berlioz and Marie set out on another

German expedition; concerts were given at Hanover (April 1st), Brunswick (April 3rd), and Dresden (April 22nd, 26th, 29th, and May 1st). Marie did him a great deal of harm by her venomous jealousy of other composers, particularly of Wagner. It so happened that most of the intelligent musicians in Germany who admired Berlioz were also ardent partisans of the other great innovator of the day; and Marie's angry screechings against the man in whom she saw nothing but a dangerous rival and a false friend to Hector tried the temper and the tact of people like Bülow severely.

Faust was published in October 1854, and about the same time Berlioz completed what he then intended to be the final pages of his autobiography. He first added the chapter (LXX) dealing with the failure of *Faust* in 1846, the story of his visit to Russia, and Chapter LXXIV, dealing with his experiences with Jullien in London in 1847–48. Chapter LXII had been written before this. He went to the Côte in September 1854 to arrange with his co-inheritors for the sale of the father's property, added Chapter LXXVI, in which he describes the death of Harriet and pours out the flood of his hatred for the French public that had no use for him, gave the seemingly complete work the date "October 18th, 1854," and the next day legalised his position with Marie Recio by a marriage.

On December 10th the complete *L'Enfance du Christ* received its first performance, in the Salle Herz in Paris. The work was repeated on the 24th, and again on the following 28th January, on which occasion Berlioz also produced a new cantata, *Le Dix Décembre*, which afterwards received the title of *L'Impériale.*

At the end of January 1855 Berlioz went once more to the appreciative Hanover, where *L'Enfance du Christ* was given on February 3rd. A week later he and Marie were in Weimar with Liszt, from whom and the Princess von Sayn-Wittgenstein the composer received the impulse that was to lead to the composition of *Les Troyens.*

POSTSCRIPT

LETTER TO M. ———, ACCOMPANYING THE MS. OF MY MEMOIRS, IN REPLY TO HIS REQUEST FOR NOTES FOR MY BIOGRAPHY[1]

SIR, you wish to know the grounds for the opposition I have encountered in Paris as a composer for five-and-twenty years. They are many in number, but happily they have now partially disappeared.[2]

The kindly feeling of the whole press (always excepting the *Revue des Deux Mondes,* whose musical critic is a monomaniac, and whose editor honours me with his hatred), on the occasion of my latest work, *L'Enfance du Christ,* seems to prove the fact. In that work many people imagined that they could detect a radical change in my style and manner. This opinion is entirely without foundation. The subject naturally lent itself to a gentle and simple style of music, and for that reason alone was more in accordance with their taste and intelligence. Time would probably have developed these qualities, but I

[1] He took good care not to make use of them. His book is full of absurd anecdotes and extravagant eulogies. [B.]

[2] They have returned in full force, and the opposition is more inveterate than ever. [B.]

should have written *L'Enfance du Christ* in the same style twenty years ago.

The principal reason for the long war waged against me lies in the antagonism existing between my musical feeling and that of the great mass of the Parisian public. Many looked upon me as a madman, because I considered them children or simpletons. All music deviating from the beaten track of the manufacturers of opéras-comiques necessarily seemed to these people the music of madmen, just as Beethoven's Ninth Symphony and colossal pianoforte sonatas are to them the compositions of a lunatic.

In the next place, the professors of the Conservatoire were against me, stirred up by Cherubini and Fétis, whose self-love and faith had alike been rudely disturbed by my heterodoxy in the matter of harmony and rhythm. In music I am a sceptic, or, to speak more correctly, I belong to the religion of Beethoven, Weber, Gluck, and Spontini, who believed and proved through their works, that *everything is good* or that *everything is bad;* the effect produced by a combination being that which alone ought to sanction or condemn it. Nowadays even the professors most obstinately bent on maintaining the authority of the old rules allow themselves more or less latitude in their works.

Among my adversaries were also the partisans of the Italian sensualist school, whose doctrines and whose gods I have often attacked and blasphemed.

I am more prudent now. I still abhor those operas which the public accept as masterpieces of dramatic art, though to my mind they are vile caricatures of passion and feeling; but I have acquired sufficient self-control not to speak of them. Still, my position as a critic continues to make me many enemies. And those who hate me most fiercely are not so often those whom I have blamed as those of whom I have not spoken, or have praised faintly. Others will never forgive certain pleasantries of mine. Eighteen or twenty years ago I was imprudent enough to make fun of a very dull little work of Rossini's. It consists of three pieces, entitled *La Foi, l'Espérance, et la Charité.* After hearing them, I said that *"his Hope had deceived ours, his Faith would never remove mountains, and as for his Charity, it would never ruin him."* It is not difficult to imagine the fury of the Rossinists, although I had also written a long laudatory analysis of *Guillaume Tell,* and repeated *ad nauseam* that the *Barbiere* was one of the finest works of this century.

Panseron having sent me an absurd prospectus, announcing in very vulgar French the opening of a musical consulting office, where amateur composers might have their songs corrected for the sum of a hundred francs, I published the affair in the *Journal des Débats,* printing the prospectus in full, under the title of :

Consulting Room for Secret Melodies.

Some years ago M. Caraffa had an opera performed, entitled *La Grande Duchesse,* of which but two representations were given. Being obliged to give an account of the second, I confined myself to quoting Bossuet's celebrated words over Henrietta Maria of England : "*Madame se meurt. Madame est morte.*" M. Caraffa never forgave me. — I must confess, also, that I have sometimes used words in the course of conversation which might fairly be taken for regular sword thrusts. One evening I was at d'Ortigue's house with several others, among them M. de Lamennais and a clerk in the Ministry of the Interior ; the conversation turned upon the discontent felt by everyone with his own circumstances. M. P——, the clerk, was not at all dissatisfied with his : " I would rather be what I am," said he, " than anything else." " For my part," said I thoughtlessly, " I am not like you ; I would rather be anything than what you are." My interlocutor had sufficient self-command to make no retort, but I am quite sure that our roars of laughter, especially those of Lamennais, must have rankled in his heart.

For some years past I have had fresh enemies owing to my supposed superiority in conducting an orchestra. Nearly every conductor in Germany has been made my enemy through the players, owing to their extraordinary success under my baton, their too eager demonstrations and their careless expressions in my favour. It was the same in Paris for a long time. You will see in my memoirs the effects of this kind of thing on Girard and Habeneck. In London, Costa does me secret injuries wherever he can.

You will admit that I have had a fine phalanx to fight, without mentioning the singers and the virtuosi, whom I always call brusquely to order when they take irreverent liberties with the music, or the envious beings who are always ready to be exasperated at anything more brilliant than themselves.

Yet this life of combat is not without a certain charm when opposition has come down to reasonable proportions, as it has now. I often find it pleasanter to smash through a gate than to jump it.

But this is the natural result of my passion for music — a passion which is always at white heat, and never satisfied for more than a moment or two. With this passion love of money has never, under any circumstances, anything to do; on the contrary, I had never any difficulty in making any kind of sacrifice in pursuit of the beautiful, or in keeping clear of the miserable commonplaces which are the delight of the crowd. Offer me a fortune to compose some of the most popular works of the day, and I should refuse it angrily. It is my nature. It is not difficult to understand what results from such an organisation as this, placed in an atmosphere like that of the musical world in Paris twenty years ago.

I should have no difficulty in sketching the reverse side of the picture, though it might be at the expense of modesty. The sympathy I have encountered in France, England, Germany, and Russia has consoled me for many troubles. I might even mention some very singular instances of enthusiasm, such as Paganini's royal gift and the cordially artistic letter accompanying it.

But I will confine myself to repeating a charming saying of Lipinski's at Dresden three years ago. After a splendid performance of my *Faust*, Lipinski brought me a musician who wished to congratulate me, but did not know a word of French. As I was equally ignorant of German, Lipinski was about to act as interpreter, when he was interrupted by the artist himself, who rushes forward, takes me by the hand, stammers out some words, and bursts into a flood of tears. Lipinski then, turning to me and pointing to his friend's emotion, said simply: " You understand! "

I will quote another saying, quite antique in its turn. It was at Brunswick, where a selection from *Romeo and Juliet* was to be given in the theatre. On the morning of the concert a stranger,[1] sitting next me at the *table d'hôte,* informed me that he had taken a long journey in order to hear my work.

" You should write an opera on that subject," said he. " From the way in which you have treated it as a symphony, and your evident

[1] Baron von Donop, chamberlain to the Prince of Lippe-Detmold. [B.]

sympathy with Shakespeare, you would do something marvellous in an opera."

"Alas!" I answered, "where am I to find artists capable of singing and playing the two principal parts? They don't exist; and even supposing they did, thanks to the musical manners and customs now prevalent in all the lyrical theatres, if I were to succeed in getting my work put into rehearsal I should certainly be dead before the first production."

That evening my amateur went to the concert, and in conversation during the interval repeated what I had said as to an opera. His neighbour was silent for a moment; then, violently striking the ledge of the box, he exclaimed: "Very well! Let him die! but let him write the opera!"

Allow me, Sir, to assure you of my warm gratitude for your kind feeling towards me, and for your desire to avenge me (according to your own expression) on so much injustice. I believe that vengeance must be left to time. He is the great avenger, and the people and things of which I have so long had, and still have, to complain are not worthy of your anger.

Hitherto I have said nothing of my manner of writing from the technical point of view; you may perhaps like a few details on the subject.

Generally speaking, my style is very bold, but it has not the slightest tendency to subvert any of the constituent elements of art. On the contrary, it is my endeavour to add to their number. I never dreamt of making music *without melody*, as so many in France are stupid enough to say. Such a school now exists in Germany, and I hold it in detestation. It is easy to see that, without confining myself to a short air for the theme of a piece, as the great masters often do, I have always taken care that my compositions shall be rich in melody. The value of the melodies, their distinction, novelty, and charm, may of course be disputed. It is not for me to estimate them; but to deny their existence is unfair and absurd. But as they are often on a very large scale, an immature or unappreciative mind cannot properly distinguish their forms; or they may be joined to other secondary melodies, which are invisible to that class of mind; and lastly, such melodies are so unlike the little absurdities to which that term is applied by the lower stratum of the musical world, that it finds it impossible to give the same name to both.

The prevailing characteristics of my music are passionate expression, intense ardour, rhythmical animation, and unexpected turns. When I say passionate expression, I mean an expression determined on enforcing the inner meaning of its subject, even when that subject is the contrary of passion, and when the feeling to be expressed is gentle and tender, or even profoundly calm. This is the sort of expression that has been discovered in the *Enfance du Christ,* the *Ciel* scene in the *Damnation de Faust,* and the *Sanctus* of the *Requiem.*

A propos to the *Requiem,* I will mention a class of ideas which I have been almost the only modern composer to deal with, and the mere import of which has entirely escaped the older writers. I refer to the enormous compositions which some critics have called architectural or monumental music, and which made Heine speak of me as a " colossal nightingale or gigantic lark; a creature of the antediluvian world." " Berlioz's music," he continues, "has for me, generally, something primitive, if not antediluvian, about it. It makes me think of vast mammoths or other extinct monsters; of fabulous empires filled with fabulous crimes, of enormous impossibilities heaped one on the other. He is a magician, and he calls up Babylon, the hanging gardens of Semiramis, the marvels of Nineveh, the audacious temples of Mizraim, as we see them in the pictures of the Englishman Martin."

In the same paragraph of his *Lutèce* he continues his comparison of me with the eccentric painter, and declares that I have *little melody* and *no simplicity.* Three weeks after the appearance of *Lutèce,* the first performance of the *Enfance du Christ* took place, and the next day I received a letter from Heine, written from his bed of suffering, in which he expresses his deep regret at having judged me so falsely. " *I hear on all sides,*" he writes, " *that your oratorio is a perfect bouquet of sweet flowers of melody, and a masterpiece of simplicity. I shall never forgive myself for having been so unjust to a friend.*" I called on him, and as he was beginning again to blame himself I said: " But why did you act so like an ordinary critic in allowing yourself to express a positive opinion about an artist of whose works as a whole you know so little? You are always thinking of the *Sabbat,* the *Marche au Supplice,* the *Dies Iræ,* and the *Lacrymosa.* And yet I think I have done, and can do, things of a totally different character from those." The musical problems I have tried to solve in these works, and which led Heine astray, are exceptional, and require exceptional methods. In the *Requiem,* for example, I employ four distinct brass orchestras, answering each other at certain distances round the main orchestra and chorus. In the *Te Deum*, the organ at one end of the church answers the orchestra and two choirs at the other, whilst a third large choir represents the mass of the people, taking part from time to time in a vast sacred concert. But it is more especially the form of the pieces, the breadth of style, and the deliberateness of certain progressions, the goal of which is not at once perceived, that give those works their strange gigantic physiognomy and colossal aspect. The result of this immensity of form is, that either one entirely misses the drift of the whole, or is crushed by a tremendous emotion. At many performances of the *Requiem* I have seen one man listening in terror, shaken to the very depths of his soul, while his next neighbour could not catch an idea, though trying with all his might to do so. The latter was in the position of the tourists who go inside the statue of St. Carlo Borromeo at Como, and are afterwards told, to their surprise, that the room in which they have just been sitting is the inside of the saint's head.

My " architectural " works are : the *Symphonie funèbre et triomphale,* for two orchestras and chorus ; the *Te Deum,* the *Judex crederis* of which is, without doubt, my most grandiose creation ; the cantata for two choirs (*L'Impériale*), performed at the concerts in the Palace of Industry in 1855, and, above all, the *Requiem.* As for such of my compositions as are conceived on an ordinary scale, and require no exceptional means of execution, it is just their inward fire, their expression, and their rhythmical originality, that have been most injurious to them, on account of the kind of execution they demand. To render them properly, the performers, and especially the conductor, ought to *feel* as I do. They require a combination of extreme precision and irresistible *verve,* a regulated vehemence, a dreamy tenderness, and an almost morbid melancholy, without which the principal features of my figures are either altered or completely effaced. It is therefore, as a rule, exceedingly painful to me to hear my compositions conducted by anyone but myself. I thought I should have had a fit when I heard the *King Lear* overture conducted at Prague by a Kapellmeister of indisputable talent. It was *all-but* right ; but then, the *all-but* made it entirely wrong. You will see in the chapter on *Benvenuto Cellini* how I suffered from Habeneck's unintentional mistakes, during the long protracted massacre of my work in rehearsal.

If you ask me which of my pieces I prefer, my answer is that of most artists : the love-scene in *Romeo and Juliet.* One day, at Hanover, at the end of that piece, I felt myself pulled from behind; and turning round, found that the musicians round the desk were kissing my coat-tails. But I should take good care never to play that movement in certain concert-rooms, or to certain audiences. . . .

With regard to French prejudice against me, I might also remind you of the story of the Shepherds' Chorus in *L'Enfance du Christ,* performed at two concerts under the name of Pierre Ducré, an imaginary composer of the eighteenth century. How its *simple melody* was praised! How many said: " Berlioz could never have written a thing like that! "

One evening in a drawing-room, a song bearing Schubert's name was sung to an amateur who was imbued with a pious horror of my music. " How good! " he exclaimed; " what melody, what feeling, clearness and sense! Berlioz could never have composed that! " It was Cellini's song in the second act of my opera.

A dilettante once complained at a party that he had been humbugged in a most unpleasant way under the following circumstances:

" I went one morning," he said, " to a rehearsal of the concert of the Société Sainte-Cécile, conducted by M. Seghers. I heard a brilliant orchestral piece, extremely spirited, but differing essentially, both in style and instrumentation, from any symphony that I knew. I went up to M. Seghers, and said: ' What is that fascinating overture you have just been playing? '

" ' That is the overture to the *Carnaval romain,* by Berlioz.'

" ' You will admit ' " . . . I said.

" ' Yes, yes,' " said one of my friends, cutting him short, " ' we agree that it is a shame to take in an honest man in that way.' "

In France, as elsewhere, I have been unanimously regarded as an expert in the art of instrumentation, especially since the publication of my treatise on the subject. But I am accused of making excessive use of Sax's instruments — no doubt because I have often praised him as an able and skilful maker. But I have never employed them till now, except in one scene of the *Prise de Troie,* an opera of which no one has yet seen a single page. I have also been reproached with being excessively noisy, and with a love for the big-drum, which I only use in a very few pieces, where there is good reason for it. In fact, I alone, of all the critics, have obstinately protested, for twenty years past, against the revolting abuse of noise, and the senseless use of the big-drum, trombones, etc., in small theatres, small orchestras, small operas, and small songs, where even the side-drum is now employed.

Rossini, in the *Siege of Corinth,* was the man who really introduced noisy instrumentation into France; but French critics never mention him in connection with this subject; nor do they ever reproach Auber, Halévy, Adam, and a score of others with their odious exaggeration of Rossini's system; but they do reproach me, and, more absurd still, Weber (see Michaut's *Life of Weber* in the *Biographie universelle*) — Weber, who only employed the big-drum *once* in his orchestra, and used all instruments with matchless reserve and skill!

As far as I myself am concerned I think that the cause of this absurd mistake is due to my having been so often seen to conduct immense orchestras at the great festivals. For instance, Prince Metternich once said to me, at Vienna:

" Is it not you who compose music for five hundred players? "

To which I answered:

" Not always, monseigneur; I sometimes write for four hundred and fifty."

But what matter? my scores are now published, and it is easy to check my statements. And if not, again what matter?

> I remain, my dear Sir,
> Yours faithfully,
> HECTOR BERLIOZ

Paris, May 25th, 1858.

SUPPLEMENT

I HAVE FINISHED — THE INSTITUTE — CONCERTS AT THE PALAIS DE L'INDUSTRIE — JULLIEN — THE DIAPASON OF ETERNITY — "LES TROYENS" IN PARIS — "BÉATRICE ET BÉNÉDICT" AT BADEN AND WEIMAR — — EXCURSION TO LÖWENBERG — CONCERTS AT THE CONSERVATOIRE — FESTIVAL AT STRASBURG — DEATH OF MY SECOND WIFE — CEMETERIES — TO THE DEVIL WITH EVERYTHING!

IT is nearly ten years since I finished the foregoing memoirs, and these years have been nearly as gravely eventful for me as those

already described. Some account of them should therefore be given
once and for all.

My career is ended — " Othello's occupation's gone." I compose
no more music, conduct no more concerts, no longer write either prose
or verse. I have resigned my post as critic. All my musical undertak-
ings are finished; I have no desire to do anything more. And all I now
do is to read, meditate, struggle against deadly weariness, and suffer
ceaseless agonies from incurable neuralgia. To my great surprise I
have been elected member of the Academy,[1] and if my occasional
speeches in my place there produce no result, I am at any rate on the
most friendly, and even charming, terms with my colleagues.

I could tell many anecdotes of Gluck's Orfeo and Alceste,[2] which
I was commissioned to produce at the Théâtre-Lyrique and the Opéra
respectively; but I have already said enough on this subject in my book,
Á travers Chants, and what there is to add, I prefer to keep to myself.

Through Prince Napoleon I received an offer to organise a huge
concert in the Industrial Exhibition, on the day of the grand distribution of prizes by the Emperor.[3] I accepted this hard task, at the same
time declining all pecuniary responsibility. This was undertaken by
M. Ber, a clever and enterprising contractor. He treated me with generosity; and on this occasion the concerts (for there were several more
after the official ceremony) brought me in nearly eight thousand
francs. I had placed twelve hundred musicians in a gallery behind the
throne, where they were scarcely heard. But on the day itself the musical effect was of so little importance that I was interrupted in the middle of the cantata — L'Impériale — which I had written for the
occasion, and was forced to stop the orchestra at the most interesting
point, because the Prince had to make his speech, and the music was
going on too long. . . . The next day the paying public was admitted,
and seventy-five thousand francs were taken. Meantime we had lowered the orchestra and arranged it at the bottom of the hall, where
it produced an excellent effect. This time the cantata was not interrupted, and I got to the end of my grand musical firework. An engineer from Brussels constructed an electric metronome for me, with
five branches. By the simple movement of one finger of my left hand,

---

[1] This goal, so dear to the heart of a Frenchman, he reached on June 21st, 1856.

[2] Orfeo was revived at Carvalho's Théâtre-Lyrique on November 18th, 1859, Alceste at the
Opéra on October 21st, 1861.

[3] November 15th, 1855.

whilst using the baton with my right, I managed to mark the time at five distinct and distant points in the vast space occupied by the performers. Five sub-conductors received the time from me through the electric wires, and communicated it to the groups under their direction, and the ensemble was marvellous. Since then most of the lyrical theatres have adopted the electric metronome for the choruses behind the scenes, when their leaders can neither see the conductor nor hear the orchestra. The Opéra alone held out against it till I was conducting the rehearsals of *Alceste,* when I insisted on the precious contrivance being adopted.

The effects produced at these concerts were very fine, especially in pieces where the harmony was broad and the tempo moderate, such as the chorus, *Jamais, dans ces beaux lieux,* from *Armide;* the *Tibi omnes,* from my *Te Deum;* and the *Apothéose* from the *Symphonie funèbre et triomphale.*

Four or five years after this sort of musical congress, Jullien, whom I have already mentioned in connection with the opera at Drury Lane, came to Paris to give a series of grand concerts in the circus at the Champs-Élysées. His bankruptcy prevented him from signing the necessary engagements; but I was happy enough to obtain his certificate for him, and with it the power of contracting. The poor man, on seeing me thus give up my own claims on him, was so deeply moved as to embrace me, in the bankruptcy court, with a burst of tears. But from that moment his mind, which no one, either in London or Paris, would believe to be affected, went from bad to worse. For many years before he had laid claim to an extraordinary discovery in acoustics, which he imparted to everybody. Putting a finger in each ear, he listened to the dull sound thus produced in the head by the blood passing through the carotid arteries, and firmly believed that it was a colossal A produced *by the terrestrial globe revolving in space.* Then whistling a D, an E flat, or an F, or any high note whatsoever, he would exclaim enthusiastically: " It is the A, the real A, the A of the spheres, the diapason of eternity ! "

One day he came to me in great haste, with a very wild air. He had *seen God,* he said, *in a blue cloud,* and God had commanded him to make my fortune. The first step was to buy the score of *Les Troyens,* which I had lately finished, and for which he offered me thirty-five thousand francs. The next, in spite of my resistance, was to pay off his Drury Lane debt. " I have money, I have money," he cried, taking handfuls of gold and bank-notes out of his pocket. " Look, look, there it is; pay yourself." I had great difficulty in making him take back his money, saying: " Another time, my dear Jullien, we will settle this affair, and see about the mission entrusted to you. For that you must be in a calmer condition than you now are." The fact was that he had already received considerable sums for his concerts at the Champs-Élysées, from a contractor whom he had inspired with the greatest confidence. The following week, after having created a public scandal by playing the piccolo on the Boulevard des Italiens, in his cabriolet, and inviting the people in the street to his concerts, Jullien died raving mad. How many musicians are there at the present moment, just as mad as he, who are taken quite seriously!

At this time I had completed the dramatic work of which I have just spoken, and which is mentioned in a note to one of the preceding chapters. Four years previously I happened to be at Weimar with the Princess Wittgenstein, a devoted friend of Liszt's, a woman of rare intelligence and feeling, who has often comforted me in my fits of depression. Something led me to speak of my admiration for Virgil and of an idea I had formed of a grand opera on the Shakespearean model, to be founded on the second and fourth books of the *Æneid*. I added that I was too well acquainted with the necessary difficulties of such an undertaking ever to attempt it. " Indeed," replied the Princess, " your passion for Shakespeare, combined with your love of the antique, ought to produce something grand and uncommon. You must write this opera, or lyric poem, or whatsoever you choose to call it. You must begin it, and you must finish it." I continued my objections, but she would hear none of them. " Listen," said she. " If you are shirking the inevitable difficulties of the piece, if you are so weak as to be afraid to brave everything for Dido and Cassandra, never come to see me again, for I will not receive you." This was quite enough to decide me. On my return to Paris I began the poem of *Les Troyens*. I next attacked the score, and after three years and a half of corrections, changes, additions, etc., I finished it. While thus polishing and repolishing my work, after having read the poem to many different persons and profited by their remarks to the best of my ability, I wrote the following letter to the Emperor.

" SIRE,

" I have just completed a grand opera, of which I have written both words and music. In spite of the boldness and variety of the means employed, the resources at our disposal in Paris are quite sufficient for its performance.[1] Permit me, Sire, to read you the poem, and afterwards to entreat your patronage of the work, if it is so fortunate as to deserve it. The Opéra is now under the management of one [2] of my old friends, who entertains the most extraordinary opinions about my style in music — a style which he does not know and cannot appreciate. The two conductors under his orders are my enemies. Defend me, Sire, from my friend. As for my enemies, as the Italian proverb says, I can defend myself. If your Majesty, after having heard my poem, does not think it worthy of representation, I will accept your decision with sincere and unqualified respect; but I cannot submit my work to the estimation of persons whose judgment is obscured by prejudice, and whose opinion therefore is not of the slightest value to me. They would make the insufficiency of the poem a pretext for refusing the music. I was tempted for a moment to ask the favour of reading my libretto of *Les Troyens* to your Majesty during the leisure your Majesty enjoyed recently at Plombières; but the score was not then finished, and had the result proved unfavourable I might have been too much discouraged to proceed, though desirous of completing my great work with untiring ardour and the most assiduous and loving care. Now, let discouragement and trouble come if they will, nothing can destroy the fact that it is in existence. It is grand and powerful, and, in spite of the apparently complicated methods employed, very simple. Unfortunately it is not common, but this is a defect that your Majesty will pardon, and the Parisian public is beginning to understand that the highest aim of art does not consist in producing tricks of sound. Allow me therefore, Sire, to say, like one of the personages in the poem from whence I have taken my subject, *Arma cito properate viro!* I believe that I shall take Latium.

" With the most profound respect and devotion, I am, your Majesty's humble and obedient servant,

" HECTOR BERLIOZ

"Member of the Institute."

"Paris, March 28th, 1858."

[1] *Les Troyens* was not at that time divided into two operas; it formed a single one, lasting five hours. [B.]

[2] Alphonse Royer. [B.]

I did not take Latium. It is true that the people at the Opéra took good care not to *properare arma viro,* and the Emperor never read the letter, since M. de Morny dissuaded me from sending it. "The Emperor," he said, "would not have thought it *a proper one.*" And finally, when *Les Troyens* was given after a fashion, His Majesty did not even condescend to come and see it.

One evening, at the Tuileries,[1] I managed to have a moment's conversation with the Emperor, who authorised me to bring him the libretto, promising to read it if he could find an hour's leisure. But what leisure has the Emperor of the French? I sent my manuscript to his Majesty, who did not read it, but despatched it to the Office of the direction of theatres. There my work was slandered, and treated as absurd; a rumour was circulated that it would take eight hours, and require two companies, each as large as that of the Opéra, and three hundred extra singers, etc. A year later, however, they seemed disposed to have something to say to it. One day Alphonse Royer told me, from the Minister, that he was going to make them begin upon it at the Opéra, and wished to give me entire satisfaction.

THIS SPONTANEOUS PROMISE WAS NO BETTER KEPT THAN ALL THE REST, AND FROM THAT TIME FORTH, ETC.

And thus it happened that after a long and useless delay, tired of submitting to such annoyance, I yielded to M. Carvalho's entreaties, and consented to let him try to bring out *Les Troyens à Carthage*[2] at the Théâtre-Lyrique, although it was manifestly impossible for him to do it justice. He had just obtained an annual subvention of a hundred thousand francs. But in spite of this the undertaking was beyond his powers; his theatre was not large enough, his singers not sufficiently skilled, his chorus and orchestra inadequate. We both made considerable sacrifices. I paid for the musicians necessary to complete the orchestra out of my own pocket. More than once I even altered the scoring, in order to proportion it to his resources. Madame Charton-Demeur, the only woman who could sing Dido's part, treated me in a most generous and friendly manner, by accepting much less money from Carvalho than was offered her by the Madrid Theatre. In spite of everything, however, the performance was an imperfect one, as it could hardly fail to be. Madame Charton did admirably at times.

[1] September 6th, 1858.
[2] The second part of the entire work (*Les Troyens*) to which I added an instrumental introduction (the *Lamento*) and a prologue. [B.]

Monjauze, as Æneas, was occasionally spirited and animated, but the *mise en scène*, which Carvalho insisted on arranging, was quite unlike what I had directed; it was absurd in some parts and ridiculous in others. At the first representation, the scene-shifter came nearly spoiling everything and upsetting the whole piece by his awkwardness in the hunting scene. At the Opéra, this tableau would have produced a strikingly wild and beautiful effect; here it was contemptible, it took fifty-five minutes to make the change to the next scene, and the result was that the whole scene in which the storm and the royal hunt take place was suppressed at the second representation.

I have already said that, in order properly to organise the performance of so great a work, I should have to be as absolutely master of the theatre as I am of the orchestra when rehearsing a symphony. I require the help of everybody, and must be obeyed by all without the slightest demur; otherwise my energy is exhausted after a few days by the opposition, the puerile opinions, and still more puerile terrors by which I am beset. I end by resigning, and letting everything go to the devil. I cannot describe the way in which Carvalho, while protesting that he desired only to conform to my wishes, positively tortured me into giving my consent to the cuts he thought necessary. When he dared not ask for these himself, he used to apply to me through our common friends. One would write me that such and such a passage was dangerous; another implored me — also by letter — to suppress something else. And the criticisms of points of detail were enough to drive me mad.

" Your rhapsodist with his four-stringed lyre is intended, I know, to account for the four notes struck by the harp in the orchestra. You wanted to show off a little archæology."

" Well? "

" That is dangerous. People will laugh."

" It certainly is a great matter for laughter. Ha! ha! ha! a tetrachord! An antique lyre, striking only four notes! ha! ha! ha! "

" There is one word in your prologue that alarms me."

" What is that? "

" The word *triomphaux.*"

" And why should that alarm you? Is it not the plural of *triomphal*, as *chevaux* is of *cheval*, *originaux* of *original*, *madrigaux* of *madrigal*, *municipaux* of *municipal?* "

" Yes, but it is not a word in common use."

" By Jove! if for an epic subject I am only to employ words in use at the music-halls and vaudeville theatres, there will be a great many forbidden expressions, and the style of the work will be remarkably poor."

" People will laugh at it, you will see."

" Ha! ha! ha! *Triomphaux!* that is funny! *Triomphaux!* it is very nearly as ludicrous as *tarte à la crème* in Molière. Ha! ha! ha! "

" Æneas must not appear on the stage in a helmet."

" Why not? "

" Because Mangin, who sells pencils in the street, also wears a helmet; a helmet of the Middle Ages, certainly, but still a helmet; and the gods in the top gallery will begin to laugh and call out ' Hello! here's Mangin! ' "

" Oh, of course, a Trojan hero must not wear a helmet, because people will laugh. Ha! ha! ha! a helmet! ha! ha! Mangin! "

" Look here, will you do me a favour? "

" Well, what now? "

" Suppress Mercury; the wings to his heels and head will make people laugh. No one has ever seen wings except on the shoulders."

" Oh! human beings have been seen with wings on their shoulders? I did not know that. However, I can understand that wings on the heels, and still more on the head, will make people laugh; ha! ha! ha! And so, as we don't often meet Mercury in the streets of Paris, let him be suppressed."

Who can understand what I underwent from these idiotic misgivings? I say nothing of Carvalho's musical ideas; he wanted me to alter the tempi of certain pieces, to add sixteen, eight, four bars here, or suppress two or three there, to suit some stage business of his own contrivance. In his eyes, the *mise en scène* of an opera is not made for the music, but the music for the *mise en scène.* Just as if in writing my score I had not carefully calculated everything in terms of the theatre, in the light of an experience of forty years at the Opéra. The actors, at any rate, took care not to torment me, and I must do them the justice to say that they sang their parts just as they were given them, without changing a single note. This may seem incredible, but it is true, and I thank them.

The first representation of *Les Troyens à Carthage* took place on the day promised, November the 4th, 1863. The work still required three or four serious general rehearsals; nothing went with certainty, particularly on the stage. But Carvalho was at his wits' end to keep up his repertory, the house had been empty every night, and he wanted to extricate himself from this unfortunate position as quickly as possible. Everybody knows that in such cases managers are ferocious. My friends and I expected a stormy evening and all sorts of hostile demonstrations, but nothing of the kind happened. My enemies dared not show themselves; a solitary hiss was heard at the end, when I was called for, and that was all. The individual who had hissed evidently determined to continue his insults, for he returned with a comrade, and hissed exactly at the same place at the third, fifth, seventh, and tenth performances. Others held forth in the lobbies with comical vehemence, heaping curses on my head, saying that such music could not and ought not to be *allowed.* Five papers insulted me, in terms expressly chosen to wound my feelings as an artist. But on the other hand, more than fifty articles appeared during the first fortnight, in a tone of appreciative criticism, by Messrs. Gasperini, Fiorentino, d'Ortigue, Léon Kreutzer, Damcke, Joannes Weber, and many others, written with an enthusiasm and ability that filled me with delight such as I had not felt for a long time past. Besides this I received a great many letters, some eloquent, others *naïf,* but all in earnest, and all touching me deeply.

I saw people in tears at several of the performances, and during the two months following the first appearance of the work I was often stopped in the street by strangers asking permission to shake hands with me, and thanking me for having produced it. This was surely ample compensation for the insults of my enemies — people whose enmity was due less to my criticisms than to my musical tendencies, and whose hatred, indeed, was such as to honour me, resembling as it did the hatred of the street-walker for the honest woman. The muse of the former is generally a Lais, a Phryne, or an Aspasia — though rarely an Aspasia, for *she* had too much intelligence; while noble souls and lovers of great art adore a Juliet, a Desdemona, a Cordelia, an Ophelia, an Imogen, a Virgilia, a Miranda, a Dido, a Cassandra, an Alceste, sublime names that evoke images of poetic love, modesty and devotion, while the others suggest only beastliness and prostitution.

I confess that I was myself powerfully impressed when I heard certain passages in the *Troyens* well performed. Æneas's song,

Ah! quand viendra l'instant des suprêmes adieux,

and still more, Dido's solo,

> Je vais mourir,
> Dans ma douleur immense submergée,

quite overcame me. Madame Charton rendered this passage in a grandly dramatic manner:

> Enée, Enée,
> Ah! mon âme te suit!

and shrieked in despair, as she struck her breast and tore her hair, just as Virgil intended:

> Terque quaterque manu pectus percussa decorem
> Flaventesque abscissa comas.

It is curious that not one of my barking critics should have reproached me with having presumed to create that vocal effect; and yet I think it is certainly worthy of their anger. Of all the passionately sad music I have ever composed, I know nothing to compare to Dido's part in that scene and the following air, except those of Cassandra, in certain parts of the *Prise de Troie,* which has never yet been performed. . . .

Ah, my noble Cassandra, my heroic virgin, I must needs resign myself to never hearing thee! . . . And I am like the young Chorebus:

> Insano Cassandræ incensus amore.

The following pieces were suppressed in *Les Troyens à Carthage* at the Théâtre-Lyrique, both at rehearsal and after the first representation:

1. The entry of the builders.
2. That of the sailors.
3. That of the labourers.
4. The instrumental interlude (hunting scene and tempest).
5. Scene and duet between Anna and Narbal.
6. Second *air de ballet.*
7. The strophes of Iopas.
8. The sentinels' duet.
9. The song of Hylas.
10. The grand duet of Æneas and Dido: *Errante sur tes pas.*

As for the first three of these, Carvalho thought the general effect cold; and the stage was too small for such processions. The *mise en scène* of the hunting interlude was wretched. Instead of a real water-fall, there was a painted one; the dancing satyrs were represented by little girls of twelve, and the blazing branches which they ought to have waved were forbidden for fear of fire. There were no dishevelled nymphs flying through the forest crying " Italy! " the chorus-singers who represented them were placed in the wings, and could not be heard in the theatre; the thunderbolt was scarcely audible, notwithstanding the weakness of the orchestra. And always after this contemptible parody, the scene-shifter took at least forty minutes to change the scene. I myself therefore requested that the interlude might be suppressed. In spite of my furious resistance, Carvalho insisted obstinately on cutting out the scene between Narbal and Anna; also the *air de ballet* and the sentinels' duet, which seemed to him too familiar for the epic style. The strophes of Iopas were omitted by my own advice, as the singer was incapable of doing them justice. In the duet between Æneas and Dido, I soon discovered that Madame Charton's voice was unequal to so violent a scene, and it fatigued her so much that she had not strength enough left to sing the terrible recitative in the fifth act, *Dieux immortels! il part!* and her last aria and the scene of the funeral pile. Lastly, the song of Hylas, which took at the first performances, and was very well sung by young Cabel, disappeared whilst I was absent with an attack of bronchitis. Cabel was required for the piece played the day after *Les Troyens,* and as his engagement only bound him to sing fifteen times in the month, they would have had to pay him two hundred francs for each extra night. Carvalho therefore suppressed the song for the sake of economy, without giving me notice. I was so stupefied by this long torture that, instead of offering any further opposition, I consented to the suppression of several pieces in the piano score, which Carvalho wished should agree as nearly as possible with the representation. Happily the full score is not yet published. I spent a month in setting it to rights, and carefully dressing its wounds. It will appear in its original form, exactly as I wrote it.

To see a work of that nature prepared for sale, with the cuts and trimmings of the publisher! Is there any torture like that? A score lying dismembered in the music-sellers' windows, like the body of a calf on a butcher's stall, with its fragments offered for sale like cat's-meat!

In spite, however, of all Carvalho's *corrections* and *improvements,* the *Troyens à Carthage* only ran twenty-one nights. As the receipts did not come up to his expectations, he consented to cancel the engagement of Madame Charton. She accordingly left for Madrid, and the work disappeared from the bills, to my great relief. My fees from these twenty-one representations were considerable, owing to my having written both words and music, and as I had disposed of the pianoforte arrangement both in Paris [1] and London, I found to my intense delight that the interest of the sum total was about equal to my annual salary from the *Journal des Débats.* I therefore at once resigned my post as critic. At last, after thirty years' bondage, I am free! No more feuilletons to write, no more commonplaces to excuse, no more mediocrities to praise, no more indignation to suppress; no more lies, no more comedies, no more mean compromises — I am free! I need never again set foot in a lyrical theatre, nor speak of, nor listen to, nor even laugh at the queer musical messes dished up there. *Gloria in excelsis Deo, et in terra pax hominibus bonae voluntatis.*

The *Troyens* was at any rate the means of releasing the wretched feuilletonist from his bondage.

Between the completion and representation of the opera I wrote, by M. Bénazet's [2] desire, both words and music of an opéra-comique in two acts, *Béatrice et Bénédict.* It was very successfully played, under my own direction, at the new Baden-Baden Theatre, August 9th, 1862.[3] Some months later, at the request of the Grand Duchess, it was got up with equal success at Weimar, after being translated into German by Herr Richard Pohl. I was invited to conduct the first two performances,[4] and overwhelmed, as usual, with all sorts of kind attention by their Highnesses. The Prince of Hohenzollern-Hechingen

---

[1] Choudens paid him 15,000 francs for the French rights. Berlioz left the *Débats* in March 1864. M. Boschot reconstructs his future budget thus:

From the property left him by his father (of the value of about 130,000 francs), an annual income of about	6,000 fcs.	
From his chair at the Institute,	1,500	"
As Librarian of the Conservatoire,	1,200	"
	8,700	"

In addition there would be the interest on the 20,000 or 30,000 francs brought him by the *Troyens* and by various concerts in France and abroad, and the performing rights of his versions of *Orfeo, Alceste* and *Der Freischütz.* All in all he would have a modest but assured income of about 9,000 or 10,000 francs per annum.

[2] Manager at Baden. [B.]

[3] The score had been finished in the preceding February. A second performance followed on August 13th.

[4] In April 1863.

was equally gracious, and sent his Kapellmeister to me at Weimar to invite me to conduct a concert at Löwenberg, his present residence. He requested me to draw up an instrumental programme consisting entirely of my own works, with which his orchestra was quite familiar.

" Monseigneur," I answered, " I am at your orders, but since your orchestra is familiar with my symphonies and overtures, will you kindly arrange the programme yourself, and I will conduct whatever you please ? "

The Prince, therefore, chose the *King Lear* overture, the banquet and love-scene from *Romeo and Juliet,* the *Carnaval romain* overture, and the entire symphony of *Harold.* As the Prince had no harp, he extended his invitation to Madame Pohl, the Weimar harpist, and she and her husband took the journey very willingly.

The Prince was much changed since my trip to Hechingen in 1842, being such a martyr to gout that he could not leave his bed, and was not able even to attend the concert. This was a real grief to him, and he did not attempt to conceal it.

" You are not a conductor," he said, " you are the orchestra itself, and it is very hard that I cannot profit by your stay here."

He has had a fine concert-room built in the castle, excellent for sound, and there a select audience of six hundred sincere and erudite lovers of musical art assembles some ten or twelve times a year. The concerts are gratuitous, attended by people from the neighbourhood, and even from Burtzlau and Dresden, and a great many distant châteaux. The orchestra contains only forty-five musicians, but I cannot describe their intelligence, attention, and good training, or the rare talent and patience with which they are directed by the conductor, Herr Seifrids. Moreover, they are not compelled to teach, and are not wearied, as our artists are, either by church or theatre duty, but are entirely at the service of the Prince. I stayed in his house, and the first day of the rehearsal a servant came to tell me that " the orchestra was waiting." I went along a gallery, entered the concert-room for the first time, and there found the forty-five performers in silence, instrument in hand; no tuning up, no noise whatever — all were ready. On the conductor's desk was the score of *King Lear.* I lift my arm, I commence: all start together with *verve* and precision; the wildest rhythmical eccentricities in the allegro are attacked without the slightest hesitation, and I say to myself as I conduct the overture — for the first time for ten or twelve years — " Why, it is overwhelming ! Did

I really write that?" It was the same with all the rest, and at last I said to the musicians, "This is a good joke, gentlemen, we are only rehearsing for amusement. I have no remarks to make."

The Kapellmeister played the solo viola in *Harold* to perfection, with a fine tone and a rhythmical control that filled me with delight; in the other works he took up his violin again. Richard Pohl played the cymbals. I may truly say that I never heard a more fascinating performance of *Harold*. But, oh! the adagio from *Romeo and Juliet* — how exquisitely they made it sing! We were at Verona, not at Löwenberg. . . . We played the piece without a single interruption, and at the end Herr Seifrids rose, stood silent for a moment, vainly striving to master his emotion, and then exclaimed: "No, there is nothing more beautiful."

Then the whole orchestra burst forth with shouts and applause on the violins, basses, drums. . . . I bit my lip. . . . Messengers from time to time passed to and from the sick room, describing the incidents of the rehearsal to the poor disconsolate Prince. The room was crowded on the day of the concert by a brilliant and impassioned audience, who had evidently long been familiar with all the pieces. After the *Pilgrims' March,* one of the Prince's officers mounted the platform, and, amid the applause of the whole audience, decorated me with the cross of the order of Hohenzollern. The secret had been so religiously kept that I had not the slightest idea that I was to receive it. Accordingly I was greatly delighted, and played the orgie from *Harold* in my own frantic fashion, without a thought of the public — grinding my teeth throughout.

The next day the musicians gave me a grand dinner and a ball. I had to reply to a great many toasts, Richard Pohl serving as my interpreter, and reproducing my words in German, sentence by sentence.

I could say much more about this delightful trip, but will content myself with recalling the exquisite courtesy I received from all the Prince's entourage, more especially the family of Colonel Broderotti, one of his officers. I may add that both he and they spoke French with a grace that was beyond all value to me, for I do not know a word of German, and it pains me to hear French badly spoken. I had to leave two days after the artists' ball, and the Prince, who was still confined to his bed, embraced me at parting, saying: "Farewell, my dear Berlioz. You are going to your friends at Paris; tell them they are my friends too."

To return to the opera of *Béatrice*. I had taken the book from *Much Ado about Nothing*, and added the songs and the episode of the musician. The duet, *Vous soupirez, madame!* the trio between Hero, Beatrice, and Ursula, *Je vais d'un cœur aimant*, and Beatrice's big song, *Dieu! que viens-je d'entendre?* (which was sung at Baden by Madame Charton with feeling, *verve*, immense fire, and rare beauty of style), produced a tremendous effect. Critics, come expressly from Paris, praised the music warmly, especially the song and the duet. Some thought that there was a great deal of rubbish in the rest of the score, and that the spoken dialogue was stupid. It is copied almost word for word from Shakespeare. . . .

This work is difficult of performance, especially in the men's parts; but I think it one of the most spirited and original I ever wrote. Unlike *Les Troyens*, its production entails no expense. However, they will take good care not to ask me to give it in Paris, and they will do well, for it is not Parisian music.

M. Bénazet, with his usual generosity, paid me two thousand francs for the words of each act, and the same for the music; that is to say, eight thousand francs in all, and gave me an additional thousand for directing the performance the following year. The piano edition has been engraved, and the full score is shortly to be published, with those of *Benvenuto Cellini, La Prise de Troie,* and *Les Troyens à Carthage,* if I am rich enough. Choudens, when he purchased *Les Troyens,* gave me a written promise to publish the full score within a year of the issue of the piano score; but THIS PROMISE WAS NO BETTER KEPT THAN ALL THE OTHERS, AND FROM THAT TIME FORTH I NEVER HEARD A WORD MORE ABOUT IT, ETC.

The duet in *Béatrice et Bénédict* is often sung in Germany, and is very popular. *À propos* thereto, I remember on my last visit to Weimar that the Grand Duke used sometimes to invite me to sup with him in private, and ask me numberless questions about my life at Paris and various other details. He was astonished and disgusted when I opened his eyes to the realities of our musical world. One evening, however, I made him laugh. He asked me when and where I had written *Vous soupirez, madame.*

"You must surely have composed it by moonlight, in some romantic spot?"

"Monseigneur," said I, "it contains one of those impressions of nature that artists hoard up, and which burst forth afterwards from the soul when they are wanted, no matter where. I sketched it one day while listening to a speech from one of my colleagues at the Institute."

" By Jove ! " exclaimed the Grand Duke, " the orator must surely have been wonderfully eloquent."

The duet was also performed at one of the concerts at the Conservatoire,[1] where it excited a most unexampled enthusiasm. It was encored with applause enough to bring down the house, and my faithful foes did not dare to utter a single hiss. It must be said also that the singing of Mesdames Viardot and Vandenheufel-Duprez was simply delicious. The orchestra played with marvellous grace and delicacy, and it was a performance that one sometimes hears . . . in one's dreams.

The Concert Society was kind enough this year to do the second part of my sacred trilogy, *L'Enfance du Christ.*[2] It was admirably performed, and also produced a great effect, but the public, for some reason or other, departed from its usual habit of encoring *Le Repos de la Sainte Famille,* and my opponents condescended to insult the room by a few hisses. The Conservatoire is now under the direction of my friend, M. Georges Hainl; it has ceased its hostilities, and occasionally performs fragments from my works. I have made over to it all the music in my possession, separate orchestral and choral parts, engraved and MS., containing all that is necessary for a grand performance of every one of my works, the operas alone excepted. This musical library will be of great value by-and-by; meantime it could not possibly be in better hands.

I must not forget the Strasburg festival, to which I was invited a year and a half ago, to direct the performance of *L'Enfance du Christ.*[3] A huge hall had been built to accommodate six thousand persons and five hundred performers. One would have supposed that this oratorio, being in a uniformly soft and tender style, would have been almost inaudible in so vast a room. To my astonishment it aroused profound emotion, and the unaccompanied mystic chorus at the end, *O mon âme,* drew tears from many. I am happy when I see my audience weep. This chorus produces nothing like the same effect in Paris. But then it is very badly performed there.

[1] On March 22nd, 1863. It was given again at the Conservatoire concert of April 5th, and at a performance at the Opéra-Comique (for the benefit of the descendants of Rameau) on April 8th.

[2] At the Conservatoire concert of April 10th, 1864.

[3] June 22nd, 1863. The occasion was the inauguration of the Kehl bridge.

I hear that during the past year several of my works have been played in America, Russia, and Germany; so much the better. My musical career will become all that I could wish by the time I am a hundred and forty!

I married again [1] . . . I was *obliged* to do so; and after eight years my second wife died suddenly from heart disease.[2] Some months after her interment in the great Montmartre cemetery, my friend Edouard Alexandre, the celebrated maker of the Alexandre organs, who has always treated me with the most unfailing kindness, thinking her tomb too unpretending, insisted on purchasing the freehold of a piece of ground for me and my family. A vault was built, and I was compelled to be present at the removal of my wife's remains to her new resting-place. It was a terribly sad moment, and I suffered keenly; but it was nothing in comparison with what fate had reserved for me. My experiences in this respect were destined to be terrible. Soon afterwards I received an official notice that the smaller cemetery at Montmartre, where my first wife, Henrietta Smithson, was buried, was about to be abolished, and that I must remove her loved remains.

I gave the necessary orders in both cemeteries, and one dark, gloomy morning set forth alone for the sad spot.[3] A municipal officer was waiting, to be present at the disinterment. The grave had already been opened, and on my arrival the gravedigger jumped in. The coffin was still entire, though it had been ten years underground; the lid alone was injured by the damp. The man, instead of lifting it out, tore away the rotten lid, which cracked with a hideous noise, and brought the contents of the coffin to light. He then bent down, took up the head, which was already parted from the trunk — the bald, uncrowned, decayed head of the *poor Ophelia* — and laid it in a new coffin awaiting it at the edge of the grave. Then, bending down a second time, he lifted with difficulty the headless trunk and limbs — a blackish mass to which the shroud still adhered, resembling a heap of pitch in a damp sack. I remember the dull sound . . . and the odour. . . .

The municipal officer stood a few feet off, looking at the sad spectacle. Seeing me leaning against the trunk of a cypress, he called out: " Don't stay there, M. Berlioz; come here, come here! " And as

---

[1] He had married Marie Recio in September 1854.
[2] June 13th, 1862. She was only forty-eight.
[3] February 3rd, 1864.

though something grotesque were to be added to the horrible scene, he added, with a mistake in the word: " Ah, poor *inhumanity!* "

A few moments later we followed the hearse down the hill to the new vault in the larger Montmartre cemetery. There both the dead sleep tranquilly, awaiting the time when my own corruption shall be brought to the same charnel-house.

I am in my sixty-first year; I have neither hopes, nor illusions, nor great thoughts left. My son is nearly always absent; I am solitary. My contempt for the folly and meanness of men, my hatred of their detestable ferocity, are at their height, and I say hourly to death: " When you will! "

Why does he delay?

As is evident from the text of the "Supplement," this chapter was added in 1864, ten years after the first closing of the *Mémoires* with Chapter LXXVI. A few details have to be added to complete the story of Berlioz's external life during those years.

For several summers he went to Baden, performing his music before audiences that wanted a momentary intellectual relief from the exacting business of gaming and gallantry. He was in Weimar in the summers of 1855 and 1856, in Brussels in March 1855 (when he dined with his old enemy Fétis), in Gotha in February 1856, and in Bordeaux in June 1859 — always for the purpose of conducting his own music.

The gigantic *Te Deum* was produced in the church of St. Eustache, Paris, on April 30th, 1855, and the score was published shortly afterwards, together with those of *Lélio* and *Benvenuto Cellini*. In 1861 he wrote *Le Temple universel*, a work for double chorus, one singing in English, the other in French. It was given in Paris on September 13th and 17th of the same year. Of his literary works, *Les Grotesques de la musique* was published in March 1859, and the volume of essays entitled *À travers Chants* was put together in the autumn of 1862. The *Troyens* was sketched out in April 1856, the poem written between then and the following July, and the score completed on April 7th 1858.

His sister Adèle died on March 2nd, 1860.

Not long after the death of Marie, he found temporary consolation in the love of a mysterious young woman of twenty-six, of whom we know nothing but her name — Amélie. She seems to have taken pity on the desolate and unhappy old man; on her shoulder he could sob out his miseries and despairs. He speaks of her in a letter of March 3rd, 1863 to his old friend Humbert Ferrand: "Once more it is a matter of a love — a love that came smiling to me, unsought by me, and that I fought against for a time. But I was conquered by my loneliness and by the inexorable need of tenderness that is killing me: I let myself be loved, then I myself loved even more, and a separation was seen by both of us to be necessary, a final separation, without compensation, absolute as death itself. . . . That is all. I recover little by little; but my health is woeful. Let us speak no more about it."

He makes the Princess von Sayn-Wittgenstein his confidant in a letter of August 30th, 1864. "We consented, out of prudence, not to see or write to each other again, to live completely separated. Is not that an effort? We saw each other at a distance in a theatre; a sign with the head . . . that was all. . . . She was already dying, and I knew nothing of it. . . . Six weeks later she was dead, and of that also I knew nothing. Not till six months later. . . . Enough, enough."

The only other reference to "Amélie" is in the *Soixante Ans de Souvenirs* (1886) of Berlioz's friend Ernest Legouvé. He tells us that one autumn he and Berlioz met in Baden, where *Béatrice et Bénédict* was in rehearsal. Berlioz, looking very old and sad, showed him an unsigned letter from a woman who, he said, was young and intelligent, and who loved him. Legouvé tried to enliven him with felicitations; but Berlioz broke out in a despairing cry of "I am sixty!" And in reply to some questions of Legouvé he added: "Sometimes I sink into a seat and weep without apparent cause. The frightful thought assails me — She divines it! And then with the tenderness of an angel she says to me, 'Unhappy and ungrateful one, what can I do to convince you? Consider: is it to my interest to tell you that I love you? Have I not forgotten everything for you? Do I not risk a thousand dangers for you?' And she takes my head in her hands, and her tears fall on my neck. And yet, in spite of all this, always at the bottom of my heart I hear the dreadful words, 'I am sixty! She cannot love me! She does not love me!' Ah, my friend, what torture! To make one's own hell in a paradise!"

Legouvé says he believes this conversation took place "about 1865." But this does not fit in with the date of the death of "Amélie" as revealed in the letter of August 1864 to the Princess; and in any case Berlioz was not in Baden in either 1865 or 1864. Legouvé must be referring to the production of *Béatrice et Bénédict* in Baden in August 1863.

It is significant that Berlioz says nothing of his relations with Wagner during the years covered by this chapter. Each of them was conducting in London in the summer of 1855. They met one evening at Sainton's house, and the two unhappy great men were drawn to each other afresh by their very misery. But Marie was an implacable enemy of Wagner, and some of the London critics made all the mischief they could between the two composers by reprinting the disparaging remarks of the German about the French composer in the *Opera and Drama* of 1851. When Wagner came to Paris in September 1859, talk of a Paris production of *Tannhäuser* being then in the air, Berlioz, egged on by Marie, saw in his German colleague nothing but a rival of his own for the favours of the Opéra. He knew the difficulty he would have in any case in getting *Les Troyens* performed, and the difficulty would become a virtual impossibility if, as the result of the Emperor's patronage, *Tannhäuser* were to be given at the Opéra, for the establishment could not face the expense of more than one production of that colossal kind. Wagner was willing to be friendly, and sent Berlioz the recently published score of *Tristan* in January 1860, just before the concerts he gave in the Théâtre Ventadour. Quite apart from all personal considerations, Berlioz was honestly unable to grasp a work so radically different in intention and in style from his own. (It must be remembered, too, that he did not know German.) The *Tristan* prelude was played at Wagner's concert of January 25th. Berlioz, in the *Débats* of February 8th, published the famous criticism in which he avowed his inability to comprehend "this strange piece" even after repeated readings of the score. In saying this he was perfectly within his rights; but he went further, and criticised what he imagined to be the Wagnerian system on the oasis of the extremely imperfect knowledge of it he had been able to pick up from the writings of anti-Wagnerian critics hardly any better informed than himself. Wagner replied in a dignified open letter on February 22nd.

Even then the two innovators and reformers might have come together and understood each other both as artists and as men had it not been for Marie, whose venomous remarks were certainly communicated to Wagner by zealous friends of both parties. As it was, he made an attempt at a rapprochement to Berlioz in a pleasant letter of May 22nd, but by then the situation was hopeless. Writing to Liszt on this same 22nd May, Wagner says philosophically that once again he had seen, "with anatomical certainty, how a malignant woman can ruin a brilliant man to her heart's delight and make him quite ridiculous"; and he asks ruefully whether "der liebe Gott would not have done better to have left women out of his scheme of creation, for they are rarely of much use, while as a rule they work us mischief without in the end doing themselves any good."

Marie Recio seems to have been a thoroughly unpleasant person. One day Berlioz told Legouvé, with tears in his eyes, how she had called on poor discarded Harriet with no other object than that of insulting and gloating over her. "A few days ago," said Berlioz, "my wife heard a ring at her bell. Opening the door, she found in front of her a young, elegant and pretty woman, who said to her, with a smile, 'Can I see Madame Berlioz?' 'I am she,' replied my wife. 'You are wrong,' said the other; 'I want to see Mme Berlioz.' 'I am she, madame.' 'No, I don't mean you. You are talking about the old Mme Berlioz, the discarded one. *I* mean the young one, the pretty one, the one he prefers. Well, *that* one is myself.' And she walked away, banging the door on the poor creature, leaving her half fainting in her misery." Legouvé asked him why he had not thrown Marie out after this atrocious confession. All that Berlioz could say, in a broken voice, was, "How could I? I love her." As Legouvé says, Harriet was amply avenged. "The woman who displaced her had a pretty but feeble voice; she was crazy to sing in opera. Berlioz was forced to use his influence as feuilletonist to get her an engagement; that honest, stern, inflexible pen of his had to stoop to flattering and manipulating managers and composers to obtain a début for her. She was hissed; and then he had to write an article transforming her failure into a success. Driven out of the theatre, she insisted on singing in Berlioz's own concerts — singing *his* music! And he had to give way — he, who was driven crazy by a note out of tune, made really ill by a wrong rhythm, had to consent to hear his own works misrepresented, to conduct the very piece in which the composer was assassinated!"

After the scandalous *Tannhäuser* fiasco of March 1861 Berlioz turned over to his colleague d'Ortigue the difficult task of a notice in the *Débats*, but in private and in his letters he gave voice to his unholy joy over the failure of his rival. This is perhaps the least creditable episode in his whole career. It has to be remembered, by way of excuse for him, that, apart from his obsession at that time with his own *Troyens*, and his despair at seeing the chances of its production indefinitely postponed by the production of *Tannhäuser*, he was a constantly sick man, suffering such unremitting agonies from his "intestinal neuralgia" that, as he says in one of his letters, he sometimes walked the streets in a daytime sleep, while one of his feuilletons would cost him four days of weary work. Prematurely aged, disappointed, disillusioned, he saw himself neglected at every turn by the Parisians, while at the Opéra he had against him every established and entrenched interest. The bulk of what energy of body and spirit was left to him went into desperate attempts to get the *Troyens* floated, and into a sick hatred of the humanity that had treated him so ill.

THE LAST CHAPTER OF ALL

VISIT TO DAUPHINY — SECOND PILGRIMAGE TO MEY-LAN — A DAY AT LYONS — I SEE MADAME F—— AGAIN — CONVULSIONS OF HEART

SELDOM have I been more dreadfully depressed than I was in the early part of last September (1864). Most of my friends had left Paris, according to custom. Stephen Heller alone remained — at once a charming humorist and a learned musician, who has written so many admirable pianoforte works, and whose melancholy spirit and religious zeal for the true divinities of art have always had a powerful attraction for me.

Fortunately my son arrived from Mexico and was able to spare me a few days. He also was in low spirits, and we three often compared notes on our melancholy. One day we dined at Asnières. Towards evening, as we walked along the banks of the Seine and talked of Shakespeare and Beethoven, I remember we got into a state of immense excitement, in which my son only shared as far as Shakespeare was concerned, he being still unacquainted with Beethoven. We all agreed finally, however, that it was good to be alive, to worship the beautiful, and that, if we could not destroy its opposite, we must rest satisfied with despising and forgetting it as far as possible.

The sun was setting. After walking for some time, we sat down on the grassy bank of the river, opposite the island of Neuilly. We amused ourselves by watching the swallows skimming along the Seine, when I suddenly recognised the spot. I looked at my son . . . I thought of his mother. Thirty-six years before, in one of my fits of despair while wandering about Paris, I had thrown myself down in the snow on this very spot, and all but fallen asleep. Then I recollected Hamlet's cold speech, when told that the funeral convoy was that of Ophelia, whom he no longer loves: " What! the *fair Ophelia?* " " One winter's day, ages ago," I said to my two companions, " I was very nearly drowned just here, in trying to cross the Seine on the ice. I had been wandering aimlessly about the fields all day." . . .

Louis sighed.

The following week he had to return, his leave being up. A sudden and intense desire then seized me to revisit Vienne, Grenoble, and especially Meylan and my nieces, and . . . someone else, if I could find out her address.

My brother-in-law Suat and his two daughters, to whom I had written the day before I started, met me at the Vienne station, and soon brought me to Estressin, a place some distance off in the country, where they spend three or four months every summer. It was a great delight to these charming girls, one of whom was nineteen and the other twenty-one; but their pleasure was somewhat troubled when I went into the drawing-room of the house at Vienne and there caught sight of the picture of their mother, my sister Adèle, who had been dead four years. It upset me terribly, and my emotion was witnessed with painful surprise both by them and their father. To *them,* the room, the furniture, and the portrait had been daily familiar, long habit had, alas! already dimmed their recollection; time had done its work.

Poor Adèle! What a heart she had, and what kindly indulgence for all my asperities of temper, even for my most trifling whims! . . .

One morning, when we were all together at the Côte-Saint-André, after my return from Italy, it was pouring with rain; and I said to her:

" Adèle, will you come out for a walk? "

" Willingly, dear; just wait till I put on my goloshes."

" Look at those two lunatics," said my eldest sister; " isn't it like them to go and paddle about the country in such weather? "

However, I took a large umbrella, and Adèle and I, paying no attention to the jeers of the family, went down into the plain, and walked arm-in-arm for five or six miles, under the umbrella, without saying a word. We did love one another.

I passed a very quiet fortnight with my nieces and their father. I had begged my brother-in-law to find out all he could about Madame F—— at Vienne, and to get her address at Lyons. This he succeeded in doing. Being unable, therefore, to restrain myself any longer, I started at once for Grenoble, and thence turned my steps towards Meylan, as I had done sixteen years before.

A kind of secret impatience made me hasten my steps. There is old St. Eynard already lifting his half-uncovered head above the other mountains on the horizon. Again I shall behold the small white house with its surroundings, and to-morrow — to-morrow! . . . I shall be at Lyons, and I shall see Estelle herself. Can it be possible?

Once at Meylan, I did not lose my way this time in climbing up the mountain, and soon found the fountain, the avenue of trees, and the house. Everything was as present to me as if I had been there only the day before. It was but sixteen years ago. I pass before the avenue, and press on to the tower without a glance behind me. Luxuriant vegetation covered the neighbouring hills, the vines were spreading out their ripe branches. On reaching the foot of the tower, I turned as before, and took in the whole of the lovely valley at a glance. Hitherto I had contented myself with murmuring, in a low voice, " Estelle! Estelle! Estelle! " but now, overwhelmed by emotion, I fell to the ground, and there lay for a long time, listening with a mortal sadness to the echoes in my brain which at each pulsation of my arteries seemed to say: The past! the past! Time! Never! never! . . . never!

I arose, I snatched a stone from the tower wall which must have seen *her,* which perhaps *she* had touched; I tore off a branch from a neighbouring oak. On my way down I recognised, in the corner of a field, the rock so anxiously sought for in 1848, on which she had once stood. Yes, there it was!

I ascend it; my feet stand where hers once stood! no doubt of it — I fill the space once occupied by her lovely form. I bear away a tiny fragment from my granite altar.

But the sweet peas! this cannot be their season for flowering, or else they have been destroyed, for my search for them is vain. But there is the cherry tree; how it has grown! I take a piece of the bark; I embrace the trunk, and press it convulsively to my heart!

Beautiful tree! thou must surely remember her; thou canst understand me.

Having descended the hill without meeting a soul on the way, I suddenly made up my mind at the avenue gate to go in and see the house and gardens. The present owners will hardly think me a burglar. And if they do! I enter the garden. An old lady makes a sudden movement of alarm at my unexpected appearance round one of the alleys.

"Excuse me, madame," I murmured almost inaudibly, "and kindly allow me . . . to visit . . . your garden; it . . . recalls . . . memories."

"Pray come in, and walk about where you please."

"Oh, I only want to go once round."

A few paces farther on I came upon a young girl mounted on a ladder, gathering pears. I bowed as I passed. I crossed a wilderness of shrubs that almost stopped my way, such is the state of dilapidation to which the little garden is reduced. I cut a branch of syringa, which I hid in my breast, and came away. As I passed before the open door, I stopped for a moment on the threshold to look in. The young girl followed me; she had come down from her pear tree, and had doubtless heard from her mother of my absurd visit. She accosted me with courtesy, and said:

"Pray come in."

"Thanks, mademoiselle; I accept your kind offer."

And there I was at last in the little room looking out on the plain below, from which *she* had pointed out to me, then a boy of twelve, the beauties of the romantic valley. Everything was just as it had been; the drawing-room close by had the old furniture. I gnawed my pocket-handkerchief in my agitation. The young lady looked at me in some alarm.

"Do not be astonished, mademoiselle; it is forty-nine years since I saw these things." . . . And I made my escape sobbing. What could the ladies have thought of this strange scene, the significance of which they will never understand?

He has said this before, the reader will say. Too true. The same memories and regrets, the same yearning towards the past, the same pitiable eagerness to retain the ever-flying present, the same useless struggle with time, the same madness in attempting to realise the impossible, the same imperative craving for boundless affection. How should I *not* repeat myself? The sea repeats herself; all her waves are alike. . . .

That same evening I was at Lyons. I passed a strange sleepless night, musing over my intended visit to Madame F——. I determined to go to her house at twelve o'clock. Whilst awaiting the hour, which seemed as if it would never arrive, and thinking it very possible that she might not at first wish to receive me, I wrote the following letter for her to read before hearing the name of her visitor:

" MADAME,

" I have been again at Meylan. This second pilgrimage to the spot haunted by the dreams of my childhood was even more painful than that which I made sixteen years ago, when I ventured to write to you at Vif. Now I venture still further, and ask you to receive me. You will have nothing to fear from the emotions of a heart revolted by the restraint of a pitiless reality. I shall know how to control myself. Spare me a few moments. I implore you to let me see you once again.
                                                    " HECTOR BERLIOZ.

"September 23rd, 1864."

I could not wait till twelve o'clock. At half-past eleven I rang at her door, and gave the letter to her maid, together with my card. She was at home. To give the letter would have been all that was necessary; but I did not know what I was doing. On seeing my name, however, Madame F—— at once ordered me to be shown in, and came out to meet me. I recognised the divine stateliness of her step; but, oh heavens! how changed she was! her complexion slightly bronzed — her hair going gray. And yet at the sight of her my heart did not feel one moment's indecision; my whole soul went out to its idol, as though she were still in her dazzling loveliness. She leads me into her sitting-room, holding my letter in her hand. I can neither breathe nor speak. Then, with a sweet dignity:

" We are very old acquaintances, M. Berlioz." . . .
Silence.
" We were two children." . . .
Silence.
At length the dying man recovers his speech.
" Pray read my letter, madame, it . . . will explain my visit."
She opens and reads it, then laying it upon the chimney-piece:

" You have been at Meylan again! No doubt it was a chance visit? You did not take the journey on purpose? "

" Can you suppose I was there by chance? No, indeed! I have long wished to see it again."

Silence.

" You have had a very eventful life, M. Berlioz."

" How do you know, madame? "

" I have read your biography."

" Which? "

" By Méry, I think. I bought it some years ago."

" Oh, do not attribute to Méry, who is one of my friends, and a clever artist and a clever man, such a pack of fables and absurdities. There shall be a true biography of me; I will write it myself."

" Ah, no doubt! You write so well."

" It was not to my style that I was alluding, madame, but to the correctness and sincerity of my story. As for my feelings towards yourself, I have spoken of them without reserve in my book; but I have not mentioned your name."

Silence.

" I have also," continued Madame F——, " heard much about you from one of your friends who married a niece of my husband's."

" Indeed, I asked him to find out the fate of the letter which I made bold to write to you sixteen years ago. I wanted at least to know if you had received it. But I never saw him again. He is now dead, and I could learn nothing."

Silence.

Madame F——: " As for my life, it has been very simple and very sad. I have lost several of my children. The others I have educated. My husband died when they were quite little. . . . I have done my duty as a mother as best I could."

Silence.

" I was much touched, M. Berlioz, by the feelings you avowed for me, and most grateful."

At these kind words, my heart began to beat violently. I gazed at her with hungry eyes, reconstructing in my imagination her vanished youth and beauty; and at last I said:

" Give me your hand, madame."

She gave it to me immediately. I carried it to my lips, and I thought I could feel my heart melting, and every nerve thrilling.

" May I hope," said I, after a long silence, " that you will sometimes allow me to write to you, and occasionally to visit you ? "

" Certainly; but I shall not be much longer at Lyons. One of my
sons is going to be married, and I am to live with him at Geneva."

Not daring to prolong my visit further, I arose. She accompanied
me to the door, where she said once more:

" Farewell, M. Berlioz, farewell. I am deeply grateful for the
feelings you have preserved towards me."

And bowing to her, I again took her hand, laid it for a few moments against my forehead, and then tore myself forcibly away.

I was wandering about the neighbourhood of her house, now
knocking up against the trees of the Brotteaux, now stopping to watch
the tumultuous course of the Rhone from the Morand bridge, then
resuming my fevered walk, not knowing why I went to one side rather
than the other, when I met M. Strakosch, the brother-in-law of
Adelina Patti.

" Berlioz! how fortunate! Adelina will be delighted to see you.
She is giving performances here. Would you like a box for the *Barber
of Seville* to-morrow night ? "

" Thanks, but I shall probably be leaving this evening."

" Well, at any rate, come and dine with us to-night; you know how
pleased we always are to see you."

" I can't promise, it will depend. . . . I am not very well. . . .
Where are you stopping ? "

" At the Grand Hotel."

" So am I. Well, if I am not too unsociable this evening, I will dine
with you, but don't expect me."

I had got an idea, a pretext for seeing Madame F—— once more.
I hastened to her house, and learnt that she had just gone out. Then
I charged her maid to tell her that I had a box for the theatre on the
following evening, that if Madame F—— would kindly accept it, and
come and hear Mdlle. Patti, I would stay at Lyons, and have the honour of accompanying her to this performance, but that otherwise I
should leave this very evening; I therefore begged she would let me
have an answer before six o'clock. I went home. Twenty minutes
passed, in which I vainly tried to read a book of travel I had bought
at Grenoble. Not a word of it could I understand. I walked about my
room. I threw myself on my bed. I opened the window. I went down,
and going out soon found myself before the door of her house, No. 56,

Avenue de Noailles. I had gone there mechanically. I could restrain myself no longer, and again I rang the bell. No one came to the door. A gloomy idea immediately began to torment me; had she suspected my intention of returning, and denied herself to me? It was an absurd notion, but it tortured me notwithstanding. An hour afterwards I came back, and this time I sent the porter's little boy to ring Madame F——'s bell.

He was not let in either.

What was to be done? Stay there on guard before the house? It would have been ridiculous. How unlucky! Where was I to go? — home? — into the Rhône? . . . Perhaps she is really out, and does not want to avoid me.

An hour later I again mounted her staircase. I heard her door closing above, and the sound of women's voices in German. I continued to ascend; I met an unknown lady coming down, then a second, and finally a third. It was she, holding a letter in her hand.

" Oh, M. Berlioz, you have come for an answer."

" Yes, madame."

" I had written to you, and was just going with these ladies to leave my note at the Grand Hotel. Unhappily I cannot accept your kind invitation, for I have an engagement in the country, and must start at twelve o'clock. I beg you a thousand pardons for having kept you waiting so long, but I have only just come in and heard of your offer."

As she made a movement to put the letter in her pocket I exclaimed: " Pray give it to me."

" Oh, but it is not worth while."

" I entreat you; you meant it for me."

" Very well, there it is."

She gave me the letter, and I saw her handwriting for the first time.

" Then I shall not see you again? " said I, when we were in the street.

" You leave this evening? "

" Yes, madame. Good-bye."

" Good-bye, and a pleasant journey."

I pressed her hand, and saw her depart with the two German ladies.

And then — will it be believed? — I felt almost joyful; I had seen her a second time, I had spoken to her again, once more I had pressed her hand, and I had had a letter from her which she ended by assuring me of her *affectionate feelings*. It was an unlooked-for treasure, and I turned my steps towards the hotel in the hope of dining fairly quietly with Mdlle. Patti. On seeing me enter the salon she uttered a cry of delight, clapping her hands like a child.

". Oh, how delightful! there he is! there he is! " And the fascinating *diva* rushed up to me after her usual fashion and presented her virgin forehead to be kissed. I sat down to table with her, her father, her brother-in-law, and some friends. During dinner she overwhelmed me with charming civilities, continually repeating: " There's something the matter with him. What are you thinking about? I don't like you to be in trouble." When the hour for my departure arrived, they determined to go down with me to the station; the charming creature herself, one of her lady friends, and her brother-in-law came with me in the carriage. We were all allowed on to the platform. Adelina would not leave me till the last moment, when the signal was given for the train to start. When we had to part, the mad creature jumped up and put her arms round my neck.

" Good-bye, good-bye till next week. We shall be returning to Paris on Tuesday; you will come and see us on Thursday. It's settled, isn't it? You won't fail? "

And so I departed.

What would I not have given to receive such marks of affection from Madame F——, and to have been greeted by Mdlle. Patti with cold politeness! . . .

During all the coaxings and caresses of the melodious Hebe, I felt as if a marvellous bird of paradise were whirling round my head, perching on my shoulder, pecking at my hair, and singing its gayest songs. I was dazzled, but not touched. The fact was I had no *love* for the young, beautiful, radiant, and celebrated artist who, at the age of twenty-two, had brought all the musical world of Europe and America to her feet; whereas my whole soul went out to the aged, saddened, and obscure woman, to whom art was unknown, as it had ever done, ever will do to my dying day.

Balzac, nay, Shakespeare himself, the great painter of the passions, never dreamt of the possibility of such a thing as this. Only one poet, Thomas Moore, believed that it was possible, and described that rare feeling in these exquisite lines, which recur to my mind as I write:

Believe me, if all those endearing young charms,
    Which I gaze on so fondly to-day,
Were to change by to-morrow, and fleet in my arms
    Like fairy-gifts fading away,
Thou wouldst still be adored, as this moment thou **art,**
    Let thy loveliness fade as it will;
And around the dear ruin each wish of my heart
    Would entwine itself verdantly still.

It is not while beauty and youth are thine own,
    And thy cheeks unprofan'd by a tear,
That the fervour and faith of a soul can be known,
    To which time will but make thee more dear;
No, the heart that has truly lov'd never forgets,
    But as truly loves on to the close,
As the sunflower turns on her god, when he sets,
    The same look which she turn'd when he rose.

How many times during that sad night in the train I repeated to myself: " Fool! why did you go away? Better to have stayed. If you had stayed, you would have seen her again to-morrow morning. What necessity was there to go back to Paris? " None, of course, except the fear of being indiscreet and troublesome. . . . What should I have done at Lyons during those long hours when, though only a few steps away, I could not see her? It would have been torture.

After some days of misery in Paris, I wrote her a letter. It will be seen by it, and those which follow, no less than by her answers, what a wretched state my mind was in, and how calm she was. My feelings, now that I have not even the consolation of writing to her, may be easily imagined. It would have been too sweet an ending to my life to have cultivated this futile love into a romantic friendship. But I was to be crushed and lacerated to the very end.

FIRST LETTER.

"Paris, September 27th, 1864.

" MADAME,

" Your greeting was characterised by a simple and dignified kindliness of which few women would have been capable under such circumstances. A thousand blessings on you! Nevertheless, I have suffered cruelly since I left you. In vain do I tell myself that nothing could have been kinder than your reception, that any other would have been either unsuitable or inhuman; my wretched heart bleeds as though it had been wounded. I ask myself the reason, and this is what I find: It is *absence;* it is that I saw too little of you, that I did not say a quarter of what I had to say, and that I went away almost as though there were to be an eternal separation between us. And yet you gave me your hand — I pressed it to my forehead and my lips, and I restrained my tears, as I had resolved to do. But I feel an imperious, inexorable necessity for further speech with you, which I hope you will not refuse me. Remember that I have loved you for forty-nine years, that I have loved you from childhood, notwithstanding the storms that have devastated my life. The proof of this is the deep emotion I now feel; if it had really ceased to exist, even for a day, it could never have revived under existing circumstances.

"Has any woman ever listened to such a declaration as this? Don't take me for a fool who is the sport of his imagination. I am not a fool; it is simply that I am gifted with a keen sensitiveness, combined, believe me, with great quickness of insight. But my true affections are intensely powerful, and of an unalterable constancy. I have loved you, I still love you, I shall always love you. And yet I am sixty-one years of age. I know the world, and have no illusions left. Grant me then — not as a sister of charity ministering to a sick man, but as a noble-hearted woman healing the sorrows of which she is the unconscious cause — the three things which alone can restore my peace of mind: permission to write to you occasionally, an assurance that my letters shall be answered, and a promise that you will invite me to visit you at least once a year. My visits might be inopportune, and therefore troublesome, if they were made without your permission, and so I will never go either to Geneva or elsewhere unless you write the word ' Come.'

"Who could find anything unsuitable or odd in this? What can be more pure than such a relationship? Are we not both free? Who could be heartless or senseless enough to blame us? No one, not even your sons, who are, as I know, most distinguished young men. I must, however, confess that it would be dreadful to see you only in the presence of others. If you bid me come, I must be able to converse with you as I did at our first interview last Friday — an interview which I dared not prolong, and the sad charm of which I could not enjoy because of my terrible efforts to restrain my emotions.

"Oh! madame, madame, I have but one aim left in the world —

that of obtaining your affection. Suffer me to try and attain it. I will be discreet and reserved; our correspondence shall not be more frequent than you desire. It shall never become a wearisome task to you; a few lines from your hand will suffice. My visits can only be few and far between, but I shall know that in thought we are no longer apart, and that after the many years in which I have been nothing to you, I have at last the hope of becoming your friend. And a devoted friend such as I shall be is rare. I shall surround you with tenderness profound and sweet, and with an entire affection in which the innocent effusions of the child will mingle with the feelings of the man. Perhaps you will find some charm in it, perhaps you will one day say, ' I am your friend,' and admit that I am deserving of your friendship.

" Farewell, madame; I have just re-read your note of the 23rd, and at the end I perceive the assurance of your affectionate sentiments. This is not a commonplace formality, is it? — is it?

" Yours eternally,
" HECTOR BERLIOZ.

" P.S. — I am sending you three books; perhaps you will not mind looking at them in your spare moments. You understand it is a pretext of the author's to lead you to think a little of him."

FIRST ANSWER FROM MADAME F——.

"Lyons, September 29th, 1864.

" MONSIEUR,

" I should feel guilty towards both myself and you if I did not at once reply to your last letter, and to your dream of the relation which you wish to establish between us. I am going to speak — my hand on my heart.

" I am but an old, a very old woman, six years older than you; my heart is withered by days of anguish, physical and mental distress of all sorts, which have left me without illusions as to the joys and sentiments of this world. Twenty years have passed since I lost my best friend. I have sought no other; only kept up such as arose from old relationships and natural family ties. Since the fatal day on which I was left a widow I have said good-bye to all pleasures and amusements, in order to devote myself entirely to my children and my home. This has been my life for the past twenty years; it has become a habit with me, the charm of which cannot now be broken, for in such close intimacy alone can I find peace for the few days remaining to me on this earth, and everything that troubled their uniformity would be painful and burdensome.

"In your letter of the 27th you tell me that your only wish is to become my friend through an interchange of letters. Do you seriously think that this is possible? I scarcely know you. I saw you for a few minutes last Friday, the first time for forty-nine years. I cannot, therefore, rightly estimate either your tastes, your disposition, or your qualities, which alone can form a foundation of friendship. When two individuals have the same way of feeling and seeing things, there is a possibility of sympathy between them; but when they are separated, correspondence alone cannot establish what you look for from me. For my part, I believe it to be impossible. Besides, I must confess that I am extremely lazy about writing; my mind is as inert as my fingers. I have the greatest difficulty in fulfilling even my most necessary duties in this respect. I could not, therefore, promise to keep up a sustained correspondence with you. I should break my promise too often. So I forewarn you. If you like to write to me sometimes, I shall receive your letters, but do not look for exact or speedy answers.

"You also wish me sometimes to ask you to come and see me. That is no more possible than to say, 'You will find me alone.' On Friday I chanced to be alone when I received you; but when I shall be living with my son and his wife at Geneva, if I am by myself when you come, well and good; but if they are with me at the time, you will have to put up with their presence, for I should be extremely displeased if it were otherwise.

"I have told you my thoughts and feelings with perfect frankness. I think I ought to remind you that there are certain dreams and illusions which should be abandoned when we come to white hairs, and with them to the disenchantment of all fresh feelings, even those of friendship, which can have no charm unless they are the result of relations established in the happy days of youth. To my mind, it is not a moment for commencing them when the weight of years is beginning to be felt, and when their number has taught us how easy it is to be deceived. I confess that I have arrived at that point. My future shortens every day. Why form relations to be born to-day and perish to-morrow? Why give occasion to fresh regrets?

"In all that I have just said, do not think I have any intention of offending against your remembrance of me. I respect its persistency, and am much touched by it. You are still very young in heart, but with me it is otherwise. I am altogether old. I am good for nothing, except to keep, believe me, a large place in my memory for you. I shall always hear of your future triumphs with pleasure. Farewell, monsieur. Again I sign myself affectionately yours,

" EST. F——.

" I received the three volumes you so kindly sent me yesterday morning. Many thanks for them."

SECOND LETTER.

"Paris, October 2nd, 1864.

" MADAME,

" Your letter is a masterpiece of sad reason. I waited till to-day to answer it, in the hope of being able to master the overwhelming emotion it created in me.

" Yes, you are right. You cannot form new friendships. You must avoid everything that can trouble your existence, etc. But, believe me, I would not have troubled it, and the friendship, for which I asked so humbly at some more or less distant period, would never have become *burdensome* to you. (You will admit that that word in your letter must have seemed to me cruel!) I am content with what you deign to bestow on me, *some affectionate feeling, a place in your memory, and a little interest in the events of my career*. I thank you, madame. I put myself at your feet. I kiss your hands respectfully. You tell me that sometimes, at long and uncertain intervals, I may expect an answer to my letters. I thank you again for your promise. What I urge with tears and entreaties is to be allowed to have news of you. You speak with such courage of years and old age that I dare to imitate you. I hope to die first, that I may be able with certainty to send you a last farewell. If it should be otherwise, let me be told that you have left this sad world. Let your son tell me — and forgive me for the request. My letters must not be addressed at hazard. Give me what you would not deny to any stranger — your address at Geneva.

" I shall not go to see you this month at Lyons; it is plain that you would think such a visit an indiscretion. Neither will I go to Geneva for at least a year; the fear of troubling you will restrain me. But your address! your address! As soon as you know it send it to me, for pity's sake. If your silence be meant as pitiless refusal, a formal prohibition of the very slightest intercourse with you, if you thus roughly thrust me aside as though I were dangerous or unworthy, you will put the finishing touch to a sorrow which you might so easily have alleviated. Then, madame, may God and your own conscience forgive you! I shall remain in the cold darkness into which you will have plunged me, suffering, desolate, and devoted to you till death.

"HECTOR BERLIOZ."

(What contradictions and disorder there are in this letter!)

MADAME F——'S SECOND ANSWER.

"Lyons, October 14th, 1864.

"MONSIEUR,

"As I do not know when I shall be able to write to you, I hasten to send you a few lines, so that you may not think I have any intention of treating you as either *dangerous or unworthy*. My son is coming to me to-morrow, to be married on the 19th, and my house will be full for some days. As his mother and as mistress of the house, I shall have a great many things to do, and shall not therefore find it possible to get a moment's peace or leisure. Immediately after the marriage I must make preparations for my journey to Geneva, which will not be by any means a light undertaking for me, as my health does not always allow me to do what I should like. I shall leave about the beginning of November, and when I am settled in my new home you shall have my address, which I cannot give you to-day, because I do not know it myself. I would have waited for my son's arrival to ascertain it, did I not fear that you might misinterpret my long silence.— Affectionately yours,

"EST. F——."

THIRD LETTER.

"Paris, October 15th, 1864.

"MADAME,

"I thank you, I thank you. I will wait. My best wishes for the happiness of the newly married pair. Dear madame, may the sweetest happiness fill your heart at this solemn moment. How good you are!

"Do not doubt me. I shall be discreet in my adoration.— Ever your devoted,

"HECTOR BERLIOZ."

After twelve weary days, I received a letter announcing the marriage of M. Charles F——. The address was in his mother's handwriting, which filled me with a delight that few will understand. I was in the seventh heaven, and wrote immediately.

FOURTH LETTER.

"Paris, October 28th, 1864.

" Life is beautiful when illuminated by certain feelings. I have received the letter of announcement, addressed by you, dear madame — I recognise the hand. . . . You thought of the poor exile. . . . What angel shall reward you for the good you have done me!

" Yes, life is beautiful, but death would be more beautiful still! To be at your feet, my head in your lap, your hands in mine, and thus to die! . . .

" HECTOR BERLIOZ."

But the days succeeded each other, and I received no tidings. I found out at Lyons that Madame F—— had left for Geneva three weeks before. Did she mean to conceal the address which she had expressly promised to send me? which I did not want to know against her will? . . . Was I to have the grief of seeing her break her word? During those last anxious days I came to believe, as I said above, that I should no longer have even the comfort of writing to her, and I felt utterly discouraged.

But one morning, while sadly musing over my fire, they brought me a card, on which I read these words: " M. et Mdme. Charles F——." It was her son and daughter-in-law, whom she had charged to pay me a visit during their stay in Paris. What a delightful surprise! *She* had sent them! I was quite overwhelmed at finding him the living image of Mdlle. Estelle at eighteen. . . . The young wife appeared alarmed at my emotion; her husband seemed less surprised. They evidently knew all. Madame F—— had shown them my letters.

" Was she then so very beautiful? " exclaimed the young lady suddenly.

" Oh! " . . .

" Yes," interrupted her husband. " I remember once seeing my mother dressed for a ball, when I was five years old. It quite dazzled me, and I recollect it to this day."

At last I succeeded in mastering myself, and speaking more like a reasonable being to my two kind visitors. Madame Charles was a Dutch Creole from Java. She had lived at Sumatra and Borneo, understood Malay, and had seen Rajah Brooke of Saráwak. How I should have catechised her if I had been in my usual frame of mind!

I had the pleasure of often seeing the young couple during their stay in Paris, and of procuring them some pleasant amusements. We often spoke of *her,* and when we grew a little more intimate the young wife even went so far as to scold me for writing to her mother-in-law.

"You frighten her," said she; "that is not the way you ought to write. You must remember that she scarcely knows you at all, and that you are both about the same age. I quite understand her tone when she shows me one of your letters and says: 'What answer do you expect me to make to that?' You must accustom yourself to be more calm; then your visits to Geneva will be delightful, and we shall be so pleased to do the honours of the town; for you *are* coming, we reckon on you."

"Oh, certainly; can you doubt it, since Madame F—— allows me?"

I tried accordingly to control myself, and when the young couple went off again, did not even send a letter by them to their mother.

However, as the second act of the *Troyens* was about to be performed at one of the Conservatoire concerts, I sent her a copy of the poem, marking a page with withered leaves, and begging her to read it on December 18th, at half-past two, when the performance was to take place at Paris. Madame Charles was to return to watch some business in which her husband, who could not leave Geneva, was interested, and she was greatly delighted at the idea of attending this concert, the announcement of which had made some sensation in the musical world.

A fortnight passed without her return, and without any letter, and still I persisted in not writing. At last, when I could bear it no longer, on the 17th she came back and brought me the following letter:

"Geneva, December 16th, 1864.

"MONSIEUR,

"I should have written much sooner, to thank you for the warm welcome you gave to my son and his wife, if I had not been constantly unwell, and for that reason very idle. However, I cannot let my daughter-in-law leave without expressing my gratitude for the pleasure you procured for them, which made their evenings so agreeable. Suzanne has promised to tell you all about our life at Geneva, where I, for my part, should be quite as happy as I was at Lyons, were it not for my regret at being separated from two of my sons, and from real friends who were fond of me, and whom in my turn I loved dearly. Thank you once more for the libretto of the *Troyens,* and for your delicate attention in sending me leaves from the Meylan trees, which recall my youth and all its pleasures.

"On Sunday my son and I will read your work, and take part in your success and in Suzanne's pleasure at hearing your music.

"Believe me ever, yours affectionately,

"Est. F——.' "

This was my answer:

"Paris, Monday, December 19th, 1864.

"Last September, as I passed through Grenoble, I paid a visit to one of my cousins, who was living at St. Georges, a hamlet buried among the gloomy mountains on the left bank of the Drac, inhabited by a most miserable population. My cousin's sister-in-law devotes herself to the alleviation of all this misery; she is the gracious Providence of the country. On the day I arrived at St. Georges she heard that a distant hovel had been destitute of bread for three weeks. She went off there immediately, and said to the mother:

"'How now, Jeanne, you are in want, and you never told me; and yet you know how willing we are to help you as much as possible.'

"'Oh, mademoiselle, we are not in want; we have still some potatoes and cabbages left. But the children will not eat them. They cry for bread. You know how unreasonable children are.'

"Well, madame! dear madame, you also did a good deed in writing to me. I had determined to be silent, and not weary you with my letters, and so I waited for your daughter-in-law's return for tidings of you. She delayed her coming, and I felt stifled, like a man who keeps his head under water and will not draw it out. People like me are *unreasonable,* you know.

"And yet, believe me, I know the truth only too well, and did not need the lesson which you have driven home with such cruel force.

. . . No, I do not wish to give you the smallest annoyance; I will write as seldom as possible. You can answer or not, as you please. I will go and see you once a year, as though merely to pay a pleasant visit. You know what I feel, and you will be grateful to me for what I conceal.

"I fancy you are sad, and that makes me doubly. . . .

"But from this day forth I shall restrict myself to a certain mode of speaking, and to indifferent subjects.

"You have perhaps heard that the performance of my music did not take place yesterday at the Conservatoire. The committee tormented me in so many different ways, asking now for the suppression of one piece, then of another, that I was fairly exasperated; the singers were deprived of their chances of success, and were furious too; and I therefore withdrew the whole thing.

"Thank you for having so kindly transported yourself in thought to the concert-room at half-past two, and for your good wishes for my success.

"At the very time when I was thus harassed in Paris, they were keeping my birthday (December 11th) at Vienna, where a part of my *Damnation of Faust* was performed, and two hours later the conductor sent me the following telegram: 'A thousand good wishes for your birthday. Soldiers' and students' chorus performed at the Männergesang-Verein concert. Immense applause. Encored.' The cordiality of these German artists touched me far more than my success; and I am sure that you understand it. Kindness is a cardinal virtue.

"Two days afterwards, a Parisian stranger wrote me a most beautiful letter about the *Troyens,* which he characterised in terms that I dare not repeat. My son has just arrived at St. Nazaire, after a tedious voyage to Mexico, where he had an opportunity of distinguishing himself. He is now first lieutenant of the *Louisiana* first-rate. He tells me that he must leave again almost directly, and cannot possibly come to Paris. I must therefore go to him at St. Nazaire. He is a fine fellow, who has the misfortune to take after me in everything, and can never make up his mind to the platitudes and horrors of the world. We love each other like twins.

"This is all my news at present. My old mother-in-law, whom I have promised never to forsake, takes the greatest care of me, and never troubles me with questions as to the cause of my bad spirits. I read, or rather re-read, Shakespeare, Virgil, Homer, *Paul and Virginia*, books of travels, etc. I am utterly depressed; I suffer horribly from neuralgia, to which I have been a martyr for the last nine years, and which has entirely baffled all the doctors. In the evening, when my sufferings of body, heart, and spirit become too keen, I take some laudanum, and sleep after a fashion. If I am less suffering, and want the society of a few friends, I go to some friends in my neighbourhood — M. Damcke, a German composer of uncommon merit, a learned professor whose wife is an angel of goodness; both of them hearts of gold. According to my humour, we either make music or talk, or else they roll a great sofa to the fire, where I lie stretched the whole evening, brooding over my bitter thoughts. That is all, madame. I no longer compose, as I think I have told you. The state of the musical world of Paris, and of many other places, the way in which the arts are cultivated, artists favoured, masterpieces treated, makes me quite sick with indignation. That, at any rate, is a proof that I am not yet dead. . . . The day after to-morrow I hope to have the pleasure of escorting Madame Charles to the Théâtre-Italien (she is charming in spite of her home-thrusts), with a Russian friend of hers. We are going to sit out the second performance of Donizetti's *Poliuto* — to the end, if possible. Madame Charton (Paolina) has given me a box.

" Farewell, madame! May you know nothing but sweet thoughts, repose of soul, and the happiness you must feel from the assured affection of your sons and of your friends. But give an occasional thought to poor children who are unreasonable.

" Your devoted servant,
" HECTOR BERLIOZ.

" P.S. — It was very generous of you to make the young couple come and see me. I was struck by the likeness of M. Charles to Mdlle. Estelle, and I forgot myself so far as to tell him so, although such compliments to a man are not quite proper."

Some time after receiving this letter, she wrote me one in which these words occurred: " Believe me, I have some pity for unreasonable children. I have always found that the best way to make them calm and reasonable was to amuse them and give them pictures. I take the liberty of sending you one which will recall to you the reality of the present, and destroy the illusions of the past."

It was her portrait! Adorable creature! . . .[1]

And here I end. I can live more peacefully now. I shall sometimes write to her; she will answer me. I shall go and see her. I know where she is, and I shall never be left in ignorance of the changes that may occur in her life; her son has promised to keep me informed of them. By degrees, in spite of her dread of new friendships, she may perhaps find her affectionate feelings towards me growing stronger. Already I am sensible of a change for the better in my life. The past is not wholly past. My sky is not without its star, and with moistened eyes I watch it beaming on me from afar. True, she does not love me; why, indeed, should she? But she might have remained in total ignorance of me, and now she knows that I adore her.

I must try to console myself for not having known her sooner, as I console myself for not having known Virgil, whom I should have loved so well, or Gluck or Beethoven . . . or Shakespeare, who perhaps might have loved me. (Nevertheless, I am really inconsolable.)

Which of the two powers, Love or Music, can elevate man to the sublimest heights? . . . It is a great problem, and yet it seems to me that this is the answer: " Love can give no idea of music; music can

[1] We possess, in all, thirty-seven letters from Berlioz to Mme Fornier. They were first published in the *Revue bleue* of 1903, and then as a booklet — *Une page d'amour romantique.*

He had had 1,200 copies of his now finished *Mémoires* printed at his own expense in the first half of 1865: a few were sent to his intimates, the remainder being stored in his room at the Conservatoire Library. He visited Geneva in August of that year; he had already sent Mme Fornier a copy of the book. He complained that he could never see her alone; in part this is to be accounted for by the fact that she was living in the house of her married son, but one suspects also that the level-headed old woman, in whom romance had completely died, meant to take no chances with the too ardent Berlioz. After reading the *Mémoires*, by the way, she informed him that his imagination had played him false with regard to the little pink shoes over which he had rhapsodised in one of the early chapters of the book: Estelle had never possessed shoes of that colour.

He had asked her if he might name her in full in the *Mémoires*, seeing that these would not be published till after both of them were dead. She refused him permission to do this, and in obedience to a request of hers in 1866 he burnt all her letters, preserving only the envelopes.

Later a slight cloud came over their relations for a time. She began to talk about money in her letters, for she had had losses; and Berlioz had to tell her that he was desolated at his inability to help: "my son," he wrote, "who is now a captain, is richer than I am — though that is not saying much."

After her reverse of fortune she went to live with one of her sons at Saint-Symphorien d'Ozon, a few miles from Vienne. There he saw her for the last time on September 9th, 1867.

give an idea of love." . . . Why separate them? They are the two wings of the soul.

When I see the way in which certain people look on love, and what they seek in works of art, I am involuntarily reminded of hogs, rooting and grunting for truffles amongst the loveliest flowers, or under the grandest trees.

But I must try to think no more of art. . . . Stella! Stella! I can now die without anger or bitterness.

January 1st, 1865.

> Life's but a walking shadow; a poor player,
> That struts and frets his hour upon the stage,
> And then is heard no more: it is a tale
> Told by an idiot, full of sound and fury,
> Signifying nothing.
>
> SHAKESPEARE (*Macbeth*).

EDITOR'S CODA

The last four years of Berlioz's life are mainly a record of increasing disappointment, deepening pessimism, and rapidly deteriorating health. Now and then a work of his would be given in Paris, but he could be under no delusion as to his position there: a small public was enthusiastic enough when it had an opportunity of hearing him, but the doors of the opera houses were closed on him for ever, and the main Parisian public of that epoch had no great taste for concert works such as his. It flocked to the theatre for Meyerbeer, Auber, Offenbach, Gounod, Ambroise Thomas and the rest of them; but to *Les Troyens* it was indifferent.

Outside France he was still admired and courted. In December 1866 he was invited to Vienna to conduct a performance of *Faust* for the Gesellschaft der Musikfreunde, and was treated with all possible deference and courtesy. In the following February he conducted a concert at Cologne, where he again renewed acquaintance with Hiller. In December 1867 he went once more to Russia, at the invitation of the Grand Duchess Helena, who had been in Paris for the Great Exhibition in the preceding September. He was to conduct six concerts in St. Petersburg — one of them of his own works — for a fee of 15,000 francs and a travelling allowance of 1000 francs, with free lodging in one of the imperial palaces and a carriage at his disposal. He conducted two additional concerts at Moscow, to audiences of ten thousand people. The strain of the concerts and the travelling proved too much for him, although he spent in bed most of the time not taken up by the rehearsals and the performances. He had hardly returned to Paris when he once more felt the need to renew the memories of his youth in the south. He went to Nice at the beginning of March 1868. At Monte-Carlo an attack of cerebral congestion brought about a fall on the rocks; he was picked up by some workmen, dazed and bleeding. A few days later he had a second attack in Nice. He returned about the middle of the month to Paris, conscious now that his end was near.

Death had for years been busy in his circle, but three blows in particular had been hard for him to bear. His son Louis died of yellow fever at Havana on June 5th, 1867, at the age of thirty-three: Berlioz thereupon burnt or destroyed many of his papers and most of his relics of the past, saving only a guitar that had been given him by Paganini and the baton given him by Mendelssohn. His old journalistic colleague d'Ortigue died of apoplexy on November 20th, 1866. When Berlioz returned to Paris after the catastrophe of Nice, it was to learn of the final misfortune that descended upon Humbert Ferrand, the gentle and faithful companion of almost a lifetime. Ferrand had been ruined, and was living in retirement in the provinces. He had adopted, some time before, a boy of the name of Blanc Gounet, to whom he clung in spite of every evidence of the youth's unworthiness. At last, in May 1868, Gounet strangled Mme. Ferrand and decamped with what remained of her jewels. He was guillotined, and poor broken Ferrand died shortly afterwards.

For the last few years Berlioz had been little more than a walking spectre, cared for by his patient mother-in-law and a few friends such as Damcke, Massart and Reyer. Eaten away by his incessant intestinal neuralgia, he could find relief from his pains only in doses of opium that left his brain perpetually clouded. Towards the end it cost him two days' labour to write a letter. In November 1868 he took up a pen to write a dedication to Reyer in the latter's copy of *Benvenuto Cellini*, paused helplessly for some time, then made the pitiful confession that he had forgotten the name of this friend of twenty years' standing. He took finally to his bed in the early days of 1869, sank into a deeper and deeper lethargy, and passed away on the 8th March, 1869.

$\mathcal{I}ndex$

A CATALOGUE OF SELECTED DOVER BOOKS
IN ALL FIELDS OF INTEREST

LEATHER TOOLING AND CARVING, Chris H. Groneman. One of few books concentrating on tooling and carving, with complete instructions and grid designs for 39 projects ranging from bookmarks to bags. 148 illustrations. 111pp. 7⅞ x 10.
23061-9 Pa. $2.50

THE CODEX NUTTALL, A PICTURE MANUSCRIPT FROM ANCIENT MEXICO, as first edited by Zelia Nuttall. Only inexpensive edition, in full color, of a pre-Columbian Mexican (Mixtec) book. 88 color plates show kings, gods, heroes, temples, sacrifices. New explanatory, historical introduction by Arthur G. Miller. 96pp. 11⅜ x 8½.
23168-2 Pa. $7.50

AMERICAN PRIMITIVE PAINTING, Jean Lipman. Classic collection of an enduring American tradition. 109 plates, 8 in full color—portraits, landscapes, Biblical and historical scenes, etc., showing family groups, farm life, and so on. 80pp. of lucid text. 8⅜ x 11¼.
22815-0 Pa. $4.00

WILL BRADLEY: HIS GRAPHIC ART, edited by Clarence P. Hornung. Striking collection of work by foremost practitioner of Art Nouveau in America: posters, cover designs, sample pages, advertisements, other illustrations. 97 plates, including 8 in full color and 19 in two colors. 97pp. 9⅜ x 12¼.
20701-3 Pa. $4.00
22120-2 Clothbd. $10.00

THE UNDERGROUND SKETCHBOOK OF JAN FAUST, Jan Faust. 101 bitter, horrifying, black-humorous, penetrating sketches on sex, war, greed, various liberations, etc. Sometimes sexual, but not pornographic. Not for prudish. 101pp. 6½ x 9¼.
22740-5 Pa. $1.50

THE GIBSON GIRL AND HER AMERICA, Charles Dana Gibson. 155 finest drawings of effervescent world of 1900-1910: the Gibson Girl and her loves, amusements, adventures, Mr. Pipp, etc. Selected by E. Gillon; introduction by Henry Pitz. 144pp. 8¼ x 11⅜.
21986-0 Pa. $3.50

STAINED GLASS CRAFT, J.A.F. Divine, G. Blachford. One of the very few books that tell the beginner exactly what he needs to know: planning cuts, making shapes, avoiding design weaknesses, fitting glass, etc. 93 illustrations. 115pp.
22812-6 Pa. $1.50

CREATIVE LITHOGRAPHY AND HOW TO DO IT, Grant Arnold. Lithography as art form: working directly on stone, transfer of drawings, lithotint, mezzotint, color printing; also metal plates. Detailed, thorough. 27 illustrations. 214pp.
21208-4 Pa. $3.00

DESIGN MOTIFS OF ANCIENT MEXICO, Jorge Enciso. Vigorous, powerful ceramic stamp impressions — Maya, Aztec, Toltec, Olmec. Serpents, gods, priests, dancers, etc. 153pp. 6⅛ x 9¼.
20084-1 Pa. $2.50

AMERICAN INDIAN DESIGN AND DECORATION, Leroy Appleton. Full text, plus more than 700 precise drawings of Inca, Maya, Aztec, Pueblo, Plains, NW Coast basketry, sculpture, painting, pottery, sand paintings, metal, etc. 4 plates in color. 279pp. 8⅜ x 11¼.
22704-9 Pa. $4.50

CHINESE LATTICE DESIGNS, Daniel S. Dye. Incredibly beautiful geometric designs: circles, voluted, simple dissections, etc. Inexhaustible source of ideas, motifs. 1239 illustrations. 469pp. 6⅛ x 9¼.
23096-1 Pa. $5.00

JAPANESE DESIGN MOTIFS, Matsuya Co. Mon, or heraldic designs. Over 4000 typical, beautiful designs: birds, animals, flowers, swords, fans, geometric; all beautifully stylized. 213pp. 11⅜ x 8¼.
22874-6 Pa. $5.00

PERSPECTIVE, Jan Vredeman de Vries. 73 perspective plates from 1604 edition; buildings, townscapes, stairways, fantastic scenes. Remarkable for beauty, surrealistic atmosphere; real eye-catchers. Introduction by Adolf Placzek. 74pp. 11⅜ x 8¼.
20186-4 Pa. $2.75

EARLY AMERICAN DESIGN MOTIFS, Suzanne E. Chapman. 497 motifs, designs, from painting on wood, ceramics, appliqué, glassware, samplers, metal work, etc. Florals, landscapes, birds and animals, geometrics, letters, etc. Inexhaustible. Enlarged edition. 138pp. 8⅜ x 11¼.
22985-8 Pa. $3.50
23084-8 Clothbd. $7.95

VICTORIAN STENCILS FOR DESIGN AND DECORATION, edited by E.V. Gillon, Jr. 113 wonderful ornate Victorian pieces from German sources; florals, geometrics; borders, corner pieces; bird motifs, etc. 64pp. 9⅜ x 12¼.
21995-X Pa. $2.75

ART NOUVEAU: AN ANTHOLOGY OF DESIGN AND ILLUSTRATION FROM THE STUDIO, edited by E.V. Gillon, Jr. Graphic arts: book jackets, posters, engravings, illustrations, decorations; Crane, Beardsley, Bradley and many others. Inexhaustible. 92pp. 8⅛ x 11.
22388-4 Pa. $2.50

ORIGINAL ART DECO DESIGNS, William Rowe. First-rate, highly imaginative modern Art Deco frames, borders, compositions, alphabets, florals, insectals, Wurlitzer-types, etc. Much finest modern Art Deco. 80 plates, 8 in color. 8⅜ x 11¼.
22567-4 Pa. $3.00

HANDBOOK OF DESIGNS AND DEVICES, Clarence P. Hornung. Over 1800 basic geometric designs based on circle, triangle, square, scroll, cross, etc. Largest such collection in existence. 261pp.
20125-2 Pa. $2.50

150 MASTERPIECES OF DRAWING, edited by Anthony Toney. 150 plates, early 15th century to end of 18th century; Rembrandt, Michelangelo, Dürer, Fragonard, Watteau, Wouwerman, many others. 150pp. 8⅜ x 11¼.   21032-4 Pa. $3.50

THE GOLDEN AGE OF THE POSTER, Hayward and Blanche Cirker. 70 extraordinary posters in full colors, from Maîtres de l'Affiche, Mucha, Lautrec, Bradley, Cheret, Beardsley, many others. 9⅜ x 12¼.   22753-7 Pa. $4.95
21718-3 Clothbd. $7.95

SIMPLICISSIMUS, selection, translations and text by Stanley Appelbaum. 180 satirical drawings, 16 in full color, from the famous German weekly magazine in the years 1896 to 1926. 24 artists included: Grosz, Kley, Pascin, Kubin, Kollwitz, plus Heine, Thöny, Bruno Paul, others. 172pp. 8½ x 12¼.   23098-8 Pa. $5.00
23099-6 Clothbd. $10.00

THE EARLY WORK OF AUBREY BEARDSLEY, Aubrey Beardsley. 157 plates, 2 in color: Manon Lescaut, Madame Bovary, Morte d'Arthur, Salome, other. Introduction by H. Marillier. 175pp. 8½ x 11.   21816-3 Pa. $3.50

THE LATER WORK OF AUBREY BEARDSLEY, Aubrey Beardsley. Exotic masterpieces of full maturity: Venus and Tannhäuser, Lysistrata, Rape of the Lock, Volpone, Savoy material, etc. 174 plates, 2 in color. 176pp. 8½ x 11. 21817-1 Pa. $4.00

DRAWINGS OF WILLIAM BLAKE, William Blake. 92 plates from Book of Job, Divine Comedy, Paradise Lost, visionary heads, mythological figures, Laocoön, etc. Selection, introduction, commentary by Sir Geoffrey Keynes. 178pp. 8½ x 11.
22303-5 Pa. $3.50

LONDON: A PILGRIMAGE, Gustave Doré, Blanchard Jerrold. Squalor, riches, misery, beauty of mid-Victorian metropolis; 55 wonderful plates, 125 other illustrations, full social, cultural text by Jerrold. 191pp. of text. 8⅛ x 11.
22306-X Pa. $5.00

THE COMPLETE WOODCUTS OF ALBRECHT DÜRER, edited by Dr. W. Kurth. 346 in all: Old Testament, St. Jerome, Passion, Life of Virgin, Apocalypse, many others. Introduction by Campbell Dodgson. 285pp. 8½ x 12¼.   21097-9 Pa. $6.00

THE DISASTERS OF WAR, Francisco Goya. 83 etchings record horrors of Napoleonic wars in Spain and war in general. Reprint of 1st edition, plus 3 additional plates. Introduction by Philip Hofer. 97pp. 9⅜ x 8¼.   21872-4 Pa. $3.00

ENGRAVINGS OF HOGARTH, William Hogarth. 101 of Hogarth's greatest works: Rake's Progress, Harlot's Progress, Illustrations for Hudibras, Midnight Modern Conversation, Before and After, Beer Street and Gin Lane, many more. Full commentary. 256pp. 11 x 14.   22479-1 Pa. $7.00
23023-6 Clothbd. $13.50

PRIMITIVE ART, Franz Boas. Great anthropologist on ceramics, textiles, wood, stone, metal, etc.; patterns, technology, symbols, styles. All areas, but fullest on Northwest Coast Indians. 350 illustrations. 378pp.   20025-6 Pa. $3.50

MOTHER GOOSE'S MELODIES. Facsimile of fabulously rare Munroe and Francis "copyright 1833" Boston edition. Familiar and unusual rhymes, wonderful old woodcut illustrations. Edited by E.F. Bleiler. 128pp. 4½ x 6⅜. 22577-1 Pa. $1.00

MOTHER GOOSE IN HIEROGLYPHICS. Favorite nursery rhymes presented in rebus form for children. Fascinating 1849 edition reproduced in toto, with key. Introduction by E.F. Bleiler. About 400 woodcuts. 64pp. 6⅞ x 5¼. 20745-5 Pa. $1.00

PETER PIPER'S PRACTICAL PRINCIPLES OF PLAIN & PERFECT PRONUNCIATION. Alliterative jingles and tongue-twisters. Reproduction in full of 1830 first American edition. 25 spirited woodcuts. 32pp. 4½ x 6⅜. 22560-7 Pa. $1.00

MARMADUKE MULTIPLY'S MERRY METHOD OF MAKING MINOR MATHEMATICIANS. Fellow to Peter Piper, it teaches multiplication table by catchy rhymes and woodcuts. 1841 Munroe & Francis edition. Edited by E.F. Bleiler. 103pp. 4⅝ x 6.
22773-1 Pa. $1.25
20171-6 Clothbd. $3.00

THE NIGHT BEFORE CHRISTMAS, Clement Moore. Full text, and woodcuts from original 1848 book. Also critical, historical material. 19 illustrations. 40pp. 4⅝ x 6. 22797-9 Pa. $1.00

THE KING OF THE GOLDEN RIVER, John Ruskin. Victorian children's classic of three brothers, their attempts to reach the Golden River, what becomes of them. Facsimile of original 1889 edition. 22 illustrations. 56pp. 4⅝ x 6⅜.
20066-3 Pa. $1.25

DREAMS OF THE RAREBIT FIEND, Winsor McCay. Pioneer cartoon strip, unexcelled for beauty, imagination, in 60 full sequences. Incredible technical virtuosity, wonderful visual wit. Historical introduction. 62pp. 8⅜ x 11¼. 21347-1 Pa. $2.50

THE KATZENJAMMER KIDS, Rudolf Dirks. In full color, 14 strips from 1906-7; full of imagination, characteristic humor. Classic of great historical importance. Introduction by August Derleth. 32pp. 9¼ x 12¼. 23005-8 Pa. $2.00

LITTLE ORPHAN ANNIE AND LITTLE ORPHAN ANNIE IN COSMIC CITY, Harold Gray. Two great sequences from the early strips: our curly-haired heroine defends the Warbucks' financial empire and, then, takes on meanie Phineas P. Pinchpenny. Leapin' lizards! 178pp. 6⅛ x 8⅜. 23107-0 Pa. $2.00

WHEN A FELLER NEEDS A FRIEND, Clare Briggs. 122 cartoons by one of the greatest newspaper cartoonists of the early 20th century — about growing up, making a living, family life, daily frustrations and occasional triumphs. 121pp. 8½ x 9½.
23148-8 Pa. $2.50

THE BEST OF GLUYAS WILLIAMS. 100 drawings by one of America's finest cartoonists: The Day a Cake of Ivory Soap Sank at Proctor & Gamble's, At the Life Insurance Agents' Banquet, and many other gems from the 20's and 30's. 118pp. 8⅜ x 11¼. 22737-5 Pa. $2.50

THE BEST DR. THORNDYKE DETECTIVE STORIES, R. Austin Freeman. The Case of Oscar Brodski, The Moabite Cipher, and 5 other favorites featuring the great scientific detective, plus his long-believed-lost first adventure — 31 New Inn — reprinted here for the first time. Edited by E.F. Bleiler. USO 20388-3 Pa. $3.00

BEST "THINKING MACHINE" DETECTIVE STORIES, Jacques Futrelle. The Problem of Cell 13 and 11 other stories about Prof. Augustus S.F.X. Van Dusen, including two "lost" stories. First reprinting of several. Edited by E.F. Bleiler. 241pp. 20537-1 Pa. $3.00

UNCLE SILAS, J. Sheridan LeFanu. Victorian Gothic mystery novel, considered by many best of period, even better than Collins or Dickens. Wonderful psychological terror. Introduction by Frederick Shroyer. 436pp. 21715-9 Pa. $4.00

BEST DR. POGGIOLI DETECTIVE STORIES, T.S. Stribling. 15 best stories from EQMM and The Saint offer new adventures in Mexico, Florida, Tennessee hills as Poggioli unravels mysteries and combats Count Jalacki. 217pp. 23227-1 Pa. $3.00

EIGHT DIME NOVELS, selected with an introduction by E.F. Bleiler. Adventures of Old King Brady, Frank James, Nick Carter, Deadwood Dick, Buffalo Bill, The Steam Man, Frank Merriwell, and Horatio Alger — 1877 to 1905. Important, entertaining popular literature in facsimile reprint, with original covers. 190pp. 9 x 12. 22975-0 Pa. $3.50

ALICE'S ADVENTURES UNDER GROUND, Lewis Carroll. Facsimile of ms. Carroll gave Alice Liddell in 1864. Different in many ways from final Alice. Handlettered, illustrated by Carroll. Introduction by Martin Gardner. 128pp. 21482-6 Pa. $1.50

ALICE IN WONDERLAND COLORING BOOK, Lewis Carroll. Pictures by John Tenniel. Large-size versions of the famous illustrations of Alice, Cheshire Cat, Mad Hatter and all the others, waiting for your crayons. Abridged text. 36 illustrations. 64pp. 8¼ x 11. 22853-3 Pa. $1.50

AVENTURES D'ALICE AU PAYS DES MERVEILLES, Lewis Carroll. Bué's translation of "Alice" into French, supervised by Carroll himself. Novel way to learn language. (No English text.) 42 Tenniel illustrations. 196pp. 22836-3 Pa. $2.50

MYTHS AND FOLK TALES OF IRELAND, Jeremiah Curtin. 11 stories that are Irish versions of European fairy tales and 9 stories from the Fenian cycle — 20 tales of legend and magic that comprise an essential work in the history of folklore. 256pp. 22430-9 Pa. $3.00

EAST O' THE SUN AND WEST O' THE MOON, George W. Dasent. Only full edition of favorite, wonderful Norwegian fairytales — Why the Sea is Salt, Boots and the Troll, etc. — with 77 illustrations by Kittelsen & Werenskiöld. 418pp. 22521-6 Pa. $4.00

PERRAULT'S FAIRY TALES, Charles Perrault and Gustave Doré. Original versions of Cinderella, Sleeping Beauty, Little Red Riding Hood, etc. in best translation, with 34 wonderful illustrations by Gustave Doré. 117pp. 8⅛ x 11. 22311-6 Pa. $2.50

EARLY NEW ENGLAND GRAVESTONE RUBBINGS, Edmund V. Gillon, Jr. 43 photographs, 226 rubbings show heavily symbolic, macabre, sometimes humorous primitive American art. Up to early 19th century. 207pp. 8⅜ x 11¼.
21380-3 Pa. $4.00

L.J.M. DAGUERRE: THE HISTORY OF THE DIORAMA AND THE DAGUERREOTYPE, Helmut and Alison Gernsheim. Definitive account. Early history, life and work of Daguerre; discovery of daguerreotype process; diffusion abroad; other early photography. 124 illustrations. 226pp. 6⅙ x 9¼.
22290-X Pa. $4.00

PHOTOGRAPHY AND THE AMERICAN SCENE, Robert Taft. The basic book on American photography as art, recording form, 1839-1889. Development, influence on society, great photographers, types (portraits, war, frontier, etc.), whatever else needed. Inexhaustible. Illustrated with 322 early photos, daguerreotypes, tintypes, stereo slides, etc. 546pp. 6⅛ x 9¼.
21201-7 Pa. $5.95

PHOTOGRAPHIC SKETCHBOOK OF THE CIVIL WAR, Alexander Gardner. Reproduction of 1866 volume with 100 on-the-field photographs: Manassas, Lincoln on battlefield, slave pens, etc. Introduction by E.F. Bleiler. 224pp. 10¾ x 9.
22731-6 Pa. $5.00

THE MOVIES: A PICTURE QUIZ BOOK, Stanley Appelbaum & Hayward Cirker. Match stars with their movies, name actors and actresses, test your movie skill with 241 stills from 236 great movies, 1902-1959. Indexes of performers and films. 128pp. 8⅜ x 9¼.
20222-4 Pa. $2.50

THE TALKIES, Richard Griffith. Anthology of features, articles from Photoplay, 1928-1940, reproduced complete. Stars, famous movies, technical features, fabulous ads, etc.; Garbo, Chaplin, King Kong, Lubitsch, etc. 4 color plates, scores of illustrations. 327pp. 8⅜ x 11¼.
22762-6 Pa. $6.95

THE MOVIE MUSICAL FROM VITAPHONE TO "42ND STREET," edited by Miles Kreuger. Relive the rise of the movie musical as reported in the pages of Photoplay magazine (1926-1933): every movie review, cast list, ad, and record review; every significant feature article, production still, biography, forecast, and gossip story. Profusely illustrated. 367pp. 8⅜ x 11¼.
23154-2 Pa. $6.95

JOHANN SEBASTIAN BACH, Philipp Spitta. Great classic of biography, musical commentary, with hundreds of pieces analyzed. Also good for Bach's contemporaries. 450 musical examples. Total of 1799pp.
EUK 22278-0, 22279-9 Clothbd., Two vol. set $25.00

BEETHOVEN AND HIS NINE SYMPHONIES, Sir George Grove. Thorough history, analysis, commentary on symphonies and some related pieces. For either beginner or advanced student. 436 musical passages. 407pp.
20334-4 Pa. $4.00

MOZART AND HIS PIANO CONCERTOS, Cuthbert Girdlestone. The only full-length study. Detailed analyses of all 21 concertos, sources; 417 musical examples. 509pp.
21271-8 Pa. $4.50

THE FITZWILLIAM VIRGINAL BOOK, edited by J. Fuller Maitland, W.B. Squire. Famous early 17th century collection of keyboard music, 300 works by Morley, Byrd, Bull, Gibbons, etc. Modern notation. Total of 938pp. 8⅜ x 11.
ECE 21068-5, 21069-3 Pa., Two vol. set $14.00

COMPLETE STRING QUARTETS, Wolfgang A. Mozart. Breitkopf and Härtel edition. All 23 string quartets plus alternate slow movement to K156. Study score. 277pp. 9⅜ x 12¼.
22372-8 Pa. $6.00

COMPLETE SONG CYCLES, Franz Schubert. Complete piano, vocal music of Die Schöne Müllerin, Die Winterreise, Schwanengesang. Also Drinker English singing translations. Breitkopf and Härtel edition. 217pp. 9⅜ x 12¼.
22649-2 Pa. $4.50

THE COMPLETE PRELUDES AND ETUDES FOR PIANOFORTE SOLO, Alexander Scriabin. All the preludes and etudes including many perfectly spun miniatures. Edited by K.N. Igumnov and Y.I. Mil'shteyn. 250pp. 9 x 12.
22919-X Pa. $5.00

TRISTAN UND ISOLDE, Richard Wagner. Full orchestral score with complete instrumentation. Do not confuse with piano reduction. Commentary by Felix Mottl, great Wagnerian conductor and scholar. Study score. 655pp. 8⅛ x 11.
22915-7 Pa. $10.00

FAVORITE SONGS OF THE NINETIES, ed. Robert Fremont. Full reproduction, including covers, of 88 favorites: Ta-Ra-Ra-Boom-De-Aye, The Band Played On, Bird in a Gilded Cage, Under the Bamboo Tree, After the Ball, etc. 401pp. 9 x 12.
EBE 21536-9 Pa. $6.95

SOUSA'S GREAT MARCHES IN PIANO TRANSCRIPTION: ORIGINAL SHEET MUSIC OF 23 WORKS, John Philip Sousa. Selected by Lester S. Levy. Playing edition includes: The Stars and Stripes Forever, The Thunderer, The Gladiator, King Cotton, Washington Post, much more. 24 illustrations. 111pp. 9 x 12.
USO 23132-1 Pa. $3.50

CLASSIC PIANO RAGS, selected with an introduction by Rudi Blesh. Best ragtime music (1897-1922) by Scott Joplin, James Scott, Joseph F. Lamb, Tom Turpin, 9 others. Printed from best original sheet music, plus covers. 364pp. 9 x 12.
EBE 20469-3 Pa. $6.95

ANALYSIS OF CHINESE CHARACTERS, C.D. Wilder, J.H. Ingram. 1000 most important characters analyzed according to primitives, phonetics, historical development. Traditional method offers mnemonic aid to beginner, intermediate student of Chinese, Japanese. 365pp.
23045-7 Pa. $4.00

MODERN CHINESE: A BASIC COURSE, Faculty of Peking University. Self study, classroom course in modern Mandarin. Records contain phonetics, vocabulary, sentences, lessons. 249 page book contains all recorded text, translations, grammar, vocabulary, exercises. Best course on market. 3 12" 33⅓ monaural records, book, album.
98832-5 Set $12.50

MANUAL OF THE TREES OF NORTH AMERICA, Charles S. Sargent. The basic survey of every native tree and tree-like shrub, 717 species in all. Extremely full descriptions, information on habitat, growth, locales, economics, etc. Necessary to every serious tree lover. Over 100 finding keys. 783 illustrations. Total of 986pp.
20277-1, 20278-X Pa., Two vol. set $8.00

BIRDS OF THE NEW YORK AREA, John Bull. Indispensable guide to more than 400 species within a hundred-mile radius of Manhattan. Information on range, status, breeding, migration, distribution trends, etc. Foreword by Roger Tory Peterson. 17 drawings; maps. 540pp.
23222-0 Pa. $6.00

THE SEA-BEACH AT EBB-TIDE, Augusta Foote Arnold. Identify hundreds of marine plants and animals: algae, seaweeds, squids, crabs, corals, etc. Descriptions cover food, life cycle, size, shape, habitat. Over 600 drawings. 490pp.
21949-6 Pa.$5.00

THE MOTH BOOK, William J. Holland. Identify more than 2,000 moths of North America. General information, precise species descriptions. 623 illustrations plus 48 color plates show almost all species, full size. 1968 edition. Still the basic book. Total of 551pp. 6½ x 9¼.
21948-8 Pa. $6.00

AN INTRODUCTION TO THE REPTILES AND AMPHIBIANS OF THE UNITED STATES, Percy A. Morris. All lizards, crocodiles, turtles, snakes, toads, frogs; life history, identification, habits, suitability as pets, etc. Non-technical, but sound and broad. 130 photos. 253pp.
22982-3 Pa. $3.00

OLD NEW YORK IN EARLY PHOTOGRAPHS, edited by Mary Black. Your only chance to see New York City as it was 1853-1906, through 196 wonderful photographs from N.Y. Historical Society. Great Blizzard, Lincoln's funeral procession, great buildings. 228pp. 9 x 12.
22907-6 Pa. $6.00

THE AMERICAN REVOLUTION, A PICTURE SOURCEBOOK, John Grafton. Wonderful Bicentennial picture source, with 411 illustrations (contemporary and 19th century) showing battles, personalities, maps, events, flags, posters, soldier's life, ships, etc. all captioned and explained. A wonderful browsing book, supplement to other historical reading. 160pp. 9 x 12.
23226-3 Pa. $4.00

PERSONAL NARRATIVE OF A PILGRIMAGE TO AL-MADINAH AND MECCAH, Richard Burton. Great travel classic by remarkably colorful personality. Burton, disguised as a Moroccan, visited sacred shrines of Islam, narrowly escaping death. Wonderful observations of Islamic life, customs, personalities. 47 illustrations. Total of 959pp.
21217-3, 21218-1 Pa., Two vol. set$10.00

INCIDENTS OF TRAVEL IN CENTRAL AMERICA, CHIAPAS, AND YUCATAN, John L. Stephens. Almost single-handed discovery of Maya culture; exploration of ruined cities, monuments, temples; customs of Indians. 115 drawings. 892pp.
22404-X, 22405-8 Pa., Two vol. set $8.00

CONSTRUCTION OF AMERICAN FURNITURE TREASURES, Lester Margon. 344 detail drawings, complete text on constructing exact reproductions of 38 early American masterpieces: Hepplewhite sideboard, Duncan Phyfe drop-leaf table, mantel clock, gate-leg dining table, Pa. German cupboard, more. 38 plates. 54 photographs. 168pp. 8⅜ x 11¼.   23056-2 Pa. $4.00

JEWELRY MAKING AND DESIGN, Augustus F. Rose, Antonio Cirino. Professional secrets revealed in thorough, practical guide: tools, materials, processes; rings, brooches, chains, cast pieces, enamelling, setting stones, etc. Do not confuse with skimpy introductions: beginner can use, professional can learn from it. Over 200 illustrations. 306pp.   21750-7 Pa. $3.00

METALWORK AND ENAMELLING, Herbert Maryon. Generally conceeded best all-around book. Countless trade secrets: materials, tools, soldering, filigree, setting, inlay, niello, repoussé, casting, polishing, etc. For beginner or expert. Author was foremost British expert. 330 illustrations. 335pp.   22702-2 Pa. $3.50

WEAVING WITH FOOT-POWER LOOMS, Edward F. Worst. Setting up a loom, beginning to weave, constructing equipment, using dyes, more, plus over 285 drafts of traditional patterns including Colonial and Swedish weaves. More than 200 other figures. For beginning and advanced. 275pp. 8¾ x 6⅜ .   23064-3 Pa. $4.00

WEAVING A NAVAJO BLANKET, Gladys A. Reichard. Foremost anthropologist studied under Navajo women, reveals every step in process from wool, dyeing, spinning, setting up loom, designing, weaving. Much history, symbolism. With this book you could make one yourself. 97 illustrations. 222pp.   22992-0 Pa. $3.00

NATURAL DYES AND HOME DYEING, Rita J. Adrosko. Use natural ingredients: bark, flowers, leaves, lichens, insects etc. Over 135 specific recipes from historical sources for cotton, wool, other fabrics. Genuine premodern handicrafts. 12 illustrations. 160pp.   22688-3 Pa. $2.00

THE HAND DECORATION OF FABRICS, Francis J. Kafka. Outstanding, profusely illustrated guide to stenciling, batik, block printing, tie dyeing, freehand painting, silk screen printing, and novelty decoration. 356 illustrations. 198pp. 6 x 9.
                                                                                                  21401-X Pa. $3.00

THOMAS NAST: CARTOONS AND ILLUSTRATIONS, with text by Thomas Nast St. Hill. Father of American political cartooning. Cartoons that destroyed Tweed Ring; inflation, free love, church and state; original Republican elephant and Democratic donkey; Santa Claus; more. 117 illustrations. 146pp. 9 x 12.
                                                                                                  22983-1 Pa. $4.00
                                                                                                  23067-8 Clothbd. $8.50

FREDERIC REMINGTON: 173 DRAWINGS AND ILLUSTRATIONS. Most famous of the Western artists, most responsible for our myths about the American West in its untamed days. Complete reprinting of *Drawings of Frederic Remington* (1897), plus other selections. 4 additional drawings in color on covers. 140pp. 9 x 12.
                                                                                                  20714-5 Pa. $3.95

HOW TO SOLVE CHESS PROBLEMS, Kenneth S. Howard. Practical suggestions on problem solving for very beginners. 58 two-move problems, 46 3-movers, 8 4-movers for practice, plus hints. 171pp. 20748-X Pa. $2.00

A GUIDE TO FAIRY CHESS, Anthony Dickins. 3-D chess, 4-D chess, chess on a cylindrical board, reflecting pieces that bounce off edges, cooperative chess, retrograde chess, maximummers, much more. Most based on work of great Dawson. Full handbook, 100 problems. 66pp. 7⅞ x 10¾. 22687-5 Pa. $2.00

WIN AT BACKGAMMON, Millard Hopper. Best opening moves, running game, blocking game, back game, tables of odds, etc. Hopper makes the game clear enough for anyone to play, and win. 43 diagrams. 111pp. 22894-0 Pa. $1.50

BIDDING A BRIDGE HAND, Terence Reese. Master player "thinks out loud" the binding of 75 hands that defy point count systems. Organized by bidding problem—no-fit situations, overbidding, underbidding, cueing your defense, etc. 254pp. EBE 22830-4 Pa. $2.50

THE PRECISION BIDDING SYSTEM IN BRIDGE, C.C. Wei, edited by Alan Truscott. Inventor of precision bidding presents average hands and hands from actual play, including games from 1969 Bermuda Bowl where system emerged. 114 exercises. 116pp. 21171-1 Pa. $1.75

LEARN MAGIC, Henry Hay. 20 simple, easy-to-follow lessons on magic for the new magician: illusions, card tricks, silks, sleights of hand, coin manipulations, escapes, and more —all with a minimum amount of equipment. Final chapter explains the great stage illusions. 92 illustrations. 285pp. 21238-6 Pa. $2.95

THE NEW MAGICIAN'S MANUAL, Walter B. Gibson. Step-by-step instructions and clear illustrations guide the novice in mastering 36 tricks; much equipment supplied on 16 pages of cut-out materials. 36 additional tricks. 64 illustrations. 159pp. 6⅝ x 10. 23113-5 Pa. $3.00

PROFESSIONAL MAGIC FOR AMATEURS, Walter B. Gibson. 50 easy, effective tricks used by professionals —cards, string, tumblers, handkerchiefs, mental magic, etc. 63 illustrations. 223pp. 23012-0 Pa. $2.50

CARD MANIPULATIONS, Jean Hugard. Very rich collection of manipulations; has taught thousands of fine magicians tricks that are really workable, eye-catching. Easily followed, serious work. Over 200 illustrations. 163pp. 20539-8 Pa. $2.00

ABBOTT'S ENCYCLOPEDIA OF ROPE TRICKS FOR MAGICIANS, Stewart James. Complete reference book for amateur and professional magicians containing more than 150 tricks involving knots, penetrations, cut and restored rope, etc. 510 illustrations. Reprint of 3rd edition. 400pp. 23206-9 Pa. $3.50

THE SECRETS OF HOUDINI, J.C. Cannell. Classic study of Houdini's incredible magic, exposing closely-kept professional secrets and revealing, in general terms, the whole art of stage magic. 67 illustrations. 279pp. 22913-0 Pa. $2.50

THE MAGIC MOVING PICTURE BOOK, Bliss, Sands & Co. The pictures in this book move! Volcanoes erupt, a house burns, a serpentine dancer wiggles her way through a number. By using a specially ruled acetate screen provided, you can obtain these and 15 other startling effects. Originally "The Motograph Moving Picture Book." 32pp. 8¼ x 11. 23224-7 Pa. $1.75

STRING FIGURES AND HOW TO MAKE THEM, Caroline F. Jayne. Fullest, clearest instructions on string figures from around world: Eskimo, Navajo, Lapp, Europe, more. Cats cradle, moving spear, lightning, stars. Introduction by A.C. Haddon. 950 illustrations. 407pp. 20152-X Pa. $3.00

PAPER FOLDING FOR BEGINNERS, William D. Murray and Francis J. Rigney. Clearest book on market for making origami sail boats, roosters, frogs that move legs, cups, bonbon boxes. 40 projects. More than 275 illustrations. Photographs. 94pp. 20713-7 Pa. $1.25

INDIAN SIGN LANGUAGE, William Tomkins. Over 525 signs developed by Sioux, Blackfoot, Cheyenne, Arapahoe and other tribes. Written instructions and diagrams: how to make words, construct sentences. Also 290 pictographs of Sioux and Ojibway tribes. 111pp. 6⅛ x 9¼. 22029-X Pa. $1.50

BOOMERANGS: HOW TO MAKE AND THROW THEM, Bernard S. Mason. Easy to make and throw, dozens of designs: cross-stick, pinwheel, boomabird, tumblestick, Australian curved stick boomerang. Complete throwing instructions. All safe. 99pp. 23028-7 Pa. $1.50

25 KITES THAT FLY, Leslie Hunt. Full, easy to follow instructions for kites made from inexpensive materials. Many novelties. Reeling, raising, designing your own. 70 illustrations. 110pp. 22550-X Pa. $1.25

TRICKS AND GAMES ON THE POOL TABLE, Fred Herrmann. 79 tricks and games, some solitaires, some for 2 or more players, some competitive; mystifying shots and throws, unusual carom, tricks involving cork, coins, a hat, more. 77 figures. 95pp. 21814-7 Pa. $1.25

WOODCRAFT AND CAMPING, Bernard S. Mason. How to make a quick emergency shelter, select woods that will burn immediately, make do with limited supplies, etc. Also making many things out of wood, rawhide, bark, at camp. Formerly titled Woodcraft. 295 illustrations. 580pp. 21951-8 Pa. $4.00

AN INTRODUCTION TO CHESS MOVES AND TACTICS SIMPLY EXPLAINED, Leonard Barden. Informal intermediate introduction: reasons for moves, tactics, openings, traps, positional play, endgame. Isolates patterns. 102pp. USO 21210-6 Pa. $1.35

LASKER'S MANUAL OF CHESS, Dr. Emanuel Lasker. Great world champion offers very thorough coverage of all aspects of chess. Combinations, position play, openings, endgame, aesthetics of chess, philosophy of struggle, much more. Filled with analyzed games. 390pp. 20640-8 Pa. $3.50

CATALOGUE OF DOVER BOOKS

SLEEPING BEAUTY, illustrated by Arthur Rackham. Perhaps the fullest, most delightful version ever, told by C.S. Evans. Rackham's best work. 49 illustrations. 110pp. 7⅞ x 10¾. 22756-1 Pa. $2.00

THE WONDERFUL WIZARD OF OZ, L. Frank Baum. Facsimile in full color of America's finest children's classic. Introduction by Martin Gardner. 143 illustrations by W.W. Denslow. 267pp. 20691-2 Pa. $2.50

GOOPS AND HOW TO BE THEM, Gelett Burgess. Classic tongue-in-cheek masquerading as etiquette book. 87 verses, 170 cartoons as Goops demonstrate virtues of table manners, neatness, courtesy, more. 88pp. 6½ x 9¼. 22233-0 Pa. $1.50

THE BROWNIES, THEIR BOOK, Palmer Cox. Small as mice, cunning as foxes, exuberant, mischievous, Brownies go to zoo, toy shop, seashore, circus, more. 24 verse adventures. 266 illustrations. 144pp. 6⅝ x 9¼. 21265-3 Pa. $1.75

BILLY WHISKERS: THE AUTOBIOGRAPHY OF A GOAT, Frances Trego Montgomery. Escapades of that rambunctious goat. Favorite from turn of the century America. 24 illustrations. 259pp. 22345-0 Pa. $2.75

THE ROCKET BOOK, Peter Newell. Fritz, janitor's kid, sets off rocket in basement of apartment house; an ingenious hole punched through every page traces course of rocket. 22 duotone drawings, verses. 48pp. 6⅞ x 8⅜. 22044-3 Pa. $1.50

PECK'S BAD BOY AND HIS PA, George W. Peck. Complete double-volume of great American childhood classic. Hennery's ingenious pranks against outraged pomposity of pa and the grocery man. 97 illustrations. Introduction by E.F. Bleiler. 347pp. 20497-9 Pa. $2.50

THE TALE OF PETER RABBIT, Beatrix Potter. The inimitable Peter's terrifying adventure in Mr. McGregor's garden, with all 27 wonderful, full-color Potter illustrations. 55pp. 4¼ x 5½. USO 22827-4 Pa. $1.00

THE TALE OF MRS. TIGGY-WINKLE, Beatrix Potter. Your child will love this story about a very special hedgehog and all 27 wonderful, full-color Potter illustrations. 57pp. 4¼ x 5½. USO 20546-0 Pa. $1.00

THE TALE OF BENJAMIN BUNNY, Beatrix Potter. Peter Rabbit's cousin coaxes him back into Mr. McGregor's garden for a whole new set of adventures. A favorite with children. All 27 full-color illustrations. 59pp. 4¼ x 5½. USO 21102-9 Pa. $1.00

THE MERRY ADVENTURES OF ROBIN HOOD, Howard Pyle. Facsimile of original (1883) edition, finest modern version of English outlaw's adventures. 23 illustrations by Pyle. 296pp. 6½ x 9¼. 22043-5 Pa. $2.75

TWO LITTLE SAVAGES, Ernest Thompson Seton. Adventures of two boys who lived as Indians; explaining Indian ways, woodlore, pioneer methods. 293 illustrations. 286pp. 20985-7 Pa. $3.00

HOUDINI ON MAGIC, Harold Houdini. Edited by Walter Gibson, Morris N. Young. How he escaped; exposés of fake spiritualists; instructions for eye-catching tricks; other fascinating material by and about greatest magician. 155 illustrations. 280pp. 20384-0 Pa. $2.50

HANDBOOK OF THE NUTRITIONAL CONTENTS OF FOOD, U.S. Dept. of Agriculture. Largest, most detailed source of food nutrition information ever prepared. Two mammoth tables: one measuring nutrients in 100 grams of edible portion; the other, in edible portion of 1 pound as purchased. Originally titled Composition of Foods. 190pp. 9 x 12. 21342-0 Pa. $4.00

COMPLETE GUIDE TO HOME CANNING, PRESERVING AND FREEZING, U.S. Dept. of Agriculture. Seven basic manuals with full instructions for jams and jellies; pickles and relishes; canning fruits, vegetables, meat; freezing anything. Really good recipes, exact instructions for optimal results. Save a fortune in food. 156 illustrations. 214pp. 6⅛ x 9¼. 22911-4 Pa. $2.50

THE BREAD TRAY, Louis P. De Gouy. Nearly every bread the cook could buy or make: bread sticks of Italy, fruit breads of Greece, glazed rolls of Vienna, everything from corn pone to croissants. Over 500 recipes altogether. including buns, rolls, muffins, scones, and more. 463pp. 23000-7 Pa. $3.50

CREATIVE HAMBURGER COOKERY, Louis P. De Gouy. 182 unusual recipes for casseroles, meat loaves and hamburgers that turn inexpensive ground meat into memorable main dishes: Arizona chili burgers, burger tamale pie, burger stew, burger corn loaf, burger wine loaf, and more. 120pp. 23001-5 Pa. $1.75

LONG ISLAND SEAFOOD COOKBOOK, J. George Frederick and Jean Joyce. Probably the best American seafood cookbook. Hundreds of recipes. 40 gourmet sauces, 123 recipes using oysters alone! All varieties of fish and seafood amply represented. 324pp. 22677-8 Pa. $3.00

THE EPICUREAN: A COMPLETE TREATISE OF ANALYTICAL AND PRACTICAL STUDIES IN THE CULINARY ART, Charles Ranhofer. Great modern classic. 3,500 recipes from master chef of Delmonico's, turn-of-the-century America's best restaurant. Also explained, many techniques known only to professional chefs. 775 illustrations. 1183pp. 6⅝ x 10. 22680-8 Clothbd. $17.50

THE AMERICAN WINE COOK BOOK, Ted Hatch. Over 700 recipes: old favorites livened up with wine plus many more: Czech fish soup, quince soup, sauce Perigueux, shrimp shortcake, filets Stroganoff, cordon bleu goulash, jambonneau, wine fruit cake, more. 314pp. 22796-0 Pa. $2.50

DELICIOUS VEGETARIAN COOKING, Ivan Baker. Close to 500 delicious and varied recipes: soups, main course dishes (pea, bean, lentil, cheese, vegetable, pasta, and egg dishes), savories, stews, whole-wheat breads and cakes, more. 168pp. USO 22834-7 Pa. $1.75

COOKIES FROM MANY LANDS, Josephine Perry. Crullers, oatmeal cookies, chaux au chocolate, English tea cakes, mandel kuchen, Sacher torte, Danish puff pastry, Swedish cookies — a mouth-watering collection of 223 recipes. 157pp.
22832-0 Pa. $2.00

ROSE RECIPES, Eleanour S. Rohde. How to make sauces, jellies, tarts, salads, pot-pourris, sweet bags, pomanders, perfumes from garden roses; all exact recipes. Century old favorites. 95pp. 22957-2 Pa. $1.25

"OSCAR" OF THE WALDORF'S COOKBOOK, Oscar Tschirky. Famous American chef reveals 3455 recipes that made Waldorf great; cream of French, German, American cooking, in all categories. Full instructions, easy home use. 1896 edition. 907pp. 6⅝ x 9⅜. 20790-0 Clothbd. $15.00

JAMS AND JELLIES, May Byron. Over 500 old-time recipes for delicious jams, jellies, marmalades, preserves, and many other items. Probably the largest jam and jelly book in print. Originally titled May Byron's Jam Book. 276pp.
USO 23130-5 Pa. $3.00

MUSHROOM RECIPES, André L. Simon. 110 recipes for everyday and special cooking. Champignons à la grecque, sole bonne femme, chicken liver croustades, more; 9 basic sauces, 13 ways of cooking mushrooms. 54pp.
USO 20913-X Pa. $1.25

FAVORITE SWEDISH RECIPES, edited by Sam Widenfelt. Prepared in Sweden, offers wonderful, clearly explained Swedish dishes: appetizers, meats, pastry and cookies, other categories. Suitable for American kitchen. 90 photos. 157pp.
23156-9 Pa. $2.00

THE BUCKEYE COOKBOOK, Buckeye Publishing Company. Over 1,000 easy-to-follow, traditional recipes from the American Midwest: bread (100 recipes alone), meat, game, jam, candy, cake, ice cream, and many other categories of cooking. 64 illustrations. From 1883 enlarged edition. 416pp. 23218-2 Pa. $4.00

TWENTY-TWO AUTHENTIC BANQUETS FROM INDIA, Robert H. Christie. Complete, easy-to-do recipes for almost 200 authentic Indian dishes assembled in 22 banquets. Arranged by region. Selected from Banquets of the Nations. 192pp.
23200-X Pa. $2.50

Prices subject to change without notice.
Available at your book dealer or write for free catalogue to Dept. GI, Dover Publications, Inc., 180 Varick St., N.Y., N.Y. 10014. Dover publishes more than 150 books each year on science, elementary and advanced mathematics, biology, music, art, literary history, social sciences and other areas.